OECD Factbook 2011

ECONOMIC, ENVIRONMENTAL
AND SOCIAL STATISTICS

Please cite this publication as:
OECD (2011), *OECD Factbook 2011: Economic, Environmental and Social Statistics*, OECD Publishing.
http://dx.doi.org/10.1787/factbook-2011-en

ISBN 978-92-64-11150-9 (print)
ISBN 978-92-64-00000-0 (PDF)
ISBN 978-92-64-12418-9 (HTML)

Series/Periodical:
ISSN 1995-3879 (print)
ISSN 1814-7364 (online)

The statistical data for Israel are supplied by and under the responsibility of the relevant Israeli authorities. The use of such data by the OECD is without prejudice to the status of the Golan Heights, East Jerusalem and Israeli settlements in the West Bank under the terms of international law.

Photo credits:
Chapter 3: © Image Source/Getty Images | Chapter 4: © Stockbyte/Getty Images | Chapter 5: © Lawrence Lawry/Photodisc/Getty Images | Chapter 6: © Larry Lee Photography/Corbis | Chapter 7: © Cocoon/Digital Vision/Getty Images | Chapter 8: © Comstock Images/Comstock Images/Getty Images | Chapter 9: © Digital Vision/Getty Images | Chapter 10: © Jacobs Stock Photography/Getty Images | Chapter 11 : © OCDE.

Corrigenda to OECD publications may be found on line at: *www.oecd.org/publishing/corrigenda*.

OECD Factbook 2011

FOREWORD

For 50 years, the OECD has been at the forefront in the production of reliable, comparable, timely and trusted statistics. These statistics are the raw material upon which the analytical work conducted at the OECD but also in many other organisations, governments and academia worldwide depends. Importantly, OECD statistics are a means to inform the public at large and lie at the core of rigorous, evidence-based, policy-making. The ongoing fallout from the financial crisis has highlighted, even more than in the past, the need for reliable statistics to help policy makers put the world economy on a more sustainable and inclusive development path. Statistics are like a compass, setting the route for the destination we want to reach: when the compass fails, or when we do not know how to use it, we are left with no guidance on where we are now and on how to steer policies towards where we want to be in the future.

The *OECD Factbook* is the most comprehensive statistical publication of the Organisation. It is an essential tool to evaluate trends in the most important factors shaping the development trajectories of OECD and emerging countries. It offers a user-friendly point of entry to the full range of statistics available the Organisation. The importance of a comprehensive but parsimonious compilation of key statistics and indicators is all the more important at a time when more and more data are available everywhere, a phenomenon that some observers have characterised as a "data deluge".

This year's edition of the *OECD Factbook* provides not only a snapshot of the most recent statistics produced by the Organisation but also celebrates its 50th Anniversary through a special chapter that focuses on longer-term developments. While the coverage of this chapter is necessarily limited, it is a useful reminder of the pioneering role that the OECD has played in developing indicators in domains that were not always on the radar screen of official statistics. This was the case in the 1960s for statistics in research and development and in science and technology; and in later decades for a whole battery of social and environmental indicators that have since become international references.

Today, like in the past 50 years, the OECD is committed to responding to the ever-rising demand for quality data by policy-makers and citizens to help address new and emerging issues. This requires both adapting existing statistical standards and guidelines to the continuous developments in our economies and societies and developing credible measures in new dimensions, in close collaboration with all producers of official statistics.

As in past editions, the *OECD Factbook* includes statistics for selected emerging economies. Data for Brazil, India, Indonesia, China and South Africa are reported in this publication when available and deemed to be comparable with those for OECD countries. These emerging countries today play a central role in the world economy, a role that is set to become even more important in the future. The OECD recognises the importance of partnering with these countries based on mutual interest and learning from each other's experiences; to that end, it aims to integrate these countries in the full range of its databases. This reflects our ambition to increase the OECD's impact and relevance on a global scale, an ambition that is demonstrated by the extension of our membership to four new countries in 2010 (Chile, Estonia, Israel and Slovenia), by the ongoing accession negotiation with the Russian Federation, and by the role that the OECD is playing to support the work of the G20.

The *OECD Factbook* is written in a non-technical language, providing users with a one-stop resource of country-based data, helping them to assess a country's performance relative to others, and encouraging readers to explore further the goldmine of OECD data and publications. All data in the *OECD Factbook* are available online through StatLinks at the bottom of each table and chart in this report, as well as through the data and metadata available through OECD.Stat, the corporate platform for data dissemination, in the form of thematic databases and Country Statistical Profiles.

I hope that this publication will help citizens, researchers, analysts and policy-makers in their daily work, and that readers will provide their feedback to us, so as to improve future editions of the *OECD Factbook*.

Martine Durand

OECD Chief Statistician and Director of Statistics

ACKNOWLEDGEMENTS

This publication would not have been possible without the cooperation of statistical authorities from OECD countries and other major economies represented in the *OECD Factbook*. The *OECD Factbook* truly represents the wealth of OECD-wide statistical activities and reflects the work of statisticians throughout the Organisation and its agencies – the *International Energy Agency* (IEA), the *Nuclear Energy Agency* (NEA), the *OECD Development Centre* and the *International Transport Forum*.

This report has been prepared by several colleagues in the OECD Statistics Directorate: David Brackfield has acted as editor, Katia Sarrazin had overall technical responsibility and Federico Giovannelli was responsible for producing the Special Chapter – "OECD turns 50". Eileen Capponi and Damian Garnys, from the OECD's Public Affairs and Communications Directorate, have provided editorial assistance; while Nigel Wilkie, Joseph Crowther and Seamus Walsh, in the Information Technology and Network Service Section of the OECD Executive Directorate, have provided assistance with the new production system.

TABLE OF CONTENTS

Science and technology

Environment

Education

Public finance

Health

READER'S GUIDE

Main Features:

- Tables and charts are preceded by short texts that explain how the statistics are defined (**Definition**) and that identify any problems there may be in comparing the performance of one country with another (**Comparability**). To avoid misunderstandings, the tables and charts must be read in conjunction with the texts that accompany them.
- Tables and charts are also available as Excel files.
- While media comment on statistics usually focuses on the short term – what has happened to employment, prices, GDP and so on in the last few months – the *OECD Factbook* takes a longer view; the text and charts mostly describe developments during the fourteen year period from 1997 to 2010. This long-term perspective provides a good basis for comparing the successes and failures of policies in raising living standards and social conditions in countries.
- To facilitate cross-country comparisons, many indicators in the *OECD Factbook* have been standardised by relating them to each country's gross domestic product (GDP). In cases where GDP needs to be converted to a common currency, purchasing power parities (PPPs) have been used rather than exchange rates. When PPPs are used, differences in GDP levels across countries reflect only differences in the volume of goods and services, *i.e.* differences in price levels are eliminated.

Conventions

Unless otherwise specified:

- *OECD total* refers to all the OECD countries listed in a table or chart; when the indicator is a ratio or a mean, *OECD total* is the weighted average of country values.
- *OECD average* refers to the unweighted, arithmetic average of the listed OECD countries.
- For each country, the average value in different periods only takes into account the years for which data are available. The *average annual growth rate* of an indicator over a period of time is the geometric average of the growth rates of that indicator across the period (i.e. the annual compound growth rate).
- Each table and chart specifies the period covered. The mention, *XXXX or latest available year* (where XXXX is a year or a period) means that data for later years are not taken into account.

Signs, abbreviations and acronyms

..	Missing value, not applicable or not available
0	Less than half of the unit precision level of the observation
–	Absolute zero
|	Break in series
USD	US dollars

DAC	Development Assistance Committee
ILO	International Labor Organisation
IMF	International Monetary Fund
ITF	International Transport Forum
ITU	International Telecommunications Union
NAFTA	North American Free Trade Agreement
UN	United Nations
UNCTAD	United Nations Conference on Trade and Development
UNECE	United Nations Economic Commission for Europe
UNODC	United Nations Office on Drugs and Crime
WTO	World Trade Organisation

For most of the charts, the OECD *Factbook* uses ISO codes for countries

AFG	Afghanistan	**EU27**	European Union (total or average)	**MEX**	Mexico
AUS	Australia	**FIN**	Finland	**NLD**	Netherlands
AUT	Austria	**FRA**	France	**NOR**	Norway
BEL	Belgium	**G7M**	Major seven	**NZL**	New Zealand
BRA	Brazil	**GBR**	United Kingdom	**OECD**	OECD total or OECD average
CAN	Canada	**GRC**	Greece	**POL**	Poland
CHE	Switzerland	**HUN**	Hungary	**PRT**	Portugal
CHL	Chile	**IDN**	Indonesia	**PSE**	Palestinian Administrated Areas
CHN	China	**IND**	India	**RUS**	Russian Federation
CIV	Côte d'Ivoire	**IRL**	Ireland	**SDN**	Sudan
CZE	Czech Republic	**IRQ**	Iraq	**SVK**	Slovak Republic
DAC	DAC total	**ISL**	Iceland	**SVN**	Slovenia
DEU	Germany	**ISR**	Israel	**SWE**	Sweden
DNK	Denmark	**ITA**	Italy	**TUR**	Turkey
EA17	Euro area	**JPN**	Japan	**USA**	United States
ESP	Spain	**KOR**	Korea	**VNM**	Vietnam
EST	Estonia	**LUX**	Luxembourg	**WLD**	World
ETH	Ethiopia	**FIN**	Finland	**ZAF**	South Africa

StatLinks

This publication includes the unique OECD **StatLink** service, which enables users to download Excel® versions of tables and charts. **StatLinks** are provided at the bottom of each table and chart. **StatLinks** behave like Internet addresses: simply type the **StatLink** in your Internet browser to obtain the corresponding data in Excel® format.

For more information about OECD **StatLinks**, please visit: *www.oecd.org/statistics/statlink*.

Accessing OECD publications

- OECD publications cited in the *OECD Factbook* are available through OECDiLibrary (*www.oecdilibrary.org*), the OECD electronic library.
- All the OECD working papers can be downloaded from OECDiLibrary.
- All OECD databases mentioned in the book can also be accessed through OECDiLibrary.
- In addition, print editions of all OECD books can be purchased via the OECD online bookshop (*www.oecdbookshop.org*).

OECD *Glossary of Statistical Terms*

The online *OECD Glossary of Statistical Terms* (available at *www.oecd.org/statistics/glossary*) is the perfect companion for the *OECD Factbook*. It contains almost 7 000 definitions of statistical terms, acronyms and concepts in an easy to use format. These definitions are primarily drawn from existing international statistical guidelines and recommendations that have been prepared over the last few decades by organisations such as the United Nations, ILO, OECD, Eurostat, IMF and national statistical institutes.

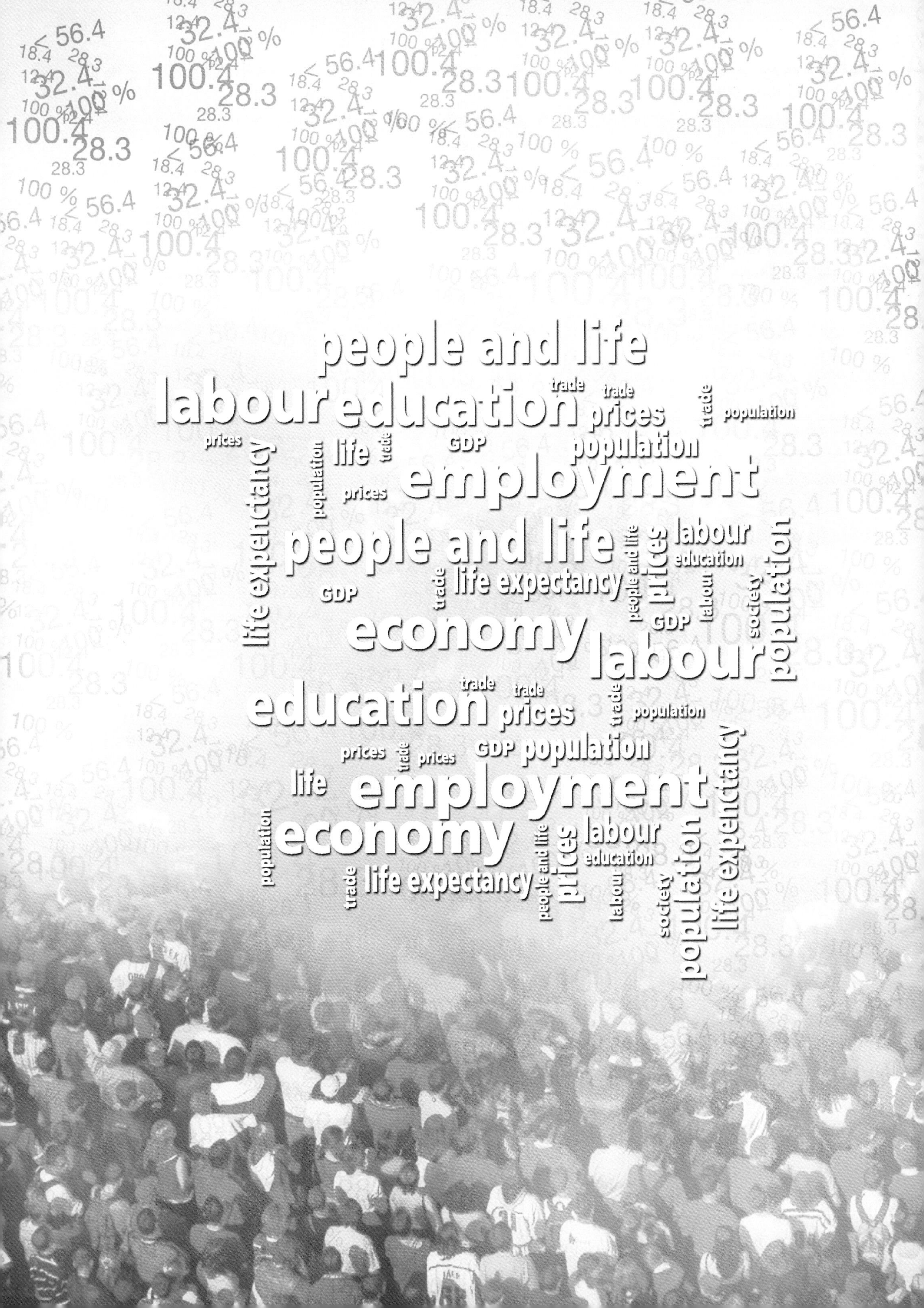

people and life
labour
education
trade
trade
prices
trade
population
prices
life
trade
GDP
population
life expectancy
population
prices
employment
people and life
people and life
prices
labour
education
GDP
trade
life expectancy
labour
society
population
economy
GDP
labour
trade
trade
education
prices
trade
population
prices
trade
prices
GDP
population
life
employment
life expectancy
population
economy
people and life
prices
labour
education
trade
life expectancy
labour
society
population

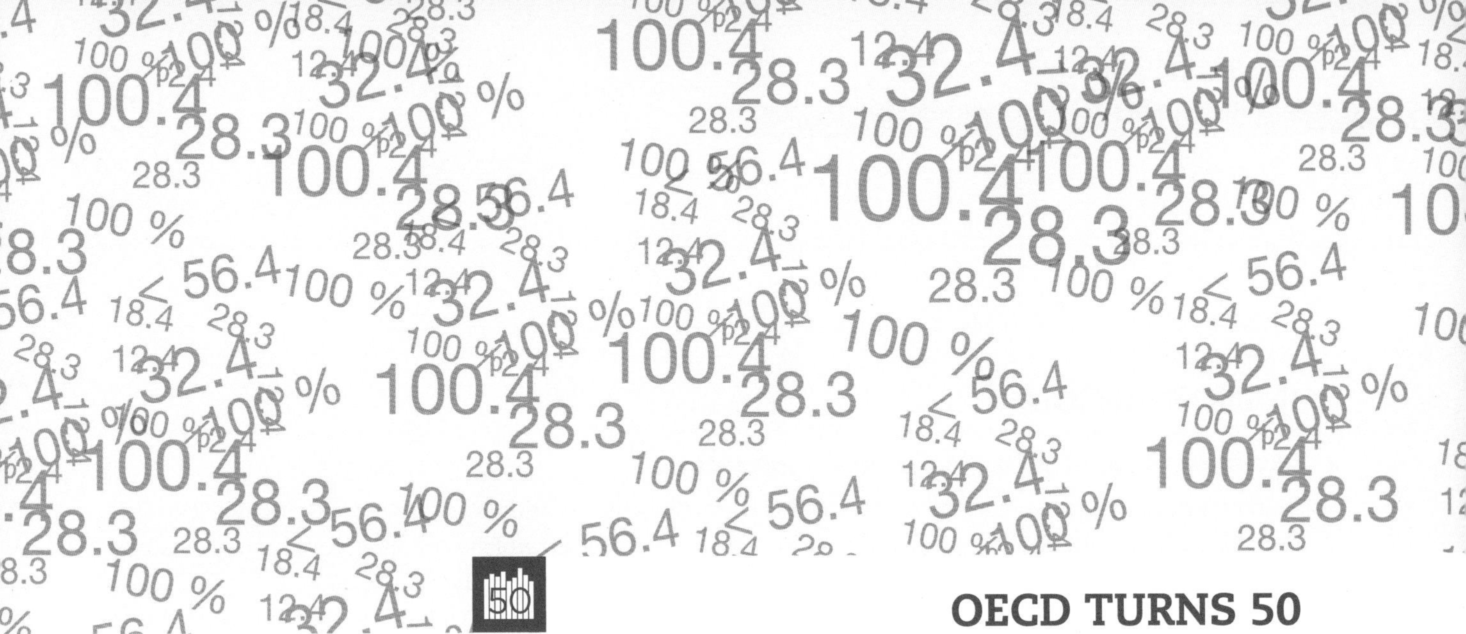

OECD TURNS 50

INTRODUCTION

OECD past and present – the importance of statistics

Statistics have always been at the heart of OECD work. Since its creation 50 years ago, the Organisation has been providing statistics to assess and benchmark the performance of its member countries. It has also been continuously pushing forward the frontiers of statistical knowledge by developing new tools to measure the economic and social challenges of the day. Over the past 50 years, the OECD has produced reliable, comparable, timely and respected statistics that lay the foundations of the policy advice provided by the Organisation to its member countries and to countries in the rest of the world. The compilation and dissemination of such statistics has brought the OECD to the forefront of international statistical providers and intrinsically linked its name with that of a trustworthy producer of statistics.

This year's "Special Focus" of the OECD Factbook is an occasion to celebrate the 50th Anniversary of the Organisation by highlighting its continuous commitment in producing high-quality, internationally-comparable statistics. This special chapter presents the evolution of selected economic and social statistics for OECD countries over the past five decades.

The structure of this chapter slightly differs from that of the rest of the publication. As most of the data presented in this special chapter are also presented (with a shorter-term perspective) in the following chapters of this publication, this special chapter does not include headings on "Definition", "Comparability" and "Overview" used elsewhere, but rather describes the key patterns highlighted by each of the indicators considered. Definitions and comparability issues surrounding these indicators can be found in the main body of the publication and further references are provided under the heading on "Sources".

Presenting consistent series of data spanning five decades is challenging, particularly for countries that joined the OECD recently, whose statistical systems were not as developed fifty years ago as they are today, or that simply did not exist then. It is also difficult due to the progressive increase in the number of OECD members, which – as shown in the Figure – increased from 19 in 1961 to 34 today. In some cases, estimates have been used to compile data for the OECD average or total, while consistent long-term series are generally available for the major seven economies, which constitute the bulk of the OECD area. In other cases, presenting consistent time-series has required making use of specific indicators, tailored to the goal of allowing long-term comparisons. This is the case for the indicator of educational attainment shown in this chapter, which draws on the data on educational attainment for different age cohorts that were included in the most recent issue of *Education at a Glance*.

Patterns highlighted by these long-term series are, by and large, well known but the size of these changes, and their different intensity among OECD countries, deserve attention. The OECD population has increased by almost half over the past 50 years, but its share in the world total has continued to shrink, and is projected to be less than 15% of the world population by 2040s. Life-expectancy at birth, the most commonly used measure of people's health conditions, has increased on average by more than 11 years since 1960 but this has also implied, in a context characterised by falling fertility rates, that the share of the dependent population, after having fallen for the past 50 years, is now rising and is expected to exceed 40% by 2040s. Many more people are completing higher education than in the past, with almost half of the cohort now aged 25 to 34 expected to attain tertiary education by the time they will reach their middle age. Over this 50-year period, international trade in both goods and services has grown exponentially, price inflation for most OECD countries is at historically low levels, and gross domestic product per capita has attained levels never reached before despite a continuous easing in its growth rate. However, with faltering GDP growth, unemployment rates for a number of countries are higher today than in the 1960s, and the share of people in paid jobs has levelled off for a number of countries since the 1970s and 1980s. The long-term perspective provided by the selected series included in this special chapter provides the common background for some of challenges that OECD countries are facing today… and in the next 50 years.

Number of OECD countries

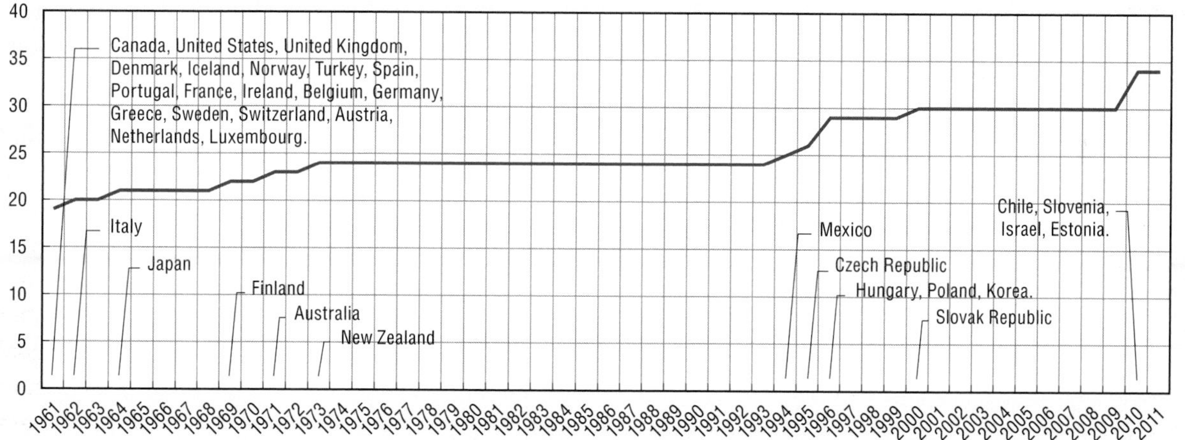

StatLink http://dx.doi.org/10.1787/888932501821

POPULATION

Population growth is measured as the difference between births, deaths and net migration. During the last 50 years population growth in the OECD area has fallen to almost zero in 2011. The world population has more than doubled over the past 50 years. Projections for the next four decades show that world population will exceed 9 billion people in the 2040s while the population for the OECD total (if the OECD remains at 34 members) will reach 1.4 billion, *i.e.* around 15% of the world total.

Looking at the variations across OECD countries, the population in Japan is expected to shrink to less than 100 million by 2040s (*i.e.* around 80% of today's level), whereas the population of the United States, after having risen by around 10% in the last decade will increase by less than 1% in the next 30 years.

Among the emerging economies, India is expected to outpace both China and the OECD area in terms of population size by 2020, reaching approximately 1.7 billion people in the 2040s. However, the overall pattern among these countries is that of declining growth rates of the population since the 1980s, which are projected to turn negative over the next 40 years in China and the Russian Federation.

Policymakers need to take into account demographic trends in order to optimise government spending, for instance, on health care or education. In this respect, beyond population size, its composition also matters. The figure on the next page shows data on the share of dependant population, where the word "dependent" refers to people aged less than 15 and over 65. In the OECD area, the share of the dependent population has been falling from around 38% in the 1960s to 33% in the 2000s. This share has been increasing in the 2010s and is projected to be close to 41% of the total population in the 2040s.

Within the OECD area, the United States has experienced a decline in its share of dependent population, followed by a flattening out at around 35% in the 2000s, and then by a ratio rising to 39% in the 2040s. In Japan, the upward trend in this share started earlier and was much steeper, with the share of the dependent population projected to be at around 47% of the total population by the 2040s. Higher shares of the dependent population are also expected in the other emerging economies with the exception of India, where this share is projected to continue to fall until at least 2050.

Sources

For more information, see:

Population and migration

- Total population
- Dependent population

Population evolution over decades

Average population levels, thousands

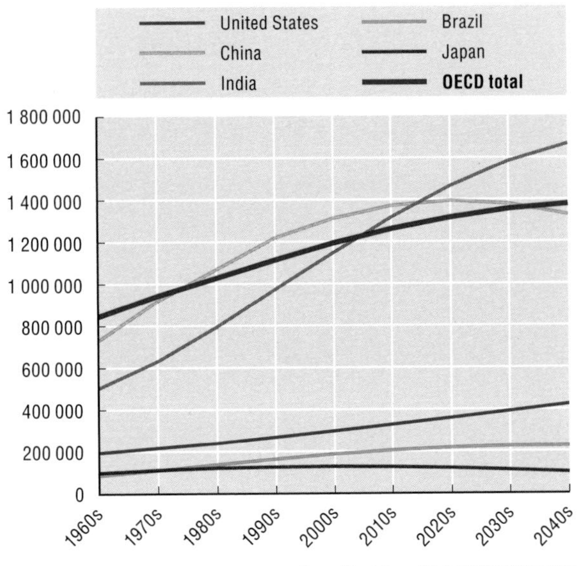

StatLink http://dx.doi.org/10.1787/888932501840

Population growth rates over decades

Average growth, percentage

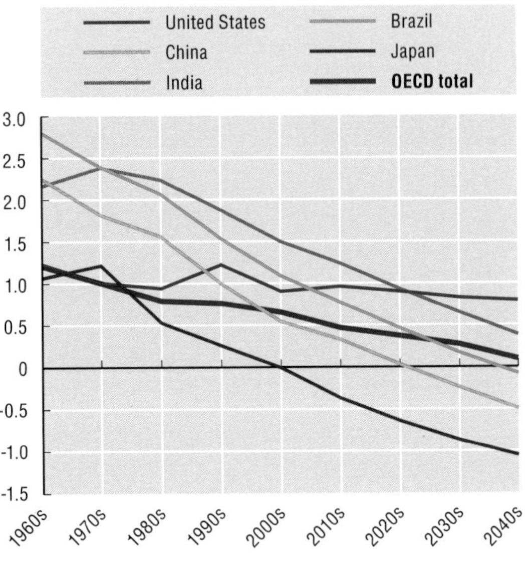

StatLink http://dx.doi.org/10.1787/888932501859

Population evolution over decades

Average population levels, thousands

	1960s	1970s	1980s	1990s	2000s	2010s	2020s	2030s	2040s
Australia	11 476	13 929	15 956	18 199	20 699	23 802	27 066	30 083	32 793
Austria	7 291	7 560	7 586	7 929	8 229	8 545	8 758	8 906	8 977
Belgium	9 457	9 789	9 882	10 141	9 458	10 697	10 914	11 026	10 964
Canada	20 231	23 248	26 106	29 415	32 485	35 129	37 740	39 880	41 367
Chile	8 723	10 473	12 240	14 453	16 341	17 916	19 150	19 908	20 181
Czech Republic	9 765	10 086	10 338	10 309	10 310	10 296	10 209	9 954	9 620
Denmark	4 774	5 059	5 123	5 245	5 438	5 539	5 638	5 690	5 653
Estonia	1 297	1 432	1 533	1 443	1 348	1 332	1 313	1 277	1 256
Finland	4 563	4 708	4 901	5 108	5 265	5 454	5 622	5 713	5 738
France	48 776	52 715	55 438	57 956	55 009	63 964	66 334	68 356	69 630
Germany	76 032	78 458	78 230	81 522	74 101	82 806	81 879	79 583	76 259
Greece	8 602	9 175	9 945	10 640	9 999	11 390	11 374	11 175	10 820
Hungary	10 173	10 556	10 612	10 309	10 085	9 929	9 717	9 356	8 921
Iceland	193	218	243	269	302	318	336	348	354
Ireland	2 881	3 196	3 513	3 637	4 185	4 592	4 949	5 220	5 423
Israel	2 613	3 488	4 276	5 618	7 009	1 732	2 040	..	..
Italy	52 247	55 434	56 600	56 859	52 686	59 096	58 611	57 708	56 454
Japan	98 815	111 866	121 093	125 599	127 575	125 047	118 796	110 127	99 910
Korea	29 042	35 535	40 936	45 236	48 364	49 239	49 031	47 535	44 260
Luxembourg	330	356	370	411	419	503	549	592	629
Mexico	45 175	59 797	76 595	92 246	104 287	112 602	118 833	122 306	122 575
Netherlands	12 353	13 693	14 564	15 497	14 673	16 625	16 897	16 990	16 863
New Zealand	2 649	3 079	3 295	3 691	4 144	4 432	4 714	4 926	5 029
Norway	3 741	4 008	4 167	4 373	4 669	4 922	5 241	5 527	5 755
Poland	31 466	34 185	37 177	38 242	38 172	37 361	36 770	35 900	34 366
Portugal	8 907	9 155	9 981	10 063	9 460	10 763	10 873	10 889	10 774
Slovak Republic	4 381	4 767	5 169	5 357	5 395	5 414	5 386	5 237	5 000
Slovenia	1 632	1 754	1 887	1 965	1 802	2 044	2 048	2 016	1 974
Spain	32 200	35 915	38 404	39 486	43 667	45 289	45 505	44 990	43 669
Sweden	7 768	8 206	8 392	8 788	9 093	9 463	9 879	10 161	10 382
Switzerland	5 864	6 294	6 508	7 025	7 493	8 148	8 587	8 833	8 951
Turkey	31 575	40 284	50 565	60 189	68 968	76 936	85 950	93 377	96 061
United Kingdom	54 397	56 186	56 664	58 115	59 991	64 757	69 025	72 573	75 650
United States	194 937	217 243	239 203	267 792	297 130	327 188	359 054	391 155	423 819
OECD total	844 328	941 851	1 027 492	1 113 127	1 193 825	1 260 223	1 314 223	1 354 611	1 377 852
Brazil	85 531	109 744	137 424	163 194	186 515	203 829	216 408	223 086	223 938
China	728 598	917 147	1 067 884	1 218 183	1 310 596	1 370 044	1 393 373	1 377 811	1 326 826
India	503 214	631 086	794 036	973 280	1 148 322	1 315 473	1 464 325	1 583 115	1 665 657
Indonesia	105 817	135 887	169 590	200 654	228 360	252 756	272 408	285 976	292 498
Russian Federation	126 656	134 735	144 108	148 247	144 070	142 023	138 684	133 525	128 535
South Africa	20 108	26 044	33 319	41 535	47 943	51 532	53 818	55 506	56 474
World	3 378 950	4 112 880	4 912 312	5 763 199	6 546 516	7 319 198	8 030 252	8 632 917	9 120 303

StatLink http://dx.doi.org/10.1787/888932501878

Share of the dependent population (people aged less than 15 and over 65)

Average percentage of the total population

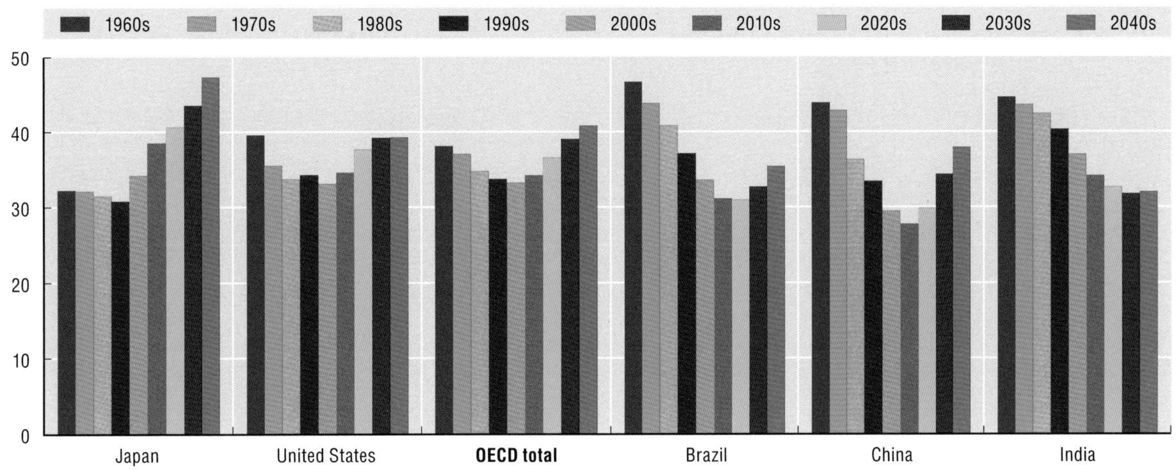

StatLink http://dx.doi.org/10.1787/888932501897

LIFE EXPECTANCY

Life expectancy at birth is one of the most widely used indicator of health status. Over the past few decades, progress in medicine, living standards and lifestyles have contributed to reduce mortality and increase the life-span that people can expect to live.

Life expectancy at birth in OECD countries has improved greatly over the past 50 years, with women and men living longer than ever before. Since 1960, life expectancy has increased on average across OECD countries by more than 11 years, reaching nearly 80 years in 2009. The increase has been particularly noticeable in those OECD countries that started with relatively low levels, such as Korea where life expectancy has increased by 28 years between 1960 and 2009. There have also been huge gains in life expectancy in Turkey and Mexico as well as in Chile, one of the countries that recently joined the OECD. Japan has also achieved large gains and is now leading the OECD league, with a life expectancy of 83 years. In 2000, only two OECD countries had a life expectancy at birth of 80 years or more; by 2009, 22 OECD countries had reached this milestone.

These gains in life expectancy reflect large declines in mortality at all ages. Infant mortality rates have declined sharply in all countries. Deaths from cardiovascular diseases (comprising mostly heart attack and stroke) have also fallen dramatically. Although cardiovascular diseases remain the leading cause of death in OECD countries, mortality rates have been cut by more than half since 1960. Falls in important risk factors for heart and cardiovascular diseases, including smoking, combined with improvements in medical treatment, have played a major role in reducing cardiovascular mortality rates.

The gender gap in life expectancy was 5.5 years, on average across OECD countries, in 2009, with average life expectancies reaching 82.2 years for women and 76.7 years for men. While this gender gap tended to widen in the 1960s and the 1970s, it has narrowed in most OECD countries since the 1980s because of stronger gains in longevity for men. This can be partly attributed to the narrowing of differences between men and woman in risk-increasing behaviours.

Sources

For more information, see:

Health

- Life expectancy

Life expectancy at birth, OECD average

Number of years

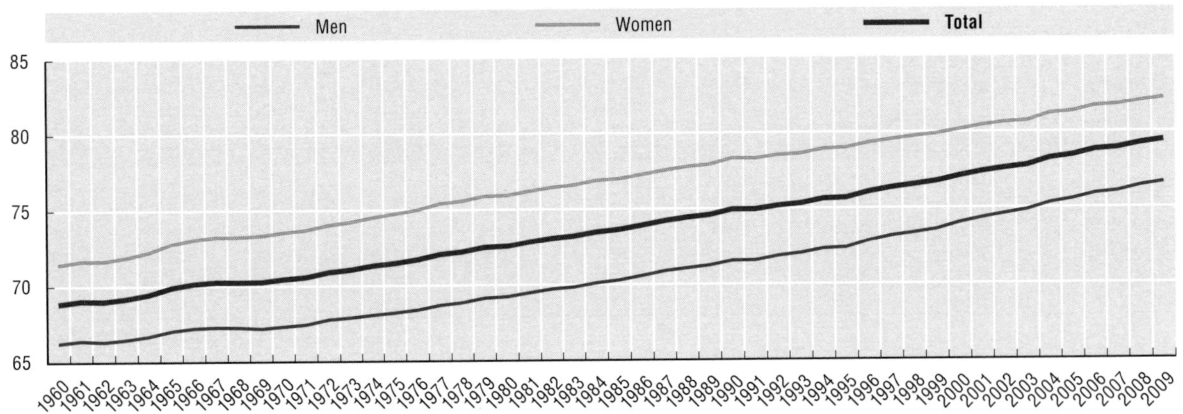

StatLink http://dx.doi.org/10.1787/888932501916

Life expectancy at birth, United States

Number of years

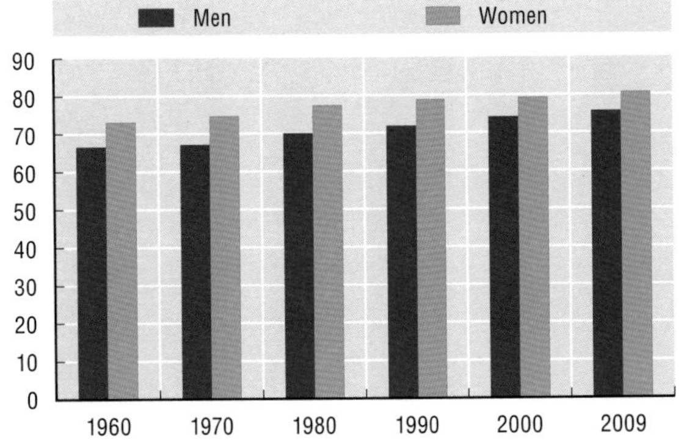

StatLink http://dx.doi.org/10.1787/888932501935

Life expectancy at birth, France

Number of years

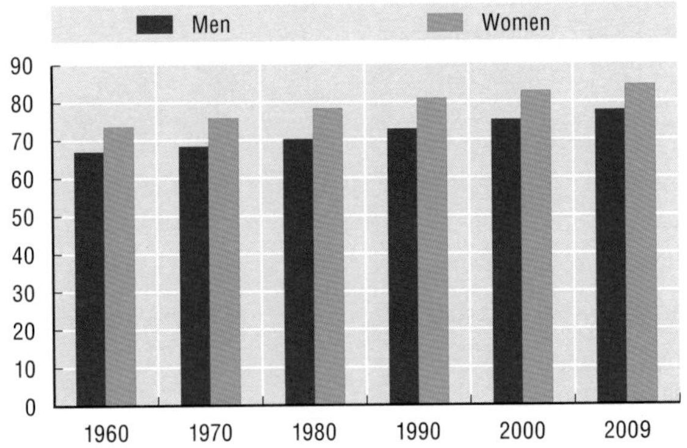

StatLink http://dx.doi.org/10.1787/888932501954

Life expectancy at birth, Germany
Number of years

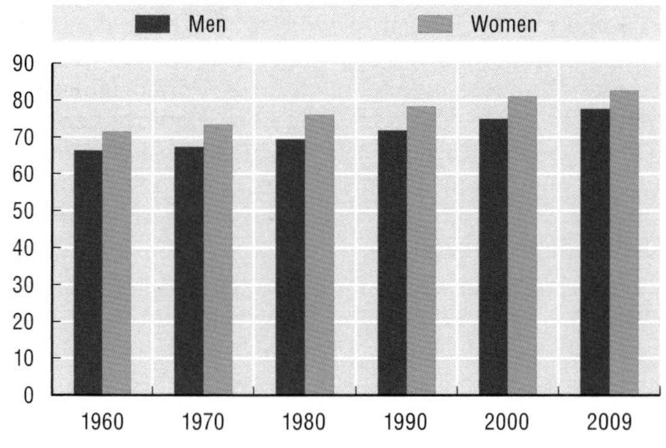

StatLink http://dx.doi.org/10.1787/888932501973

Life expectancy at birth, Japan
Number of years

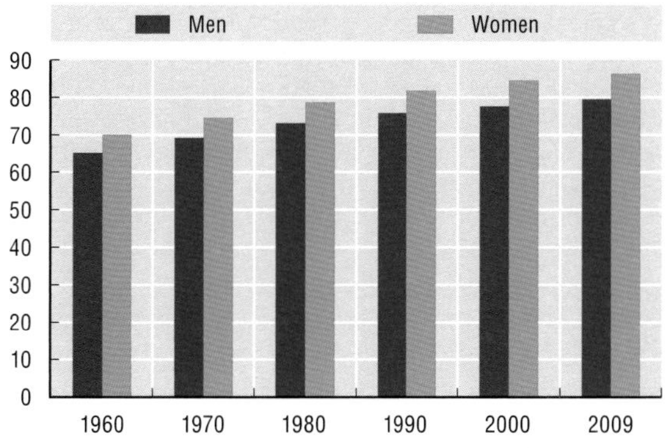

StatLink http://dx.doi.org/10.1787/888932501992

Life expectancy at birth
Number of years

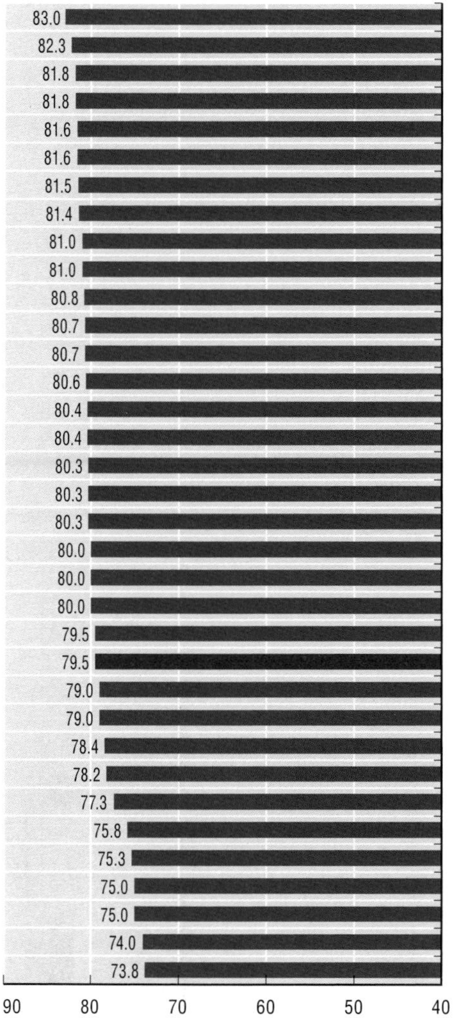

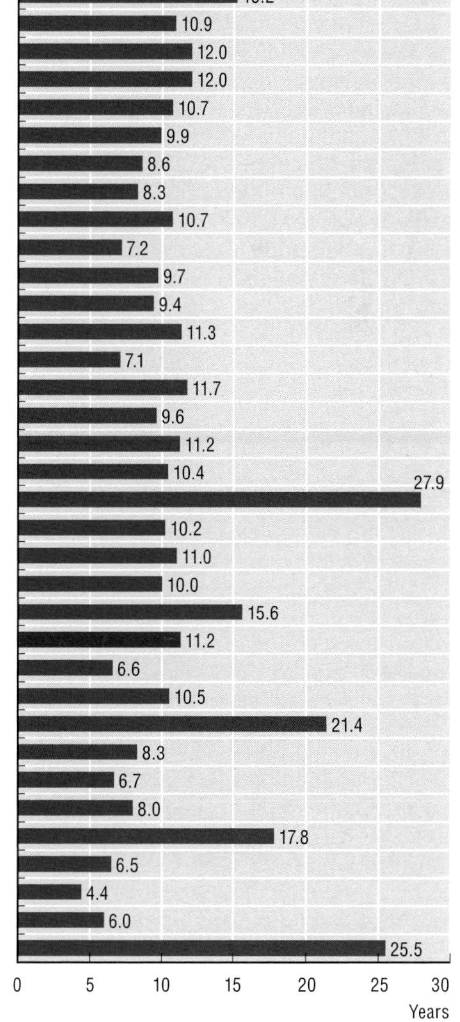

Country	Life expectancy at birth, 2009 or latest available year	Years gained, 1960-2009 or latest available year
Japan	83.0	15.2
Switzerland	82.3	10.9
Italy	81.8	12.0
Spain	81.8	12.0
Australia	81.6	10.7
Israel	81.6	9.9
Iceland	81.5	8.6
Sweden	81.4	8.3
France	81.0	10.7
Norway	81.0	7.2
New Zealand	80.8	9.7
Canada	80.7	9.4
Luxembourg	80.7	11.3
Netherlands	80.6	7.1
Austria	80.4	11.7
United Kingdom	80.4	9.6
Germany	80.3	11.2
Greece	80.3	10.4
Korea	80.3	27.9
Belgium	80.0	10.2
Finland	80.0	11.0
Ireland	80.0	10.0
Portugal	79.5	15.6
OECD average	79.5	11.2
Denmark	79.0	6.6
Slovenia	79.0	10.5
Chile	78.4	21.4
United States	78.2	8.3
Czech Republic	77.3	6.7
Poland	75.8	8.0
Mexico	75.3	17.8
Estonia	75.0	6.5
Slovak Republic	75.0	4.4
Hungary	74.0	6.0
Turkey	73.8	25.5

StatLink http://dx.doi.org/10.1787/888932502011

GDP

Gross Domestic Product (GDP) combines in a single figure the value added created by economic actors in a given economy (i.e. firms, non-profit institutions, government bodies and households) during a given period. Since its official establishment in 1961, the OECD has recorded the effects of diverse economic and financial shocks (for example due to wars, oil price movements, financial crises, etc.) on the evolution of GDP for OECD countries over these last 50 years.

Over the last five decades, the GDP growth rate for the OECD total saw the largest fluctuations during the first and the second oil shocks (1973 and 1979), the first and the second Gulf War (in the 1980s and start of the 1990s), as well as during the financial crisis in 2000 and the latest crisis that started in 2007.

Indeed, as regards the recent financial crisis, the annual growth rate for the OECD area, adjusted for inflation, registered a 3.5% fall in 2009, the largest on record, going back to 1961. Over the past five decades, the Organisation's member economies have grown at different speeds. Analysing the G7 countries presented here for example we see that Japan recorded high GDP growth rates compared to the other G7 economies from the 1960s to the mid 1980s. However, from the 1990s onwards all G7 economies saw mixed GDP growth compared to the two decades before, with all G7 economies recording lower growth in the decade of 2000s compared to the 1990s.

Comparing OECD countries with the emerging economies of Brazil, China, India, Indonesia, the Russian Federation and South Africa underlines how these countries have grown at a faster speed than the OECD average in the recent past and continue to do so throughout the recent financial crisis, unlike most of the OECD economies.

GDP per capita is often used as an indicator of a country's material living standards, and the table opposite presents a harmonised view of country GDP per capita adjusted for Purchasing Power Parities (PPPs) in US dollars. The OECD average is also included as a benchmark. For the G7 countries the table highlights that the United States has always been above the other G7 member countries and the OECD average for the last 50 years. The table shows that G7 countries saw strong growth in GDP per capita from 1970 to around 2005 when the situation levelled off somewhat and even dipped in 2009.

Looking at GDP per capita for all OECD member countries and the five selected emerging economies, there is a wide spread of material living standards as measured by GDP per capita across countries. In 2009, the lowest country is India at 3 039 USD and Luxembourg the highest at 84 848 USD (care must be paid to the result for Luxembourg as the large number of frontier workers overstate disposable income levels). Of the four new countries that joined the OECD in 2010, none were measured above the OECD average (33 023 USD) in 2009; only Israel at 27 661 USD and Slovenia at 27 462 USD come close. In 1970 only two countries ranked above the United States for GDP per capita, Luxembourg and Switzerland, while in 2009 this number had not changed but Norway replaced Switzerland.

Sources

For more information, see:

Production and income

- Size of GDP
- Evolution of GDP

OECD Gross Domestic Product

Volume, market prices

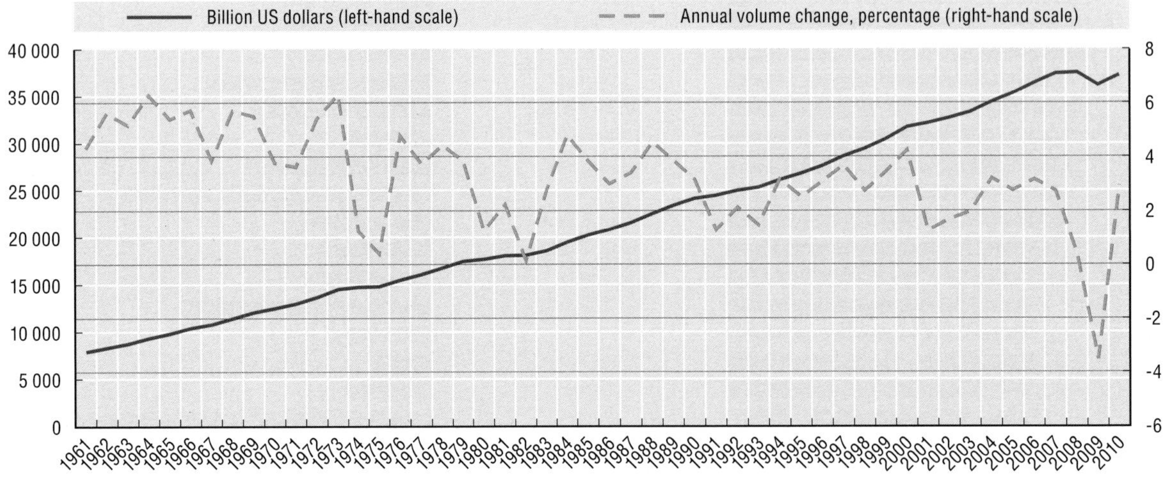

StatLink http://dx.doi.org/10.1787/888932502030

GDP per capita

US dollars, current prices and PPPs

	1970	1975	1980	1985	1990	1995	2000	2005	2006	2007	2008	2009
Australia	4 541	6 774	10 302	14 113	17 598	22 113	28 047	35 115	37 109	39 087	39 058	39 918
Austria	3 807	6 277	10 551	14 591	19 450	23 494	28 770	33 409	36 269	37 802	39 849	38 814
Belgium	3 830	6 197	10 226	13 826	18 680	22 442	27 624	32 141	34 159	35 597	36 879	36 300
Canada	4 356	6 868	11 066	15 504	19 569	22 737	28 485	35 106	36 854	38 353	38 883	37 808
Chile	..	..	..	..	..	7 460	9 294	12 194	13 036	13 897	14 568	14 321
Czech Republic	..	..	..	..	11 871	12 809	14 992	20 366	22 350	24 579	25 845	25 563
Denmark	4 216	6 194	9 959	14 719	18 455	22 984	28 822	33 196	36 026	37 731	39 494	37 680
Estonia	..	..	..	..	..	6 272	9 862	16 531	19 134	21 262	21 802	19 876
Finland	3 271	5 471	8 963	12 910	17 583	18 780	25 651	30 690	33 095	36 149	37 795	35 229
France	3 563	5 747	9 487	12 890	17 266	20 241	25 241	29 554	31 406	33 151	33 963	33 373
Germany	3 773	5 797	9 778	13 606	18 382	22 485	25 949	31 366	33 713	35 623	37 171	36 332
Greece	2 912	4 992	8 171	10 300	12 569	14 674	18 410	24 572	27 095	28 250	30 077	29 303
Hungary	..	..	..	..	..	9 014	12 134	16 938	18 329	19 187	20 700	20 275
Iceland	3 692	6 506	11 990	16 384	21 296	23 212	28 840	35 025	35 808	37 179	39 166	36 647
Ireland	2 293	3 734	6 200	8 711	12 995	17 912	28 695	38 623	42 268	45 294	42 644	39 562
Israel	..	..	..	..	..	18 909	23 496	23 390	24 960	26 583	27 679	27 661
Italy	3 386	5 299	9 206	12 872	17 589	21 104	25 594	28 144	30 224	31 898	33 269	32 413
Japan	3 109	4 983	8 387	12 897	18 913	22 537	25 608	30 312	31 865	33 577	33 805	32 018
Korea	612	1 224	2 397	4 450	8 160	12 803	17 197	22 783	24 286	26 191	26 877	27 133
Luxembourg	5 503	8 280	12 981	18 816	30 397	38 923	53 646	68 372	78 523	84 577	89 742	84 848
Mexico	1 736	2 796	4 740	6 014	6 939	7 536	10 046	12 461	13 673	14 582	15 291	14 388
Netherlands	4 014	6 240	9 867	13 140	17 623	21 544	29 406	35 111	38 064	40 744	42 887	40 804
New Zealand	4 109	6 344	8 609	12 485	14 495	17 523	21 039	25 219	27 007	28 567	29 077	29 149
Norway	3 249	5 494	9 563	14 298	17 881	23 588	36 126	47 319	53 288	55 042	60 480	54 568
Poland	..	..	..	..	5 988	7 480	10 567	13 786	15 067	16 762	18 062	18 925
Portugal	1 921	3 149	5 349	7 035	11 001	13 467	17 749	21 294	22 870	24 206	24 957	25 055
Slovak Republic	..	..	..	..	..	8 310	10 982	16 175	18 401	20 919	23 245	22 869
Slovenia	..	..	..	..	..	13 027	17 549	23 472	25 428	27 214	29 221	27 462
Spain	2 685	4 578	6 797	9 172	13 264	15 983	21 320	27 377	30 348	32 252	33 173	32 247
Sweden	4 570	7 038	10 552	14 844	19 301	21 857	27 948	32 701	35 680	38 486	39 475	37 155
Switzerland	6 326	8 895	13 796	18 741	24 439	26 613	31 618	35 478	39 116	42 756	45 586	44 840
Turkey	1 239	1 997	2 880	4 161	5 841	7 124	9 170	11 391	12 887	13 897	14 962	14 218
United Kingdom	3 558	5 390	8 349	11 949	16 315	19 709	26 071	32 724	34 971	35 719	36 817	35 151
United States	4 997	7 516	12 153	17 546	23 003	27 606	35 050	42 466	44 595	46 337	46 901	45 674
EU27 total	..	..	..	..	..	17 456	21 919	26 895	29 068	30 773	32 114	31 269
OECD total	3 411	5 263	8 531	12 091	16 252	19 482	24 359	29 562	31 516	33 133	34 002	33 023
Brazil	..	..	3 741	4 540	5 335	6 466	7 204	8 603	9 166	9 900	10 528	10 453
China	..	..	251	502	796	1 514	2 378	4 102	4 749	5 554	6 189	6 786
India	..	..	416	619	870	1 133	1 518	2 153	2 402	2 677	2 862	3 039
Indonesia	..	..	727	1 059	1 539	2 265	2 441	3 207	3 449	3 727	3 987	4 155
Russian Federation	..	..	..	..	..	5 596	6 798	11 826	14 981	16 787	20 342	19 023
South Africa	..	..	3 928	4 784	5 456	5 779	6 640	8 654	9 336	10 049	10 453	10 238

StatLink http://dx.doi.org/10.1787/888932502068

G7 GDP growth

Average annual volume change in per cent

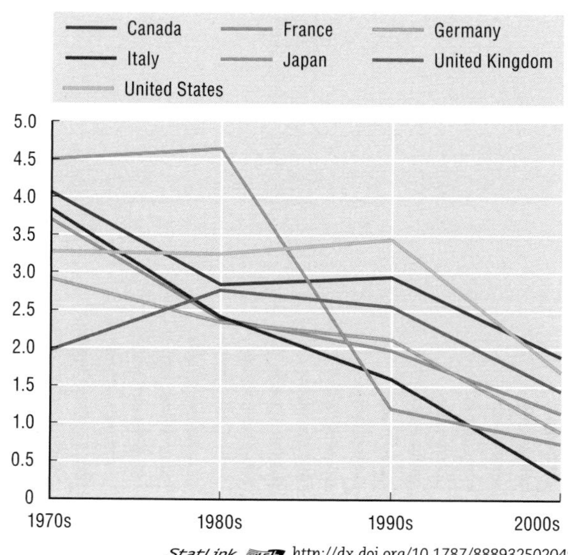

StatLink http://dx.doi.org/10.1787/888932502049

GDP growth

Average annual volume change in per cent

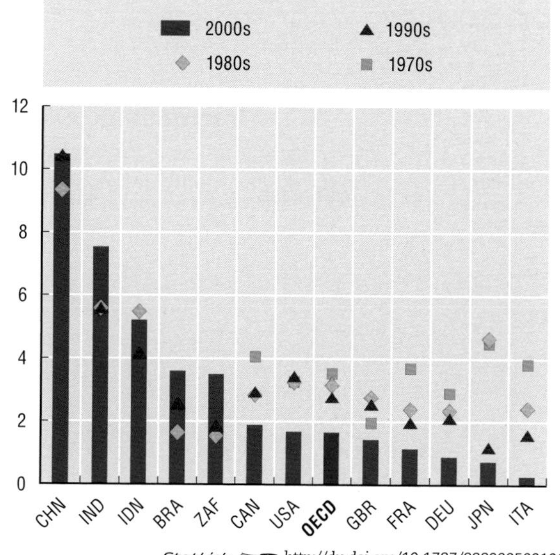

StatLink http://dx.doi.org/10.1787/888932502106

TRADE

Trade, defined as the transfer of goods and services across countries, represents a fundamental component of economic activity and is an indicator of globalisation. The progressive reduction of trade barriers over the past decades has boosted international trade and encouraged economic integration (*e.g.* in the European Union). In most OECD countries, international trade in goods and services, calculated as a share of GDP, expanded between the 1970s and the 2000s.

For example, in Ireland exports increased dramatically from 41% to 86% of GDP, and during the same period imports consistently increased, from 51% to 73% of GDP. Trade-to-GDP ratios have always been below 20% in Japan and the United States, on average from the 1970s to now. Israel and Norway are the only countries that import less now, as a percentage of GDP, than they did 50 years ago when the OECD was founded and this can most likely be explained through aid flows (for Israel) and oil wealth (for Norway). The offset to consistently increasing imports, as a percentage of GDP, for nearly all OECD countries, is the huge level of export growth as seen in the big exporting countries of China, Germany and the United States.

In general, trade in goods has constantly expanded on average in the OECD area since the Organisation's creation in the 1960s, with a period of particularly strong growth between 2001 and 2008. In 2008/2009 the financial crisis resulted in the first major decline in OECD trade, in stark contrast with the small declines recorded following the different economic shocks over the past 50 years. In comparison the decline in trade in the emerging economies, such as China for example, was much more limited after the financial crisis.

Looking at the G7 countries and average annual growth in imports and exports over the last 50 years, strong average growth rates have been recorded during the 1960s and especially in the 1970s for both exports and imports of goods. In countries like Japan and Germany, exports grew on average more than imports, except in the 1970s, leading to large trade surpluses in these countries. On the other hand, the United States has consistently experienced faster import growth than exports, resulting in a large and widening trade deficit during most of the last 50 years.

Sources

For more information, see:

Globalisation

- Share of international trade in GDP
- International trade in goods

International imports in goods and services

Average percentage of GDP over decades

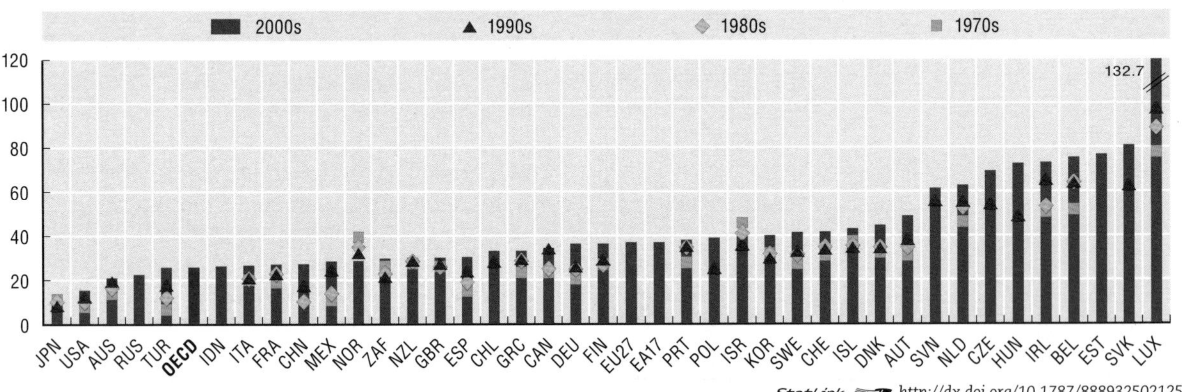

StatLink http://dx.doi.org/10.1787/888932502125

International exports in goods and services

Average percentage of GDP over decades

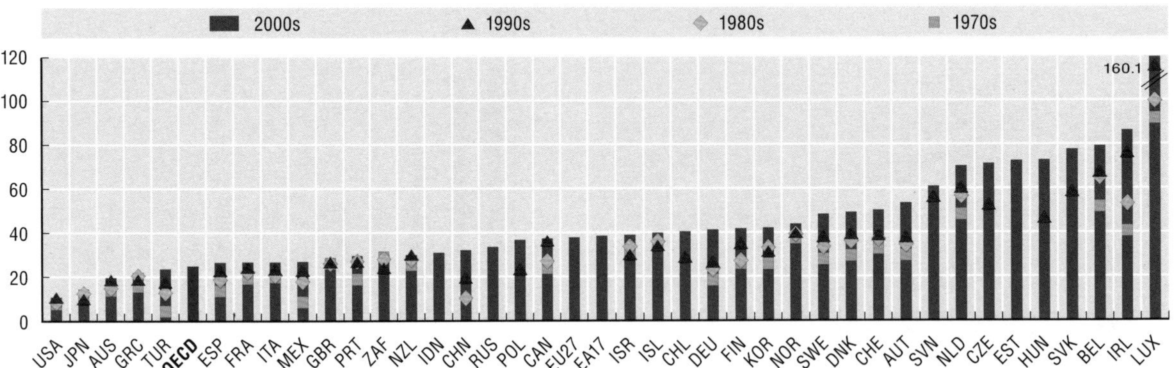

StatLink http://dx.doi.org/10.1787/888932502144

Imports and exports of goods

Billion US dollars

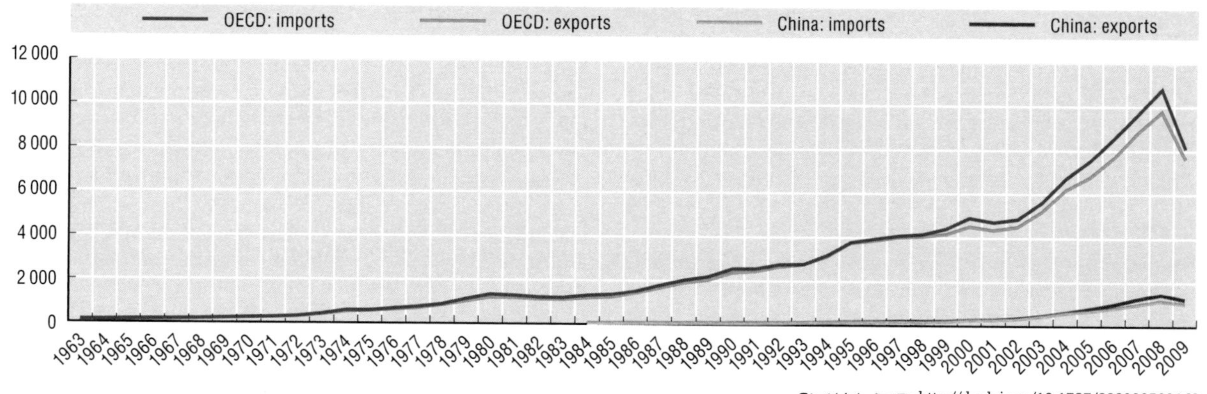

StatLink http://dx.doi.org/10.1787/888932502163

Imports and exports of goods

Average annual percentage change

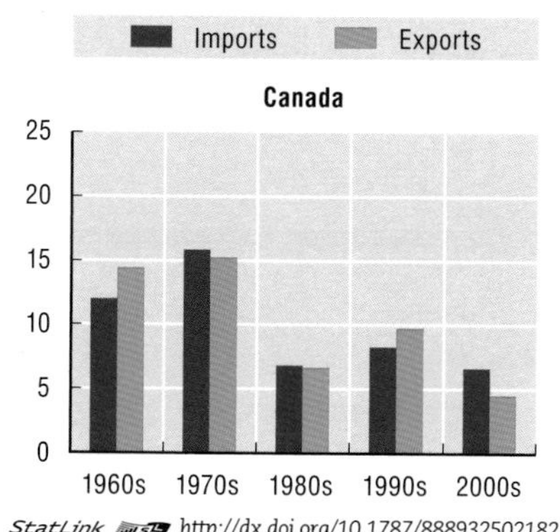

StatLink http://dx.doi.org/10.1787/888932502182

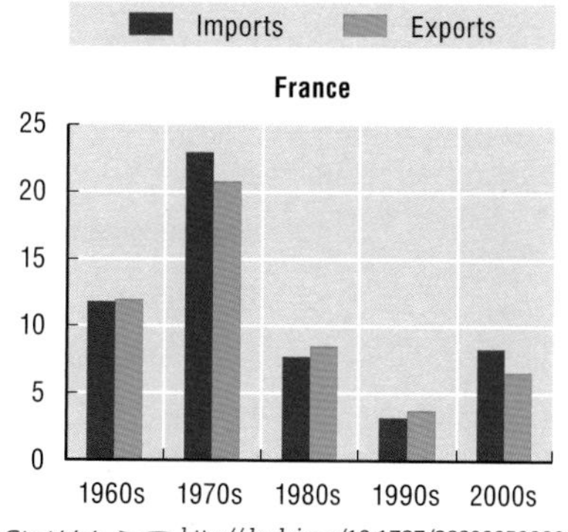

StatLink http://dx.doi.org/10.1787/888932502201

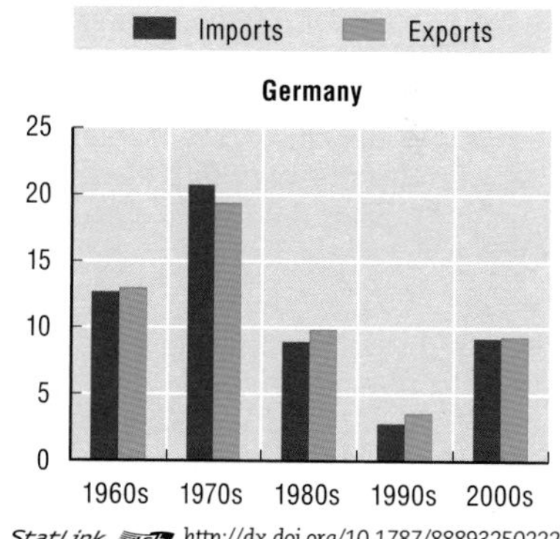

StatLink http://dx.doi.org/10.1787/888932502220

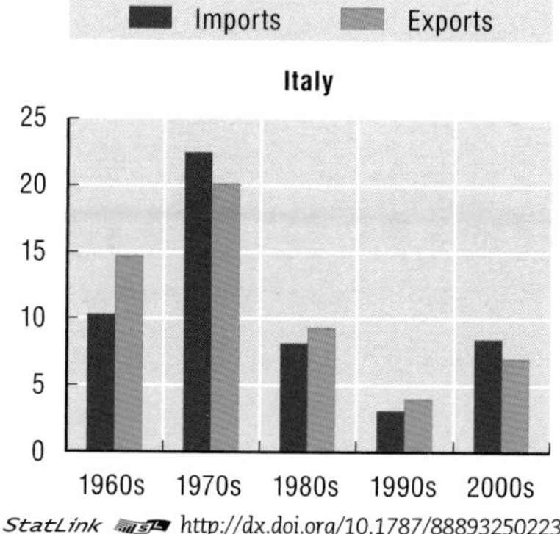

StatLink http://dx.doi.org/10.1787/888932502239

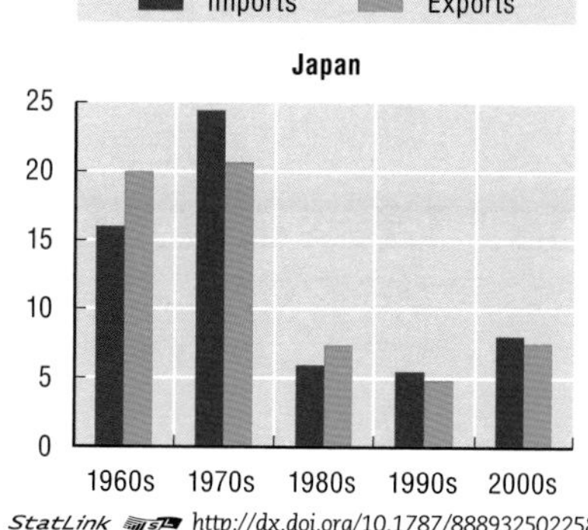

StatLink http://dx.doi.org/10.1787/888932502258

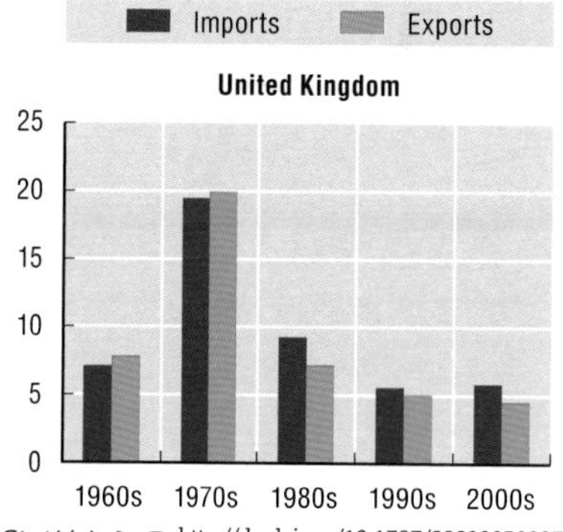

StatLink http://dx.doi.org/10.1787/888932502277

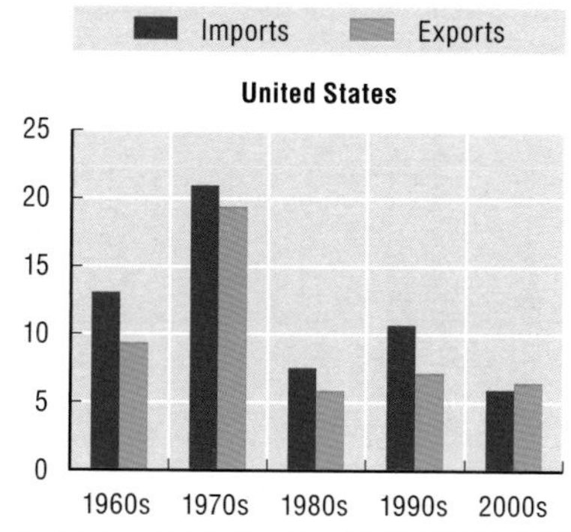

StatLink http://dx.doi.org/10.1787/888932502296

PRICES

Inflation represents the increase of the price level of goods and services over a certain period of time. In order to measure inflation for a basket of goods and services, a range of different price indices exist such as consumer price indices (CPI), producer price indices (PPI) and GDP deflators. The OECD has long contributed to the harmonised measurement of price statistics by providing a platform where countries have been able to share views and best practices on price measures.

The consumer price index (CPI) is one of the most recognisable and widely used economic indicators in the world. Compiled by measuring the price variation of a specific basket of goods and services purchased by a defined group of consumers (namely households), the CPI provides a measure of inflation that is directly relevant to the public at large.

In recent decades, inflation in most OECD countries has been at comparable levels to those seen in the 1960s. The 1970s and in particular the 1980s saw relatively high inflation rates in many OECD countries, while the 1990s witnessed a period of a return to lower inflation in most OECD countries. Some countries, notably the former transition economies such as Poland and Slovenia recorded significantly high inflation over the 1990s as they moved to market-based economies. High rates were also observed in Mexico in this period reflecting in part the Mexican Peso crisis. Similarly, the high rates for Turkey in the 2000s also in part reflect the currency crisis in the beginning of that decade.

Whereas price indices such as the CPI compare prices of a basket of products of a given country over time, Purchasing Power Parities (PPPs) compare the prices of a basket of products in a given year across countries. PPPs take the form of currency conversion rates but, unlike market exchange rates, PPPs allow meaningful comparisons of economic data in real terms across countries. A conversion with market exchange rates does not reflect differences in price levels across countries as market exchange rate are determined by many factors, for instance international capital movements.

The comparison of PPPs and market exchange rates yields a measure of comparative price levels. If market exchange rates between two countries equal PPPs, the exchange rate exactly reflects price differences between the two countries and it can be said that the two countries show the same price level. If, however, market exchange rates are different from PPPs, price levels will also be different. Because comparative price levels depend on market exchange rates, they can be subject to significant variations over time. In 1970, for example, the United Kingdom's market exchange rate was around 0.42£/US dollar whereas the PPP conversion rate was estimated at 0.26£/US dollar. By implication, the United Kingdom's relative price level compared to the United States stood at about 63%. In 2010, the British currency depreciated to about 0.65£/US dollar, close to the PPP conversion rate, implying a relative price level in 2010 that is about equal between the United Kingdom and the United States.

Sources

For more information, see:

Prices

- Consumer price indices
- Rates of conversion

CPI: all items

Annual growth in percentage

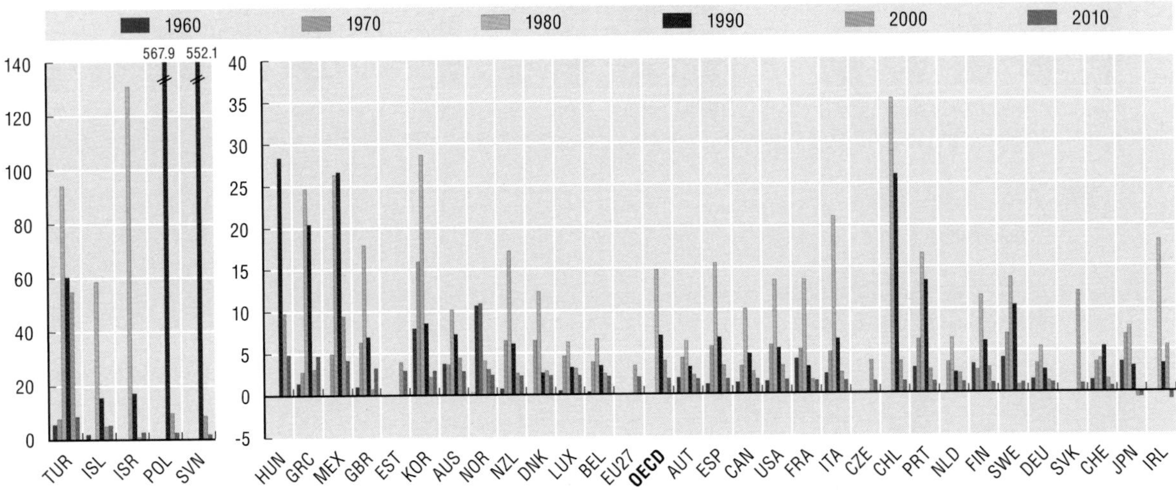

StatLink http://dx.doi.org/10.1787/888932502315

Comparative price level

PPPs to exchange rates ratio

	1970	1975	1980	1985	1990	1995	2000	2005	2006	2007	2008	2009	2010
Canada	93	107	99	89	108	89	83	100	107	113	116	105	119
France	79	115	132	74	124	131	87	115	113	122	130	122	117
Germany	71	104	120	67	118	137	89	108	105	114	119	112	108
Italy	60	75	89	60	114	94	75	108	105	112	115	108	107
Japan	64	91	109	87	131	186	144	118	107	102	113	123	127
United Kingdom	63	78	115	69	108	101	96	116	115	129	118	100.1	101
United States	100	100	100	100	100	100	100	100	100	100	100	100	100

StatLink http://dx.doi.org/10.1787/888932502334

Purchasing power parities

National currency units per US dollar

	1970	1975	1980	1985	1990	1995	2000	2005	2006	2007	2008	2009	2010
Canada	0.971	1.09	1.16	1.21	1.25	1.22	1.23	1.21	1.21	1.21	1.23	1.20	1.22
France	0.670	0.751	0.851	1.020	1.028	0.995	0.939	0.923	0.903	0.892	0.887	0.878	0.881
Germany	1.33	1.31	1.12	1.01	0.971	1.01	0.967	0.867	0.838	0.830	0.813	0.806	0.814
Italy	0.194	0.252	0.391	0.590	0.703	0.790	0.817	0.867	0.834	0.816	0.788	0.779	0.812
Japan	229	269	247	208	189	175	155	130	125	120	117	115	111
United Kingdom	0.263	0.353	0.496	0.535	0.611	0.641	0.636	0.636	0.627	0.645	0.639	0.642	0.652
United States	1	1	1	1	1	1	1	1	1	1	1	1	1

StatLink http://dx.doi.org/10.1787/888932502353

Exchange rates

National currency units per US dollar

	1970	1975	1980	1985	1990	1995	2000	2005	2006	2007	2008	2009	2010
Canada	1.048	1.017	1.169	1.365	1.167	1.372	1.485	1.212	1.134	1.074	1.067	1.143	1.030
France	0.847	0.653	0.644	1.370	0.830	0.761	1.085	0.804	0.797	0.731	0.683	0.720	0.755
Germany	1.871	1.258	0.929	1.505	0.826	0.733	1.085	0.804	0.797	0.731	0.683	0.720	0.755
Italy	0.323	0.337	0.442	0.986	0.619	0.841	1.085	0.804	0.797	0.731	0.683	0.720	0.755
Japan	360.00	296.79	226.74	238.54	144.79	94.06	107.77	110.22	116.30	117.75	103.36	93.57	87.78
United Kingdom	0.417	0.452	0.430	0.779	0.563	0.634	0.661	0.550	0.543	0.500	0.544	0.642	0.647
United States	1	1	1	1	1	1	1	1	1	1	1	1	1

StatLink http://dx.doi.org/10.1787/888932502372

Consumer prices

Average annual growth in percentage over decades

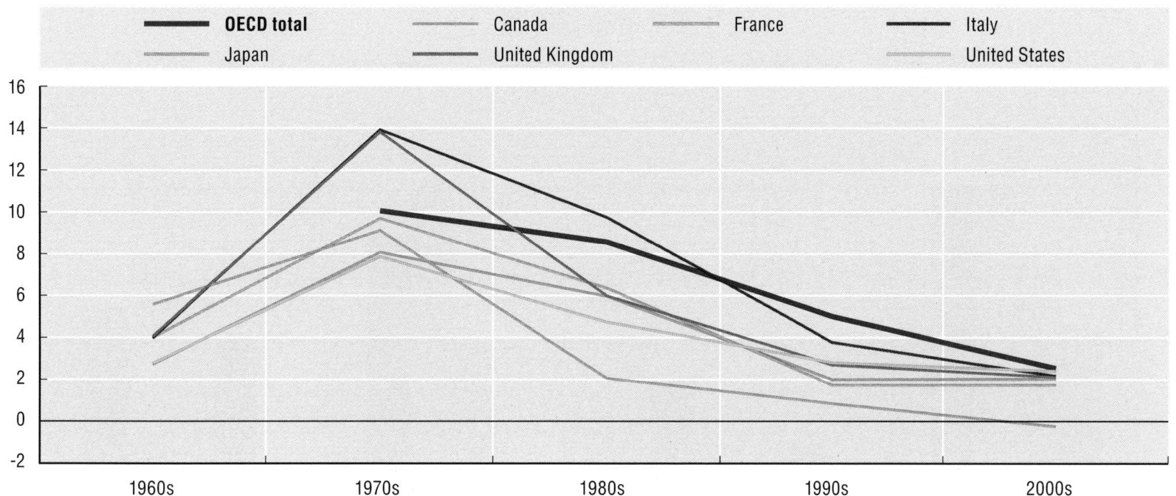

StatLink http://dx.doi.org/10.1787/888932502391

LABOUR

Labour is one of the most important aspects influencing our daily lives and well-being. Indeed, people spend a large part of their lives at work, with earnings representing the main source of their sustenance and the workplace also being a site where individuals socially interact.

Unemployment rates, one of the most commonly used indicators of the labour market, is computed as the percentage of the labour force without work but who is actively searching for jobs and currently available for work. When looking at the major OECD countries, long-term patterns differ significantly among countries. Japan, for example, recorded growing unemployment rates over the last five decades, even though its level is still below that attained by Canada, the United Kingdom and the United States. In the United States, conversely, the unemployment rate has increased in the 1960s, 1970s and 1980s, reaching an historical peak of more than 10%, and then declined in the 1990s and in the early 2000s, followed by a dramatic rise since the onset of the jobs crisis in late 2007.

In the selected OECD countries presented here, unemployment rates for women have evolved over the past 50 years in a way that mirror those for men. One noticeable feature highlighted by the data shown here is that the unemployment rate for men have tended to become higher than that of woman during the 2000s. This pattern is particularly noticeable for the United States but is also visible in Japan, Canada and the United Kingdom.

A complementary indicator of labour market conditions is provided by the employment rates, *i.e.* the percentage of the working age population having a paid job. In all of the countries shown here, the general pattern is one of rising employment rates for women accompanied by stable or declining rates for men. As a result of these patterns, the gap in employment rates between women and men has been falling over the past four decades in all the countries presented here, although remaining significant in most of them. For instance, in Italy the gap between the employment rate of women and that of men has almost halved over the last 40 years, from 46 percentage points in the 1970s to 24 points in the 2000s. The same pattern can be observed in the other countries presented here. For example, in Canada this gender gap has halved between the 1970s and the 2000s, narrowing such gap to the lowest level among the countries shown here.

Sources

For more information, see:

Labour

- Employment rates
- Unemployment rates

Average unemployment rates: total

Percentage

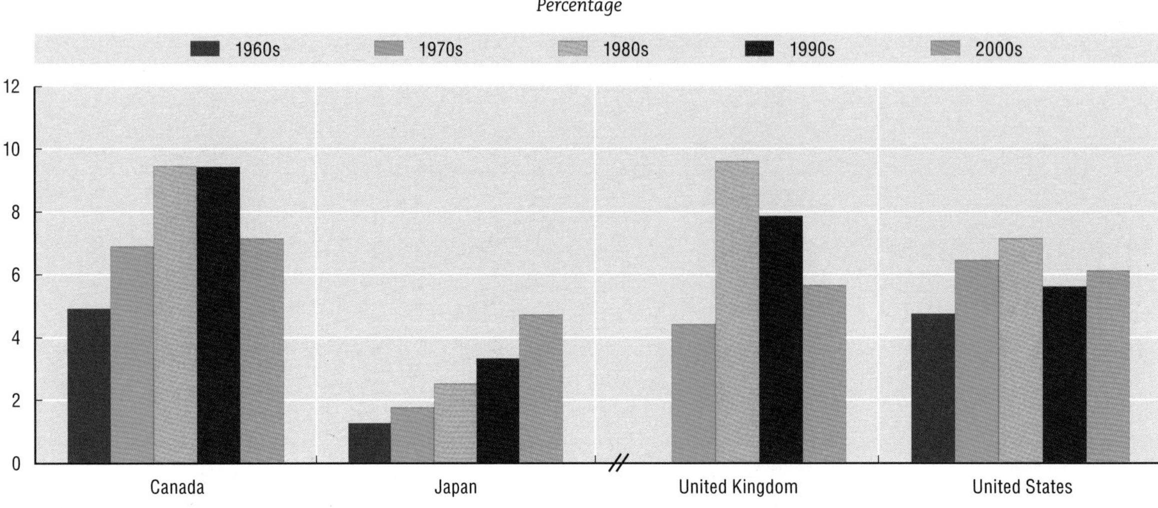

StatLink http://dx.doi.org/10.1787/888932502410

Average unemployment rates, Canada

Percentage

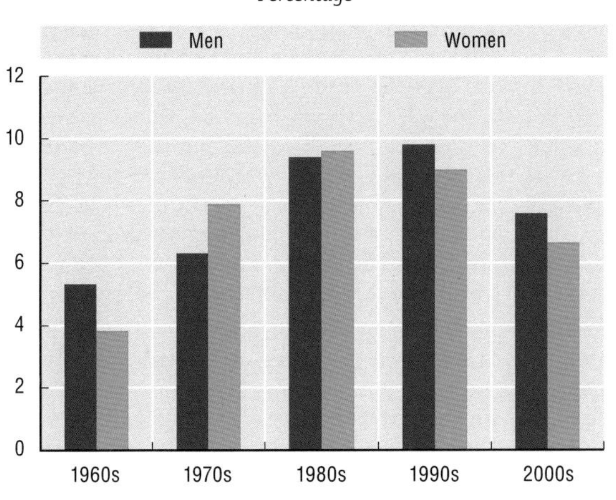

StatLink http://dx.doi.org/10.1787/888932502429

Average unemployment, Japan

Percentage

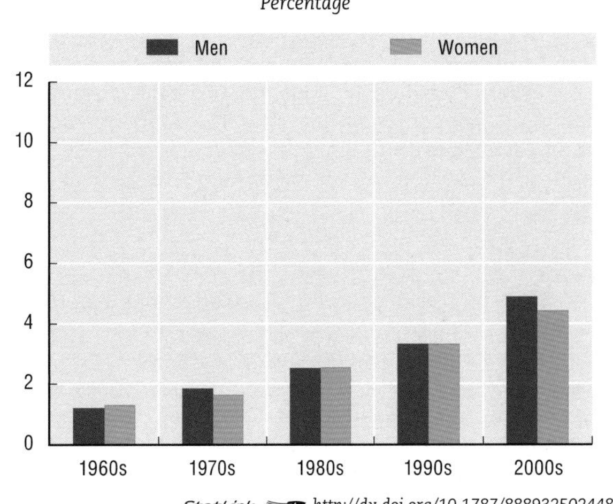

StatLink http://dx.doi.org/10.1787/888932502448

Average unemployment, United Kingdom

Percentage

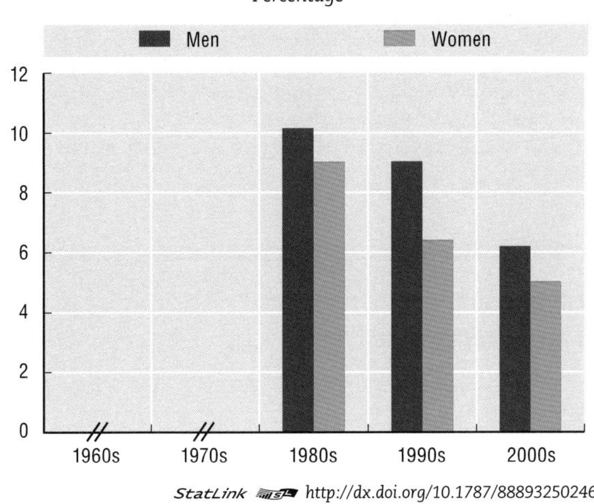

StatLink http://dx.doi.org/10.1787/888932502467

Average unemployment, United States

Percentage

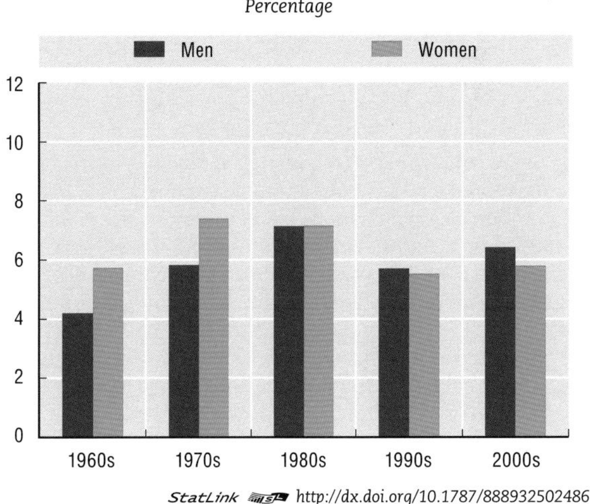

StatLink http://dx.doi.org/10.1787/888932502486

Average employment rates: share of persons of working age in employment

Percentage

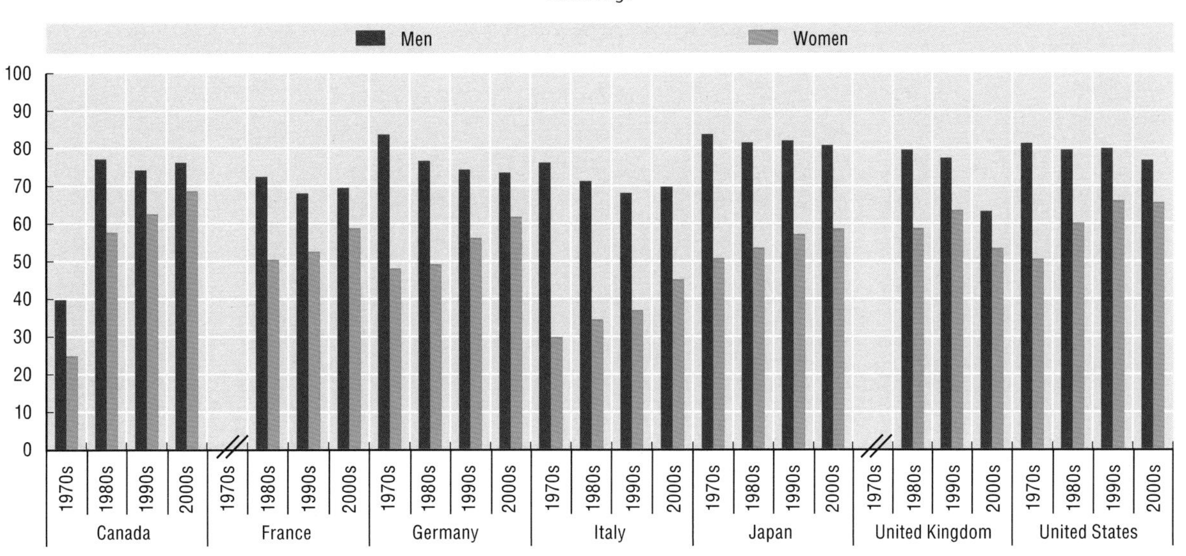

StatLink http://dx.doi.org/10.1787/888932502505

EDUCATION

In the last 50 years, OECD countries have transformed their views on educational outcomes, moving past the simplistic "more is better" approach to one that takes into account the quality of the competencies that the students acquire during their education. Since its inception, the OECD has emphasised the role of education and human capital in helping to drive both economic and social development. This focus has seen the pool of human capital expand and develop significantly in OECD countries since 1961.

Measuring changes in educational qualifications over time is not easy, as data on educational attainment was not sufficiently standardised until the 1990s. However, age-based attainment levels can be used to estimate how many people earned education qualifications over their lifetimes. For example, the number of people aged 55-64 who have a degree can be used as proxy for the number of people who graduated three or four decades ago. This method somewhat overestimates the qualification rates among older compared to younger groups of people, because it measures the attainment of the former group after those individuals have had a chance to acquire qualifications later in life. However, now that consistent attainment data have existed for over a decade, it is possible to control for this "lifelong learning" effect by comparing the qualifications held by the same cohort at different times during their lives.

The figure below presents estimates of the long-term changes in educational qualifications based on this method. It provides information on qualifications held by adults born as far apart as 1933 (now aged 78) and 1984 (now aged 27), with each year shown representing an age cohort in a ten-year period starting with that year (*e.g.* 1933 represents people born from 1933 to 1942, and 1975 represents people born from 1975 to 1984). The oldest adults among them (those aged 78 in 2011) completed their initial education in the 1950s, the youngest adults (those aged 27) in the 2000s. These data show that the rise in educational attainment at both the upper secondary level (upper line) and at the tertiary level (lower line) has been large and continuous over the entire half-century. On average, the proportion of people with at least an upper secondary education has risen from 45% to 81%, and the proportion of those with tertiary qualifications from 13% to 37%. The figure implies that, if people now aged 25-34 (37% of whom already have tertiary qualifications) make the progress seen to date in the next two decades, half of this cohort could have tertiary qualifications by the time they reach their middle age.

Information about changes in educational attainment across countries is provided by the figure on the next page, which shows progress in the share of people having attained upper secondary education, with countries grouped in three panels based on the attainment level achieved in the earlier period ("high" attainment, in the upper panel, "medium" attainment in the central panel, and "low attainment" in the lower panel). The figure shows that gains in educational attainment at the upper secondary level have been stronger in countries starting from low levels in the initial year (*e.g.* Korea), and weaker in those starting from higher levels (*e.g.* the United States). It is also significant that countries in which college enrolment expanded the most over the past decades still see rising earnings differentials for college graduates, suggesting that an increase in the supply of highly educated workers does not lead to a decrease in their pay, as is the case among low-skilled workers.

Sources

For more information, see:

Education

- Education attainment

Educational attainment by age and birth cohort, OECD average

Percentage

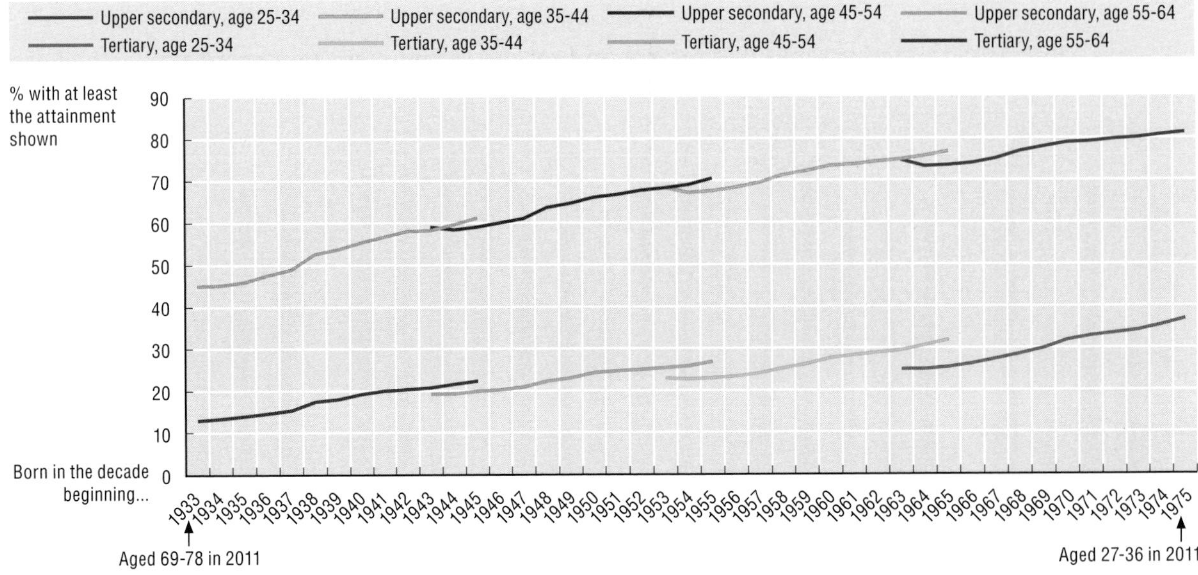

StatLink http://dx.doi.org/10.1787/888932502524

Progress in attainment of upper secondary education over half a century

Historically high attainment, percentage

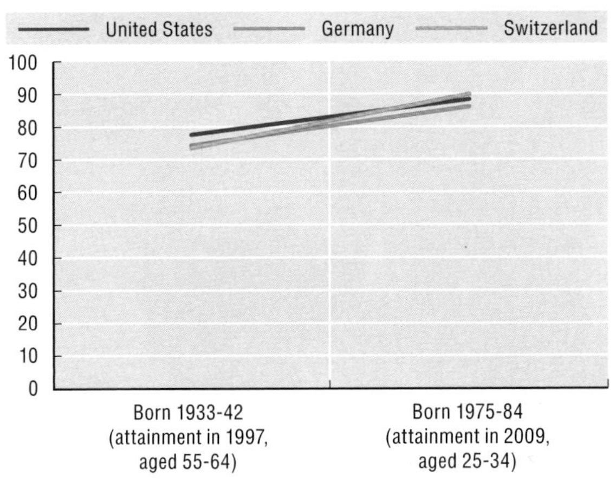

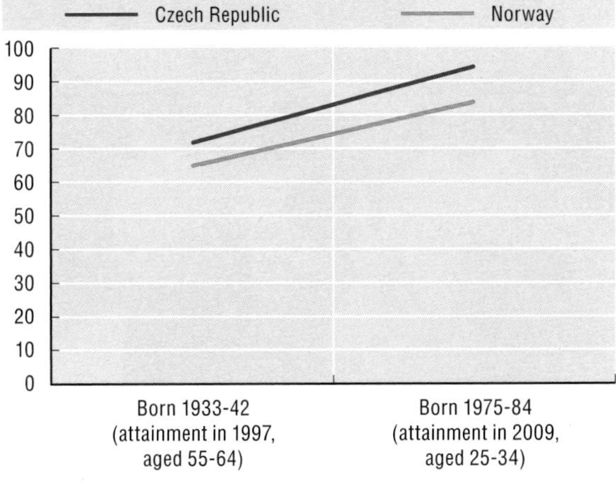

StatLink http://dx.doi.org/10.1787/888932502543

Progress in attainment of upper secondary education over half a century

Historically medium attainment, percentage

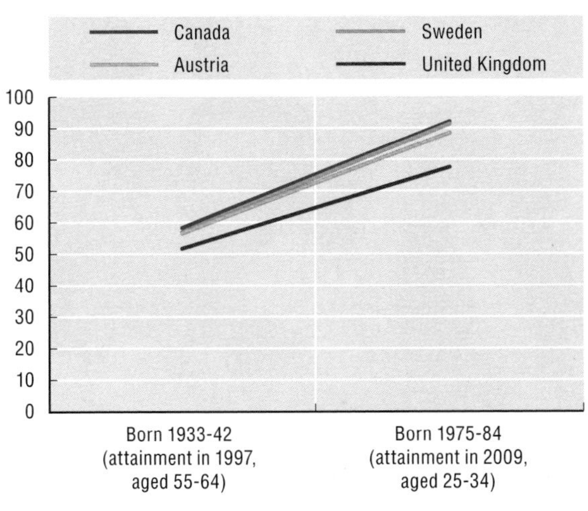

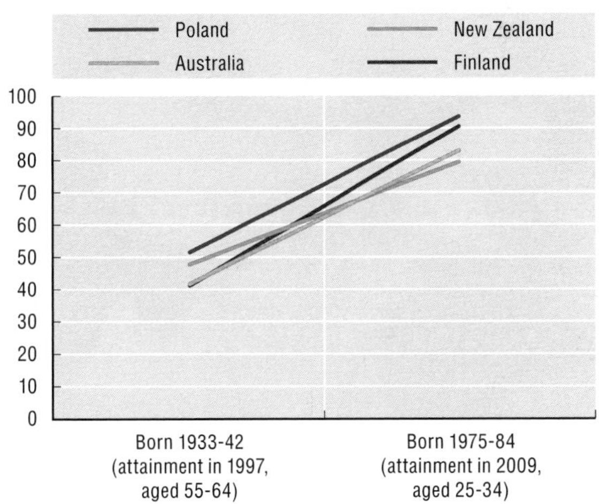

StatLink http://dx.doi.org/10.1787/888932502562

Progress in attainment of upper secondary education over half a century

Historically low attainment, percentage

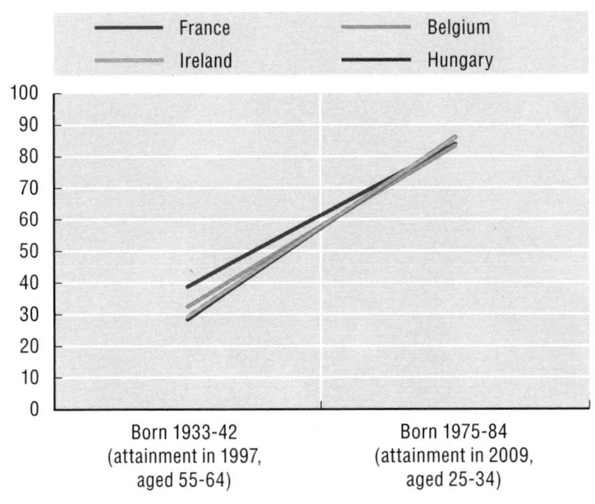

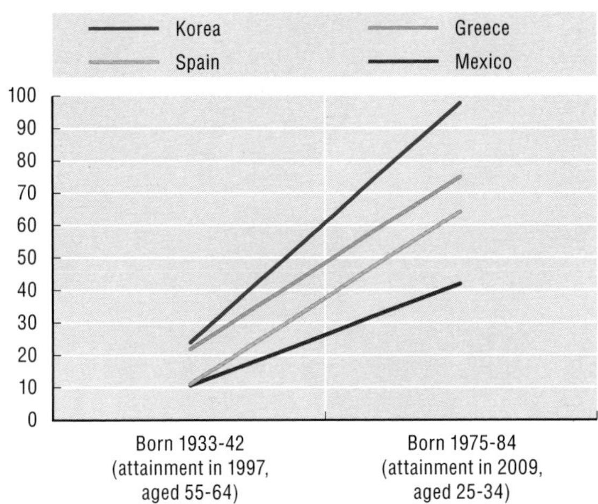

StatLink http://dx.doi.org/10.1787/888932502581

POPULATION AND MIGRATION

POPULATION

TOTAL POPULATION

DEPENDENT POPULATION

POPULATION BY REGION

ELDERLY POPULATION BY REGION

INTERNATIONAL MIGRATION

IMMIGRANT POPULATION

TRENDS IN MIGRATION

MIGRATION AND EMPLOYMENT

MIGRATION AND UNEMPLOYMENT

TOTAL POPULATION

The size and growth of a country's population are both causes and effects of economic and social developments. The pace of population growth has slowed in all OECD countries.

Definition

Data refer to the resident population. For countries with overseas colonies, protectorates or other territorial possessions, their populations are generally excluded. Growth rates are the annual changes in the population resulting from births, deaths and net migration during the year.

The total fertility rate is the total number of children that would be born to each woman if she were to live to the end of her child-bearing years and give birth to children in agreement with the prevailing age-specific fertility rates.

Comparability

For most OECD countries, population data are based on regular, ten-yearly censuses, with estimates for intercensal years derived from administrative data. In several European countries, population estimates are based entirely on administrative records. Population data are fairly comparable.

For some countries the population figures shown here differ from those used for calculating GDP and other economic statistics on a per capita basis, although differences are normally small.

Population projections are taken from national sources where these are available, but for some countries they are based on UN or Eurostat projections; the projection for the world comes from UN. All population projections require assumptions about future trends in life expectancy, fertility rates and migration. Often, a range of projections is produced using different assumptions about these future trends. The estimates shown here correspond to the median or central variant.

Overview

In 2010, OECD countries accounted for 18% of the world's population of 6.9 billion. China accounted for 19% and India for 18%. Within the OECD, in 2009, the United States accounted for 25% of the OECD total, followed by Japan (10%), Mexico (9%), Germany (7%) and Turkey (6%).

In the three years to 2010, growth rates above the OECD population average (0.6% per year) were recorded in Israel, Mexico and Turkey (high birth rate countries) and in Australia, Canada, Chile, Korea, Luxembourg, Norway, Spain, Sweden, Switzerland, and the United States (high net immigration). New Zealand and Ireland also recorded population growth rates above the OECD total which can be attributed to both a birth rate equal to the replacement rate and a positive net migration rate. In Japan, Hungary and Germany, populations declined mostly due to low birth rates. Growth rates were very low, although still positive, in Estonia, Poland, Portugal, the Slovak Republic, and Slovenia. The population of OECD countries is expected to grow by less than 0.2 per cent per year until 2050.

Total fertility rates in OECD countries have declined dramatically over the past few decades, falling on average from 2.7 in 1970 to 1.6 children per woman of childbearing age in the 2000s. In all OECD countries, fertility rates declined for young women and increased at older ages. A modest recovery in total fertility rates started in 2002, to an average level of 1.7 in 2009. In 2009, the total fertility rate was below its replacement level of 2.1 in all OECD countries except Iceland, Ireland, Israel, New Zealand, and Turkey.

Sources

- For OECD member countries: National Sources, United Nations and Eurostat.
- For Brazil, China, India, Indonesia, the Russian Federation and South Africa: Population Division of the Department of Economic and Social Affairs of the United Nations Secretariat, *World Population Prospects: The 2010 Revision*, United Nations, New York.
- Fertility rates: OECD (2011), *Society at a Glance: OECD Social Indicators*, OECD Publishing.

Further information

Analytical publications

- Bagnoli, P., T. Goeschl and E. Kovacs (2008), *People and Biodiversity Policies: Impacts, Issues and Strategies for Policy Action*, OECD Publishing.
- OECD (2011), *Doing Better for Families*, OECD Publishing.

Statistical publications

- Maddison, A. (2003), *The World Economy: Historical Perspectives*, Development Centre Studies, OECD Publishing.
- OECD (2011), *Society at a Glance: OECD Social Indicators*, OECD Publishing.

Methodological publications

- d'Addio, A.C. and M.M. d'Ercole (2005), "Trends and Determinants of Fertility Rates: The Role of Policies", *OECD Social Employment and Migration Working Papers*, No. 27.
- OECD (2011), *Labour Force Statistics*, OECD Publishing.

Online databases

- *OECD Employment and Labour Market Statistics.*
- *United Nations World Population Prospects.*

Websites

- Doing better for families (supplementary material), *www.oecd.org/social/family/doingbetter.*
- OECD Family Database, *www.oecd.org/els/social/family/database.*
- World Bank – World Development Indicators, *http://data.worldbank.org/indicator.*

Population levels

Thousands

	1999	2000	2001	2002	2003	2004	2005	2006	2007	2008	2009	2010	2020	2050
Australia	18 926	19 153	19 413	19 651	19 895	20 127	20 395	20 698	21 015	21 499	21 955	22 342	25 288	33 959
Austria	7 992	8 012	8 042	8 082	8 118	8 169	8 225	8 268	8 301	8 337	8 363	8 388	8 651	8 986
Belgium	10 226	10 251	10 287	10 333	10 376	10 421	10 479	10 548	10 626	10 710	10 796 |	..	10 801	10 897
Canada	30 401	30 686	31 019	31 354	31 640	31 941	32 245	32 576	32 930	33 316	33 720	34 109	36 344	41 896
Chile	15 197	15 398	15 572	15 746	15 919	16 093	16 267	16 433	16 598	16 763	16 929	17 094	18 549	20 205
Czech Republic	10 283	10 273	10 224	10 201	10 202	10 207	10 234	10 267	10 323	10 430	10 491	10 517	10 287	9 457
Denmark	5 319	5 337	5 355	5 374	5 387	5 401	5 416	5 435	5 457	5 489	5 519	5 544	5 582	5 621
Estonia	1 376	1 370	1 364	1 359	1 354	1 349	1 346	1 344	1 342	1 341	1 340	1 340	1 328	1 250
Finland	5 165	5 176	5 188	5 201	5 213	5 228	5 246	5 266	5 289	5 313	5 339	5 363	5 538	5 747
France	58 677	59 062	59 476	59 894	60 304	60 734	61 182	61 597	61 965	62 304	62 636 |	..	65 102	69 993
Germany	82 100	82 212	82 350	82 488	82 534	82 516	82 469	82 376	82 266	82 110	81 902 |	..	82 635	74 422
Greece	10 883	10 917	10 950	10 988	11 024	11 062	11 104	11 149	11 193	11 237	11 283 |	..	11 426	10 605
Hungary	10 238	10 211	10 188	10 159	10 130	10 107	10 087	10 071	10 050	10 038	10 023	10 000	9 856	8 718
Iceland	277	281	285	288	289	293	296	304	311	319	319	318	327	355
Ireland	3 742	3 790	3 847	3 917	3 980	4 045	4 134	4 240	4 339	4 422	4 459	4 471	4 774	5 482
Israel	6 125	6 289	6 439	6 570	6 690	6 809	6 930	7 054	7 180	7 309	7 486	7 619	9 022	..
Italy	56 916	56 942	56 977	57 157	57 605	58 175	58 607	58 942	59 375	59 832	60 193 |	..	59 001	55 710
Japan	126 686	126 926	127 291	127 435	127 619	127 687	127 768	127 770	127 771	127 692	127 510	..	122 735	95 152
Korea	46 617	47 008	47 357	47 622	47 859	48 039	48 138	48 297	48 456	48 607	48 747	50 516	49 326	42 343
Luxembourg	430	436	442	446	452	458	465	473	480	484	494 |	..	523	644
Mexico	97 115	98 439	99 716	100 909	102 000	103 002	103 947	104 874	105 791	106 683	107 551	108 396	115 762	121 856
Netherlands	15 812	15 926	16 046	16 149	16 225	16 282	16 320	16 346	16 382	16 446	16 530	..	16 762	16 789
New Zealand	3 835	3 858	3 881	3 949	4 027	4 088	4 134	4 185	4 228	4 269	4 316	4 368	4 565	5 046
Norway	4 462	4 491	4 514	4 538	4 565	4 592	4 623	4 661	4 709	4 768	4 829	4 889	5 061	5 854
Poland	38 270	38 256	38 251	38 232	38 195	38 180	38 161	38 132	38 116	38 116	38 153	38 187	37 038	33 576
Portugal	10 172	10 226	10 293	10 368	10 441	10 502	10 549	10 584	10 608	10 622	10 632 |	..	10 832	10 674
Slovak Republic	5 395	5 401	5 380	5 379	5 379	5 383	5 387	5 391	5 398	5 407	5 418	5 431	5 417	4 880
Slovenia	1 982	1 985	1 988	1 991	1 994	1 997	2 001	2 005	2 010	2 015	2 020	..	2 053	1 954
Spain	39 927	40 264	40 721	41 314	42 005	42 692	43 398	44 068	44 874	45 593	45 929	46 073	45 568	42 703
Sweden	8 858	8 872	8 896	8 925	8 958	8 994	9 030	9 081	9 148	9 220	9 299	9 379	9 658	10 490
Switzerland	7 144	7 184	7 227	7 285	7 339	7 390	7 437	7 484	7 551	7 648	7 744	7 822	8 379	8 981
Turkey	63 366	64 259	65 135	66 009	66 873	67 734	68 582	69 421 |	70 256	71 079	71 897	72 698	80 257	96 496
United Kingdom	58 684	58 886	59 113	59 323	59 557	59 846	59 402	59 744	60 124	60 520	60 930	61 349	66 754	76 959
United States	279 040	282 166	285 050	287 746	290 242	292 936	295 619	298 432	301 394	304 177	306 656	309 051	341 387	439 010
OECD total	1 141 640	1 149 942	1 158 276	1 166 381	1 174 389	1 182 480	1 189 624	1 197 515 |	1 205 856	1 214 115	1 221 410 |	1 228 199	1 286 590	1 383 862
Brazil	171 936	174 425	176 877	179 289	181 633	183 873	185 987	187 958	189 798	191 543	193 247	194 947	210 433	222 843
China	1 259 477	1 269 117	1 277 904	1 285 934	1 293 397	1 300 552	1 307 594	1 314 581	1 321 482	1 328 276	1 334 909	1 341 335	1 387 792	1 295 604
India	1 036 259	1 053 898	1 071 374	1 088 694	1 105 886	1 122 991	1 140 043	1 157 039	1 173 972	1 190 864	1 207 740	1 224 614	1 386 909	1 692 008
Indonesia	210 611	213 395	216 204	219 026	221 839	224 607	227 303	229 919	232 462	234 951	237 415	239 871	262 570	293 456
Russian Federation	147 287	146 758	146 162	145 520	144 881	144 307	143 843	143 510	143 295	143 163	143 064	142 958	141 022	126 188
South Africa	44 137	44 760	45 390	46 015	46 631	47 227	47 793	48 331	48 842	49 319	49 752	50 133	52 573	56 757
World	6 044 932	6 122 770	6 200 003	6 276 722	6 353 196	6 429 758	6 506 649	6 583 959	6 661 638	6 739 611	6 817 737	6 895 889	7 656 528	9 306 128

StatLink http://dx.doi.org/10.1787/888932502600

World population

Thousands, year 2009

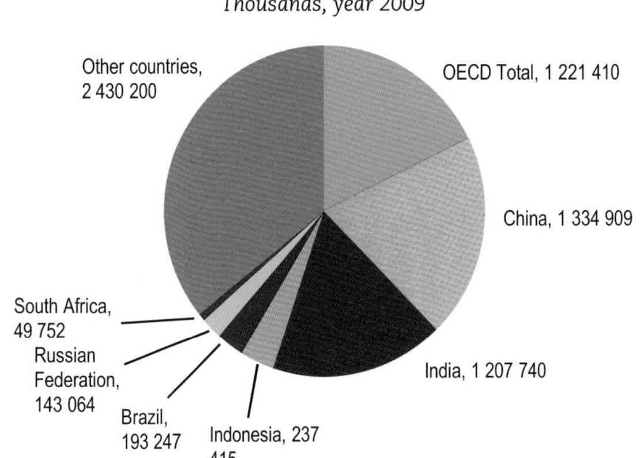

StatLink http://dx.doi.org/10.1787/888932502619

OECD population

Thousands, year 2009

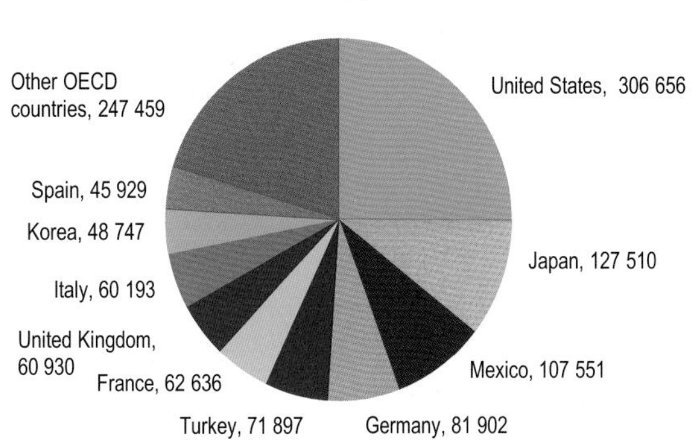

StatLink http://dx.doi.org/10.1787/888932502638

Population growth rates

Annual growth in percentage

	1997	1998	1999	2000	2001	2002	2003	2004	2005	2006	2007	2008	2009	2010
Australia	1.13	1.05	1.15	1.20	1.36	1.23	1.24	1.17	1.33	1.49	1.53	2.30	2.12	1.76
Austria	0.11	0.11	0.19	0.24	0.38	0.50	0.45	0.63	0.68	0.52	0.40	0.43	0.32	0.30
Belgium	0.24	0.21	0.23	0.24	0.34	0.45	0.42	0.43	0.55	0.66	0.74	0.79	0.81	..
Canada	1.00	0.83	0.82	0.94	1.09	1.08	0.91	0.95	0.95	1.03	1.09	1.17	1.21	1.15
Chile	1.37	1.36	1.34	1.32	1.13	1.12	1.10	1.09	1.08	1.02	1.01	1.00	0.99	0.98
Czech Republic	-0.11	-0.08	-0.12	-0.10	-0.47	-0.23	0.01	0.05	0.27	0.32	0.55	1.04	0.59	0.25
Denmark	0.43	0.32	0.34	0.34	0.33	0.36	0.24	0.26	0.27	0.34	0.42	0.58	0.55	0.44
Estonia	-1.13	-0.96	-0.76	-0.45	-0.40	-0.40	-0.37	-0.32	-0.24	-0.19	-0.14	-0.07	-0.03	-0.01
Finland	0.30	0.27	0.23	0.21	0.23	0.24	0.24	0.29	0.34	0.38	0.43	0.47	0.48	0.46
France	0.31	0.33	0.48	0.66	0.70	0.70	0.68	0.71	0.74	0.68	0.60	0.55	0.53	..
Germany	0.15	0.02	0.06	0.14	0.17	0.17	0.06	-0.02	-0.06	-0.11	-0.13	-0.19	-0.25	..
Greece	0.63	0.54	0.44	0.32	0.30	0.34	0.33	0.35	0.38	0.40	0.40	0.40	0.41	..
Hungary	-0.20	-0.23	-0.28	-0.26	-0.23	-0.28	-0.29	-0.22	-0.20	-0.16	-0.21	-0.12	-0.15	-0.23
Iceland	0.74	1.06	1.24	1.43	1.39	0.88	0.60	1.15	1.12	2.86	2.32	2.56	-0.03	-0.39
Ireland	1.05	1.06	1.04	1.28	1.52	1.82	1.60	1.64	2.19	2.56	2.34	1.92	0.84	0.26
Israel	2.53	2.43	2.59	2.68	2.38	2.03	1.82	1.78	1.78	1.78	1.79	1.79	2.42	1.78
Italy	0.05	0.03	0.02	0.05	0.06	0.32	0.78	0.99	0.74	0.57	0.74	0.77	0.60	..
Japan	0.24	0.25	0.16	0.19	0.29	0.11	0.14	0.05	0.06	0.00	0.00	-0.06	-0.14	..
Korea	0.94	0.72	0.71	0.84	0.74	0.56	0.50	0.38	0.21	0.33	0.33	0.31	0.29	3.63
Luxembourg	1.26	1.25	1.36	1.35	1.20	1.05	1.22	1.43	1.54	1.61	1.56	0.79	2.01	..
Mexico	1.45	1.39	1.38	1.36	1.30	1.20	1.08	0.98	0.92	0.89	0.87	0.84	0.81	0.79
Netherlands	0.52	0.62	0.67	0.72	0.76	0.64	0.47	0.35	0.23	0.16	0.22	0.39	0.52	..
New Zealand	1.32	0.89	0.53	0.59	0.59	1.75	1.99	1.50	1.14	1.23	1.04	0.96	1.10	1.20
Norway	0.54	0.60	0.69	0.65	0.51	0.54	0.59	0.59	0.68	0.81	1.04	1.25	1.27	1.25
Poland	0.01	-0.02	-0.03	-0.04	-0.01	-0.05	-0.10	-0.04	-0.05	-0.08	-0.04	0.00	0.10	0.09
Portugal	0.33	0.38	0.42	0.53	0.66	0.73	0.70	0.58	0.45	0.33	0.23	0.13	0.09	..
Slovak Republic	0.18	0.14	0.08	0.10	-0.39	-0.02	0.00	0.07	0.09	0.07	0.12	0.17	0.21	0.23
Slovenia	0.22	0.18	0.16	0.15	0.15	0.14	0.15	0.16	0.19	0.21	0.24	0.25	0.25	..
Spain	0.26	0.35	0.52	0.84	1.14	1.46	1.67	1.64	1.65	1.54	1.83	1.60	0.74	0.31
Sweden	0.06	0.06	0.08	0.16	0.27	0.33	0.37	0.39	0.40	0.56	0.74	0.79	0.86	0.86
Switzerland	0.24	0.30	0.48	0.56	0.59	0.80	0.74	0.69	0.64	0.63	0.90	1.28	1.26	1.01
Turkey	1.50	1.43	1.44	1.41	1.36	1.34	1.31	1.29	1.25	1.22	1.20 |	1.17	1.15	1.11
United Kingdom	0.26	0.28	0.36	0.34	0.39	0.36	0.39	0.49	-0.74	0.58	0.64	0.66	0.68	0.69
United States	1.21	1.18	1.15	1.12	1.02	0.95	0.87	0.93	0.92	0.95	0.99	0.92	0.81	0.78
OECD total	0.72	0.68	0.69	0.73	0.72	0.70	0.69	0.69	0.60	0.66	0.70 |	0.68	0.60	0.56
Brazil	1.54	1.52	1.49	1.45	1.41	1.36	1.31	1.23	1.15	1.06	0.98	0.92	0.89	0.88
China	0.96	0.90	0.84	0.77	0.69	0.63	0.58	0.55	0.54	0.53	0.52	0.51	0.50	0.48
India	1.83	1.79	1.75	1.70	1.66	1.62	1.58	1.55	1.52	1.49	1.46	1.44	1.42	1.40
Indonesia	1.39	1.35	1.33	1.32	1.32	1.31	1.28	1.25	1.20	1.15	1.11	1.07	1.05	1.03
Russian Federation	-0.21	-0.26	-0.31	-0.36	-0.41	-0.44	-0.44	-0.40	-0.32	-0.23	-0.15	-0.09	-0.07	-0.07
South Africa	1.65	1.50	1.43	1.41	1.41	1.38	1.34	1.28	1.20	1.13	1.06	0.98	0.88	0.77
World	1.38	1.35	1.32	1.29	1.26	1.24	1.22	1.21	1.20	1.19	1.18	1.17	1.16	1.15

StatLink http://dx.doi.org/10.1787/888932502657

Population growth rates

Average annual growth in percentage

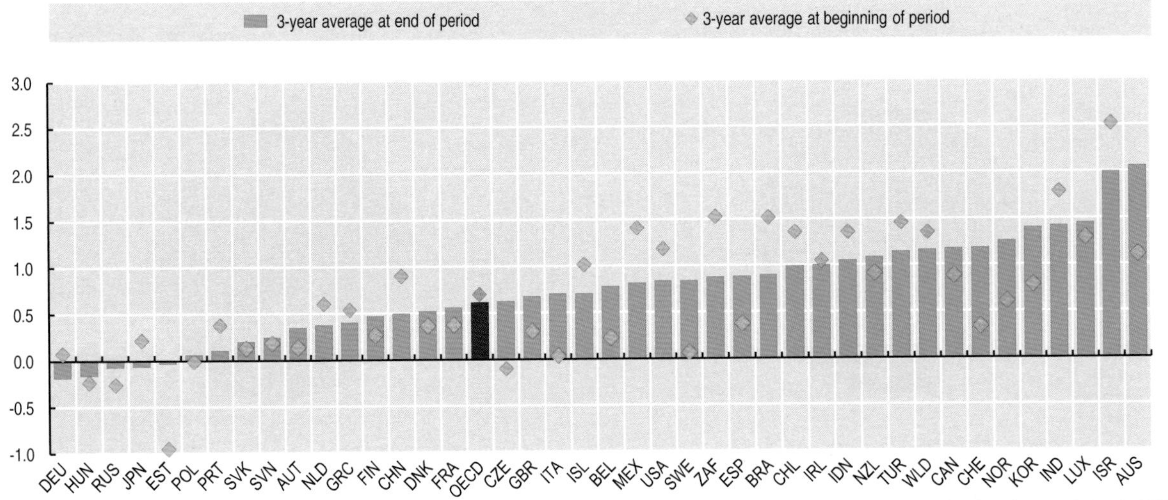

StatLink http://dx.doi.org/10.1787/888932502676

Total fertility rates

Number of children born to women aged 15 to 49

	1970	1997	1998	1999	2000	2001	2002	2003	2004	2005	2006	2007	2008	2009
Australia	2.86	1.78	1.76	1.76	1.76	1.73	1.76	1.75	1.76	1.79	1.82	1.92	1.96	1.90
Austria	2.29	1.39	1.37	1.34	1.36	1.33	1.39	1.38	1.42	1.41	1.41	1.38	1.41	1.39
Belgium	2.25	1.61	1.60	1.62	1.72	1.76	1.65	1.72	1.76	1.77	1.80	1.81	1.82	1.83
Canada	2.33	1.58	1.54	1.51	1.49	1.51	1.50	1.53	1.53	1.54	1.59	1.66	1.68	..
Chile	3.95	2.26	2.22	2.16	2.13	2.10	2.03	1.98	1.93	1.93	1.91	1.97	2.00	..
Czech Republic	1.91	1.17	1.16	1.13	1.14	1.15	1.17	1.18	1.23	1.28	1.33	1.44	1.50	1.49
Denmark	1.95	1.75	1.72	1.74	1.77	1.75	1.72	1.76	1.78	1.80	1.85	1.85	1.89	1.84
Estonia	..	1.32	1.28	1.32	1.39	1.34	1.37	1.37	1.47	1.50	1.55	1.64	1.66	1.63
Finland	1.83	1.75	1.71	1.73	1.73	1.73	1.72	1.76	1.80	1.80	1.84	1.83	1.85	1.86
Slovenia	2.21	1.25	1.23	1.21	1.26	1.21	1.21	1.20	1.25	1.26	1.31	1.31	1.53	1.53
France	2.48	1.73	1.76	1.79	1.87	1.88	1.86	1.87	1.90	1.92	1.98	1.96	1.99	1.99
Greece	2.39	1.31	1.29	1.28	1.27	1.26	1.27	1.29	1.31	1.34	1.41	1.42	1.51	1.53
Hungary	1.97	1.38	1.33	1.29	1.33	1.31	1.31	1.28	1.28	1.32	1.35	1.32	1.35	1.33
Iceland	2.81	2.04	2.05	1.99	2.08	1.95	1.93	1.99	2.03	2.05	2.07	2.09	2.14	2.22
Ireland	3.87	1.94	1.95	1.91	1.90	1.96	1.98	1.98	1.95	1.88	1.90	2.03	2.10	2.07
Israel	..	2.93	2.98	2.94	2.95	2.89	2.89	2.95	2.90	2.84	2.88	2.90	2.96	2.96
Italy	2.43	1.23	1.21	1.23	1.26	1.25	1.27	1.29	1.33	1.32	1.35	1.37	1.42	1.41
Japan	2.13	1.39	1.38	1.34	1.36	1.33	1.32	1.29	1.29	1.26	1.32	1.34	1.37	1.37
Korea	4.53	1.52	1.45	1.41	1.47	1.30	1.17	1.18	1.15	1.08	1.12	1.25	1.19	1.15
Luxembourg	1.98	1.71	1.67	1.71	1.78	1.66	1.63	1.62	1.66	1.62	1.64	1.61	1.60	1.59
Mexico	6.77	2.74	2.71	2.73	2.77	2.60	2.46	2.34	2.25	2.20	2.17	2.13	2.10	2.08
Netherlands	2.57	1.56	1.63	1.65	1.72	1.71	1.73	1.75	1.73	1.71	1.72	1.72	1.77	1.79
New Zealand	3.17	1.96	1.89	1.97	1.98	1.97	1.89	1.93	1.98	1.97	2.01	2.17	2.18	2.14
Norway	2.50	1.86	1.81	1.85	1.85	1.78	1.75	1.80	1.83	1.84	1.90	1.90	1.96	1.98
Poland	2.20	1.47	1.41	1.37	1.37	1.32	1.25	1.22	1.23	1.24	1.27	1.31	1.39	1.40
Portugal	2.83	1.47	1.48	1.51	1.56	1.46	1.47	1.44	1.40	1.41	1.36	1.33	1.37	1.32
Slovak Republic	2.40	1.43	1.37	1.33	1.29	1.20	1.19	1.20	1.24	1.25	1.24	1.25	1.32	1.41
Germany	2.03	1.37	1.36	1.36	1.38	1.35	1.34	1.34	1.36	1.34	1.33	1.37	1.38	1.36
Spain	2.90	1.18	1.16	1.19	1.23	1.24	1.26	1.31	1.33	1.35	1.38	1.40	1.46	1.40
Sweden	1.94	1.53	1.51	1.50	1.55	1.57	1.65	1.72	1.75	1.77	1.85	1.88	1.91	1.94
Switzerland	2.10	1.48	1.47	1.48	1.50	1.38	1.39	1.39	1.42	1.42	1.44	1.46	1.48	1.50
Turkey	5.00	2.63	2.56	2.48	2.27	2.37	2.17	2.08	2.10	2.10	2.10	2.12	2.10	2.12
United Kingdom	2.43	1.72	1.71	1.68	1.64	1.63	1.64	1.71	1.77	1.79	1.84	1.90	1.96	1.94
United States	2.48	1.97	2.00	2.01	2.06	2.03	2.01	2.04	2.05	2.05	2.10	2.12	2.08	2.01
OECD average	2.73	1.69	1.67	1.66	1.68	1.65	1.63	1.64	1.65	1.65	1.68	1.71	1.75	1.74
Brazil	..	2.45	2.43	2.41	2.39	2.34	2.27	2.20	2.13	2.06	1.99	1.93	1.86	..
China	5.51	1.80	1.79	1.78	1.77	1.76	1.76	1.76	1.76	1.76	1.76	1.76	1.77	..
India	5.47	3.50	3.43	3.35	3.28	3.21	3.14	3.07	3.00	2.93	2.86	2.80	2.74	..
Russian Federation	1.97	1.22	1.23	1.16	1.20	1.22	1.29	1.32	1.34	1.29	1.30	1.41	1.49	1.54
South Africa	5.65	3.00	2.97	2.93	2.90	2.86	2.81	2.75	2.70	2.65	2.59	2.54	2.48	2.43

StatLink http://dx.doi.org/10.1787/888932502695

Total fertility rates

Number of children born to women aged 15 to 49

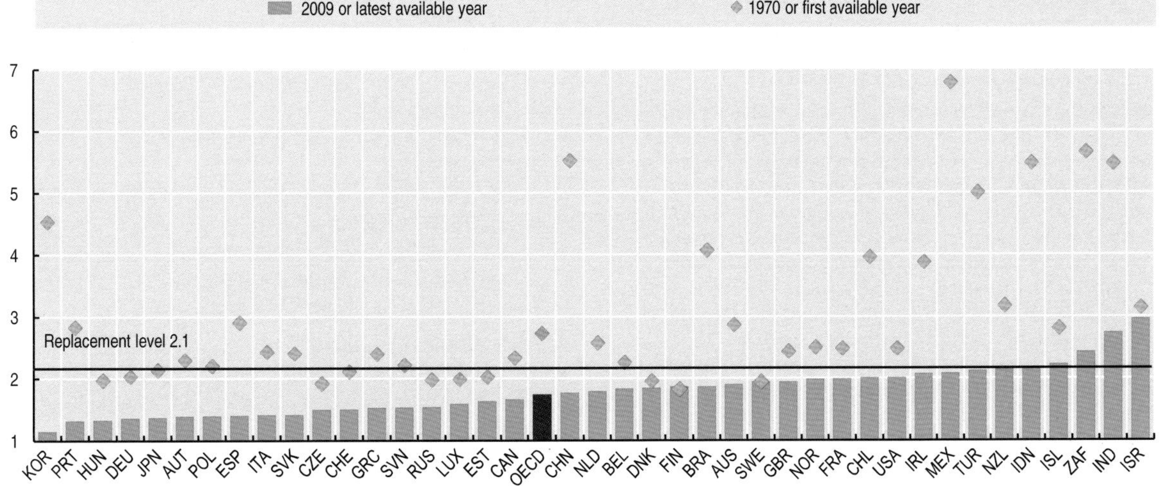

StatLink http://dx.doi.org/10.1787/888932502714

DEPENDENT POPULATION

Demographic trends in OECD countries have implied a sharp increase in the share of the dependent population (*i.e.* the sum of the elderly and youth population) in the total population, and this increase is expected to continue in the future. These trends have a number of implications for government and private spending on pensions, health-care and education and, more generally, for economic growth and welfare.

Definition

Population is defined as the resident population, *i.e.* all persons, regardless of citizenship, who have a permanent place of residence in the country. Population projections by age and gender are taken from national sources where these are available; for other countries they are based on Eurostat and UN projections.

The elderly population refers to people aged 65 and over and the youth population to people aged less than 15. The share of dependent population is calculated as the sum of the elderly and youth population expressed as a ratio of the total population.

Comparability

All population projections require assumptions about future trends in life expectancy, fertility rates and migration, and these assumptions may differ across countries. Often, a range of projections is produced. The estimates shown here correspond to the median or central variant of these projections.

Overview

The share of dependent population reflects the combined effect of fertility rates and life expectancy. In 2010, countries with a share of dependent population more than 2 percentage points above the OECD total (33% on average) were Israel, Japan, France, Sweden, and Italy. Korea at 27% has the lowest recorded share of dependent population in the OECD and is closely followed by the Slovak Republic, Poland, the Czech Republic and Slovenia. There is a wide variation among the emerging countries, with this share ranging between 36% in India and 28% in the Russian Federation and China.

By 2050, the share of dependent population is projected to increase in all OECD countries, while declining only in India and South Africa. The share of the dependent population is projected to be above 45% in Japan, Korea, Spain and Italy by 2050.

The youth population accounted for around 19% of the OECD total (on average) in 2010 with a steady decline since the 1970s. This fall is projected to continue as a result of lower fertility rates. By 2050 Japan and Korea are projected to have youth populations of 9% of the total, while only the United States (19%), Iceland (18%) and Estonia (18%) have projected youth populations close to the current OECD total.

In 2010, the share of the elderly in the total population ranged between less than 7% in South Africa, India, Indonesia and Mexico, to above 18% in Greece, Germany, Italy, and Japan. By 2050, this share is projected to be below 11% in South Africa, and to exceed one third of the total population in Greece, Italy, Spain, Korea and Japan. A number of countries are projected to have large increases in their elderly population between 2010 and 2050. For example, the Slovak Republic, Spain, and Korea all see projected growth in the share at the elderly in the total population in excess of 17 percentage points. However, some countries see smaller projected increases between 2010 and 2050. For example, Sweden, South Africa, Estonia and the United States all see project growth to be less than 8 percentage points for this period.

Sources

- OECD (2011), *Labour Force Statistics*, OECD Publishing.
- Eurostat, United Nations, national sources and OECD estimates.

Further information

Analytical publications

- Burniaux, J., R. Duval and F. Jaumotte (2004), "Coping with Ageing", *OECD Economics Department Working Papers*, No. 371.
- OECD (2011), *OECD Employment Outlook*, OECD Publishing.
- OECD (2011), *OECD Pensions at a Glance*, OECD Publishing.
- OECD (2007), *Ageing and the Public Service: Human Resource Challenges*, OECD Publishing.
- OECD (2006), *Ageing and Employment Policies*, OECD Publishing.
- OECD (2003), *Ageing, Housing and Urban Development*, OECD Publishing.
- OECD (2001), *Ageing and Transport Mobility Needs and Safety Issues*, OECD Publishing.
- Oliveira Martins J., *et al.* (2005), "The Impact of Ageing on Demand, Factor Markets and Growth", *OECD Economics Department Working Papers*, No. 420.

Methodological publications

- OECD (2005), *Main Economic Indicators – Sources and Methods: Labour and Wage Statistics*, OECD Publishing.

Online databases

- *OECD Employment and Labour Market Statistics.*

Share of the dependent population

As a percentage of total population

	Youth population (aged less than 15)							Elderly population (aged 65 and over)						
	2000	2005	2010	2020	2030	2040	2050	2000	2005	2010	2020	2030	2040	2050
Australia	20.7	19.7	18.9	18.4	17.6	16.9	16.7	12.4	12.9	13.5	16.8	19.7	21.3	22.2
Austria	17.0	16.0	14.8	14.4	14.3	13.8	13.6	15.4	16.2	17.6	19.3	23.4	26.4	27.4
Belgium	17.6	17.1	16.3	15.7	15.4	14.8	14.7	16.8	17.2	17.6	20.7	24.9	27.4	27.7
Canada	19.2	17.7	16.5	15.3	14.7	13.8	13.6	12.6	13.1	14.1	18.2	23.1	25.0	26.3
Chile	27.8	24.9	22.3	20.2	18.7	17.3	16.6	7.2	7.9	9.0	11.9	16.5	19.8	21.6
Czech Republic	16.4	14.8	14.3	13.7	12.7	12.2	12.4	13.8	14.1	15.4	20.1	22.7	26.5	31.2
Denmark	18.5	18.8	18.1	16.9	17.2	17.3	16.8	14.8	15.1	16.3	20.0	22.6	24.5	23.8
Estonia	18.0	15.3	15.2	18.1	17.2	16.0	17.8	15.1	16.6	17.0	18.3	20.4	21.8	23.8
Finland	18.2	17.4	16.6	16.6	16.1	15.5	15.6	14.9	15.9	17.3	22.8	26.2	27.0	27.6
France	18.9	18.4	18.3	17.5	16.7	16.5	16.3	16.1	16.5	16.7	20.3	23.4	25.6	26.2
Germany	15.6	14.3	13.6	13.0	12.7	12.0	11.9	16.4	18.9	20.4	22.7	27.8	31.1	31.5
Greece	15.3	14.4	14.2	14.0	12.6	12.1	12.3	16.6	18.3	18.9	21.3	24.8	29.4	32.5
Hungary	16.8	15.5	14.7	15.1	14.4	13.7	13.9	15.1	15.7	16.7	20.1	21.5	23.9	26.9
Iceland	23.3	22.1	20.9 |	19.7	19.0	18.2	18.1	11.6	11.7	12.1 |	15.5	19.2	20.9	21.5
Ireland	21.8	20.6	21.5	19.7	16.8	16.1	16.0	11.2	11.1	11.4	14.9	18.5	22.4	26.3
Israel	28.6	28.3	28.0	27.4	27.0	..	..	9.8	9.9	9.9	12.0	13.1	..	..
Italy	14.3	14.1	14.0	13.1	12.1	12.4	12.7	18.3	19.6	20.5	23.3	27.3	32.2	33.6
Japan	14.6	13.8	13.0	10.8	9.7	9.3	8.6	17.4	20.2	23.1	29.2	31.8	36.5	39.6
Korea	21.1	19.2	15.9	12.4	11.4	10.3	8.9	7.2	9.1	10.9	15.6	24.3	32.5	38.2
Luxembourg	18.9	18.5	17.8	17.0	17.3	16.9	16.6	14.1	14.1	14.6	16.6	20.0	22.3	22.1
Mexico	34.1	31.3	28.1	23.2	20.8	18.5	16.8	4.7	5.2	5.9	8.1	11.8	16.7	21.2
Netherlands	18.6	18.4	17.5	15.9	16.1	16.2	16.0	13.6	14.2	15.5	19.8	23.4	25.0	23.5
New Zealand	22.8	21.5	20.5	18.1	16.9	16.3	15.6	11.8	12.0	13.0	17.1	21.9	25.2	26.2
Norway	20.0	19.6	18.8	17.5	17.5	16.9	16.4	15.2	14.7	15.0	18.0	20.6	22.9	23.2
Poland	19.5	16.5	15.1	14.5	14.1	12.8	13.0	12.2	13.2	13.5	18.5	22.7	25.0	29.6
Portugal	16.1	15.6	15.2	13.7	12.4	12.2	12.1	16.2	17.1	18.0	20.8	24.4	28.6	32.0
Slovak Republic	19.5	16.8	15.3	14.6	13.4	12.6	13.2	11.4	11.7	12.4	17.3	21.6	25.0	30.1
Slovenia	15.9	14.2	13.8	14.5	13.5	13.1	14.3	14.0	15.5	16.4	20.3	24.6	27.5	30.2
Spain	14.8	14.5	15.0	14.1	11.6	11.3	11.4	16.8	16.7	17.0	20.0	25.1	31.6	35.7
Sweden	18.4	17.4	16.6	17.2	17.1	16.4	16.6	17.3	17.3	18.3	21.2	22.8	24.0	23.6
Switzerland	17.4	16.1	14.6	14.4	14.0	13.2	13.1	15.3	15.9	17.5	20.5	24.7	27.4	28.3
Turkey	29.4	27.7	25.8	22.9	..	..	..	6.8	6.6	7.7	9.5	..	..	..
United Kingdom	19.0	18.2	17.6	17.8	16.9	16.3	16.3	15.8	15.5	16.0	19.0	21.9	23.7	24.1
United States	21.4	20.6	20.1 |	20.0	19.5	19.3	19.3	12.4	12.4	13.1 |	16.1	19.3	20.0	20.2
OECD total	20.5	19.4	18.5	17.3	..	..	..	13.1	13.8	14.7	17.9	..	..	..
Brazil	29.5	27.5	25.5	20.7	18.1	15.9	14.7	5.6	6.3	7.0	9.6	13.7	17.7	22.5
China	25.5	21.9	19.5	16.7	14.6	13.6	13.5	7.0	7.6	8.2	12.0	16.5	23.3	25.6
India	34.7	32.6	30.6	27.1	23.8	21.1	19.0	4.2	4.6	4.9	6.3	8.3	10.5	13.5
Indonesia	30.7	28.8	27.0	23.5	20.1	17.9	16.5	4.6	5.1	5.6	7.0	10.5	14.9	19.2
Russian Federation	18.2	15.1	15.0	17.3	15.8	15.4	16.9	12.4	13.8	12.8	15.2	19.1	20.1	23.1
South Africa	33.7	31.7	30.1	27.6	25.2	23.1	21.1	3.7	4.1	4.6	6.2	7.8	8.5	10.1

StatLink http://dx.doi.org/10.1787/888932502733

Share of the dependent population

As a percentage of total population

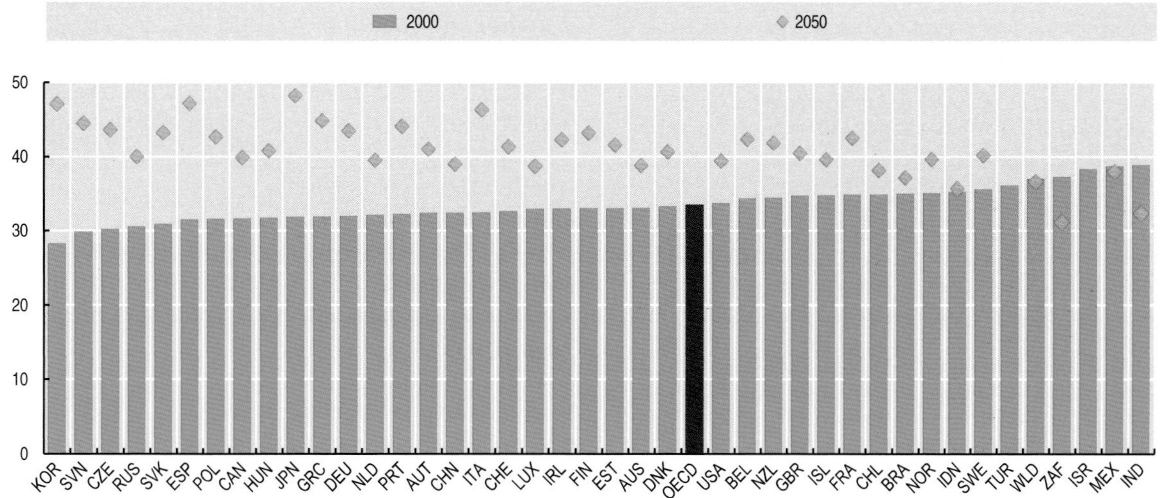

StatLink http://dx.doi.org/10.1787/888932502752

POPULATION BY REGION

Population is unevenly distributed among regions within countries. Differences in climatic and environmental conditions discourage human settlement in some areas and favour concentration of the population around a few urban centres. This pattern is reinforced by higher economic opportunities and wider availability of services stemming from urbanisation itself.

Definition

The number of inhabitants of a given region, *i.e.* its total population, can be measured as either its average annual population or as the population at a specific date during the year considered. The average population during a calendar year is generally calculated as the arithmetic mean of the population on 1 January of two consecutive years, although some countries estimate it on a date close to 1 July.

Comparability

The main problem with economic analysis at the sub-national level is the unit of analysis, *i.e.* the region. The word "region" can mean very different things both within and among countries, with significant differences in area and population.

The smallest OECD region (Melilla, Spain) has an area of 13 square kilometres whereas the largest region (Northwest Territories and Nunavut, Canada) has an area of over 3 million square kilometres. Similarly, the population across OECD regions ranges from about 400 inhabitants in Balance ACT (Australia) to more than 47 million in Kanto (Japan).

To address this issue, the OECD has classified regions within each member country to facilitate comparability at the same territorial level. The classification is based on two territorial levels: the higher level (TL2) consists of 362 larger regions and the lower level (TL3) consists of 1 794 smaller regions. These two levels are used as a framework for implementing regional policies in most countries. In Brazil, China, India and the Russian Federation only TL2 large regions have been identified. This classification (which, for European Union countries, is largely consistent with the Eurostat NUTS classification) facilitates comparability of regions at the same territorial level.

All the regional data shown here refer to small regions with the exception of Brazil, China, India, the Russian Federation and South Africa.

In addition, the OECD has established a regional typology to take into account geographical differences and enable meaningful comparisons between regions belonging to the same type. Regions have been classified as predominantly rural, intermediate and predominantly urban on the basis of the percentage of population living in local rural units.

The metropolitan database identifies 90 large metropolitan regions (with a population of 1.5 million or more) in OECD countries on the basis of the TL3 territorial classification. For Canada, Mexico and the United States national definitions are applied.

Overview

In 2009, 10% of regions accounted for approximately 40% of the total population in OECD countries. The concentration of population was highest in Australia, Canada, Iceland and the United States, where differences in climatic and environmental conditions discourage human settlement in some areas.

In large metropolitan regions, population growth has been faster than the growth of the total OECD population (1.3 times higher), suggesting that migration, besides demographic dynamics, has increased the size of urban regions. Growth of population within countries, though, has varied. Compared to the national rate, the growth rate of the population in large metropolitan regions has been particularly intense in Ireland, Turkey, New Zealand and Canada.

In 2009, almost half of the total OECD population (47%) lived in predominantly urban regions, which accounted for less than 6% of the total area. More than 60% of the population lived in predominantly urban regions in the Netherlands, Belgium and the United Kingdom.

Predominantly rural regions accounted for one-fourth of total population and 80% of land area. In Ireland, Finland, Norway, Slovenia and Sweden the share of national population in rural regions was twice as high as the OECD average.

Sources

- OECD (2011), *OECD Regions at a Glance*, OECD Publishing.

Further information

Analytical publications

- OECD (2011), *OECD Regional Outlook 2011*, OECD Publishing.
- OECD (2011), *OECD Territorial Reviews*, OECD Publishing.
- OECD (2006), *The New Rural Paradigm: Policies and Governance*, OECD Publishing.

Statistical publications

- OECD (2011), *Labour Force Statistics*, OECD Publishing.

Online databases

- *OECD Regional Database.*

Websites

- Regional Development, *www.oecd.org/gov/regionaldevelopment*.
- Regional Statistics and Indicators, *www.oecd.org/gov/regional/statisticsindicators*.

Share of national population in the ten per cent of regions with the largest population

Percentage

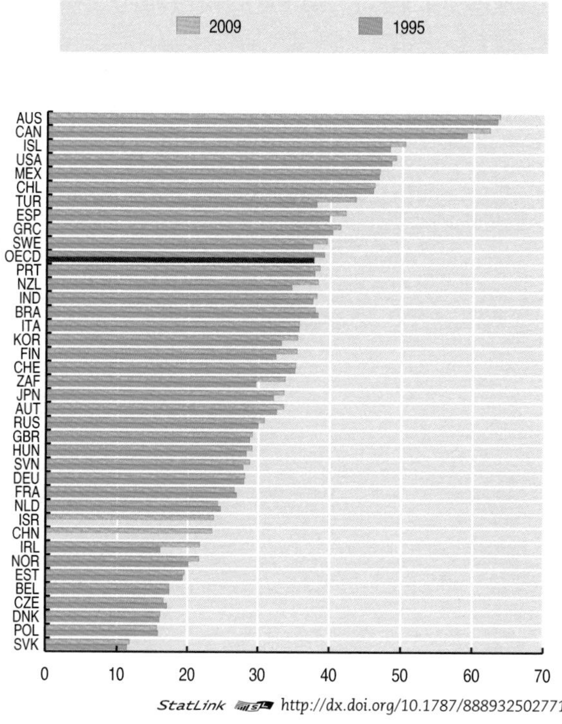

StatLink http://dx.doi.org/10.1787/888932502771

Total population: metropolitan regions and country average

Percentage, annual change 1997-2008

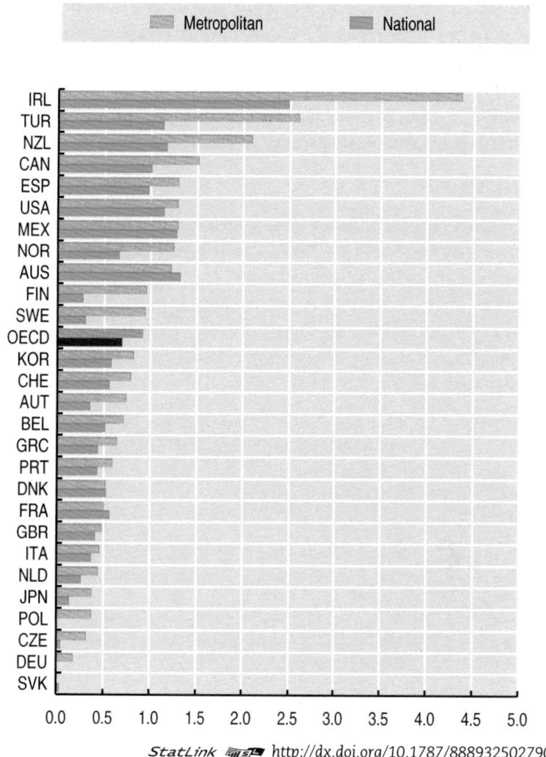

StatLink http://dx.doi.org/10.1787/888932502790

Distribution of the national population into urban, intermediate and rural regions

Percentage, 2009

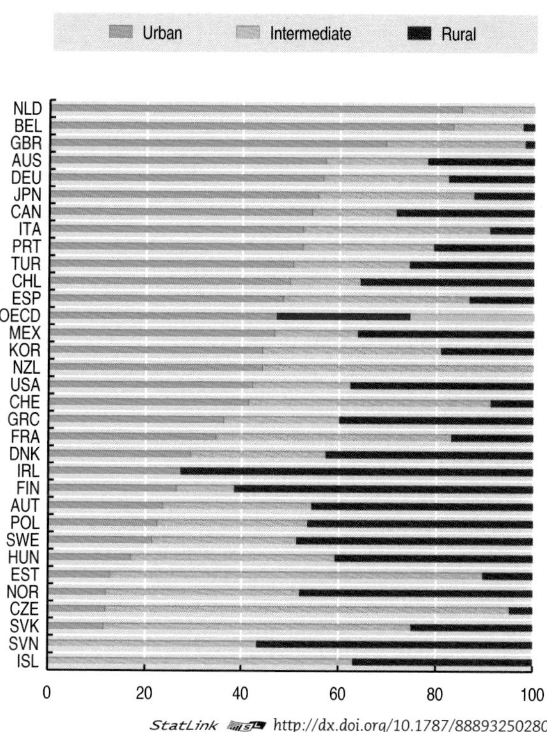

StatLink http://dx.doi.org/10.1787/888932502809

Distribution of the national area into urban, intermediate and rural regions

Percentage, 2009

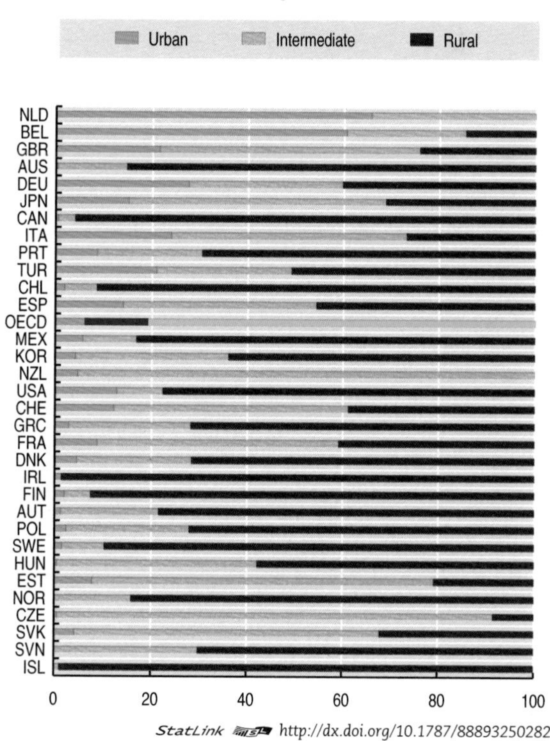

StatLink http://dx.doi.org/10.1787/888932502828

ELDERLY POPULATION BY REGION

In all OECD countries, populations aged 65 years and over have dramatically increased over the last 30 years, both in size and as a percentage of total population. As elderly people tend to be concentrated in few areas within each country, a small number of regions will have to face a number of specific social and economic challenges and opportunities raised by ageing population.

Definition

The elderly population is the number of inhabitants of a given region aged 65 or older. The population can be either the average annual population or the population at a specific date during the year considered. The average population during a calendar year is generally calculated as the arithmetic mean of the population on 1 January of two consecutive years.

The elderly dependency rate is defined as the ratio between the elderly population and the working age (15-64 years) population.

Comparability

As for the other regional statistics, the comparability of elderly population data is affected by differences in the definition of the regions and the different geography of rural and urban communities (see Population by region), both within and among countries.

All the regional data shown here refer to small regions with the exception of Brazil, China, India, the Russian Federation and South Africa.

Overview

In most OECD countries the population is ageing. Due to higher life expectancy and low fertility rates, the elderly population (those aged 65 years and over), accounts for 14% of OECD population in 2008. The proportion of elderly population is remarkably lower in the emerging economies (Brazil, China, India, and South Africa) and Mexico and Turkey.

The elderly population in OECD countries has increased more than 1.5 times faster than the total population between 1995 and 2008. The rate of ageing within a country can be quite different, as an increase in the geographic concentration of the elderly may arise from inward migration of the elderly or by ageing "in place" because the younger generations have moved out of the regions.

The ratio of the elderly to the working age population, the elderly dependency rate, is steadily growing in OECD countries. The elderly dependency rate gives an indication of the balance between the economically active and the retired population. In 2008 this ratio was around 22% in OECD countries, with substantial differences between countries (34% in Japan versus 9% in Mexico). Differences among regions within the same countries were also large. The higher the regional elderly dependency rate, the higher the challenges faced by regions in generating wealth and sufficient resources to provide for the needs of the population. Concerns may arise on the financial self-sufficiency of these regions to generate taxes to pay for these services.

Sources

- OECD (2011), *OECD Regions at a Glance*, OECD Publishing.

Further information

Analytical publications

- OECD (2011), *OECD Regional Outlook 2011*, OECD Publishing.
- Oliveira Martins J., et al. (2005), *The Impact of Ageing on Demand, Factor Markets and Growth*, *OECD Economics Department Working Papers*, No. 420.

Online databases

- *OECD Regional Database*.

Websites

- Regional Development, *www.oecd.org/gov/regionaldevelopment*.
- Regional Statistics and Indicators, *www.oecd.org/gov/regional/statisticsindicators*.

Elderly population

As a percentage of total population

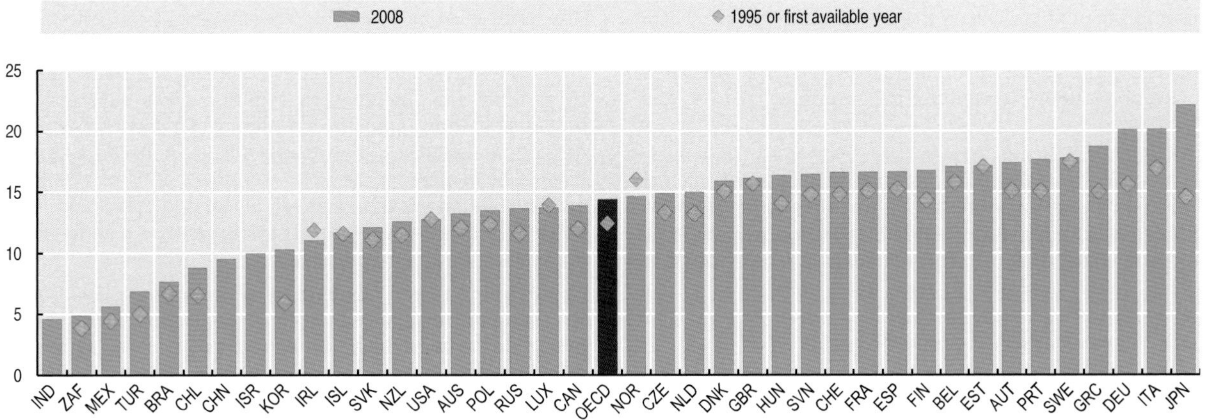

StatLink http://dx.doi.org/10.1787/888932502847

Regional elderly population

Average annual growth in percentage, 1995-2008

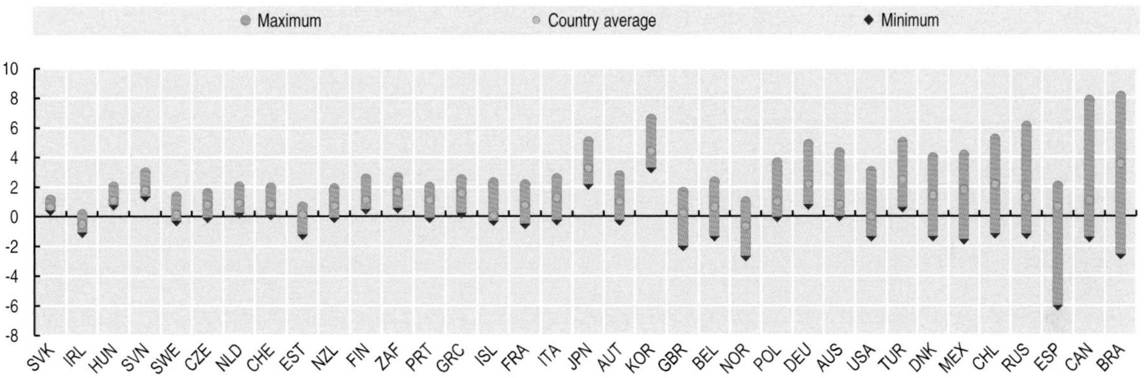

StatLink http://dx.doi.org/10.1787/888932502866

Elderly dependency rate in urban and rural regions

Percentage, 2008

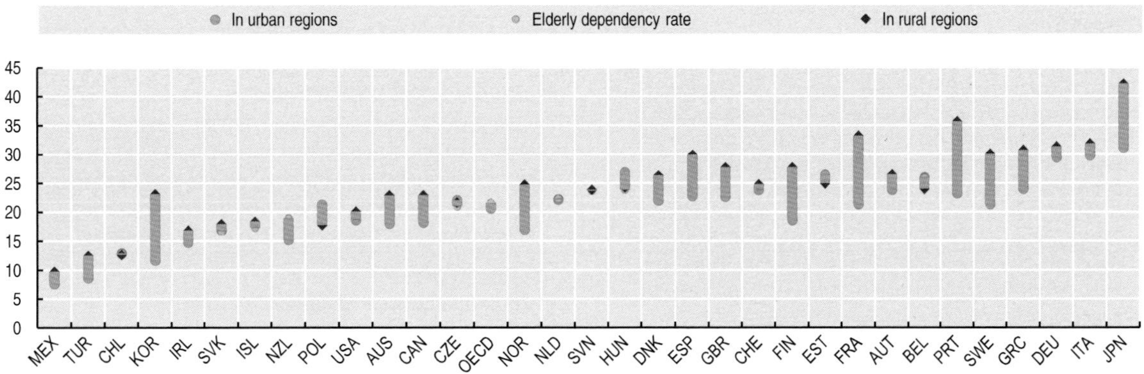

StatLink http://dx.doi.org/10.1787/888932502885

IMMIGRANT POPULATION

National views on the appropriate definition of the immigrant population vary from country to country. Despite this, it is possible to provide an internationally comparable picture of the size of the immigrant population, based either on nationality or country-of-birth criteria.

Definition

Nationality and place of birth are the two criteria most commonly used to define the "immigrant" population. The foreign-born population covers all persons who have ever migrated from their country of birth to their current country of residence. The foreign population consists of persons who still have the nationality of their home country. It may include persons born in the host country.

Comparability

The difference across countries between the size of the foreign-born population and that of the foreign population depends on the rules governing the acquisition of citizenship in each country. In some countries, children born in the country automatically acquire the citizenship of their country of birth (*jus soli*, the right of soil) while in other countries, they retain the nationality of their parents (*jus sanguinis*, the right of blood). In still others, they retain the nationality of their parents at birth but receive that of the host country at their majority. Differences in the ease with which immigrants may acquire the citizenship of the host country explain part of the gap between the two series. For example, residency requirements vary from as little as three years in Canada to as much as ten years in some countries. The naturalisation rate is high in settlement countries such as Australia, Canada, New Zealand and in some European countries including Belgium, Sweden and the Netherlands. In general, the foreign-born criterion gives substantially higher percentages for the immigrant population than the definition based on nationality. This is because many foreign-born persons acquire the nationality of the host country and no longer appear as foreign nationals. The place of birth, however, does not change, except when there are changes in country borders.

The definitions and coverage used to estimate the size of the foreign-born and foreign populations differ slightly from one country to another but it results in relatively minor differences.

Most of the data published in this database are taken from the contributions of national correspondents who are part of the Continuous Reporting System on Migration (SOPEMI). Consequently, these data have not necessarily been harmonised at international level.

The foreign-born population data shown here include persons born abroad as nationals of their current country of residence. The prevalence of such persons among the foreign-born can be significant in some countries, in particular France and Portugal (repatriations from former colonies).

Overview

The foreign-born population is especially high in Luxembourg, Australia, Switzerland, Israel, New Zealand, and Canada. It has increased in the past decade in all countries for which data are available with the exception of the two most recent members of the OECD, namely Estonia and Israel. The proportion of foreign-born in the population as a whole at least doubled over the decade in Spain, Ireland and Norway. Other countries, such as Finland, South Africa and Chile report a low share of foreign-born in the total population but have seen a spectacular increase in recent years. By contrast, the foreign population tends to increase more slowly, because inflows of foreign nationals tend to be counterbalanced by persons acquiring the nationality of the host country.

Sources

- OECD (2011), *International Migration Outlook*, OECD Publishing.

Further information

Analytical publications

- OECD (2008), *A Profile of Immigrant Populations in the 21st Century: Data from OECD Countries*, OECD Publishing.

Methodological publications

- Lemaître, G. and C. Thoreau, (2006), *Estimating the foreign-born population on a current basis*, OECD Publishing.
- OECD (2005), "Counting Immigrants and Expatriates in OECD Countries – a New Perspective", *Trends in International Migration 2004*, OECD Publishing.

Online databases

- *OECD International Migration Statistics.*

Websites

- Database on Immigrants in OECD Countries (DIOC), *www.oecd.org/els/migration/dioc.*

Foreign-born and foreign populations

	As a percentage of total population												As a percentage of all foreign-born
	Foreign-born population						Foreign population						Foreign-born nationals
	1995	2000	2005	2007	2008	2009	1995	2000	2005	2007	2008	2009	2009 or latest available year
Australia	23.0	23.0	24.2	25.1	25.8	26.5	..	..	..	..	..	..	67.8
Austria	..	10.4	14.5	15.0	15.3	15.5	8.5	8.8	9.7	10.1	10.4	10.7	42.9
Belgium	9.7	10.3	12.1	13.0	..	..	9.0	8.4	8.6	9.1	9.5	9.8	44.0
Canada	16.7	17.4	18.7	19.2	19.4	19.6	..	..	..	..	..	..	75.0
Chile	..	1.2	1.5	1.8	1.9	2.1	..	..	..	..	..	..	..
Czech Republic	..	4.2	5.1	6.2	6.5	6.4	1.5	1.9	2.7	3.8	4.2	4.1	57.5
Denmark	4.8	5.8	6.5	6.9	7.3	7.5	4.2	4.8	5.0	5.5	5.8	6.0	42.0
Estonia	..	18.4	17.5	16.9	16.7	16.6	..	..	..	17.3	16.7	16.4	..
Finland	2.1	2.6	3.4	3.8	4.1	4.4	1.3	1.8	2.2	2.5	2.7	2.9	41.8
France	..	10.1	11.0	11.3	11.4	11.6	..	..	..	6.0	..	..	55.7
Germany	11.5	12.5	12.6	12.8	12.9	12.9	8.8	8.9	8.8	8.2	8.2	8.2	..
Greece	..	..	..	..	..	..	..	2.9	5.2	5.7	6.5	7.4	27.6
Hungary	2.7	2.9	3.3	3.8	3.9	4.1	1.4	1.1	1.5	1.7	1.8	2.0	..
Ireland	..	8.7	12.6	15.7	16.7	17.2	2.7	3.3	6.3	..	..	..	31.8
Israel	..	32.2	29.1	27.6	26.9	26.2	..	..	..	..	..	..	..
Italy	..	..	..	..	..	..	1.7	2.4	4.6	5.8	6.6	7.1	39.1
Japan	..	..	..	..	..	..	1.1	1.3	1.6	1.7	1.7	1.7	..
Korea	..	..	..	..	..	..	0.2	0.4	1.0	1.7	1.8	1.9	..
Luxembourg	30.9	33.2	35.0	36.2	37.3	36.9	33.4	37.3	39.6	43.2	44.5	43.8	10.3
Mexico	0.4	0.5	0.6	0.7	0.7	0.8	..	..	..	..	..	0.2	..
Netherlands	9.1	10.1	10.6	10.7	10.9	11.1	4.7	4.2	4.2	4.2	4.4	4.4	70.2
New Zealand	..	17.2	20.3	21.6	22.3	22.7	..	..	..	..	..	..	..
Norway	5.5	6.8	8.2	9.5	10.3	10.9	3.8	4.0	4.8	5.7	6.4	6.9	47.4
Poland	..	..	..	..	..	..	..	..	..	0.2	0.2	0.1	90.5
Portugal	5.2	5.1	6.3	6.1	6.1	6.3	1.7	2.1	4.1	4.2	4.2	4.3	57.1
Slovak Republic	..	..	4.6	6.8	8.2		0.4	0.5	0.5	0.8	1.0	1.2	..
Slovenia	..	..	..	..	..	..	..	..	..	3.4	3.5	4.0	..
Spain	..	4.9	11.1	13.5	14.2	14.3	..	..	..	11.7	12.4	12.4	18.4
Sweden	10.6	11.3	12.5	13.4	13.9	14.4	6.0	5.4	5.3	5.7	6.0	6.4	64.5
Switzerland	21.4	21.9	23.8	24.9	25.8	26.3	18.9	19.3	20.3	20.8	21.4	21.7	29.6
Turkey	..	1.9	..	..	..	..	..	..	..	..	..	..	..
United Kingdom	6.9	7.9	9.4	10.3	11.0	11.3	3.4	4.0	5.2	6.4	6.8	7.1	42.6
United States	9.9	11.0	13.0	13.6	13.7	12.7	..	..	..	7.5	7.3	6.9	48.9
Brazil	0.4	0.4	0.4	..	..	0.4	..	..	..	..	..	..	..
China	0.0	0.0	0.0	..	..	0.1	..	..	..	..	..	..	..
India	0.7	0.6	0.5	..	..	0.4	..	..	..	..	..	..	..
Indonesia	0.1	0.1	0.1	..	..	0.1	..	..	..	..	..	..	..
Russian Federation	7.9	8.1	8.4	..	..	8.7	..	8.2	..	..	..	..	..
South Africa	2.7	2.3	2.6	..	..	3.7	..	1.0	..	..	..	..	1.3

StatLink http://dx.doi.org/10.1787/888932502904

Foreign-born population

As a percentage of total population

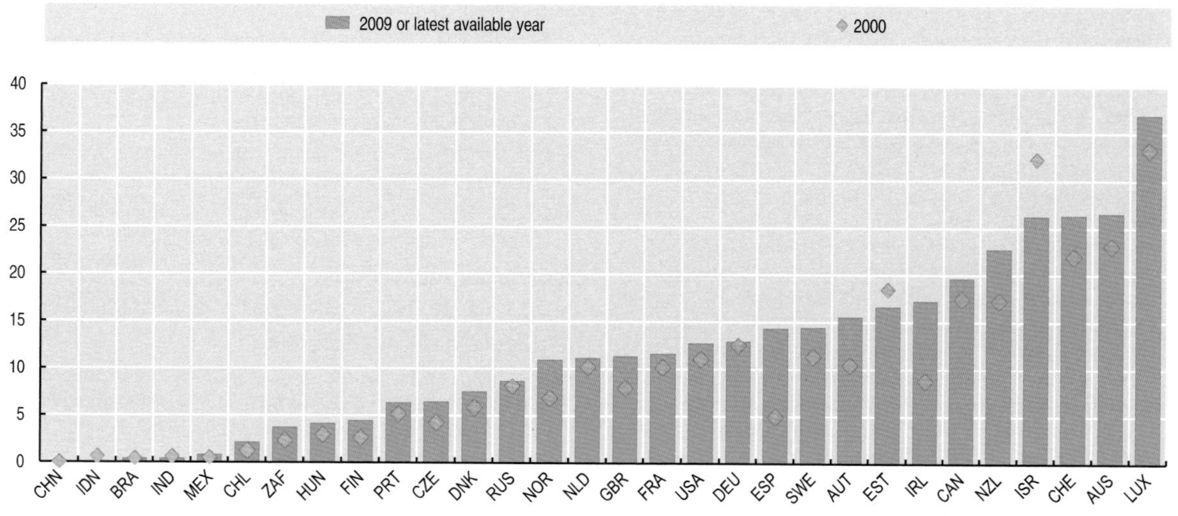

StatLink http://dx.doi.org/10.1787/888932502923

TRENDS IN MIGRATION

Migration movements include not only entries of persons of foreign nationality, on which public attention tends to be focused, but also include movements of nationals and of emigrants. Net migration summarises the overall effect of these movements. Migration currently represents, in almost all OECD countries, the main source of increases in population.

Definition

Net migration is defined as the total number of immigrant nationals and foreigners minus the total of emigrant foreigners and nationals. Arrivals and departures for purposes such as tourism and business travel are not included in the statistics.

The net migration rate is expressed per 1 000 inhabitants. The three-year averages referred to concern the years 2007 to 2009 (end of period); and 1997 to 1999 (beginning of period).

Comparability

The main sources of information on migration vary across countries. This may pose problems for the comparability of available data on inflows and outflows of migrants. However, since comparability problems generally relate to the extent to which short-term movements are covered, taking the difference between arrivals and departures tends to eliminate the movements that are the main source of non-comparability.

Despite this feature, net migration data should be interpreted with care, because unauthorised movements are not taken into account in the inflows and these unauthorised movements are significant in some OECD countries. In addition, the data on outflows are of uneven quality, with departures being only partially recorded in many countries or having to be estimated in others.

The net migration rate is used to describe the contribution of international migration to population change, the other component being natural increase, defined as the difference between the number of births and the number of deaths in a given year.

Overview

Mexico, Estonia, Japan and Poland are the only countries among those shown here that recorded negative or zero net migration in the three years to 2009. Ireland, Iceland, Luxembourg and Spain top the league showing net migration rates above 10 per thousand in recent years. Some of the former emigration countries that figure prominently among those experiencing high net migration in the past decade have shown lower or even negative net migration rates in the last two years.

For the second consecutive year, net migration rates have decreased, to reach the levels of the late 1990s, with the decrease being especially evident in the country's most hit by the economic crisis (*e.g.* Iceland). With the retirement of baby-boomers in the near future and the entry of smaller youth cohorts in the labour market, labour supply needs may well require a further rise in net migration in the future.

There are nonetheless a number of countries where net migration rates remain higher than was the case five to ten years ago. These include Switzerland, Australia, Norway and Spain.

Sources

- OECD (2011), *Labour Force Statistics*, OECD Publishing.

Further information

Analytical publications

- OECD (2011), *International Migration Outlook*, OECD Publishing.
- OECD (2008), *A Profile of Immigrant Populations in the 21st Century: Data from OECD Countries*, OECD Publishing.
- OECD (2006), *From Immigration to Integration: Local Solutions to a Global Challenge*, OECD Publishing.
- OECD (2004), *Migration for Employment: Bilateral Agreements at a Crossroads*, OECD Publishing.
- OECD (2004), *Trade and Migration: Building Bridges for Global Labour Mobility*, OECD Publishing.
- OECD (2003), *Migration and the Labour Market in Asia: Recent Trends and Policies – 2002 Edition*, OECD Publishing.
- OECD (2001), *Migration Policies and EU Enlargement: The Case of Central and Eastern Europe*, OECD Publishing.

Statistical publications

- OECD (2011), *OECD Employment Outlook*, OECD Publishing.

Methodological publications

- Dumont, J. and G. Lemaître (2005), "Counting Immigrants and Expatriates in OECD Countries: A New Perspective", *OECD Social, Employment and Migration Working Papers*, No. 25.

Online databases

- *OECD International Migration Statistics*.

Net migration rate

Per 1 000 inhabitants

	1997	1998	1999	2000	2001	2002	2003	2004	2005	2006	2007	2008	2009	2010
Australia	3.9	4.8	5.5	5.8	7.0	5.6	5.5	5.3	6.7	8.8	10.3	14.0	12.7	..
Austria	0.2	1.1	2.5	2.2	4.1	4.1	4.9	6.2	5.4	2.9	4.2	4.1	2.5	..
Belgium	1.9	2.1	2.7	2.5	3.4	4.0	3.9	4.2	4.5	4.8	..	..	..	..
Canada	5.2	3.9	5.2	6.5	8.1	7.0	6.7	6.6	7.0	6.9	7.1	8.1	7.7	7.2
Chile	0.9	0.8	0.7	0.4	0.4	0.4	0.4	0.4	0.4	0.4	0.4	0.4	0.4	0.4
Czech Republic	1.2	0.9	0.9	0.6	-0.8	1.2	2.5	1.8	3.5	3.4	8.1	6.9	2.7	1.5
Denmark	2.3	2.1	1.7	1.7	2.2	1.7	1.1	0.9	1.2	1.8	4.2	5.3	4.0	4.0
Estonia	-1.8	-0.8	-0.4	-0.7	-1.4	-1.1	-1.6	-1.4	-2.4	-2.5	-0.5	-0.6	..	..
Finland	0.8	0.6	0.6	0.4	1.2	1.0	1.2	1.3	1.7	1.9	2.5	2.6	2.6	2.4
France	0.7	0.8 |	1.0	1.2	1.4	1.6	1.7	1.7	1.6	1.9	1.1	1.2	1.1	..
Germany	1.1	0.6	2.5	2.0	3.3	2.7	1.7	1.0	1.0	0.3	0.5	..	..	..
Greece	5.7	5.1	4.1 |	2.7	3.5	3.5	3.3	3.7	3.5	3.6	3.6	3.2	..	..
Hungary	1.7	1.7	1.7	1.7 |	1.0	0.4	1.6	1.8	1.7	2.1	1.4	1.7	1.7	1.2
Iceland	0.3	3.2	4.0	6.1	3.4	-1.0	-0.5	1.8	13.0	17.3	16.5	3.6	-15.2	..
Ireland	5.1	4.5	6.4	8.4	10.0	8.4	7.8	11.6	15.9	..	..	..	..	..
Israel	9.2	8.2	11.9	9.8	6.2	3.3	1.6	2.0	2.4	2.4	2.1	1.7	..	..
Italy	2.2	1.6	1.8	3.1	2.2 |	6.1	10.6	9.6	5.2	6.4	..	..	..	..
Japan	0.1	0.3	-0.1	0.3 |	-0.4	0.5	-0.3	-0.4	0.0	0.0	-0.4	-1.0	..	..
Luxembourg	9.0	9.6	10.9	8.2	2.5	5.8	12.0	9.6	13.1	11.4	12.5	15.8	13.3	..
Mexico	-5.4	-5.5	-5.7	-6.4	-5.6	-5.5	-5.6	-5.6	-5.6	-5.3	-5.3	-5.2	-5.2	-5.1
Netherlands	1.8	2.7	2.6	3.4	3.2	1.5	-	-1.0	-1.7	-1.9	-0.4	1.6	2.1	..
New Zealand	2.0	-1.7	-2.3	-2.9	2.5	9.7	8.7	3.7	1.7	3.6	1.4	0.9	4.9	2.3
Norway	2.5	3.2	4.3	2.0	1.8	3.7	2.4	2.8	3.9	5.1	8.5	9.0	8.1	8.6
Poland	-0.3	-0.3	-0.4 |	-0.5	-0.4	-0.5	-0.4	-0.2	-0.3	-0.9	-0.5	-0.4	0.0	..
Portugal	2.9	3.2	3.7	4.6	6.3	6.8	6.1	4.5	3.6	2.5	1.9	0.8	1.4	..
Slovak Republic	0.3	0.2	0.3	0.3	0.2	0.2	0.3	0.5	0.6	0.7	1.3	1.3	0.8	0.6
Slovenia	1.2	-1.1	1.2	1.3	1.5	0.9	1.7	1.0	3.2	3.1	7.1	9.2	..	..
Spain	1.6	3.1	4.9	8.9	10.1	15.7	14.5	14.7	15.0	14.2	16.0	10.1	..	..
Sweden	0.7	1.2	1.6	2.8	3.3	3.5	3.2	2.8	3.0	5.6	5.9	6.1	6.8	5.3
Switzerland	-1.0	0.2	2.3	2.8	5.8	6.7	5.9	5.4	4.8	5.2	9.9	12.8	8.5	..
Turkey	1.6	1.6	1.6	-	-	-	-	-	-	..	..	..	..	..
United States	4.8	4.2	4.4	4.6	3.8	3.7	3.0	3.1	3.3	3.2	2.8	2.9	2.8	..
Brazil	..	..	..	..	..	..	..	..	..	..	..	..	-0.2	..
China	..	..	..	..	..	..	..	..	..	..	..	..	-0.3	..
India	..	..	..	..	..	..	..	..	..	..	..	..	-0.2	..
Indonesia	..	..	..	..	..	..	..	..	..	..	..	..	-0.6	..
Russian Federation	3.5	2.9	1.8	2.5	1.9	1.6	0.6	0.7	0.9	1.1	1.8	1.8	..	..
South Africa	..	..	..	..	..	..	..	..	..	..	..	..	2.8	..

StatLink http://dx.doi.org/10.1787/888932502942

Net migration rate

Per 1 000 inhabitants, annual average

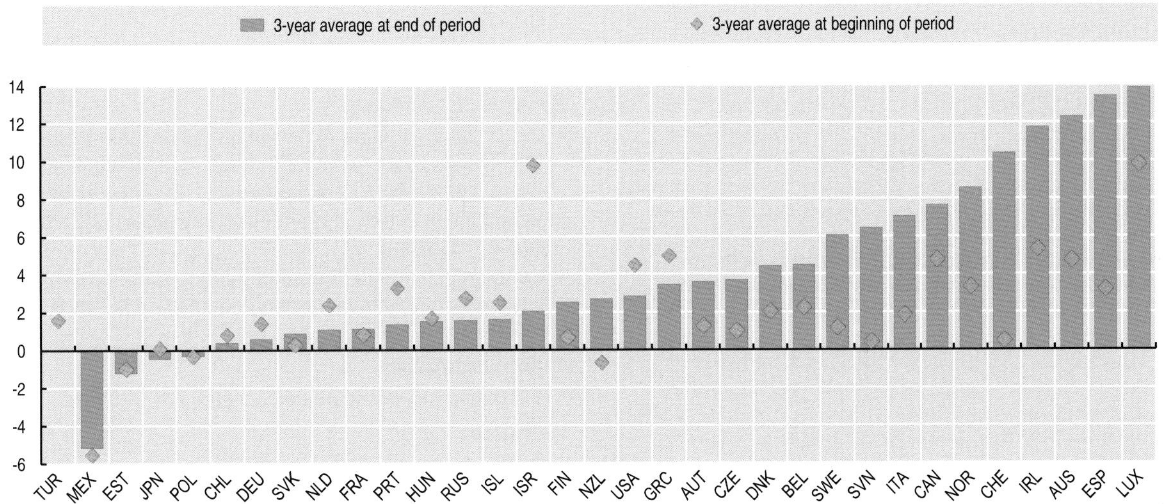

StatLink http://dx.doi.org/10.1787/888932502961

MIGRATION AND EMPLOYMENT

In most OECD countries, employment rates for immigrants are lower than for native-born persons. However, the situation is more diverse if one disaggregates employment rates by educational attainment.

Definition

The employment rate is calculated as the share of employed persons aged 15-64 in the total population (active and inactive persons) of the same age. In accordance with ILO definitions, employed persons are those who worked at least one hour or who had a job but were absent from work during the reference week. The educational classification shown is based on the International Standard Classification of Education (ISCED) categories. Generally speaking, "low" corresponds to less than upper secondary education; "intermediate" to upper secondary education; and "high" to tertiary education. Tertiary education includes high-level vocational education feeding into technical or semi-professional occupations.

Comparability

Data for European countries are from the European Union Labour Force Survey. Data for the United States and Canada are from the Current Population Survey and the Canadian Labour Force Survey, respectively. Even if employment levels can at times be affected by changes in survey design (this occurred in France in 2004) and by survey implementation problems (*e.g.* non-response), data on employment rates are generally consistent over time. However, comparability of education levels between immigrants and the native-born population and across countries is only approximate. The educational qualifications of other countries may not fit exactly into national educational categories because the duration of study or the programme content for what appear to be equivalent qualifications may not be the same. Likewise, the reduction of the ISCED classification into three categories may result in some loss of information regarding the duration of study, the programme orientation, etc. For example, high educational qualifications can include programmes of durations varying from two years (in the case of short, university-level technical programmes) to seven years or more (in the case of PhDs).

Data for Brazil, Indonesia and the Russian Federation refer to 2000; data for South Africa refer to 2007.

Overview

Labour market outcomes of immigrants and natives vary significantly across OECD countries, and differences by educational attainment are even larger. In all OECD countries, the employment rate increases with educational level. While people with tertiary education find work more easily and are less exposed to unemployment, access to tertiary education does not necessarily guarantee equal employment rates for immigrants and native-born persons. In all OECD countries, employment rates are higher for native-born persons with high educational qualification than for foreign-born persons with the same qualification. The gap is particularly high for countries such as Poland, Germany and Austria. This difference can be partly explained by language proficiency problems and difficulties with the recognition or acceptance of competences and diplomas acquired abroad.

The situation is more diverse for persons with low educational attainment. In South Africa, Luxembourg, the United States, Hungary and some southern European countries such as Greece and Slovenia, foreign-born immigrants with low educational qualifications have much higher employment rates than their native-born counterparts. The reverse is true in Indonesia, Brazil, the Netherlands, the United Kingdom and Denmark. The higher employment rate of foreign-born persons with low educational attainment in some countries may reflect the strong demand for workers in low-skilled jobs which are no longer taken up by the in-coming cohorts of native-born workers.

Sources

- OECD (2011), *International Migration Outlook*, OECD Publishing.

Further information

Analytical publications

- OECD (2008), *A Profile of Immigrant Populations in the 21st Century: Data from OECD Countries*, OECD Publishing.
- OECD (2008), *Jobs for Immigrants (Vol. 2): Labour Market Integration in France, Belgium, the Netherlands and Portugal*, OECD Publishing.
- OECD (2007), *Jobs for Immigrants (Vol. 1): Labour Market Integration in Australia, Denmark, Germany and Sweden*, OECD Publishing.

Online databases

- *OECD International Migration Statistics.*

Websites

- OECD International Migration Statistics (supplementary material), *www.oecd.org/els/migration/statistics.*

Employment rates of native-born and foreign-born population by educational attainment

As a percentage of total population, 2009 or latest available year

	Native-born				Foreign-born			
	Low	Medium	High	Total	Low	Medium	High	Total
Austria	48.9	77.5	88.3	73.1	50.0	70.8	76.4	64.7
Belgium	39.2	66.7	83.4	63.2	36.4	55.9	72.8	52.2
Canada	48.0	72.5	82.9	72.3	46.1	65.8	75.9	68.5
Czech Republic	22.3	71.3	81.9	65.4	35.9	69.8	85.4	65.8
Denmark	62.9	79.3	88.1	76.6	55.5	68.9	78.5	67.3
Estonia	27.7	66.5	82.4	62.9	28.5	64.9	80.3	67.8
Finland	42.1	72.0	84.3	68.7	46.0	68.0	77.2	64.5
France	45.3	68.8	81.2	64.9	48.1	60.7	70.4	57.4
Germany	43.3	75.4	88.7	72.5	49.6	70.0	78.3	63.3
Greece	49.8	59.9	82.3	60.7	65.4	64.9	71.6	66.0
Hungary	25.5	61.5	78.1	55.2	41.1	65.8	79.2	65.5
Iceland	71.2	79.7	88.7	78.4	71.6	77.0	84.7	77.7
Ireland	40.0	65.1	82.5	61.8	39.6	59.8	74.4	62.0
Italy	43.2	66.3	77.6	56.9	56.0	68.6	70.4	62.8
Luxembourg	35.6	66.6	84.9	61.9	56.5	64.7	82.3	69.0
Netherlands	63.1	81.7	88.8	78.0	52.6	69.9	76.7	64.5
Norway	60.8	80.4	90.7	77.1	55.9	73.5	82.0	69.0
Portugal	62.8	65.7	84.4	66.0	64.6	70.3	83.4	69.8
Slovenia	39.0	70.0	88.5	67.7	53.8	70.3	80.6	66.1
Spain	49.2	62.1	80.4	60.0	48.6	62.3	70.2	57.4
Sweden	51.4	80.2	89.5	74.2	45.6	68.6	75.9	62.1
Switzerrland	58.7	81.3	91.5	80.5	66.1	76.8	84.1	75.9
Turkey	36.1	48.1	69.0	41.2	39.3	48.8	70.5	44.2
United Kingdom	56.3	72.9	84.8	70.3	48.7	67.4	79.8	66.6
United States	37.4	72.2	84.3	70.0	58.3	70.6	78.8	69.0
Brazil	49.3	67.4	80.8	54.0	29.7	54.2	70.9	44.0
Indonesia	66.4	62.2	78.8	66.1	35.8	47.1	77.8	57.4
Russian Federation	30.1	61.3	79.1	57.9	32.4	62.1	76.4	60.7
South Africa	27.8	43.9	79.9	36.3	60.8	64.3	75.3	63.7

StatLink http://dx.doi.org/10.1787/888932502980

Gap in employment rate between native-born and foreign-born population by educational attainment

Percentage points, 2009 or latest available year

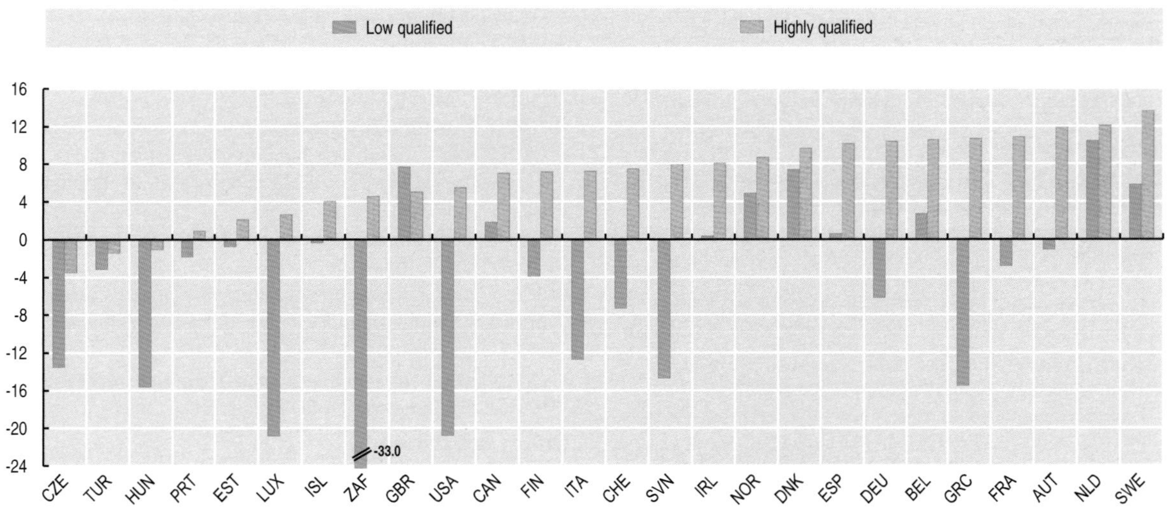

StatLink http://dx.doi.org/10.1787/888932502999

MIGRATION AND UNEMPLOYMENT

Immigrant workers are more affected by unemployment in traditional European immigration countries. Conversely, in South Africa, Hungary, the United States and Estonia, the unemployment rate depends less on the place of birth. Some groups, such as young immigrants, women or older immigrants have greater difficulties in finding jobs.

Definition

The unemployment rate is the share of the unemployed in the total labour force (the sum of employed and unemployed persons). In accordance with the ILO standards, unemployed persons consist of those persons who report that they are without work during the reference week, that they are available for work and that they have taken active steps to find work during the four weeks preceding the interview.

Comparability

Data for the European countries are from the European Union Labour Force Survey. Data for Australia are taken from the National Labour Force Survey; those for Canada from the Canadian Labour Force Survey; and those for the United States from the Current Population Survey. Even if unemployment levels can at times be affected by changes in the survey design (this occurred in France in 2004) and by survey implementation problems (*e.g.* non-response), data on unemployment rates are generally consistent over time.

Data for Brazil, Indonesia and the Russian Federation refer to 2000; data for South Africa refer to 2007.

Unemployment rates of foreign- and native-born populations

As a percentage of total labour force, 2009

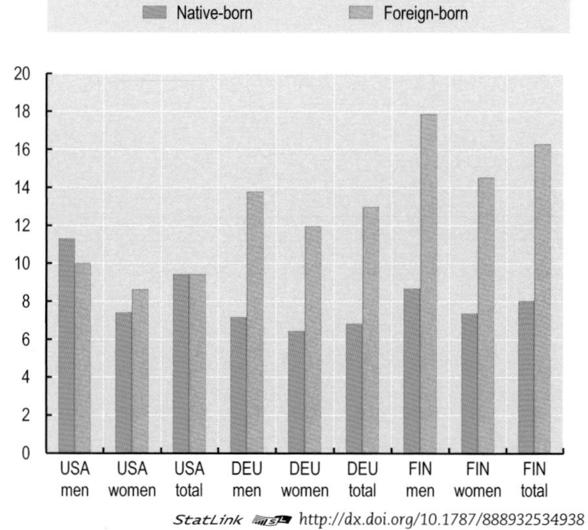

StatLink http://dx.doi.org/10.1787/888932534938

Overview

In 2009, unemployment rates increased both for foreign- and native-born persons in most OECD countries. However immigrants in most European OECD countries were much more affected by unemployment than the native population. In Ireland, Finland, Estonia, Belgium, Sweden and France, the unemployment rate of immigrants was above 15%. It was close to 30% in Spain. The unemployment rate was more than twice the level observed for the native-born population in Norway, the Netherlands, Belgium, Austria, Luxembourg, Switzerland, Sweden and Finland. In other countries, especially in the settlement countries (Australia, Canada, the United States) and in recent immigration countries (Greece and Portugal), the unemployment rate does not vary much by birth status. In Indonesia, South Africa and Brazil, the native population was more affected by unemployment than immigrants.

Recent years have seen some sizable increases in the unemployment rates of the foreign-born (both men and women) in a number of countries, such as Spain, Ireland, the United States, Portugal and Luxembourg. At the same time, labour market conditions have improved for immigrants in the Czech Republic, Switzerland, Norway, the Netherlands, Finland and Germany.

More than 15% of immigrant women are unemployed in Finland, Belgium, France, Greece and Germany. The unemployment rate of immigrant women is at least twice as high as that of native women in Norway, Belgium, Luxembourg, Switzerland, the Netherlands, Sweden, Austria and Denmark. In all OECD countries with the exception of South Africa, immigrant women have a higher unemployment rate than native women.

Sources

- OECD (2011), *International Migration Outlook*, OECD Publishing.

Further information

Analytical publications

- OECD (2008), *A Profile of Immigrant Populations in the 21st Century: Data from OECD Countries*, OECD Publishing.
- OECD (2008), *Jobs for Immigrants (Vol. 2): Labour Market Integration in France, Belgium, the Netherlands and Portugal*, OECD Publishing.
- OECD (2007), *Jobs for Immigrants (Vol. 1): Labour Market Integration in Australia, Denmark, Germany and Sweden*, OECD Publishing.
- OECD (2006), *From Immigration to Integration: Local Solutions to a Global Challenge*, OECD Publishing.

Online databases

- *OECD International Migration Statistics*.

Websites

- OECD International Migration Statistics (supplementary material), *www.oecd.org/els/migration/statistics*.

Unemployment rates of foreign- and native-born populations

As a percentage of total labour force

	Men						Women						Total	
	Native-born			Foreign-born			Native-born			Foreign-born			Native-born	Foreign-born
	2000	2005	2009	2000	2005	2009	2000	2005	2009	2000	2005	2009	2009	2009
Australia	..	4.9	5.6		5.2	6.5	..	5.2	5.0	..	5.5	6.9	5.3	6.7
Austria	4.3	3.9	3.9	8.7	10.8	10.7	4.2	4.6	3.9	7.2	10.5	8.2	3.9	9.5
Belgium	4.2	6.5	6.4	14.7	15.7	16.3	7.4	8.4	7.0	17.5	18.9	16.1	6.6	16.2
Canada	..	..	9.3	..	..	10.7	..	..	6.4	..	..	9.6	7.9	10.2
Czech Republic	..	6.4	5.9	..	9.7	8.5	..	9.7	7.7	..	15.8	11.0	6.7	9.6
Denmark	3.7	4.2	6.4	10.7	9.0	10.3	4.9	4.9	5.0	6.6	10.4	10.1	5.7	10.2
Estonia	15.3	8.9	17.3	13.4	9.4	17.7	11.8	6.3	10.5	11.1	11.4	12.3	14.0	14.8
Finland	10.3	9.3	8.7	36.6	22.4	17.9	12.0	9.4	7.4	..	22.7	14.6	8.1	16.3
France	7.7	7.5	8.4	14.5	12.5	15.3	11.3	9.0	9.1	19.7	16.8	14.9	8.8	15.1
Germany	6.9	10.2	7.2	12.9	18.4	13.8	8.0	9.8	6.5	12.1	16.8	12.0	6.8	13.0
Greece	7.5	6.2	6.5	9.5	6.7	10.4	17.0	15.4	13.2	21.4	15.6	14.5	9.3	12.0
Hungary	7.3	7.1	10.4	..	..	8.6	5.8	7.4	9.8	..	6.4	9.6	10.1	9.1
Iceland	8.4	6.2	6.6	6.5	6.8	9.4	14.9	9.7	8.8	21.2	14.5	13.0	7.5	11.0
Ireland	4.4	4.5	14.4	5.4	6.0	18.2	4.1	3.5	7.2	6.1	6.0	11.7	11.2	15.4
Luxembourg	1.4	3.0	2.8	2.5	4.2	6.1	3.0	4.5	3.8	3.3	7.5	8.8	3.3	7.3
Netherlands	1.8	3.6	3.2	5.4	10.8	8.8	3.0	4.4	3.4	7.6	10.0	7.4	3.3	8.1
Norway	3.4	4.0	2.9	6.8	12.5	10.2	3.2	3.9	2.2	..	8.5	6.6	2.6	8.4
Portugal	3.1	7.0	9.0	6.0	8.3	13.2	4.9	9.1	10.5	6.9	10.4	13.0	9.7	13.1
Slovenia	6.6	6.2	5.9	10.0	6.2	7.5	7.1	7.1	5.8	7.9	7.8	7.2	5.9	7.4
Spain	9.4	6.8	15.3	11.8	9.1	29.5	20.4	11.9	16.9	20.0	13.8	24.9	16.0	27.4
Sweden	5.1	7.0	7.5	13.5	15.1	16.2	4.3	6.9	6.9	11.2	13.7	14.5	7.2	15.4
Switzerland	..	2.7	2.9	..	7.8	6.2	..	3.7	3.4	..	9.7	7.8	3.1	6.9
Turkey	..	..	12.7	..	..	14.7	..	..	12.8	..	..	16.6	12.8	15.1
United Kingdom	5.9	4.7	8.8	9.6	7.4	8.3	4.6	3.7	6.2	7.8	7.1	8.5	7.6	8.4
United States	4.5	6.3	11.3	4.4	5.0	10.0	4.2	5.2	7.4	5.4	5.2	8.6	9.4	9.4
Brazil	5.3	..	..	5.8	..	..	9.7	..	..	10.3	..	..	7.9	7.0
Indonesia	4.8	..	..	1.1	..	..	5.3	..	..	4.2	..	..	5.0	1.7
Russian Federation	12.7	..	..	10.8	..	..	12.3	..	..	13.2	..	..	12.5	11.9
South Africa	..	..	25.3	..	..	11.3	..	..	31.4	..	..	25.0	28.5	16.6

StatLink http://dx.doi.org/10.1787/888932503018

Foreign-born unemployment rate relative to native-born unemployment rate

Ratio, 2009 or latest available year

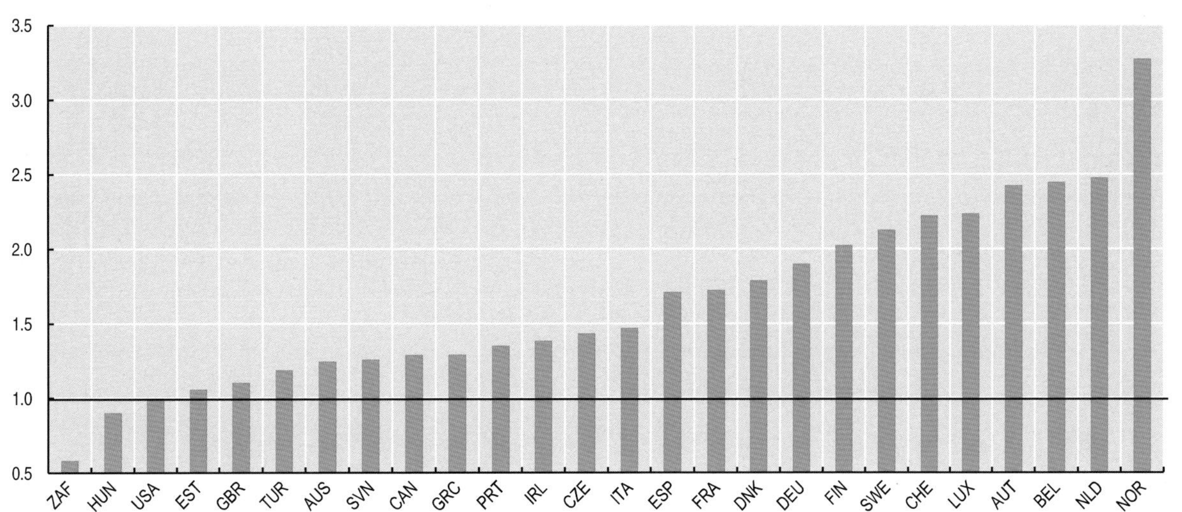

StatLink http://dx.doi.org/10.1787/888932503037

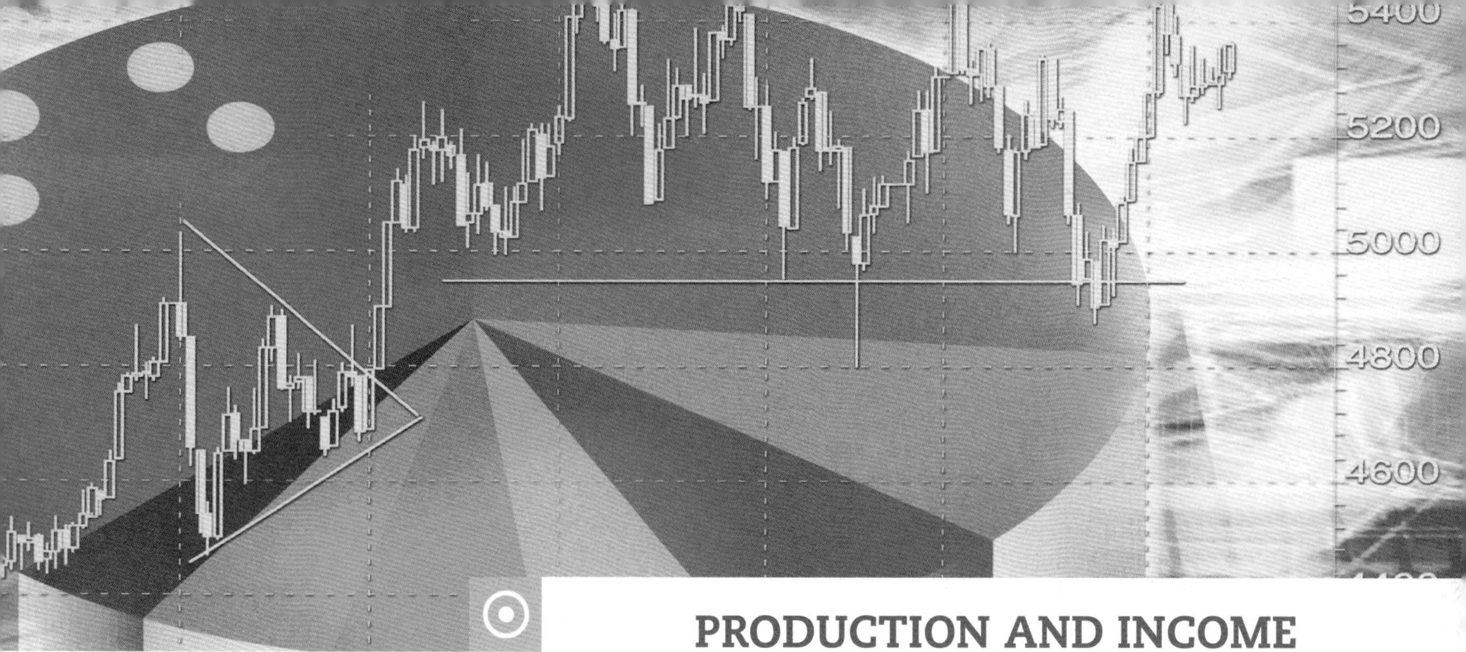

PRODUCTION AND INCOME

SIZE OF GDP

Gross domestic product (GDP) is the standard measure of the value of the goods and services produced by a country during a period. Per capita GDP is a broad indicator of economic living standards.

Each country calculates GDP in its own currency. In order to compare countries, these estimates have to be converted into a common currency. Often, the conversion is made using exchange rates, but these can give a misleading comparison of the volumes of goods and services produced. Comparisons of GDP between countries are best made using purchasing power parities (PPPs) to convert each country's GDP into a common currency. PPPs are currency converters that equalise the purchasing power of the different currencies (see also Rates of conversion).

Definition

What does gross domestic product mean? "Gross" signifies that no deduction has been made for the depreciation of machinery, buildings and other capital products used in production. "Domestic" means that it refers to production by the resident institutional units of each country. As many products are used to produce other products, GDP measures production in terms of value added.

GDP can be measured in three different ways: as output less intermediate consumption (*i.e.* value added) plus taxes on products (such as VAT) less subsidies on products; as income earned from production, obtained by summing employee compensation, the gross operating surplus of enterprises and government, the gross mixed income of unincorporated enterprises and net taxes on production and imports (VAT, payroll tax, import duties, etc, less subsidies); or as final expenditure on the goods and services produced, obtained by summing final consumption expenditures, gross fixed capital formation, changes in inventories and exports less imports.

Comparability

All OECD countries follow the 1993 *System of National Accounts*, except Australia which follows the 2008 SNA. This implies that data are highly comparable across countries. Because of a relatively large number of frontier workers, data on GDP per capita for Luxembourg and, to a lesser extent, Switzerland, are to some extent overstated compared with other countries. GDP data for Australia and New Zealand refer to fiscal years.

For some countries, data for the latest year have been estimated by the OECD. For several countries, historical data have also been estimated by the OECD (by linking the new and old series when countries revise their methodologies but only supply revised data for recent years). Relatively minor differences in the measured per capita GDP can result in a different country order that may not be statistically or economically significant.

Overview

Among OECD countries, the United States has, by far, the largest GDP in USD current prices and PPPs, followed by Japan and, at some distance, the four largest EU members – Germany, the United Kingdom, France and Italy. The next four OECD countries are Mexico, Spain, Korea and Canada. China's GDP is close to 70% of that of the US, while those of India and the Russian Federation are equivalent to 28% and 19%.

Per capita GDP for the OECD as a whole was 34 025 USD in 2010. Six OECD countries had per capita GDP in excess of 40 000 USD in 2010 – Luxembourg, Norway, the United States, Switzerland, the Netherlands and Australia. About half of all OECD countries had per capita GDP between 30 000 and 45 000 USD in 2010, while 14 countries had per capita GDP below 30 000 USD, with Turkey, Chile and Mexico at the bottom of the distribution.

Sources

- OECD (2011), *National Accounts of OECD Countries*, OECD Publishing.
- For Brazil and India: IMF (2009), *World Economic Outlook (WEO)*, IMF, Washington DC.

Further information

Analytical publications

- OECD (2011), *OECD Economic Outlook*, OECD Publishing.
- OECD (2011), *Towards Green Growth*, OECD Publishing.
- OECD (2011), *Towards Green Growth – Monitoring Progress: OECD Indicators*, OECD Publishing.
- OECD (2003), *The Sources of Economic Growth in OECD Countries*, OECD Publishing.

Statistical publications

- Maddison, A. (2003), *The World Economy: Historical Perspectives*, OECD Publishing.
- OECD (2011), *OECD Latin American Economic Outlook*, OECD Publishing.
- OECD (2011), *National Accounts at a Glance*, OECD Publishing.
- OECD, African Development Bank and United Nations Economic Commission for Africa (UNECA) (2011), *African Economic Outlook*, OECD Publishing.

Methodological publications

- OECD (2000), *OECD Glossaries, System of National Accounts, 1993 – Glossary*, OECD Publishing.
- United Nations, OECD, International Monetary Fund and Eurostat (eds.) (2010), *System of National Accounts 2008*, United Nations, Geneva.

Online databases

- *OECD National Accounts Statistics.*
- *OECD Economic Outlook: Statistics and Projections.*

Websites

- OECD Economic Outlook – Sources and Methods, *www.oecd.org/eco/sources-and-methods*.
- The World Economy (supplementary material), *www.theworldeconomy.org*.

Gross domestic product

Billion US dollars, current prices and PPPs

	1997	1998	1999	2000	2001	2002	2003	2004	2005	2006	2007	2008	2009	2010
Australia	449.7	478.6	511.8	540.5	571.0	601.8	642.1	678.7	721.3	774.5	831.0	848.7	884.7	915.7
Austria	198.5	208.0	215.9	230.5	231.6	244.3	252.3	266.3	274.8	299.9	313.8	332.2	324.6	332.9
Belgium	242.5	248.4	259.0	283.0	292.9	310.0	313.7	324.5	336.6	360.1	378.1	394.9	391.7	407.4
Canada	731.9	770.5	825.0	874.1	909.8	937.8	989.3	1 049.1	1 132.0	1 200.5	1 263.0	1 295.9	1 275.6	1 327.3
Chile	127.5	133.1	134.1	143.1	151.2	157.0	166.8	181.9	198.4	214.2	230.7	244.2	242.4	257.5
Czech Republic	142.5	143.7	147.2	154.0	165.4	172.1	183.5	197.0	208.4	229.5	253.7	269.6	268.2	266.1
Denmark	133.5	138.6	143.3	153.9	157.7	165.3	164.0	174.5	179.9	195.9	206.0	216.9	208.1	219.3
Estonia	11.2	11.7	12.1	13.5	14.6	16.3	18.1	19.9	22.3	25.7	28.5	29.2	26.6	27.6
Finland	107.6	116.2	121.9	132.8	137.6	143.1	143.8	156.1	161.0	174.3	191.2	200.8	188.1	196.6
France	1 298.3	1 366.0	1 424.2	1 532.8	1 627.9	1 704.9	1 692.4	1 761.9	1 860.7	1 991.0	2 114.4	2 178.5	2 152.4	2 194.1
Germany	1 934.5	1 989.1	2 063.8	2 132.7	2 211.3	2 275.4	2 357.3	2 466.8	2 586.5	2 776.8	2 930.5	3 052.5	2 974.7	3 071.3
Greece	172.9	178.8	185.4	201.0	218.2	237.3	250.3	266.5	272.8	302.1	316.2	338.0	330.6	318.7
Hungary	103.7	111.0	115.2	123.9	138.3	150.0	156.2	164.9	170.9	184.6	192.9	207.8	203.2	203.3
Iceland	7.1	7.6	7.9	8.1	8.7	8.9	8.9	9.9	10.4	10.9	11.6	12.5	11.7	11.1
Ireland	79.7	89.0	97.2	109.2	117.9	130.0	138.0	148.5	160.7	180.1	197.7	189.5	176.8	178.0
Israel	118.5	124.8	130.8	147.8	151.0	154.6	149.0	161.0	162.1	176.1	190.9	202.3	205.8	217.3
Italy	1 284.6	1 350.1	1 377.2	1 457.4	1 545.6	1 532.0	1 563.2	1 594.9	1 649.4	1 781.5	1 893.9	1 990.5	1 951.0	1 908.6
Japan	3 059.8	3 031.0	3 071.1	3 250.3	3 330.1	3 417.2	3 509.9	3 708.5	3 872.8	4 071.4	4 290.2	4 316.6	4 082.6	4 301.9
Korea	678.8	647.3	727.3	808.4	859.6	936.0	965.8	1 039.1	1 096.7	1 173.0	1 269.1	1 306.4	1 322.7	1 417.5
Luxembourg	17.1	18.4	21.1	23.4	23.8	25.7	27.4	29.8	31.8	37.1	40.6	43.8	42.2	45.4
Mexico	799.6	849.3	894.1	987.1	1 009.2	1 047.7	1 108.7	1 186.6	1 293.8	1 432.2	1 540.9	1 629.6	1 545.9	1 646.4
Netherlands	376.0	400.1	425.8	468.2	493.9	515.8	514.3	540.5	572.9	622.0	667.3	705.1	674.4	705.6
New Zealand	70.8	72.3	77.5	81.4	85.9	90.4	94.8	100.4	104.6	113.4	121.2	124.5	126.3	130.7
Norway	123.2	121.5	133.0	162.2	167.4	168.2	174.8	194.0	218.7	248.4	259.0	288.4	263.4	277.0
Poland	339.6	362.4	382.6	404.3	418.9	442.1	457.8	496.9	526.1	574.6	638.9	688.5	722.0	754.1
Portugal	150.3	158.9	169.9	181.5	190.1	197.9	202.5	207.9	224.6	242.1	256.8	265.1	266.4	272.4
Slovak Republic	52.5	55.6	56.2	59.3	64.9	69.7	73.1	78.9	87.1	99.2	112.9	125.6	123.9	127.3
Slovenia	29.5	31.1	33.1	34.9	36.7	39.4	41.0	44.5	47.0	51.1	54.9	59.1	56.1	56.4
Spain	700.4	750.4	791.5	858.4	920.0	994.3	1 039.5	1 108.2	1 188.1	1 337.4	1 447.3	1 512.5	1 481.1	1 477.8
Sweden	207.8	216.1	230.1	248.0	251.1	261.3	272.5	292.4	295.3	324.0	352.1	364.0	345.5	365.9
Switzerland	202.6	210.4	215.2	227.9	233.9	245.2	246.3	257.4	266.1	295.6	325.7	351.5	349.8	361.9
Turkey	510.8	535.4	517.7	589.2	561.0	572.1	587.8	688.6	781.2	894.6	976.4	1 063.5	1 022.3	1 116.0
United Kingdom	1 307.4	1 362.7	1 423.0	1 535.2	1 630.2	1 713.7	1 777.7	1 902.6	1 971.3	2 118.7	2 178.4	2 260.5	2 172.0	2 233.9
United States	8 278.9	8 741.0	9 301.0	9 898.8	10 233.9	10 590.2	11 089.2	11 812.3	12 579.7	13 336.2	13 995.0	14 296.9	14 043.9	14 582.4
Euro area	6 675.8	6 992.9	7 273.7	7 722.2	8 149.7	8 465.4	8 658.0	9 044.7	9 525.0	10 320.1	10 983.9	11 471.6	11 217.3	11 372.5
EU27 total	9 119.5	9 536.2	9 928.9	10 587.4	11 163.0	11 642.8	11 967.2	12 603.8	13 234.7	14 362.3	15 275.6	16 014.6	15 645.1	15 919.7
OECD total	24 049.0	25 029.4	26 242.0	28 056.7	29 161.4	30 268.1	31 372.5	33 311.0	35 266.1	37 848.3	40 070.9	41 405.4	40 456.5	41 925.3
Brazil	1 125.0	1 138.1	1 157.8	1 233.8	1 278.3	1 333.5	1 377.8	1 494.7	1 584.6	1 701.0	1 857.7	1 996.3	2 001.6	2 172.1
China	2 286.2	2 492.3	2 721.2	3 013.6	3 337.5	3 700.2	4 157.8	4 697.9	5 364.3	6 242.4	7 338.7	8 219.0	9 057.4	10 085.7
India	1 329.1	1 415.2	1 483.0	1 582.3	1 681.0	1 786.0	1 949.5	2 161.6	2 434.4	2 756.4	3 118.0	3 382.9	3 644.5	4 060.4
Indonesia	517.8	454.9	465.2	500.7	530.7	563.6	603.2	650.2	705.2	768.2	841.0	911.0	961.4	1 029.9
Russian Federation	842.0	806.0	869.8	998.6	1 073.2	1 166.7	1 335.7	1 473.9	1 696.7	2 138.6	2 387.5	2 888.8	2 699.5	2 812.4
South Africa	263.1	267.5	277.8	295.6	310.6	327.2	344.1	371.7	405.8	442.5	480.8	508.9	504.9	524.0

StatLink http://dx.doi.org/10.1787/888932503056

Gross domestic product

Billion US dollars, current prices and PPPs, 2010

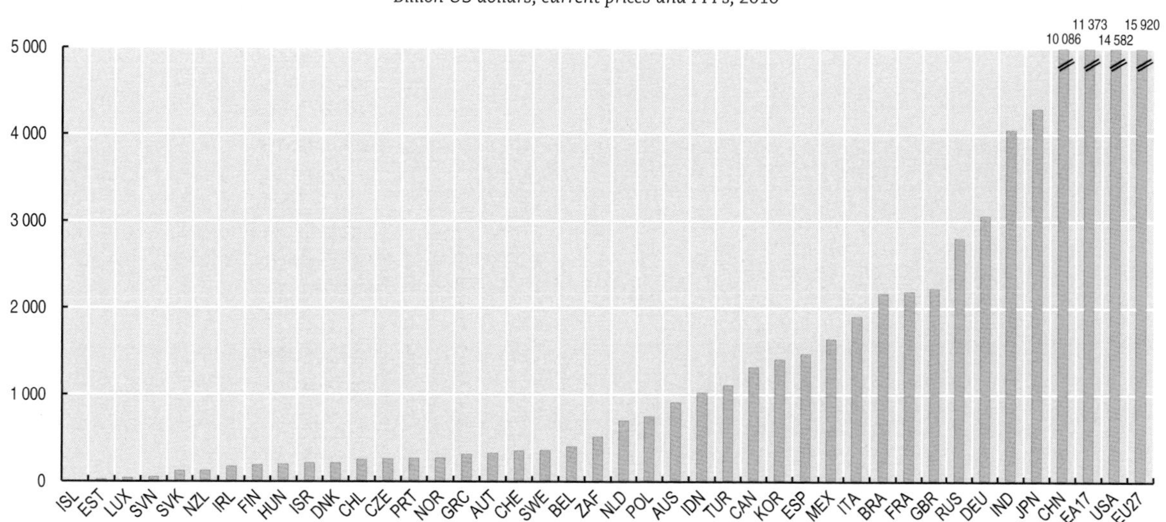

StatLink http://dx.doi.org/10.1787/888932503075

GDP per capita

US dollars, current prices and PPPs

	1997	1998	1999	2000	2001	2002	2003	2004	2005	2006	2007	2008	2009	2010
Australia	24 170	25 443	26 888	28 047	29 235	30 441	32 091	33 516	35 115	37 109	39 087	39 058	39 918	40 644
Austria	24 910	26 075	27 011	28 770	28 799	30 231	31 081	32 598	33 409	36 269	37 802	39 849	38 814	39 768
Belgium	23 825	24 348	25 333	27 624	28 489	30 014	30 242	31 152	32 141	34 159	35 597	36 879	36 300	37 435
Canada	24 473	25 551	27 138	28 485	29 332	29 911	31 269	32 846	35 106	36 854	38 353	38 883	37 808	38 914
Chile	8 616	8 877	8 824	9 294	9 713	9 973	10 476	11 300	12 194	13 036	13 897	14 568	14 321	15 064
Czech Republic	13 827	13 962	14 312	14 992	16 174	16 872	17 992	19 304	20 366	22 350	24 579	25 845	25 563	25 299
Denmark	25 256	26 139	26 926	28 822	29 438	30 756	30 428	32 301	33 196	36 026	37 731	39 494	37 680	39 545
Estonia	7 954	8 417	8 752	9 862	10 693	11 967	13 370	14 758	16 531	19 134	21 262	21 802	19 876	20 608
Finland	20 932	22 551	23 596	25 651	26 518	27 509	27 592	29 855	30 690	33 095	36 149	37 795	35 229	36 664
France	21 700	22 750	23 612	25 241	26 616	27 676	27 281	28 195	29 554	31 406	33 151	33 963	33 373	33 835
Germany	23 576	24 249	25 142	25 949	26 855	27 587	28 567	29 901	31 366	33 713	35 623	37 171	36 332	37 567
Greece	16 041	16 506	17 032	18 410	19 929	21 598	22 702	24 088	24 572	27 095	28 250	30 077	29 303	28 189
Hungary	10 073	10 812	11 250	12 134	13 576	14 765	15 424	16 317	16 938	18 329	19 187	20 700	20 275	20 325
Iceland	26 092	27 824	28 632	28 840	30 444	31 084	30 768	33 698	35 025	35 808	37 179	39 166	36 647	34 905
Ireland	21 764	23 955	25 887	28 695	30 524	33 052	34 525	36 512	38 623	42 268	45 294	42 644	39 562	39 778
Israel	20 335	20 897	21 352	23 496	23 455	23 535	22 271	23 650	23 390	24 960	26 583	27 679	27 661	28 510
Italy	22 580	23 725	24 196	25 594	27 127	26 804	27 138	27 416	28 144	30 224	31 898	33 269	32 413	31 563
Japan	24 254	23 966	24 245	25 608	26 156	26 805	27 487	29 021	30 312	31 865	33 577	33 805	32 018	33 772
Korea	14 772	13 984	15 601	17 197	18 151	19 656	20 181	21 630	22 783	24 286	26 191	26 877	27 133	29 004
Luxembourg	40 882	43 264	49 072	53 646	53 932	57 559	60 724	65 022	68 372	78 523	84 577	89 742	84 848	89 633
Mexico	8 515	8 918	9 261	10 046	10 136	10 398	10 884	11 535	12 461	13 673	14 582	15 291	14 388	15 204
Netherlands	24 093	25 478	26 933	29 406	30 788	31 943	31 703	33 209	35 111	38 064	40 744	42 887	40 804	42 478
New Zealand	18 667	18 919	20 165	21 039	22 024	22 775	23 438	24 492	25 219	27 007	28 567	29 077	29 149	29 813
Norway	27 959	27 413	29 800	36 126	37 092	37 052	38 299	42 258	47 319	53 288	55 042	60 480	54 568	56 648
Poland	8 870	9 467	9 996	10 567	10 950	11 563	11 985	13 015	13 786	15 067	16 762	18 062	18 925	19 747
Portugal	14 891	15 686	16 703	17 749	18 465	19 088	19 392	19 796	21 294	22 870	24 206	24 957	25 055	25 609
Slovak Republic	9 745	10 324	10 408	10 982	12 072	12 967	13 599	14 660	16 175	18 401	20 919	23 245	22 869	23 448
Slovenia	14 841	15 687	16 707	17 549	18 441	19 759	20 514	22 276	23 472	25 428	27 214	29 221	27 462	27 545
Spain	17 694	18 890	19 824	21 320	22 591	24 067	24 748	25 958	27 377	30 348	32 252	33 173	32 247	32 076
Sweden	23 488	24 418	25 976	27 948	28 231	29 278	30 418	32 506	32 701	35 680	38 486	39 475	37 155	39 013
Switzerland	28 483	29 500	30 028	31 618	32 103	33 391	33 266	34 537	35 478	39 116	42 756	45 586	44 840	46 480
Turkey	8 295	8 571	8 171	9 170	8 613	8 667	8 790	10 166	11 391	12 887	13 897	14 962	14 218	15 320
United Kingdom	22 419	23 304	24 249	26 071	27 578	28 888	29 849	31 791	32 724	34 971	35 719	36 817	35 151	35 917
United States	30 330	31 653	33 298	35 050	35 866	36 755	38 128	40 246	42 466	44 595	46 337	46 901	45 674	47 024
Euro area	21 395	22 365	23 200	24 538	25 779	26 630	27 068	28 097	29 410	31 698	33 541	34 842	33 950	34 328
EU27 total	18 990	19 831	20 610	21 919	23 049	23 977	24 543	25 731	26 895	29 068	30 773	32 114	31 269	31 737
OECD total	21 328	22 047	22 956	24 359	25 132	25 901	26 657	28 111	29 562	31 516	33 133	34 002	33 023	34 025
Brazil	6 869	6 846	6 861	7 204	7 354	7 560	7 698	8 231	8 603	9 166	9 900	10 528	10 453	11 239
China	1 849	1 998	2 163	2 378	2 615	2 881	3 217	3 614	4 102	4 749	5 554	6 189	6 786	7 519
India	1 344	1 405	1 447	1 518	1 585	1 657	1 779	1 942	2 153	2 402	2 677	2 862	3 039	3 339
Indonesia	2 572	2 226	2 243	2 441	2 552	2 674	2 825	3 005	3 207	3 449	3 727	3 987	4 155	4 394
Russian Federation	5 688	5 453	5 895	6 798	7 336	8 010	9 214	10 223	11 826	14 981	16 787	20 342	19 023	19 833
South Africa	6 179	6 178	6 322	6 640	6 897	7 184	7 478	8 000	8 654	9 336	10 049	10 453	10 238	10 498

StatLink http://dx.doi.org/10.1787/888932503094

GDP per capita

US dollars, current prices and PPPs, 2010

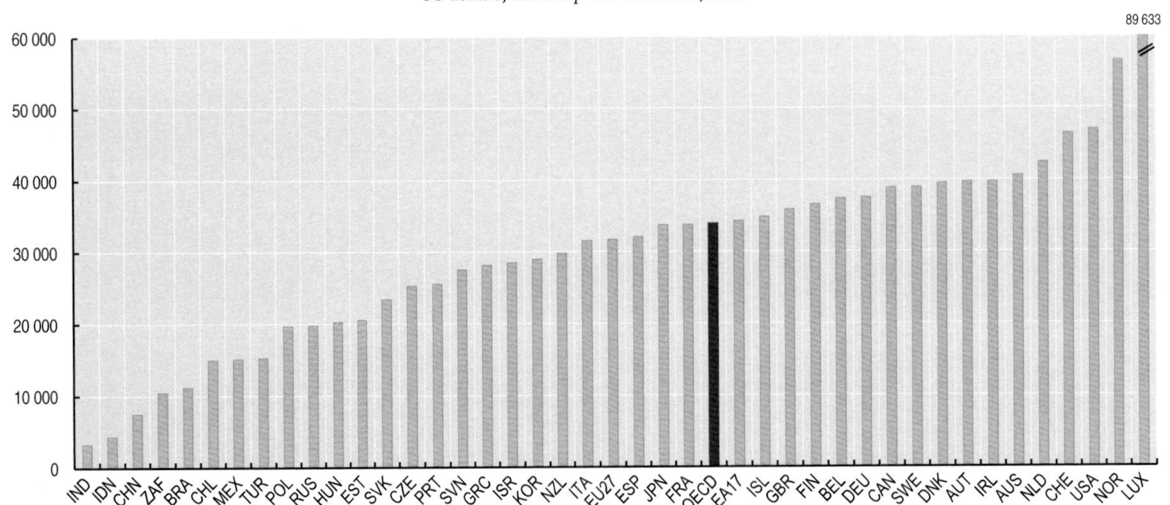

StatLink http://dx.doi.org/10.1787/888932503113

Volume index of GDP per capita

OECD = 100 in 2000, at 2000 price levels and PPPs

	1997	1998	1999	2000	2001	2002	2003	2004	2005	2006	2007	2008	2009	2010
Australia	106.9	111.2	114.2	115.1	118.0	120.4	123.9	126.1	128.1	130.6	133.1	132.1	132.5	..
Austria	107.0	110.7	114.2	118.1	118.3	119.6	120.0	122.3	124.5	128.3	132.6	134.9	129.2	131.6
Belgium	104.3	106.1	109.6	113.4	113.9	114.9	115.3	118.6	119.9	122.4	125.0	125.2	120.9	122.5
Canada	103.8	107.2	112.2	116.9	117.7	119.9	121.0	123.6	126.2	128.4	129.8	129.0	124.2	..
Chile	37.1	37.8	37.0	38.2	39.0	39.4	40.5	42.5	44.4	45.9	47.6	48.8	47.5	..
Czech Republic	58.9	58.5	59.3	61.5	63.4	64.7	67.0	70.0	74.2	79.0	83.4	84.6	80.6	82.3
Denmark	110.2	112.2	114.7	118.3	118.7	118.9	119.0	121.5	124.1	127.8	129.3	127.1	119.8	121.8
Estonia	33.8	36.4	36.6	40.5	43.7	47.4	51.1	55.0	60.4	66.9	71.7	68.1	58.7	60.5
Finland	92.3	96.6	100.2	105.3	107.5	109.1	111.1	115.3	118.3	123.0	129.0	129.6	118.4	121.6
France	95.0	97.9	100.6	103.6	104.8	105.0	105.2	107.1	108.2	110.1	112.0	111.3	107.6	108.6
Germany	99.3	101.4	103.3	106.5	107.7	107.5	107.2	108.5	109.4	113.2	116.3	117.7	112.5	116.7
Greece	68.6	70.5	72.6	75.6	78.5	80.9	85.5	88.9	90.6	94.9	98.5	99.2	96.7	92.2
Hungary	43.2	45.4	47.4	49.8	51.8	54.1	56.4	59.1	61.1	63.4	64.0	64.7	60.4	61.3
Iceland	106.4	112.0	115.1	118.4	121.4	120.5	122.6	130.6	138.8	141.1	146.2	144.5	134.5	..
Ireland	92.8	99.2	108.8	117.8	122.6	128.4	131.8	135.5	140.5	144.4	148.9	141.1	129.7	128.1
Israel	88.7	90.1	90.7	96.5	94.2	91.7	91.5	94.5	97.4	101.1	104.6	107.1	106.1	..
Italy	98.6	99.9	101.4	105.1	106.9	107.1	106.2	106.8	106.7	108.2	109.0	106.8	100.6	101.4
Japan	105.1	102.7	102.4	105.1	105.0	105.1	106.4	109.3	111.4	113.7	116.4	115.1	108.0	..
Korea	63.6	59.5	65.4	70.6	72.9	77.6	79.4	82.8	85.9	90.0	94.3	96.2	96.2	101.9
Luxembourg	183.1	192.5	205.8	220.2	223.2	229.9	230.6	237.5	246.6	254.8	267.4	266.7	252.2	256.3
Mexico	37.1	38.5	39.4	41.2	40.7	40.5	40.6	41.9	42.8	44.6	45.7	46.0	42.9	..
Netherlands	108.9	112.5	117.0	120.7	122.1	121.4	121.3	123.6	125.8	129.9	134.6	136.7	130.6	132.3
New Zealand	80.8	81.1	84.9	86.4	88.6	91.3	93.1	95.1	97.1	98.1	99.9	97.9	97.5	..
Norway	139.8	142.7	144.6	148.3	150.5	151.9	152.6	157.6	160.8	163.1	165.9	164.9	160.2	158.7
Poland	37.9	39.8	41.6	43.4	43.9	44.6	46.3	48.8	50.6	53.8	57.5	60.4	61.4	63.7
Portugal	65.0	68.0	70.5	72.9	73.8	73.8	72.6	73.3	73.5	74.3	75.9	75.8	73.9	74.8
Slovak Republic	42.7	44.5	44.5	45.1	46.8	49.0	51.3	53.9	57.4	62.3	68.7	72.6	69.0	71.6
Slovenia	63.5	65.8	69.3	72.0	74.1	76.8	79.0	82.4	85.6	90.3	95.9	99.3	90.4	91.1
Spain	77.5	80.6	84.0	87.5	89.7	90.8	92.1	93.6	95.4	97.7	99.4	98.6	94.3	93.8
Sweden	101.0	105.2	110.0	114.7	115.9	118.4	120.7	125.3	128.7	133.5	136.9	135.0	126.7	132.8
Switzerland	122.1	125.0	126.1	129.8	129.9	129.5	128.1	130.5	133.1	136.9	140.8	142.0	137.7	..
Turkey	36.9	37.5	35.8	37.6	35.0	36.7	38.1	41.2	44.1	46.5	48.1	47.9	45.1	..
United Kingdom	97.0	100.2	103.4	107.0	109.2	111.1	113.8	116.6	118.4	121.0	123.4	122.5	115.8	116.6
United States	130.5	134.7	139.7	143.9	144.0	145.2	147.4	151.3	154.5	157.2	158.6	157.1	151.6	..
Euro area	92.4	94.8	97.3	100.7	102.2	102.6	102.8	104.3	105.5	108.1	110.6	110.4	105.5	107.1
EU27 total	82.1	84.4	86.8	90.0	91.5	92.4	93.3	95.2	96.6	99.3	101.8	101.9	97.2	98.7
OECD total	92.2	94.1	96.7	100.0	100.6	101.5	102.8	105.5	107.6	110.2	112.4	112.0	107.5	..
China	8.0	8.5	9.1	9.8	10.5	11.4	12.4	13.6	15.1	16.9	19.2	20.9	22.7	..
Indonesia	11.1	9.5	9.4	10.0	10.2	10.6	10.9	11.3	11.8	12.3	12.9	13.5	13.9	14.4
Russian Federation	25.0	23.7	25.3	27.9	29.4	31.0	33.4	36.0	38.5	41.8	45.6	48.0	44.3	..
South Africa	..	..	..	..	..	..	28.7	29.9	31.2	32.6	34.1	34.7	33.7	34.2

StatLink http://dx.doi.org/10.1787/888932503132

Growth of GDP per capita in volume terms

Average annual growth in percentage

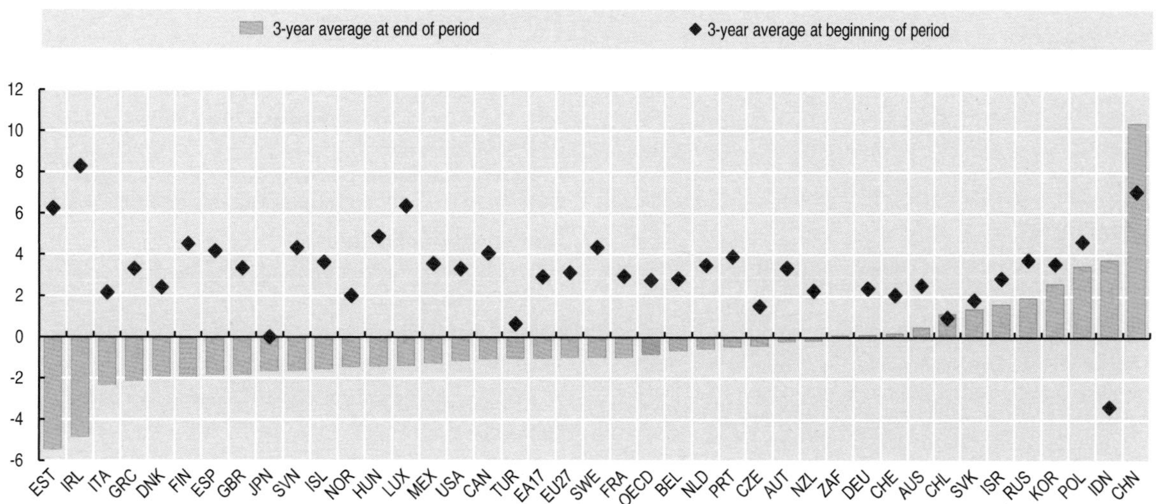

StatLink http://dx.doi.org/10.1787/888932503151

EVOLUTION OF GDP

Measuring GDP growth is important but GDP can grow simply via inflation. Abstracting from price changes to measure real GDP growth provides a sounder basis for assessing growth in economic production.

Definition

In order to calculate the growth rate of GDP free of the direct effects of inflation, data at fixed, or constant, prices should be used. Price relativities change over time, and the 1993 *System of National Accounts* (SNA) recommends that the fixed prices used should be representative of the periods for which the growth rates are calculated. This means that new fixed prices should be introduced frequently, typically every year. The growth rates of GDP between successive periods are linked together to form chain volume indices. All OECD countries derive their "volume" estimates in this way, except for Mexico who only revises its fixed weights every ten years. Such practices tend to lead to biased growth rates, usually upward. For the definition of GDP, please refer to the definition under "Size of GDP" in this chapter.

The GDP growth rates for OECD total are averages of the growth rates of individual countries, weighted by the relative size of each country's GDP in US dollars. Conversion to US dollars is done using purchasing power parities.

Comparability

The GDP statistics used to compute volume GDP growth rates have been compiled according to the 1993 *System of National Accounts* for all countries except Australia which uses the 2008 SNA. GDP estimates at current prices are generally regarded as highly comparable across countries. However, there is more variability in how countries calculate their volume estimates of GDP, particularly in respect of services, government consumption and some types of capital expenditures, although this doesn't necessarily imply lower comparability in estimated GDP growth rates.

Three-year averages refer to the years 2008 to 2010 (end of period); and 1997 to 1999 (beginning of period).

Overview

The average annual rate of volume GDP growth for the OECD total in the three years to 2010 was minus 0.1%. This mainly reflects the strong fall of 3.5% in 2009 at the height of the recent economic crisis. This compares to significantly higher GDP growth rates in India, Indonesia, and China, which all had average annual growth of 5% or more over the period. Estonia, Ireland and Iceland, which contracted between 3 and 6%, recorded the lowest average annual GDP growth rates between 2007 and 2010.

Real GDP growth

Annual growth in percentage

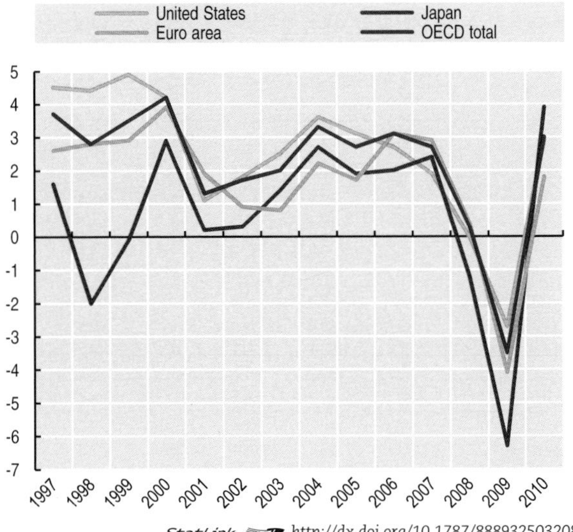

StatLink http://dx.doi.org/10.1787/888932503208

Sources

- OECD (2011), *National Accounts of OECD Countries*, OECD Publishing.
- For non-member countries: national sources.

Further information

Analytical publications

- Goldstein, A., *et al.* (2006), *The Rise of China and India: What's in it for Africa?*, Development Centre Studies, OECD Publishing.
- OECD (2011), *Economic Policy Reforms*, OECD Publishing.
- OECD (2011), *OECD Economic Outlook*, OECD Publishing.

Statistical publications

- OECD (2011), *National Accounts at a Glance*, OECD Publishing.

Online databases

- *OECD National Accounts Statistics.*
- *OECD Economic Outlook: Statistics and Projections.*

Websites

- OECD Economic Outlook – Sources and Methods, *www.oecd.org/eco/sources-and-methods.*

Real GDP growth

Annual growth in percentage

	1997	1998	1999	2000	2001	2002	2003	2004	2005	2006	2007	2008	2009	2010
Australia	4.6	5.2	4.0	2.1	3.9	3.3	4.2	3.0	3.1	3.6	3.8	1.4	2.3	2.6
Austria	2.1	3.6	3.3	3.7	0.5	1.6	0.8	2.5	2.5	3.6	3.7	2.2	-3.9	2.0
Belgium	3.7	1.9	3.5	3.7	0.8	1.4	0.8	3.2	1.7	2.7	2.9	1.0	-2.8	2.2
Canada	4.2	4.1	5.5	5.2	1.8	2.9	1.9	3.1	3.0	2.8	2.2	0.5	-2.5	3.1
Chile	6.6	3.3	-0.7	4.5	3.3	2.2	4.0	6.0	5.6	4.6	4.6	3.7	-1.7	5.2
Czech Republic	-0.7	-0.8	1.3	3.6	2.5	1.9	3.6	4.5	6.3	6.8	6.1	2.5	-4.1	2.3
Denmark	3.2	2.2	2.6	3.5	0.7	0.5	0.4	2.3	2.4	3.4	1.6	-1.1	-5.2	2.1
Estonia	11.7	6.7	-0.3	10.0	7.5	7.9	7.6	7.2	9.4	10.6	6.9	-5.1	-13.9	3.1
Finland	6.2	5.0	3.9	5.3	2.3	1.8	2.0	4.1	2.9	4.4	5.3	0.9	-8.2	3.1
France	2.2	3.4	3.3	3.7	1.8	0.9	0.9	2.5	1.8	2.5	2.3	-0.1	-2.7	1.5
Germany	1.8	2.0	2.0	3.2	1.2	0.0	-0.2	1.2	0.8	3.4	2.7	1.0	-4.7	3.6
Greece	3.6	3.4	3.4	4.5	4.2	3.4	5.9	4.4	2.3	5.2	4.3	1.0	-2.0	-4.5
Hungary	3.9	4.8	4.1	4.9	3.8	4.1	4.0	4.5	3.2	3.6	0.8	0.8	-6.7	1.2
Iceland	4.9	6.3	4.1	4.3	3.9	0.1	2.4	7.7	7.5	4.6	6.0	1.4	-6.9	-3.5
Ireland	11.5	8.4	10.9	9.7	5.7	6.5	4.4	4.6	6.0	5.3	5.6	-3.5	-7.6	-1.0
Israel	3.3	4.1	3.3	9.1	-0.1	-0.6	1.5	5.1	4.9	5.7	5.3	4.2	0.8	4.6
Italy	1.9	1.4	1.5	3.7	1.8	0.5	-	1.5	0.7	2.0	1.5	-1.3	-5.2	1.3
Japan	1.6	-2.0	-0.1	2.9	0.2	0.3	1.4	2.7	1.9	2.0	2.4	-1.2	-6.3	3.9
Korea	5.8	-5.7	10.7	8.8	4.0	7.2	2.8	4.6	4.0	5.2	5.1	2.3	0.3	6.2
Luxembourg	5.9	6.5	8.4	8.4	2.5	4.1	1.5	4.4	5.4	5.0	6.6	1.4	-3.6	3.5
Mexico	6.8	5.0	3.8	6.6	0.0	0.8	1.4	4.1	3.3	5.1	3.4	1.5	-6.0	5.5
Netherlands	4.3	3.9	4.7	3.9	1.9	0.1	0.3	2.2	2.0	3.4	3.9	1.9	-3.9	1.8
New Zealand	2.9	1.2	5.2	2.5	3.5	4.9	3.9	3.6	3.2	2.2	2.9	-1.1	0.8	2.5
Norway	5.4	2.7	2.0	3.3	2.0	1.5	1.0	3.9	2.7	2.3	2.7	0.7	-1.7	0.3
Poland	7.1	5.0	4.5	4.3	1.2	1.4	3.9	5.3	3.6	6.2	6.8	5.1	1.7	3.8
Portugal	4.4	5.0	4.1	3.9	2.0	0.7	-0.9	1.6	0.8	1.4	2.4	0.0	-2.5	1.3
Slovak Republic	4.4	4.4	0.0	1.4	3.5	4.6	4.8	5.1	6.7	8.5	10.5	5.8	-4.8	4.0
Slovenia	5.0	3.5	5.3	4.3	2.9	3.8	2.9	4.4	4.0	5.8	6.8	3.7	-8.1	1.2
Spain	3.9	4.5	4.7	5.0	3.6	2.7	3.1	3.3	3.6	4.0	3.6	0.9	-3.7	-0.1
Sweden	2.7	4.2	4.7	4.5	1.3	2.5	2.3	4.2	3.2	4.3	3.3	-0.6	-5.3	5.7
Switzerland	2.1	2.6	1.3	3.6	1.2	0.4	-0.2	2.5	2.6	3.6	3.6	2.1	-1.9	2.6
Turkey	7.5	3.1	-3.4	6.8	-5.7	6.2	5.3	9.4	8.4	6.9	4.7	0.7	-4.8	8.9
United Kingdom	3.3	3.6	3.5	3.9	2.5	2.1	2.8	3.0	2.2	2.8	2.7	-0.1	-4.9	1.4
United States	4.5	4.4	4.9	4.2	1.1	1.8	2.5	3.6	3.1	2.7	1.9	0.0	-2.7	2.9
Euro area	2.6	2.8	2.9	3.9	1.9	0.9	0.8	2.2	1.7	3.1	2.9	0.4	-4.1	1.8
EU27 total	2.7	3.0	3.1	3.9	2.0	1.2	1.3	2.5	2.0	3.2	3.0	0.5	-4.2	1.8
OECD total	3.7	2.8	3.5	4.2	1.3	1.7	2.0	3.3	2.7	3.1	2.7	0.3	-3.5	3.0
Brazil	3.4	0.0	0.3	4.3	1.3	2.7	1.1	5.7	3.2	4.0	6.1	5.2	-0.6	7.5
China	9.3	7.8	7.6	8.4	8.3	9.1	10.0	10.1	11.3	12.7	14.2	9.6	9.2	10.3
India	10.3	5.3	3.3	4.4	3.9	4.6	6.9	8.1	9.2	9.7	9.9	6.2	6.8	10.4
Indonesia	4.7	-13.1	0.8	5.4	3.6	4.5	4.8	5.0	5.7	5.5	6.3	6.0	4.6	6.1
Russian Federation	1.4	-5.3	6.4	10.0	5.1	4.7	7.3	7.2	6.4	8.2	8.5	5.2	-7.9	4.0
South Africa	2.6	0.5	2.4	4.2	2.7	3.7	2.9	4.6	5.3	5.6	5.6	3.6	-1.7	2.8

StatLink http://dx.doi.org/10.1787/888932503170

Real GDP growth

Average annual growth in percentage

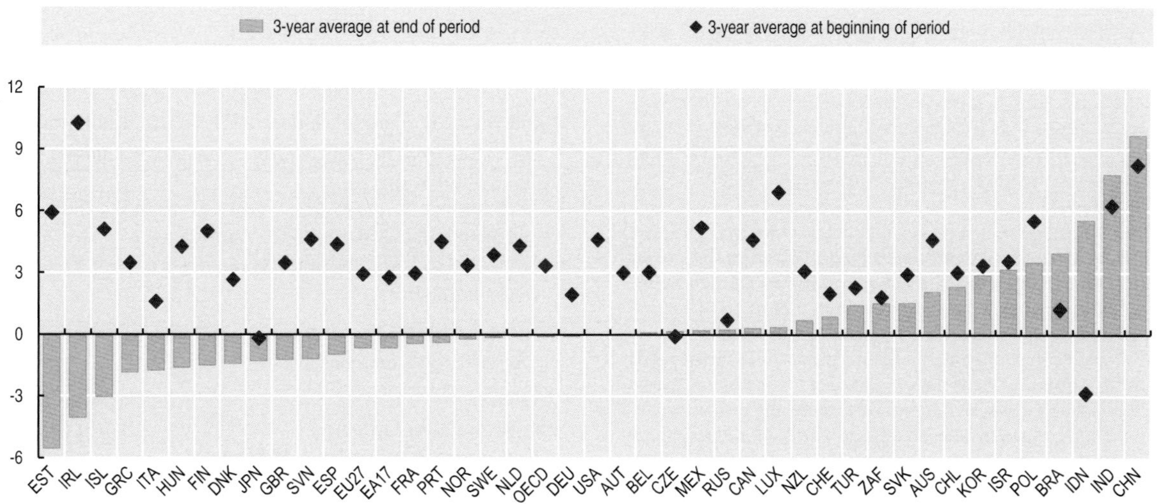

StatLink http://dx.doi.org/10.1787/888932503189

GDP BY REGION

Disparities in economic performance across OECD countries are often smaller than those prevailing among regions of the same country. Further, these regional disparities have persisted over time, even when economic disparities among countries were falling.

Definition

Regional inequalities in economic performance are here measured by regional GDP per capita. GDP per capita is calculated by dividing the GDP of a country or a region by the population (number of inhabitants) living there, and is measured according to the definitions of the 1993 *System of National Accounts*.

The Gini index is a measure of inequality among all regions of a given country. The index takes on values between 0 and 1, with zero interpreted as no disparity. It assigns equal weight to each region regardless of its size; therefore differences in the values of the index among countries may be partially due to differences in the average size of regions in each country.

Comparability

As for the other regional statistics, comparability is affected by differences in the meaning of the word "region". The word "region" can mean very different things both within and among countries, with significant differences in terms of area and population. To address this issue, the OECD has classified regions within each member country based on two levels: territorial level 2 (TL2, large regions) and territorial level 3 (TL3, small regions). All the data shown here refer to small regions with the exception of Australia, Brazil, Canada, Chile, China, India, Mexico, the Russian Federation, South Africa, Turkey and the United States.

Part of the observed differences in GDP per capita within a country are due to commuting, which tends to increase GDP per capita in those regions where people are employed and reduce the GDP per capita of those regions where commuters reside.

"2007 or latest available year" refers to 2007 in all countries except the Russian Federation (2008), China (2008), New Zealand (2003) and Turkey (2006). "1995-2007 or latest available period" refers to data from 1995 to 2007 in all countries except Estonia (1996-2007), Norway (1997-2007), Poland (1999-2007), Turkey (2004-06), China (2004-07), India (2000-07), and the Russian Federation (2005-07).

Overview

Regional disparities in the economic performance within countries are often substantial. Large differences are found in the Russian Federation, Mexico, the United Kingdom, India, the United States and China. Regional inequalities within countries remain large also when using a measure of regional productivity (for example GDP per worker).

GDP growth at the national level appears largely due to a small number of regions. On average, 40% of OECD growth was accounted for by just 10% of regions over the period 1995-2007. At country level, the regional contribution to growth was very concentrated in Greece, Hungary, Sweden, Finland and Japan where the 10% of regions with the highest GDP increase were responsible for more than half of the national growth in 1995-2007.

The Gini index is a measure of inequality which assigns equal weight to each region of a country regardless of its size, while the number of people living in regions with low GDP per capita (under the national median), provide an indication of the different economic implications of disparities within a country. For example, while regional disparities as measured by the Gini index in GDP per capita are of the same magnitude in the Slovak Republic, Turkey and Estonia, the percentage of national population living in regions with low GDP per capita varies from almost 60% in the Slovak Republic to 23% in Estonia.

Sources

- *OECD Regional Database.*
- OECD (2011), *OECD Regions at a Glance*, OECD Publishing.

Further information

Analytical publications

- OECD (2011), *OECD Territorial Reviews*, OECD Publishing.
- OECD (2011), *Regional Outlook 2011*, OECD Publishing.
- OECD (2009), *How Regions Grow: Trends and Analysis*, OECD Publishing.
- OECD (2009), *Regions Matter: Economic Recovery, Innovation and Sustainable Growth*, OECD Publishing.
- OECD (2005), *Local Governance and the Drivers of Growth*, OECD Publishing.

Online databases

- *OECD Regional Database.*

Websites

- Regional Development, *www.oecd.org/gov/regionaldevelopment.*
- Regional Statistics and Indicators, *www.oecd.org/gov/regional/statisticsindicators.*

Range in regional GDP per capita

As a percentage of national GDP per capita, 2007 or latest available year

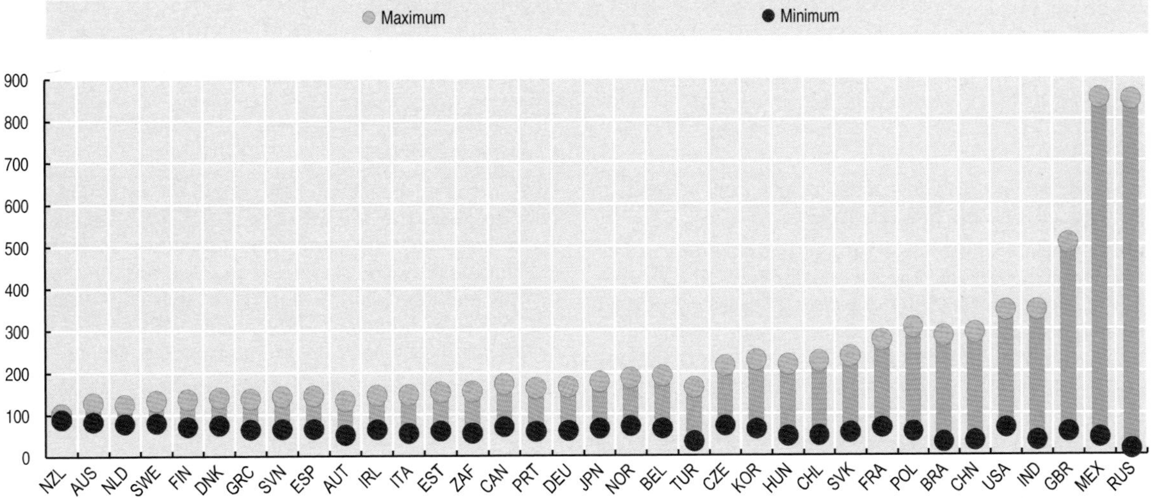

StatLink http://dx.doi.org/10.1787/888932503227

Share of GDP increase of each country due to the 10% of most dynamic regions

Percentage, 1995-2007 or latest available period

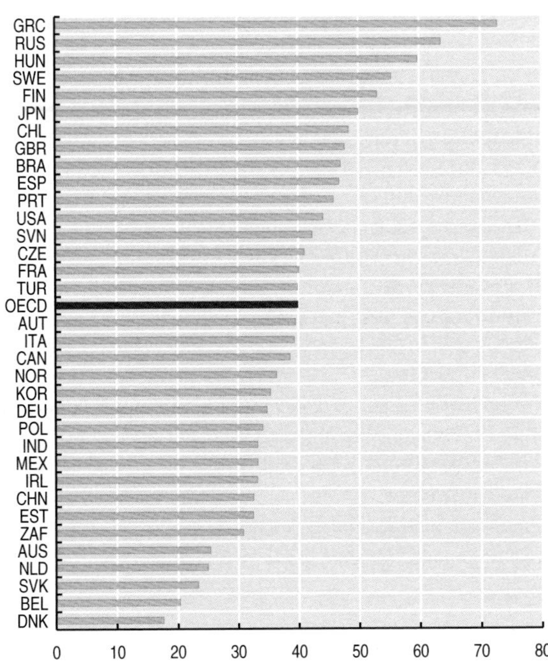

StatLink http://dx.doi.org/10.1787/888932503246

Gini index of regional GDP per capita and share of the population in regions with low GDP per capita

2007 or latest available year

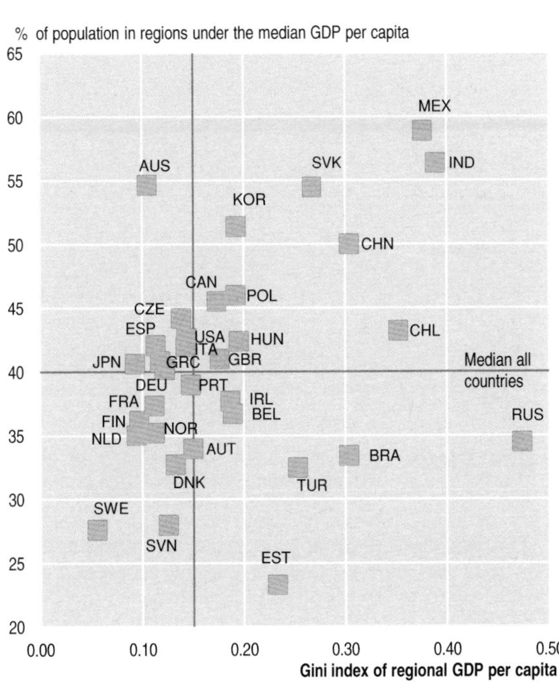

StatLink http://dx.doi.org/10.1787/888932503265

NATIONAL INCOME PER CAPITA

While per capita gross domestic product is the indicator most commonly used to compare living standards across countries, two other measures are preferred by many analysts. These are per capita gross national income (GNI) and net national income (NNI).

Definition

GNI is defined as GDP plus net receipts from abroad of wages and salaries and property income.

Wages and salaries from abroad are those that are earned by residents, *i.e.* by persons who essentially live and consume inside the economic territory of a country but work abroad (this happens in border areas on a regular basis) or by persons who live and work abroad for only short periods (seasonal workers). Guest-workers and other migrant workers who live abroad for one year or more are considered to be resident in the country where they are working. Such persons may send part of their earnings to relatives at home; these remittances, however, are treated as transfers between resident and non-resident households rather than net receipts from abroad of wages and salaries.

Property income from abroad includes interest, dividends and all or part of the retained earnings of foreign enterprises owned fully or partly by residents. In most countries, net receipts of property income account for most of the difference between GDP and GNI. Note that retained earnings of foreign enterprises owned by residents may not actually return to the residents concerned as, in some countries, there are restrictions on the repatriation of profits. Receipt of retained earnings is an imputation; since there is no actual transaction, an outflow of the same amount is recorded as a financial transaction (a reinvestment of earnings abroad). Countries with large stocks of outward foreign direct investment may be shown as having large receipts of property income from abroad and therefore high GNI even though much of the property income may never return to the country, but instead add to the foreign direct investment.

Overview

In the chart, countries are ranked according to GNI per capita, which is usually around 15-19% higher than NNI per capita. The country rankings are not greatly affected by the choice of income measure. The only countries that would be more than one place lower in the ranking if NNI per capita were used instead of GNI are Australia, Belgium, and Japan; the only countries that would be more than one place higher in the ranking if NNI per capita were used are Ireland, Israel and the United Kingdom.

Depreciation, which is deducted from GNI to obtain NNI, is the decline in the market value of fixed capital assets – dwellings, buildings, machinery, transport equipment such as physical infrastructure, software, etc. – through wear and tear and obsolescence.

Comparability

Both income measures are compiled according to the definitions of the 1993 *System of National Accounts* (SNA). There are, however, practical difficulties in measuring international flows of wages and salaries and property income and depreciation. Because of these difficulties, GDP per capita is the most widely used indicator of income despite being theoretically inferior to either GNI or NNI.

Note that data for Australia, which follows the 2008 SNA, and New Zealand refer to fiscal years.

Sources

- OECD (2011), *National Accounts of OECD Countries*, OECD Publishing.

Further information

Analytical publications

- OECD (2011), *OECD Economic Outlook*, OECD Publishing.
- OECD (2011), *Perspectives on Global Development 2010: Shifting Wealth*, OECD Publishing.
- OECD (2003), *The Sources of Economic Growth in OECD Countries*, OECD Publishing.

Statistical publications

- OECD (2011), *National Accounts at a Glance*, OECD Publishing.
- Maddison, A. (2003), *The World Economy: Historical Perspectives*, Development Centre Studies, OECD Publishing.

Methodological publications

- OECD (2000), *System of National Accounts, 1993 – Glossary*, OECD Publishing.
- United Nations, OECD, International Monetary Fund and Eurostat (eds.) (2010), *System of National Accounts 2008*, United Nations, Geneva.

Online databases

- *OECD National Accounts Statistics.*
- *OECD Economic Outlook: Statistics and Projections.*

Websites

- OECD Economic Outlook – Sources and Methods, *www.oecd.org/eco/sources-and-methods.*
- The World Economy (supplementary material), *www.theworldeconomy.org.*

Gross national income per capita

US dollars, current prices and PPPs

	1997	1998	1999	2000	2001	2002	2003	2004	2005	2006	2007	2008	2009	2010
Australia	23 427	24 665	26 130	27 284	28 462	29 601	31 194	32 296	33 786	35 511	37 455	37 646	38 376	..
Austria	24 620	25 722	26 529	28 282	28 183	29 854	30 778	32 353	33 083	35 876	37 343	39 297	38 409	39 464
Belgium	24 292	24 777	25 826	28 257	28 946	30 417	30 708	31 490	32 350	34 463	35 946	37 423	36 632	37 787
Canada	23 705	24 701	26 220	27 743	28 502	29 162	30 532	32 176	34 448	36 492	37 863	38 431	37 277	..
Chile	8 385	8 704	8 585	8 968	9 388	9 577	9 844	10 374	11 115	11 401	12 317	13 444	13 293	..
Czech Republic	13 612	13 702	13 975	14 654	15 630	16 103	17 217	18 243	19 452	21 240	22 859	24 003	24 051	23 639
Denmark	24 899	25 843	26 699	28 213	29 022	30 393	30 241	32 450	33 659	36 698	38 137	40 016	38 364	40 281
Estonia	7 749	8 316	8 632	9 539	10 257	11 475	12 677	14 049	15 902	18 134	19 795	20 626	19 414	19 682
Finland	20 555	22 031	23 290	25 455	26 482	27 555	27 383	30 081	30 831	33 409	36 165	37 992	35 905	37 181
France	21 909	23 001	24 041	25 665	27 022	27 850	27 545	28 546	29 968	31 968	33 729	34 562	33 897	34 453
Germany	23 406	23 998	24 873	25 706	26 588	27 246	28 367	30 187	31 738	34 413	36 250	37 765	36 845	38 115
Greece	16 391	16 858	17 160	18 460	20 055	21 655	22 567	23 917	24 184	26 513	27 408	29 097	28 501	27 415
Hungary	9 545	10 228	10 623	11 545	12 903	14 002	14 711	15 470	16 022	17 343	17 865	19 369	19 260	..
Iceland	25 497	27 225	28 071	28 043	29 487	31 033	30 286	32 328	33 764	33 719	35 140	30 732	29 928	..
Ireland	19 440	21 241	22 285	24 737	25 811	27 435	29 522	31 276	33 280	37 035	39 240	36 957	32 860	..
Israel	19 592	20 124	20 364	21 929	22 403	22 589	21 345	23 033	23 146	24 836	26 553	27 122	27 012	..
Italy	22 435	23 562	24 091	25 403	26 949	26 594	26 915	27 258	28 056	30 172	31 698	32 757	31 926	31 140
Japan	24 572	24 295	24 557	25 935	26 593	27 252	27 965	29 581	31 027	32 771	34 700	34 927	32 896	..
Korea	14 672	13 749	15 407	17 109	18 109	19 668	20 198	21 694	22 762	24 323	26 239	27 077	27 254	29 012
Luxembourg	39 346	39 800	44 091	46 745	47 907	47 736	47 076	56 807	58 719	59 725	68 035	67 354	59 711	..
Mexico	8 256	8 644	9 028	9 811	9 926	10 216	10 692	11 376	12 243	13 402	14 317	15 053	14 153	..
Netherlands	24 414	25 214	27 226	30 040	31 021	32 236	32 063	34 098	35 280	39 087	41 421	42 073	39 701	42 618
New Zealand	17 507	18 047	18 954	19 815	20 876	21 618	22 304	23 100	23 570	25 147	26 444	27 012	27 942	..
Norway	27 666	27 104	29 550	35 638	37 125	37 166	38 537	42 339	47 646	53 327	54 866	60 213	54 239	56 784
Poland	8 804	9 403	9 940	10 529	10 924	11 524	11 869	12 655	13 523	14 685	16 161	17 699	18 256	..
Portugal	14 799	15 567	16 537	17 380	17 992	18 782	19 205	19 585	20 977	22 180	23 438	24 065	24 040	24 738
Slovak Republic	9 758	10 332	10 349	10 920	12 070	12 919	12 924	14 070	15 718	17 834	20 266	22 617	22 508	23 176
Slovenia	14 891	15 727	16 761	17 560	18 480	19 649	20 357	22 019	23 273	25 127	26 636	28 425	26 891	27 074
Spain	17 533	18 704	19 638	21 141	22 227	23 703	24 461	25 613	26 991	29 843	31 496	32 248	31 501	31 651
Sweden	22 977	24 059	25 739	27 713	28 026	29 163	30 793	32 500	32 936	36 139	39 364	40 870	37 825	39 728
Switzerland	29 912	31 109	31 961	33 942	33 582	34 469	35 778	37 001	38 822	42 092	43 176	42 537	46 459	..
United Kingdom	22 355	23 527	24 141	26 023	27 743	29 315	30 255	32 246	33 272	35 160	36 183	37 484	35 648	36 427
United States	30 467	32 024	33 652	35 658	36 410	37 002	38 307	40 583	43 063	45 575	46 675	47 026	45 567	..
Euro area	21 290	22 190	23 076	24 402	25 568	26 331	26 833	28 039	29 306	31 703	33 432	34 544	33 627	34 121
EU27 total	18 908	19 749	20 519	21 827	22 940	23 848	24 456	25 751	26 910	29 107	30 754	32 017	31 118	31 695
OECD total	21 311	22 082	22 978	24 451	25 204	25 896	26 659	28 198	29 732	31 801	33 227	34 010	32 949	..
China	..	..	..	..	..	..	..	3 608	4 121	4 776	5 595	6 232	..	..
Russian Federation	5 565	5 214	5 661	6 622	7 234	7 857	8 934	10 002	11 531	14 538	16 392	19 750	18 421	..
South Africa	..	..	..	..	..	..	7 208	7 821	8 481	9 152	9 706	10 112	10 009	10 460

StatLink http://dx.doi.org/10.1787/888932503284

Gross and net national income per capita

US dollars, current prices and PPPs, 2010 or latest available year

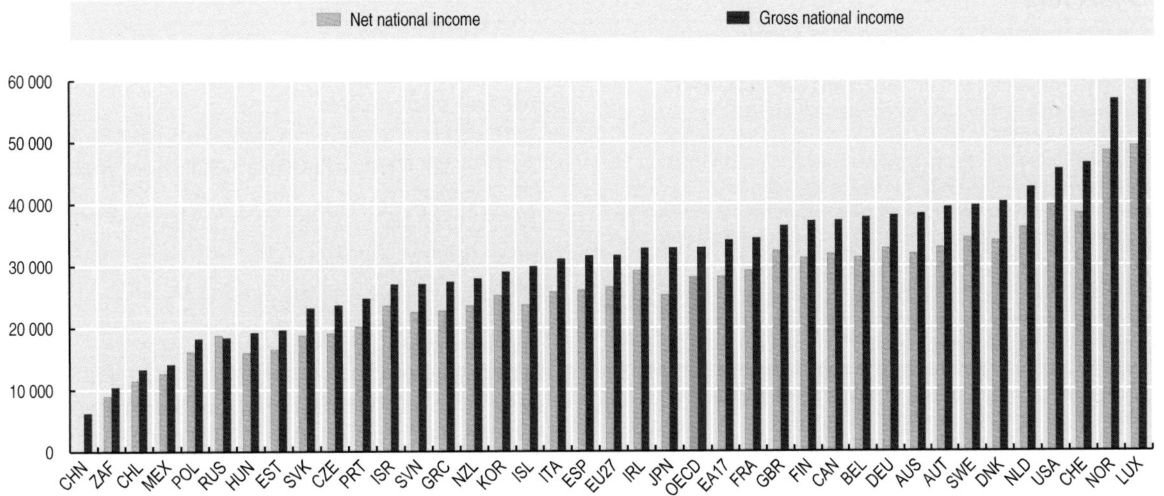

StatLink http://dx.doi.org/10.1787/888932503303

HOUSEHOLD DISPOSABLE INCOME

Household disposable income is closer to the concept of income generally used in economics and is an important indicator of well-being and living standards. Ignoring changes in net worth that arise from capital transfers or holding gains, household disposable income can be seen as the maximum amount that households can afford to spend on consumption goods or services without having to reduce their financial or non-financial assets or to increase their liabilities.

Definition

Household disposable income is the sum of household final consumption expenditure and savings (minus the change in net equity of households in pension funds). It also corresponds to the sum of wages and salaries, mixed income, net property income, net current transfers and social benefits other than social transfers in kind, less taxes on income and wealth and social security contributions paid by employees, the self-employed and the unemployed.

The figures shown here for the household sector include the disposable income of non-profit institutions serving households (NPISH). The price deflator used to obtain real values is consistent with that used to deflate the final consumption expenditure of households and NPISH.

Comparability

Household disposable income is compiled according to the definitions of the 1993 *System of National Accounts*. There are, however, practical difficulties in measuring some income components, such as remittances. Data for Australia are based on the 2008 SNA but this has little impact on the comparability of household disposable income statistics shown here.

Real household disposable income

Annual growth in percentage

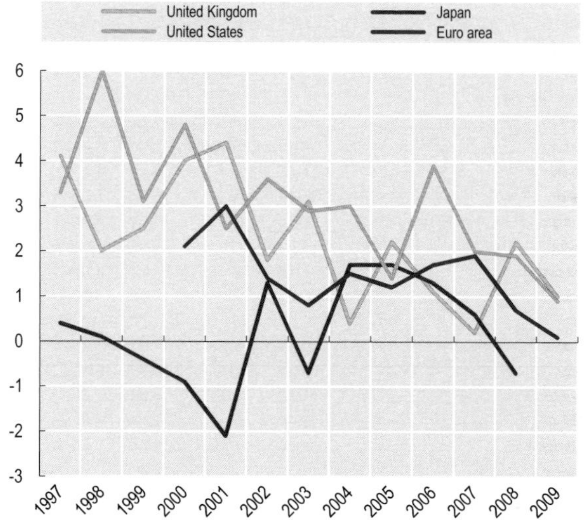

StatLink http://dx.doi.org/10.1787/888932534957

Overview

Over the period 2008-2010, household disposable income in real terms increased for all OECD countries with the exceptions of Hungary, Italy, Mexico and Denmark, where declines partly reflect significant falls in household disposable income in 2009. Of the 27 countries where information is available, falls in household disposable income were also recorded in Chile, the Czech Republic, Estonia, and Germany. All other (19) countries saw increases in real household disposable income in 2009. The Slovak Republic and Australia both showed increases of over 5% for this three year average period.

Across OECD countries, comparisons of growth of real household disposable income over the three years to 2010 compared to growth in the three years to 1999 show a mixed picture, with some countries showing higher growth and others showing slower growth.

Among the major seven countries, only Japan and Canada saw higher growth in real household disposable income over the two periods shown in the graph.

Sources

- OECD (2011), *National Accounts at a Glance*, OECD Publishing.
- OECD (2011), *National Accounts of OECD Countries*, OECD Publishing.

Further information

Statistical publications

- OECD (2011), *OECD Pensions at a Glance*, OECD Publishing.
- OECD (2011), *Society at a Glance: OECD Social Indicators*, OECD Publishing.
- OECD (2011), *Taxing Wages*, OECD Publishing.

Methodological publications

- OECD (2007), *Understanding National Accounts*, OECD Publishing.
- OECD (2000), *System of National Accounts, 1993 – Glossary*, OECD Publishing.
- United Nations, OECD, International Monetary Fund and Eurostat (eds.) (2010), *System of National Accounts 2008*, United Nations, Geneva.

Online databases

- *OECD Social Expenditure Statistics.*

Real household disposable income

Annual growth in percentage

	1997	1998	1999	2000	2001	2002	2003	2004	2005	2006	2007	2008	2009	2010
Australia	3.2	2.6	3.8	3.4	3.1	0.9	4.4	3.7	4.8	5.9	3.3	7.5	..	..
Austria	-1.6	2.4	3.8	1.9	0.0	1.2	1.9	2.4	2.6	2.6	2.3	0.9	0.0	..
Belgium	0.6	2.1	2.4	1.8	3.1	-0.4	-0.3	-0.2	0.4	2.8	2.0	2.0	1.8	..
Canada	2.2	2.8	2.9	4.8	2.8	1.8	2.1	3.8	2.5	5.7	3.8	3.8	1.4	..
Chile	3.8	4.9	-0.9	3.5	3.2	2.2	3.4	7.8	7.7	7.0	7.1	4.9	-0.3	..
Czech Republic	2.2	-2.6	2.1	1.0	0.9	2.8	5.3	0.8	5.3	6.8	6.6	3.2	-1.0	..
Denmark	-0.1	2.7	-3.8	0.5	3.7	2.0	2.4	2.7	2.2	1.8	0.1	0.0	-1.1	..
Estonia	9.5	2.3	-1.8	11.0	6.0	7.7	6.9	3.3	10.9	11.5	12.6	0.1	-7.9	..
Finland	5.2	2.5	4.5	0.6	3.2	2.3	6.0	4.8	1.1	2.7	3.7	2.2	2.2	2.6
France	1.4	3.2	3.0	3.3	3.1	3.7	0.6	2.1	1.4	2.5	3.1	0.2	1.8	..
Germany	0.3	1.2	2.2	1.9	2.1	-0.4	0.5	0.2	0.6	1.1	-0.1	1.5	-1.0	..
Greece	..	..	..	..	4.1	2.6	4.7	3.1	1.9	5.4	9.2	-1.8	2.7	..
Hungary	-0.1	2.7	1.3	3.1	6.0	8.3	6.0	5.5	3.4	2.1	-2.1	-2.5	-5.4	..
Ireland	..	..	..	..	..	..	2.4	6.9	4.3	4.5	3.9	2.4	2.2	..
Italy	-	-1.1	1.0	0.3	3.0	1.1	0.1	0.6	0.5	0.7	0.9	-1.0	-3.0	..
Japan	0.4	0.1	-0.4	-0.9	-2.1	1.3	-0.7	1.7	1.7	1.3	0.6	-0.7	..	..
Korea	1.6	-4.0	2.8	0.4	0.9	3.4	4.9	4.7	2.3	2.6	2.7	1.3	0.9	..
Luxembourg	..	..	..	..	..	..	..	..	..	..	4.0	5.1	1.6	..
Mexico	..	..	..	..	..	..	..	4.0	4.6	5.5	3.4	3.1	-8.1	..
Netherlands	4.0	3.5	2.1	2.2	5.6	-0.6	-2.5	0.6	-0.3	0.5	2.6	-0.1	0.1	..
New Zealand	2.3	5.4	7.8	-4.1	3.7	-0.5	8.4	5.8	2.4	2.1	..	..	..	..
Norway	3.7	5.7	2.5	3.8	-	8.0	4.4	3.6	7.6	-6.4	6.3	3.6	4.5	..
Poland	7.1	5.5	3.5	1.7	4.1	-1.0	1.2	3.4	1.5	4.4	4.7	3.5	4.8	..
Portugal	2.7	4.6	6.6	3.6	1.6	1.0	0.3	1.7	0.7	-0.4	1.9	1.6	3.3	0.7
Slovak Republic	4.9	4.7	-1.3	2.0	3.0	5.1	-0.7	3.9	6.2	3.7	9.2	5.3	2.2	..
Slovenia	5.0	1.6	3.4	4.4	4.8	3.5	0.6	4.1	5.1	3.2	4.3	2.7	0.1	..
Spain	..	..	..	..	3.0	3.1	3.2	3.1	4.1	3.2	2.6	2.5	1.9	..
Sweden	-0.6	1.7	3.0	5.2	6.5	3.2	1.0	1.3	2.1	3.8	5.4	3.2	1.6	1.4
Switzerland	1.3	2.8	2.7	3.7	2.7	-1.2	-0.7	2.1	2.6	3.0	3.6	-0.2	..	..
United Kingdom	4.1	2.0	2.5	4.0	4.4	1.8	3.1	0.4	2.2	1.1	0.2	2.2	1.0	..
United States	3.3	6.0	3.1	4.8	2.5	3.6	2.9	3.0	1.4	3.9	2.0	1.9	0.9	..
Euro area	..	..	..	2.1	3.0	1.4	0.8	1.5	1.2	1.7	1.9	0.7	0.1	..
EU27 total	..	..	..	2.5	3.4	1.6	1.5	1.4	1.7	1.8	1.8	1.3	0.4	..
Russian Federation	..	..	..	..	..	..	7.7	9.4	11.9	13.6	14.1	9.4	..	..

StatLink http://dx.doi.org/10.1787/888932503322

Real household disposable income

Average annual growth in percentage

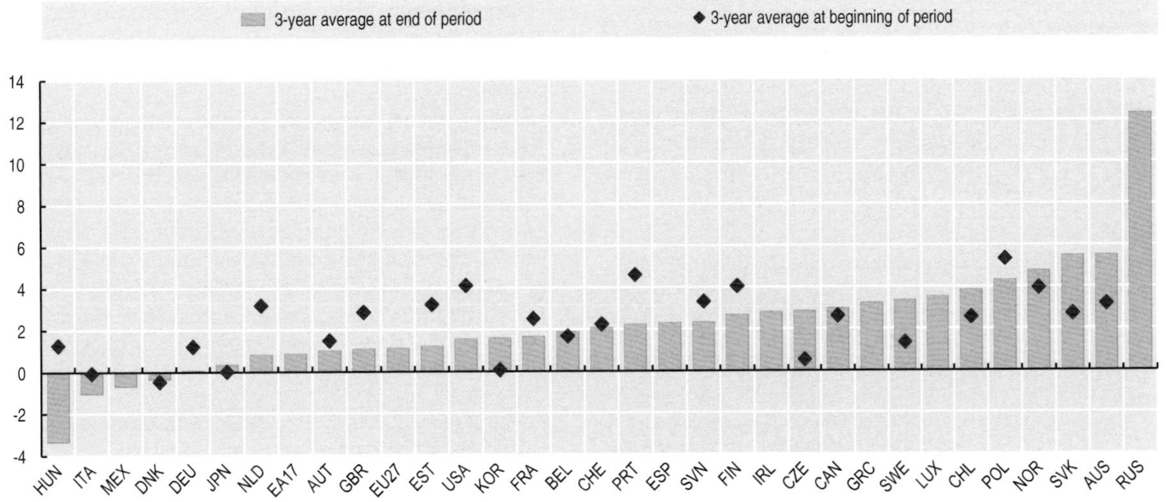

StatLink http://dx.doi.org/10.1787/888932503341

HOUSEHOLD SAVINGS

Household savings are the main domestic source of funds to finance capital investment, which is a major driver of long-term economic growth.

Definition

In the national accounts, household savings are estimated by subtracting household consumption expenditure from household disposable income and by adding the change in net equity of households in pension funds (since this component is also a determinant of household disposable income but with an opposite sign).

Household disposable income consists essentially of income from employment and from the operation of unincorporated enterprises, plus receipts of interests, dividends and social benefits minus payments of income taxes, interest and social security contributions. Enterprise income includes imputed rents paid by owner-occupiers of dwellings.

Household consumption expenditure consists mainly of cash outlays for consumer goods and services. It also includes the imputed expenditures that owner occupiers pay, as occupiers, to themselves as owners of their dwellings and the production of goods such as agricultural products for own-final use.

Household saving rates may be measured on either a net or a gross basis. The net saving rates shown here are measured after deducting consumption of fixed capital (depreciation), in respect of assets used in enterprises operated by households and in respect of owner-occupied dwellings. This consumption of fixed capital is deducted from both savings and the disposable income of households.

Households include households plus non-profit institutions serving households. The household saving rate is calculated as the ratio of household savings to household disposable income (plus the change in net equity of households in pension funds).

Comparability

Data are compiled according to the 1993 *System of National Accounts* (SNA). Because savings are a residual between two large aggregates (household disposable income and household consumption expenditure), both of which are subject to estimation errors, measures of household savings are also subject to large errors and to revisions over time.

Data for Australia (which are compiled according to the 2008 SNA) and New Zealand refer to fiscal years.

Overview

Household saving rates differ significantly across countries. In 2010 or the most recent available year (2009 in most cases), saving rates of above 10% were recorded in Austria, Belgium, France, Germany, Ireland, Slovenia, Spain, Sweden, Switzerland and the Russian Federation. Savings rates were negative in Denmark, Greece, New Zealand, and South Africa. Of the 29 countries where data is available for 2009, 23 countries saw increases in their savings rate compared to 2008.

These differences are partly due to institutional differences between countries. These include the extent to which old-age pensions are funded by government rather than through personal savings, and the extent to which governments provide insurance against sickness and unemployment. The age composition of the population is also relevant, as the elderly tend to run down financial assets acquired during their working life. This implies that a country with a high share of retired persons will usually have a low household saving rate.

Over the last 10-15 years covered in the graph, household saving rates have decreased markedly in Japan and, to a much lesser extent, in Canada. Rates have remained broadly stable in Germany and France. The United States saw its household saving rate fall from 1996 to around 2006; after that year, the household saving rate started to pick up and is now above its 1996 level.

Sources

- OECD (2011), *National Accounts of OECD Countries*, OECD Publishing.

Further information

Analytical publications

- Fournier, J. and I. Koske (2010), *A Simple Model of the Relationship Between Productivity, Saving and the Current Account, OECD Economics Department Working Papers*, No. 816.
- Harvey, R. (2004), "Comparison of Household Saving Ratios: Euro Area/United States/Japan", *OECD Statistics Brief*, No. 8, June, *www.oecd.org/std/statisticsbrief*.
- Hüfner, F. and I. Koske (2010), "Explaining Household Saving Rates in G7 Countries: Implications for Germany", *OECD Economics Department Working Papers*, No. 754.
- de Laiglesia, J. and C. Morrison (2008), "Household Structures and Savings: Evidence from Household Surveys", *OECD Development Centre Working Papers*, No. 267.

Statistical publications

- OECD (2011), *National Accounts at a Glance*, OECD Publishing.

Websites

- OECD Economic Outlook – Sources and Methods, *www.oecd.org/eco/sources-and-methods*.

Household net saving rates

As a percentage of household disposable income

	1997	1998	1999	2000	2001	2002	2003	2004	2005	2006	2007	2008	2009	2010
Australia	5.6	3.4	2.8	2.6	2.6	0.2	-0.9	-1.5	0.4	1.3	0.5	4.5	..	..
Austria	7.7	8.5	9.8	9.2	8.0	8.0	9.1	9.3	9.7	10.4	11.6	11.8	11.1	..
Belgium	13.2	12.7	13.1	12.3	13.7	12.9	12.2	10.8	10.2	11.0	11.4	11.9	13.5	..
Canada	5.0	4.9	4.1	4.8	5.3	3.5	2.7	3.2	2.2	3.6	2.9	3.7	4.7	..
Chile	5.3	6.1	6.8	6.1	6.6	6.4	6.1	6.8	6.7	7.3	7.3	7.4	7.2	..
Czech Republic	6.0	4.1	3.4	3.3	2.2	3.0	2.4	0.5	3.2	4.8	6.3	5.7	4.5	..
Denmark	-2.8	-1.2	-5.6	-4.0	2.1	2.1	2.4	-1.3	-4.2	-2.3	-4.0	-3.3	-0.5	..
Estonia	-0.1	-2.8	-5.4	-3.0	-4.0	-6.4	-7.1	-12.8	-11.1	-13.1	-8.1	-2.5	7.6	..
Finland	2.5	0.6	2.4	0.5	0.3	0.5	1.4	2.7	0.9	-1.1	-0.9	-0.2	3.9	4.3
France	12.6	12.2	11.9	11.8	12.5	13.7	12.5	12.4	11.4	11.4	11.9	11.6	12.5	..
Germany	10.1	10.1	9.5	9.2	9.4	9.9	10.3	10.4	10.5	10.6	10.8	11.7	11.1	..
Greece	..	..	..	-4.5	-5.5	-7.6	-6.2	-6.9	-9.7	-9.5	-3.0	-8.3	-3.2	..
Hungary	14.2	13.4	9.9	8.9	8.5	6.4	4.3	6.8	7.0	7.7	5.4	3.2	5.6	..
Ireland	..	..	..	..	..	2.4	2.4	5.5	3.6	2.2	-	3.8	12.1	..
Italy	15.1	11.4	10.2	8.4	10.5	11.2	10.3	10.2	9.9	9.1	8.4	8.2	7.1	..
Japan	10.9	11.7	10.2	8.8	5.1	5.1	3.9	3.6	3.9	3.7	2.5	2.3	..	..
Korea	16.1	23.2	16.1	9.3	5.2	0.4	5.2	9.2	7.2	5.2	2.9	2.9	3.6	..
Luxembourg	..	..	..	..	..	..	..	..	..	3.8	4.3	5.0	6.4	..
Mexico	..	..	..	..	..	..	11.4	10.1	10.1	10.1	9.6	10.2	10.0	..
Netherlands	13.3	12.2	9.0	6.9	9.7	8.7	7.6	7.4	6.4	6.1	6.9	5.7	6.8	..
New Zealand	-3.5	-3.3	1.0	-4.6	-3.6	-9.1	-6.9	-5.6	-7.6	-8.0	..	..	..	..
Norway	3.0	5.7	4.7	4.3	3.1	8.2	8.9	7.2	10.1	0.1	1.5	3.7	7.3	..
Poland	11.7	12.1	10.5	10.0	11.9	8.3	7.7	7.0	7.3	7.5	6.1	0.8	7.8	..
Portugal	3.8	3.3	3.9	3.8	3.7	3.3	3.7	2.8	2.7	0.4	-0.7	-0.8	3.4	2.0
Slovak Republic	9.2	7.6	6.2	6.0	3.8	3.3	1.1	0.3	1.1	0.4	2.4	1.5	..	..
Slovenia	8.3	7.2	4.3	7.0	9.0	9.9	7.6	9.2	11.5	11.9	9.9	9.8	10.2	..
Spain	..	..	..	5.9	5.6	5.6	6.0	4.9	4.7	4.2	3.6	6.6	11.9	..
Sweden	3.4	2.8	2.8	4.3	8.4	8.2	7.2	6.1	5.5	6.6	8.8	11.2	12.9	10.8
Switzerland	10.7	10.7	10.8	11.7	11.9	10.7	9.4	9.0	10.1	11.4	12.6	11.8	..	..
United Kingdom	5.8	3.4	0.9	0.1	1.5	-0.1	0.4	-1.6	-1.2	-2.2	-3.2	-2.8	1.2	..
United States	4.7	5.4	3.2	3.0	2.8	3.7	3.8	3.4	1.5	2.5	2.1	4.2	6.2	..
Euro area	..	..	9.2	8.3	9.0	9.5	9.2	9.0	8.4	8.0	8.2	8.4	9.6	..
EU27 total	..	..	7.2	6.4	7.3	7.2	6.9	6.3	6.0	5.6	5.3	5.4	7.8	..
Russian Federation	..	..	..	..	..	..	..	..	11.0	12.4	12.1	10.9	..	..
South Africa	2.0	1.4	1.2	1.0	0.4	0.7	0.6	0.4	0.1	-0.8	-1.0	-1.0	-0.3	-0.3

StatLink http://dx.doi.org/10.1787/888932503360

Household net saving rates

As a percentage of household disposable income

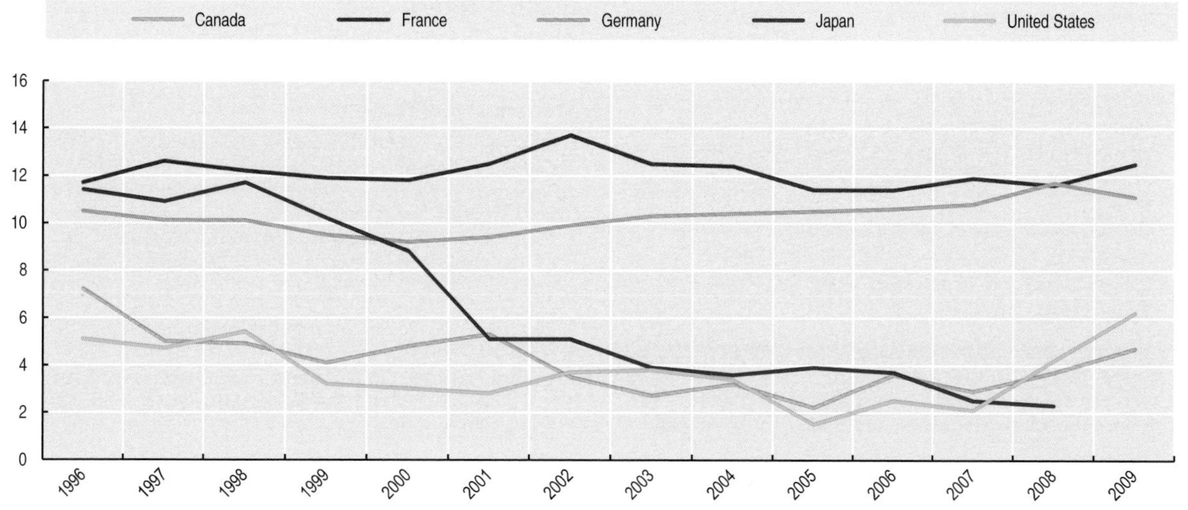

StatLink http://dx.doi.org/10.1787/888932503379

INVESTMENT RATES

The share of total GDP that is devoted to investment in fixed assets is an important determinant of future economic growth. However, not all types of investment contribute to future GDP growth in the same way, and future GDP growth may also depend on expenditures that are conventionally considered as consumption (*e.g.* education, health).

Definition

Gross fixed capital formation (*i.e.* investment or GFCF) reflects the acquisition, less disposal, of fixed assets, *i.e.* products that are expected to be used in production for several years. Acquisitions include both purchases of assets (new or second-hand) and the construction of assets by producers for their own use. Disposals include sales of assets for scrap as well as sales of used assets in a working condition to other producers. New Zealand, Mexico and some central European countries import substantial quantities of used assets, which are included in GFCF.

Fixed assets consist of machinery and equipment; dwellings and other buildings; roads, bridges, airfields and dams; orchards and tree plantations; improvements to land such as fencing, levelling and draining; draught animals and other animals that are kept for the milk and wool that they produce; computer software and databases; entertainment, literary or artistic originals; and expenditures on mineral exploration. What all these things have in common is that they contribute to future production. This may not be obvious in the case of dwellings but, in the national accounts, flats and houses are considered to produce services that are consumed by owners or tenants over the life of the building.

Investment figures shown here relate to annual growth in the volume of total investment.

Overview

Investment over the period 2007-2009 fell on average by 4% per year for the OECD as a whole, largely reflecting the retrenchment in investment that occurred at the height of the recent crisis, with investment volumes falling by 12% in 2009. Australia was the only country in the OECD to record investment growth (3%) in 2009. Iceland, Estonia, Ireland, and Slovenia all recorded falls in investment of over 20% in 2009.

Comparability

When the *System of National Accounts (SNA)* was revised in 1993, the scope of GFCF was widened to include mineral exploration, computer software and entertainment, as well as literary and artistic originals. Comparability of these items has improved in recent years but the coverage of the various items differs across countries. This applies particularly in the case of own-account production of software. Data for Australia (based on the 2008 SNA) and New Zealand refer to fiscal years. The 2008 SNA recognises that expenditures on research and development and expenditures on weapons systems can be included as investment. This implies that, all other things equal, 2008 SNA levels of investment will be higher than 1993 SNA levels.

Sources

- OECD (2011), *National Accounts of OECD Countries*, OECD Publishing.
- For Brazil: National sources and OECD (2011), *Main Economic Indicators*, OECD Publishing.

Further information

Analytical publications

- OECD (2011), *OECD Economic Outlook*, OECD Publishing.

Statistical publications

- OECD (2011), *National Accounts at a Glance*, OECD Publishing.

Methodological publications

- Ahmad, N. (2004), "Towards More Harmonised Estimates of Investment in Software", *OECD Economic Studies*, No. 37, 2003/2.
- OECD (2000), *System of National Accounts, 1993 – Glossary*, OECD Publishing.
- United Nations, OECD, International Monetary Fund and Eurostat (eds.) (2010), *System of National Accounts 2008*, United Nations, Geneva.

Websites

- OECD Economic Outlook – Sources and Methods, *www.oecd.org/eco/sources-and-methods*.

Gross fixed capital formation

Annual growth in percentage

	1997	1998	1999	2000	2001	2002	2003	2004	2005	2006	2007	2008	2009	2010
Australia	9.1	4.5	7.8	-8.4	9.5	14.0	8.0	6.5	8.8	5.4	10.4	0.8	2.5	..
Austria	-	3.6	1.0	5.5	-1.7	-4.4	4.7	0.7	1.2	1.8	3.9	4.1	-8.8	-1.3
Belgium	5.9	3.3	2.6	5.1	1.0	-4.5	0.1	7.9	6.5	2.7	6.2	2.6	-5.4	-1.3
Canada	15.2	2.4	7.3	4.7	4.0	1.6	6.2	7.8	9.3	7.1	3.5	1.4	-11.7	..
Chile	10.5	1.9	-18.2	8.9	4.3	1.5	5.7	10.0	23.9	2.3	11.2	19.4	-15.9	18.8
Czech Republic	-5.7	-0.9	-3.3	5.1	6.6	5.1	0.4	3.9	1.8	6.0	10.8	-1.5	-7.9	-3.1
Denmark	10.3	8.1	-0.1	7.6	-1.4	0.1	-0.2	3.9	4.7	14.3	0.4	-3.3	-14.3	-4.0
Estonia	23.6	21.4	-15.5	16.7	9.9	24.0	18.6	5.2	15.3	23.2	6.0	-15.0	-32.9	-9.2
Finland	10.5	11.1	3.3	6.4	2.9	-3.7	3.0	4.9	3.6	1.9	10.7	-0.4	-14.6	0.8
France	0.5	7.4	8.5	6.8	2.2	-1.9	2.2	3.4	4.4	4.0	6.3	0.3	-9.0	-1.2
Germany	1.0	4.0	4.7	3.0	-3.7	-6.1	-0.3	-0.3	0.9	8.0	4.7	2.5	-10.1	6.0
Greece	6.8	10.6	11.0	8.0	4.8	9.5	11.8	0.4	-6.3	10.6	5.5	-7.5	-11.2	-16.5
Hungary	4.3	9.7	4.9	6.8	4.7	10.3	2.6	7.6	6.5	-3.5	3.7	3.2	-9.2	-6.9
Iceland	9.3	34.4	-4.1	11.8	-4.3	-14.0	11.1	28.1	35.7	22.4	-11.1	-19.7	-50.9	-8.1
Ireland	16.4	14.1	13.5	6.2	0.2	2.8	6.5	9.4	14.9	4.5	2.8	-14.3	-31.1	..
Israel	-0.7	-4.0	-	3.4	-3.5	-6.7	-4.2	0.5	3.4	13.6	14.7	3.9	-5.8	..
Italy	1.6	4.2	3.9	6.3	2.7	3.7	-1.2	2.3	0.8	2.9	1.7	-3.8	-11.9	2.5
Japan	-0.3	-7.2	-0.8	1.2	-0.9	-4.9	-0.5	1.4	3.1	0.5	-1.2	-3.6	-11.7	..
Korea	-1.5	-22.0	8.7	12.3	0.3	7.1	4.4	2.1	1.9	3.4	4.2	-1.9	-1.0	7.0
Luxembourg	10.4	6.1	22.0	-4.7	8.8	5.5	6.3	2.7	2.5	3.8	17.9	1.4	-19.2	2.6
Mexico	21.0	10.3	7.7	11.4	-5.6	-0.6	0.4	8.0	7.5	9.9	6.9	5.9	-11.3	..
Netherlands	8.5	6.8	8.7	0.6	0.2	-4.5	-1.5	-1.6	3.7	7.5	5.5	5.1	-12.7	-4.8
New Zealand	0.2	-2.4	10.6	0.4	6.8	7.8	12.9	7.6	5.2	-2.3	4.7	-5.2	-12.0	..
Norway	15.8	13.6	-5.4	-3.5	-1.1	-1.1	0.2	10.2	13.3	11.7	12.5	2.5	-6.8	-7.4
Poland	21.8	14.0	6.6	2.7	-9.7	-6.3	-0.1	6.4	6.5	14.9	17.6	9.6	-1.1	-2.0
Portugal	14.2	11.8	6.0	3.9	0.6	-3.2	-7.1	-	-0.5	-1.3	2.6	-0.3	-11.3	-4.9
Slovak Republic	14.0	9.4	-15.7	-9.6	12.9	0.2	-2.7	4.8	17.6	9.3	9.1	1.0	-19.9	3.6
Slovenia	13.2	8.6	14.7	2.6	1.3	0.3	7.6	5.0	3.0	10.4	13.2	7.9	-23.0	-7.1
Spain	5.0	11.3	10.4	6.6	4.8	3.4	5.9	5.1	7.0	7.2	4.5	-4.8	-16.0	-7.6
Sweden	0.6	8.8	8.7	5.7	0.5	-1.3	1.6	5.7	8.1	9.2	8.9	1.4	-16.3	7.1
Switzerland	2.1	6.4	1.5	4.2	-3.5	-0.5	-1.2	4.5	3.8	4.7	5.1	0.5	-4.9	4.6
Turkey	14.8	-3.9	-16.2	17.5	-30.0	14.7	14.2	28.4	17.4	13.3	3.1	-6.2	-19.0	29.9
United Kingdom	6.8	13.7	3.0	2.7	2.6	3.6	1.1	5.1	2.4	6.4	7.8	-5.0	-15.4	3.7
United States	8.8	9.9	9.1	6.9	-1.1	-3.0	2.9	6.2	5.3	2.3	-1.4	-5.1	-15.5	..
Euro area	2.7	6.0	6.0	4.9	0.6	-1.6	1.3	2.3	3.2	5.4	4.7	-0.8	-11.4	-0.8
EU27 total	3.5	7.3	5.4	4.6	0.8	-0.7	1.3	3.1	3.5	6.1	5.8	-0.8	-12.0	-0.7
OECD total	5.6	3.9	5.2	5.3	-0.7	-1.0	2.2	4.7	4.9	4.3	2.6	-2.1	-12.0	..
Indonesia	8.6	-33.0	-18.2	16.7	6.5	4.7	0.6	14.7	10.9	2.6	9.3	11.9	3.3	8.5
Russian Federation	-9.6	-12.4	8.1	16.6	10.9	3.1	13.9	12.0	10.2	17.9	21.1	9.5	-16.1	..
South Africa	5.7	4.8	-7.6	3.9	2.8	3.5	10.2	12.9	11.0	12.1	14.0	14.1	-2.2	-3.7

StatLink http://dx.doi.org/10.1787/888932503398

Gross fixed capital formation

Average annual growth in percentage

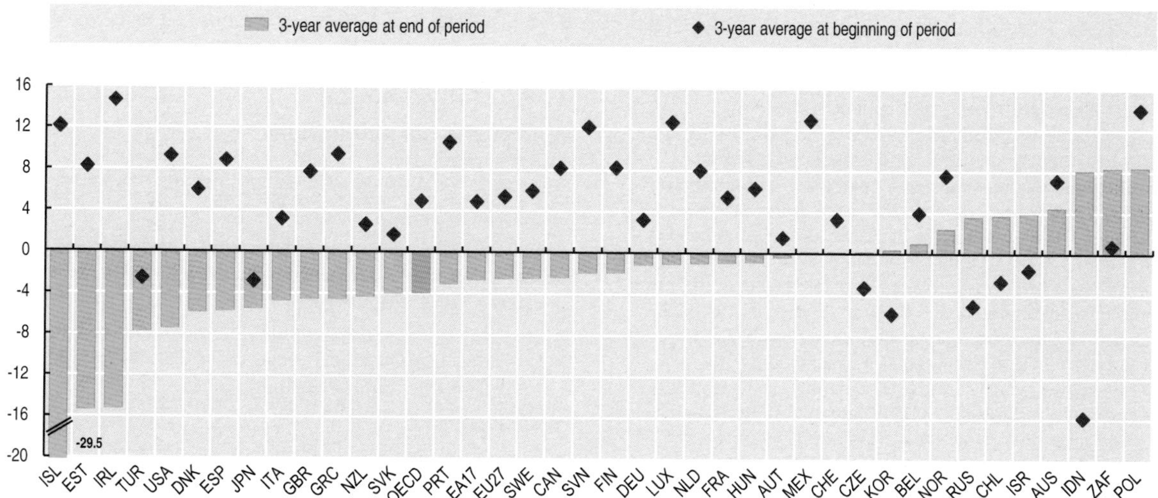

StatLink http://dx.doi.org/10.1787/888932503417

LABOUR PRODUCTIVITY LEVELS

Productivity is a measure of the efficiency with which available resources are used in production. Labour productivity, together with use of labour resources, is one of the main determinants of living standards.

Definition

Labour productivity is measured as GDP per hour worked. The estimates shown here are based on OECD *Annual National Accounts* data on GDP at current prices, converted to a common currency using OECD Purchasing Power Parities (PPPs) for 2010.

Differences in GDP per capita with respect to the United States can be decomposed into differences in labour productivity levels and differences in the extent of labour utilisation, measured as the number of hours worked per capita.

Comparability

Comparisons of productivity and income levels across countries first require comparable data on output. All OECD countries have implemented the 1993 *System of National Accounts*. However, there are differences such as the measurement of software investment that can affect the comparability of GDP across countries, although these differences are usually small. Second, in a number of countries, employment data are derived from labour force surveys that may not be entirely consistent with national account concepts; this reduces the comparability of labour utilisation across countries. Third, the measure of labour inputs also requires hours worked data, which are derived either from labour force surveys or from business surveys. Several OECD countries estimate hours worked from a combination of these sources or integrate these sources in a system of labour accounts, which is comparable to the national accounts. The *OECD Productivity Database* uses consistent estimates of employment and hours worked. Nonetheless, the cross-country comparability of hours worked remains limited, generating a margin of uncertainty in estimates of productivity levels.

A final problem relates to the conversion of output from national currency into a common unit. Market exchange rates cannot be used directly, as they are volatile and reflect a range of factors. The preferred alternative is to use Purchasing Power Parities (PPPs), which measure the prices of the same basket of consumption goods in different countries.

Data for EA17 exclude Cyprus and Malta.

Overview

In 2010, labour productivity per hour worked ranged from over 70 USD in Luxembourg and Norway to less than 20 USD in Chile and Mexico. Gaps in GDP per capita relative to the United States ranged from around 70% in Chile, Mexico and Turkey to around 15% or less in Australia, Canada and several European countries. In Norway and Luxembourg, GDP per capita levels were higher than in the United States. Much of the differences in GDP per capita reflect differences in labour productivity, with gaps relative to the United States ranging between 60% or more in Chile, Mexico and Poland and 8% or less in Belgium, France and Ireland; Luxembourg and Norway, experienced higher labour productivity than in the United States.

Cross-country differences in labour utilisation were significantly smaller than in the case of GDP per capita and per hour. In Belgium, Ireland and France, lower labour utilisation accounted for 94%, 84% and 73%, respectively, of the gap in living standard relative to the United States (*i.e.* for Belgium 20 points out of the 21 points gap in GDP per capita for Ireland 13 points out of 16 and for France, 21 points out of 29) while in Turkey the contribution of lower labour utilisation was only 16%. Several non-EU countries, such as Australia, Canada, Iceland, Israel, Japan, Korea and New Zealand, recorded higher levels of labour utilisation than in the United States which contributed to narrow their gap in GDP per capita. Cross-country differences in labour utilisation reflect high unemployment and low participation rates of the working age population, on the one hand, and lower working hours among employed people, on the other hand.

Sources

- OECD (2011), *OECD National Accounts Statistics* (database).
- OECD (2011), *OECD Productivity Statistics* (database).

Further information

Methodological publications

- OECD (2004), "Clocking In (and Out): Several Facets of Working Time", *OECD Employment Outlook: 2004 Edition*, OECD Publishing. See also Annex I.A1.
- OECD (2001), *Measuring Productivity – OECD Manual Measurement of Aggregate and Industry-level Productivity Growth*, OECD Publishing.
- Pilat, D. and P. Schreyer (2004), "The OECD Productivity Database – An Overview", *International Productivity Monitor*, No. 8, Spring, CSLS, Ottawa, pp. 59-65.

Websites

- OECD Compendium of Productivity Indicators, *www.oecd.org/statistics/productivity/compendium*.
- OECD Productivity, *www.oecd.org/statistics/productivity*.

GDP per hour worked

US dollars, current prices and PPPs, 2010

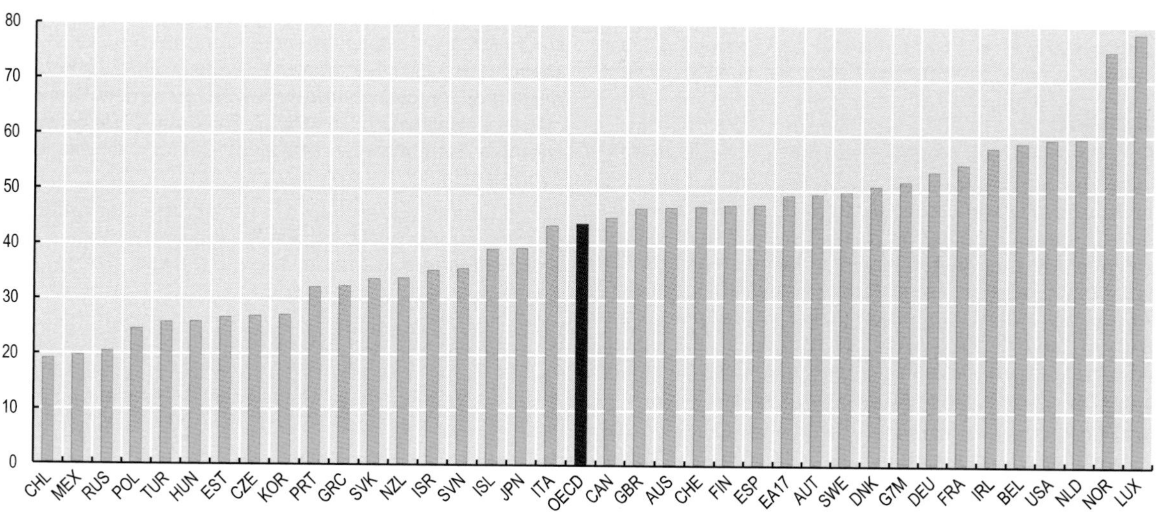

80
70
60
50
40
30
20
10
0
CHL
MEX
RUS
POL
TUR
HUN
EST
CZE
KOR
PRT
GRC
SVK
NZL
ISR
SVN
ISL
JPN
ITA
OECD
CAN
GBR
AUS
CHE
FIN
ESP
EA17
AUT
SWE
DNK
G7M
DEU
FRA
IRL
BEL
USA
NLD
NOR
LUX

StatLink http://dx.doi.org/10.1787/888932503436

Levels of GDP per capita and labour productivity

Percentage point differences with respect to the United States, 2010

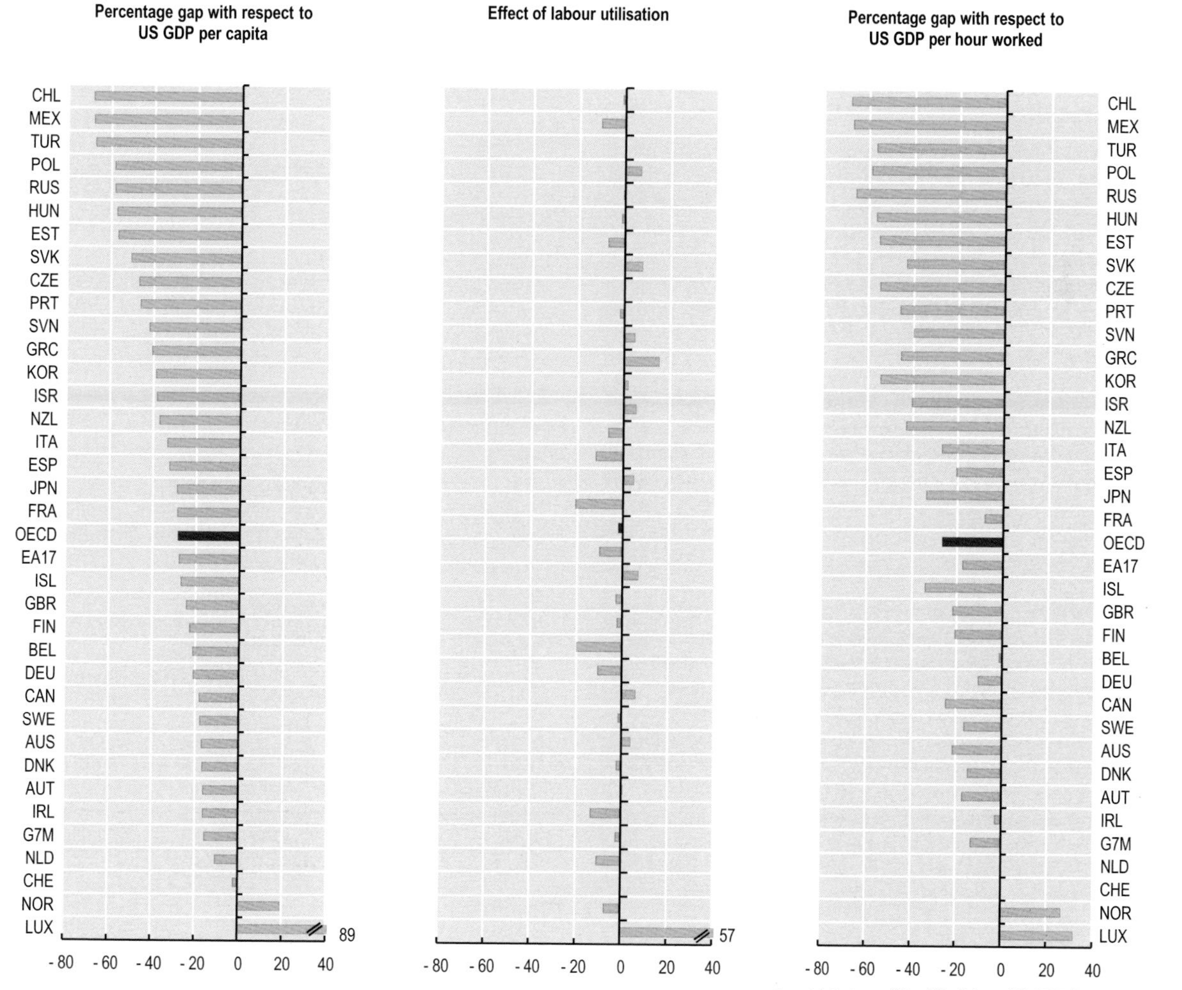

Percentage gap with respect to US GDP per capita
Effect of labour utilisation
Percentage gap with respect to US GDP per hour worked
CHL
MEX
TUR
POL
RUS
HUN
EST
SVK
CZE
PRT
SVN
GRC
KOR
ISR
NZL
ITA
ESP
JPN
FRA
OECD
EA17
ISL
GBR
FIN
BEL
DEU
CAN
SWE
AUS
DNK
AUT
IRL
G7M
NLD
CHE
NOR
LUX
89
57
-80
-60
-40
-20
0
20
40

StatLink http://dx.doi.org/10.1787/888932503455

LABOUR PRODUCTIVITY GROWTH

Labour productivity growth is a key dimension of economic performance and an essential driver of changes in living standards.

Definition

Labour productivity is defined as GDP per hour worked. Growth in per capita GDP is broken down into the contribution of labour productivity growth, on one side, and changes in labour utilisation (measured as hours worked per capita), on the other. Changes in living standards can result from changes in labour productivity (GDP per hours worked) and in labour utilisation (hours worked per person employed and employment per capita). High labour productivity growth can reflect greater use of capital and/or falling employment of low-productivity workers.

The indicators shown here are based on measures of GDP and population coming from the *OECD Annual National Accounts*. Actual hours worked are derived from either the *OECD Annual National Accounts* or from the *OECD Employment Outlook*. Hours worked reflect regular hours worked by full-time and part-time workers, paid and unpaid overtime, hours worked in additional jobs, and time not worked because of public holidays, annual paid leaves, strikes and labour disputes, bad weather, economic conditions and other reasons.

For zone aggregates, GDP estimates have been converted to constant US dollars using 2000 constant Purchasing Power Parities (PPPs).

Comparability

Although National Accounts data are based on common definitions, methods used by countries may differ in some respects. In particular, data on hours worked are based on a range of primary sources. In most countries, the data are drawn from Labour Force Surveys, but other countries rely upon establishment surveys, administrative sources or a combination of both. For several EU countries, hours data are OECD estimates based on the Spring European Labour Force Survey, supplemented by information from other sources on hours not worked. Annual working hours for non-European countries are provided by national statistical offices. In general, these data are most suited for comparing changes rather than levels of hours worked across countries.

The estimates shown here are not adjusted for differences in the business cycle; cyclically adjusted estimates might show different patterns.

Data for EA17 exclude Cyprus and Malta.

Overview

Over the period 2001-07, average growth in GDP per capita was rather contrasted across countries with highest rates recorded by Korea and several countries from Eastern Europe, the slowest growth was showed by Italy, Mexico and Spain. Growth in income over the same period was essentially driven by growth in labour productivity.

The downturn of 2008-09 contributed to slowdown economies' growth performance and, in some cases (*i.e.* Estonia, Iceland and Ireland) led to a significant decline in the labour utilisation.

In 2010, income and productivity growth bounced back strongly in the majority of countries as they moved out of recession, while the labour market's recovery was much slower and unemployment remained high in most countries.

Sources

- OECD (2011), *OECD Productivity Statistics* (database).

Further information

Analytical publications

- Ahmad, N., F. Lequiller, P. Marianna, D. Pilat, P. Schreyer and A. Wölfl (2003), "Comparing Labour Productivity Growth in the OECD Area: The Role of Measurement", *OECD Science, Technology and Industry Working Papers*, No. 2003/14.

Methodological publications

- Ark, B. van (2004), "The Measurement of Productivity: What Do the Numbers Mean?", in Klomp, L. (ed.), *Fostering Productivity: Patterns, Determinants and Policy Implications (Contributions to Economic Analysis, Volume 263)*, Emerald Group Publishing Limited, pp. 29-61.
- OECD (2004), "Clocking In (and Out): Several Facets of Working Time", *OECD Employment Outlook: 2004 Edition*, OECD Publishing. See also Annex I.A1.
- OECD (2001), *Measuring Productivity – OECD Manual: Measurement of Aggregate and Industry-level Productivity Growth*, OECD Publishing.
- Pilat, D. and P. Schreyer (2004), "The OECD Productivity Database – An Overview", *International Productivity Monitor*, No. 8, Spring, CSLS, Ottawa, pp. 59-65.
- Schreyer, P. and D. Pilat (2001), "Measuring Productivity", *OECD Economic Studies*, OECD Publishing.

Websites

- OECD Compendium of Productivity Indicators, *www.oecd.org/statistics/productivity/compendium*.
- OECD Productivity, *www.oecd.org/statistics/productivity*.

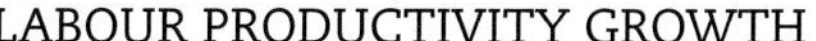

Growth in GDP per hour worked

Average annual growth in percentage

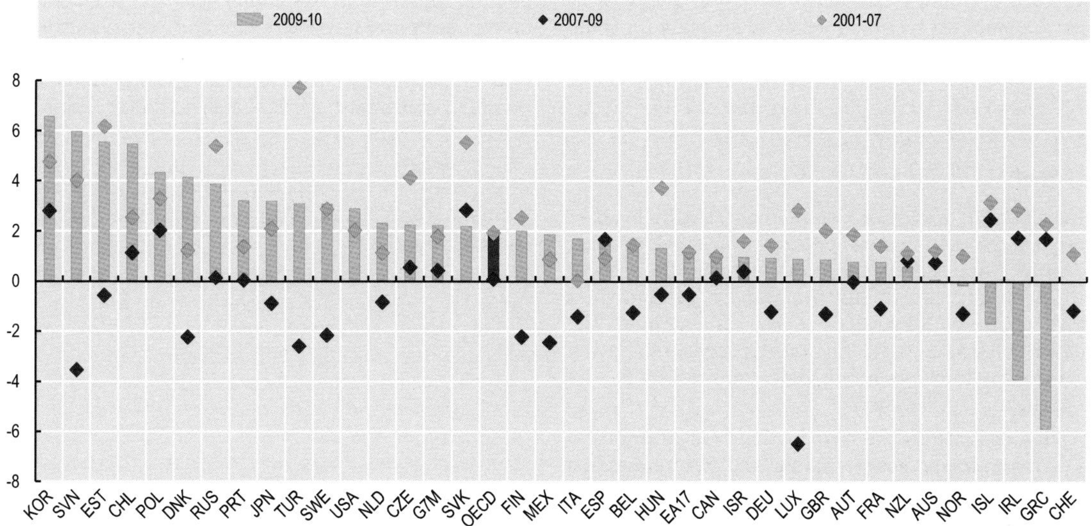

StatLink http://dx.doi.org/10.1787/888932503474

Contribution of labour productivity and labour utilisation to GDP per capita

Percentage change, annual rate

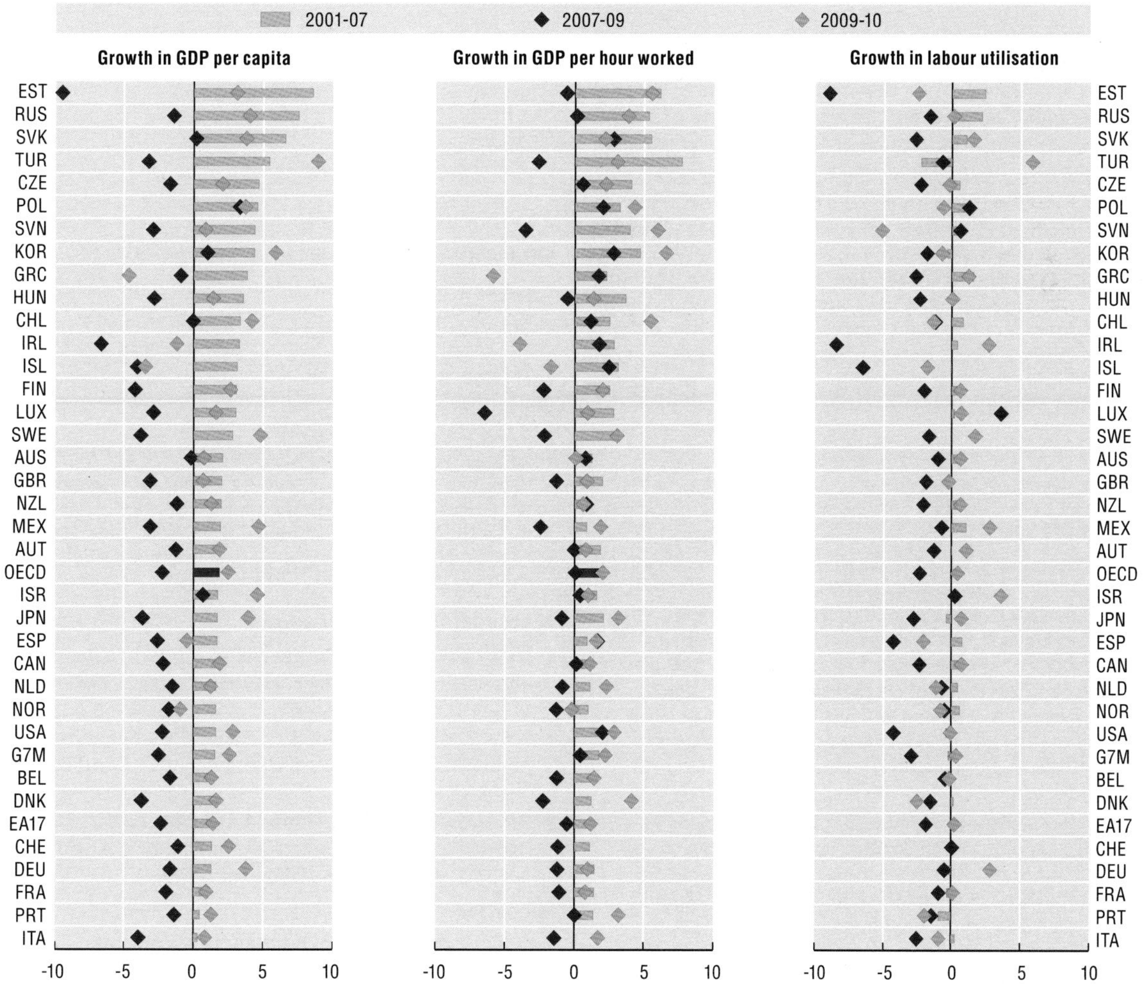

2001-07 ◆ 2007-09 ◆ 2009-10

Growth in GDP per capita **Growth in GDP per hour worked** **Growth in labour utilisation**

StatLink http://dx.doi.org/10.1787/888932503493

PRODUCTIVITY AND GROWTH ACCOUNTING

Economic growth can be increased either by raising the labour and capital inputs used in production, or by greater overall efficiency in how these inputs are used together, *i.e.* higher multi-factor productivity (MFP). Growth accounting involves breaking down GDP growth into the contribution of labour inputs, capital inputs and MFP growth.

Definition

Growth accounting explains output growth by the rates of change of labour and capital inputs and by MFP growth, computed as a residual. In these calculations, the growth rates of labour and capital inputs are weighted with their respective share in total costs. Thus, for example, the contribution of labour to GDP growth is measured as the speed with which labour input grows, multiplied by the share of labour in total costs.

In the tables and graphs, the contribution of capital to GDP growth is broken down into Information and Communication Technologies (ICT) capital (which includes hardware, communication and software) and non-ICT capital (transport equipment and non-residential construction; products of agriculture, metal products and machinery other than hardware and communication equipment; and other products of non-residential gross fixed capital formation).

Comparability

The appropriate measure for capital input in the growth accounting framework is the flow of productive services that can be drawn from the cumulative stock of past investments in capital assets. These services are estimated by the OECD using the rate of change of the "productive capital stock". This measure takes into account wear and tear and retirements, *i.e.*, reductions in the productive capacity of the fixed assets. The price of capital services for each type of asset is measured as their rental price. In principle, the latter could be directly observed if markets existed for capital services. In practice, however, rental prices have to be imputed for most assets, using the implicit rent that capital goods' owners "pay" themselves (or "user costs of capital"). Accurate price indices in measuring volume investment, capital services and user costs should be constant quality deflators that reflect price changes for a given performance of the ICT investment goods. There are differences how countries deal with quality adjustment with possible consequences for the international comparability of price and volume measures of ICT investment. The OECD uses a set of "harmonised" deflators assuming that the ratios between ICT and non-ICT asset prices evolve in a similar manner across countries, using the United States as the benchmark.

The measure of total hours worked is an incomplete measure of labour input because it does not account for changes in the skill composition of workers over time, such as those due to higher educational attainment and work experience. Adjustment for such attributes would provide a more accurate indication of the contribution of labour to production. In the absence of these adjustments, as is the case in the series shown here, more rapid output growth due to a rise in skills of the labour force are captured by the MFP residual, rather than being attributed to labour. This should be kept in mind when interpreting rates of MFP growth.

Overview

From 1985 to 2009, GDP growth in most OECD countries was for a large part driven by growth in capital and MFP. However, data shows large variations in terms of contributions of labour, capital and MFP to GDP growth. In many countries, growth in capital accounted for around one third of GDP growth from 1985 to 2009. Over the same period, ICT capital services represented between 0.2 and 0.6 percentage points of growth in GDP. The GDP-contribution from ICT capital was largest in Sweden, Denmark, the United Kingdom and the United States, and smallest in Ireland and Finland.

In contrast, growth in labour input was important for a few countries over 1985-2009, notably Australia, Spain, Ireland and Canada. However, Japan, Finland and Germany experienced negative GDP contributions of labour inputs. Over the same period, MFP growth was a significant source of GDP growth in Korea, Ireland and Finland, while its contribution was very small in Italy, Canada and Spain.

Sources

- *OECD Productivity Statistics.*

Further information

Analytical publications

- OECD (2011), *OECD Science, Technology and Industry Scoreboard 2011*, OECD Publishing.
- OECD (2004), *Understanding Economic Growth A Macro-level, Industry-level, and Firm-level Perspective*, OECD Publishing.
- OECD (2003), *The Sources of Economic Growth in OECD Countries*, OECD Publishing.

Methodological publications

- OECD (2001), *Measuring Productivity – OECD Manual Measurement of Aggregate and Industry-level Productivity Growth*, OECD Publishing.
- Schreyer, P. (2004), "Capital Stocks, Capital Services and Multi-factor Productivity Measures", *OECD Economic Studies*, Vol. 2003/2.
- Schreyer, P., P.-E. Bignon and J. Dupont (2003), "OECD Capital Services Estimates: Methodology and a First Set of Results", *OECD Statistics Working Papers*, No. 2003/6.

Websites

- OECD Compendium of Productivity Indicators, *www.oecd.org/statistics/productivity/compendium*.
- OECD Productivity, *www.oecd.org/statistics/productivity*.

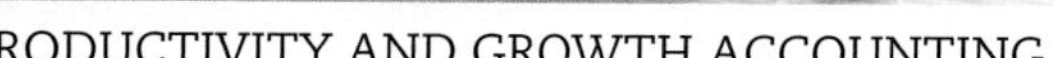

Contributions to GDP growth

Average annual growth in percentage, 1985-2009 (or closest comparable period)

	Labour input	ICT capital				Non-ICT capital	Multi-factor productivity	GDP growth
		IT equipment	Communication equipment	Software	Total			
Australia	1.36	0.30	0.09	0.14	0.53	0.58	0.75	3.22
Austria	0.65	0.19	0.04	0.1	0.27	0.30	1.26	2.48
Belgium	0.21	0.33	0.06	0.07	0.46	0.28	1.31	2.27
Canada	1.02	0.21	0.07	0.14	0.43	0.65	0.32	2.42
Denmark	0.24	0.35	0.02	0.19	0.56	0.43	0.74	1.99
Finland	-0.21	0.08	0.04	0.12	0.23	0.28	1.81	2.09
France	0.05	0.12	0.05	0.16	0.32	0.38	1.15	1.90
Germany	-0.27	0.16	0.05	0.08	0.29	0.28	0.85	1.14
Ireland	1.16	0.11	0.05	0.06	0.23	0.60	2.86	4.82
Italy	0.33	0.11	0.08	0.07	0.26	0.49	0.15	1.23
Japan	-0.36	0.22	0.05	0.13	0.40	0.49	1.45	1.97
Korea	0.63	0.11	0.11	0.15	0.38	1.32	3.76	6.07
Netherlands	0.85	0.23	0.07	0.14	0.44	0.39	1.10	2.78
New Zealand	0.73	0.19	0.15	0.16	0.51	0.40	0.68	2.32
Portugal	0.47	0.23	0.12	0.01	0.36	0.48	1.29	2.61
Spain	1.27	0.16	0.11	0.12	0.39	0.80	0.44	2.90
Sweden	0.19	0.28	0.04	0.24	0.56	0.37	0.85	1.97
Switzerland	0.36	0.17	0.07	0.14	0.38	0.39	0.54	1.68
United Kingdom	0.45	0.29	0.07	0.2	0.56	0.40	1.26	2.68
United States	0.73	0.25	0.1	0.19	0.55	0.32	1.02	2.62

StatLink http://dx.doi.org/10.1787/888932503512

Contributions to GDP growth

Average annual growth in percentage, 1985-2009 (or closest comparable period)

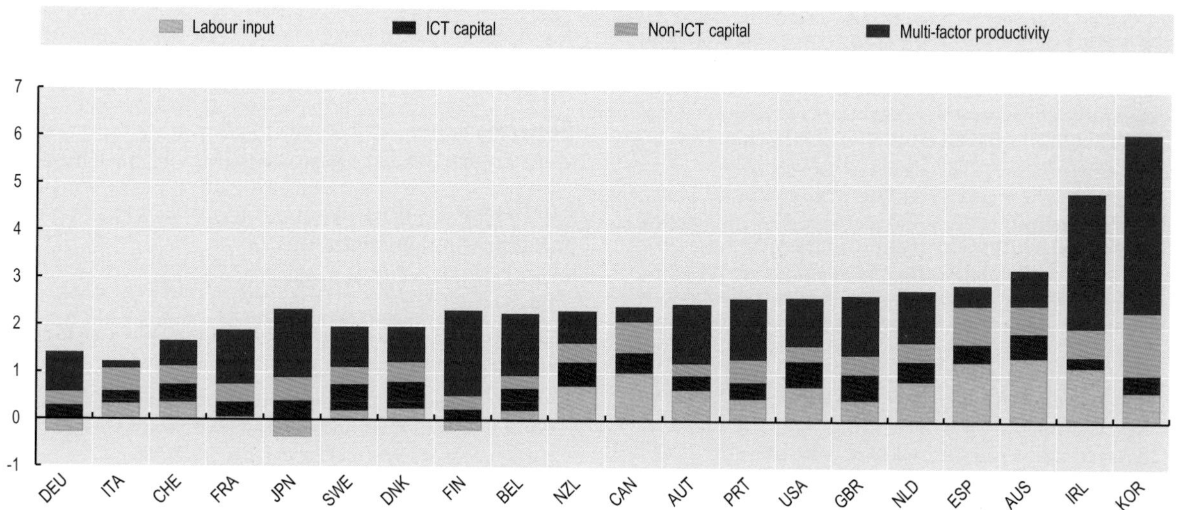

StatLink http://dx.doi.org/10.1787/888932503531

UNIT LABOUR COSTS

Unit labour costs are a key determinant of the competitiveness of the productive system of a country in both domestic and foreign markets. Unit labour costs reflect the combined evolution of compensation of employees per unit of labour input and of labour productivity, and can be an indicator of inflationary pressure on producer prices.

Definition

Unit labour costs measure the average cost of labour per unit of output produced. They are calculated as the ratios of total labour costs to real output. Equivalently, they may be expressed as the ratio of total labour costs per hours worked by employee (or per employee, if hours data is not available) to output per total hours worked (or per person employed if hours data is not available).

Data are taken from the *OECD System of Unit Labour Cost and Related Indicators*, which provides annual and quarterly information for OECD countries as well as for selected non-members countries. Labour productivity estimates are produced as a by-product of calculating unit labour cost. Data are presented as annual growth rates in unit labour costs for the economy as a whole.

Comparability

These indicators are compiled according to a specific methodology to ensure comparability across countries. The primary data source for these indicators is the *OECD National Accounts Database*, where data are compiled on a similar basis across countries according to the 1993 *System of National Accounts*. Due to the high level of comparability, cross country comparisons of developments in the annual growth of unit labour costs can be made with a strong degree of confidence.

Overview

Unit labour costs in the total economy increased at an annual average rate of 2.0% for the OECD area as a whole over the decade since 2000. Annual average growth rates in unit labour costs ranged from negative values in Japan to values exceeding 5% in Estonia, Mexico, South Africa and Turkey.

Annual average growth in unit labour costs for other geographical regions, i.e. G7, euro area and OECD total, was smaller than for the EU27 at 1.4%, 2.0% and 2.0%, respectively. Before the global financial crisis, the annual growth rates of unit labour costs were positive in all years between 2001 and 2008, except in ten countries (Austria, the Czech Republic, Finland, Germany, Israel, Japan, the Netherlands, Poland, Sweden and Switzerland). In the 2009-2010 period, the annual growth rates in unit labour costs were negative or slightly positive in most countries. Estonia experienced the largest decrease of unit labour costs in 2010, at -8.3%.

During this ten-year period, only eight countries (the Czech Republic, Germany, Israel, Korea, Japan, Poland, the Slovak Republic and Sweden) displayed stronger growth in labour productivity than in unit labour costs. Weaker growth in labour productivity than in unit labour costs were recorded in all geographical regions compiled, with the widest margin in the euro area (0.4% labour productivity growth and 2.0% unit labour cost growth) and EU27 (1.1% and 2.5%).

Sources

- OECD (2011), *Main Economic Indicators*, OECD Publishing.

Further information

Analytical publications

- OECD (2011), *National Accounts at a Glance*, OECD Publishing.
- OECD (2011), *OECD Economic Surveys*, OECD Publishing.

Methodological publications

- McKenzie, R. and D. Brackfield (2008), "The OECD System of Unit Labour Cost and Related Indicators", *OECD Statistics Working Papers*, No. 2008/04.

Online databases

- *Labour, Main Economic Indicators.*

Websites

- OECD Compendium of Productivity Indicators, *www.oecd.org/statistics/productivity/compendium*.
- OECD Productivity, *www.oecd.org/statistics/productivity*.

Unit labour costs, total economy

Annual growth in percentage

	1997	1998	1999	2000	2001	2002	2003	2004	2005	2006	2007	2008	2009	2010
Australia	0.9	-0.3	1.5	3.2	0.9	2.3	1.9	4.4	4.0	4.9	..	..	..	..
Austria	-1.6	-0.2	0.3	-0.1	1.0	0.3	1.1	-0.6	1.2	0.4	0.5	2.1	5.1	0.1
Belgium	0.4	1.2	1.6	0.6	3.7	2.4	0.8	-	1.4	2.0	2.2	4.1	4.4	-0.3
Canada	1.5	1.2	-0.4	2.0	2.2	1.0	2.5	2.3	2.3	3.7	3.1	3.2	..	..
Czech Republic	10.7	7.6	2.4	2.1	6.5	5.8	4.7	1.0	-0.8	0.1	2.8	4.6	3.3	..
Denmark	1.1	3.8	1.6	0.2	4.2	3.7	2.2	1.1	2.8	2.3	4.5	6.0	4.2	..
Estonia	8.5	4.3	3.5	2.4	2.5	2.8	4.9	4.8	3.0	9.4	17.5	15.2	2.1	-8.3
Finland	-0.9	1.5	0.5	-	3.5	1.2	1.6	-	2.3	0.5	-0.2	5.9	8.3	-1.4
France	-0.1	-0.4	0.7	1.6	2.3	2.9	1.9	0.9	1.9	2.0	1.3	2.4	..	..
Germany	-1.0	0.1	0.6	0.3	0.4	0.3	0.7	-0.9	-0.9	-1.8	-0.7	2.3	6.4	-1.5
Greece	10.0	4.3	4.2	1.5	-0.1	9.2	1.2	1.3	3.5	3.0	3.8	5.4	4.8	-0.8
Hungary	17.6	10.6	5.2	11.3	11.4	9.5	6.3	4.2	3.3	2.0	5.9	4.4	2.3	-1.6
Iceland	4.1	8.3	6.3	4.3	6.9	7.8	1.6	2.2	5.1	10.2	7.2	4.3	-0.8	..
Ireland	-	4.8	1.3	3.1	3.8	0.1	4.7	3.4	6.0	4.1	3.2	4.3	-3.5	..
Israel	8.9	5.0	6.6	0.8	3.9	1.1	-2.5	-2.4	0.8	3.7	1.1	2.2	0.4	..
Italy	3.0	-1.9	1.8	-0.4	3.3	3.4	4.4	1.5	3.1	1.8	2.1	3.9	4.3	-0.2
Japan	0.6	0.5	-2.7	-2.4	-1.3	-3.8	-3.1	-3.1	-2.1	-0.6	-2.4	1.8	..	..
Korea	0.8	3.3	-6.3	-0.2	5.5	1.2	5.3	1.3	2.4	0.2	0.7	2.2	..	..
Luxembourg	0.6	-0.9	1.0	3.4	5.7	2.3	1.5	1.6	1.9	0.8	1.4	5.4	6.4	-0.6
Mexico	21.8	17.1	17.6	11.1	10.6	6.8	6.1	2.1	3.2	2.5	3.2	4.2	8.8	..
Netherlands	1.1	2.7	2.0	3.1	4.7	4.5	2.3	0.3	-0.3	0.7	1.6	2.6	5.2	-1.3
New Zealand	1.8	1.5	-2.5	0.3	3.1	2.0	3.2	4.7	4.5	4.5	4.3	6.6	2.1	..
Norway	2.5	7.3	4.3	2.0	4.3	3.5	1.6	1.5	3.2	7.3	8.4	8.2	4.1	3.4
Poland	17.3	13.5	3.9	5.4 |	3.2	-1.8	-2.8	-2.0	0.7	-0.8	2.6	7.8	1.7	..
Portugal	4.1	4.3	2.9	4.5	3.5	3.1	3.5	0.8	3.7	0.6	0.8	2.9	3.1	-1.4
Slovak Republic	9.0	5.5	4.2	11.0	0.9	4.3	5.4	4.0	4.7	0.5	0.4	3.3	5.0	-1.5
Slovenia	5.4	5.0	5.2	6.5	8.7	5.6	4.3	3.7	1.0	0.8	2.4	6.3	8.5	0.3
Spain	2.0	2.1	2.0	2.7	3.1	3.0	3.2	2.5	3.5	3.2	3.7	4.6	0.8	..
Sweden	0.5	0.1	-1.2	4.5	5.3	0.6	0.4	-1.2	0.6	-0.7	4.1	2.6	5.2	-2.0
Switzerland	-0.4	-0.7	1.2	1.0	4.7	2.1	0.4	-2.3	1.1	0.6	1.6	3.5	5.0	..
Turkey	88.8	73.1	82.4 |	33.1	49.9	30.0	21.2 |	2.2	0.9	4.9	..	..	..	..
United Kingdom	2.4	3.7	2.3	2.8	3.6	2.5	3.0	1.7	2.4	2.2	2.8	2.4	6.1	2.0
United States	1.1	2.2	1.3	3.6	2.0	0.7	2.4	1.6	2.4	3.1	2.8	2.6	-0.4	..
Euro area	-1.4	-0.1	1.8	1.0	2.1	2.3	2.1	0.6	1.3	1.0	1.4	3.2	4.0	..
EU27 total	2.1	1.8	1.6	2.5	3.2	2.6	2.5	0.8	2.0	1.2	2.0	3.5	4.6	..
Major seven	0.9	1.2	0.5	1.7	1.5	0.4	1.4	0.5	1.3	1.8	1.5	2.5	..	..
OECD total	4.0	3.8	3.0	2.8	3.3	1.6	2.1	0.8	1.6	1.9	1.8	2.9	..	..
South Africa	7.5	8.8	5.7	4.7	4.4	7.3	6.3	5.3	4.2	5.4	7.5	9.2	10.1	7.6

StatLink http://dx.doi.org/10.1787/888932503550

Unit labour costs and labour productivity, total economy

Average annual growth in percentage, 2000-10 or latest available period

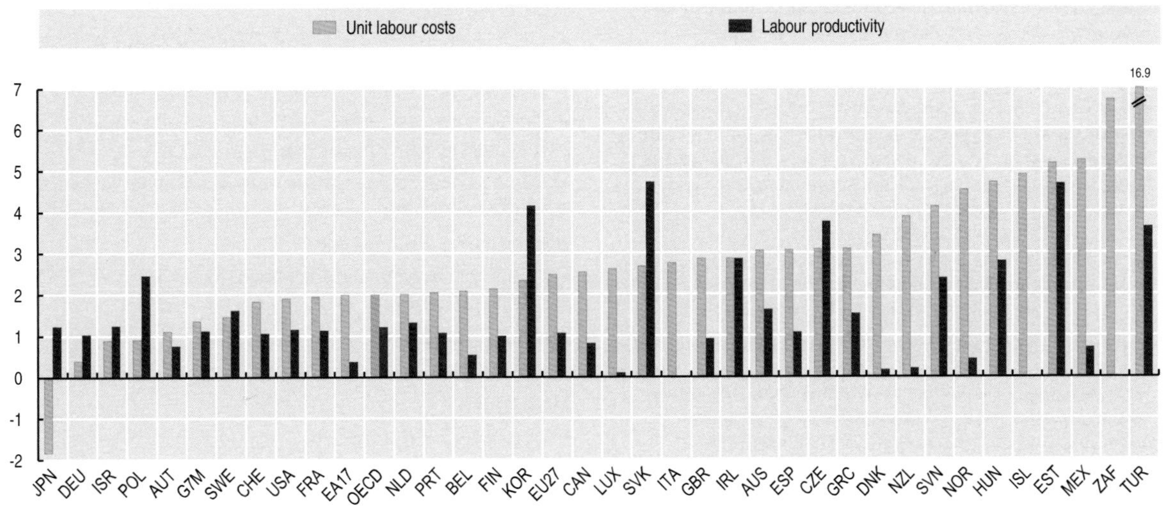

StatLink http://dx.doi.org/10.1787/888932503569

VALUE ADDED BY ACTIVITY

The structure of total value added has changed considerably over recent decades. The share of agriculture is now relatively small in almost all OECD countries. The share of industry has also fallen while services now account for well over 60% of total gross value added in most OECD countries.

Definition

Gross value added is defined as output minus intermediate consumption. This also equals the sum of employee compensation, gross operating surplus of government and corporations, gross mixed income of unincorporated enterprises and other taxes less other subsidies on production. The shares of each sector are calculated by dividing the value added in each sector by total value added. Total value added is less than GDP because it excludes value-added tax (VAT) and other product taxes.

Agriculture consists of agriculture, hunting and forestry and fishing. Industry consists of mining and quarrying, manufacturing, and production and distribution of electricity, gas and water. Other service activities include education, health and other personal services, public administration and defence.

Comparability

All OECD countries follow the international 1993 *System of National Accounts* (SNA), except Australia which follows the 2008 SNA. This assures good comparability between countries in terms of definitions of value added and sectoral coverage. However, part of the decline in the share of industry and of the rise in that of services reflects the outsourcing of service activities that were previously carried out internally within industrial enterprises. For example, if cleaning and security services were earlier provided by employees of a manufacturing enterprise, their salaries would have formed part of value added of industry; if these services are now purchased from specialised producers, the salaries of these employees will now be included in the value added of service industries.

Data for Australia (which are compiled according to the 2008 SNA) and New Zealand refer to fiscal years.

Overview

The share of agriculture in total value added within the OECD fell by 0.5% between 2000 and 2010 to a level of 1.8% continuing its long term decline. In only three countries (Turkey, Iceland and New Zealand) agriculture accounts for more than 5% of total value added, compared to seven countries in 2000. The share of industry in total value added has also continued its decline in recent decades, with its share for the OECD area falling by nearly 1.5% between 2000 and 2010. However Chile, Estonia, Hungary, Iceland, Korea and Poland experienced rises over the period. The share of industry also fell in non-member countries but remains at considerably higher levels than in most OECD countries, with the share for China and Indonesia remaining close to 40%. Norway and Chile, where mining and quarrying are large contributors to activity, come closest to these rates in the OECD.

Conversely the share of financial intermediation, real estate, renting and business activities increased by 1.5% over the period, bringing the average share for OECD countries up to 28.6% in 2010; this share ranges from a low of just over 18% in Poland to over 48% in Luxembourg.

Sources

- OECD (2011), *National Accounts of OECD Countries*, OECD Publishing.

Further information

Analytical publications

- Lal, K. (2003), "Measurement of Output, Value Added, GDP in Canada and the United States: Similarities and Differences", *OECD Statistics Working Papers*, No. 2003/4.
- OECD (2002), *Measuring the Non-Observed Economy: A Handbook*, OECD Publishing.
- OECD (1996), *Services: Measuring Real Annual Value Added*, OECD Publishing.

Statistical publications

- OECD (2011), *National Accounts at a Glance*, OECD Publishing.

Online databases

- *STAN: OECD Structural Analysis Statistics.*

Websites

- OECD National Accounts, *www.oecd.org/std/national-accounts.*
- OECD National Accounts Archive, *www.oecd.org/std/national-accounts/papers.*

Value added by activity

As a percentage of total value added

	Agriculture, hunting and forestry; fishing		Industry, including energy		Construction		Wholesale and retail trade, repairs; hotels and restaurants; transport		Financial intermediation; real estate, renting and business activities		Other services activities	
	2000	2010 or latest available year	2000	2010 or latest available year	2000	2010 or latest available year	2000	2010 or latest available year	2000	2010 or latest available year	2000	2010 or latest available year
Australia	3.9	2.3	20.2	19.8	5.7	7.9	21.7	20.0	29.1	31.5	19.4	18.5
Austria	2.0	1.5	23.3	22.3	7.5	6.9	24.6	23.4	21.5	24.0	21.1	21.9
Belgium	1.4	0.7	22.1	16.6	5.0	5.3	21.2	21.8	27.8	30.3	22.5	25.3
Canada	2.3	1.7	28.2	24.6	5.0	6.9	20.3	21.1	25.0	26.0	19.2	19.7
Chile	5.3	3.2	27.4	34.8	6.6	8.1	21.1	17.0	23.1	20.7	16.9	16.2
Czech Republic	3.9	2.4	31.6	30.5	6.5	7.2	25.8	24.0	16.2	18.4	16.0	17.5
Denmark	2.6	1.3	21.3	17.8	5.5	4.3	21.8	20.7	22.3	26.8	26.4	29.3
Estonia	4.8	3.5	22.0	22.7	5.6	5.7	28.3	25.2	22.4	23.8	17.0	19.1
Finland	3.5	2.9	28.4	22.3	6.2	6.6	20.2	19.8	21.0	24.1	20.7	24.2
France	2.8	1.8	17.8	12.5	5.2	6.5	18.9	19.2	30.7	34.1	24.8	27.0
Germany	1.3	0.9	25.1	23.7	5.2	4.1	18.2	17.2	27.5	30.5	22.8	23.6
Greece	6.6	3.3	13.9	13.8	7.0	4.1	30.1	33.3	20.6	20.5	21.7	25.1
Hungary	5.4	3.5	26.6	26.8	5.0	4.0	20.1	20.4	20.9	23.3	22.0	22.1
Iceland	9.1	7.2	17.4	20.2	8.7	5.0	22.0	18.6	18.9	25.1	23.9	23.9
Ireland	3.2	1.0	34.3	26.3	7.5	5.6	17.9	17.2	21.3	27.2	15.8	22.8
Israel	1.7	2.1	19.2	16.5	5.8	4.9	18.2	16.8	30.5	36.5	24.6	23.3
Italy	2.8	1.9	23.4	19.4	5.0	6.0	23.9	22.2	24.7	28.4	20.1	22.2
Japan	1.7	1.4	24.0	19.9	7.1	6.1	20.2	18.9	24.9	27.9	22.1	25.7
Korea	4.6	2.6	31.1	32.8	6.9	6.5	21.4	19.0	19.3	19.0	16.6	20.2
Luxembourg	0.7	0.3	12.6	8.1	5.7	4.9	21.8	22.1	43.8	48.4	15.4	16.2
Mexico	4.2	3.6	29.4	26.7	6.4	7.1	29.8	27.6	19.0	20.9	12.7	14.2
Netherlands	2.6	1.9	19.3	18.4	5.6	5.3	23.1	20.5	27.3	27.7	22.1	26.1
New Zealand	8.5	5.4	19.9	18.4	4.4	5.4	21.8	21.4	27.8	30.5	17.6	18.9
Norway	2.1	1.6	37.8	35.7	4.1	4.9	18.8	15.3	16.9	19.7	20.3	22.8
Poland	5.0	3.5	24.0	24.7	7.7	7.0	27.3	27.3	18.1	18.1	18.0	19.3
Portugal	3.7	2.4	20.4	17.0	7.6	6.0	25.3	25.5	20.3	23.1	22.7	26.0
Slovak Republic	4.5	3.8	29.1	25.8	7.0	9.0	25.2	24.2	17.1	19.1	17.0	18.0
Slovenia	3.3	2.4	29.0	24.3	6.7	6.7	20.4	22.2	20.2	23.4	20.0	21.3
Spain	4.4	2.7	20.9	15.6	8.3	10.1	26.1	25.3	19.5	22.8	20.8	23.5
Sweden	2.1	1.9	24.5	21.1	4.3	5.5	18.9	19.6	24.9	24.6	25.3	27.4
Switzerland	1.6	1.1	21.8	21.0	5.5	5.7	21.4	22.0	24.0	23.6	25.7	26.5
Turkey	10.8	9.4	24.6	21.5	5.4	4.6	29.1	30.1	19.5	22.2	10.6	12.3
United Kingdom	1.0	0.7	22.0	15.7	5.3	6.1	22.9	20.6	27.0	33.7	21.8	23.2
United States	1.2	1.0	18.4	15.9	5.0	4.1	20.0	18.0	31.7	34.2	23.7	26.8
Euro area	2.5	1.7	22.2	18.5	5.7	5.9	21.2	20.6	26.3	29.0	22.2	24.3
EU27 total	2.4	1.7	22.4	18.7	5.6	6.0	21.6	20.9	25.9	28.8	22.1	23.9
OECD total	2.3	1.8	22.0	20.6	5.7	5.9	21.4	20.7	27.1	28.6	21.7	22.5
China	15.1	10.3	40.4	39.7	5.6	6.6	8.2	8.5	8.3	10.7	22.5	24.2
Indonesia	15.6	15.3	40.4	36.8	5.5	10.3	20.8	20.2	8.3	7.2	9.3	10.2
Russian Federation	6.4	4.7	31.1	27.3	6.6	5.5	33.1	30.3	4.6	17.6	18.3	14.6
South Africa	3.3	2.5	29.3	27.0	2.5	3.8	24.3	23.1	18.6	21.3	22.0	22.4

StatLink http://dx.doi.org/10.1787/888932503588

Value added in industry, including energy

As a percentage of total value added

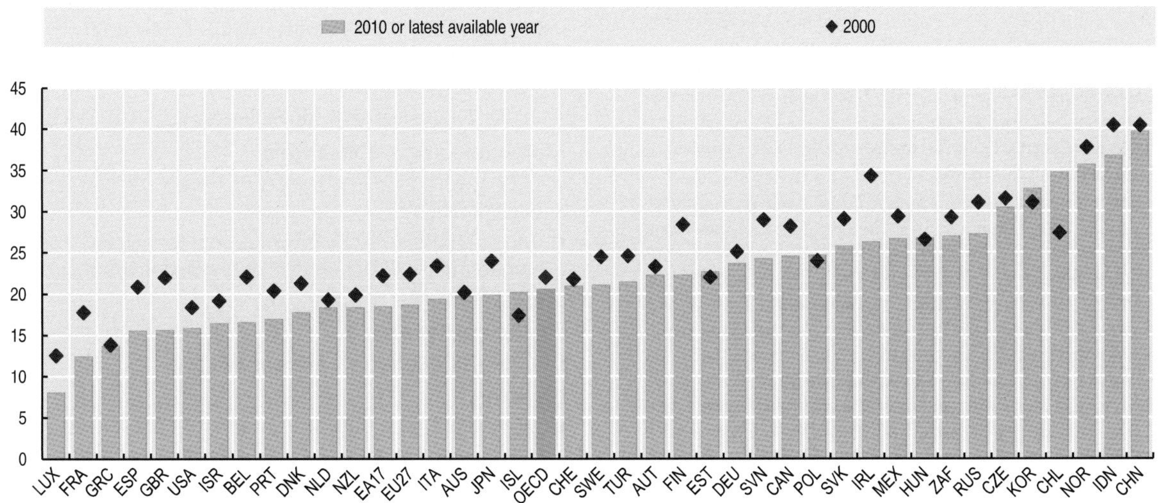

StatLink http://dx.doi.org/10.1787/888932503607

REAL VALUE ADDED BY ACTIVITY

GDP growth has not been evenly spread across economic activities. Some economic activities have grown faster than others and some have declined in importance. A convenient way to show how the patterns of economic growth have changed is to distinguish between the various sectors of the economy, such as agriculture, industry and services.

Definition

Gross value added is defined as output minus intermediate consumption. It also equals the sum of employee compensation, net operating surplus, net mixed income, depreciation of capital assets and other taxes less other subsidies on production. The growth rates shown here refer to volume estimates of gross value added.

Agriculture consists of agriculture; hunting and forestry; and fishing. Industry consists of mining and quarrying; manufacturing; production and distribution of electricity, gas and water. Other services consist of education, health and other personal services, public administration; and defence. The graphs show annual growth rates or real value-added in the relevant sector in 2000 and 2009.

Comparability

All OECD countries follow the 1993 *System of National Accounts* (SNA), except Australia which follows the 2008 SNA. This assures good comparability between countries as regards definitions and coverage. However part of the decline of industry and of the rise of service activities reflects the outsourcing of service activities that were previously carried out internally within industrial enterprises; because of this, the trends shown here overstate real changes in these activities. For example, if cleaning and security services were earlier provided by employees of a manufacturing enterprise, their salaries would have formed part of value added by industry; if these services are now purchased from specialised producers, the salaries of these employees will form part of the value added of the service sector.

Data for Australia (which are compiled according to 2008 SNA) and New Zealand refer to fiscal years.

Overview

The table shows how the various sectors of the economy fared in 2010, as the recent crisis continued to have an impact on production and demand. Hardest hit in 2010 were the agriculture and construction sectors, however, all sectors recorded growth rates below those recorded in 2000.

In the construction sector for 2010, falls in the growth rate greater than 10% were recorded in Estonia, the Netherlands, Slovenia, the United States, the Russian Federation, Ireland and Hungary (with these last two countries recording falls of more than 30%). The construction sector for 2010 in China (19%) and Turkey (17%) appear unaffected by the ongoing crisis.

The picture was more mixed for the industry sector in 2010 with the Russian Federation, France, Canada, Greece and Japan all seeing falls in excess of 10%, however, most of the remaining OECD countries and emerging economics saw some bounce back from the previous years in the growth rate for the industry sector. The OECD total for 2010 was however still below that recorded in 2000.

The wholesale and retail trade, hotels, repairs and transport sector recorded 4% growth for the OECD total in 2010, however, this rates hides some large differences between countries, with for example 10 OECD countries recording negative growth during this period.

Other services activities, which includes government, health and education output continued to record steady growth with the OECD total for 2010 being equal to the 2% recorded in 2000. Of the major seven countries only Germany recorded higher growth in this sector in 2010 compared to 2000; but only very marginally. In the same sense, while the remaining major seven countries saw less growth in this sector in 2010 compared with 2000, the differences could all be considered minor. The picture for agricultural activities was mixed, with some countries seeing significant growth (*e.g.* Denmark with over 15%) and some seeing significant falls (*e.g.* Hungary with over 15%).

Sources

- OECD (2011), *National Accounts of OECD Countries*, OECD Publishing.

Further information

Analytical publications

- OECD (2011), *OECD Economic Outlook*, OECD Publishing.

Statistical publications

- Maddison (2003), *The World Economy: Historical Perspectives*, Development Centre Studies, OECD Publishing.
- OECD (2011), *National Accounts at a Glance*, OECD Publishing.
- OECD (2009), *Quarterly National Accounts*, OECD Publishing.

Methodological publications

- OECD (2000), *System of National Accounts, 1993 – Glossary*, OECD Publishing.
- United Nations, OECD, International Monetary Fund and Eurostat (eds.) (2010), *System of National Accounts 2008*, United Nations, Geneva.

Online databases

- STAN: *OECD Structural Analysis Statistics.*

Websites

- OECD National Accounts, *www.oecd.org/std/national-accounts.*
- The World Economy (supplementary material), *www.theworldeconomy.org.*

Real value added by activity

Annual growth in percentage

	Agriculture, hunting and forestry; fishing		Industry, including energy		Construction		Wholesale and retail trade, repairs; hotels and restaurants; transport		Financial intermediation; real estate, renting and business activities		Other services activities	
	2000	2010 or latest available year	2000	2010 or latest available year	2000	2010 or latest available year	2000	2010 or latest available year	2000	2010 or latest available year	2000	2010 or latest available year
Australia	3.8	-1.2	3.5	3.8	-14.4	0.5	2.3	1.8	5.2	2.9	6.4	1.7
Austria	-5.4	0.1	6.3	5.7	0.6	-6.4	2.9	1.3	7.5	3.5	-0.2	1.6
Belgium	4.2	-0.7	4.8	3.9	5.8	0.5	0.4	2.6	4.6	1.3	3.4	1.7
Canada	-1.8	-9.5	8.4	-11.0	5.2	-6.6	6.0	-3.5	5.2	0.9	2.6	2.0
Chile	6.6	-2.5	4.9	0.9	-0.7	3.6	6.0	11.2	4.0	5.7	3.0	2.5
Czech Republic	4.1	-5.4	9.7	7.5	-4.1	-1.4	0.9	2.3	2.9	4.7	0.9	-0.9
Denmark	8.3	15.5	3.9	2.7	1.0	-9.1	7.1	5.7	6.4	0.9	1.3	1.3
Estonia	16.2	8.6	17.7	18.3	18.3	-10.1	7.3	0.7	9.8	2.6	2.0	-1.4
Finland	8.1	6.0	12.4	6.3	0.4	4.9	4.8	5.4	3.9	0.4	2.1	0.2
France	-1.4	3.4	4.2	-10.3	5.0	-4.5	4.4	-3.3	5.7	-1.6	0.8	0.9
Germany	-0.4	-0.4	6.3	10.3	-3.3	1.5	4.6	3.3	3.7	1.9	2.0	1.9
Greece	-3.7	12.3	5.3	-11.6	5.7	-3.2	7.6	-6.4	5.1	-2.4	1.4	-5.0
Hungary	-3.1	-15.4	4.7	8.9	17.2	-8.3	-0.5	0.4	8.4	0.1	4.2	-0.3
Iceland	-1.8	2.8	5.5	-0.8	13.8	-35.2	8.8	-7.3	9.6	-11.6	2.5	-1.5
Ireland	-0.5	8.4	8.8	0.5	5.1	-31.3	10.0	-8.9	12.0	-2.5	7.4	-1.7
Israel	6.6	9.5	13.7	-4.1	-1.3	-0.9	6.8	-2.1	17.0	2.3	1.4	2.9
Italy	-2.4	1.0	3.5	4.8	4.7	-3.4	6.0	2.7	4.7	0.6	0.8	-0.1
Japan	2.1	-10.9	4.7	-19.4	-3.5	-0.6	-0.9	-11.3	4.1	-3.0	2.1	-0.2
Korea	1.1	-4.3	16.9	14.0	-4.4	-0.1	13.1	6.7	4.2	1.3	2.0	2.7
Luxembourg	-13.0	8.8	7.9	12.8	1.9	3.0	8.1	8.7	11.0	0.5	0.8	3.0
Mexico	0.4	-0.2	6.4	-7.7	4.2	-6.5	11.1	-9.7	5.5	-3.4	2.9	1.8
Netherlands	2.1	1.1	5.4	7.8	3.5	-10.7	7.0	4.5	2.5	-0.6	1.9	2.2
New Zealand	2.7	0.1	2.4	-4.4	-6.5	-7.9	5.0	-2.3	2.2	3.5	3.3	1.7
Norway	-2.7	11.8	4.0	-3.5	-1.2	0.0	3.7	1.8	6.6	1.9	1.0	2.3
Poland	-4.1	-1.4	6.3	9.1	-0.4	3.8	4.5	4.0	5.4	-2.2	3.2	1.1
Portugal	-4.6	-1.6	3.3	2.7	5.9	-4.2	6.4	2.0	1.9	1.6	3.8	0.9
Slovak Republic	2.0	-16.0	-3.2	1.8	25.8	-0.5	-2.6	5.7	-2.4	9.6	6.4	8.6
Slovenia	1.3	-1.7	8.9	6.7	-1.2	-14.4	4.3	2.7	5.1	0.8	2.3	1.8
Spain	7.3	-1.3	4.2	1.3	5.9	-6.3	3.7	1.2	7.9	-1.2	4.3	1.3
Sweden	2.7	-0.8	7.7	15.3	1.4	8.9	5.9	7.8	5.8	2.8	1.9	0.8
Switzerland	7.8	-0.5	0.7	3.2	-0.4	4.1	4.4	2.2	6.5	4.9	2.3	0.2
Turkey	7.1	1.6	6.6	12.9	4.9	17.1	9.8	11.0	4.2	6.0	1.6	0.8
United Kingdom	-0.8	-3.5	1.8	2.1	0.7	7.1	5.1	1.3	6.7	1.2	2.1	0.8
United States	12.8	6.5	2.6	-5.5	3.3	-15.8	6.3	-2.9	6.1	-1.2	1.2	-0.4
Euro area	0.2	0.2	5.2	6.1	2.3	-4.3	4.9	1.9	4.8	1.0	1.8	1.3
EU27 total	-0.3	-0.1	4.8	6.0	1.9	-2.7	4.9	2.0	5.2	0.9	1.9	1.2
OECD total	3.6	-1.9	4.8	3.2	1.1	-0.1	5.2	3.8	5.5	3.2	1.8	1.7
China	2.4	4.2	9.8	8.7	5.7	18.6	9.4	12.1	6.7	14.4	11.0	6.4
Indonesia	1.9	2.9	5.9	4.3	5.6	7	6.6	10.3	4.6	5.7	2.3	6.0
Russian Federation	-1.5	0.2	8.1	-10.0	12.7	-17.2	11.0	-8.3	8.0	-1.3	0.1	-1.6
South Africa	4.7	0.9	4.9	4.9	5.6	1.5	8.1	2.5	3.2	1.9	0.6	2.3

StatLink http://dx.doi.org/10.1787/888932503626

Real value added in industry, including energy

Annual growth in percentage

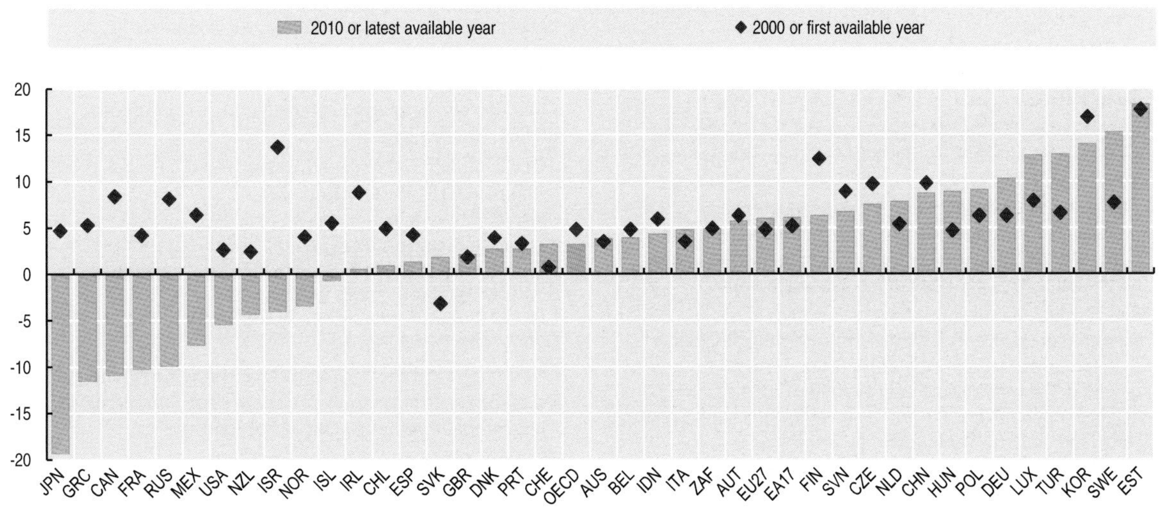

StatLink http://dx.doi.org/10.1787/888932503645

SMALL AND MEDIUM-SIZED ENTERPRISES

Small firms, and especially recent start-ups, can be very dynamic and innovative. A few very high-performance new and small firms can make an important contribution to employment creation and economic growth. Although the majority of small firms have more modest economic impacts individually, taken together they make an important contribution.

Definition

An enterprise is a legal entity possessing the right to conduct business on its own; for example to enter into contracts, own property, incur liabilities and establish bank accounts. It may consist of one or more establishments situated in a geographically separate area. In this section, small enterprises refer to those with less than 20 persons engaged. Data on the number of small enterprises and the number of employees working in them refer to the manufacturing sector.

Employees include all persons covered by a contractual arrangement, working in the enterprise and receiving compensation for their work. They include salaried managers, students who have a formal commitment whereby they contribute to the unit's process of production in return for remuneration and/or education services, and employees engaged under a contract designed to encourage the recruitment of unemployed persons. They also include persons on sick leave, paid leave or vacation, while excluding working proprietors, active business partners, unpaid family workers and home-workers, irrespective of whether or not they are on the payroll.

Comparability

Most countries present information using the enterprise as the statistical unit. Japan, Korea and Mexico are exceptions, as data refer to establishments. As most enterprises correspond to a single establishment, these differences do not significantly distort comparisons. An area where considerable differences do arise concerns the coverage of data on enterprises/establishments. In many countries, this information is based on business registers, economic censuses or surveys that may have a size cut-off. All countries have thresholds of one sort or another, often depending on tax legislation and legal provisions reducing administrative burdens on small enterprises. For Ireland, only enterprises with three or more persons engaged are reflected, while the data for Japan and Korea do not include establishments with fewer than 4 and 5 persons engaged respectively. Also, it is typically difficult, if not impossible, to cover enterprises operating in the underground economy. These differences, however, do not prevent meaningful comparisons across countries.

Employment data for Australia and Switzerland refer to the total number of persons engaged rather than to the number of employees. Data refer to 2007 in the case of France, Greece, Japan, and Norway; to 2006 for Australia and Korea; 2005 for Iceland; 2003 for Mexico; and 2001 for Switzerland.

Because data do not follow the same enterprise over time, they do not show the contribution that small enterprises make to economic and employment growth as they move from the start-up phase to some optimal size.

Overview

The contribution of small enterprises varies considerably across countries. In most economies, the share of enterprises with less than 20 persons engaged exceeds 70% of the total, ranging between 69% in Ireland and above 95% in Greece. Small enterprises account for a smaller share of the total number of employees, ranging between around 9% in the United States and the Czech Republic and around 35% in Greece.

Some larger economies are characterised by a lower proportion of small enterprises, partly reflecting the greater scope for growth in larger markets (due to the existence of a greater pool of workers and larger demand) but also due to a statistical phenomenon (*i.e.* when an enterprise opens a new establishment in the same economy within which it is registered, it will move from being a small to a large enterprise).

Sources

- OECD (2010), *OECD Studies on SMEs and Entrepreneurship*, OECD Publishing.
- OECD (2010), *Structural and Demographic Business Statistics* (database).

Further information

Analytical publications

- OECD (2011), *Entrepreneurship at a Glance 2011*, OECD Publishing.
- OECD (2009), *The Impact of the Global Crisis on SME and Entrepreneurship Financing and Policy Responses*, OECD Publishing.
- OECD (2008), *Enhancing the Role of SMEs in Global Value Chains*, OECD Publishing.
- OECD (2008), *Removing Barriers to SME Access to International Markets*, OECD Publishing.

Statistical publications

- OECD (2010), *Structural and Demographic Business Statistics 2009*, OECD Publishing.
- OECD and Eurostat (2009), *Measuring Entrepreneurship – a collection of indicators, OECD-Eurostat Entrepreneurship Indicators Programme*, OECD Publishing.

Methodological publications

- OECD and Eurostat (2008), *Eurostat-OECD Manual on Business Demography Statistics*, OECD Publishing.

Number of employees and number of enterprises in manufacturing

Breakdown by size-class of enterprise, 2008 or latest available year

	As a percentage of total number of employees in manufacturing							As a percentage of total number of enterprises in manufacturing						
Number of persons engaged	Less than 20	20 or more	Less than 10	10-19	20-49	50-249	250 or more	Less than 20	20 or more	Less than 10	10-19	20-49	50-249	250 or more
Australia	28.9	71.1	19.3	9.6	13.9	..	..	94.2	5.8	88.5	5.7	3.8	..	..
Austria	13.4	86.6	6.8	6.6	11.0	26.8	48.7	83.9	16.1	72.0	11.9	8.6	5.8	1.8
Belgium	13.1	86.9	6.6	6.4	13.3	25.6	48.1	89.0	11.0	81.3	7.6	6.5	3.6	0.9
Czech Republic	11.4	88.6	5.7	5.7	10.6	29.8	48.3	94.1	5.9	90.5	3.6	3.0	2.3	0.6
Denmark	12.0	88.0	5.6	6.4	14.0	27.7	46.3	81.5	18.5	70.8	10.7	10.6	6.5	1.4
Estonia	17.4	82.6	9.4	8.0	16.2	39.1	27.4	77.5	22.5	65.0	12.5	12.4	8.8	1.3
Finland	13.5	86.5	7.4	6.1	10.6	23.5	52.4	89.2	10.9	81.6	7.5	5.9	3.9	1.1
France	17.9	82.1	10.7	7.3	12.1	22.2	47.8	91.3	8.7	84.1	7.2	5.1	2.8	0.8
Germany	12.8	87.2	5.0	7.8	7.5	25.5	54.3	81.4	18.6	61.1	20.3	7.9	8.6	2.1
Greece	35.3	64.7	30.4	4.9	12.1	25.6	27.1	97.8	2.3	96.5	1.2	1.3	0.8	0.2
Hungary	16.5	83.5	9.8	6.8	11.1	26.0	46.4	91.4	8.6	84.9	6.5	4.6	3.2	0.8
Iceland	..	..	..	..	..	..	..	88.9	11.1	80.2	8.7	6.7	3.8	0.7
Ireland	12.2	87.8	5.8	6.4	12.9	30.4	44.6	69.4	30.7	50.2	19.2	16.5	11.3	2.9
Israel	17.3	82.7	9.8	7.6	13.3	30.5	38.9	82.3	17.7	69.8	12.5	9.8	6.7	1.1
Italy	30.0	70.0	14.3	15.7	18.4	24.9	26.8	92.3	7.7	81.3	11.0	5.3	2.1	0.3
Japan	19.2	80.8	8.6	10.7	17.6	31.0	32.2	69.6	30.4	45.4	24.2	18.4	10.2	1.8
Korea	25.8	74.2	11.3	14.5	20.9	26.8	26.5	76.1	23.9	49.5	26.6	16.5	6.7	0.8
Luxembourg	..	..	..	..	..	..	..	76.2	23.8	63.3	12.9	11.3	9.3	3.3
Mexico	13.7	86.3	9.4	4.3	7.3	21.6	57.3	92.8	7.2	89.7	3.1	..	..	..
Netherlands	17.9	82.1	8.8	9.1	16.3	31.6	34.2	87.0	13.0	77.8	9.2	7.7	4.4	0.9
New Zealand	23.3	76.7	12.5	10.9	15.8	24.9	36.0	83.6	16.4	67.7	15.9	10.5	5.0	0.9
Norway	17.5	82.5	9.3	8.2	14.6	28.2	39.6	88.2	11.8	79.6	8.6	6.9	4.1	0.9
Poland	13.9	86.2	9.5	4.3	10.0	30.7	45.5	91.6	8.5	87.6	3.9	4.1	3.5	0.9
Portugal	30.7	69.3	18.4	12.3	19.6	30.7	19.0	90.5	9.5	81.7	8.8	6.2	3.0	0.3
Slovak Republic	10.9	89.1	3.5	7.5	7.5	26.5	55.1	72.3	27.7	42.1	30.2	10.6	13.0	4.1
Slovenia	15.2	84.8	9.3	5.9	9.7	29.4	45.8	91.8	8.2	86.2	5.6	4.0	3.4	0.9
Spain	27.4	72.6	15.2	12.2	19.8	24.3	28.4	89.5	10.5	79.3	10.3	7.3	2.7	0.5
Sweden	15.5	84.5	9.0	6.6	10.7	24.4	49.4	92.6	7.4	87.2	5.4	4.0	2.7	0.7
Switzerland	22.7	77.3	14.9	7.8	13.0	29.2	35.1	87.8	12.2	79.1	8.7	6.7	4.5	0.9
Turkey	23.6	76.4	..	..	14.4	26.2	35.8	94.1	5.9	..	..	3.5	2.0	0.4
United Kingdom	17.5	82.5	10.5	7.0	12.0	26.8	43.6	85.4	14.6	74.7	10.7	8.1	5.3	1.3
United States	8.9	91.1	4.3	4.6	..	..	..	74.1	25.9	58.5	15.6	..	..	..
Brazil	15.2	84.8	6.9	8.3	12.7	21.6	50.5	82.7	17.3	66.2	16.5	10.8	5.4	1.2

StatLink http://dx.doi.org/10.1787/888932503664

Manufacturing enterprises with less than 20 persons engaged

As a percentage of total number of employees or total number of enterprises, 2008 or latest available year

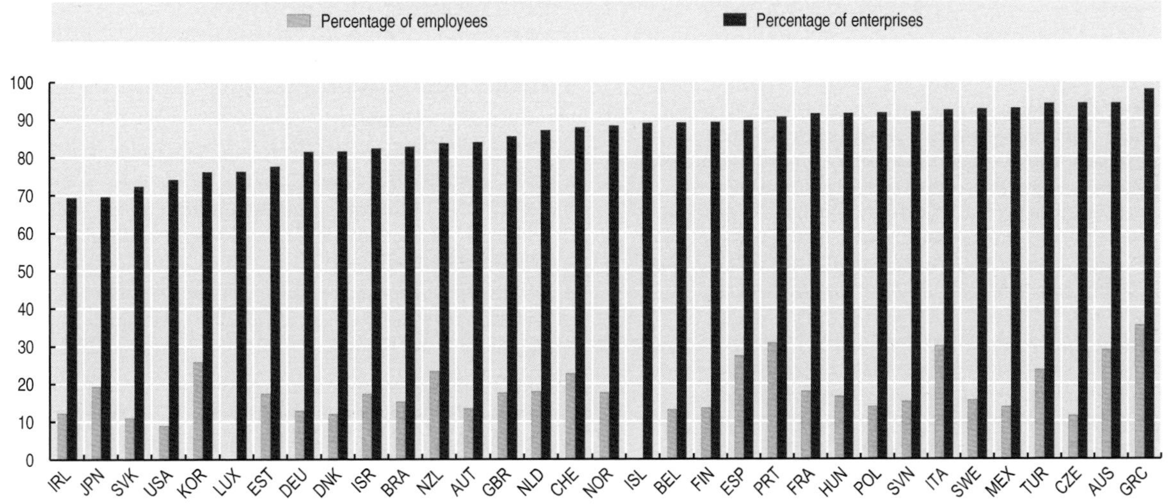

StatLink http://dx.doi.org/10.1787/888932503683

INCOME INEQUALITY

Income inequalities are one of the most visible manifestations of differences in living standards within each country. High income inequalities typically imply a waste of human resources, in the form of a large share of the population out of work or trapped in low-paid and low-skilled jobs.

Definition

Income is defined as household disposable income in a particular year. It consists of earnings, self-employment and capital income and public cash transfers; income taxes and social security contributions paid by households are deducted. The income of the household is attributed to each of its members, with an adjustment to reflect differences in needs for households of different sizes (*i.e.* the needs of a household composed of four people are assumed to be twice as large as those of a person living alone).

Income inequality among individuals is measured here by four indicators. The Gini coefficient is based on the comparison of cumulative proportions of the population against cumulative proportions of income they receive, and it ranges between 0 in the case of perfect equality and 1 in the case of perfect inequality. The P90/P10 ratio is the ratio of the upper bound value of the ninth decile (*i.e.* the 10% of people with highest income) to that of the first decile; the P90/P50 ratio is the ratio of the upper bound value of the ninth decile to the median income; and the P50/P10 ratio is the ratio of median income to the upper bound value of the first decile.

Comparability

Data used here were provided by national experts applying common methodologies and standardised definitions. In many cases, experts have made several adjustments to their source data to conform to standardized definitions. While this approach improves comparability, full standardisation cannot be achieved. Also, small differences between periods and across countries are usually not significant.

Results refer to different years. "Late-2000s" data refer to the income in 2008 in all countries except Japan (2006); Denmark, Hungary and Turkey (2007); and Chile (2009). "Mid-1990s" data refer to the income earned between 1993 and 1996 in all countries for which data are available except Poland and Switzerland (2000); Estonia, Iceland, the Slovak Republic and Slovenia (2004); and Korea (2006). "Mid-1980s" data refer to the income earned between 1983 and 1987 in all countries for which data are available except Greece (1988); Portugal (1990); and the Czech Republic (1992). "Mid-1980s" data refer to the western Lander of Germany. "Late-2000s" data for Austria, Belgium, Ireland, Portugal and Spain are based on EU-SILC and are not deemed to be fully comparable with those for earlier years; therefore these countries are not included in the "Mid-1980s to Late-2000s" changes.

Overview

There is considerable variation in income inequality across OECD countries. Inequality as measured by the Gini coefficient is lowest in Slovenia, Denmark and Norway and highest in Chile, Mexico and Turkey. It is above-average in Israel, Portugal and the United States, and below-average in the remaining Nordic and many Continental European countries. The Gini coefficient for the most unequal country (Chile) is double the value of the most equal country (Slovenia). Overall, the different measures of income inequalities provide similar ranking across countries.

From the mid-1980s to the late-2000s, inequality rose in 15 out of 19 countries. The increase was strongest in Finland, New Zealand and Sweden. Declines occurred in France, Greece, and Turkey. Income inequality generally rose faster from the mid-1980s to the mid-1990s than in the following period.

Sources

- OECD (2011), *Divided We Stand: Why Inequality Keeps Rising*, OECD Publishing.
- OECD (2010), *OECD Social Expenditure Statistics* (database).

Further information

Analytical publications

- OECD (2011), *Society at a Glance: OECD Social Indicators*, OECD Publishing.
- OECD (2010), *Tackling Inequalities in Brazil, China, India and South Africa: The Role of Labour Market and Social Policies*, OECD Publishing.
- OECD (2008), *Growing Unequal?: Income Distribution and Poverty in OECD Countries*, OECD Publishing.

Websites

- OECD Income Distribution and Poverty, *www.oecd.org/els/social/inequality*.
- OECD Ministerial Meeting on Social Policy, *www.oecd.org/social/ministerial*.
- OECD Social and Welfare Statistics, *www.oecd.org/social/statistics*.

Income inequality

Different summary measures, level and rank from low to high inequality, late-2000s

	Gini coefficient		Interdecile ratio P90/P10		Interdecile ratio P90/P50		Interdecile ratio P50/P10	
	Level	Rank	Level	Rank	Level	Rank	Level	Rank
Australia	0.34	26	4.5	24	2.0	23	2.1	20
Austria	0.26	9	3.2	9	1.8	9	1.8	8
Belgium	0.26	6	3.3	11	1.7	6	1.9	16
Canada	0.32	23	4.2	21	1.9	19	2.1	19
Chile	0.49	34	8.5	33	3.2	34	2.7	33
Czech Republic	0.26	4	2.9	2	1.7	7	1.7	2
Denmark	0.25	2	2.8	1	1.6	1	1.7	4
Estonia	0.32	21	4.3	22	2.0	26	2.3	25
Finland	0.26	8	3.2	7	1.7	5	1.9	10
France	0.29	12	3.4	14	1.9	17	1.8	7
Germany	0.30	15	3.5	15	1.8	14	1.9	14
Greece	0.31	18	4.0	19	2.0	21	2.2	21
Hungary	0.27	10	3.1	6	1.7	8	1.8	6
Iceland	0.30	16	3.2	10	1.8	11	1.7	3
Ireland	0.29	13	3.7	17	1.9	16	2.2	22
Israel	0.37	30	6.2	32	2.3	30	2.7	32
Italy	0.34	27	4.3	23	2.0	27	2.1	18
Japan	0.33	24	5.0	29	2.0	24	2.4	29
Korea	0.32	20	4.8	27	1.9	18	2.4	28
Luxembourg	0.29	11	3.4	13	1.8	12	1.9	9
Mexico	0.48	33	9.7	34	3.0	33	2.9	34
Netherlands	0.29	14	3.3	12	1.8	13	1.9	12
New Zealand	0.33	25	4.2	20	2.1	28	2.1	17
Norway	0.25	3	3.0	3	1.6	2	1.8	5
Poland	0.31	19	4.0	18	2.0	22	2.4	27
Portugal	0.35	29	4.9	28	2.3	31	2.2	24
Slovak Republic	0.26	5	3.1	5	1.8	10	1.9	13
Slovenia	0.24	1	3.0	4	1.6	3	1.9	11
Spain	0.32	22	4.6	25	2.0	20	2.3	26
Sweden	0.26	7	3.2	8	1.7	4	1.7	1
Switzerland	0.30	17	3.7	16	1.9	15	1.9	15
Turkey	0.41	32	6.2	31	2.5	32	2.7	30
United Kingdom	0.34	28	4.6	26	2.0	25	2.2	23
United States	0.38	31	5.9	30	2.2	29	2.7	31
OECD average	0.31	–	4.3	–	2.0	–	2.1	–

StatLink http://dx.doi.org/10.1787/888932503702

Trends in income inequality

Percentage point changes in the Gini coefficient

Mid-1980s to late-2000s = Mid-1980s to mid-1990s + Mid-1990s to late-2000s

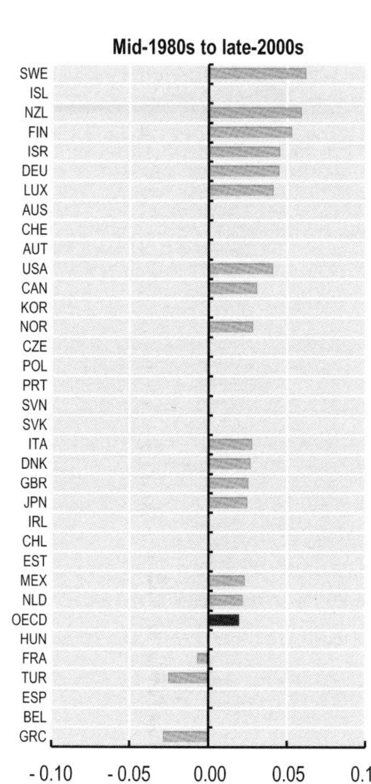

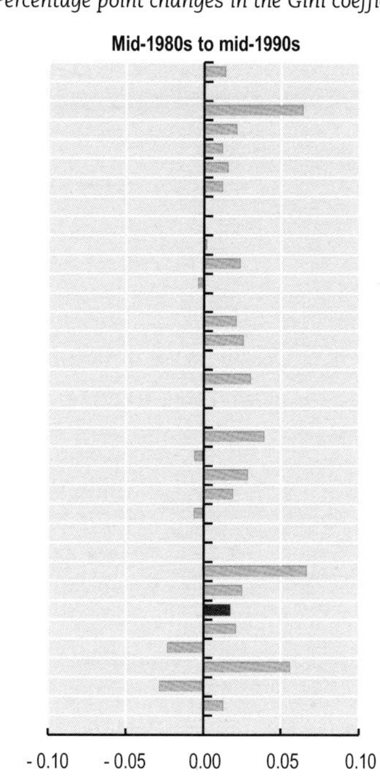

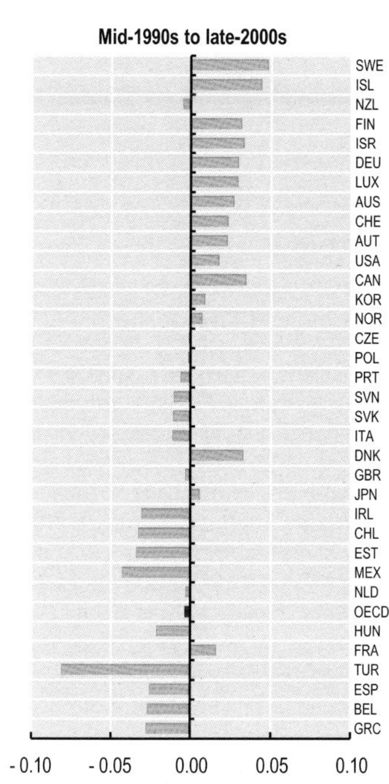

StatLink http://dx.doi.org/10.1787/888932503721

POVERTY RATES AND GAPS

Avoiding economic hardship is a primary objective of social policy. As perceptions of "a decent standard of living" vary across countries and over time, no commonly agreed measure of "absolute" poverty across OECD countries exists. A starting point for measuring poverty is therefore to look at "relative" poverty, whose measure is based on the income that is most typical in each country in each year.

Definition

Relative income poverty is measured here by the poverty rate and the poverty gap. The poverty rate is the ratio of the number of people whose income falls below the poverty line and the total population; the poverty line is here taken as half the median household income. However, two countries with the same poverty rates may differ in terms of the relative income-level of the poor. To measure this dimension, the poverty gap, *i.e.* the percentage by which the mean income of the poor falls below the poverty line, is also presented.

Income is defined as household disposable income in a particular year. It consists of earnings, self-employment and capital income and public cash transfers; income taxes and social security contributions paid by households are deducted. The income of the household is attributed to each of its members, with an adjustment to reflect differences in needs for households of different sizes (*i.e.* the needs of a household composed of four people are assumed to be twice as large as those of a person living alone).

Comparability

Data used here were provided by national experts applying common methodologies and standardised definitions. In many cases, experts have made several adjustments to their source data to conform to standardised definitions. While this approach improves comparability, full standardisation cannot be achieved. Also, small differences between periods and across countries are usually not significant.

Measurement problems are especially severe at the bottom end of the income scale. Further, as large proportions of the population are clustered around the poverty line used here, small changes in their income can lead to large swings in poverty measures. Small differences between periods and across countries are usually not significant. Exact years for each country are provided under the section on "Measures of income inequality".

Results refer to different years. "Late-2000s" data refer to the income in 2008 in all countries except Japan (2006); Denmark, Hungary and Turkey (2007); and Chile (2009). "Mid-1990s" data refer to the income earned between 1993 and 1996 in all countries for which data are available except Poland and Switzerland (2000); Estonia, Iceland, the Slovak Republic and Slovenia (2004); and Korea (2006). "Mid-1980s" data refer to the income earned between 1983 and 1987 in all countries for which data are available except Greece (1988); Portugal (1990); and the Czech Republic (1992). "Mid-1980s" data refer to the western Lander of Germany. "Late-2000s" data for Austria, Belgium, Ireland, Portugal and Spain are based on EU-SILC which are not deemed to be fully comparable with those for earlier years; therefore these countries were not included in the "Mid-1980s to Late-2000s" changes.

Overview

Across OECD countries, the average poverty rate was about 11% in the late-2000s. There is considerable diversity across countries: poverty rates are 20% or more in Israel and Mexico, but below 7% in the Czech Republic, Denmark, Hungary and Iceland. On average, in OECD countries, the mean income of poor people is 27% below the poverty line (poverty gap), with larger gaps in Korea, Mexico, Spain and the United States and lower ones in Belgium, Luxembourg, Finland and the Netherlands. In general, countries with higher poverty rates also have higher poverty gaps but this is not universal; for example Norway combines low poverty rates and high poverty gaps, while the opposite occurs in Estonia.

From the mid-1980s to the late-2000s, poverty rates rose in 16 out of 19 countries for which longer-run data are available, resulting in an overall increase of 2 percentage points for the OECD as a whole. The largest rise was experienced by Israel, and the largest decline was registered in Greece.

Sources

- OECD (2011), *Divided We Stand: Why Inequality Keeps Rising*, OECD Publishing.
- OECD (2010), *OECD Social Expenditure Statistics* (database).

Further information

Analytical publications

- OECD (2011), *Society at a Glance: OECD Social Indicators*, OECD Publishing.
- OECD (2008), *Growing Unequal?: Income Distribution and Poverty in OECD Countries*, OECD Publishing.
- Atkinson, A.B., and A. Brandolini (2004), "*Global World Income Inequality: Absolute, Relative or Intermediate?*", paper presented at the 28th General Conference of the International Association for Research in Income and Wealth, Cork, 22-28 August.
- Förster, M. (1994), "Measurement of Low Incomes and Poverty in a Perspective of International Comparisons", *OECD Labour Market and Social Policy Occasional Papers*, No. 14.

Websites

- OECD Social and Welfare Statistics, *www.oecd.org/social/statistics*.
- OECD Income Distribution and Poverty, *www.oecd.org/els/social/inequality*.

Poverty rates and poverty gaps

Late-2000s

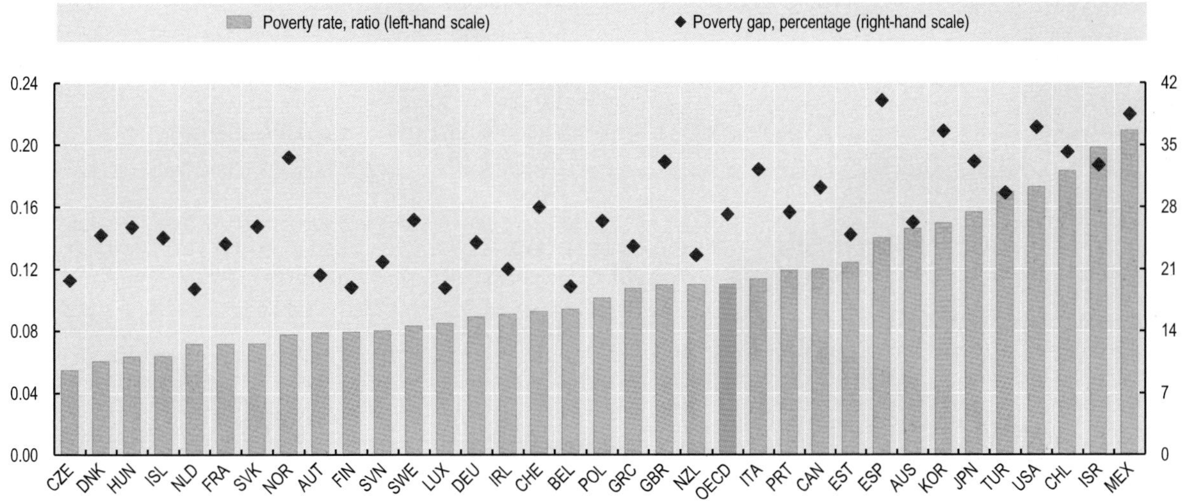

Poverty rate, ratio (left-hand scale)
Poverty gap, percentage (right-hand scale)
0.00 0.04 0.08 0.12 0.16 0.20 0.24
0 7 14 21 28 35 42
CZE DNK HUN ISL NLD FRA SVK NOR AUT FIN SVN SWE LUX DEU IRL CHE BEL POL GRC GBR NZL OECD ITA PRT CAN EST ESP AUS KOR JPN TUR USA CHL ISR MEX

StatLink http://dx.doi.org/10.1787/888932503740

Trends in poverty rates

Percentage point changes in income poverty rate at 50% median level

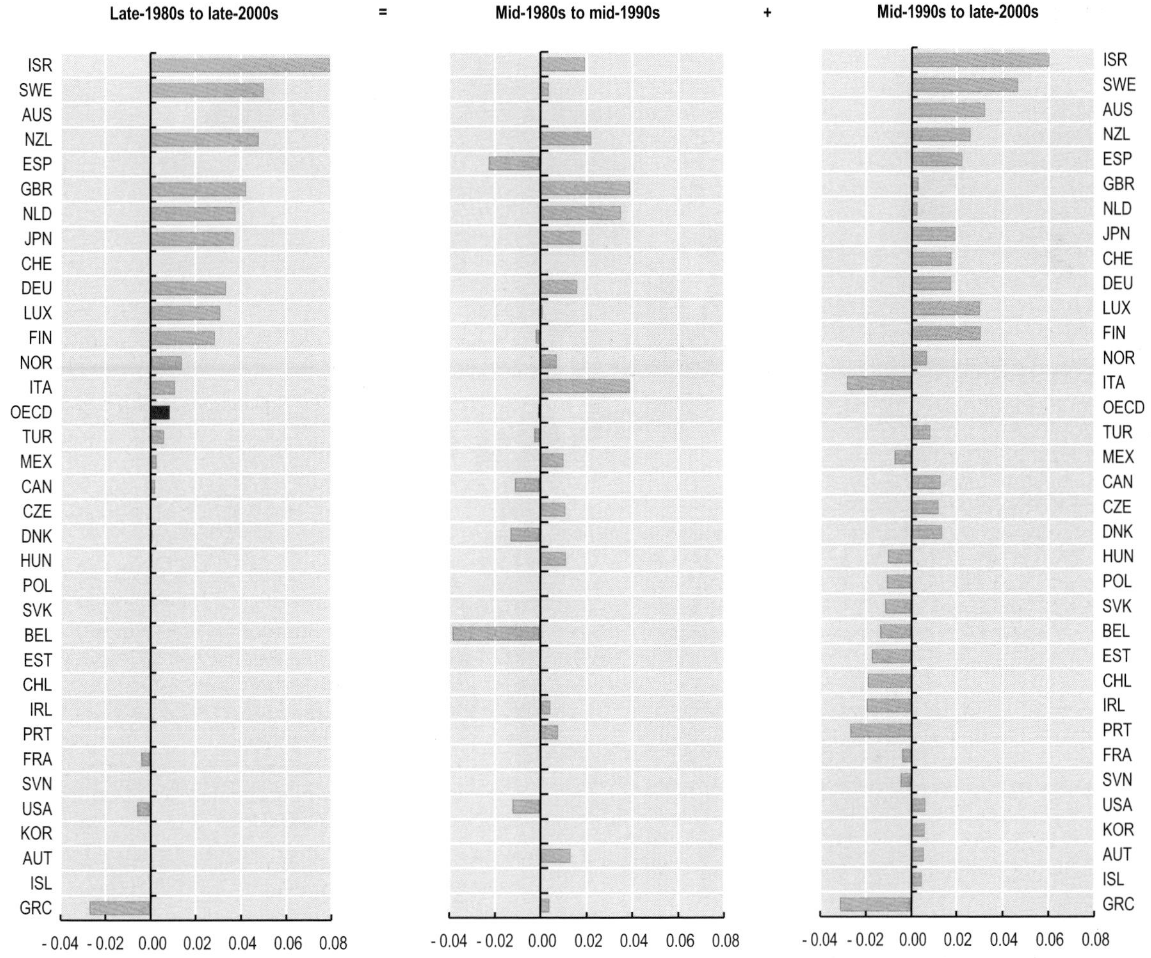

Late-1980s to late-2000s
=
Mid-1980s to mid-1990s
+
Mid-1990s to late-2000s
ISR SWE AUS NZL ESP GBR NLD JPN CHE DEU LUX FIN NOR ITA OECD TUR MEX CAN CZE DNK HUN POL SVK BEL EST CHL IRL PRT FRA SVN USA KOR AUT ISL GRC
- 0.04 - 0.02 0.00 0.02 0.04 0.06 0.08

StatLink http://dx.doi.org/10.1787/888932503759

GLOBALISATION

TRADE

SHARE OF INTERNATIONAL TRADE IN GDP
INTERNATIONAL TRADE IN GOODS
INTERNATIONAL TRADE IN SERVICES
TRADING PARTNERS
AFRICA'S TRADE PARTNERS

FDI AND BALANCE OF PAYMENTS

FOREIGN DIRECT INVESTMENT
BALANCE OF PAYMENTS

SHARE OF INTERNATIONAL TRADE IN GDP

International trade is a principal channel of economic integration. International trade tends to be more important for countries that are small in terms of geographic size or population and surrounded by neighbouring countries with open trade regimes than for countries that are large, relatively self-sufficient, or geographically isolated and penalised by high transport costs. Other factors that help explain differences in the importance of international trade across countries are history, culture, trade policy, the structure of the economy (especially the weight of non-tradable services in GDP), re-exports and the presence of multinational firms (which leads to much intra-firm trade).

Definition

The importance of international trade in different countries is measured here by the share of trade in goods and services, for exports and imports, in GDP. The rates shown correspond to imports and exports of both goods and services at current prices as a percentage of GDP. Goods consist of merchandise imports and exports. Services cover transport, travel, communications, construction, IT, financial, other business, personal and government services, as well as royalties and license fees.

The data are taken from OECD national accounts statistics compiled according to the *1993 System of National Accounts.*

Comparability

The ratios shown in this table are compiled using common standards and definitions. Data for Australia and New Zealand refer to fiscal years.

International imports in goods and services

As a percentage of GDP

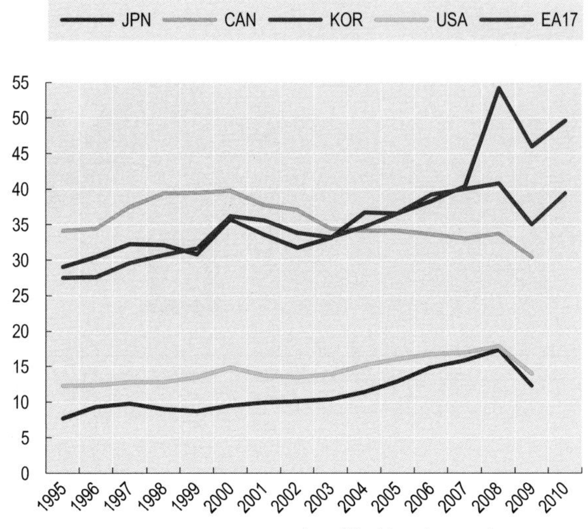

StatLink http://dx.doi.org/10.1787/888932534976

Overview

Before the recent economic crisis international trade in goods and services, both for imports and exports, showed a steady increase throughout the OECD area, with the OECD total increasing (on average) by between 4 and 5 percentage points for both measures between 2004 and 2008, with imports slightly outpacing exports. In 2009 however, in the midst of the recent crisis, the ratio for both imports and exports in GDP fell markedly, wiping out nearly all of the increases recorded after 2004. The GDP ratio for imports in 2009 at 25.0% was only marginally higher than in 2004. This pattern was mirrored by the export-to-GDP ratio for the OECD total, which increased on average from 23.7% to 24.7% over the same period.

Estimates for 2010 show a return to pre-crisis ratios in many countries, with strong rebounds in Belgium, the Czech Republic, Estonia, Hungary, the Netherlands and the Slovak Republic.

Sources

- OECD (2011), *National Accounts of OECD Countries*, OECD Publishing.

Further information

Statistical publications

- OECD (2011), *International Trade by Commodity Statistics*, OECD Publishing.
- OECD (2011), *Main Economic Indicators*, OECD Publishing.
- OECD (2011), *Monthly Statistics of International Trade*, OECD Publishing.
- OECD (2011), *National Accounts at a Glance*, OECD Publishing.
- OECD (2011), *Statistics on International Trade in Services*, OECD Publishing.

Methodological publications

- Lindner, A., *et al.* (2001), "Trade in Goods and Services: Statistical Trends and Measurement Challenges", *OECD Statistics Brief*, No. 1, October.
- OECD, *et al.* (2002), *Manual on Statistics of International Trade in Services*, United Nations.

Websites

- OECD International Trade and Balance of Payments Statistics, *www.oecd.org/std/its*

International trade in goods and services

As a percentage of GDP

	Imports							Exports						
	2004	2005	2006	2007	2008	2009	2010	2004	2005	2006	2007	2008	2009	2010
Australia	20.6	21.1	20.9	21.8	22.1	20.2	..	18.0	19.5	19.7	19.7	22.7	19.8	..
Austria	48.1	50.2	51.7	53.6	53.4	46.0	50.5	51.9	54.2	56.8	59.3	59.2	50.5	55.3
Belgium	71.8	76.2	78.5	79.5	84.8	70.2	78.2	76.7	80.2	82.3	83.4	85.7	73.0	81.4
Canada	34.1	34.1	33.6	33.0	33.7	30.4	..	38.4	37.8	36.1	35.0	35.3	28.7	..
Chile	31.6	32.8	30.7	33.2	41.1	31.2	33.3	40.8	41.3	45.8	47.2	44.7	39.0	40.5
Czech Republic	70.1	69.0	73.0	75.1	72.5	63.6	74.5	70.1	72.2	76.4	80.1	77.1	69.1	79.3
Denmark	40.5	44.1	48.9	49.9	51.9	44.1	44.9	45.4	49.0	52.1	52.2	55.1	47.9	50.5
Estonia	80.1	84.2	82.9	78.1	75.6	58.6	71.6	73.1	77.7	72.7	67.6	71.5	64.7	78.3
Finland	33.4	37.7	40.8	40.7	43.0	35.2	36.2	39.9	41.8	45.5	45.8	47.0	37.5	38.9
France	25.7	27.0	28.1	28.4	29.1	25.2	27.8	26.1	26.4	27.0	26.9	26.9	23.3	25.5
Germany	33.3	35.8	39.7	39.8	41.0	35.9	40.8	38.4	41.1	45.4	46.9	47.5	40.8	46.1
Greece	32.4	31.5	33.0	34.6	36.3	29.6	29.4	22.4	22.4	22.5	22.7	23.4	18.8	21.0
Hungary	66.4	68.3	78.4	79.7	81.1	72.2	79.1	62.9	66.1	77.3	80.8	81.6	77.4	86.5
Iceland	39.7	44.0	50.0	45.3	47.1	44.3	45.9	34.1	31.7	32.2	34.6	44.3	52.9	56.5
Ireland	68.9	69.9	69.7	71.5	74.4	75.4	..	83.8	81.6	79.3	80.5	83.4	90.7	..
Israel	41.2	42.9	42.2	43.7	41.5	32.2	..	41.3	42.7	42.7	42.4	40.1	34.7	..
Italy	24.6	26.0	28.6	29.2	29.4	24.3	28.5	25.4	25.9	27.7	29.0	28.7	23.8	26.8
Japan	11.4	12.9	14.9	15.9	17.4	12.3	..	13.3	14.3	16.1	17.6	17.5	12.6	..
Korea	36.7	36.6	38.3	40.4	54.2	46.0	49.6	40.9	39.3	39.7	41.9	53.0	49.7	52.4
Luxembourg	128.2	130.3	139.1	143.6	145.9	134.6	141.5	152.3	155.8	169.9	175.9	178.4	167.6	176.7
Mexico	28.4	28.6	29.3	29.6	30.3	29.2	..	26.6	27.2	28.1	28.0	28.1	27.7	..
Netherlands	59	61.1	65.1	66.0	68.4	62.0	70.3	66.4	69.6	72.8	74.2	76.6	69.2	78.4
New Zealand	29.3	29.6	30.0	29.2	32.1	26.5	..	28.6	27.4	28.6	28.3	30.8	27.9	..
Norway	28.5	28.2	28.4	30.4	29.6	28.1	28.6	42.0	44.6	46.4	45.8	48.5	41.6	41.9
Poland	39.8	37.8	42.2	43.6	43.9	39.4	42.3	37.5	37.1	40.4	40.8	39.9	39.5	41.5
Portugal	36.5	37.2	39.7	40.2	42.5	35.5	38.1	28.1	27.8	31.0	32.2	32.4	28.0	31.0
Slovak Republic	77.3	80.9	88.4	87.8	85.6	71.0	81.9	74.5	76.3	84.4	86.7	83.3	70.6	80.9
Slovenia	59.1	62.6	67.1	71.3	70.5	57.0	63.0	57.8	62.2	66.5	69.6	67.4	58.3	63.6
Spain	29.9	31.0	32.7	33.6	32.2	25.5	28.4	25.9	25.7	26.3	26.9	26.5	23.4	26.3
Sweden	37.8	40.6	43.0	44.4	46.8	41.9	44.1	46.0	48.4	51.1	51.9	53.5	48.4	50.0
Switzerland	39.4	42.3	44.2	46.0	45.1	40.7	42.1	46.3	49.0	52.5	56.2	56.4	51.7	54.2
Turkey	26.2	25.4	27.6	27.5	28.3	24.4	26.6	23.6	21.9	22.7	22.3	23.9	23.3	21.1
United Kingdom	28	29.8	31.6	29.7	31.9	30.1	32.8	25.3	26.4	28.5	26.6	29.3	28.0	29.4
United States	15.2	16.1	16.8	17.0	17.9	14.0	..	10.0	10.4	11.0	11.9	12.9	11.2	..
Euro area	34.7	36.6	39.2	40.0	40.8	35.0	39.4	36.7	38.1	40.4	41.4	41.9	36.3	40.7
EU27 total	34.6	36.5	39.2	39.6	41.0	35.6	39.7	35.7	37.1	39.6	40.1	41.3	36.6	40.5
OECD total	24.7	25.8	27.5	28.0	29.5	25.0	..	23.7	24.4	25.9	26.8	28.0	24.7	..
China	31.4	31.5	31.4	29.6	27.3	22.3	..	34.0	37.1	39.1	38.4	35.0	26.7	..
Russian Federation	22.2	21.5	21.0	21.5	22.0	20.4	..	34.4	35.2	33.7	30.2	31.2	27.7	..
South Africa	26.7	27.9	32.5	34.2	38.6	28.3	27.5	26.4	27.4	30.0	31.5	35.6	27.4	27.4

StatLink http://dx.doi.org/10.1787/888932503778

International trade to GDP ratios

As percentage of GDP, 2010 or latest available year

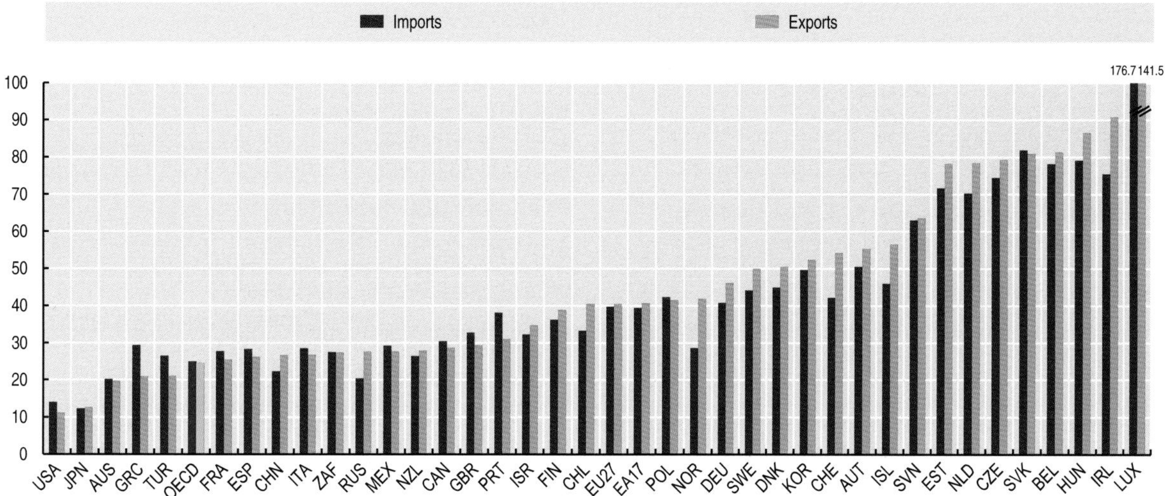

StatLink http://dx.doi.org/10.1787/888932503797

INTERNATIONAL TRADE IN GOODS

Since its creation, the OECD has sought to promote international trade, considering it an effective way of enhancing economic growth and raising living standards. Member countries benefit from increased trade as do OECD's trade partners in the rest of the world.

Definition

According to United Nations guidelines, international merchandise trade statistics record all goods which add to, or subtract from, the stock of material resources of a country by entering (as imports) or leaving (as exports) its economic territory. Goods being transported through a country or temporarily admitted or withdrawn (except for goods for inward or outward processing) are not included in merchandise trade statistics.

Comparability

All OECD countries use the United Nations guidelines so far as their data sources allow. There are some, generally minor, differences across countries in the coverage of certain types of transactions such as postal trade, imports and exports of military equipment under defence agreements, sea products traded by domestic vessels on the high seas and goods entering or leaving bonded customs areas.

Exports are usually valued free on board (f.o.b.), with the exception of the United States which values exports free alongside ship (f.a.s.), which is lower than f.o.b. by the cost of loading the goods on board. Imports are valued by most countries at cost, insurance and freight (c.i.f.) *i.e.* the cost of the goods plus the costs of insurance and freight to bring the goods to the borders of the importing country. Canada, however, reports imports at f.o.b. values. The trade balances shown in the table are, therefore, not strictly comparable because imports are not valued in the same way by all countries.

The introduction by the European Union of the single market in 1993 resulted in some loss of accuracy for intra-EU trade because custom documents were no longer available to record all imports and exports. Note that while the OECD data mostly follow the UN recommendations, trade statistics reported by Eurostat follow Community definitions, and are not strictly comparable with those reported here.

OECD total includes all 34 member economies only from 1999.

Overview

Over the three years 2008-10, Australia, India, Indonesia, China, Brazil and Poland experienced an annual average growth of exports exceeding 5%. This represents a higher growth rate compared to the three years average 1998-2000, except for China.

The three year average growth of trade in goods at end of period compared to the three year at beginning of period reveals the impact of the crisis on trade data. Over the last three year period, Indonesia, Brazil, China, India, Australia and Poland recorded an annual average growth of imports exceeding 5%. Imports of goods over the three years to 2010 recorded a growth inferior to 5% for Iceland, Ireland, Estonia, Greece and Finland.

Sources

- OECD (2011), *International Trade by Commodity Statistics*, OECD Publishing.
- *United Nations Commodity Trade Statistics Database.*

Further information

Analytical publications

- OECD (2006), *The Development Dimension – Aid for Trade: Making it Effective*, OECD Publishing.
- OECD (2006), *Trade Based Money Laundering*, OECD Publishing.
- OECD (2005), *Trade and Structural Adjustment: Embracing Globalisation*, OECD Publishing.

Statistical publications

- OECD (2011), *Monthly Statistics of International Trade*, OECD Publishing.

Methodological publications

- Lindner, A., *et al.* (2001), "Trade in Goods and Services: Statistical Trends and Measurement Challenges", *OECD Statistics Brief*, No 1, October.
- OECD (2011), *International Trade by Commodity Statistics*, OECD Publishing.
- United Nations (2004), *International Merchandise Trade Statistics: Compilers Manual*, United Nations.

Online databases

- *International Trade by Commodity Statistics.*
- *Monthly Statistics of International Trade.*

Trade balance: exports of goods minus imports of goods

Billion US dollars

	1997	1998	1999	2000	2001	2002	2003	2004	2005	2006	2007	2008	2009	2010
Australia	1.0	-5.0	-9.5	-4.0	2.4	-4.5	-14.6	-17.3	-12.8	-9.3	-16.9	-4.7	-5.1	18.6
Austria	-6.9	-6.2	-6.2	-5.2	-4.4	-0.1	-2.3	-0.4	-2.2	-0.2	0.5	-2.6	-5.1	..
Belgium	12.3	14.4	14.3	13.5	11.6	17.7	20.7	21.0	13.8	15.4	17.3	6.5	18.2	21.0
Canada	18.1	13.3	23.2	37.6	39.4	30.2	31.8	43.4	46.1	37.9	39.2	46.9	-5.8	-5.3
Chile	-1.4	-2.2	1.7	1.6	2.6	2.0	3.6	9.4	10.4	22.5	23.5	8.0	13.7	..
Czech Republic	-4.4	-2.2	-2.0	-3.2	-3.1	-2.2	-2.5	-0.9	1.7	1.7	4.1	2.3	7.8	..
Denmark	3.7	1.7	4.7	5.2	5.8	6.4	8.4	7.9	8.3	6.3	4.9	5.9	10.5	12.3
Estonia	-1.5	-1.5	-1.1	-1.2	-1.2	-1.5	-2.3	-2.5	-2.8	-4.6	-4.9	-3.6	-0.9	..
Finland	10.0	10.8	10.2	11.7	10.7	11.0	10.9	10.2	6.8	7.8	8.3	4.7	2.0	1.2
France	16.8	14.7	9.5	-8.5	-4.3	1.1	-4.4	-20.5	-41.6	-50.9	-71.8	-100.6	-76.4	-87.5
Germany	67.1	72.3	69.3	54.8	85.7	125.6	146.8	193.6	197.3	199.7	269.5	261.9	189.4	204.3
Greece	-15.8	-19.4	-18.8	-18.8	-17.9	-21.8	-31.2	-37.6	-37.4	-42.8	-52.6	-63.8	-47.1	-41.8
Hungary	-2.1	-2.7	-3.0	-4.0	-3.2	-3.3	-4.7	-4.8	-3.6	-2.9	-0.1	-0.6	5.3	7.3
Iceland	-0.2	-0.6	-0.5	-0.7	-0.3	0.0	-0.4	-0.8	-1.9	-2.5	-1.9	-0.8	0.5	0.7
Ireland	14.4	19.9	24.0	25.6	26.4	36.0	38.7	42.0	39.7	32.2	35.3	42.2	54.3	57.8
Israel	-6.5	-4.2	-5.2	-4.3	-4.2	-3.6	-2.4	-2.3	-2.3	-1.0	-2.5	-3.8	0.6	..
Italy	29.9	26.5	14.7	1.9	8.1	7.6	2.1	-1.7	-11.9	-25.4	-11.6	-13.6	-8.0	-39.1
Japan	82.2	107.5	107.2	99.6	54.0	79.1	88.5	110.5	79.1	67.7	92.1	18.9	28.7	75.7
Korea	-8.5	39.0	23.9	11.8	9.3	10.4	15.0	29.4	23.2	16.1	14.6	-13.3	40.4	..
Luxembourg	..	..	-2.8	-2.8	-2.9	-2.9	-3.7	-4.6	-4.9	-5.5	-6.1	-7.8	-5.9	-6.5
Mexico	0.5	-8.0	-5.7	-5.8	-7.6	-7.9	-5.6	-8.8	-7.6	-6.1	-11.2	-17.3	-4.7	-3.2
Netherlands	15.5	10.9	2.7	5.4	5.6	11.9	18.3	32.8	36.9	38.7	55.6	47.8	50.0	..
New Zealand	-0.8	-0.6	-2.4	-0.6	0.4	-0.7	-2.0	-2.8	-4.5	-4.0	-3.9	-3.8	-0.6	0.8
Norway	12.8	2.9	11.3	25.5	26.0	24.7	28.1	34.0	48.3	57.9	56.1	82.2	45.7	54.1
Poland	-16.6	-18.8	-18.5	-17.2	-14.2	-14.1	-14.4	-14.4	-12.2	-16.1	-25.4	-38.6	-10.5	..
Portugal	-11.1	-12.8	-15.3	-15.6	-15.4	-14.2	-15.3	-19.2	-23.1	-23.3	-26.9	-34.2	-26.5	-26.5
Slovak Republic	-2.1	-2.4	-1.1	-0.9	-2.1	-2.2	-0.7	-1.6	-2.4	-3.1	-2.1	-2.4	0.4	-1.2
Slovenia	-1.0	-1.1	-1.5	-1.4	-0.9	-0.6	-1.1	-1.7	-1.7	-2.0	-2.9	-4.7	-1.6	-2.2
Spain	-18.2	-25.8	-36.4	-39.5	-38.8	-40.0	-53.4	-76.5	-96.8	-115.9	-137.5	-139.5	-64.4	..
Sweden	18.3	16.4	16.3	14.2	12.8	15.9	18.2	22.8	18.9	20.3	16.2	16.5	10.7	9.7
Switzerland	0.2	-1.2	0.4	-2.0	-2.1	4.2	4.2	6.8	4.4	6.5	10.9	17.2	17.1	19.3
Turkey	-22.3	-19.0	-14.1	-26.7	-10.1	-15.5	-22.1	-34.4	-43.3	-54.0	-62.8	-70.0	-38.8	-71.6
United Kingdom	-26.3	-46.9	-53.2	-56.6	-65.4	-78.8	-85.8	-119.1	-131.4	-150.1	-184.7	-177.0	-132.2	-153.9
United States	-210.5	-263.9	-366.4	-477.7	-449.1	-509.1	-581.4	-707.4	-828.0	-882.0	-854.6	-864.9	-545.2	-689.4
EU27 total	..	..	..	..	..	..	..	..	-157.8	-230.1	-263.5	-358.4	-143.5	..
OECD total	-53.4	-94.1 |	-230.1	-388.4	-346.2	-339.3	-414.8	-515.8	-737.5	-871.0	-832.3	-1 006.7	-477.1	..
Brazil	-12.1	-9.7	-3.7	-0.7	2.7	13.2	24.9	33.8	44.9	46.5	40.0	24.7	25.3	20.3
China	40.4	43.6	29.2	24.1	22.5	30.4	25.5	32.1	102.0	177.5	263.9	298.1	196.1	181.8
India	-6.6	-9.2	-13.1	-10.6	-6.8	-7.4	-13.1	-23.1	-40.5	-57.0	-72.7	-133.9	-89.6	..
Indonesia	11.8	21.5	24.7	28.6	25.4	25.9	28.5	25.1	28.0	39.7	39.6	7.8	19.7	22.1
Russian Federation	19.7	28.6	42.6	69.2	58.0	60.5	76.3	106.0	142.7	163.4	152.5	200.9	131.0	155.6
South Africa	..	..	0.0	-0.5	0.4	-3.2	-2.9	-7.3	-8.0	-15.9	-15.8	-13.6	-9.9	-8.7

StatLink http://dx.doi.org/10.1787/888932503816

Trade balance: exports of goods minus imports of goods

Billion US dollars

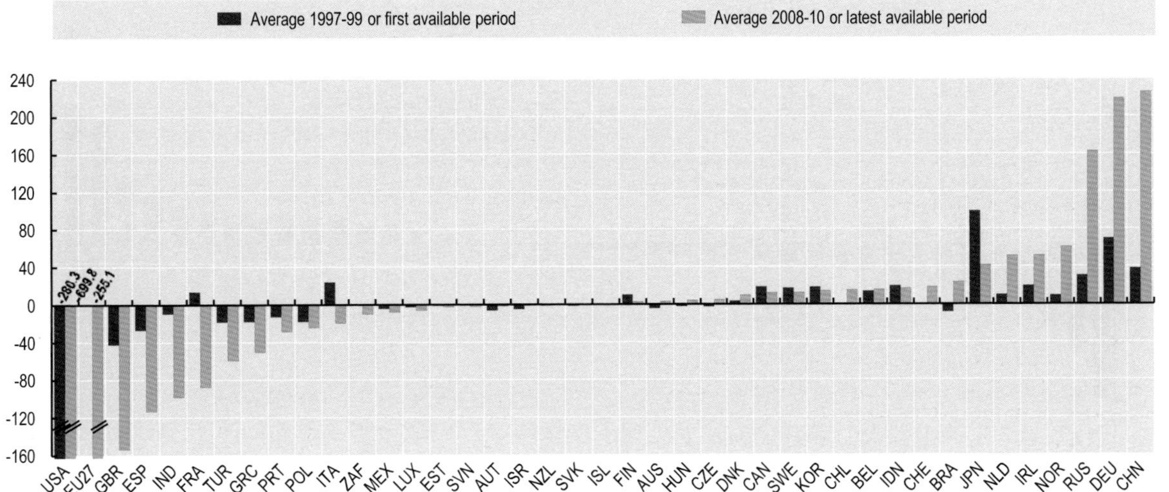

StatLink http://dx.doi.org/10.1787/888932503835

Imports of goods

Billion US dollars

	1997	1998	1999	2000	2001	2002	2003	2004	2005	2006	2007	2008	2009	2010
Australia	61.8	60.8	65.5	67.8	60.9	69.5	84.8	103.8	118.9	132.7	157.8	191.6	158.9	193.3
Austria	63.6	67.1	68.7	67.4	69.0	71.4	91.5	111.3	120.0	134.3	156.1	175.4	136.4	..
Belgium	158.3	164.9	164.6	171.7	178.7	198.1	234.8	285.4	320.2	353.7	413.6	470.7	351.8	390.1
Canada	197.1	201.3	215.6	240.0	221.6	222.4	240.2	273.8	314.4	350.3	380.6	408.8	321.0	392.0
Chile	18.1	17.1	13.9	16.6	16.1	15.4	17.0	22.0	29.5	34.4	42.4	56.1	38.2	..
Czech Republic	27.2	30.5	28.8	32.2	36.5	40.7	51.2	66.7	76.5	93.4	116.8	140.3	102.9	..
Denmark	44.5	46.2	44.3	44.4	44.3	49.3	56.2	66.8	75.0	85.3	104.3	109.8	82.0	84.5
Estonia	4.4	4.8	4.1	5.1	5.2	5.9	7.9	9.1	11.0	14.6	16.7	17.3	11.3	..
Finland	31.0	32.4	31.6	34.1	32.2	33.6	41.6	50.7	58.5	69.4	81.8	92.2	60.9	68.2
France	266.6	285.8	292.8	304.0	293.9	303.8	362.5	434.2	476.0	529.9	611.1	695.5	540.5	599.2
Germany	445.3	471.6	473.5	495.4	486.3	490.1	601.8	718.2	779.8	922.2	1 059.3	1 204.2	938.0	1 066.8
Greece	27.0	30.3	29.5	29.8	28.2	32.5	44.9	52.8	54.9	63.7	76.1	89.3	67.2	63.3
Hungary	21.2	25.7	28.0	32.1	33.7	37.6	47.7	60.2	65.9	77.0	94.7	108.8	77.3	87.4
Iceland	2.0	2.5	2.5	2.6	2.3	2.3	2.8	3.6	5.0	6.0	6.7	6.2	3.6	3.9
Ireland	39.2	44.4	46.5	50.7	51.1	52.3	54.2	62.3	70.3	76.6	86.7	85.0	62.6	60.5
Israel	29.0	27.5	31.1	35.7	33.3	33.1	34.2	41.0	45.0	47.8	56.6	65.2	47.4	..
Italy	208.1	215.6	220.3	238.1	236.1	246.6	297.4	355.3	384.8	442.6	511.9	553.2	414.7	486.6
Japan	338.8	280.6	309.9	379.7	348.6	337.6	383.5	455.2	515.9	579.1	622.2	762.5	552.0	694.1
Korea	144.6	93.3	119.8	160.5	141.1	152.1	178.8	224.5	261.2	309.4	356.8	435.3	323.1	..
Luxembourg	..	..	10.6	10.6	11.2	11.5	13.6	16.8	17.6	19.6	22.3	25.4	18.7	20.4
Mexico	109.8	125.3	142.0	171.1	165.1	168.7	170.5	196.8	221.8	256.1	283.2	308.6	234.4	301.5
Netherlands	158.3	156.8	167.9	174.7	169.9	163.4	209.0	257.7	283.2	331.5	421.3	458.2	352.6	..
New Zealand	14.5	12.5	14.3	13.9	13.3	15.0	18.6	23.2	26.2	26.4	30.9	34.4	25.6	30.2
Norway	35.8	37.5	34.2	34.4	33.0	34.9	39.9	48.5	55.5	64.3	80.3	90.6	69.0	77.3
Poland	42.3	47.0	45.9	48.8	50.2	55.1	68.0	88.2	101.5	125.6	164.2	210.5	147.1	..
Portugal	35.1	37.0	39.8	39.9	39.5	40.0	47.1	54.9	61.2	66.7	78.2	90.1	69.9	75.2
Slovak Republic	11.7	13.1	11.1	12.7	14.7	16.6	22.6	29.5	34.2	44.8	60.2	72.6	55.2	65.9
Slovenia	9.4	10.1	10.1	10.1	10.1	10.9	13.9	17.6	19.6	23.0	29.5	34.0	23.8	26.4
Spain	124.4	137.2	147.9	152.9	155.0	165.9	209.7	259.3	289.6	330.0	391.2	418.7	287.5	..
Sweden	63.2	68.6	68.5	73.1	63.5	67.1	84.2	100.5	111.4	127.1	152.8	167.3	120.2	148.4
Switzerland	75.9	80.1	79.9	82.5	84.2	83.7	96.4	110.0	126.6	141.4	161.2	183.6	155.4	176.3
Turkey	48.6	45.9	40.7	54.5	41.4	51.3	69.3	97.5	116.8	139.6	170.1	202.0	140.9	185.5
United Kingdom	307.5	320.3	323.8	339.4	338.0	359.4	393.5	468.1	515.8	598.4	624.7	638.6	484.7	558.6
United States	898.0	944.4	1 059.2	1 258.1	1 180.1	1 202.3	1 305.1	1 525.3	1 732.3	1 919.0	2 017.1	2 164.8	1 601.9	1 966.5
EU27 total	..	..	..	..	..	..	..	..	1 465.1	1 671.9	1 966.6	2 287.7	1 670.9	..
OECD total	4 062.3	4 138.0 |	4 386.9	4 884.6	4 688.2	4 840.2	5 594.6	6 690.7	7 496.2	8 535.9	9 639.4	10 766.6	8 075.4	..
Brazil	65.1	60.8	51.7	55.9	55.6	47.2	48.3	62.8	73.6	91.3	120.6	173.2	127.6	181.6
China	142.4	140.2	165.7	225.1	243.6	295.2	412.8	561.2	660.0	791.5	956.1	1 132.6	1 005.6	1 396.0
India	41.4	42.4	50.0	52.9	50.7	57.5	72.4	99.0	140.9	178.2	218.6	315.7	266.4	..
Indonesia	41.7	27.3	24.0	33.5	31.0	31.3	32.6	46.5	57.7	61.1	74.5	129.2	96.8	135.7
Russian Federation	67.6	43.7	30.3	33.9	41.9	46.2	57.3	75.6	98.7	137.8	199.7	267.1	170.8	217.4
South Africa	..	-	-	26.8	25.6	26.2	34.5	47.6	55.0	68.5	79.9	87.6	63.8	80.1

StatLink http://dx.doi.org/10.1787/888932503854

Imports of goods

Average annual growth in percentage

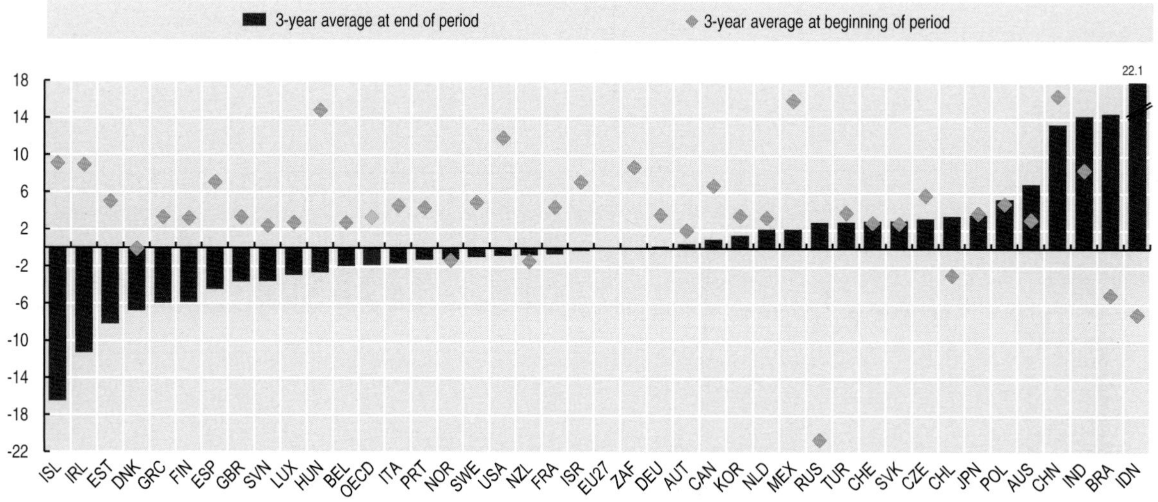

StatLink http://dx.doi.org/10.1787/888932503873

Exports of goods

Billion US dollars

	1997	1998	1999	2000	2001	2002	2003	2004	2005	2006	2007	2008	2009	2010
Australia	62.8	55.8	56.0	63.8	63.3	65.0	70.2	86.4	106.0	123.3	140.9	186.9	153.8	211.8
Austria	56.7	60.9	62.4	62.3	64.7	71.3	89.2	110.8	117.7	134.2	156.7	172.8	131.4	..
Belgium	170.7	179.3	178.9	185.2	190.3	215.8	255.5	306.4	334.0	369.1	430.9	477.2	370.0	411.1
Canada	215.1	214.6	238.9	277.6	261.1	252.6	272.1	317.2	360.6	388.2	419.9	455.6	315.3	386.7
Chile	16.7	14.8	15.6	18.2	18.7	17.4	20.6	31.5	39.9	57.0	66.0	64.0	51.9	..
Czech Republic	22.7	28.3	26.8	29.1	33.4	38.5	48.7	65.8	78.2	95.1	120.9	142.6	110.7	..
Denmark	48.2	47.9	49.0	49.6	50.1	55.7	64.6	74.7	83.3	91.6	109.2	115.6	92.5	96.8
Estonia	2.9	3.2	3.0	3.8	4.0	4.3	5.6	6.5	8.2	10.0	11.7	13.7	10.4	..
Finland	41.0	43.2	41.8	45.8	42.8	44.7	52.5	60.9	65.2	77.3	90.1	96.9	62.9	69.4
France	283.4	300.5	302.3	295.6	289.6	304.9	358.1	413.7	434.4	479.0	539.4	594.9	464.1	511.7
Germany	512.4	543.8	542.8	550.2	572.0	615.6	748.5	911.8	977.1	1 122.0	1 328.8	1 466.1	1 127.5	1 271.1
Greece	11.2	10.9	10.7	11.0	10.3	10.8	13.7	15.2	17.5	20.9	23.5	25.5	20.1	21.6
Hungary	19.1	23.0	25.0	28.1	30.5	34.3	43.0	55.5	62.3	74.1	94.6	108.2	82.6	94.7
Iceland	1.9	1.9	2.0	1.9	2.0	2.2	2.4	2.8	3.1	3.5	4.8	5.4	4.1	4.6
Ireland	53.6	64.2	70.5	76.3	77.4	88.3	92.9	104.3	110.0	108.8	122.0	127.1	116.9	118.3
Israel	22.5	23.3	25.8	31.4	29.1	29.5	31.8	38.6	42.8	46.8	54.1	61.3	47.9	..
Italy	238.0	242.1	235.1	239.9	244.3	254.2	299.5	353.5	373.0	417.2	500.2	539.6	406.7	447.5
Japan	421.0	388.1	417.1	479.2	402.6	416.7	472.0	565.7	594.9	646.7	714.3	781.4	580.7	769.8
Korea	136.2	132.3	143.7	172.3	150.4	162.5	193.8	253.8	284.4	325.5	371.5	422.0	363.5	..
Luxembourg	..	..	7.8	7.9	8.3	8.6	10.0	12.2	12.7	14.2	16.2	17.7	12.8	13.9
Mexico	110.2	117.3	136.3	165.3	157.5	160.8	164.9	188.0	214.2	250.0	272.0	291.3	229.7	298.3
Netherlands	173.8	167.6	170.5	180.1	175.5	175.3	227.3	290.5	320.1	370.2	476.8	506.0	402.6	..
New Zealand	13.7	11.9	11.9	13.3	13.7	14.4	16.5	20.3	21.7	22.4	26.9	30.6	24.9	30.9
Norway	48.5	40.4	45.5	59.9	59.0	59.6	67.9	82.5	103.8	122.2	136.4	172.7	114.7	131.4
Poland	25.7	28.2	27.4	31.6	36.1	41.0	53.5	73.8	89.4	109.6	138.8	171.9	136.6	..
Portugal	24.0	24.2	24.5	24.4	24.1	25.8	31.8	35.7	38.1	43.4	51.3	55.9	43.4	48.8
Slovak Republic	9.6	10.7	10.1	11.8	12.6	14.5	22.0	27.9	31.9	41.7	58.0	70.2	55.6	64.7
Slovenia	8.4	9.1	8.5	8.7	9.3	10.4	12.8	15.9	17.9	21.0	26.6	29.3	22.3	24.2
Spain	106.2	111.4	111.5	113.3	116.1	125.9	156.3	182.7	192.8	214.1	253.8	279.2	223.1	..
Sweden	81.5	85.0	84.8	87.4	76.3	82.9	102.4	123.2	130.3	147.4	169.1	183.9	131.0	158.1
Switzerland	76.2	78.9	80.3	80.5	82.1	87.9	100.7	116.8	130.9	147.9	172.1	200.8	172.5	195.6
Turkey	26.2	27.0	26.6	27.8	31.3	35.8	47.3	63.1	73.5	85.5	107.3	132.0	102.1	114.0
United Kingdom	281.2	273.4	270.7	282.9	272.6	280.6	307.7	349.0	384.4	448.4	440.0	461.6	352.4	404.7
United States	687.5	680.4	692.8	780.3	731.0	693.2	723.7	817.9	904.3	1 037.0	1 162.5	1 299.9	1 056.7	1 277.1
EU27 total	..	..	..	..	..	..	..	..	1 307.3	1 441.8	1 703.1	1 929.3	1 527.4	..
OECD total	4 008.9	4 043.9	4 156.7	4 496.2	4 342.0	4 500.9	5 179.7	6 174.9	6 758.6	7 664.9	8 807.1	9 759.8	7 598.3	..
Brazil	53.0	51.1	48.0	55.1	58.3	60.4	73.2	96.7	118.5	137.8	160.6	197.9	153.0	201.9
China	182.8	183.8	194.9	249.2	266.1	325.6	438.2	593.3	762.0	968.9	1 220.1	1 430.7	1 201.6	1 577.8
India	34.8	33.2	36.9	42.4	43.9	50.1	59.4	75.9	100.4	121.2	145.9	181.9	176.8	..
Indonesia	53.4	48.8	48.7	62.1	56.3	57.2	61.1	71.6	85.7	100.8	114.1	137.0	116.5	157.8
Russian Federation	87.4	72.3	72.9	103.1	99.9	106.7	133.7	181.6	241.5	301.2	352.3	468.0	301.8	373.1
South Africa	..	..	-	26.3	26.0	23.1	31.6	40.3	47.0	52.6	64.0	74.0	53.9	71.5

StatLink http://dx.doi.org/10.1787/888932503892

Exports of goods

Average annual growth in percentage

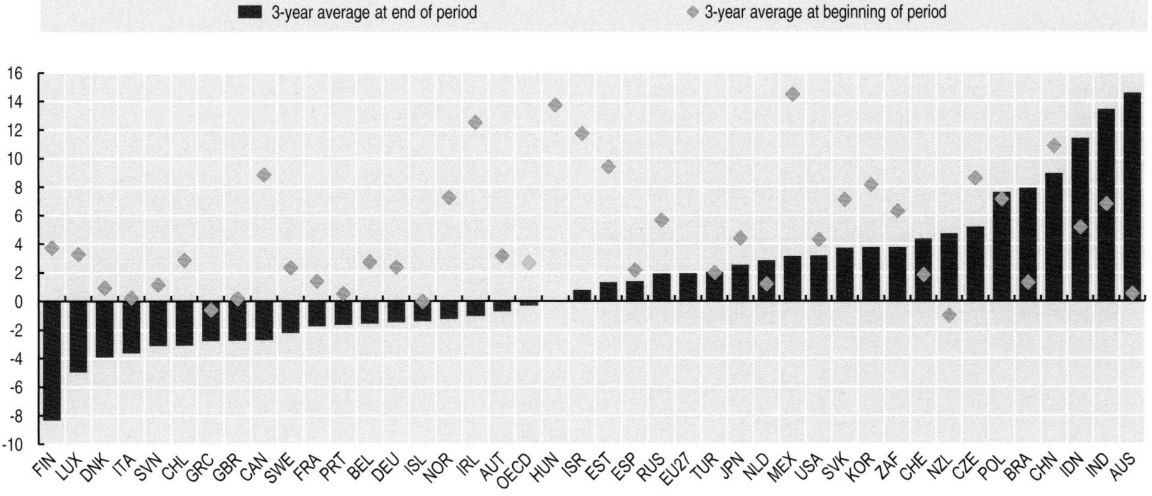

StatLink http://dx.doi.org/10.1787/888932503911

INTERNATIONAL TRADE IN SERVICES

International trade in services is growing in importance both among OECD countries and with the rest of the world. Traditional services – transport, insurance on merchandise trade, and travel – account for about half of international trade in services, but trade in newer types of services, particularly those that can be conducted via the Internet, is growing rapidly.

Definition

International trade in services is defined according to the 5th edition of the International Montetary Fund (IMF) *Balance of Payments Manual* (BPM5). Services include transport (both freight and passengers), travel (mainly expenditure on goods and services by tourists and business travellers), communications services (postal, telephone, satellite, etc.), construction services, insurance and financial services, computer and information services, royalties and license fees, other business services (merchanting, operational leasing, technical and professional services, etc.), cultural and recreational services (rents for films, fees for actors and other performers, but excluding purchases of films, recorded music, books, etc.) and government services not included in the list above.

Comparability

BPM5 was issued in 1993 and countries began to implement it in the next two or three years. All OECD countries now report international trade in services broadly according to the BPM5 framework.

Overview

The impact of the recent crisis is reflected in lower imports and exports of services averages at end of period shown in the graphs compared to beginning of period. As a percent average over the three years ending 2010, Turkey, Chile, Switzerland, Australia and the Czech Republic recorded an export of services growth of over 5%. India has shown a three year average growth of over 20% at beginning and at end of period. Over the three years ending 2010, Switzerland, Chile, Poland, Turkey, the Czech Republic and Australia recorded an import growth of services of over 5%. India, in both the initial and final period, recorded a growth of over 20%. Austria, Iceland and the United Kingdom recorded a decrease of imports of services of over 5% during the same period. Averaged over the three years to 2010, trade in services recorded large surpluses for the United States and the United Kingdom while substantial deficits were recorded in Germany, Japan and Canada.

Sources

- OECD (2011), *Main Economic Indicators*, OECD Publishing.
- OECD (2011), *OECD Statistics on International Trade in Services*, OECD Publishing.

Further information

Analytical publications

- OECD (2008), *Export Credit Financing Systems in OECD Member Countries and Non-Member Economies*, OECD Publishing.
- OECD (2007), *Infrastructure to 2030 (Vol. 2): Mapping Policy for Electricity, Water and Transport*, OECD Publishing.
- OECD and The World Bank (2006), *Liberalisation and Universal Access to Basic Services: Telecommunications, Water and Sanitation, Financial Services, and Electricity*, OECD Trade Policy Studies, OECD Publishing.
- OECD (2005), *Trade and Structural Adjustment: Embracing Globalisation*, OECD Publishing.
- OECD (2004), *Promoting Trade in Services: Experience of the Baltic States*, OECD Publishing.

Statistical publications

- OECD (2011), *International Trade by Commodity Statistics*, OECD Publishing.
- OECD (2011), *Statistics on International Trade in Services*, OECD Publishing.
- OECD (2008), *Measuring Globalisation: Activities of Multinationals, Volume II, Services*, OECD Publishing.

Methodological publications

- International Monetary Fund (IMF) (2010), *Balance of Payments and International Investment Position Manual*, 6th edition, IMF, Washington DC.
- OECD, *et al.* (2002), *Manual on Statistics of International Trade in Services*, United Nations.

Websites

- OECD International Trade in Services, *www.oecd.org/std/trade-services*.

Services trade balance: exports of services minus imports of services

Billion US dollars

	1997	1998	1999	2000	2001	2002	2003	2004	2005	2006	2007	2008	2009	2010
Australia	-0.3	-1.4	-0.5	0.5	0.4	0.9	1.3	0.0	-0.1	0.3	-0.7	-4.3	-0.4	-2.9
Austria	3.9	5.1	6.1	6.5	6.3	7.3	8.9	9.9	11.6	12.2	15.3	20.8	17.9	13.3
Belgium	1.3	0.8 |	1.4	2.1	1.8	2.0	1.8	3.6	5.0	6.3	5.8	4.8	9.8	7.0
Canada	-6.4	-4.3	-4.5	-3.9	-5.0	-4.6	-8.2	-8.5	-9.9	-12.5	-17.5	-20.2	-19.4	-22.1
Chile	-0.1	-0.5	-0.7	-0.7	-0.8	-0.7	-0.6	-0.7	-0.6	-0.6	-1.0	-1.0	-1.4	-1.0
Czech Republic	1.8	1.9	1.2	1.4	1.5	0.7	0.5	0.6	1.5	2.0	2.4	3.9	3.4	3.5
Denmark	0.1	-0.3	2.0	2.4	3.4	2.0	3.5	3.3	6.2	7.1	7.4	10.1	4.4	9.2
Estonia	0.6	0.6	0.6	0.6	0.6	0.6	0.8	1.1	1.0	1.1	1.3	1.8	1.9	1.7
Finland	-1.6	-1.0 |	-1.1	-1.4	-0.2	0.6	-0.7	0.6	-0.7	-1.1	0.6	1.5	1.8	2.0
France	16.7	17.3 |	18.6	17.2	15.3	15.5	14.1	15.1	15.3	15.4	19.8	25.1	16.0	15.3
Germany	-48.1	-51.6 |	-57.9	-55.0	-54.1	-43.2	-50.7	-51.1	-48.8	-38.3	-39.4	-39.3	-26.4	-29.1
Greece	7.1	7.0 |	7.6	8.2 |	8.2	10.1	13.0	19.2	19.1	19.3	22.7	25.1	17.6	17.5
Hungary	1.7	1.7 |	1.3	0.8	1.1	0.0	-1.2	0.1	1.4	1.6	1.4	1.5	1.9	3.2
Iceland	0.0	0.0	-0.1	-0.1	0.0	0.0	-0.1	-0.2	-0.5	-0.7	-0.7	-0.3	0.4	0.4
Ireland	-9.0 |	-9.9 |	-11.4	-13.0	-11.9	-13.0	-12.5	-12.7	-11.6	-8.5	-1.5	-11.2	-11.7	-11.3
Israel	0.2	0.8	2.1	3.5	1.0	1.3	2.5	3.3	3.8	4.6	3.6	4.4	4.8	6.6
Italy	2.0	4.0 |	1.2	1.1	0.0	-2.9	-2.7	1.5	-0.7	-1.6	-9.7	-13.2	-13.7	-11.8
Japan	-54.1	-49.3	-54.0	-47.6	-43.8	-42.0	-33.7	-37.9	-25.0	-20.1	-20.6	-20.7	-20.4	-16.8
Korea	-2.4	1.7	-0.2	-2.0	-3.0	-6.4	-5.8	-6.0	-10.0	-13.3	-12.0	-5.7	-6.6	-11.2
Luxembourg	4.0	4.2 |	5.4	6.8	6.4	8.1	9.9	13.0	16.2	20.8	27.2	29.1	24.9	30.1
Mexico	-0.7	-0.9	-1.8	-2.3	-3.6	-4.0	-4.6	-4.6	-4.7	-5.7	-6.3	-7.4	-8.4	-9.6
Netherlands	3.3	2.5 |	2.6	-2.1	-2.5	-1.0	-0.7	4.3	6.8	9.4	12.1	13.0	7.9	10.2
New Zealand	-0.6	-0.7	-0.2	-0.1	0.1	0.7	1.2	1.0	0.4	0.2	0.3	-0.5	-	-0.4
Norway	1.4	0.7	1.0	2.7	2.6	1.6	1.1	1.0	0.7	1.8	1.4	0.3	1.7	-1.9
Poland	3.2	4.2	1.4	1.4	0.8	0.8	0.2	0.1	0.7	0.7	4.8	5.0	4.8	3.5
Portugal	1.5	1.9 |	2.0	2.0	2.6	3.2	4.1	5.0	4.9	6.3	8.9	9.7	8.3	8.9
Slovak Republic	0.2	0.2	0.2	0.4	0.5	0.5	0.2	0.3	0.3	0.8	0.5	-0.7	-1.7	-1.0
Slovenia	0.8	0.6	0.4	0.5	0.5	0.6	0.6	0.9	1.1	1.2	1.4	2.2	1.5	1.4
Spain	18.2	19.8 |	20.4	19.4	20.6	21.3	26.3	27.0	27.6	27.9	31.6	37.7	35.4	37.0
Sweden	-1.3	-1.6	-1.4	-1.5	-0.6	-0.5	1.7	5.5	7.3	9.7	15.6	16.6	13.5	15.9
Switzerland	14.9	15.9	16.7	17.9	17.3	18.1	21.5	24.4	26.9	31.3	37.8	45.8	38.9	46.3
Turkey	10.9	13.5	7.5	11.4	9.1	7.9	10.5	12.8	15.2	13.6	13.3	17.3	16.7	14.2
United Kingdom	27.5	24.9	25.2	22.7	24.8	29.5	36.9	52.1	46.8	64.0	93.6	101.4	82.1	76.2
United States	90.2	82.1	72.1	67.5	57.6	54.8	47.4	56.3	69.6	80.2	121.1	135.9	132.0	151.4
Euro area	5.0	0.7 |	-8.9	-8.1	-2.5	16.0	25.4	39.6	48.1	52.2	64.3	61.5	44.7	43.4
OECD total	86.7 |	90.2 |	63.3	65.3 |	57.1	69.5	86.7	140.1	177.2	235.2	340.4	388.4	337.6	362.5
Brazil	-9.3	-9.0	-7.0	-7.2	-7.8	-5.0	-4.9	-4.7	-8.3	-9.7	-13.2	-16.7	-19.2	..
China	-3.4	-2.8	-5.3	-5.6	-5.9	-6.8	-8.6	-9.7	-9.4	-8.8	-7.9	-11.8	-29.4	..
India	1.3	2.1	2.2	3.4	2.9	4.4	6.4	13.0	20.0	29.4	39.3	46.9	..	..
Indonesia	-9.7	-7.6	-7.8	-10.4	-10.4	-10.4	-12.1	-8.8	-9.1	-9.9	-11.8	-13.0	-9.7	-9.5
Russian Federation	-5.9	-4.1	-4.3	-6.7	-9.1	-9.9	-10.9	-12.7	-13.8	-13.6	-18.9	-24.3	-19.9	..
South Africa	-0.6	-0.3	-0.5	-0.8	-0.4	-0.5	0.4	-0.5	-0.8	-2.0	-2.7	-4.2	-2.8	..

StatLink http://dx.doi.org/10.1787/888932503930

Services trade balance: exports of services minus imports of services

Billion US dollars

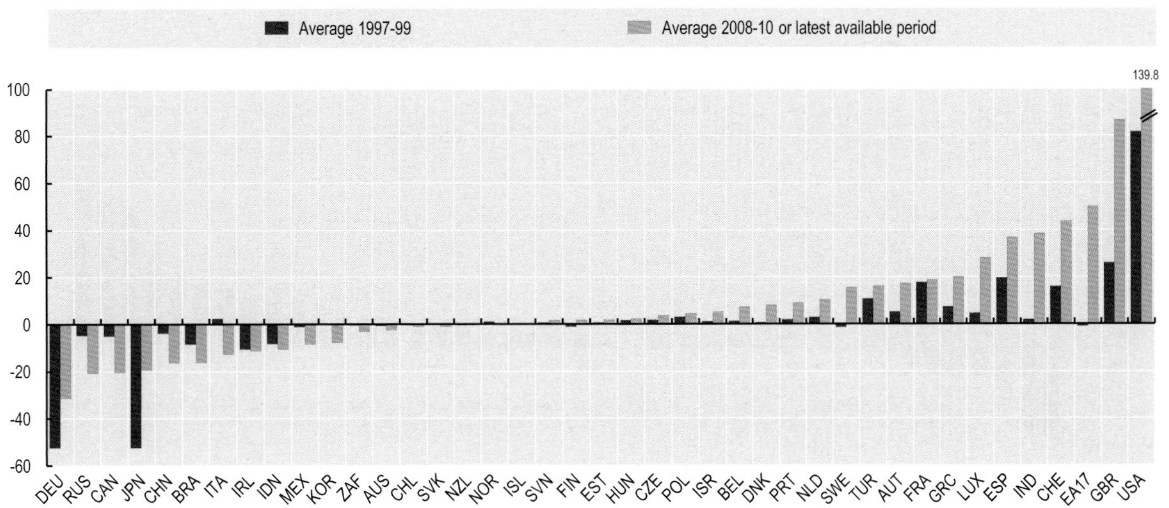

StatLink http://dx.doi.org/10.1787/888932503949

Imports of services

Billion US dollars

	1997	1998	1999	2000	2001	2002	2003	2004	2005	2006	2007	2008	2009	2010
Australia	19.7	18.5	19.2	19.2	17.5	18.5	22.1	28.2	30.8	32.4	40.2	48.0	41.5	51.3
Austria	17.8	18.0	17.3	16.5	17.6	18.8	23.8	28.0	30.7	33.6	39.1	42.8	37.0	27.8
Belgium	27.9	30.0 |	31.2	32.3	33.6	35.7	42.8	49.1	51.2	53.2	68.6	82.8	73.8	78.5
Canada	38.0	38.1	40.6	44.1	43.8	45.0	52.3	58.7	65.7	72.7	82.5	88.1	79.2	91.3
Chile	4.0	4.4	4.6	4.8	5.0	5.1	5.7	6.8	7.8	8.5	9.9	11.8	10.1	11.8
Czech Republic	5.4	5.7	5.9	5.4	5.6	6.4	7.3	9.0	10.2	11.9	14.4	17.8	16.8	18.2
Denmark	14.2	15.6	18.4	22.1	23.5	25.1	27.9	33.3	37.3	45.1	54.0	62.3	50.8	50.7
Estonia	0.7	0.9	0.9	0.9	1.0	1.1	1.4	1.7	2.2	2.5	3.1	3.3	2.5	2.8
Finland	8.3	7.8 |	7.6	9.1	9.4	9.8	12.1	14.6	17.7	18.6	22.6	30.3	25.6	22.9
France	64.2	67.5 |	63.1	65.7	67.1	72.9	87.5	99.7	107.0	113.2	129.5	141.1	127.0	126.9
Germany	130.7	135.6 |	141.9	138.2	142.7	145.5	174.0	198.1	212.5	225.5	261.5	292.4	257.6	265.9
Greece	4.0	4.5 |	9.7	11.5 |	11.6	9.8	11.2	14.0	14.7	16.4	20.2	24.8	19.9	20.2
Hungary	4.1	4.2 |	4.4	4.8	5.6	6.8	9.2	10.2	11.5	12.1	15.8	18.8	16.7	15.9
Iceland	0.8	1.0	1.0	1.2	1.1	1.1	1.5	1.8	2.5	2.6	3.0	2.4	2.0	2.2
Ireland	15.2 |	23.9 |	26.1	31.4	35.4	42.8	54.5	65.4	71.5	80.2	94.6	110.6	104.3	105.1
Israel	9.0	9.3	10.3	11.9	11.8	10.9	11.2	12.8	13.7	14.7	17.6	19.9	17.1	18.0
Italy	74.1	65.7 |	57.5	55.4	57.6	62.8	74.3	83.2	90.0	100.4	121.7	129.2	109.0	110.1
Japan	123.4	111.7	114.9	116.8	108.2	107.8	108.8	133.7	134.0	134.5	149.3	163.3	144.8	154.4
Korea	29.6	24.6	27.3	33.6	33.2	37.0	40.8	50.5	59.7	70.2	85.0	96.4	80.2	93.9
Luxembourg	8.7	9.9 |	11.5	13.2	13.3	12.4	15.5	21.0	24.2	29.9	37.8	40.2	34.5	37.4
Mexico	11.8	12.4	13.5	16.0	16.2	16.7	17.1	18.6	20.8	22.0	23.8	25.4	23.2	25.1
Netherlands	45.8	47.2 |	49.5	51.4	53.8	57.0	63.9	69.5	73.3	75.3	84.2	92.2	85.0	85.2
New Zealand	4.8	4.4	4.5	4.5	4.3	4.8	5.7	7.2	8.2	7.9	9.1	9.6	7.8	9.1
Norway	14.3	14.8	15.4	15.0	15.8	17.8	20.6	24.3	29.2	31.2	38.9	44.5	36.7	42.3
Poland	5.7	6.6	7.0	9.0	9.0	9.3	10.9	13.4	15.5	19.9	24.2	30.5	24.2	29.0
Portugal	6.2	6.9 |	7.3	7.0	6.8	7.1	8.3	9.7	10.3	12.1	14.3	16.5	14.4	14.3
Slovak Republic	2.1	2.3	1.8	1.8	2.0	2.3	3.0	3.5	4.1	4.7	6.5	9.2	8.0	6.8
Slovenia	1.9	2.0	1.9	1.7	1.6	1.8	2.2	2.6	2.9	3.2	4.2	5.2	4.4	4.4
Spain	25.6	28.6 |	32.0	33.2	35.2	38.8	48.0	59.2	67.1	78.6	96.5	105.4	87.4	87.2
Sweden	19.7	21.3	23.2	24.6	24.2	24.8	28.6	33.0	35.0	39.2	47.3	53.8	45.7	48.5
Switzerland	11.2	12.3	13.1	12.8	12.3	12.9	14.8	19.5	22.8	23.5	28.0	32.0	35.0	33.3
Turkey	8.3	9.7	8.9	8.1	6.1	6.1	7.4	10.1	11.7	12.0	15.6	17.8	16.7	19.4
United Kingdom	79.8	89.9	98.6	101.1	101.6	112.0	130.3	154.8	169.7	183.7	213.1	213.5	173.1	175.5
United States	165.9	180.7	195.8	219.0	217.0	226.4	244.3	282.4	302.5	336.7	367.2	398.3	370.3	394.2
Euro area	241.4	262.8 |	274.2	276.5	285.5	294.5	347.2	412.8	455.6	501.6	612.3	688.5	606.8	629.5
OECD total	997.8 |	1 030.0 |	1 081.8	1 148.1 |	1 154.5	1 214.1	1 389.6	1 626.4	1 768.5	1 929.0	2 245.0	2 483.8	2 183.1	2 291.1
Brazil	15.3	16.7	14.2	16.7	17.1	14.5	15.4	17.3	24.4	29.1	37.2	47.1	47.0	..
China	28.0	26.7	31.6	36.0	39.3	46.5	55.3	72.1	83.8	100.8	130.1	158.9	158.9	..
India	7.8	9.6	12.3	13.3	14.5	15.0	17.5	25.2	32.6	40.3	47.7	56.2	..	..
Indonesia	16.6	12.1	12.4	15.6	15.9	17.0	17.4	20.9	22.0	21.4	24.3	28.2	22.8	26.3
Russian Federation	20.0	16.5	13.4	16.2	20.6	23.5	27.1	33.3	38.7	44.7	58.1	75.5	61.4	..
South Africa	6.0	5.7	5.8	5.8	5.2	5.5	8.0	10.3	12.1	14.2	16.5	17.0	14.8	..

StatLink http://dx.doi.org/10.1787/888932503968

Imports of services

Average annual growth in percentage

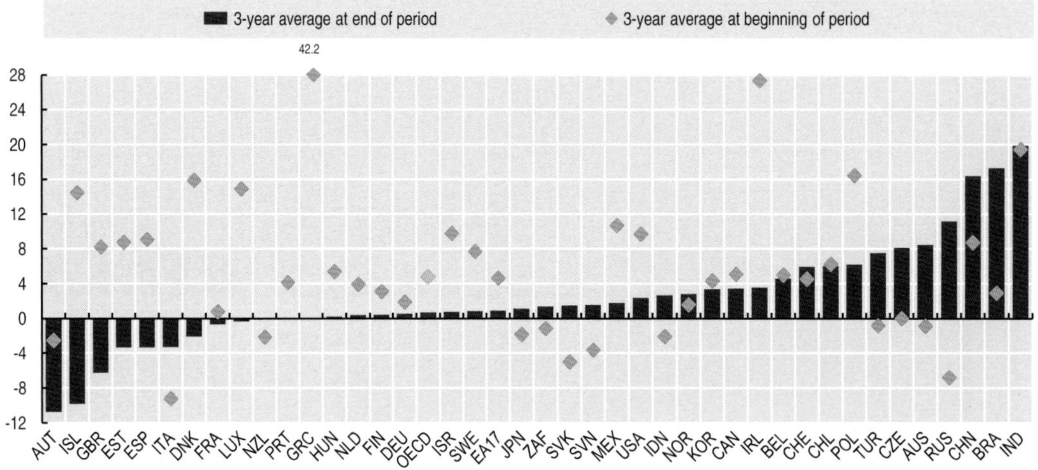

StatLink http://dx.doi.org/10.1787/888932503987

Exports of services

Billion US dollars

	1997	1998	1999	2000	2001	2002	2003	2004	2005	2006	2007	2008	2009	2010
Australia	19.3	17.1	18.7	19.7	17.9	19.4	23.4	28.2	30.7	32.7	39.6	43.7	41.0	48.4
Austria	21.8	23.1	23.4	23.0	23.9	25.9	32.6	37.9	42.4	45.7	54.3	63.4	54.7	41.2
Belgium	29.1	30.8 |	32.6	34.3	35.4	37.7	44.6	52.7	56.1	59.5	74.5	87.5	83.5	85.5
Canada	31.6	33.9	36.1	40.2	38.8	40.4	44.1	50.3	55.8	60.3	65.0	67.9	59.8	69.2
Chile	3.9	4.0	3.9	4.1	4.1	4.4	5.1	6.0	7.1	7.8	9.0	10.8	8.6	10.8
Czech Republic	7.2	7.6	7.1	6.9	7.1	7.1	7.8	9.6	11.8	13.9	16.8	21.7	20.2	21.6
Denmark	14.3	15.3	20.4	24.5	26.9	27.1	31.4	36.6	43.5	52.2	61.4	72.4	55.2	59.9
Estonia	1.3	1.5	1.5	1.5	1.6	1.7	2.2	2.8	3.2	3.6	4.4	5.1	4.4	4.5
Finland	6.7	6.7 |	6.5	7.7	9.2	10.4	11.5	15.2	17.0	17.5	23.2	31.9	27.5	24.9
France	80.9	84.8 |	81.7	82.8	82.4	88.3	101.5	114.8	122.3	128.6	149.3	166.2	143.0	142.2
Germany	82.6	84.0 |	84.0	83.2	88.6	102.3 |	123.3	147.0	163.7	187.2	222.1	253.1	231.2	236.7
Greece	11.2	11.5 |	17.4	19.6 |	19.8	19.9	24.2	33.2	33.9	35.6	42.9	49.8	37.5	37.7
Hungary	5.7	5.9	5.6	5.6	6.6	6.9	8.0	10.3	12.9	13.7	17.3	20.2	18.6	19.1
Iceland	0.8	1.0	0.9	1.0	1.1	1.1	1.4	1.6	2.0	1.9	2.3	2.1	2.3	2.5
Ireland	6.2 |	14.1 |	14.7	18.4	23.5	29.8	42.0	52.7	59.9	71.6	93.0	99.3	92.6	97.1
Israel	9.2	10.1	12.3	15.4	12.9	12.2	13.7	16.1	17.5	19.2	21.1	24.3	22.0	24.7
Italy	76.1	69.7 |	58.7	56.5	57.7	59.9	71.7	84.7	89.4	98.8	112.0	116.1	95.3	98.3
Japan	69.3	62.4	60.9	69.2	64.5	65.7	73.3	94.7	106.1	114.4	126.2	141.3	113.4	136.0
Korea	27.2	26.4	27.1	31.5	30.2	30.6	35.0	44.5	49.7	56.8	73.0	90.6	73.6	82.7
Luxembourg	12.7	14.2 |	16.9	20.0	19.8	20.5	25.4	33.9	40.5	50.7	64.8	69.1	59.3	67.5
Mexico	11.1	11.5	11.7	13.7	12.7	12.7	12.5	14.0	16.1	16.2	17.5	18.0	14.8	15.4
Netherlands	49.0	49.7 |	52.1	49.3	51.3	56.0	63.2	73.7	80.1	84.7	96.4	105.2	92.9	95.4
New Zealand	4.2	3.7	4.3	4.4	4.4	5.4	6.9	8.2	8.7	8.1	9.4	9.1	7.8	8.7
Norway	15.7	15.5	16.4	17.8	18.4	19.4	21.7	25.2	29.9	33.1	40.4	44.8	38.4	40.4
Poland	8.9	10.8	8.4	10.4	9.8	10.0	11.2	13.5	16.3	20.6	28.9	35.5	29.0	32.5
Portugal	7.7	8.8 |	9.2	9.1	9.4	10.3	12.4	14.7	15.2	18.4	23.2	26.1	22.6	23.2
Slovak Republic	2.3	2.4	2.1	2.2	2.5	2.8	3.3	3.7	4.4	5.4	7.0	8.5	6.3	5.8
Slovenia	2.7	2.6	2.3	2.2	2.1	2.4	2.8	3.5	4.0	4.5	5.7	7.4	6.0	5.8
Spain	43.9	48.4 |	52.5	52.6	55.8	59.9	74.2	86.2	94.8	106.4	127.7	142.8	122.6	124.1
Sweden	18.4	19.7	21.7	22.7	23.0	23.3	30.2	38.4	42.4	48.8	62.7	70.2	58.9	64.2
Switzerland	26.2	28.2	29.7	30.7	29.6	30.9	36.3	43.9	49.7	54.8	65.8	77.8	73.8	79.5
Turkey	19.2	23.2	16.4	19.5	15.2	14.0	18.0	22.9	26.9	25.5	28.9	35.1	33.5	33.6
United Kingdom	107.4	114.7	123.8	124.0	126.4	141.0	167.2	206.9	216.7	247.3	306.4	312.8	254.5	251.6
United States	256.1	262.8	267.9	286.4	274.6	281.2	291.6	338.7	372.2	416.9	488.3	534.1	502.3	545.5
Euro area	246.4	263.5 |	265.3	268.3	283.0	310.5	372.6	452.5	503.7	553.8	676.5	750.0	651.5	672.9
OECD total	1 081.1 |	1 115.3 |	1 153.9	1 219.7 |	1 217.9	1 283.1	1 476.3	1 766.9	1 942.1	2 163.8	2 583.0	2 872.4	2 511.8	2 651.0
Brazil	6.0	7.6	7.2	9.5	9.3	9.6	10.4	12.6	16.0	19.5	24.0	30.5	27.7	..
China	24.6	23.9	26.2	30.4	33.3	39.7	46.7	62.4	74.4	92.0	122.2	147.1	129.5	..
India	9.1	11.7	14.5	16.7	17.3	19.5	23.9	38.3	52.6	69.7	86.9	103.1	..	..
Indonesia	6.9	4.5	4.6	5.2	5.5	6.7	5.3	12.0	12.9	11.5	12.5	15.2	13.2	16.8
Russian Federation	14.1	12.4	9.1	9.6	11.4	13.6	16.2	20.6	25.0	31.1	39.3	51.1	41.5	..
South Africa	5.4	5.4	5.2	5.0	4.8	5.0	8.4	9.9	11.3	12.2	13.8	12.8	12.0	..

StatLink http://dx.doi.org/10.1787/888932504006

Exports of services

Average annual growth in percentage

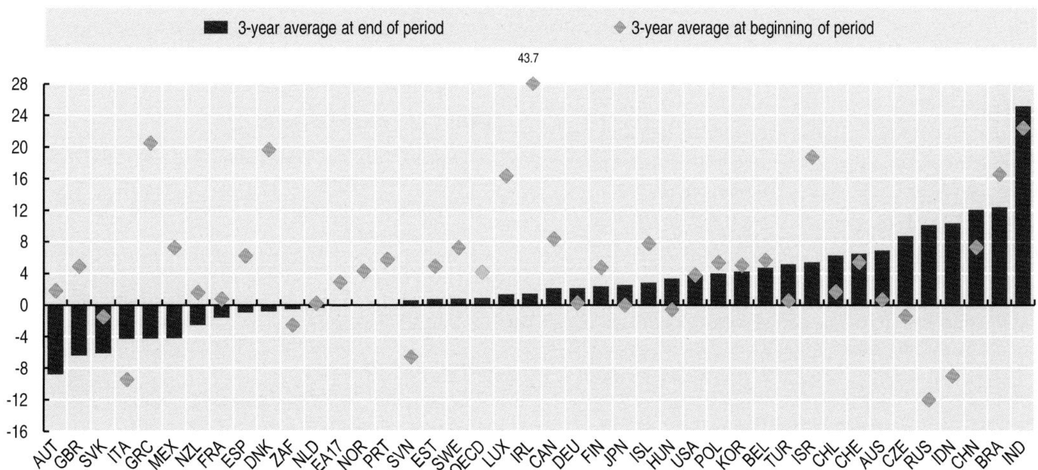

StatLink http://dx.doi.org/10.1787/888932504025

TRADING PARTNERS

The pattern of OECD merchandise trade – where imports come from and where exports go to – has undergone significant shifts over the last decade. These shifts have occurred in response to changes in the distribution of global income and to globalization – in particular, the outsourcing of manufacturing from OECD countries to the rest of the world.

Definition

The data shown here refer to total imports and exports declared by all 34 members economies of the OECD. It shows merchandise trade both within the OECD area and with selected countries of the rest of the world.

The definitions of merchandise imports and exports are explained under "International trade in goods".

Overview

Since 2000, there has been a steady decline in the share of OECD imports and exports coming from OECD countries. In 2000, imports from OECD countries accounted for 73% of total OECD imports; by 2009, this share had fallen to 65%. For exports, the share directed to other OECD countries also declined from 79% in 2000 to 72% in 2009.

OECD imports from non-OECD countries have risen from 26% to 34% of the total over the same period, while exports to these countries have increased from 20% to 28%. A large change occurred in trade between OECD countries and China. In 2000, China supplied only 5% of total OECD imports but by 2009 this share had risen to 12%. China's importance as a destination for OECD exports has increased less sharply, rising from 2% in 2000 to 6% in 2009.

Comparability

OECD countries follow common definitions and procedures in compiling their merchandise trade statistics. These statistics are therefore comparable and of good quality. The removal of customs frontiers following the creation of a common market in Europe required EU countries to adopt a system of recording trade flows through sample surveys of exporters and importers. This led to a fall in the reliability of merchandise trade statistics for trade between the EU countries. Statistics on trade between EU countries and non-EU countries, however, were not affected.

Sources

- OECD (2011), *International Trade by Commodity Statistics*, OECD Publishing.

Further information

Analytical publications

- OECD (2010), *Smart Rules for Fair Trade: 50 Years of Export Credits*, OECD Publishing.
- OECD (2006), *Aid for Trade: Making it Effective*, The Development Dimension, OECD Publishing.
- OECD (2005), *Agriculture, Trade and the Environment*, OECD Publishing.
- OECD (2005), *Environmental Requirements and Market Access*, OECD Trade Policy Studies, OECD Publishing.
- OECD (2005), *Trade and Structural Adjustment: Embracing Globalisation*, OECD Publishing.
- OECD (2004), *Trade and Competitiveness in Argentina, Brazil and Chile: Not as Easy as A-B-C*, OECD Publishing.
- OECD, The World Bank and International Organisation for Migration (2004), *Trade and Migration: Building Bridges for Global Labour Mobility*, OECD Publishing.
- OECD and World Trade Organisation (2011), *Aid for Trade at a Glance*, OECD Publishing.

Statistical publications

- OECD (2011), *Monthly Statistics of International Trade*, OECD Publishing.
- OECD (2011), *Statistics on International Trade in Services*, OECD Publishing.

Methodological publications

- OECD, *et al.* (2002), *Manual on Statistics of International Trade in Services*, United Nations.

Online databases

- *International Trade by Commodity Statistics.*
- *Monthly Statistics of International Trade.*

Websites

- OECD International Trade Statistics, *www.oecd.org/std/its*.

Partner countries and regions of OECD merchandise trade

	Imports				Exports				Merchandise trade			
	As a percentage of total OECD merchandise imports				As a percentage of total OECD merchandise imports				As a percentage of total OECD merchandise trade			
	2000	2005	2008	2009	2000	2005	2008	2009	2000	2005	2008	2009
EU27 total	39.0	40.8	36.2	41.1	43.3	45.9	41.9	45.9	41.1	43.2	38.9	43.5
Major seven	47.4	40.6	37.2	37.1	51.0	46.5	42.3	41.8	49.1	43.4	39.6	39.4
OECD total	**72.8**	**67.6**	**64.3**	**65.3**	**78.7**	**76.2**	**72.4**	**71.6**	**75.6**	**71.7**	**68.1**	**68.3**
Australia	0.8	0.8	1.0	1.0	1.0	1.0	1.0	1.0	0.9	0.9	1.0	1.0
Austria	1.0	1.2	1.2	1.3	1.4	1.5	1.5	1.6	1.2	1.4	1.4	1.5
Belgium	2.5	2.8	2.8	2.8	2.9	3.5	3.4	3.4	2.7	3.1	3.1	3.1
Canada	5.6	4.5	3.8	3.5	4.8	3.9	3.4	3.5	5.2	4.2	3.6	3.5
Chile	0.3	0.4	0.4	0.4	0.2	0.2	0.3	0.3	0.2	0.3	0.3	0.3
Czech Republic	0.5	0.8	1.0	1.1	0.6	0.9	1.1	1.1	0.6	0.9	1.1	1.1
Denmark	0.8	0.9	0.8	0.9	0.8	0.9	0.9	0.9	0.8	0.9	0.9	0.9
Estonia	0.1	0.1	0.1	0.1	0.1	0.1	0.1	0.1	0.1	0.1	0.1	0.1
Finland	0.7	0.7	0.7	0.6	0.6	0.7	0.7	0.6	0.7	0.7	0.7	0.6
France	5.1	4.8	4.5	4.7	6.0	6.1	5.9	6.1	5.5	5.4	5.2	5.4
Germany	9.1	10.2	10.0	10.1	8.7	9.0	9.1	9.1	8.9	9.6	9.6	9.6
Greece	0.1	0.2	0.1	0.1	0.6	0.6	0.6	0.6	0.3	0.4	0.4	0.4
Hungary	0.5	0.7	0.7	0.7	0.6	0.7	0.8	0.7	0.5	0.7	0.7	0.7
Iceland	0.0	0.0	0.0	0.0	0.1	0.1	0.0	0.0	0.1	0.0	0.0	0.0
Ireland	1.5	1.8	1.4	1.7	1.0	1.0	0.8	0.7	1.3	1.4	1.1	1.2
Israel	0.5	0.4	0.4	0.4	0.6	0.5	0.4	0.4	0.6	0.4	0.4	0.4
Italy	3.6	3.7	3.5	3.5	3.6	3.9	3.7	3.7	3.6	3.8	3.6	3.6
Japan	6.3	4.6	3.7	3.6	3.5	2.6	2.3	2.3	4.9	3.7	3.1	3.0
Korea	2.0	1.8	1.6	1.7	1.8	1.7	1.6	1.7	1.9	1.8	1.6	1.7
Luxembourg	0.1	0.2	0.2	0.2	0.2	0.3	0.3	0.3	0.2	0.2	0.2	0.2
Mexico	3.2	2.7	2.5	2.7	3.0	2.3	2.2	2.3	3.1	2.5	2.3	2.5
Netherlands	3.5	3.7	3.9	3.9	3.9	3.8	4.0	4.0	3.7	3.7	4.0	3.9
New Zealand	0.2	0.2	0.2	0.2	0.2	0.3	0.2	0.2	0.2	0.2	0.2	0.2
Norway	1.1	1.2	1.3	1.2	0.6	0.7	0.8	0.8	0.9	1.0	1.1	1.0
Poland	0.5	0.8	1.1	1.2	0.8	1.1	1.7	1.6	0.7	1.0	1.4	1.4
Portugal	0.5	0.5	0.4	0.4	0.8	0.8	0.7	0.8	0.6	0.6	0.6	0.6
Slovak Republic	0.2	0.4	0.5	0.5	0.2	0.4	0.6	0.6	0.2	0.4	0.5	0.5
Slovenia	0.1	0.2	0.2	0.2	0.2	0.2	0.3	0.3	0.2	0.2	0.2	0.2
Spain	1.9	2.1	2.0	2.1	2.8	3.4	3.0	2.8	2.3	2.7	2.5	2.4
Sweden	1.5	1.4	1.4	1.3	1.4	1.4	1.4	1.3	1.5	1.4	1.4	1.3
Switzerland	1.4	1.4	1.4	1.7	1.7	1.7	1.8	2.0	1.6	1.5	1.6	1.8
Turkey	0.4	0.7	0.7	0.7	0.8	0.9	1.0	1.0	0.6	0.8	0.8	0.8
United Kingdom	4.9	4.0	3.5	3.5	6.0	5.7	5.4	5.3	5.4	4.8	4.4	4.3
United States	12.8	8.7	8.0	8.3	18.4	15.3	12.4	11.8	15.5	11.8	10.1	10.0
Non-OECD	**26.1**	**31.1**	**34.7**	**33.7**	**20.2**	**22.8**	**26.5**	**27.7**	**23.3**	**27.2**	**30.8**	**30.8**
Brazil	0.8	1.0	1.1	1.0	0.8	0.7	1.0	1.0	0.8	0.9	1.0	1.0
China	5.4	9.3	10.3	11.6	2.2	4.1	4.7	5.9	3.9	6.8	7.6	8.8
India	0.6	0.8	0.9	0.9	0.5	0.8	1.0	1.2	0.6	0.8	1.0	1.0
Indonesia	1.0	0.8	0.9	0.9	0.5	0.4	0.4	0.5	0.7	0.6	0.7	0.7
Russian Federation	1.4	2.1	2.7	2.4	0.6	1.3	2.0	1.4	1.0	1.7	2.4	1.9
South Africa	0.5	0.5	0.6	0.5	0.4	0.5	0.5	0.4	0.4	0.5	0.5	0.5

StatLink http://dx.doi.org/10.1787/888932504044

Partner countries and regions of OECD merchandise trade

As a percentage of total OECD merchandise trade

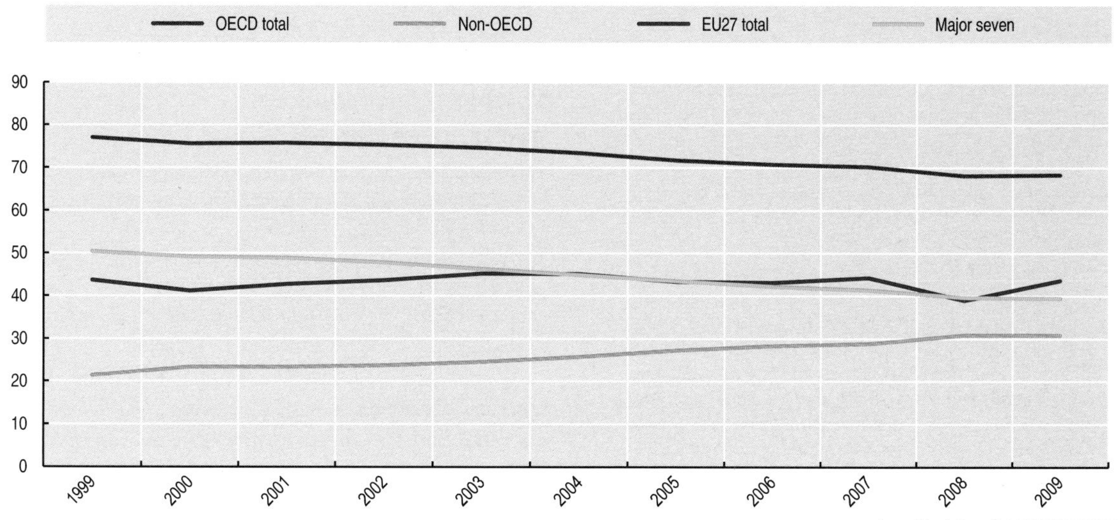

StatLink http://dx.doi.org/10.1787/888932504063

AFRICA'S TRADE PARTNERS

The 2011 edition of the *African Economic Outlook* investigates the increasing intensity and changing patterns of Africa's trade. It analyses policy options for African policy-makers to make the best out of Africa's rapid integration into the global economy.

Definition

The data shown here refer to Africa's total merchandise trade, *i.e.* imports plus exports. These data are broken down by OECD and non-OECD partners and illustrate the biggest countries in each group. The definitions of merchandise imports and exports are explained under "International trade in goods".

Comparability

All the statistics provided are based on "ComTrade SITC Revision 3" data series provided by the United Nations. They have been compiled from trade volumes declared by Africa's trading partners to maximize the availability of the data. They can be considered of reasonable quality and the most comparable series available across countries and over time.

Partner countries and regions of African merchandise trade

As a percentage of total African merchandise trade

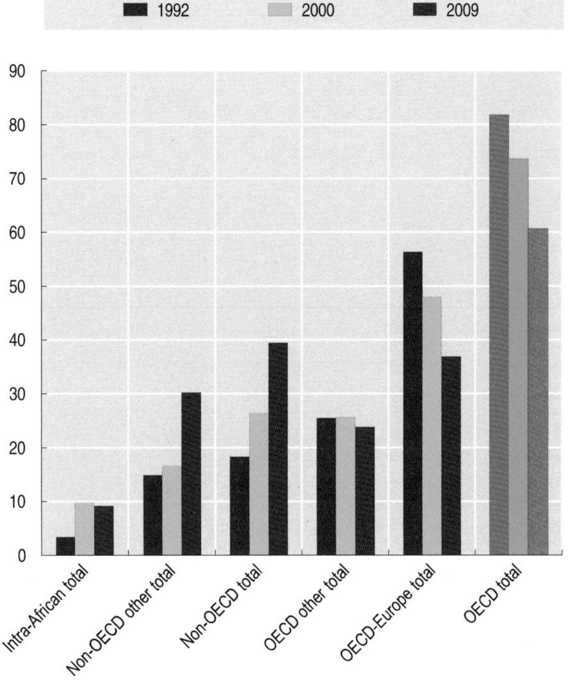

StatLink http://dx.doi.org/10.1787/888932504120

Overview

Trade between Africa and non-OECD countries has been growing rapidly during the past decade. China, India, and Brazil are leading the pack. The share of non-OECD countries in Africa's trade has risen from 26% in 2000 to 39% in 2009. Yet, OECD countries remain key trading partners for the continent and trade volume between them and Africa countries have kept growing. Trade between OECD countries and Africa has doubled in nominal value.

OECD partners still dominate African trade and continue growing, though less rapidly than other emerging partners. The United States was overtaken by China in 2009 as Africa's major trading partner, however both these countries remain far behind the level of trade volumes with the EU total. Some OECD members (for instance, those who were not members of the OECD's Development Assistance Committee a decade ago) such as Korea and Turkey, have seen their own trade with Africa surge rapidly over recent years.

Sources

- OECD Development Centre (calculations based on *United Nations ComTrade* data: SITC Rev. 3).

Further information

Analytical publications

- OECD (2011), *African Economic Outlook*, OECD Publishing.
- OECD (2010), *OECD Economic Surveys: South Africa*, OECD Publishing.
- OECD (2010), *The Mutual Review of Development Effectiveness in Africa 2009: Promise and Performance*, OECD Publishing.
- OECD (2009), *West African Studies*, OECD Publishing.
- OECD and United Nations (2011), *Economic Diversification in Africa: A Review of Selected Countries*, OECD Publishing.

Online databases

- United Nations Comtrade, *http://comtrade.un.org/db*.

Websites

- OECD Development Centre, *www.oecd.org/dev*.

Partner countries and regions of African merchandise trade

Percentage

	Imports				Exports				Merchandise trade			
	As a percentage of total African merchandise imports				As a percentage of total African merchandise imports				As a percentage of total African merchandise trade			
	1992	2000	2005	2009	1992	2000	2005	2009	1992	2000	2005	2009
OECD total	**81.5**	**70.8**	**62.2**	**58.4**	**82.0**	**75.7**	**73.2**	**62.7**	**81.8**	**73.6**	**68.5**	**60.6**
OECD-Europe total	55.1	49.9	43.9	38.5	57.3	46.6	41.4	35.3	56.3	48.0	42.5	36.8
Belgium	..	3.0	2.6	2.9	..	3.5	2.8	2.1	..	3.3	2.7	2.5
France	16.0	14.3	10.8	9.5	11.7	8.0	7.2	7.8	13.8	10.7	8.8	8.6
Germany	11.4	8.2	8.0	7.1	11.1	7.1	5.5	5.5	11.3	7.6	6.6	6.3
Italy	8.3	7.1	6.1	6.6	13.8	9.4	7.8	9.6	11.2	8.4	7.1	8.1
Netherlands	2.9	2.6	3.0	3.8	3.4	2.5	2.6	3.3	3.1	2.5	2.8	3.5
Portugal	1.4	0.8	0.8	1.4	1.8	1.1	1.4	1.1	1.6	1.0	1.1	1.3
United Kingdom	7.2	5.8	4.5	3.6	5.0	5.5	5.0	3.9	6.1	5.6	4.8	3.7
All others	7.8	8.0	8.1	3.6	10.5	9.5	9.1	2.0	9.2	8.9	8.7	2.8
OECD other total	26.3	21.0	18.3	19.9	24.7	29.1	31.8	27.5	25.5	25.6	26.0	23.8
Canada	0.9	0.9	0.7	0.8	1.0	1.2	1.9	1.9	1.0	1.1	1.4	1.4
Japan	7.4	4.2	3.5	2.8	3.7	3.2	3.2	2.6	5.4	3.6	3.3	2.7
Korea	3.0	2.8	3.5	3.8	1.1	2.0	1.1	1.3	2.0	2.4	2.1	2.5
Turkey	0.9	1.2	1.6	3.0	0.9	1.7	2.0	1.6	0.9	1.5	1.8	2.3
United States	11.2	9.0	6.5	6.9	16.0	18.6	21.1	18.2	13.7	14.5	14.8	12.7
All others	3.0	3.0	2.6	2.5	2.0	2.3	2.5	1.9	2.5	2.6	2.6	2.2
Non-OECD total	**18.5**	**29.2**	**37.8**	**41.6**	**18.0**	**24.3**	**26.8**	**37.3**	**18.2**	**26.4**	**31.5**	**39.4**
Intra-African total	4.2	11.4	10.1	9.9	2.7	8.6	9.1	8.4	3.4	9.8	9.5	9.2
South Africa	2.4	3.4	3.1	3.1	0.4	0.4	0.8	1.3	1.4	1.7	1.8	2.2
All others	1.8	8.0	7.0	6.8	2.3	8.3	8.3	7.1	2.1	8.1	7.7	7.0
Non-OECD other total	14.3	17.8	27.7	31.7	15.3	15.6	17.7	28.8	14.8	16.6	22.0	30.2
Brazil	1.3	1.1	2.6	2.6	0.6	1.9	2.2	2.4	1.0	1.6	2.3	2.5
China and Hong Kong	1.8	4.3	8.1	14.0	1.7	4.2	7.2	12.9	1.7	4.2	7.6	13.5
India	0.9	1.8	2.8	3.9	1.6	2.2	1.6	5.9	1.3	2.1	2.1	4.9
Russian Federation	..	0.9	1.1	1.6	..	0.2	0.3	0.5	..	0.5	0.7	1.0
All others	10.3	9.6	13.1	9.7	11.3	7.1	6.4	7.1	10.8	8.2	9.3	8.3
World	100.0	100.0	100.0	100.0	100.0	100.0	100.0	100.0	100.0	100.0	100.0	100.0

StatLink http://dx.doi.org/10.1787/888932504082

Africa's merchandise trade flows with OECD and Non-OECD partners

Billion US dollars

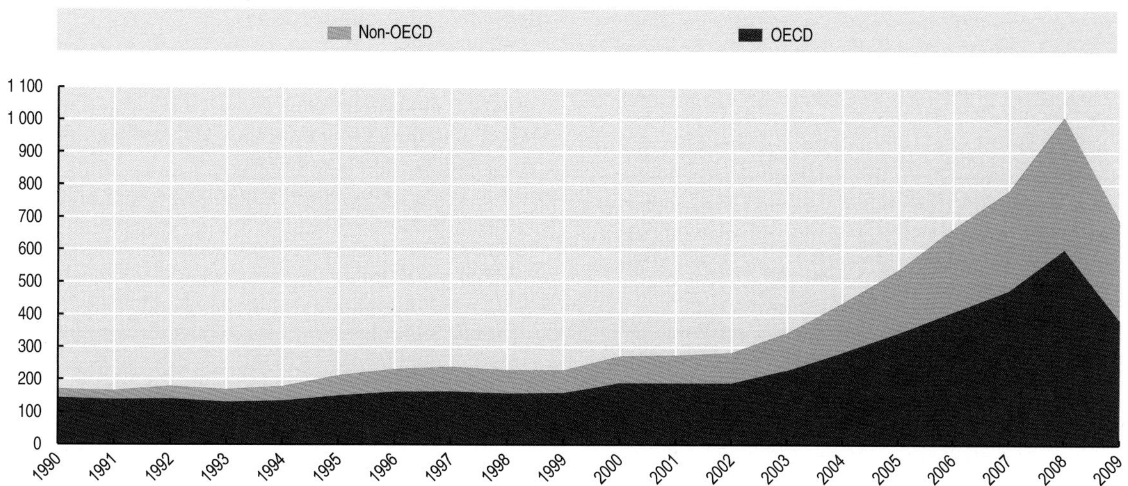

StatLink http://dx.doi.org/10.1787/888932504101

FOREIGN DIRECT INVESTMENT

Foreign direct investment (FDI) is a key element in international economic integration. FDI creates direct, stable and long-lasting links between economies. It encourages the transfer of technology and know-how between countries, and allows the host economy to promote its products more widely in international markets. FDI is also an additional source of funding for investment and, under the right policy environment, it can be an important vehicle for enterprise development.

Definition

FDI is defined as investment by a resident entity in one economy that reflects the objective of obtaining a lasting interest in an enterprise resident in another economy. The lasting interest implies the existence of a long-term relationship between the direct investor and the enterprise and a significant degree of influence by the direct investor on the management of the enterprise. The ownership of at least 10% of the voting power, representing the influence by the investor, is the basic criterion used.

Inward stocks refer to all direct investments held by non-residents in the reporting economy; outward stocks are the investments of the reporting economy held abroad. Corresponding flows relate to investment during a period of time. Negative flows generally indicate disinvestments or the impact of substantial reimbursements of inter-company loans.

The FDI index gauges the restrictiveness of a country's FDI rules through four types of restrictions: foreign equity limitations; screening or approval mechanisms; restriction on key foreign employment; operational restrictions.

The OECD FDI restrictiveness indexes presented here demonstrate that more open economies receive more FDI.

Comparability

In recent years the comparability of FDI statistics has improved significantly but asymmetries remain between inward and outward FDI.

Overview

FDI activity recovered in 2010 after two years of sharp declines following the global financial crises. FDI outflows world-wide picked up in 2010 by around 13% from 2009, to USD 1 282 billion, as compared to the sharp decline in investments in the two previous years (-40% and -12% in 2009 and 2008, respectively). OECD investors accounted for around 80% of global FDI outflows (USD 1 004 billion) representing a 10% increase from 2009 (compared to the decline in 2009 by -44% to USD 912 billion and in 2008 by -15% to USD 1 633 billion). The top three investing countries were the United States (USD 351 billion), Germany (USD 107 billion) and France (USD 84 billion). The United Kingdom, the second largest OECD investor in the pre-crisis period, was in 18th position in 2010. Investors from the European Union as a whole accounted for 34% of global outflows in 2010, at USD 437 billion (34% in 2009 and 51% in 2008).

OECD countries hosted only 53% (USD 650 billion) of global FDI inflows (as compared to 87% of inflows in 2000). The large majority of OECD inflows went to America and Europe. The United States account for 36% (USD 236 billion) of the OECD's FDI inflows in 2010. The United Kingdom, Germany and France in total accounted for 19% (USD 45 billion, USD 46 billion and USD 34 billion, respectively). OECD investors have continued diversifying the destination of their investments, with around 34% of their investments hosted outside the OECD area. The largest non-OECD recipients were China (USD 185 billion), Brazil (USD 48 billion), the Russian Federation (USD 43 billion) and India (USD 25 billion). Indonesia and South Africa received in total USD 15 billion.

Sources

- OECD (2011), *OECD International Direct Investment Statistics* (database).
- Foreign Direct Investment (supplementary material), *www.oecd.org/investment/statistics*.

Further information

Analytical publications

- OECD (2011), *OECD Investment Policy Reviews*, OECD Publishing.
- OECD (2009), *OECD Investment Policy Perspectives*, OECD Publishing.

Statistical publications

- OECD (2010), *Measuring Globalisation: OECD Economic Globalisation Indicators*, OECD Publishing.

Methodological publications

- Kalinova, B., A. Palerm and S. Thomsen (2010), *OECD's FDI Restrictiveness Index: 2010 Update*, OECD Working Papers on International Investment, No. 2010/03, OECD Publishing.
- OECD (2011), *OECD Guidelines for Multinational Enterprises, 2011 Edition*, OECD Publishing.
- OECD (2008), *OECD Benchmark Definition of Foreign Direct Investment*, Fourth edition, OECD Publishing.
- OECD (2005), *Measuring Globalisation: OECD Handbook on Economic Globalisation Indicators*, OECD Publishing.
- OECD and International Monetary Fund (2004), *Foreign Direct Investment Statistics: How Countries Measure FDI*, International Monetary Fund.

Websites

- Foreign Direct Investment Statistics – OECD Data, Analysis and Forecasts, *www.oecd.org/investment/statistics*.
- OECD International Investment, *www.oecd.org/daf/investment*.

Outward and inward FDI stocks

Million US dollars

	Outward direct investment stocks							Inward direct investment stocks						
	1990	1995	2000	2007	2008	2009	2010	1990	1995	2000	2007	2008	2009	2010
Australia	37 491	60 484	95 978	339 389	239 633	340 995	412 902	80 333	111 310	118 858	386 315	305 930	426 037	514 027
Austria	4 747	11 832	24 820	148 830	148 782	163 233	171 967	11 098	21 363	31 165	162 667	148 086	172 598	166 088
Belgium	40 636	80 690	179 773	621 228	744 607	765 019	736 725	58 388	112 960	195 219	784 631	822 547	861 547	670 013
Canada	84 813	118 106	237 647	519 320	524 274	593 580	616 134	112 850	123 182	212 723	516 283	443 191	523 247	561 111
Chile	..	..	11 154	31 688	31 820	41 339	49 838	..	..	45 753	99 413	99 359	121 395	139 538
Czech Republic	..	345	738	8 556	12 531	14 805	15 523	..	7 350	21 647	112 396	113 173	125 829	129 894
Denmark	..	..	73 117	184 789	193 268	210 650	220 981	..	..	73 585	161 281	151 683	150 251	143 482
Estonia	..	..	256	5 768	6 996	6 410	5 702	..	..	2 611	15 666	17 291	16 222	16 219
Finland	11 227	14 993	52 109	116 532	114 146	129 195	136 808	5 132	8 465	24 272	91 703	83 531	84 668	85 800
France	110 121	204 430	445 087	1 286 867	1 357 446	1 501 137	1 529 650	84 931	191 433	259 773	955 476	952 727	995 100	965 020
Germany	130 760	233 107	486 750	1 311 055	1 250 104	1 357 729	1 426 644	74 067	104 367	462 564	1 012 366	919 555	999 712	956 708
Greece	..	..	5 852	31 650	37 235	39 457	37 875	..	..	14 113	53 221	38 121	42 101	33 558
Hungary	..	278	1 279	17 320	17 593	19 093	19 559	569	11 304	22 856	95 463	88 008	98 173	89 290
Iceland	75	179	663	25 172	9 412	9 262	11 138	147	129	497	16 451	9 214	8 622	11 767
Ireland	..	..	27 925	150 060	168 937	273 318	317 708	..	..	127 088	203 683	188 302	247 466	247 094
Israel	..	758	9 091	49 833	54 410	57 371	64 969	365	5 741	22 556	60 550	62 169	69 164	77 816
Italy	60 195	106 319	180 274	417 876	442 423	486 424	475 599	60 009	65 347	121 169	376 514	327 932	364 456	337 397
Japan	201 440	238 452	278 441	542 614	680 331	740 965	831 110	9 850	33 508	50 322	132 851	203 372	200 151	214 890
Korea	..	..	..	74 777	97 910	120 440	138 980	..	..	..	121 956	94 680	117 730	127 050
Luxembourg	..	..	..	110 219	158 238	192 381	191 691	..	..	..	130 286	95 849	150 594	133 045
Mexico	..	..	..	55 859	57 016	64 035	78 379	22 424	41 130	97 170	238 164	264 459	279 793	298 472
Netherlands	105 085	172 348	305 458	942 087	889 944	956 521	954 388	68 699	115 756	243 730	766 622	645 642	660 507	594 920
New Zealand	3 320	7 676	6 065	15 836	13 397	14 737	16 101	8 065	25 728	28 070	67 775	51 979	64 801	67 706
Norway	10 889	22 521	22 937	155 169	145 059	179 881	..	12 404	19 836	25 282	132 417	118 554	150 872	..
Poland	..	539	1 018	21 318	24 092	29 304	39 029	109	7 843	34 233	178 418	164 290	185 182	201 003
Portugal	..	..	19 793	67 708	63 010	68 477	64 607	..	18 973	32 043	115 315	99 976	114 718	110 241
Slovak Republic	..	139	373	1 862	2 976	3 697	2 830	..	1 297	4 761	42 695	51 032	52 645	50 677
Slovenia	..	727	870	7 238	7 901	8 022	7 374	..	2 617	3 278	14 375	15 638	15 182	14 393
Spain	15 652	31 037	129 192	582 058	590 731	645 038	655 363	65 916	110 291	156 347	585 859	588 938	628 299	603 549
Sweden	50 720	73 143	123 260	332 208	322 952	347 557	336 086	12 636	31 089	93 998	293 384	278 710	331 932	348 667
Switzerland	66 087	142 481	232 176	652 303	734 147	839 899	889 469	34 245	57 064	86 810	353 328	446 400	497 611	543 167
Turkey	..	..	3 668	12 210	17 846	22 338	21 570	..	..	19 209	154 022	80 227	143 590	185 780
United Kingdom	236 118	330 665	923 366	1 802 757	1 524 953	1 674 159	1 689 332	233 305	226 626	463 134	1 229 880	974 503	1 056 495	1 086 132
United States	616 655	885 506	1 531 607	3 553 095	3 748 512	4 067 501	4 429 426	505 346	680 066	1 421 017	2 345 923	2 397 396	2 441 705	2 658 932
EU27 total	..	..	..	8 183 152	8 098 547	8 915 800	9 059 806	..	..	..	7 535 500	6 930 639	7 533 931	7 165 709
OECD total	1 786 030	2 736 756	5 410 736	14 195 251	14 432 632	15 983 968	16 595 457	1 460 888	2 134 773	4 515 854	12 007 347	11 342 464	12 398 396	12 383 445
of which: Manufacturing	36%	37%	27%	26%	25%	24%	..	37%	37%	30%	25%	25%	25%	..
Services	53%	57%	68%	68%	69%	71%	..	50%	57%	67%	70%	69%	69%	..
Brazil	..	..	..	139 886	155 668	164 523	189 222	..	..	..	309 668	287 697	400 808	472 576
China	..	..	..	115 960	185 694	245 800	310 800	..	..	..	703 667	915 524	1 314 800	1 476 400
India	..	..	2 609	44 080	63 338	79 266	93 915	..	..	20 278	105 790	125 207	167 236	198 427
Indonesia	..	..	..	3 193	2 802	-961	..	..	..	..	79 927	72 227	108 223	..
Russian Federation	..	2 420	20 141	370 161	205 631	302 542	369 076	..	345	32 204	491 052	215 756	378 837	493 354
South Africa	15 010	23 301	32 325	65 878	49 956	72 583	..	9 198	15 014	43 451	110 415	67 987	117 434	..

StatLink http://dx.doi.org/10.1787/888932504139

FDI stocks

As a percentage of GDP, 2010 or latest available year

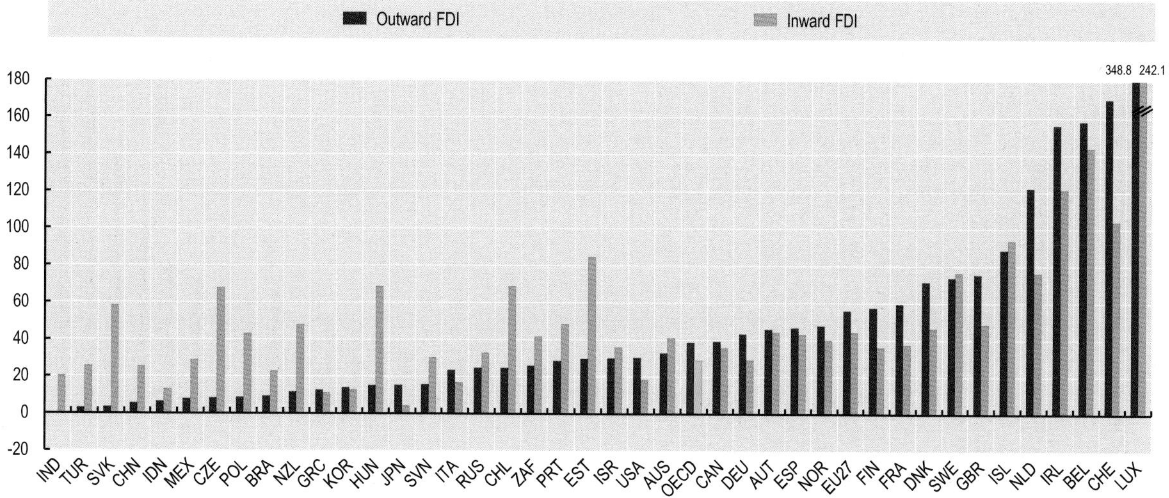

StatLink http://dx.doi.org/10.1787/888932504158

Outflows and Inflows of foreign direct investment

Million US dollars

	Outflows of foreign direct investment							Inflows of foreign direct investment						
	2004	2005	2006	2007	2008	2009	2010	2004	2005	2006	2007	2008	2009	2010
Australia	10 706	-31 058	25 411	16 785	33 455	16 260	25 788	42 472	-24 184	31 070	45 392	46 633	26 036	33 435
Austria	8 036	11 138	13 678	39 034	29 395	10 007	8 399	3 187	10 778	7 936	31 159	6 845	9 304	3 837
Belgium	34 038	32 640	50 713	80 141	220 595	3 687	48 844	43 583	34 351	58 926	93 448	193 575	56 023	71 960
Canada	43 341	27 540	44 404	57 719	79 752	41 728	38 583	-445	25 693	59 765	114 642	57 147	21 438	23 412
Chile	1 563	2 183	2 171	2 573	8 041	8 061	8 743	7 173	6 984	7 298	12 534	15 150	12 874	15 095
Czech Republic	1 014	-19	1 469	1 621	4 322	950	1 704	4 975	11 654	5 465	10 446	6 449	2 929	6 788
Denmark	-10 369	16 195	8 438	20 624	14 134	6 882	3 150	-10 447	12 873	2 715	11 815	2 228	2 966	-340
Estonia	269	691	1 107	1 746	1 112	1 549	133	958	2 869	1 797	2 725	1 729	1 839	1 540
Finland	-1 080	4 220	4 808	7 202	9 279	4 917	10 525	2 828	4 747	7 656	12 455	-1 136	356	6 935
France	56 767	114 909	110 734	164 341	154 747	102 955	84 117	32 579	84 898	71 888	96 240	64 060	34 029	33 907
Germany	20 559	75 848	118 767	170 650	76 992	78 205	106 961	-10 195	47 411	55 657	80 223	4 063	37 629	46 136
Greece	1 030	1 467	4 047	5 247	2 413	2 055	1 269	2 103	623	5 358	2 112	4 490	2 435	2 188
Hungary	1 119	2 179	3 877	3 622	2 230	1 826	1 236	4 508	7 711	7 021	5 447	6 313	1 552	1 811
Iceland	2 581	7 102	5 555	10 181	-4 206	2 286	-2 506	737	3 086	3 858	6 822	917	86	476
Ireland	18 079	14 304	15 332	21 150	18 912	26 617	17 803	-10 614	-31 670	-5 545	24 712	-16 421	25 961	26 331
Israel	4 533	2 946	15 462	8 604	7 210	1 695	7 960	2 947	4 819	15 296	8 798	10 877	4 438	5 153
Italy	19 272	41 795	42 089	90 795	66 870	21 277	21 011	16 824	19 960	39 259	40 209	-10 814	20 078	9 498
Japan	30 963	45 831	50 243	73 545	127 981	74 698	56 276	7 818	2 778	-6 503	22 548	24 417	11 938	-1 670
Korea	5 651	6 366	11 175	19 720	20 251	17 197	19 230	9 246	6 309	3 586	1 784	3 311	2 249	-150
Luxembourg	6 939	9 034	7 183	73 364	11 737	7 213	15 124	5 195	5 976	31 803	-28 265	11 195	22 478	9 211
Mexico	4 432	6 474	5 758	8 256	1 157	7 019	13 570	24 818	24 280	19 951	30 070	26 948	15 575	19 627
Netherlands	37 039	122 998	71 214	55 618	68 202	26 821	49 990	12 459	39 023	13 984	119 406	4 540	36 046	-13 526
New Zealand	-456	-1 520	182	3 702	-239	-308	591	2 425	1 524	4 689	3 440	4 984	-1 293	636
Norway	5 317	21 970	21 321	13 595	25 954	28 615	12 194	2 544	5 414	6 413	5 803	10 766	14 070	11 856
Poland	902	3 405	8 864	5 410	4 413	4 701	5 488	12 898	10 299	19 599	23 582	14 833	12 936	8 861
Portugal	7 457	2 110	7 143	5 494	2 736	817	-8 377	1 936	3 927	10 914	3 063	4 656	2 707	1 453
Slovak Republic	-21	149	512	600	529	432	328	3 033	2 427	4 700	3 583	4 685	-50	526
Slovenia	549	641	862	1 802	1 438	242	-79	829	588	644	1 515	1 944	-653	363
Spain	60 567	41 805	104 306	137 078	74 573	9 737	21 600	24 775	25 005	30 819	64 277	76 843	9 136	24 548
Sweden	22 227	27 712	26 613	38 811	31 298	26 300	31 841	12 125	11 897	28 908	27 740	37 120	10 673	6 026
Switzerland	26 282	50 994	75 863	51 036	45 312	27 867	38 263	933	-949	43 740	32 446	15 137	27 484	4 342
Turkey	780	1 064	924	2 106	2 549	1 554	1 464	2 785	10 031	20 185	22 047	19 504	8 409	9 258
United Kingdom	94 375	79 995	82 808	325 473	160 425	44 424	11 016	57 178	177 868	156 218	200 808	91 132	71 208	44 696
United States	316 222	36 236	244 922	414 039	329 080	303 605	351 350	145 966	112 638	243 151	221 166	310 091	158 581	236 227
EU27 total	379 718	604 508	686 543	1 252 600	962 403	386 789	436 725	222 661	497 651	582 109	856 592	538 747	372 736	302 022
OECD total	830 686	779 342	1 187 954	1 931 682	1 632 647	911 890	1 003 586	460 136	661 637	1 008 223	1 354 191	1 054 209	661 469	650 445
Brazil	9 807	2 517	28 202	7 067	20 457	-10 084	11 500	18 146	15 066	18 822	34 585	45 058	25 949	48 459
China	1 805	11 306	21 200	17 000	53 500	43 900	60 100	54 937	117 200	124 100	160 100	175 100	114 200	185 000
India	2 179	2 978	14 344	17 281	19 257	15 928	14 649	5 771	7 606	20 336	25 483	43 407	35 597	24 616
Indonesia	3 408	3 065	2 726	4 675	5 900	2 249	2 664	1 896	8 337	4 914	6 929	9 318	4 878	13 304
Russian Federation	13 782	12 767	23 151	45 916	55 594	43 666	52 476	15 444	12 886	29 701	55 073	75 002	36 500	42 868
South Africa	1 350	930	6 063	2 966	-3 134	1 151	450	798	6 647	-527	5 695	9 007	5 696	1 553

StatLink http://dx.doi.org/10.1787/888932504177

FDI flows

Billion US dollars, 2010

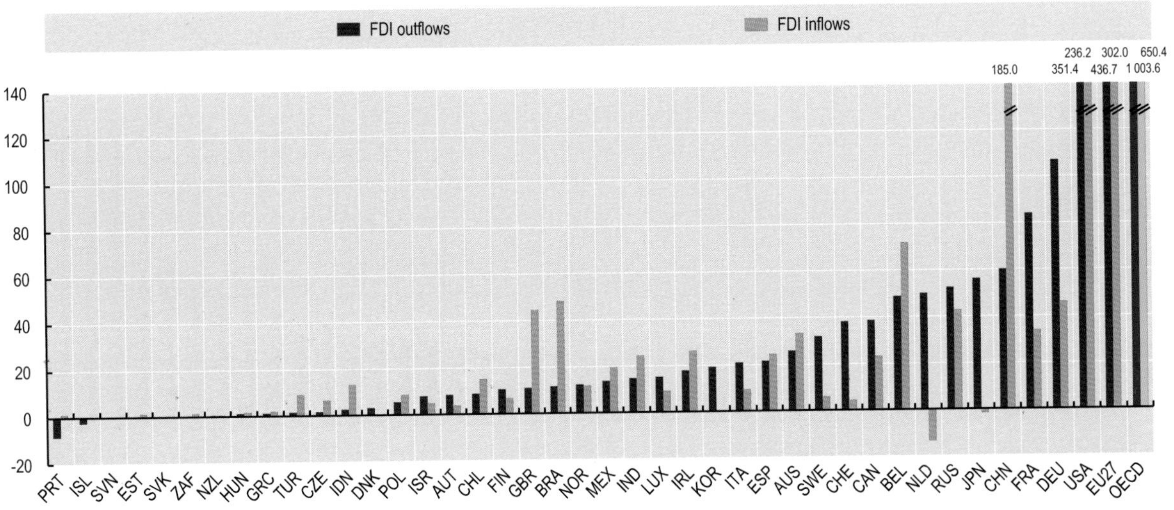

StatLink http://dx.doi.org/10.1787/888932504196

FDI regulatory restrictiveness index

2010

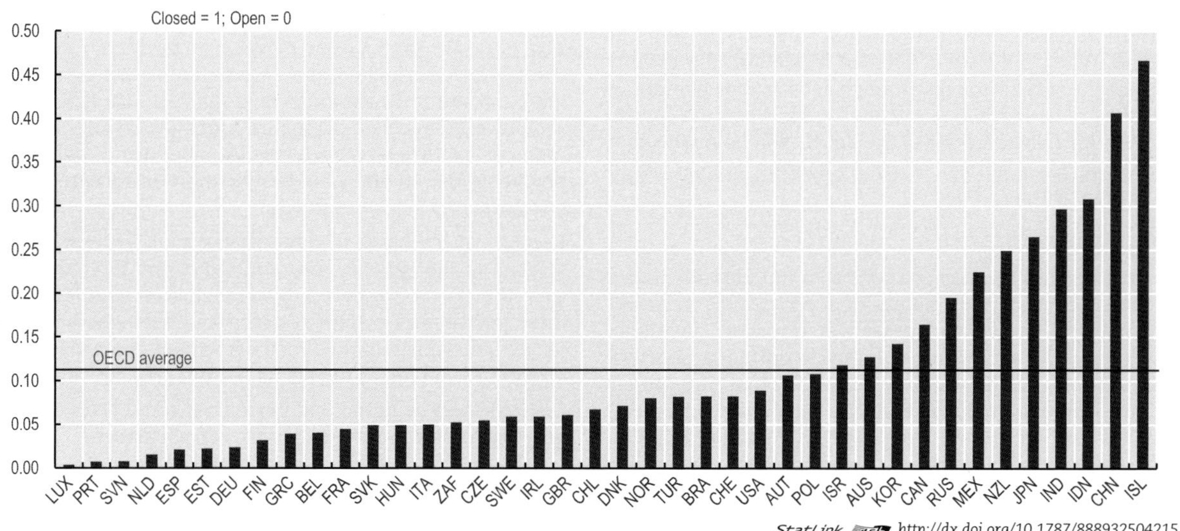

StatLink http://dx.doi.org/10.1787/888932504215

2010 FDI regulatory restrictiveness index *vs* 2009 FDI stock/GDP

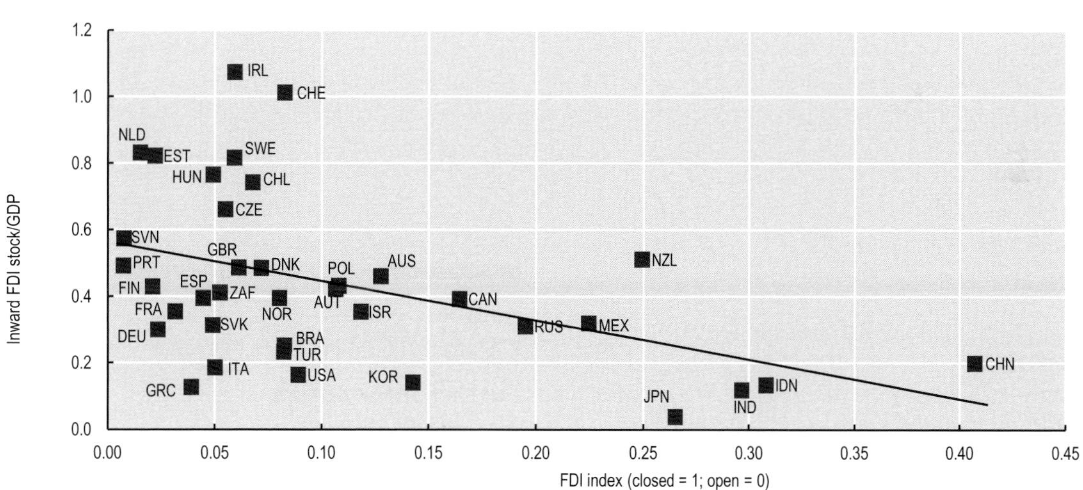

StatLink http://dx.doi.org/10.1787/888932504234

BALANCE OF PAYMENTS

The current account balance is the difference between current receipts from abroad and current payments to abroad. When the current account is positive, the country can use the surplus to repay foreign debts, to acquire foreign assets or to lend to the rest of the world. When the current account balance is negative, the deficit will be financed by borrowing from abroad or by liquidating foreign assets acquired in earlier periods.

Definition

Current account transactions consist of exports and imports of goods; exports and imports of services such as travel, international freight and passenger transport, insurance and financial services; income flows consisting of wages and salaries, dividends, interest and other investment income (*i.e.* property income in *System of National Accounts*); and current transfers such as government transfers (*i.e.* international cooperation), worker's remittances and other transfers such as gifts, inheritances and prizes won from lotteries.

Investment income includes retained earnings (*i.e.* profits not distributed as dividends to the direct investor) of foreign subsidiaries. In general, earnings of direct investment enterprises are treated as if they were remitted abroad to the direct investor, with the part that is actually retained in the country where the direct investment enterprises are located shown as direct investment income-reinvested earnings (debit) in the current account and (with the opposite sign) as inward direct investment in the financial account.

Comparability

The data are taken from balance of payments statistics compiled according to the International Monetary Fund (IMF) *Balance of Payments Manual* (BPM5). The IMF closely monitors balance of payments statistics reported by its member countries through regular meetings of balance of payments compilers. As a result, there is relatively good comparability across countries.

Because all earnings of direct investment enterprises are treated as though they are remitted to the direct investor even though a large part may in practice be retained by the direct investment enterprise in the countries where they are located, the existence of direct investment enterprises in an economy will tend to reduce its current account balance.

It should also be noted that portfolio income plays a role of growing importance for current account balances.

Overview

Current account balances as a percentage of GDP have been negative throughout the period since 1990 in Australia, Mexico, New Zealand, Spain, the United Kingdom and the United States; this is partly due to the way in which earnings of direct investment enterprises are treated. The portfolio investment balance, as well as the balance on goods, had a significant impact on trends in current account balances up to the recent crisis that affected the world economy. Countries which have recorded current account surpluses throughout the crisis period include Japan, Luxembourg, the Netherlands, Norway and Switzerland.

Since 1990, current account balances have generally moved from deficit to surplus in Austria and Germany.

Current account balances, as a percentage of GDP and averaged over the three years to 2010, recorded deficits of 5% of GDP or more in Iceland, Greece, Portugal, Spain and South Africa. Surpluses in excess of 5% were recorded by Norway, Switzerland, Sweden, Luxembourg, the Netherlands, Germany and the Russian Federation.

Sources

- OECD (2011), *Main Economic Indicators*, OECD Publishing.

Further information

Analytical publications

- OECD (2008), *Export Credit Financing Systems in OECD Member Countries and Non-Member Economies*, OECD Publishing.

Methodological publications

- International Monetary Fund (IMF) (2010), *Balance of Payments and International Investment Position Manual*, 6th edition, IMF, Washington DC.
- OECD *et al.* (2002), *Manual on Statistics of International Trade in Services*, United Nations.

Online databases

- *Main Economic Indicators.*
- *OECD Economic Outlook: Statistics and Projections.*

Websites

- OECD Economic Outlook – Sources and Methods, *www.oecd.org/eco/sources-and-methods*.

Current account balance

As a percentage of GDP

	1997	1998	1999	2000	2001	2002	2003	2004	2005	2006	2007	2008	2009	2010
Australia	-2.8	-4.6	-5.3	-3.8	-2.0	-3.6	-5.2	-6.0	-5.7	-5.3	-6.2	-4.5	-4.2	-2.6
Austria	-2.6	-1.7	-1.7	-0.5	-0.8	2.6	1.6	1.8	2.2	2.9	3.5	4.6	2.9	..
Belgium	5.5	5.2	5.1	4.0	3.4	4.3	3.5	3.2	2.1	2.0	1.7	-1.8	0.3	1.4
Canada	-1.3	-1.2	0.3	2.7	2.3	1.7	1.2	2.3	1.9	1.4	0.8	0.3	-3.0	-3.1
Chile	-4.2	-4.9	0.1	-1.5	-1.7	-0.9	-0.9	2.3	1.2	4.7	4.6	-2.1	1.7	2.2
Czech Republic	-6.3	-2.0	-2.4	-4.8	-5.3	-5.5	-6.2	-5.3	-1.3	-2.4	-3.2	-0.6	-3.2	-3.8
Denmark	0.5	-0.8	2.0	1.5	2.5	2.8	3.4	2.2	4.2	2.9	1.3	2.6	3.6	5.5
Estonia	-11.0	-8.6	-4.3	-5.3	-5.2	-10.6	-11.3	-11.4	-10.1	-15.4	-17.3	-9.6	4.5	3.5
Finland	5.5	5.6	6.2	8.1	8.6	8.9	5.2	6.3	3.6	4.6	4.2	2.9	2.7	2.9
France	2.6	2.6	3.1	1.4	1.8	1.2	0.8	0.5	-0.5	-0.5	-1.0	-2.0	-2.0	-2.1
Germany	-0.4	-0.8	-1.3	-1.8	0.0	2.0	1.9	4.6	5.0	6.2	7.5	6.2	5.6	5.6
Greece	..	..	..	-7.8	-7.2	-6.5	-6.6	-5.8	-7.5	-11.3	-14.3	-14.7	-11.0	-10.4
Hungary	-4.3	-6.9	-7.5	-8.8	-6.1	-6.8	-7.9	-8.3	-7.6	-7.6	-6.9	-7.2	0.5	2.1
Iceland	-1.8	-6.9	-6.8	-10.1	-4.6	1.5	-4.8	-9.7	-15.9	-23.6	-16.5	-24.7	-10.7	-8.0
Ireland	2.4 |	0.8	0.6	0.1	-0.6	-1.0	0.0	-0.6	-3.5	-3.6	-5.3	-5.6	-3.0	-0.7
Israel	-3.1	-0.9	-1.5	-3.2	-1.5	-1.1	0.8	1.6	3.3	5.2	2.6	0.9	3.6	3.1
Italy	2.8	1.6	0.7	-0.5	-0.1	-0.8	-1.3	-0.9	-1.7	-2.6	-2.4	-2.9	-2.1	-3.2
Japan	2.3	3.1	2.6	2.6	2.1	2.9	3.2	3.7	3.7	3.9	4.8	3.2	2.8	3.6
Korea	-1.4	12.0	5.3	2.8	1.7	1.3	2.4	4.5	2.2	1.5	2.1	0.5	3.9	2.8
Luxembourg	10.6	9.2	8.7	13.5	8.8	10.2	8.3	12.0	11.2	9.9	9.6	4.9	7.0	7.5
Mexico	-1.7	-3.5	-2.7	-2.9	-2.6	-2.0	-1.0	-0.7	-0.6	-0.5	-0.9	-1.5	-0.7	-0.6
Netherlands	6.5	3.2	3.8	1.9	2.4	2.5	5.5	7.6	7.4	9.3	6.7	4.4	4.9	7.6
New Zealand	-6.3	-3.7	-6.1	-4.6	-2.2	-3.6	-3.8	-5.7	-7.9	-8.3	-8.1	-8.7	-2.9	-2.2
Norway	6.3	0.0	5.4	14.9	16.1	12.6	12.3	12.7	16.3	17.3	14.1	17.9	13.4	12.9
Poland	..	..	..	-6.0	-3.1	-2.8	-2.5	-4.0	-1.2	-2.7	-4.7	-4.8	-2.2	-3.4
Portugal	-5.8	-6.9	-8.2	-10.4	-10.4	-8.3	-6.5	-8.3	-10.4	-10.7	-10.1	-12.6	-10.2	-9.7
Slovak Republic	-8.6	-8.9	-4.8	-3.4	-8.3	-7.9	-6.0	-7.8	-8.4	-7.9	-5.2	-5.9	-3.6	-4.0
Slovenia	0.3	-0.7	-3.7	-3.1	0.3	1.2	-0.6	-2.6	-1.7	-2.3	-4.5	-6.7	-1.7	-1.2
Spain	-0.1	-1.1	-2.9	-4.0	-4.0	-3.3	-3.5	-5.2	-7.4	-9.0	-10.0	-9.6	-5.1	-4.5
Sweden	4.1	3.8	4.1	3.8	3.7	4.0	7.0	6.6	6.7	8.4	9.2	8.8	7.0	6.3
Switzerland	9.3	9.3	10.8	12.0	8.2	8.8	13.3	13.4	14.0	14.9	9.0	1.9	11.5	14.7
Turkey	-1.1	0.7	-0.4	-3.7	2.0	-0.2	-2.5	-3.7	-4.6	-6.1	-5.9	-5.6	-2.2	-6.5
United Kingdom	-0.1	-0.4	-2.4	-2.6	-2.1	-1.7	-1.6	-2.1	-2.6	-3.4	-2.6	-1.6	-1.7	-2.5
United States	-1.7	-2.4	-3.2	-4.2	-3.7	-4.3	-4.7	-5.3	-5.9	-6.0	-5.1	-4.7	-2.7	-3.2
OECD total	0.1	-0.1	-0.6	-1.3	-1.1	-1.1	-1.0	-0.9	-1.4	-1.5	-1.3	-1.5	-0.5	..
Brazil	-3.5	-4.0	-4.4	-3.8	-4.2	-1.3	0.7	1.7	1.6	1.2	0.2	-1.7	-1.4	..
China	0.9	0.7	0.5	0.4	0.3	0.6	0.7	1.0	2.0	2.6	3.3	3.4	2.2	..
India	-0.7	-1.6	-0.7	-1.0	0.3	1.4	1.4	0.2	-1.2	-1.0	-0.9	-2.9	..	..
Indonesia	-1.9	4.1	3.7	4.8	4.3	4.0	3.4	0.6	0.1	3.0	2.4	0.0	1.9	0.9
Russian Federation	..	..	..	..	..	..	8.3	10.0	11.0	9.6	5.9	6.1	3.9	..
South Africa	-1.5	-1.7	-0.5	-0.1	0.3	0.8	-1.0	-3.0	-3.4	-5.3	-7.0	-7.1	-4.1	..

StatLink http://dx.doi.org/10.1787/888932504253

Current account balance

As a percentage of GDP

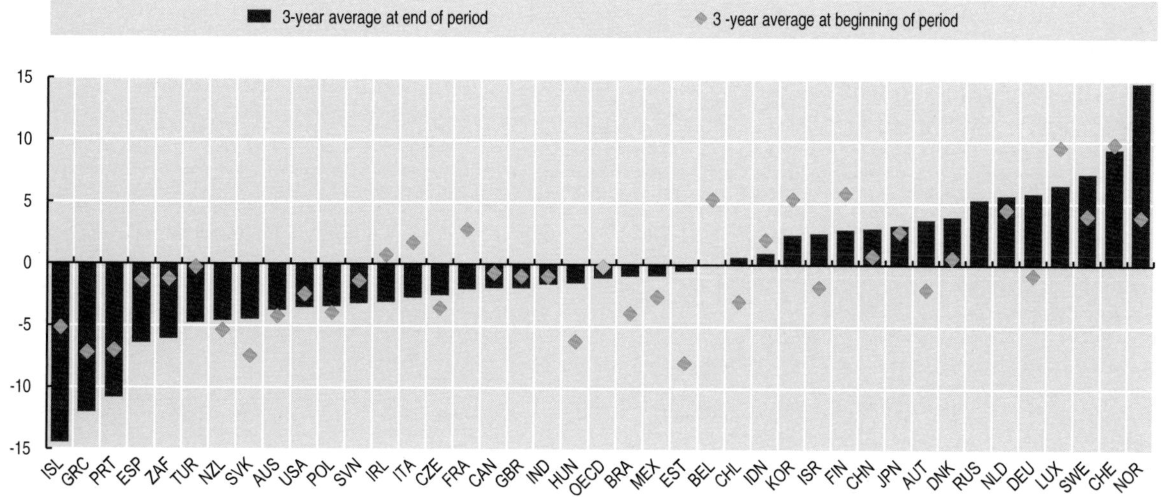

StatLink http://dx.doi.org/10.1787/888932504272

43,628,500• −
36,286,400• +
34,432,741,064• ◊
34,432,741,064• ∗
220,061,246• +
242,765• +
54,975,316• −
3,458,295,462• +
9,423,290,000• −
627,646,320• −
242,347,296• +
312,759• +
184,652,108• ◊

PRICES

PRICES, LABOUR COSTS AND INTEREST RATES

CONSUMER PRICE INDICES

PRODUCER PRICE INDICES

LABOUR COMPENSATION

LONG-TERM INTEREST RATES

PURCHASING POWER PARITIES AND EXCHANGE RATES

RATES OF CONVERSION

REAL EFFECTIVE EXCHANGE RATES

CONSUMER PRICE INDICES

Consumer price indices have a long history in official statistics. They measure the erosion of living standards through price inflation and are probably one of the best known economic statistics used by the media and general public.

Definition

Consumer price indices (CPI) measure the change in the prices of a basket of goods and services that are typically purchased by specific groups of households. The CPI shown in these tables cover virtually all households except for "institutional" households – people in prisons and military barracks, for example – and, in some countries, households in the highest income group.

The CPI for all items excluding food and energy provides a measure of underlying inflation, which is less affected by short-term effects. The index for food covers food and non-alcoholic beverages but excludes purchases in restaurants. The index for energy covers all forms of energy, including fuels for motor vehicles, heating and other household uses.

Comparability

There are a number of differences in the ways that these indices are calculated. The most important ones concern the treatment of dwelling costs, the adjustments made for changes in the quality of goods and services, the frequency with which the basket weights are updated, and the index formulae used. In particular, country methodologies for the treatment of owner-occupied housing vary significantly. The European Harmonized Indices of Consumer Prices (HICP) exclude owner-occupied housing as do national CPIs for Belgium, Chile, Estonia, France, Greece, Italy, Luxembourg, Poland, Portugal, Slovenia, Spain, Turkey, the United Kingdom and most of the countries outside the OECD area. For the United Kingdom, the national CPI is the same as the HICP. The European Union and euro area CPI refer to the HICP published by Eurostat and cover the 27 and 17 countries respectively for the entire period of the time series.

Overview

In the three years to 2010, annual inflation has been below 4.5% in all OECD countries except Hungary, Iceland, Mexico and Turkey. The CPI for the OECD total has dropped from 4.2% in the three years to 1999 to 2.0% for the three years to 2010. Over the entire period covered by the table, Japan experienced negative inflation while Hungary, Mexico, Turkey, Iceland, the Slovak Republic and Slovenia experienced substantial inflation.

Annual inflation has been significantly higher outside the OECD area, with annual increases above 10% in India and the Russian Federation in the three years to 2010.

Since 1997, consumer prices for energy have recorded large swings, with spikes in 2000, 2005, 2008 and again in 2010 (after a sharp decrease in 2009). Across OECD countries, annual inflation for food has been decreasing since 2009 after a regular increase between 2005 and 2008. When excluding these more volatile items, the underlying consumer price index (*i.e.* all items excluding food and energy) points to a progressive decline until 2010 with a period of stability at annual rates of around 2.0% between 2003 and 2008. In the three years to 2010, the CPI excluding food and energy fell in Ireland and Japan, while increasing by around 9% per year in Iceland.

Sources

- OECD (2011), *Main Economic Indicators*, OECD Publishing.

Further information

Analytical publications

- Brook, A.M. *et al.* (2004), "Oil Price Developments: Drivers, Economic Consequences and Policy Responses", *OECD Economics Department Working Papers*, No. 412.
- OECD (2011), *OECD Economic Outlook*, OECD Publishing.

Methodological publications

- International Labour Office (ILO) *et al.* (2004), *Consumer Price Index Manual: Theory and Practice*, ILO, Geneva.
- OECD (2011), *Main Economic Indicators*, OECD Publishing.
- OECD (2002), "Comparative Methodological Analysis: Consumer and Producer Price Indices", *Main Economic Indicators, Volume 2002, Supplement 2*, OECD Publishing.

Websites

- OECD Main Economic Indicators, *www.oecd.org/std/mei*.

CPI: all items

Annual growth in percentage

	1997	1998	1999	2000	2001	2002	2003	2004	2005	2006	2007	2008	2009	2010
Australia	0.3	0.9	1.5	4.5	4.4	3.0	2.8	2.3	2.7	3.5	2.3	4.4	1.8	2.8
Austria	1.3	0.9	0.6	2.3	2.7	1.8	1.4	2.1	2.3	1.4	2.2	3.2	0.5	1.8
Belgium	1.6	0.9	1.1	2.5	2.5	1.6	1.6	2.1	2.8	1.8	1.8	4.5	-0.1	2.2
Canada	1.6	1.0	1.7	2.7	2.5	2.3	2.8	1.9	2.2	2.0	2.1	2.4	0.3	1.8
Chile	6.1	5.1	3.3	3.8	3.6	2.5	2.8	1.1	3.1	3.4	4.4	8.7	0.4	1.4
Czech Republic	8.5	10.7	2.1	3.9	4.7	1.8	0.1	2.8	1.9	2.6	3.0	6.3	1.0	1.5
Denmark	2.2	1.8	2.5	2.9	2.4	2.4	2.1	1.2	1.8	1.9	1.7	3.4	1.3	2.3
Estonia	..	8.7	3.3	4.0	5.7	3.6	1.3	3.0	4.1	4.4	6.6	10.4	-0.1	3.0
Finland	1.2	1.4	1.2	3.0	2.6	1.6	0.9	0.2	0.6	1.6	2.5	4.1	0.0	1.2
France	1.2	0.6	0.5	1.7	1.6	1.9	2.1	2.1	1.7	1.7	1.5	2.8	0.1	1.5
Germany	1.9	1.0	0.6	1.4	1.9	1.5	1.0	1.7	1.5	1.6	2.3	2.6	0.4	1.1
Greece	5.5	4.8	2.6	3.2	3.4	3.6	3.5	2.9	3.5	3.2	2.9	4.2	1.2	4.7
Hungary	18.3	14.2	10.0	9.8	9.1	5.3	4.7	6.7	3.6	3.9	8.0	6.0	4.2	4.9
Iceland	1.8	1.7	3.2	5.1	6.4	5.2	2.1	3.2	4.0	6.7	5.1	12.7	12.0	5.4
Ireland	1.4	2.4	1.6	5.6	4.9	4.6	3.5	2.2	2.4	3.9	4.9	4.1	-4.5	-0.9
Israel	9.0	5.4	5.2	1.1	1.1	5.7	0.7	-0.4	1.3	2.1	0.5	4.6	3.3	2.7
Italy	2.0	2.0	1.7	2.5	2.8	2.5	2.7	2.2	2.0	2.1	1.8	3.3	0.8	1.5
Japan	1.8	0.7	-0.3	-0.7	-0.8	-0.9	-0.2	0.0	-0.3	0.2	0.1	1.4	-1.4	-0.7
Korea	4.4	7.5	0.8	2.3	4.1	2.8	3.5	3.6	2.8	2.2	2.5	4.7	2.8	2.9
Luxembourg	1.4	1.0	1.0	3.2	2.7	2.1	2.0	2.2	2.5	2.7	2.3	3.4	0.4	2.3
Mexico	20.6	15.9	16.6	9.5	6.4	5.0	4.5	4.7	4.0	3.6	4.0	5.1	5.3	4.2
Netherlands	2.2	2.0	2.2	2.3	4.2	3.3	2.1	1.2	1.7	1.2	1.6	2.5	1.2	1.3
New Zealand	1.2	1.3	-0.1	2.6	2.6	2.7	1.8	2.3	3.0	3.4	2.4	4.0	2.1	2.3
Norway	2.6	2.3	2.3	3.1	3.0	1.3	2.5	0.5	1.5	2.3	0.7	3.8	2.2	2.4
Poland	14.9	11.6	7.2	9.9	5.4	1.9	0.7	3.4	2.2	1.3	2.4	4.2	3.8	2.6
Portugal	2.3	2.8	2.3	2.9	4.4	3.6	3.3	2.4	2.3	3.1	2.5	2.6	-0.8	1.4
Slovak Republic	6.1	6.7	10.6	12.0	7.3	3.1	8.6	7.5	2.7	4.5	2.8	4.6	1.6	1.0
Slovenia	8.4	7.9	6.2	8.9	8.4	7.5	5.6	3.6	2.5	2.5	3.6	5.7	0.9	1.8
Spain	2.0	1.8	2.3	3.4	3.6	3.1	3.0	3.0	3.4	3.5	2.8	4.1	-0.3	1.8
Sweden	0.7	-0.3	0.5	0.9	2.4	2.2	1.9	0.4	0.5	1.4	2.2	3.4	-0.5	1.2
Switzerland	0.5	0.0	0.8	1.6	1.0	0.6	0.6	0.8	1.2	1.1	0.7	2.4	-0.5	0.7
Turkey	85.7	84.6	64.9	54.9	54.4	45.0	21.6	8.6	8.2	9.6	8.8	10.4	6.3	8.6
United Kingdom	1.8	1.6	1.3	0.8	1.2	1.3	1.4	1.3	2.0	2.3	2.3	3.6	2.2	3.3
United States	2.3	1.6	2.2	3.4	2.8	1.6	2.3	2.7	3.4	3.2	2.9	3.8	-0.4	1.6
Euro area	1.7	1.2	1.2	2.2	2.4	2.3	2.1	2.2	2.2	2.2	2.1	3.3	0.3	1.6
EU27 total	7.3	4.6	3.0	3.5	3.2	2.5	2.1	2.3	2.3	2.3	2.4	3.7	1.0	2.1
OECD total	4.8	4.2	3.6	4.0	3.7	2.8	2.4	2.3	2.6	2.6	2.5	3.7	0.5	1.9
Brazil	6.9	3.2	4.9	7.0	6.8	8.5	14.7	6.6	6.9	4.2	3.6	5.7	4.9	5.0
China	2.8	-0.8	-1.4	0.4	0.7	-0.8	1.2	3.9	1.8	1.5	4.8	5.9	-0.7	3.3
India	7.2	13.2	4.7	4.0	3.8	4.3	3.8	3.8	4.2	5.8	6.4	8.3	10.9	12.0
Indonesia	6.2	58.4	20.5	3.7	11.5	11.9	6.8	6.1	10.5	13.1	6.4	10.2	4.4	5.1
Russian Federation	14.7	27.8	85.7	20.8	21.5	15.8	13.7	10.9	12.7	9.7	9.0	14.1	11.7	6.9
South Africa	8.6	6.9	5.2	5.3	5.7	9.5	5.7	-0.7	2.1	3.2	6.2	10.1	7.2	4.1

StatLink http://dx.doi.org/10.1787/888932504291

CPI: all items

Average annual growth in percentage

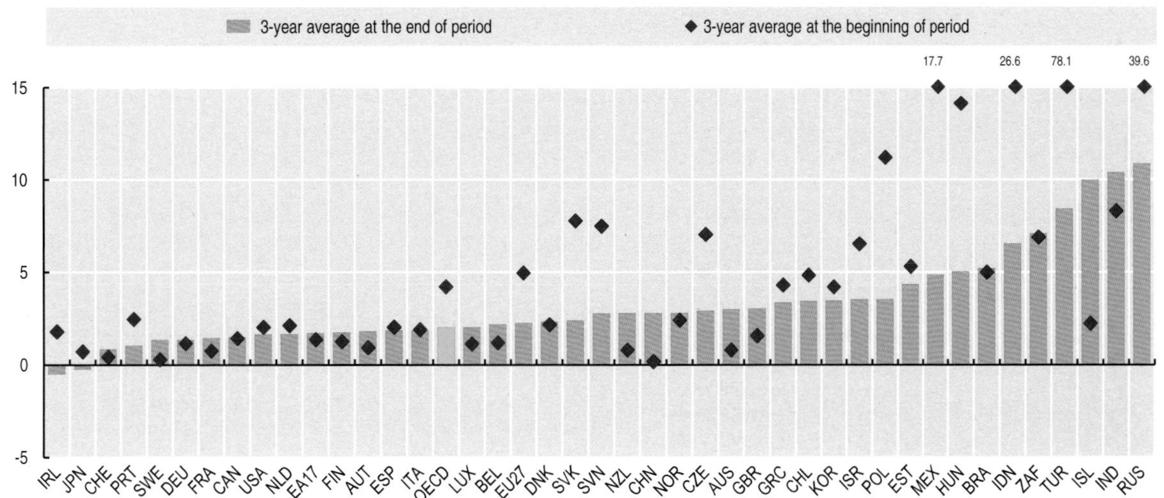

StatLink http://dx.doi.org/10.1787/888932504310

CPI: all items non-food non-energy

Annual growth in percentage

	1997	1998	1999	2000	2001	2002	2003	2004	2005	2006	2007	2008	2009	2010
Australia	-0.2	0.8	1.1	4.2	4.3	3.1	2.5	2.1	2.2	2.1	2.5	3.6	2.4	2.7
Austria	1.1	1.2	0.7	1.7	2.6	2.2	1.4	1.8	1.7	0.9	1.6	1.9	1.8	1.4
Belgium	1.3	1.4	1.3	1.5	2.3	2.2	1.7	1.6	1.9	0.9	1.6	1.8	2.1	1.3
Canada	1.6	1.4	1.5	1.7	2.1	2.7	2.4	1.3	1.3	1.3	2.0	1.0	1.7	1.2
Chile	..	..	3.8	3.1	3.3	2.7	1.6	1.2	2.4	3.0	2.4	5.2	1.2	0.5
Czech Republic	10.1	12.8	5.5	3.5	5.9	2.9	0.7	2.5	1.7	1.8	2.7	5.0	1.8	1.1
Denmark	1.8	1.7	2.5	2.1	2.2	2.5	2.4	1.4	1.3	1.3	1.4	2.2	2.4	1.9
Estonia	..	10.1	5.8	3.9	4.1	2.9	2.4	1.2	1.9	3.3	5.4	6.5	1.9	0.8
Finland	1.1	1.6	1.2	2.6	2.6	1.5	0.6	-0.2	0.2	1.3	2.6	2.5	0.4	1.2
France	0.9	0.8	0.6	0.5	1.1	2.1	2.1	2.2	1.3	0.9	1.4	1.4	1.7	0.9
Germany	1.9	1.3	0.6	0.8	1.2	1.6	0.9	1.7	1.0	0.7	1.9	1.3	1.3	0.7
Greece	7.4	5.9	2.8	2.3	3.4	3.6	3.2	3.2	3.3	2.5	2.9	2.9	2.6	3.3
Hungary	18.4	14.4	12.2	8.4	8.6	6.1	5.3	6.4	3.4	2.2	5.8	3.5	4.6	3.7
Iceland	1.1	1.9	3.3	4.7	6.5	6.2	3.0	3.2	5.1	6.3	6.6	11.4	11.4	4.7
Ireland	1.3	2.3	1.3	5.5	5.1	5.0	3.9	2.3	2.3	4.1	5.3	3.2	-4.3	-1.5
Israel	8.8	5.5	4.7	0.4	1.1	5.9	-0.3	-0.9	0.1	1.3	-0.2	2.5	4.7	2.6
Italy	2.6	2.5	1.8	2.1	2.7	2.5	2.5	2.2	2.0	1.7	1.7	2.2	1.5	1.6
Japan	1.7	0.7	-0.1	-0.5	-0.9	-0.7	-0.3	-0.4	-0.3	-0.4	-0.2	0.1	-0.6	-1.2
Korea	3.5	4.8	-0.2	1.8	3.5	3.1	3.2	2.4	2.1	2.0	2.5	3.6	3.0	1.9
Luxembourg	1.3	1.1	0.9	2.2	2.7	1.9	1.9	1.9	1.9	2.1	2.1	1.7	2.4	1.6
Mexico	21.0	15.9	16.7	10.4	6.6	3.5	4.0	3.9	3.5	3.3	3.4	4.3	4.7	4.2
Netherlands	1.9	2.1	2.3	1.9	3.7	3.4	2.1	1.6	1.3	0.5	1.5	1.8	1.8	1.7
New Zealand	0.9	1.0	-0.4	2.4	2.1	2.7	2.0	2.1	2.9	2.8	2.3	2.0	2.2	1.9
Norway	2.1	2.6	2.2	2.5	3.2	2.2	0.6	0.5	1.3	0.3	2.3	1.8	2.8	0.9
Poland	16.2	14.0	10.3	9.3	5.7	2.8	1.0	1.7	1.4	0.7	1.1	2.2	3.0	1.6
Portugal	4.0	2.7	2.9	2.8	3.6	4.4	3.3	2.5	2.5	2.7	2.3	1.8	0.8	0.6
Slovak Republic	6.6	7.5	11.8	11.5	7.0	4.2	7.3	6.7	2.7	0.5	2.2	4.1	2.8	2.1
Slovenia	..	..	..	7.3	7.3	8.1	6.3	3.9	1.7	1.4	2.8	3.7	1.8	0.2
Spain	2.6	2.6	2.5	2.9	3.5	2.8	2.9	2.4	2.5	2.8	2.5	2.3	0.8	0.6
Sweden	-0.4	-0.3	0.6	-0.3	1.8	1.6	0.3	-0.9	-0.1	0.5	3.2	1.3	-0.4	-0.4
Switzerland	0.4	0.2	0.9	1.2	1.0	0.6	0.4	0.8	0.9	0.7	0.7	1.4	1.0	0.2
Turkey	83.5	87.8	71.5	58.0	51.1	43.2	21.8	10.3	8.5	9.2	7.5	7.1	5.7	7.2
United Kingdom	1.9	1.5	0.7	0.1	1.1	1.5	1.3	1.1	1.5	1.3	1.7	1.6	1.8	2.9
United States	2.4	2.3	2.1	2.4	2.7	2.3	1.5	1.8	2.2	2.5	2.3	2.3	1.7	1.0
Euro area	1.6	1.5	1.2	1.0	1.8	2.4	1.8	1.9	1.4	1.4	1.9	1.8	1.4	1.0
EU27 total	3.3	2.4	1.5	1.2	2.1	2.5	1.8	1.8	1.5	1.4	1.9	1.9	1.6	1.3
OECD total	4.9	4.6	3.8	3.5	3.4	3.1	2.0	1.8	1.9	1.9	2.1	2.2	1.7	1.3
South Africa	..	..	..	..	..	..	5.4	-1.6	1.7	2.3	5.2	7.8	7.4	4.0

StatLink http://dx.doi.org/10.1787/888932504329

CPI: all items non-food non-energy

Average annual growth in percentage

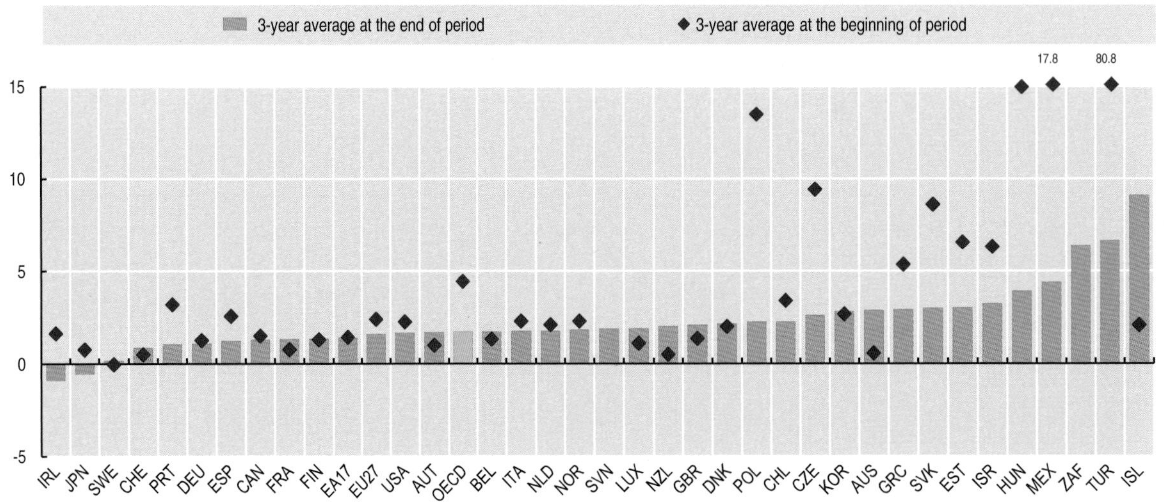

StatLink http://dx.doi.org/10.1787/888932504348

CPI: food and energy

Annual growth in percentage

	CPI: food							CPI: energy						
	2004	2005	2006	2007	2008	2009	2010	2004	2005	2006	2007	2008	2009	2010
Australia	2.0	2.0	9.4	1.8	4.3	3.4	1.3	6.6	10.2	9.7	1.2	12.7	-7.6	8.1
Austria	1.9	2.1	1.8	4.2	6.3	0.2	0.5	6.4	9.8	6.2	4.2	10.3	-9.5	7.6
Belgium	1.5	1.9	2.2	3.6	5.8	1.1	1.5	6.5	11.5	7.5	0.2	19.9	-14.0	9.4
Canada	1.8	2.3	2.3	2.6	3.9	5.5	0.9	6.8	9.7	5.2	2.3	9.8	-13.5	6.6
Chile	-1.9	2.9	2.6	9.6	17.2	4.4	2.2	6.6	10.1	8.2	8.4	14.9	-12.6	7.1
Czech Republic	3.4	-0.3	0.8	4.8	8.1	-4.0	1.5	3.4	6.5	9.8	1.7	11.0	3.1	3.8
Denmark	-1.0	0.6	2.7	4.4	7.6	-0.1	0.4	2.1	7.6	5.3	0.4	7.6	-4.5	9.0
Estonia	4.2	3.5	5.0	9.3	14.2	-4.0	3.0	8.2	13.5	8.2	7.8	23.2	-2.5	12.3
Finland	0.8	0.6	1.4	2.1	8.6	2.0	-3.4	3.8	6.8	5.9	1.8	13.5	-8.3	10.6
France	0.5	0.1	1.7	1.5	5.1	0.1	0.8	4.8	10.0	6.6	1.9	10.6	-11.5	9.6
Germany	-0.3	0.1	2.0	3.8	6.1	-1.3	1.4	4.1	9.8	8.5	4.0	9.6	-5.4	4.0
Greece	0.5	0.6	3.7	3.2	5.4	1.9	0.1	6.2	13.9	9.0	2.1	13.3	-11.8	28.8
Hungary	5.7	1.7	8.2	11.9	10.4	3.9	2.8	10.2	7.4	6.8	13.8	11.7	2.7	10.8
Iceland	1.1	-2.6	8.0	-1.1	16.0	17.5	4.2	7.5	6.1	8.0	1.7	21.7	8.2	15.5
Ireland	-0.2	-0.7	1.4	2.8	6.5	-3.5	-4.6	8.4	12.7	8.2	4.6	8.8	-7.9	9.6
Israel	-0.7	1.7	5.1	4.0	12.3	1.1	2.5	6.6	9.9	4.3	0.8	11.2	-5.3	3.9
Italy	2.2	0.0	1.7	2.9	5.4	1.8	0.2	2.3	8.7	8.1	0.9	10.1	-8.0	3.5
Japan	1.1	-1.3	0.6	0.4	2.9	0.1	-0.3	1.4	3.4	5.9	1.7	9.2	-11.2	2.7
Korea	8.0	2.6	0.5	2.5	5.0	7.6	6.4	5.4	5.2	7.0	2.8	12.9	-5.2	6.5
Luxembourg	1.8	1.6	2.4	3.4	5.4	1.4	0.8	9.0	15.3	9.4	2.5	13.2	-14.6	9.8
Mexico	7.3	5.5	3.6	6.5	8.1	8.8	3.4	7.5	6.0	7.3	3.9	6.1	2.5	5.4
Netherlands	-3.5	-1.3	1.7	1.0	5.6	1.1	-0.1	5.8	11.5	7.2	3.7	4.5	-3.9	-0.3
New Zealand	0.4	1.2	3.0	4.0	8.4	5.9	1.0	10.0	10.1	11.8	1.7	12.9	-4.7	7.0
Norway	1.8	1.6	1.4	2.7	4.2	4.2	0.2	-2.4	3.2	19.0	-11.3	18.8	-3.9	15.5
Poland	6.0	2.2	0.7	4.5	5.6	4.7	2.8	5.1	5.7	5.1	3.7	8.7	6.0	5.8
Portugal	1.1	-0.6	2.7	2.4	3.7	-3.4	-0.2	5.1	9.3	7.7	3.5	6.5	-6.7	8.9
Slovak Republic	4.8	-1.4	1.4	4.0	7.7	-3.2	1.6	14.3	7.8	15.5	2.2	3.4	1.0	-0.2
Slovenia	0.5	-0.8	2.3	7.8	10.1	0.6	1.0	6.9	11.9	8.2	3.1	10.6	-3.5	13.2
Spain	3.9	3.2	4.1	3.7	5.9	-1.1	-0.8	4.8	9.6	8.0	1.7	11.9	-9.0	12.5
Sweden	-0.4	-0.7	0.8	2.0	6.9	2.9	1.4	4.0	4.1	7.8	-1.5	11.8	-1.7	6.8
Switzerland	0.5	-0.7	0.0	0.5	3.1	-0.2	-1.1	4.2	10.4	7.1	1.9	12.4	-15.4	9.2
Turkey	6.8	4.9	9.7	12.4	12.8	8.0	10.6	4.7	14.7	11.3	6.3	22.4	5.1	10.5
United Kingdom	0.7	1.5	2.5	4.5	9.1	5.4	3.4	6.2	11.0	14.7	5.4	17.0	0.2	6.1
United States	3.8	1.9	1.8	4.2	6.4	0.5	0.3	10.9	16.9	11.2	5.5	13.9	-18.4	9.5
Euro area	1.1	0.7	2.3	2.7	5.5	0.0	0.4	4.6	10.1	7.8	2.6	10.3	-8.0	7.4
EU27 total	1.8	1.1	2.4	3.5	6.4	1.0	1.1	5.4	9.9	8.5	3.3	11.0	-5.1	7.2
OECD total	2.7	1.4	2.2	3.7	6.2	1.6	1.2	7.1	11.8	9.3	4.0	12.4	-10.4	7.8
Brazil	4.0	3.1	0.0	6.8	13.1	5.8	6.1	..	..	..	..	..	..	..
China	9.8	2.8	2.4	12.4	14.4	0.7	7.3	..	..	..	..	..	..	..
Indonesia	5.9	10.3	14.9	11.0	17.0	7.0	9.4	..	..	..	..	..	..	..
Russian Federation	10.4	13.7	9.6	9.0	20.9	11.9	7.0	..	..	..	..	..	..	..
South Africa	1.4	1.7	6.0	10.0	15.5	9.4	1.2	8.4	10.6	9.3	8.6	26.8	-2.5	15.4

StatLink http://dx.doi.org/10.1787/888932504367

Consumer price index for OECD total

Annual growth in percentage

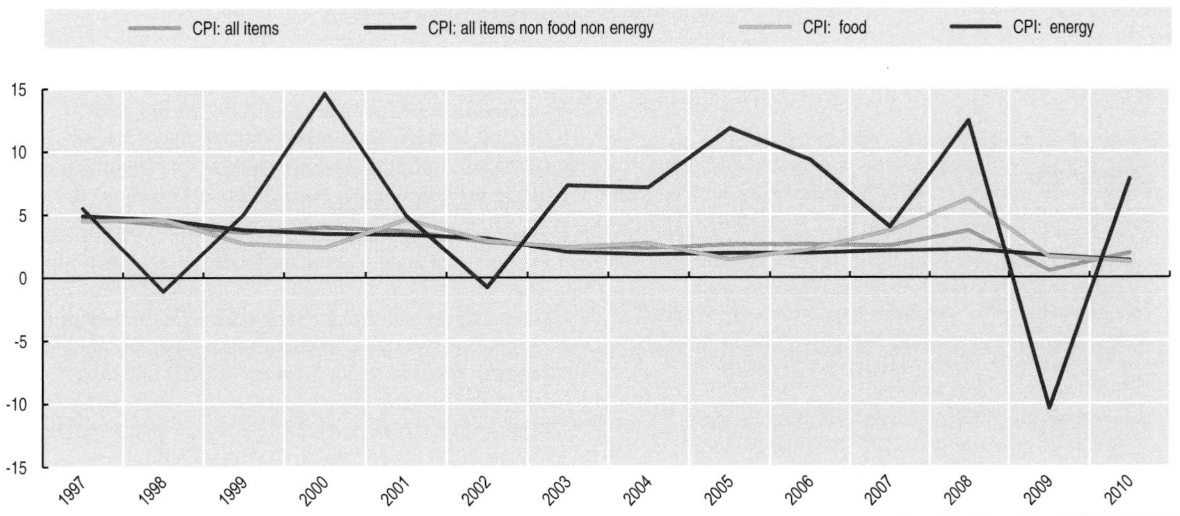

StatLink http://dx.doi.org/10.1787/888932504386

PRODUCER PRICE INDICES

A variety of price indices may be used to measure inflation in an economy. These include consumer price indices (CPI), price indices relating to specific goods and/or services, GDP deflators and producer price indices (PPI). Whereas CPIs are designed to measure changes over time in average retail prices of a fixed basket of goods and services taken as representing the consumption habits of households, PPIs aim to provide measures of average movements of prices received by the producers of various commodities. They are often seen as advanced indicators of price changes throughout the economy, including changes in the prices of consumer goods and services.

Definition

Producer price indices (PPI) measure the rate of change in prices of products sold as they leave the producer. They exclude any taxes, transport and trade margins that the purchaser may have to pay. Manufacturing covers the production of semi-processed goods and other intermediate goods as well as final products such as consumer goods and capital equipment.

The indexes shown here are weighted averages of monthly price changes in the manufacturing sector. These indexes capture the production of products intended for the domestic market.

Comparability

The precise ways in which PPIs are defined and constructed depend on their intended use. In this context, national practices may differ and these differences may affect cross-country comparability. This is especially the case for aspects such as the weighting and aggregation systems, the treatment of quality differences, the sampling and collection of individual prices, the frequency with which the weights are updated, and in the index formulae used. Differences may also arise concerning the scope of the manufacturing sector and the statistical unit used for measurement. In some countries, for example, indices may reflect price changes in the output of the manufacturing sector as opposed to manufactured products.

While the PPI series for most countries refer to domestic sales of manufacturing goods, those for Australia, Canada, Chile, New Zealand and the United States include prices applied for foreign sales (i.e. "total market").

Overview

In the three years to 2010, producer prices in the OECD area as a whole increased at an annual rate of around 2.1%, a slightly lower level to that recorded in the three years to 1999. This average stability, however, hides large differences across countries with, on one side, huge drops recorded by Mexico, Turkey, and to a smaller extent, in the Czech and Slovak Republics, Slovenia, Israel and Hungary, and increases recorded in most other countries.

During the years of the recent crisis, PPI inflation rates showed large variation across OECD countries ranging from negative rates in the Czech and Slovak Republics, Japan and Luxembourg to a rate above 17% in Iceland.

Sources

- OECD (2011), *Main Economic Indicators*, OECD Publishing.

Further information

Analytical publications

- Brook, A.M. *et al.* (2004), "Oil Price Developments: Drivers, Economic Consequences and Policy Responses", *OECD Economics Department Working Papers*, No. 412.
- OECD (2011), *OECD Economic Outlook*, OECD Publishing.

Methodological publications

- International Monetary Fund (IMF) *et al.* (2004), *Producer Price Index Manual: Theory and Practice*, IMF, Washington, DC.
- OECD, Statistical Office of the European Communities (2007), *Eurostat-OECD Methodological Guide for Developing Producer Price Indices for Services*, OECD Publishing.
- OECD (2002), *Main Economic Indicators: Comparative Methodological Analysis: Consumer and Producer Price Indices, Volume 2002, Supplement 2*, OECD Publishing.

Websites

- OECD Main Economic Indicators, *www.oecd.org/std/mei*.

PPI: domestic manufacturing

Annual growth in percentage

	1997	1998	1999	2000	2001	2002	2003	2004	2005	2006	2007	2008	2009	2010
Australia	1.2	0.7	0.7	7.1	3.1	0.2	0.5	4.0	6.0	7.9	2.3	8.3	-5.4	1.9
Austria	..	..	..	3.4	0.0	-1.4	0.3	2.2	3.7	1.8	3.4	3.4	-2.2	4.4
Belgium	1.9	-1.5	-	9.8	-1.0	0.1	0.9	4.2	6.0	5.5	3.6	5.7	-4.9	6.3
Canada	0.7	0.4	1.8	4.3	1.0	0.1	-1.2	3.2	1.6	2.3	1.5	4.3	-3.5	1.0
Chile	..	..	..	..	..	..	..	..	2.9	5.0	6.0	15.9	-4.3	0.8
Czech Republic	4.8	4.6	0.1	5.7	2.4	-1.3	-0.4	5.7	2.0	0.6	3.5	3.1	-5.5	1.5
Denmark	1.6	-0.6	0.3	4.0	2.9	1.0	0.0	1.0	3.1	3.4	4.8	5.7	-1.2	3.2
Estonia	..	..	..	..	..	-1.0	-0.6	3.4	2.3	4.8	10.1	7.6	-3.9	2.1
Finland	0.3	-1.3	-0.8	5.7	-1.5	-2.0	-1.4	0.4	4.7	5.6	4.5	8.1	-7.5	6.5
France	0.2	-1.3	-0.1	4.0	1.3	-0.6	0.8	2.8	3.0	3.3	3.0	5.3	-7.3	3.3
Germany	0.6	-0.2	-0.3	3.1	1.3	0.2	0.6	1.7	2.4	2.3	2.3	3.1	-3.4	2.5
Greece	3.8	2.9	2.4	5.9	3.4	2.1	2.1	3.8	6.4	7.9	3.5	9.7	-7.2	6.9
Hungary	..	9.1	6.9	16.1	9.4	2.0	3.7	7.3	4.3	5.7	4.3	8.6	-0.1	5.6
Iceland	..	..	..	..	..	..	..	..	..	17.5	1.8	31.0	11.3	11.8
Ireland	0.8	0.4	1.5	7.5	2.4	2.1	0.8	0.4	1.9	3.4	2.2	5.9	-3.6	1.6
Israel	6.3	4.2	7.1	3.6	-0.1	3.9	4.3	5.4	6.2	5.7	3.5	9.6	-6.3	4.0
Italy	0.8	0.6	0.2	4.0	1.1	0.8	1.4	3.3	3.1	4.0	3.3	5.0	-5.6	3.6
Japan	0.1	-1.8	-1.8	-0.4	-2.6	-2.4	-1.4	0.3	0.8	1.9	1.3	4.1	-4.7	0.0
Korea	3.4	14.5	-3.3	2.9	-2.1	-1.5	1.8	7.5	6.8	0.2	0.8	11.9	-1.6	4.3
Luxembourg	3.0	2.7	-2.3	6.4	2.5	0.9	3.3	14.8	0.0	9.0	7.6	12.9	-19.2	8.3
Mexico	17.3	14.8	15.1	8.9	4.1	3.2	6.6	8.6	4.5	6.0	5.0	8.6	5.4	4.7
Netherlands	2.2	-1.8	0.3	9.1	1.9	-0.6	1.3	3.6	4.6	4.2	5.2	7.3	-8.1	6.4
New Zealand	-0.8	0.5	1.3	8.5	5.5	0.0	-1.7	2.8	5.6	6.5	4.0	14.9	-4.8	4.3
Norway	1.5	2.6	3.0	5.0	1.9	-0.4	1.4	3.1	3.5	3.0	4.4	7.8	0.3	3.2
Poland	..	..	..	7.4	0.5	-1.7	0.8	8.0	1.4	1.9	3.6	3.4	-2.6	2.9
Portugal	3.0	-4.7	3.6	15.0	2.7	0.4	0.4	2.9	3.2	4.2	2.5	5.2	-5.6	3.5
Slovak Republic	4.9	2.3	3.9	8.6	3.8	2.5	-0.1	2.5	1.3	1.5	0.2	2.0	-5.9	0.1
Slovenia	..	5.7	2.7	8.4	9.9	4.9	2.9	4.2	3.3	2.4	4.4	5.2	-2.0	2.1
Spain	1.3	-0.4	0.9	5.7	1.7	0.6	1.4	3.7	4.7	5.0	3.4	6.0	-5.5	3.5
Sweden	0.9	-0.2	0.4	3.9	3.1	0.6	-0.9	1.8	4.0	3.9	3.3	3.9	1.0	0.3
Switzerland	..	..	..	..	..	..	..	2.0	2.0	2.7	2.8	4.4	-2.8	0.5
Turkey	80.6	66.7	57.2	56.1	66.7	48.3	23.8	11.0 |	9.6	9.3	5.6	11.8	-0.6	6.0
United Kingdom	-1.4	-2.0	-0.2	1.9	-0.6	-0.3	1.1	2.2	4.0	3.1	3.0	9.5	-1.5 |	5.5
United States	0.3	-1.1	1.7	4.1	0.8	-0.7	2.5	4.3	5.5	4.0	3.8	7.9	-4.9	5.0
Euro area	0.8	-0.5	0.1	4.5	1.1	0.1	0.9	2.7	3.2	3.5	3.0	4.8	-5.4	3.4
EU27 total	0.5	-0.6	0.1	4.3	1.1	0.1	1.0	3.0	3.4	3.5	3.2	5.2	-3.8	3.0
OECD total	2.9	1.8	2.3	5.1	2.0	0.8	1.8	3.7	4.1	3.7	3.2	6.8	-4.0	3.8
Russian Federation	..	..	69.3	38.6	13.4	8.0	16.0	19.4	13.8	11.1	13.2	21.1	-5.1	11.5
South Africa	7.2	3.8	5.3	7.6	7.1	13.3	4.6	2.0	3.7	6.4	9.8	15.2	0.7	1.9

StatLink http://dx.doi.org/10.1787/888932504405

PPI: domestic manufacturing

Average annual growth in percentage

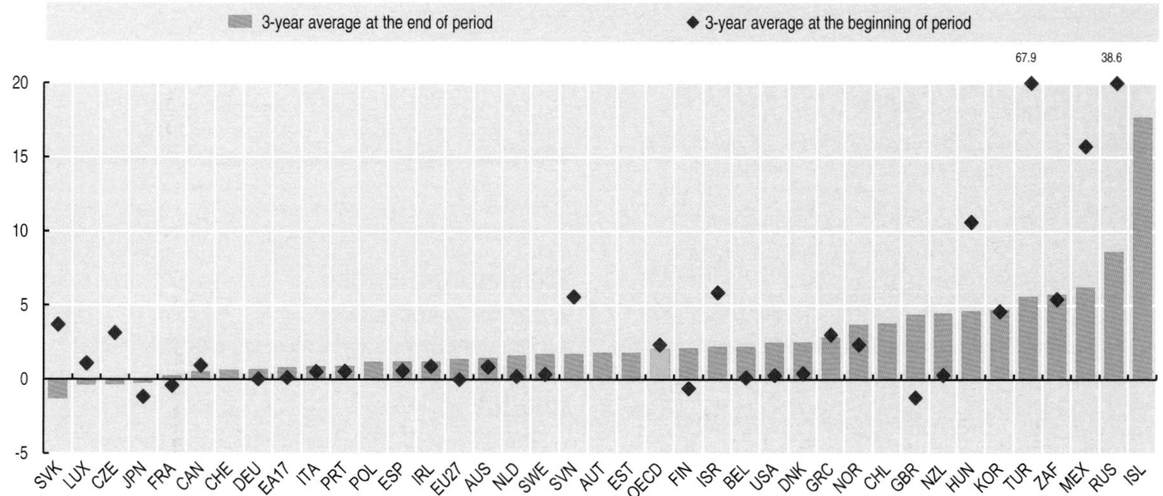

StatLink http://dx.doi.org/10.1787/888932504424

LABOUR COMPENSATION

Labour compensation per unit labour input shows the average compensation received by employees in the economy. This item is closely linked with other competitiveness indicators, *e.g.* unit labour costs, shown elsewhere in this publication.

Definition

Labour compensation per unit labour input is defined as total compensation of employees divided by total hours worked by employees in the case of Australia, Austria, Canada, the Czech Republic, Denmark, Estonia, France, Germany, Greece, Hungary, Ireland, Italy, Korea, Mexico, Norway, Poland, the Slovak Republic, Spain and Sweden. For all other countries, where data on actual hours worked by employees are not available, labour compensation per unit of labour input is defined as total compensation of employees divided by the number of employees.

The annual measures of labour compensation shown here provide one of the building blocks for international comparisons of competitiveness elaborated by the OECD.

Comparability

Compensation of employees is the sum of the gross wages and salaries and of employers' social security contributions. Data refer to the total economy.

Data on total compensation of employees, the total hours worked by them and number of employees are based on annual national accounts data. This assures a fairly good degree of comparability across countries despite differences in the ways in which countries may implement international guidelines in this field.

Differences in the definition of labour inputs (*i.e.* hours worked in some countries, number of employees in others) affect the comparability of this series across countries. For Poland, there is a break in the hours worked data in 2000-01; from 2001, hours worked for Poland are fully consistent with the 1993 *System of National Accounts*.

Labour compensation per unit labour input, total economy

Annual growth in percentage

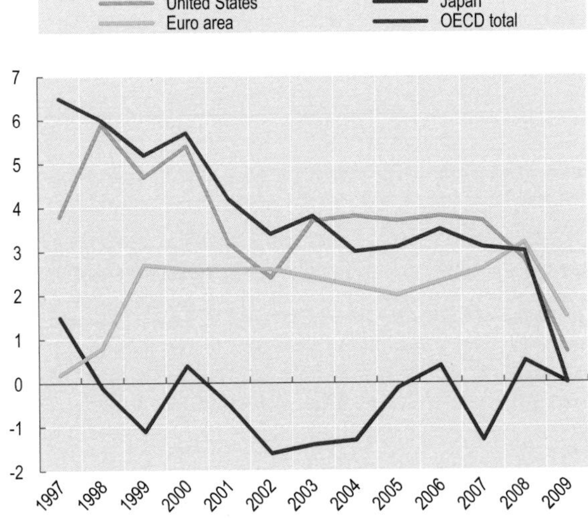

StatLink http://dx.doi.org/10.1787/888932534995

Overview

Between 2000 and 2010, labour compensation per unit of labour input in the total economy increased in all OECD countries except Japan. The average annual growth of the labour compensation over this period ranged from -1% in Japan to 24% in Turkey. About three-quarters of all OECD countries recorded annual growth rates of less than 5% in labour compensation per unit of labour. For the OECD area as a whole, labour compensation per unit of labour input grew 3.4% on average over the past ten years. The growth rates declined from 4.2% in 2001 to 3% in 2008.

Amongst individual OECD countries, the annual growth rates of labour compensation declined the most drastically in Hungary (falling from 18% in 2001 to 0% in 2010) and Turkey (from 44% in 2001 to 11% in 2006). With the exception of Australia, Japan, Poland, Spain and the United Kingdom, the annual growth rates of labour compensation exhibited a decreasing trend over the last ten years. In 2010, following the 2008 financial crisis, the annual growth rate of labour compensation per unit of labour input was negative in Estonia, Germany, Greece, Hungary and Ireland.

When looking at broader geographical regions, the average annual growth rate was 3% for EU27, 3% in the G7 countries and 2% in the euro area. Over the past 10 years, the annual growth rates of the labour compensation for these three regions have been broadly stable.

Sources

- OECD (2011), *Main Economic Indicators*, OECD Publishing.

Further information

Statistical publications

- OECD (2011), *National Accounts at a Glance*, OECD Publishing.

Websites

- Main Economic Indicators,*www.oecd.org/std/mei*.
- OECD Compendium of Productivity Indicators, *www.oecd.org/statistics/productivity/compendium*.
- OECD Productivity, *www.oecd.org/statistics/productivity*.

Labour compensation per unit labour input, total economy

Annual growth in percentage

	1997	1998	1999	2000	2001	2002	2003	2004	2005	2006	2007	2008	2009	2010
Australia	3.8	3.1	3.1	3.9	5.0	3.3	4.4	4.5	5.0	6.1	..	..	..	..
Austria	0.0	2.1	2.3	2.0	1.1	2.3	1.4	1.3	3.4	3.5	3.3	3.1	3.9	1.2
Belgium	3.2	1.3	3.5	2.1	3.7	3.8	1.8	1.7	1.8	3.3	3.4	3.6	1.8	1.2
Canada	5.2	2.9	2.3	5.3	3.1	2.2	3.1	2.7	4.7	4.8	3.8	2.8	..	..
Czech Republic	8.5	8.2	5.9	6.2	13.7	9.1	9.1	4.7	4.0	5.9	6.7	6.1	3.6	..
Denmark	1.6	3.1	2.9	3.0	3.7	4.5	3.9	3.1	3.3	3.0	4.3	3.5	3.0	2.9
Estonia	20.1	13.6	8.5	14.5	9.6	9.1	10.9	11.3	9.8	14.7	24.5	11.8	3.8	-2.7
Finland	1.6	4.5	2.1	3.8	4.6	1.7	2.7	3.7	3.7	2.9	3.7	5.1	1.7	2.0
France	2.3	2.3	2.4	5.1	3.1	6.0	3.1	1.5	3.4	4.7	1.0	2.1	..	..
Germany	1.6	1.3	2.0	3.3	2.4	2.1	2.0	0.1	0.6	1.3	0.8	2.2	3.4	-0.1
Greece	16.1	4.2	4.1	5.5	3.3	11.8	6.8	4.9	4.9	0.5	7.7	6.8	8.3	-7.3
Hungary	20.8	14.2	5.7	15.3	17.9	13.2	11.6	10.0	6.8	5.6	6.9	6.9	-1.3	-0.1
Ireland	5.0	4.9	5.1	7.0	9.2	6.2	7.0	5.3	5.6	5.4	6.4	5.0	2.3	-2.7
Israel	8.3	6.8	6.6	5.5	4.4	0.0	-1.0	1.9	2.9	6.9	1.2	2.7	0.7	..
Italy	4.9	-2.5	2.1	2.2	4.1	2.9	2.9	2.8	3.7	2.1	2.4	3.1	1.8	1.7
Japan	1.5	-0.1	-1.1	0.4	-0.5	-1.6	-1.4	-1.3	-0.1	0.4	-1.3	0.5	..	..
Korea	6.8	8.1	1.2	3.3	8.1	7.4	10.0	5.4	6.9	4.3	6.6	7.0	..	..
Luxembourg	2.6	0.9	4.0	5.3	3.5	3.1	1.1	3.3	4.6	2.6	3.7	2.1	1.8	1.6
Mexico	20.5	23.7	16.7	19.7	12.1	3.0	9.6	3.8	1.9	5.5	5.6	4.3	8.3	..
Netherlands	2.8	4.6	4.2	5.1	5.3	5.3	3.8	3.7	1.7	2.2	3.5	3.9	2.8	1.4
New Zealand	3.7	-0.6	-0.6	3.3	4.2	3.8	4.6	5.3	3.7	3.1	6.5	2.9	2.9	..
Norway	5.2	7.1	5.5	6.1	7.6	5.4	4.8	2.8	4.2	5.7	5.8	5.7	4.8	2.9
Poland	21.5	16.3	11.3	12.2 |	-14.7	2.9	1.7	1.9	1.9	1.9	4.8	9.6	5.6	..
Portugal	5.7	5.6	5.1	6.3	4.0	3.4	3.5	2.6	4.7	1.8	3.6	3.0	3.4	1.5
Slovak Republic	16.6	10.9	7.3	13.4	6.8	11.9	11.8	5.8	7.2	9.2	6.7	7.8	7.3	1.2
Slovenia	12.5	8.7	8.7	10.2	11.9	8.7	7.9	7.8	5.6	5.3	6.4	7.0	1.6	4.1
Spain	2.1	1.6	1.9	2.8	3.9	3.5	3.7	3.1	4.1	4.1	5.8	5.5	3.8	..
Sweden	4.6	2.7	0.8	8.6	5.8	4.5	4.3	2.4	3.4	2.2	3.9	1.3	2.3	1.1
Turkey	101.8	74.2	74.8 |	44.9	43.6	37.8	27.9	20.7	7.1	10.8	..	..	..	..
United Kingdom	4.0	6.7	4.5	5.4	4.8	3.6	4.7	3.7	3.3	4.3	4.9	1.9	2.8	4.2
United States	3.8	5.9	4.7	5.4	3.2	2.4	3.7	3.8	3.7	3.8	3.7	2.8	0.7	..
Euro area	0.2	0.8	2.7	2.6	2.6	2.6	2.4	2.2	2.0	2.3	2.6	3.2	1.5	..
EU27 total	4.3	3.3	3.2	4.6	3.4	4.1	3.8	2.6	3.4	3.4	3.4	3.5	3.2	..
Major seven	3.2	3.4	2.9	4.0	2.6	2.1	2.6	2.3	2.7	3.0	2.4	2.3	..	..
OECD total	6.5	6.0	5.2	5.7	4.2	3.4	3.8	3.0	3.1	3.5	3.1	3.0	..	..

StatLink http://dx.doi.org/10.1787/888932504443

Labour compensation per unit labour input, total economy

Average annual growth in percentage, 2000-10 or latest available period

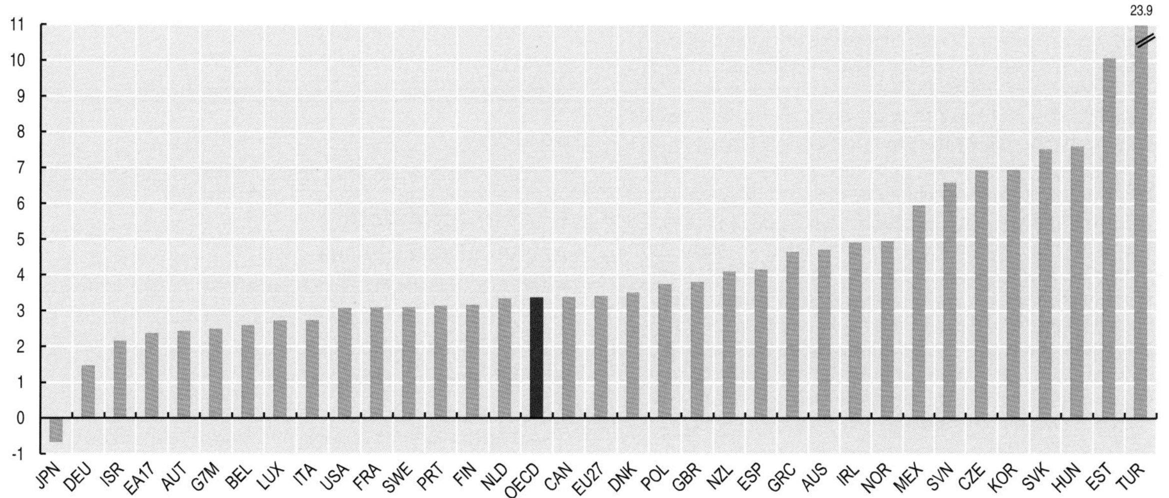

StatLink http://dx.doi.org/10.1787/888932504462

LONG-TERM INTEREST RATES

Long-term interest rates are one of the determinants of business investment. Low long-term interest rates encourage investment in new equipment and high interest rates discourage it. Investment is, in turn, a major source of economic growth.

Definition

Long-term interest rates refer to government bonds with a residual maturity of about ten years. They are not the interest rates at which the loans were issued, but the interest rates implied by the prices at which these government bonds are traded on financial markets. For example if a bond was initially bought at a price of 100 with an interest rate of 9%, but it is now trading at a price 90, the interest rate shown here will be 10% ([9/90] × 100).

The long-term interest rates shown are, where possible, averages of daily rates. In all cases, they refer to bonds whose capital repayment is guaranteed by governments.

Long-term interest rates are mainly determined by three factors: the price that lenders charge for postponing consumption; the risk that the borrower may not repay the capital; and the fall in the real value of the capital that the lender expects to occur because of inflation during the lifetime of the loan. The interest rates shown here refer to government borrowing and the risk factor is assumed to be very low. To an important extent the interest rates in this table are driven by expected inflation rates.

Comparability

Comparability of these data is considered to be high. There may be differences, however, in the size of these government bonds outstanding, and in the extent to which these rates are representatives of financial conditions in various countries.

Evolution of long-term interest rates

Percentage

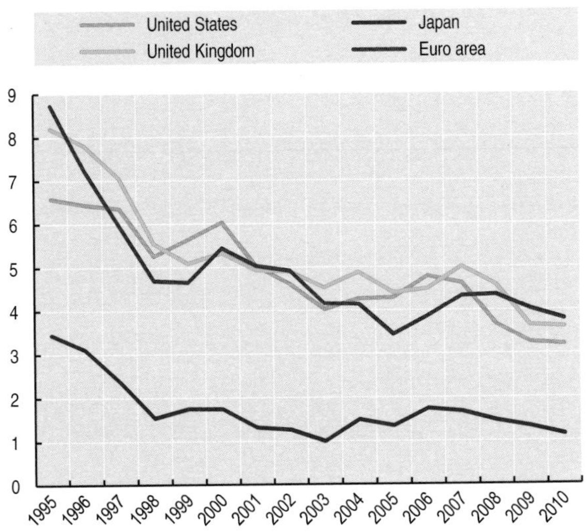

StatLink http://dx.doi.org/10.1787/888932504519

Overview

From the mid-1990s until the mid-2000s long-term interest rates fell steadily in most OECD countries. For many countries, these long-term interest rates reached an historical low level in 2005. However, the financial bubble and resulting financial crisis saw long-term interest rates rise and peak between 2007 and 2009 for a large number of countries. Since then, long-term interest rates have continued to decline in Germany, the United States and the United Kingdom but increased sharply in Greece, Ireland, Portugal, Spain and with Greece now having the highest long-term interest rate amongst OECD countries for 2010.

One of the most striking features of recent trends is the reduction in the variance of interest rates among OECD countries. This convergence of long-term interest rates mainly reflects the increasing integration of financial markets – one aspect of globalisation – and was particularly pronounced among members of the euro area. Japan and Switzerland are exceptions to this pattern, as their long-term interest rates have remained low and steady throughout the period, rather than converging towards the levels prevailing in most other OECD countries. The recent financial crisis and ongoing financial difficulties now experienced by some OECD countries may mean this convergence trend may not continue.

Sources

- OECD (2011), *Main Economic Indicators*, OECD Publishing.

Further information

Analytical publications

- OECD (2011), *OECD Economic Outlook*, OECD Publishing.
- OECD (2011), *OECD Journal: Financial Market Trends*, series, OECD Publishing.

Methodological publications

- OECD (1998), *Main Economic Indicators – Sources and Methods: Interest Rates and Share Price Indices*, OECD Publishing.

Websites

- Main Economic Indicators, *www.oecd.org/std/mei*.

Long-term interest rates

Percentage

	1997	1998	1999	2000	2001	2002	2003	2004	2005	2006	2007	2008	2009	2010
Australia	6.95	5.49	6.01	6.31	5.62	5.84	5.37	5.59	5.34	5.59	5.99	5.82	5.04	5.37
Austria	5.68	4.71	4.68	5.56	5.08	4.97	4.15	4.15	3.39	3.80	4.30	4.36	3.94	3.23
Belgium	5.59	4.70	4.71	5.57	5.06	4.89	4.15	4.06	3.37	3.81	4.33	4.40	3.82	3.35
Canada	6.14	5.28	5.54	5.93	5.48	5.30	4.80	4.58	4.07	4.21	4.27	3.60	3.23	3.24
Chile	..	..	..	..	..	..	..	..	6.05	..	6.09	7.07	5.71	6.27
Czech Republic	..	..	..	..	6.31	4.88	4.12	4.82	3.54	3.80	4.30	4.63	4.84	3.88
Denmark	6.26	5.04	4.92	5.66	5.09	5.06	4.31	4.30	3.40	3.81	4.29	4.28	3.59	2.93
Finland	5.96	4.79	4.72	5.48	5.04	4.98	4.14	4.11	3.35	3.78	4.29	4.29	3.74	3.01
France	5.58	4.64	4.61	5.39	4.94	4.86	4.13	4.10	3.41	3.80	4.30	4.23	3.65	3.12
Germany	5.66	4.58	4.50	5.27	4.80	4.78	4.07	4.04	3.35	3.76	4.22	3.98	3.22	2.74
Greece	..	8.48	6.31	6.11	5.30	5.12	4.27	4.26	3.59	4.07	4.50	4.80	5.17	9.09
Hungary	..	..	..	8.55	7.95	7.09	6.77	8.29	6.60	7.12	6.74	8.24	9.12	7.28
Iceland	8.71	7.66	8.47	11.20	10.36	7.96	6.65	7.49	7.73	9.33	9.85	11.07	8.04	5.00
Ireland	6.26	4.75	4.77	5.48	5.02	4.99	4.13	4.06	3.32	3.79	4.33	4.55	5.23	5.99
Israel	4.07	4.93	5.20	5.48	..	5.35	..	7.56	6.36	6.31	5.55	5.92	5.06	4.68
Italy	6.86	4.88	4.73	5.58	5.19	5.03	4.30	4.26	3.56	4.05	4.49	4.68	4.31	4.04
Japan	2.37	1.54	1.75	1.74	1.32	1.26	1.00	1.49	1.35	1.74	1.67	1.47	1.33	1.15
Korea	..	..	..	..	6.86	6.59	5.05	4.73	4.95	5.15	5.35	5.57	5.17	4.77
Luxembourg	5.60	4.73	4.67	5.52	4.86	4.68	3.32	2.84	2.41	3.30	..	..	..	..
Mexico	22.45	-	24.13	16.94	13.79	8.54	7.37	7.74	9.28	7.51	7.60	8.09	5.83	4.86
Netherlands	5.58	4.63	4.63	5.41	4.96	4.89	4.12	4.10	3.37	3.78	4.29	4.23	3.69	2.99
New Zealand	7.19	6.29	6.41	6.85	6.39	6.53	5.87	6.07	5.88	5.78	6.26	6.08	5.46	5.60
Norway	5.89	5.40	5.50	6.22	6.24	6.38	5.05	4.37	3.75	4.08	4.77	4.46	4.00	3.53
Poland	..	..	..	..	10.68	7.36	5.78	6.90	5.22	5.23	5.48	6.07	6.12	5.78
Portugal	6.36	4.88	4.78	5.60	5.16	5.01	4.18	4.14	3.44	3.91	4.42	4.52	4.21	5.40
Slovak Republic	..	..	..	..	8.04	6.94	4.99	5.03	3.52	4.41	4.49	4.72	4.71	3.87
Slovenia	..	..	..	..	..	..	6.40	4.68	3.81	3.85	4.53	4.61	4.38	3.83
Spain	6.40	4.83	4.73	5.53	5.12	4.96	4.13	4.10	3.39	3.78	4.31	4.36	3.97	4.25
Sweden	6.61	4.99	4.98	5.37	5.11	5.30	4.64	4.43	3.38	3.70	4.17	3.89	3.25	2.89
Switzerland	3.36 |	3.04	3.04	3.93	3.38	3.20	2.66	2.74	2.10	2.52	2.93	2.90	2.20	1.63
United Kingdom	7.05	5.55	5.09	5.33	4.93	4.90	4.53	4.88	4.41	4.50	5.01	4.59	3.65	3.61
United States	6.35	5.26	5.64	6.03	5.02	4.61	4.02	4.27	4.29	4.79	4.63	3.67	3.26	3.21
Euro area	5.96	4.70 |	4.66	5.44 |	5.03	4.92	4.16	4.14	3.44	3.86	4.33	4.36	4.03	3.79
Russian Federation	..	..	87.38	35.16	19.38	15.82	9.12	8.29	8.11	6.98	6.72	7.52	9.87	7.83
South Africa	14.70	15.12	14.90	13.79	11.41	11.50	9.62	9.53	8.07	7.94	7.99	9.10	8.70	8.62

StatLink http://dx.doi.org/10.1787/888932504481

Long-term interest rates

Percentage

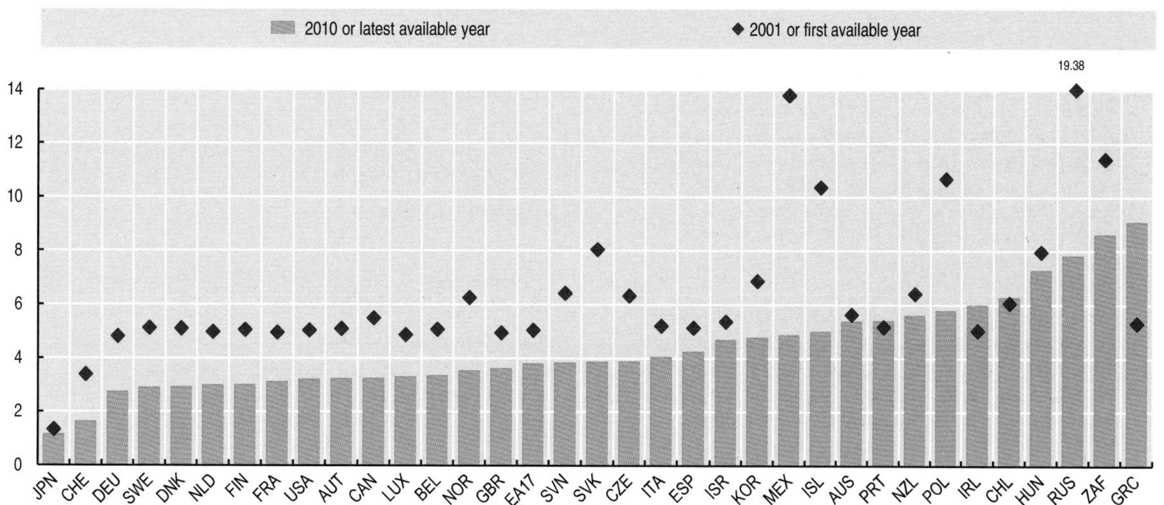

StatLink http://dx.doi.org/10.1787/888932504500

RATES OF CONVERSION

To compare a single country's real GDP over a period of years, it is necessary to remove movements that are due to price changes. In the same way, in order to compare the real GDPs of a group of countries at a single point in time, it is necessary to remove any differences in their GDPs that are due to differences in their price levels. Price indices are used to remove the effects of price changes in a single country over time; purchasing power parities (PPPs) are used to remove the effects of the different levels of prices within a group of countries at a point in time.

Definition

PPPs are currency converters that equalise price levels between countries. The PPPs shown here have been calculated by comparing the prices in OECD countries of a common basket of about 2 500 goods and services. Countries are not required to price all the items in the common basket because some of the items may be hard to find in certain countries. However, the common basket has been drawn up in such a way that each country can find prices for a wide range of the goods and services that are representative of their markets.

The goods and services to be priced cover all those that enter into final expenditure; household consumption, government services, capital formation and net exports. Prices for the different items are weighted by their shares in total final expenditures to obtain the PPPs for GDP shown here.

Comparability

The PPPs shown here have been calculated jointly by the OECD and Eurostat using standard procedures. In consultation with their member countries, OECD and Eurostat keep their methodology under review and improvements are made regularly.

Overview

Over the period 1997-2010, there were significant differences between changes in PPPs and changes in market exchange rates; even when the two indicators moved in the same direction, changes differed in their magnitude.

Market exchange rates are sometimes used to convert the GDP in different currencies to a common currency. However, comparisons of GDP based on exchange rates do not reflect the real volumes of goods and services in the GDP of the countries being compared. For many of the low-income countries, for example, the differences between GDP converted using market exchange rates and GDP converted using PPPs are considerable. For Turkey and Mexico, the difference between GDP estimates for 2010 based on either PPPs or market exchange rate is over 50%. For India, the difference is around 150%. In general, the use of market exchange rates understates the real GDP of low-income countries and overstates the real GDP of high-income countries.

Price level indices are the PPPs estimates for 2010 divided by market exchange rates for the same year, with the OECD set equal to 100. In general, there is a positive correlation between GDP levels and price level. Denmark, Norway and Switzerland, three OECD countries with high per capita income, also recorded the highest price levels in 2010, exceeding the OECD level by 35% or more, while India had price levels of around 40% of the OECD average.

Sources

- OECD (2011), "*PPP benchmark results 2008*", *OECD National Accounts Statistics* (database).
- For Brazil, China, Indonesia and South Africa: International Monetary Fund (IMF) (2011), *World Economic Outlook (WEO) Database*, IMF, Washington DC.

Further information

Analytical publications

- Bournot, S., F. Koechlin and P. Schreyer (2011), "2008 benchmark PPPs: Measurement and Uses", *OECD Statistics Brief*, No. 17.

Online databases

- OECD (2011), *OECD National Accounts Statistics* (database).
- OECD (2011), "*PPP benchmark results 2008*", *OECD National Accounts Statistics* (database).

Statistical publications

- OECD (2011), *National Accounts at a Glance*, OECD Publishing.

Websites

- Joint World Bank-OECD Seminar on Purchasing Power Parities (2001), *www.oecd.org/std/ppp/seminar2001*.
- OECD Purchasing Power Parities, *www.oecd.org/std/ppp*.

Purchasing power parities

National currency units per US dollar

	1997	1998	1999	2000	2001	2002	2003	2004	2005	2006	2007	2008	2009	2010
Australia	1.32	1.30	1.30	1.31	1.33	1.34	1.35	1.37	1.39	1.41	1.43	1.48	1.45	1.51
Austria	0.924	0.918	0.917	0.900	0.917	0.896	0.885	0.874	0.886	0.857	0.867	0.852	0.845	0.853
Belgium	0.912	0.925	0.921	0.891	0.886	0.865	0.879	0.896	0.900	0.883	0.886	0.874	0.866	0.866
Canada	1.21	1.19	1.19	1.23	1.22	1.23	1.23	1.23	1.21	1.21	1.21	1.23	1.20	1.22
Chile	273	275	278	284	289	296	307	321	334	363	372	365	372	403
Czech Republic	12.7	13.9	14.1	14.2	14.2	14.3	14.0	14.3	14.3	14.0	13.9	13.7	13.5	13.8
Denmark	8.43	8.39	8.47	8.41	8.47	8.30	8.54	8.40	8.59	8.33	8.23	8.03	7.96	7.96
Estonia	0.40	0.43	0.44	0.46	0.48	0.48	0.48	0.49	0.50	0.52	0.55	0.55	0.52	0.53
Finland	1.00	1.00	1.00	1.00	1.01	1.00	1.01	0.97	0.98	0.95	0.94	0.92	0.91	0.92
France	0.974	0.967	0.960	0.939	0.919	0.905	0.938	0.940	0.923	0.903	0.892	0.887	0.878	0.881
Germany	0.990	0.988	0.975	0.967	0.956	0.942	0.918	0.896	0.867	0.838	0.830	0.813	0.806	0.814
Greece	0.630	0.662	0.681	0.678	0.671	0.660	0.689	0.695	0.714	0.700	0.718	0.701	0.711	0.722
Hungary	85.0	94.2	101.1	107.9	110.7	114.9	120.6	126.3	128.6	128.5	131.2	128.8	128.2	133.4
Iceland	74.5	77.2	79.7	84.3	88.9	91.3	94.5	94.2	99.1	107.2	113.0	118.6	127.8	138.8
Ireland	0.854	0.882	0.930	0.962	0.993	1.004	1.015	1.006	1.010	0.985	0.958	0.950	0.903	0.865
Israel	3.16	3.35	3.50	3.44	3.42	3.46	3.63	3.53	3.72	3.70	3.62	3.59	3.73	3.73
Italy	0.816	0.808	0.818	0.817	0.808	0.845	0.854	0.872	0.867	0.834	0.816	0.788	0.779	0.812
Japan	169	167	162	155	149	144	140	134	130	125	120	117	115	111
Korea	746	774	755	746	758	770	794	796	789	775	768	786	805	827
Luxembourg	0.958	0.948	0.941	0.940	0.948	0.934	0.942	0.922	0.953	0.915	0.924	0.905	0.902	0.916
Mexico	4.35	4.96	5.63	6.10	6.31	6.55	6.81	7.22	7.13	7.22	7.33	7.47	7.69	7.95
Netherlands	0.910	0.906	0.907	0.893	0.906	0.902	0.927	0.909	0.896	0.869	0.857	0.846	0.848	0.838
New Zealand	1.45	1.45	1.43	1.44	1.47	1.47	1.50	1.51	1.54	1.49	1.50	1.49	1.49	1.51
Norway	9.09	9.39	9.33	9.13	9.18	9.11	9.12	8.98	8.90	8.69	8.77	8.71	8.85	9.01
Poland	1.52	1.66	1.74	1.84	1.86	1.83	1.84	1.86	1.87	1.84	1.84	1.85	1.86	1.87
Portugal	0.672	0.693	0.697	0.700	0.706	0.708	0.706	0.716	0.684	0.662	0.659	0.649	0.633	0.634
Slovak Republic	0.455	0.470	0.501	0.526	0.522	0.528	0.555	0.572	0.566	0.555	0.545	0.533	0.509	0.518
Slovenia	0.462	0.485	0.511	0.532	0.565	0.588	0.615	0.611	0.612	0.608	0.629	0.631	0.630	0.637
Spain	0.720	0.719	0.733	0.734	0.740	0.733	0.753	0.759	0.765	0.736	0.728	0.719	0.712	0.719
Sweden	9.30	9.37	9.29	9.14	9.35	9.35	9.34	9.10	9.38	9.09	8.88	8.80	8.94	9.04
Switzerland	1.90	1.88	1.87	1.85	1.84	1.77	1.78	1.75	1.74	1.66	1.60	1.55	1.53	1.51
Turkey	0.076	0.131	0.202	0.283	0.428	0.613	0.774	0.812	0.831	0.848	0.864	0.894	0.932	0.990
United Kingdom	0.635	0.645	0.653	0.636	0.627	0.628	0.641	0.632	0.636	0.627	0.645	0.639	0.642	0.652
United States	1.00	1.00	1.00	1.00	1.00	1.00	1.00	1.00	1.00	1.00	1.00	1.00	1.00	1.00
Brazil	0.84	0.86	0.92	0.96	1.02	1.11	1.23	1.30	1.36	1.39	1.43	1.52	1.59	1.69
China	3.45	3.39	3.30	3.29	3.29	3.25	3.27	3.40	3.45	3.47	3.62	3.82	3.76	3.95
India	11.6	12.5	13.3	13.6	13.8	14.0	14.2	14.5	14.7	14.9	15.3	16.2	16.9	18.4
Indonesia	1 340	2 322	2 612	2 775	3 102	3 233	3 338	3 531	3 934	4 347	4 698	5 432	5 829	6 237
Russian Federation	2.78	3.26	5.54	7.31	8.32	9.27	9.89	11.55	12.74	12.59	13.93	14.34	14.48	15.98
South Africa	2.61	2.78	2.93	3.12	3.28	3.58	3.70	3.81	3.87	4.00	4.19	4.47	4.75	4.99

StatLink http://dx.doi.org/10.1787/888932504538

Changes in exchange rates and purchasing power parities

Average annual growth in percentage, 2000-10

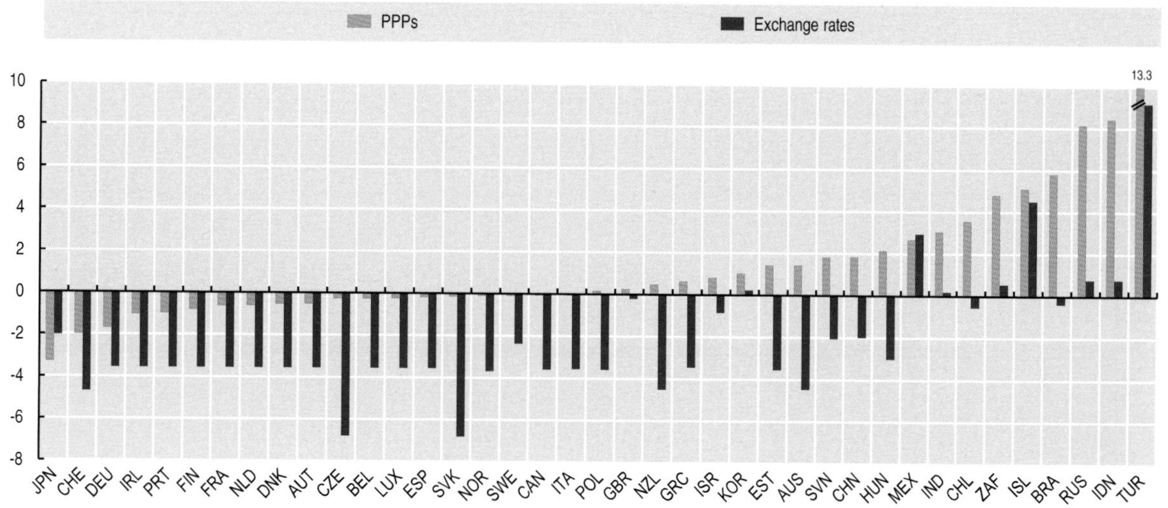

StatLink http://dx.doi.org/10.1787/888932504557

Exchange rates

National currency units per US dollar

	1997	1998	1999	2000	2001	2002	2003	2004	2005	2006	2007	2008	2009	2010
Australia	1.3474	1.5918	1.5500	1.7248	1.9334	1.8406	1.5419	1.3598	1.3095	1.3280	1.1951	1.1922	1.2822	1.0902
Austria	0.88691	0.89962	0.93863	1.08540	1.11751	1.06255	0.88603	0.80537	0.80412	0.79714	0.73064	0.68268	0.71984	0.75504
Belgium	0.88681	0.89982	0.93863	1.08540	1.11751	1.06255	0.88603	0.80537	0.80412	0.79714	0.73064	0.68268	0.71984	0.75504
Canada	1.3846	1.4835	1.4857	1.4851	1.5488	1.5693	1.4011	1.3010	1.2118	1.1344	1.0741	1.0670	1.1431	1.0302
Chile	419.30	460.29	508.78	539.59	634.94	688.94	691.40	609.53	559.77	530.28	522.46	522.46	560.86	510.25
Czech Republic	31.698	32.281	34.569	38.598	38.035	32.739	28.209	25.700	23.957	22.596	20.294	17.072	19.063	19.098
Denmark	6.6045	6.7008	6.9762	8.0831	8.3228	7.8947	6.5877	5.9911	5.9969	5.9468	5.4437	5.0981	5.3609	5.6241
Estonia	0.887	0.900	0.938	1.084	1.117	1.062	0.886	0.805	0.804	0.797	0.731	0.684	0.719	0.755
Finland	0.87314	0.89881	0.93863	1.08540	1.11751	1.06255	0.88603	0.80537	0.80412	0.79714	0.73064	0.68268	0.71984	0.75504
France	0.88980	0.89938	0.93863	1.08540	1.11751	1.06255	0.88603	0.80537	0.80412	0.79714	0.73064	0.68268	0.71984	0.75504
Germany	0.88661	0.89970	0.93863	1.08540	1.11751	1.06255	0.88603	0.80537	0.80412	0.79714	0.73064	0.68268	0.71984	0.75504
Greece	0.80134	0.86729	0.89698	1.07234	1.11751	1.06255	0.88603	0.80537	0.80412	0.79714	0.73064	0.68268	0.71984	0.75504
Hungary	186.79	214.40	237.15	282.18	286.49	257.89	224.31	202.75	199.58	210.39	183.63	172.11	202.34	207.94
Iceland	70.904	70.958	72.335	78.616	97.425	91.662	76.709	70.192	62.982	70.180	64.055	87.948	123.638	122.242
Ireland	0.83757	0.89170	0.93863	1.08540	1.11751	1.06255	0.88603	0.80537	0.80412	0.79714	0.73064	0.68268	0.71984	0.75504
Israel	3.4494	3.8001	4.1397	4.0773	4.2057	4.7378	4.5541	4.4820	4.4877	4.4558	4.1081	3.5880	3.9323	3.7390
Italy	0.87958	0.89668	0.93863	1.08540	1.11751	1.06255	0.88603	0.80537	0.80412	0.79714	0.73064	0.68268	0.71984	0.75504
Japan	120.99	130.91	113.91	107.77	121.53	125.39	115.93	108.19	110.22	116.30	117.75	103.36	93.57	87.78
Korea	951.3	1 401.4	1 188.8	1 131.0	1 291.0	1 251.1	1 191.6	1 145.3	1 024.1	954.8	929.3	1 102.1	1 276.9	1 156.1
Luxembourg	0.88681	0.89982	0.93863	1.08540	1.11751	1.06255	0.88603	0.80537	0.80412	0.79714	0.73064	0.68268	0.71984	0.75504
Mexico	7.918	9.136	9.560	9.456	9.342	9.656	10.789	11.286	10.898	10.899	10.928	11.130	13.514	12.636
Netherlands	0.88545	0.90018	0.93863	1.08540	1.11751	1.06255	0.88603	0.80537	0.80412	0.79714	0.73064	0.68268	0.71984	0.75504
New Zealand	1.5124	1.8683	1.8896	2.2012	2.3788	2.1622	1.7221	1.5087	1.4203	1.5421	1.3607	1.4227	1.6002	1.3874
Norway	7.0734	7.5451	7.7992	8.8018	8.9917	7.9838	7.0802	6.7408	6.4425	6.4133	5.8617	5.6400	6.2883	6.0442
Poland	3.2793	3.4754	3.9671	4.3461	4.0939	4.0800	3.8891	3.6576	3.2355	3.1032	2.7680	2.4092	3.1201	3.0153
Portugal	0.87445	0.89835	0.93863	1.08540	1.11751	1.06255	0.88603	0.80537	0.80412	0.79714	0.73064	0.68268	0.71984	0.75504
Slovak Republic	1.1159	1.1695	1.3730	1.5281	1.6051	1.5046	1.2206	1.0707	1.0296	0.9858	0.8197	0.7091	0.7198	0.7550
Slovenia	0.66637	0.69326	0.75851	0.92913	1.01297	1.00254	0.86427	0.80279	0.80414	0.79715	0.73064	0.68268	0.71984	0.75504
Spain	0.87997	0.89788	0.93863	1.08540	1.11751	1.06255	0.88603	0.80537	0.80412	0.79714	0.73064	0.68268	0.71984	0.75504
Sweden	7.6349	7.9499	8.2624	9.1622	10.3291	9.7371	8.0863	7.3489	7.4731	7.3783	6.7588	6.5911	7.6538	7.2075
Switzerland	1.4513	1.4498	1.5022	1.6888	1.6876	1.5586	1.3467	1.2435	1.2452	1.2538	1.2004	1.0831	1.0881	1.0429
Turkey	0.1519	0.2607	0.4188	0.6252	1.2256	1.5072	1.5009	1.4255	1.3436	1.4285	1.3029	1.3015	1.5500	1.5028
United Kingdom	0.61084	0.60382	0.61806	0.66093	0.69466	0.66722	0.61247	0.54618	0.55000	0.54349	0.49977	0.54397	0.64192	0.64718
United States	1.000	1.000	1.000	1.000	1.000	1.000	1.000	1.000	1.000	1.000	1.000	1.000	1.000	1.000
Euro area	0.88180	0.89199	0.93863	1.08540	1.11751	1.06255	0.88603	0.80537	0.80412	0.79714	0.73064	0.68268	0.71984	0.75504
Brazil	1.0780	1.1605	1.8139	1.8294	2.3496	2.9204	3.0775	2.9251	2.4344	2.1753	1.9471	1.8338	1.9994	1.7592
China	8.2898	8.2790	8.2783	8.2785	8.2771	8.2770	8.2770	8.2768	8.1943	7.9734	7.6075	6.9487	6.8314	6.7703
India	36.313	41.259	43.055	44.942	47.186	48.610	46.583	45.316	44.100	45.307	41.349	43.505	48.405	45.726
Indonesia	2 909	10 014	7 855	8 422	10 261	9 311	8 577	8 939	9 705	9 159	9 141	9 699	10 390	9 090
Russian Federation	5.785	9.705	24.620	28.129	29.169	31.349	30.692	28.814	28.284	27.191	25.581	24.853	31.740	30.368
South Africa	4.6080	5.5283	6.1095	6.9398	8.6092	10.5407	7.5648	6.4597	6.3593	6.7716	7.0454	8.2612	8.4737	7.3212

StatLink http://dx.doi.org/10.1787/888932504576

Differences in GDP when converted to US dollars using exchange rates and PPPs

PPP-based GDP minus exchange rate-based GDP as per cent of exchange rate-based GDP, 2010

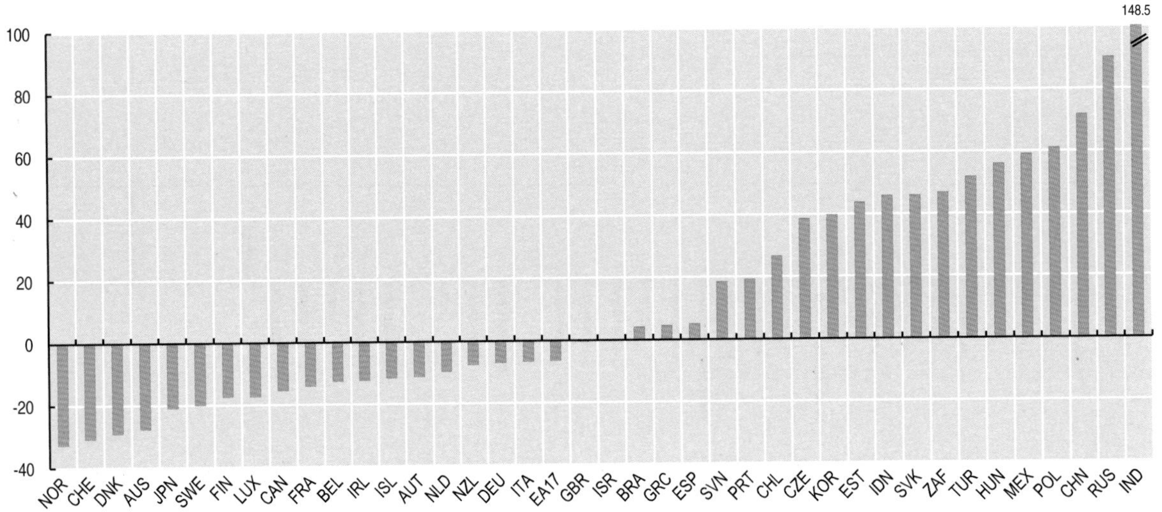

StatLink http://dx.doi.org/10.1787/888932504595

REAL EFFECTIVE EXCHANGE RATES

Effective exchange rates are a summary measure of the changes in the exchange rates of a country *vis-à-vis* its trading partners. This section shows two indicators of real effective exchange rates, namely changes in either consumer good prices or unit labour costs in manufacturing of a given country relative to those of its competitors. These indicators provide a broad interpretation of a country's price competitiveness. This competitiveness is, in turn, a major determinant of the success of different countries in raising productivity, fostering innovation and improving living standards.

There are several ways of looking at exchange rates as a measure of competitiveness. One indicator is the nominal effective exchange rate; other things being equal, a nominal depreciation of any country's currency leads, in the short run, to a decrease in the relative price of its products internationally. Potential competitiveness gains derived from nominal exchange rate depreciations however, can be eroded by local inflation. Real effective exchange rates try to eliminate this factor. A real effective exchange rate based on consumer prices try to get around this problem. However, this raises another issue, namely the assumption that the relative price of domestic tradable goods as compared with foreign tradables evolves in parallel to the relative consumer prices. Changes in relative consumer prices are therefore not the best measure of a country's competitive position, as their movement also reflects trends in the price of non-tradable goods. In an attempt to remove these differences, relative production costs can be used; these are generally measured by trade weighted relative unit labour costs in the manufacturing sector.

Definition

Nominal effective exchange rate indices are calculated by comparing, for each country, the change in its own exchange rate against the US dollar to a weighted average of changes in its competitors' exchange rates, also against the US dollar. Changes in the competitor exchange rates are weighted using a matrix measuring the importance of bilateral trade flows in the current year.

The two indicators of real effective exchange rates shown here, relative consumer price indices and relative unit labour costs in manufacturing, take into account not only changes in market exchange rates but also variations in relative prices using, respectively, consumer prices and unit labour costs in manufacturing.

The change in a country's relative consumer prices between two years is obtained by comparing the change in the country's consumer price index converted into US dollars at market exchange rates to a weighted average of changes in its competitors' consumer price indices, also expressed in US dollars. The weighted average of competitors' prices is based on a matrix for the current year expressing the importance of bilateral trade. Changes in the index of relative unit labour costs in manufacturing are calculated in the same way.

A rise in the indices represents a deterioration in that country's competitiveness. Real exchange rates are a major short-run determinant of any country's capacity to compete. Note that the indices only show changes in the international competitiveness of each country over time. Differences between countries in the levels of the indices have no significance.

Comparability

The indices shown here are constructed using a common procedure that assures a high degree of comparability both across countries and over time.

Overview

Since 2000 a number of patterns are evident. Germany experienced little variation in both measures of the real exchange rates and, to a lesser extent, so has its closest trading partner France. Japan and the United States, however, both recorded significant improvements in their competitiveness over this ten year period. For example, the Unites States saw a 36.9% depreciation and Japan a 28.8% depreciation in their real effective exchanges rates based on unit labour costs in manufacturing. Depreciation of unit labour cost-based real effective exchange rates in Turkey virtually matched that of the US, displaying less variability over last 10 years. However, unlike the United States, real effective exchange rates based on CPI have appreciated.

Following a long period of stability, Canada experienced significant deterioration of competitiveness compared to 2000 (a 80% increase in real effective exchange rates based on unit labour costs). Australia and New Zealand are not too far from Canada, although New Zealand was still more competitive in 2010 compared to 2005. At the same time, the appreciation in relative consumer prices in Canada and New Zealand is somewhat less pronounced, pointing to more stability in prices of non-tradable goods.

Sources

- OECD (2011), *OECD Economic Outlook*, OECD Publishing.

Further information

Analytical publications

- OECD (2011), *OECD Economic Surveys*, OECD Publishing.

Statistical publications

- OECD (2011), *Main Economic Indicators*, OECD Publishing.

Methodological publications

- Durand, M., C. Madaschi and F. Terribile (1998), "Trends in OECD Countries' International Competitiveness", *OECD Economics Department Working Papers*, No. 195.
- Durand, M., J. Simon and C. Webb (1992), "OECD's Indicators of International Trade and Competitiveness", *OECD Economics Department Working Papers*, No. 120.

Online databases

- *OECD Economic Outlook: Statistics and Projections.*

Websites

- OECD Economic Outlook – Sources and Methods, *www.oecd.org/eco/sources-and-methods.*

Real effective exchange rates

2005 = 100

	Based on consumer price indices							Based on unit labour costs in manufacturing						
	1990	2000	2006	2007	2008	2009	2010	1990	2000	2006	2007	2008	2009	2010
Australia	97.2	77.7	99.9	105.9	103.8	100.6	114.9	79.0	73.2	100.3	109.6	107.2	105.0	115.6
Austria	101.5	95.9	99.4	99.8	100.0	100.6	98.2	109.3	94.9	98.2	96.7	93.9	95.3	93.4
Belgium	98.8	91.1	99.7	100.5	103.3	103.4	100.4	95.7	90.2	102.5	103.9	104.6	105.9	101.4
Canada	112.1	83.6	105.6	109.6	107.3	101.9	111.8	83.5	65.7	109.4	117.4	114.7	109.1	118.0
Chile	..	104.1	104.0	102.1	103.6	100.0	106.4	..	97.7	105.5	106.7	111.4	110.4	120.9
Czech Republic	..	80.4	105.5	108.3	123.9	118.9	120.9	..	75.2	100.4	102.0	109.3	101.2	97.7
Denmark	96.7	92.1	99.7	100.2	101.8	104.9	101.2	80.9	83.7	100.9	103.2	100.9	101.2	97.8
Estonia	..	88.5	101.7	106.4	113.9	116.3	112.4	..	87.9	104.0	117.3	125.4	132.4	108.1
Finland	142.2	96.0	99.0	100.3	102.1	103.0	97.1	174.6	101.7	93.7	88.1	87.2	89.8	85.7
France	103.0	93.3	99.6	99.9	100.7	100.8	97.5	112.3	95.2	101.4	103.6	104.6	107.0	103.1
Germany	101.2	94.8	99.4	100.5	100.4	101.2	96.2	94.2	99.5	95.9	95.2	97.4	101.4	99.4
Greece	84.6	88.1	100.9	102.6	104.8	106.1	105.5	..	..	..	..	..	..	..
Hungary	..	75.1	95.4	106.3	109.0	102.4	104.1	..	79.6	92.5	98.3	100.0	92.5	86.0
Iceland	87.6	85.9	93.7	97.5	76.4	62.0	66.0	65.7	84.2	97.4	104.4	77.3	53.2	60.0
Ireland	95.1	80.6	101.8	106.9	112.7	108.8	101.4	129.5	87.8	99.6	96.0	96.0	84.4	71.0
Israel	..	128.6	99.7	100.6	112.5	109.5	114.9	..	122.1	102.6	107.2	117.3	108.7	118.2
Italy	112.4	90.6	100.0	100.5	101.3	102.4	98.4	99.7	79.1	100.9	104.0	108.3	110.2	107.1
Japan	92.5	122.4	90.5	82.9	89.3	99.9	100.8	105.4	141.4	88.0	77.6	81.9	94.8	100.4
Korea	102.4	86.4	107.8	107.1	86.7	76.0	82.4	107.8	85.0	103.9	101.6	77.4	62.5	66.2
Luxembourg	98.8	93.5	100.9	102.3	103.1	102.9	101.4	97.2	82.9	106.7	99.7	108.4	113.5	100.9
Mexico	81.6	105.1	100.0	99.1	97.4	85.4	92.4	64.0	91.3	100.7	100.7	94.3	78.7	84.4
Netherlands	94.4	86.9	99.0	99.8	100.2	101.2	96.4	98.0	88.0	98.1	97.7	100.4	99.4	93.3
New Zealand	87.1	71.6	93.2	99.7	93.1	86.7	93.7	75.4	64.5	95.4	103.5	95.9	85.8	94.5
Norway	101.8	91.0	99.9	99.7	99.7	98.1	102.7	72.4	88.5	108.4	115.1	115.1	111.0	119.4
Poland	..	94.0	102.2	105.7	115.4	97.6	103.7	..	125.8	97.9	98.7	107.7	82.7	82.6
Portugal	82.3	91.7	100.6	101.2	101.1	100.3	97.7	76.9	92.9	101.2	99.9	100.3	98.7	99.3
Slovak Republic	..	76.9	105.4	116.2	125.8	135.2	129.5	..	116.4	104.6	109.1	111.0	110.9	104.8
Slovenia	..	94.1	99.8	101.7	104.2	106.0	102.1	..	87.2	100.9	103.7	105.3	112.2	110.1
Spain	105.9	88.1	101.5	103.0	105.1	105.1	102.2	94.3	84.8	102.5	107.3	111.0	109.9	106.2
Sweden	129.0	104.2	99.6	100.5	98.1	88.8	95.0	196.8	118.1	95.2	99.3	100.2	97.8	94.7
Switzerland	99.9	96.2	97.4	93.2	97.1	101.1	105.8	78.0	86.2	99.3	97.9	101.9	108.9	115.3
Turkey	79.5	92.4	99.6	108.1	109.6	102.5	113.3	116.9	116.4	96.3	99.9	91.4	72.7	75.6
United Kingdom	97.6	104.4	100.6	102.1	89.0	80.3	81.3	82.8	98.4	102.1	104.6	90.0	83.2	87.7
United States	92.3	105.6	99.3	95.1	91.4	95.3	91.1	131.2	135.1	96.8	89.5	87.1	90.5	85.3

StatLink http://dx.doi.org/10.1787/888932504652

Real effective exchange rates based on consumer price indices

1995 = 100

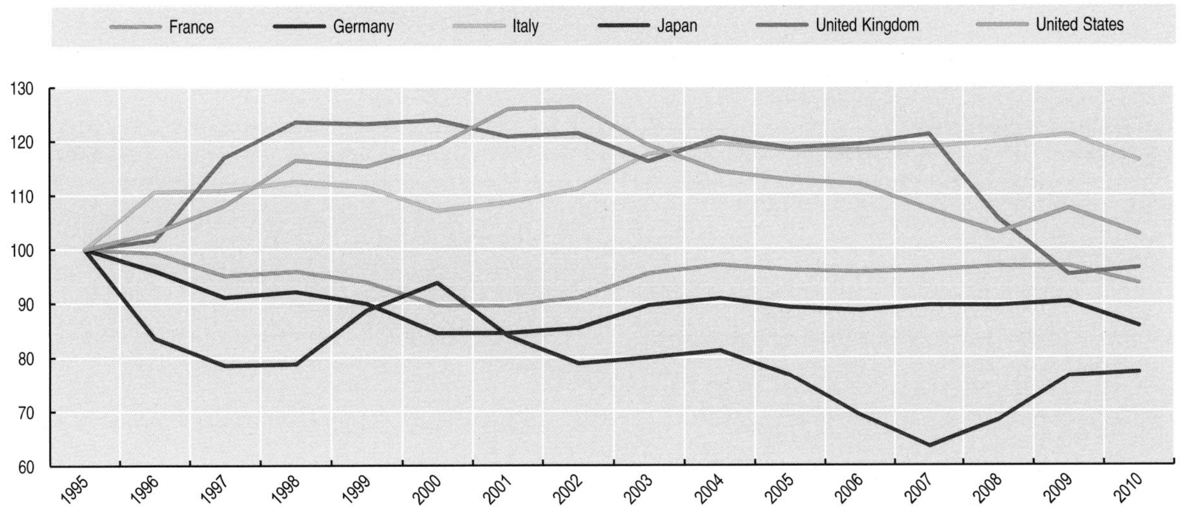

StatLink http://dx.doi.org/10.1787/888932504671

ENERGY AND TRANSPORTATION

ENERGY SUPPLY

An analysis of energy problems requires a comprehensive presentation of basic supply and demand data for all fuels in a manner which allows the easy comparison of the contribution that each fuel makes to the economy and their interrelationships through the conversion of one fuel into another. This type of presentation is suitable for the study of energy substitution, energy conservation and forecasting.

Definition

The table refers to total primary energy supply (TPES). TPES equals production plus imports minus exports minus international bunkers plus or minus stock changes. The International Energy Agency energy balance methodology is based on the calorific content of the energy commodities and a common unit of account. The unit of account adopted is the tonne of oil equivalent (toe) which is defined as 10^7 kilocalories (41.868 gigajoules). This quantity of energy is, within a few per cent, equal to the net heat content of one tonne of crude oil. The difference between the "net" and the "gross" calorific value for each fuel is the latent heat of vaporisation of the water produced during combustion of the fuel. For coal and oil, net calorific value is about 5% less than gross, for most forms of natural and manufactured gas the difference is 9-10%, while for electricity there is no difference. The International Energy Agency balances are calculated using the physical energy content method to calculate the primary energy equivalent.

Comparability

While every effort is made to ensure the accuracy of the data, quality is not homogeneous for all countries and regions. In some countries, data are based on secondary sources, and where incomplete or unavailable, the International Energy Agency has made estimates. In general, data are likely to be more accurate for production and trade than for international bunkers or stock changes. Moreover, statistics for biofuels and waste are less accurate than those for traditional commercial energy data in most countries.

Overview

Between 1971 and 2009, the world's total primary energy supply increased by 119%, reaching 12 141 Mtoe (million tonnes of oil equivalent). This equates to a compound growth rate of 2.1% per annum. By comparison, world population grew by 1.6% and gross domestic product by 3.5% per annum in real terms over the same period.

Energy supply growth was fairly constant over the period, except in 1974-1975 and in the early 1980s as a consequence of the first two oil shocks, and in the early 1990s following the dissolution of the Soviet Union. With the economic crisis in 2008/2009, world energy supply declined by 1% in 2009. However, early indicators suggest that growth in energy supply rebounded in 2010.

The share of OECD in world primary energy supply decreased from 61% in 1971 to 43% in 2009. Strong economic development in Asia led to a large increase in the share of non-OECD Asia (including China) in world energy supply, from 13% to 31% over the same period. By contrast, the combined share of non-OECD Europe and Eurasia (which includes the Former Soviet Union) decreased significantly in the late 1980s.

Sources

- IEA (2011), *Energy Balances of Non-OECD Countries*, IEA, Paris.
- IEA (2011), *Energy Balances of OECD Countries*, IEA, Paris.

Further information

Analytical publications

- IEA (2011), *Climate and Electricity Annual 2011: Data and Analyses*, IEA, Paris.
- IEA (2011), *Energy Policies of IEA Countries*, series, IEA, Paris.
- IEA (2011), *IEA Scoreboard 2011: Implementing Energy Efficiency Policy: Progress and challenges in IEA member countries*, IEA, Paris.
- IEA (2011), *World Energy Outlook*, IEA, Paris.
- IEA (2010), *Energy Technology Perspectives*, IEA, Paris.
- IEA (2009), *Energy Technology Transitions for Industry: Strategies for the Next Industrial Revolution*, IEA, Paris.

Online databases

- *IEA World Energy Statistics and Balances.*

Websites

- International Energy Agency, *www.iea.org*.

Total primary energy supply

Million tonnes of oil equivalent (Mtoe)

	1971	1990	1999	2000	2001	2002	2003	2004	2005	2006	2007	2008	2009	2010
Australia	51.6	86.2	106.2	108.1	106.8	111.5	113.1	113.7	119.6	122.3	124.9	129.4	131.1	125.8
Austria	18.8	24.8	28.6	28.6	30.3	30.6	32.3	32.5	34.0	33.8	33.3	33.5	31.7	33.1
Belgium	39.7	48.3	58.2	58.5	58.4	56.4	59.2	58.9	58.7	58.1	57.0	58.6	57.2	56.8
Canada	141.3	208.6	244.3	251.4	247.9	248.2	262.0	267.6	272.2	268.5	272.0	266.5	254.1	255.3
Chile	8.7	13.6	24.6	24.7	24.2	25.1	25.4	27.0	27.7	28.3	28.5	29.3	28.8	31.3
Czech Republic	45.4	49.6	39.0	41.0	42.1	42.5	44.4	45.5	44.9	45.8	45.8	44.6	42.0	42.3
Denmark	18.5	17.4	19.2	18.6	19.2	19.0	20.1	19.4	18.9	20.3	19.8	19.2	18.6	19.7
Estonia	..	9.9	4.8	4.7	4.9	4.7	5.2	5.3	5.2	5.0	5.6	5.4	4.7	5.5
Finland	18.2	28.4	32.5	32.3	33.0	34.8	36.9	37.1	34.2	37.3	36.8	35.3	33.2	35.6
France	158.6	223.9	249.3	251.9	260.3	261.1	265.8	269.7	270.6	267.4	264.4	267.2	256.2	264.2
Germany	305.0	351.4	335.6	337.3	347.4	339.3	342.1	343.5	338.7	341.2	331.8	334.7	318.5	331.5
Greece	8.7	21.4	25.7	27.1	28.0	28.3	29.1	29.7	30.2	30.2	30.2	30.4	29.4	27.0
Hungary	19.0	28.7	25.5	25.0	25.6	25.6	26.1	26.2	27.6	27.3	26.7	26.5	24.9	25.4
Iceland	0.9	2.1	3.0	3.1	3.2	3.3	3.3	3.4	3.5	4.2	4.9	5.3	5.2	5.4
Ireland	6.7	10.0	13.3	13.7	14.5	14.5	14.3	14.6	14.4	14.7	15.0	14.9	14.3	14.9
Israel	5.7	11.5	16.8	18.2	19.2	19.2	19.9	19.7	20.2	20.9	21.5	22.3	21.5	21.9
Italy	105.4	146.6	168.3	171.5	172.1	172.4	179.4	182.0	183.9	182.1	179.1	176.1	164.6	170.2
Japan	267.5	439.3	512.3	518.9	510.8	510.4	506.2	522.5	520.5	519.8	515.2	495.5	472.0	494.9
Korea	17.0	93.1	172.9	188.1	191.0	198.6	202.6	208.2	210.1	213.5	222.1	226.9	229.2	246.5
Luxembourg	4.1	3.4	3.1	3.3	3.5	3.6	3.8	4.3	4.4	4.3	4.2	4.2	3.9	4.2
Mexico	43.0	122.5	146.8	145.1	146.1	150.7	153.6	159.1	170.2	171.4	175.9	181.1	174.6	169.8
Netherlands	50.9	65.7	71.5	73.2	75.6	75.7	78.0	79.1	78.8	76.8	79.3	79.6	78.2	83.3
New Zealand	6.9	12.8	16.4	16.8	16.8	17.2	16.9	16.9	16.6	16.8	16.9	17.3	17.4	18.3
Norway	13.3	21.0	26.3	25.9	26.6	24.9	27.0	26.4	26.8	27.1	27.5	29.8	28.2	30.9
Poland	86.1	103.1	93.0	89.1	89.7	88.9	91.1	91.4	92.4	97.0	96.7	97.9	94.0	101.7
Portugal	6.3	16.7	24.5	24.7	24.8	25.8	25.1	25.8	26.5	24.7	25.3	24.4	24.1	23.5
Slovak Republic	14.3	21.3	17.7	17.7	18.6	18.7	18.6	18.4	18.8	18.6	17.8	18.3	16.7	17.3
Slovenia	..	5.7	6.4	6.4	6.7	6.8	6.9	7.1	7.3	7.3	7.3	7.7	7.0	7.1
Spain	42.6	90.1	116.2	121.9	125.0	128.9	133.2	139.1	141.8	141.5	143.9	138.8	126.5	128.1
Sweden	36.0	47.2	50.1	47.6	50.5	51.8	50.6	52.6	51.6	50.2	50.1	49.6	45.4	50.8
Switzerland	16.4	24.3	25.3	25.0	26.5	25.9	26.0	26.1	25.9	27.1	25.8	26.8	27.0	26.3
Turkey	19.5	52.8	70.4	76.3	70.4	74.2	77.8	80.9	84.4	93.0	100.0	98.5	97.7	104.8
United Kingdom	208.7	205.9	222.0	222.9	223.8	218.5	222.2	221.9	222.4	219.0	210.3	208.1	196.8	204.2
United States	1 587.5	1 915.0	2 210.9	2 273.3	2 230.8	2 256.0	2 261.2	2 307.8	2 318.9	2 296.7	2 337.0	2 277.0	2 162.9	2 235.0
EU27 total	..	1 636.3	1 673.6	1 685.5	1 725.2	1 720.3	1 759.9	1 778.0	1 779.4	1 779.1	1 757.2	1 751.3	1 655.8	..
OECD total	3 372.3	4 522.1	5 180.8	5 292.1	5 274.4	5 313.0	5 379.7	5 483.2	5 521.7	5 512.4	5 552.7	5 480.8	5 237.7	5 412.8
Brazil	69.8	140.2	186.7	189.2	190.3	195.8	199.1	209.7	215.4	223.0	235.4	248.6	240.2	..
China	391.7	863.0	1 085.8	1 094.9	1 091.4	1 181.7	1 345.0	1 567.9	1 696.4	1 854.0	1 964.0	2 117.5	2 257.1	..
India	156.5	316.7	448.3	457.2	464.5	477.5	489.5	518.6	537.9	565.0	596.6	619.0	675.8	..
Indonesia	35.1	101.3	152.9	155.7	160.0	166.5	166.9	178.6	181.4	187.7	188.3	191.8	202.0	..
Russian Federation	..	879.2	609.0	619.3	626.0	623.1	645.3	647.4	651.7	670.7	672.6	688.5	646.9	..
South Africa	45.1	93.9	114.3	114.4	114.9	112.4	120.8	131.4	130.4	130.7	138.8	150.0	144.0	..
World	5 532.5	8 782.3	9 836.3	10 031.8	10 074.4	10 297.6	10 645.7	11 178.5	11 468.5	11 776.2	12 049.4	12 265.1	12 140.9	..

StatLink http://dx.doi.org/10.1787/888932504690

Total primary energy supply by region

Million tonnes of oil equivalent (Mtoe)

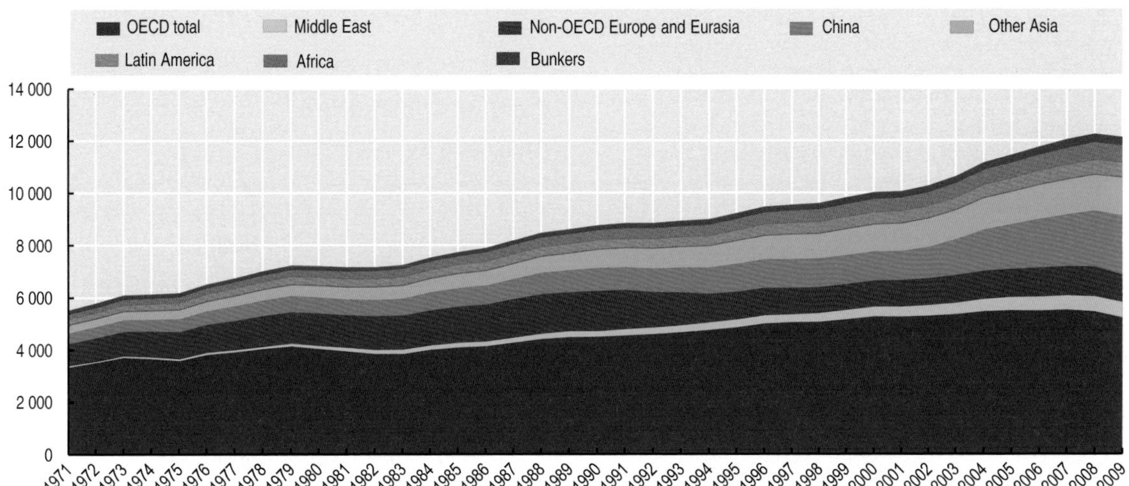

StatLink http://dx.doi.org/10.1787/888932504709

ENERGY INTENSITY

A common way to measure and compare the energy intensity of different countries, and how this changes over time, is to look at the ratio of energy supply to GDP. It should be noted that energy intensity is only a poor proxy of energy efficiency, as the latter depends on numerous elements (such as climate, output composition, outsourcing of goods produced by energy-intensive industries, etc.) that are not considered by the simple measure of energy supply to GDP shown here.

Definition

The table shows total primary energy supply (TPES) per thousand US dollars of GDP. The ratios are calculated by dividing each country's annual TPES by each country's annual GDP expressed in constant 2000 prices and converted to US dollars using purchasing power parities (PPPs) for the year 2000.

TPES consists of primary energy production adjusted for net trade, bunkers and stock changes. Production of secondary energy (*e.g.* oil/coal products, electricity from fossil fuels, etc.) is not included since the "energy equivalent" of the primary fuels used to create the secondary products or electric power has already been counted. TPES is expressed in tonnes of oil equivalent (see the International Energy Agency sources below for details on how TPES is calculated).

Comparability

Care should be taken when comparing energy intensities between countries and over time since different national circumstances (*e.g.* density of population, country size, average temperatures and economic structure) will affect the ratios. A decrease in the TPES/GDP ratio may reflect a restructuring of the economy and the transfer of energy-intensive industries such as iron and steel out of the country. The harmful effects of such outsourcing may increase the global damage to the environment if the producers abroad use less energy efficient techniques. Data for Latin America include the Caribbean islands. Data for non-OECD Europe refer to non-OECD Europe and Eurasia.

Total primary energy supply per unit of GDP

Tonnes of oil equivalent (toe) per thousand 2000 US dollar of GDP calculated using PPPs, 2009

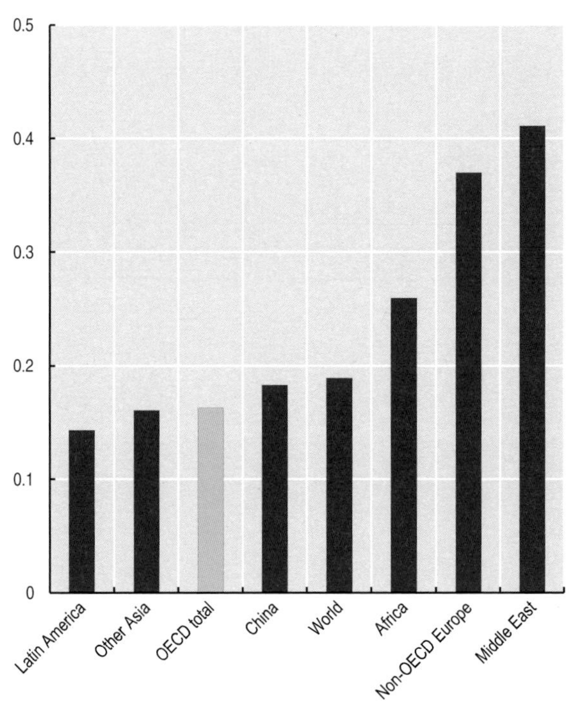

StatLink http://dx.doi.org/10.1787/888932504766

Overview

Sharp improvements in the efficiency of key end uses, shifts to electricity, and some changes in manufacturing output and consumer behaviour have occurred in many OECD countries since 1971. As a consequence, energy supply per unit of GDP fell significantly, particularly in the 1979-1990 period.

Contributing to the trend were higher fuel prices, long-term technological progress, government energy efficiency programmes and regulations.

The ratio of energy supply to GDP (TPES/GDP) fell less than the ratio of energy consumption to GDP (total final consumption/GDP, not shown here), because of increased use of electricity. The main reason for this divergence is that losses in electricity generation outweighed intensity improvements achieved in end uses such as household appliances.

Among OECD countries, the ratio of energy consumption to GDP varies considerably. Apart from energy prices, winter weather is a key element in these variations, as are raw materials processing techniques, the distance goods must be shipped, the size of dwellings, the use of private rather than public transport and other lifestyle factors.

Sources

- IEA (2011), *Energy Balances of Non-OECD Countries*, IEA, Paris.
- IEA (2011), *Energy Balances of OECD Countries*, IEA, Paris.

Further information

Analytical publications

- IEA (2011), *Energy Policies of IEA Countries*, IEA, Paris.
- IEA (2011), *IEA Scoreboard 2011: Implementing Energy Efficiency Policy: Progress and challenges in IEA member countries*, IEA, Paris.
- IEA (2011), *World Energy Outlook*, IEA, Paris.
- IEA (2010), *Energy Technology Perspectives*, IEA, Paris.
- IEA (2009), *Implementing Energy Efficiency: are IEA Countries on Track?*, IEA, Paris.

Online databases

- *IEA World Energy Statistics and Balances.*

Websites

- International Energy Agency, *www.iea.org*.

Total primary energy supply per unit of GDP

Tonnes of oil equivalent (toe) per thousand 2000 US dollars of GDP calculated using PPPs

	1971	1990	1999	2000	2001	2002	2003	2004	2005	2006	2007	2008	2009	2010
Australia	0.23	0.23	0.20	0.20	0.19	0.19	0.19	0.18	0.19	0.18	0.18	0.19	0.19	0.17
Austria	0.18	0.14	0.13	0.12	0.13	0.13	0.14	0.13	0.14	0.13	0.12	0.12	0.12	0.12
Belgium	0.29	0.21	0.21	0.21	0.20	0.19	0.20	0.20	0.19	0.18	0.18	0.18	0.18	0.18
Canada	0.41	0.32	0.29	0.29	0.28	0.27	0.28	0.28	0.27	0.26	0.26	0.25	0.25	0.24
Chile	0.20	0.18	0.18	0.17	0.16	0.17	0.16	0.16	0.16	0.15	0.15	0.15	0.15	0.15
Czech Republic	0.44	0.33	0.26	0.27	0.27	0.26	0.27	0.26	0.24	0.23	0.22	0.21	0.20	0.20
Denmark	0.23	0.15	0.13	0.12	0.12	0.12	0.13	0.12	0.12	0.12	0.11	0.11	0.12	0.12
Estonia	..	0.71	0.39	0.35	0.34	0.30	0.31	0.29	0.26	0.23	0.24	0.24	0.25	0.28
Finland	0.32	0.26	0.26	0.24	0.24	0.25	0.26	0.25	0.23	0.24	0.22	0.21	0.22	0.22
France	0.22	0.18	0.17	0.16	0.17	0.17	0.17	0.16	0.16	0.16	0.15	0.15	0.15	0.15
Germany	0.29	0.20	0.16	0.16	0.16	0.16	0.16	0.16	0.15	0.15	0.14	0.14	0.14	0.14
Greece	0.08	0.13	0.13	0.13	0.13	0.13	0.13	0.12	0.12	0.12	0.11	0.11	0.11	0.11
Hungary	0.28	0.25	0.22	0.20	0.20	0.19	0.19	0.18	0.18	0.18	0.17	0.17	0.17	0.17
Iceland	0.31	0.33	0.38	0.38	0.38	0.39	0.38	0.36	0.35	0.40	0.44	0.47	0.50	0.53
Ireland	0.27	0.18	0.13	0.13	0.13	0.12	0.11	0.11	0.10	0.10	0.09	0.10	0.10	0.11
Israel	0.15	0.14	0.12	0.12	0.13	0.13	0.13	0.13	0.12	0.12	0.12	0.12	0.11	0.11
Italy	0.15	0.12	0.12	0.12	0.12	0.12	0.12	0.12	0.12	0.12	0.11	0.11	0.11	0.11
Japan	0.22	0.15	0.16	0.16	0.16	0.16	0.15	0.15	0.15	0.15	0.14	0.14	0.14	0.14
Korea	0.21	0.22	0.23	0.23	0.23	0.22	0.22	0.21	0.21	0.20	0.20	0.20	0.20	0.20
Luxembourg	0.58	0.24	0.14	0.14	0.15	0.14	0.15	0.16	0.16	0.15	0.13	0.13	0.13	0.13
Mexico	0.13	0.17	0.16	0.15	0.15	0.15	0.15	0.15	0.16	0.15	0.15	0.15	0.16	0.14
Netherlands	0.24	0.19	0.16	0.16	0.16	0.16	0.16	0.16	0.16	0.15	0.15	0.15	0.15	0.16
New Zealand	0.16	0.21	0.21	0.21	0.20	0.19	0.18	0.18	0.17	0.17	0.16	0.17	0.17	0.17
Norway	0.23	0.19	0.17	0.16	0.16	0.15	0.16	0.15	0.15	0.15	0.14	0.16	0.15	0.16
Poland	0.41	0.37	0.24	0.22	0.22	0.21	0.21	0.20	0.20	0.19	0.18	0.17	0.16	0.17
Portugal	0.09	0.12	0.14	0.14	0.13	0.14	0.14	0.14	0.14	0.13	0.13	0.12	0.13	0.12
Slovak Republic	0.38	0.39	0.30	0.30	0.30	0.29	0.28	0.26	0.25	0.23	0.20	0.19	0.18	0.18
Slovenia	..	0.20	0.19	0.18	0.19	0.18	0.18	0.18	0.18	0.17	0.16	0.16	0.16	0.16
Spain	0.12	0.14	0.14	0.14	0.14	0.14	0.14	0.14	0.14	0.13	0.13	0.13	0.12	0.12
Sweden	0.27	0.23	0.21	0.19	0.20	0.20	0.19	0.19	0.18	0.17	0.16	0.16	0.16	0.17
Switzerland	0.11	0.12	0.12	0.11	0.12	0.11	0.11	0.11	0.11	0.11	0.10	0.10	0.10	0.10
Turkey	0.11	0.13	0.13	0.13	0.13	0.13	0.13	0.12	0.11	0.12	0.12	0.12	0.12	0.12
United Kingdom	0.27	0.17	0.15	0.15	0.14	0.14	0.13	0.13	0.13	0.12	0.11	0.11	0.11	0.12
United States	0.41	0.27	0.23	0.23	0.22	0.22	0.22	0.21	0.21	0.20	0.20	0.20	0.19	0.19
EU27 total	..	0.19	0.16	0.16	0.16	0.16	0.16	0.16	0.15	0.15	0.14	0.14	0.14	..
OECD total	0.29	0.21	0.19	0.19	0.19	0.18	0.18	0.18	0.18	0.17	0.17	0.16	0.16	0.16
Brazil	0.17	0.14	0.16	0.15	0.15	0.15	0.15	0.15	0.15	0.15	0.15	0.15	0.15	..
China	0.88	0.47	0.24	0.22	0.20	0.20	0.21	0.22	0.21	0.21	0.19	0.19	0.19	..
India	0.25	0.22	0.19	0.19	0.18	0.18	0.17	0.17	0.16	0.15	0.15	0.15	0.15	..
Indonesia	0.33	0.26	0.27	0.26	0.26	0.26	0.25	0.25	0.24	0.24	0.22	0.21	0.22	..
Russian Federation	..	0.59	0.67	0.62	0.60	0.57	0.55	0.51	0.48	0.46	0.43	0.41	0.42	..
South Africa	0.22	0.29	0.31	0.30	0.29	0.27	0.29	0.30	0.28	0.27	0.27	0.28	0.27	..
World	0.32	0.26	0.23	0.22	0.21	0.21	0.21	0.21	0.21	0.20	0.19	0.19	0.19	..

StatLink http://dx.doi.org/10.1787/888932504728

Total primary energy supply per unit of GDP

Tonnes of oil equivalent (toe) per thousand 2000 US dollars of GDP calculated using PPPs

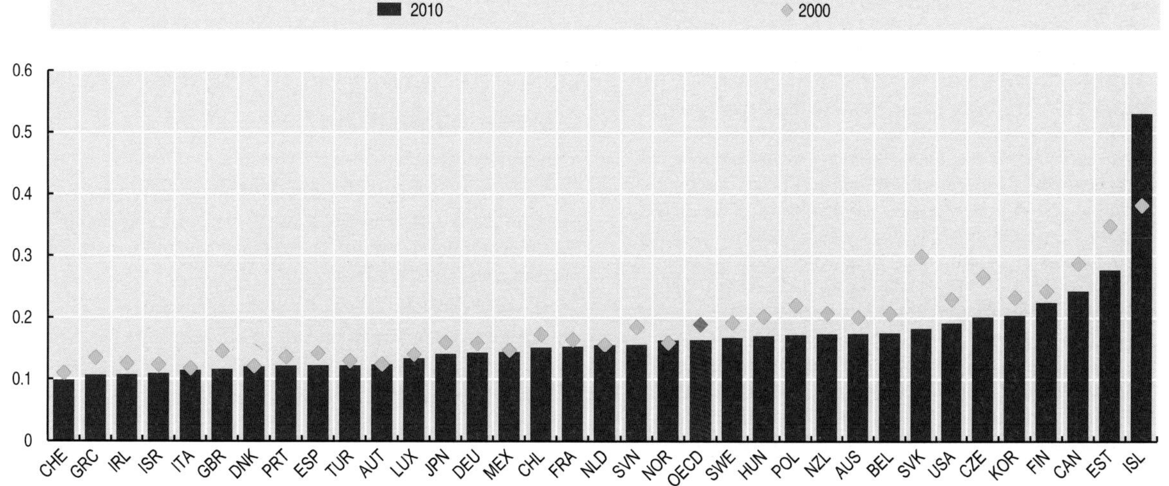

StatLink http://dx.doi.org/10.1787/888932504747

ENERGY SUPPLY PER CAPITA

Total primary energy supply per capita is a common, albeit imperfect, measure of energy efficiency in a country. For instance, neither the impact of climate on energy use (heating, cooling) nor the size of the country and the density of the population are taken into account when comparing countries. Energy analysts usually prefer to compare energy use per unit of output or per unit of GDP. However, energy supply per capita is presented here since its use is widespread.

Definition

The table refers to total primary energy supply (TPES) per head of population. The ratio is expressed in tonnes of oil equivalent (toe) per person (see the International Energy Agency sources below for details on how TPES is calculated). TPES consists of primary energy production adjusted for net trade, bunker use and stock changes. Production of secondary energy (*e.g.* oil/coal products, electricity from fossil fuels, etc.) is not included since the "energy equivalent" of the primary fuels used to create the secondary products or electric power has already been counted.

Comparability

Care should be taken when comparing energy supply per capita between countries and over time. Different national circumstances (such as density of population, country size, temperatures, economic structure and domestic energy resources) affect the ratios. Data for Latin America include the Caribbean islands. Data for non-OECD Europe refer to non-OECD Europe and Eurasia.

Overview

The level of energy supply on a per capita basis varied significantly across OECD countries. The countries with the highest ratios are those with the smallest populations. In 2010, the energy supply per capita for Iceland was 16.8 toe/capita, while that for Luxembourg was 8.3 toe/capita. The high ratio for Iceland is explained partly by the climate but also by the availability of cheap – and non-polluting – thermal energy from hot springs. In the case of Luxembourg, the high ratio is partly due to low sales taxes on petroleum products, which encourage motorists and other consumers from neighbouring countries – Belgium, France and Germany – to buy their supplies in Luxembourg.

The United States and Canada also have high energy supply per capita, with ratios of 7.2 and 7.5 toe/capita in 2010. At the other end of the scale, the countries with the lowest TPES/capita were Turkey (1.4 toe/capita) and Mexico (1.6 toe/capita).

Between 1971 and 2010, trends in energy supply per capita differ markedly across OECD countries. Compared to 1971, TPES/capita in 2010 was almost ten times higher in Korea and three times higher in Iceland, Portugal and Turkey. On the other hand, the ratio decreased over this period in five OECD countries: Luxembourg (-30%), the United Kingdom (-12%), the United States (-6%), Denmark (-5%) and the Czech Republic (-5%).

In general, the TPES/capita ratios of non-OECD countries are lower than for OECD countries. In 2009, the ratio for China (1.7 toe/capita) was four times greater than in 1971 and that of Indonesia (0.9 toe/capita) was three times greater. For the ratio India (0.6 toe/capita) doubled over the period while that of South Africa (2.9 toe/capita) and Brazil (1.2 toe/capita) grew slightly more slowly.

Total primary energy supply per capita

Tonnes of oil equivalent (toe) per capita, 2009

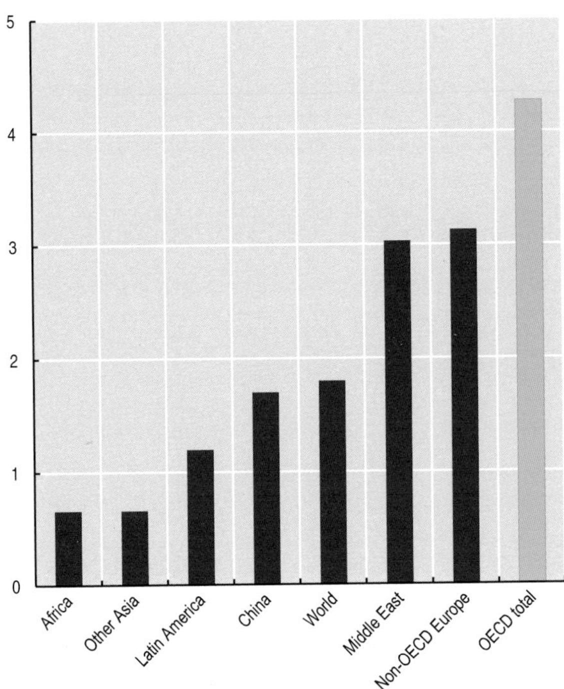

StatLink http://dx.doi.org/10.1787/888932504823

Sources

- IEA (2011), *Energy Balances of Non-OECD Countries*, IEA, Paris.
- IEA (2011), *Energy Balances of OECD Countries*, IEA, Paris.

Further information

Analytical publications

- IEA (2011), *Energy Policies of IEA Countries*, series, IEA, Paris.
- IEA (2011), *IEA Scoreboard 2011: Implementing Energy Efficiency Policy: Progress and challenges in IEA member countries*, OECD Publishing.
- IEA (2011), *World Energy Outlook*, IEA, Paris.
- IEA (2009), *Implementing Energy Efficiency: are IEA Countries on Track?*, IEA, Paris.

Online databases

- *IEA World Energy Statistics and Balances.*

Websites

- International Energy Agency, *www.iea.org*.

Total primary energy supply per capita

Tonnes of oil equivalent (toe) per capita

	1971	1990	1999	2000	2001	2002	2003	2004	2005	2006	2007	2008	2009	2010
Australia	3.91	5.02	5.58	5.61	5.47	5.64	5.65	5.62	5.82	5.86	5.88	5.98	5.93	5.67
Austria	2.51	3.23	3.58	3.57	3.76	3.78	3.97	3.98	4.13	4.08	4.01	4.02	3.79	3.94
Belgium	4.11	4.84	5.69	5.71	5.68	5.46	5.71	5.65	5.60	5.51	5.37	5.47	5.30	5.23
Canada	6.44	7.53	8.04	8.19	7.99	7.92	8.28	8.38	8.44	8.24	8.26	8.00	7.53	7.53
Chile	0.89	1.03	1.62	1.60	1.56	1.59	1.59	1.68	1.70	1.72	1.72	1.75	1.70	1.83
Czech Republic	4.62	4.78	3.79	3.99	4.11	4.17	4.35	4.46	4.39	4.46	4.43	4.28	4.00	4.04
Denmark	3.73	3.38	3.60	3.49	3.58	3.54	3.73	3.60	3.49	3.72	3.62	3.50	3.37	3.56
Estonia	..	6.24	3.49	3.44	3.60	3.46	3.83	3.91	3.83	3.75	4.19	4.06	3.54	4.09
Finland	3.94	5.69	6.28	6.23	6.37	6.68	7.07	7.09	6.53	7.08	6.95	6.64	6.21	6.65
France	3.03	3.85	4.13	4.15	4.26	4.24	4.28	4.32	4.30	4.22	4.15	4.17	3.97	4.09
Germany	3.89	4.43	4.09	4.10	4.22	4.11	4.15	4.16	4.11	4.14	4.03	4.08	3.89	4.06
Greece	0.97	2.07	2.36	2.48	2.56	2.58	2.64	2.69	2.72	2.71	2.70	2.71	2.61	2.39
Hungary	1.84	2.76	2.49	2.45	2.51	2.52	2.58	2.59	2.73	2.71	2.66	2.64	2.48	2.55
Iceland	4.38	8.19	10.69	11.03	11.36	11.40	11.33	11.50	11.76	13.68	15.74	16.46	16.38	16.79
Ireland	2.26	2.85	3.54	3.60	3.74	3.70	3.59	3.58	3.47	3.46	3.45	3.35	3.21	3.29
Israel	1.85	2.45	2.74	2.90	2.97	2.92	2.97	2.89	2.92	2.96	2.99	3.05	2.90	2.89
Italy	1.95	2.58	2.96	3.01	3.02	3.02	3.11	3.13	3.14	3.09	3.02	2.94	2.74	2.84
Japan	2.55	3.55	4.04	4.09	4.01	4.00	3.96	4.09	4.07	4.07	4.03	3.89	3.71	3.90
Korea	0.52	2.17	3.71	4.00	4.03	4.17	4.23	4.33	4.36	4.42	4.58	4.67	4.70	5.05
Luxembourg	11.88	8.93	7.25	7.53	7.91	8.12	8.46	9.29	9.40	9.15	8.72	8.58	7.95	8.31
Mexico	0.86	1.51	1.52	1.48	1.47	1.50	1.51	1.55	1.64	1.64	1.66	1.70	1.63	1.57
Netherlands	3.86	4.39	4.52	4.60	4.71	4.69	4.81	4.86	4.83	4.70	4.84	4.84	4.73	5.01
New Zealand	2.41	3.80	4.28	4.35	4.31	4.32	4.17	4.12	3.99	4.01	3.99	4.03	4.02	4.19
Norway	3.41	4.95	5.90	5.76	5.90	5.49	5.92	5.76	5.79	5.82	5.85	6.25	5.85	6.39
Poland	2.63	2.71	2.43	2.33	2.35	2.32	2.39	2.39	2.42	2.54	2.54	2.57	2.46	2.67
Portugal	0.72	1.67	2.41	2.41	2.41	2.49	2.41	2.46	2.51	2.33	2.39	2.30	2.27	2.21
Slovak Republic	3.13	4.03	3.27	3.29	3.46	3.48	3.47	3.41	3.50	3.46	3.31	3.39	3.09	3.19
Slovenia	..	2.86	3.24	3.22	3.38	3.42	3.46	3.57	3.64	3.65	3.63	3.83	3.41	3.44
Spain	1.24	2.31	2.91	3.03	3.07	3.12	3.17	3.26	3.27	3.21	3.21	3.04	2.75	2.77
Sweden	4.45	5.51	5.66	5.36	5.68	5.80	5.65	5.85	5.71	5.53	5.47	5.38	4.88	5.41
Switzerland	2.58	3.58	3.53	3.47	3.64	3.52	3.51	3.50	3.46	3.58	3.38	3.47	3.45	3.39
Turkey	0.54	0.96	1.11	1.19	1.08	1.12	1.16	1.19	1.23	1.34	1.42	1.39	1.36	1.44
United Kingdom	3.73	3.60	3.78	3.79	3.79	3.68	3.73	3.71	3.69	3.61	3.45	3.39	3.18	3.28
United States	7.64	7.65	7.92	8.05	7.82	7.83	7.77	7.86	7.83	7.68	7.74	7.47	7.03	7.20
EU27 total	..	3.46	3.47	3.49	3.56	3.54	3.61	3.63	3.62	3.60	3.54	3.51	3.31	..
OECD total	3.77	4.25	4.53	4.59	4.55	4.55	4.57	4.63	4.63	4.59	4.59	4.50	4.28	4.40
Brazil	0.71	0.94	1.09	1.09	1.08	1.09	1.10	1.14	1.16	1.19	1.24	1.30	1.24	..
China	0.47	0.76	0.87	0.87	0.86	0.92	1.04	1.21	1.30	1.41	1.49	1.60	1.70	..
India	0.28	0.37	0.45	0.45	0.45	0.46	0.46	0.48	0.49	0.51	0.53	0.54	0.58	..
Indonesia	0.29	0.57	0.75	0.76	0.77	0.79	0.78	0.83	0.83	0.85	0.84	0.84	0.88	..
Russian Federation	..	5.95	4.13	4.22	4.28	4.28	4.45	4.49	4.54	4.70	4.73	4.85	4.56	..
South Africa	2.00	2.67	2.66	2.60	2.56	2.47	2.62	2.82	2.76	2.74	2.88	3.07	2.92	..
World	1.47	1.67	1.64	1.65	1.64	1.65	1.69	1.75	1.78	1.80	1.82	1.84	1.80	..

StatLink http://dx.doi.org/10.1787/888932504785

Total primary energy supply per capita

Tonnes of oil equivalent (toe) per capita

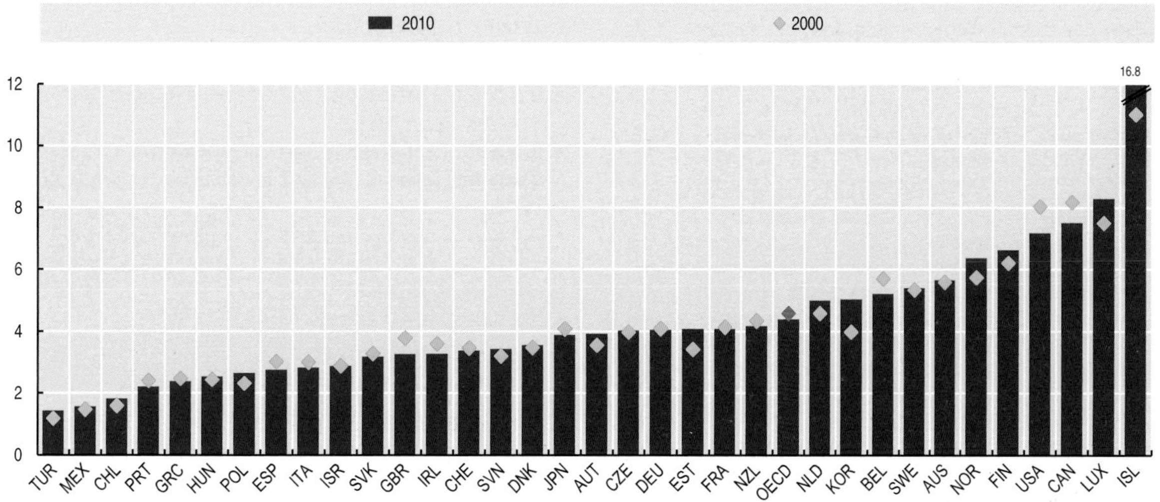

StatLink http://dx.doi.org/10.1787/888932504804

ELECTRICITY GENERATION

The amount of electricity generated by a country, and the breakdown of that production by type of fuel, reflects the natural resources, imported energy, national policies on security of energy supply, population size, electrification rate as well as the stage of development and rate of growth of the economy in each country.

Definition

The table shows data on electricity generation from fossil fuels, nuclear, hydro (excluding pumped storage), geothermal, solar, biofuels, etc. It includes electricity produced in electricity-only plants and in combined heat and power plants. Both main activity producer and autoproducer plants are included, where data are available. Main activity producers generate electricity for sale to third parties as their primary activity. Autoproducers generate electricity wholly or partly for their own use as an activity which supports their primary activity. Both types of plants may be privately or publicly owned.

Electricity generation is measured in terawatt hours, which expresses the generation of 1 terawatt (10^{12} watts) of electricity for one hour.

Comparability

Some countries, both OECD member and non-member countries, have trouble reporting electricity generation from autoproducer plants. In some OECD non-member countries it is also difficult to obtain information on electricity generated by biofuels and waste. For example, electricity generated from waste biofuel in sugar refining remains largely unreported in some of these countries.

World electricity generation by source of energy

As a percentage of world electricity generation

1971

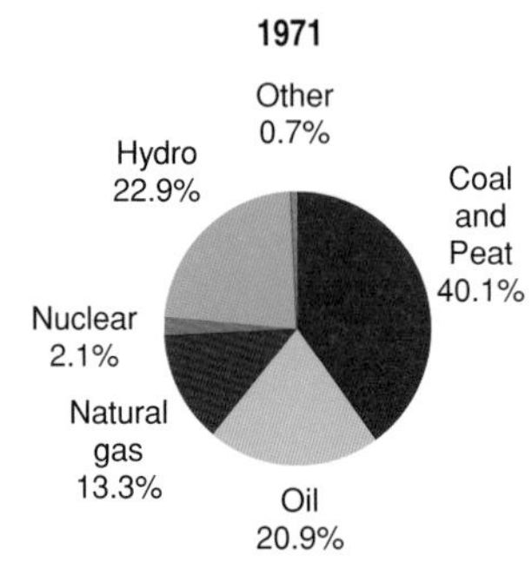

2009

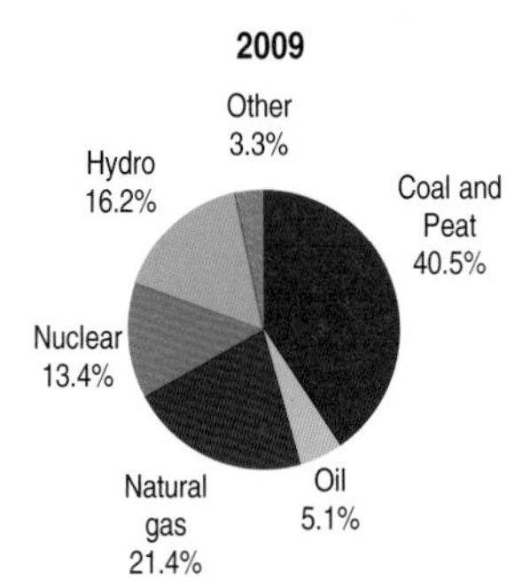

StatLink http://dx.doi.org/10.1787/888932504880

Overview

World electricity generation rose at an average annual rate of 3.6% from 1971 to 2009, greater than the 2.1% growth in total primary energy supply. This increase was largely due to more electrical appliances, the development of electrical heating in several developed countries and of rural electrification programmes in developing countries.

The share of electricity production from fossil fuels has gradually fallen, from just under 75% in 1971 to 67% in 2009. This decrease was due to a progressive move away from oil, which fell from 20.9% to 5.1%.

Oil for world electricity generation has been displaced in particular by dramatic growth in nuclear electricity generation, which rose from 2.1% in 1971 to 17.7% in 1996. However, the share of nuclear has been falling steadily since then and represented 13.4% in 2009. The share of coal remained stable, at 40-41% while that of natural gas increased from 13.3% to 21.4%. The share of hydro-electricity decreased from 22.9% to 16.2%. Due to large development programmes in several OECD countries, the share of new and renewable energies, such as solar, wind, geothermal, biofuels and waste increased. However, these energy forms remain of limited importance: in 2009, they accounted for only 3.3% of total electricity production for the world as a whole.

Sources

- IEA (2011), *Energy Balances of Non-OECD Countries*, IEA, Paris.
- IEA (2011), *Energy Balances of OECD Countries*, IEA, Paris.

Further information

Analytical publications

- IEA (2011), *Climate and Electricity Annual 2011: Data and Analyses*, IEA, Paris.
- IEA (2011), *Empowering Electricity Customers: Customer Choice and Demand Response in Competitive Markets*, IEA, Paris.
- IEA (2011), *IEA Scoreboard 2011: Implementing Energy Efficiency Policy: Progress and challenges in IEA member countries*, IEA, Paris.
- IEA (2011), *World Energy Outlook*, IEA, Paris.

Statistical publications

- IEA (2011), *Electricity Information*, IEA, Paris.

Online databases

- *IEA World Energy Statistics and Balances.*

Websites

- International Energy Agency, *www.iea.org*.

Electricity generation

Terawatt hours (TWh)

	1971	1990	1999	2000	2001	2002	2003	2004	2005	2006	2007	2008	2009	2010
Australia	53.0	154.3	203.6	209.9	224.3	227.4	226.3	236.3	245.2	247.0	250.8	257.1	260.9	256.2
Austria	28.2	49.3	59.7	59.9	60.9	60.4	57.7	61.5	63.6	61.7	62.2	64.1	65.6	67.0
Belgium	33.2	70.3	83.4	82.8	78.6	80.9	83.6	84.4	85.7	84.3	87.5	83.6	89.8	95.1
Canada	221.8	482.0	578.9	605.6	589.8	601.2	589.5	599.9	626.0	615.9	642.0	640.9	603.1	598.0
Chile	8.5	18.4	38.4	40.1	42.5	43.7	46.8	51.2	52.5	55.3	58.5	59.7	60.7	62.5
Czech Republic	36.4	62.3	64.2	72.9	74.2	76.0	82.8	83.8	81.9	83.7	87.8	83.2	81.7	85.3
Denmark	18.6	26.0	38.9	36.1	37.7	39.3	46.2	40.4	36.2	45.6	39.3	36.6	36.4	38.6
Estonia	..	17.4	8.3	8.5	8.5	8.6	10.2	10.3	10.2	9.7	12.2	10.6	8.8	13.0
Finland	21.7	54.4	69.5	70.0	74.5	74.9	84.2	85.8	70.6	82.3	81.2	77.4	72.1	80.4
France	155.8	417.2	521.3	536.1	545.7	553.9	561.8	569.1	571.5	569.3	564.4	569.5	537.4	567.6
Germany	327.2	547.7	552.5	572.3	581.9	582.0	601.5	608.5	613.4	629.4	629.5	631.2	586.4	614.1
Greece	11.6	34.8	49.4	53.4	53.1	53.9	57.9	58.8	59.4	60.2	62.7	62.9	61.1	60.8
Hungary	15.0	28.4	37.8	35.2	36.4	36.2	34.1	33.7	35.8	35.9	40.0	40.0	35.9	37.4
Iceland	1.6	4.5	7.2	7.7	8.0	8.4	8.5	8.6	8.7	9.9	12.0	16.5	16.8	17.1
Ireland	6.3	14.2	21.8	23.7	24.6	24.8	24.9	25.2	25.6	27.1	27.9	29.9	27.9	28.3
Israel	7.6	20.9	39.2	42.7	44.0	45.5	47.0	47.3	48.6	50.6	53.8	57.0	55.0	57.2
Italy	123.9	213.1	259.3	269.9	271.9	277.5	286.3	295.8	296.8	307.7	308.2	313.5	288.3	295.0
Japan	382.9	835.5	1 028.1	1 049.0	1 030.3	1 049.0	1 038.4	1 068.3	1 089.9	1 094.8	1 125.5	1 075.5	1 041.0	1 071.3
Korea	10.5	105.4	235.6	288.5	309.1	329.8	343.2	366.6	387.9	402.3	425.9	443.9	451.7	478.0
Luxembourg	1.3	0.6	0.4	0.4	0.9	2.8	2.8	3.4	3.3	3.5	3.2	2.7	3.2	3.2
Mexico	31.0	115.8	190.0	204.2	211.9	215.9	213.7	232.6	243.8	249.5	257.2	261.9	261.0	268.4
Netherlands	44.9	71.9	86.7	89.6	93.7	95.9	96.8	102.4	100.2	98.4	105.2	107.6	113.5	114.7
New Zealand	15.5	32.3	37.8	39.2	39.9	40.7	40.8	42.5	43.0	43.6	43.8	43.9	43.5	44.8
Norway	63.5	121.6	122.3	139.6	119.2	130.3	106.8	110.2	137.2	121.2	136.1	141.2	132.0	124.1
Poland	69.5	134.4	140.0	143.2	143.7	142.5	150.0	152.6	155.4	160.8	158.8	154.7	151.1	157.0
Portugal	7.9	28.4	42.9	43.4	46.2	45.7	46.5	44.8	46.2	48.6	46.9	45.5	49.5	52.7
Slovak Republic	10.9	25.5	28.1	30.8	31.9	32.2	31.0	30.5	31.4	31.3	27.9	28.8	25.9	27.3
Slovenia	..	12.4	13.3	13.6	14.5	14.6	13.8	15.3	15.1	15.1	15.0	16.4	16.4	16.2
Spain	61.6	151.2	205.9	222.2	233.2	241.6	257.9	277.2	288.9	295.5	301.8	311.1	291.0	295.3
Sweden	66.5	146.0	154.8	145.2	161.6	146.7	135.4	151.7	158.4	143.3	148.8	149.9	136.6	152.8
Switzerland	31.2	55.0	68.7	66.1	71.1	65.5	65.4	63.9	57.8	62.1	66.4	67.0	66.7	66.6
Turkey	9.8	57.5	116.4	124.9	122.7	129.4	140.6	150.7	162.0	176.3	191.6	198.4	194.8	211.2
United Kingdom	255.8	317.8	365.3	374.4	382.4	384.6	395.5	391.3	395.4	393.4	393.0	384.6	372.0	378.1
United States	1 703.4	3 202.8	3 873.6	4 025.9	3 838.8	4 026.4	4 054.6	4 148.1	4 268.9	4 275.0	4 323.9	4 343.0	4 165.4	4 337.1
EU27 total	..	2 567.8	2 914.3	2 996.7	3 077.5	3 099.0	3 187.5	3 254.2	3 274.5	3 318.9	3 333.4	3 339.4	3 178.3	..
OECD total	3 836.9	7 629.3	9 343.3	9 726.9	9 607.5	9 888.0	9 982.6	10 252.7	10 516.6	10 590.3	10 790.9	10 809.8	10 403.1	10 772.2
Brazil	51.6	222.8	334.7	349.2	328.2	346.0	365.3	387.9	403.4	419.9	445.8	463.4	466.5	..
China	138.4	621.2	1 239.8	1 356.2	1 472.4	1 641.4	1 908.5	2 201.0	2 499.7	2 864.3	3 276.3	3 458.8	3 695.9	..
India	66.4	289.4	536.6	561.2	579.9	597.3	634.0	666.6	698.2	753.2	813.9	843.3	899.4	..
Indonesia	1.8	32.7	85.8	93.4	101.4	108.3	114.1	121.3	127.8	132.7	140.9	148.4	155.5	..
Russian Federation	..	1 082.2	845.3	876.5	889.3	889.3	914.3	929.9	951.2	993.9	1 013.4	1 038.4	990.0	..
South Africa	54.6	165.4	200.4	207.8	208.2	215.7	231.2	240.9	242.1	250.9	260.5	255.5	246.8	..
World	5 245.0	11 819.1	14 708.1	15 403.4	15 511.9	16 114.5	16 701.2	17 490.9	18 256.4	18 960.6	19 801.7	20 164.0	20 052.8	..

StatLink http://dx.doi.org/10.1787/888932504842

World electricity generation by source of energy

Terawatt hours (TWh)

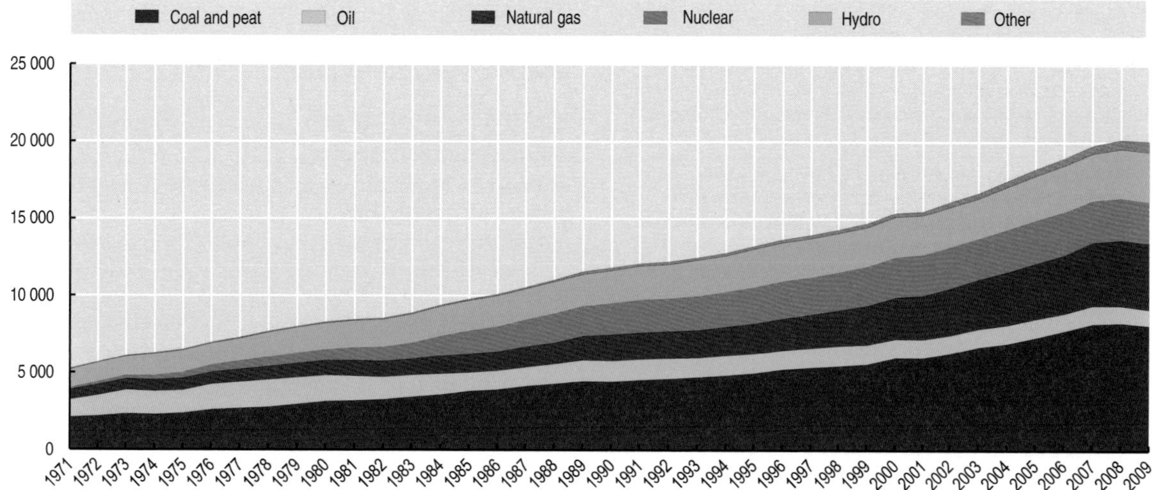

StatLink http://dx.doi.org/10.1787/888932504861

NUCLEAR ENERGY

In 2009 nuclear energy provided nearly 22% of total electricity supply in OECD countries. However, the use of nuclear energy varies widely. In all, 18 of the 34 OECD countries use nuclear energy at present, with ten generating one-third or more of their power from this source in 2009. Collectively, OECD countries produce about 83% of the world's nuclear energy. The remainder is produced in 12 non-OECD economies.

Definition

The table gives the nuclear electricity generation in terawatt hours (TWh) in each of the OECD member countries and in selected non-OECD countries. The chart shows the percentage share of nuclear in total electricity generation, in each country and in the OECD as a whole.

The table also provides information on the number of nuclear power plants in operation and under construction as of 1 June 2011.

Comparability

Some generation data are provisional and may be subject to revision. Generation data for Japan are for the fiscal year.

Nuclear electricity generation

Terawatt hours, 2009

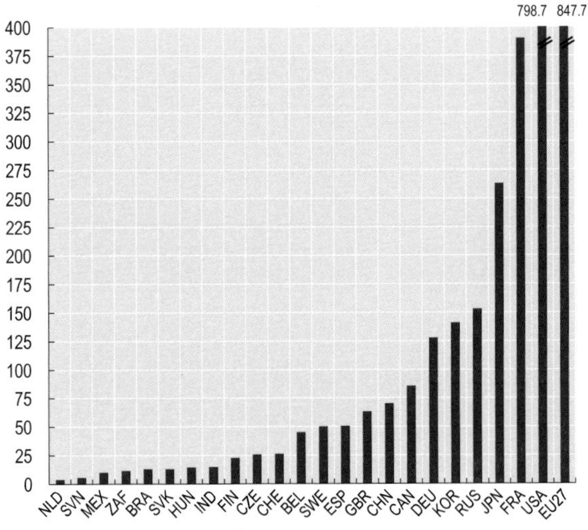

StatLink http://dx.doi.org/10.1787/888932535014

Overview

Nuclear energy expanded rapidly in the 1970s and 1980s, but in the last 20 years only small numbers of new nuclear power plants have entered operation. The role of nuclear energy in reducing greenhouse gas emissions and in increasing energy diversification and security of supply has been increasingly recognised over the last few years, leading to renewed interest in building new nuclear plants in several countries. However, the accident at the Fukushima Daiichi nuclear power plant in Japan following a major earthquake and tsunami in March 2011 has led some countries to review their nuclear programmes. Nuclear capacity may thus grow more slowly than had been expected, at least over the next few years.

Much of the future growth in nuclear capacity is expected to be in non-OECD countries. China in particular has begun a rapid expansion of nuclear capacity, starting construction of 10 additional units during 2010. India and the Russian Federation also have several new plants under construction. Among OECD countries, Finland, France, Japan, Korea, the Slovak Republic and the United States all presently have one or more nuclear plant under construction, while Poland and Turkey are actively planning their first nuclear units.

The analysis in the *Nuclear Energy Technology Roadmap*, prepared jointly by the International Energy Agency and Nuclear Energy Agency, indicates that, as part of a scenario to limit global temperature rise to two degrees, nuclear generating capacity could rise from 374 GW at present to around 1 200 GW by 2050, supplying almost 25% of global electricity. This would be a major contribution to cutting the emissions of greenhouse gases from the electricity supply sector. However, uncertainties remain concerning the successful construction and operation of the next generation of nuclear plants, public and political acceptance of nuclear energy, and the extent to which other low-carbon energy sources are successfully developed.

Sources

- NEA (2010), *Nuclear Energy Data*, OECD Publishing.
- Data for non-OECD countries provided by the *International Atomic Energy Agency* (IAEA).

Further information

Analytical publications

- International Energy Agency (IEA) (2010), *Energy Technology Perspectives*, IEA, Paris.
- IEA, Nuclear Energy Agency (NEA) (2010), *Technology Roadmap: Nuclear Energy*, IEA Technology Roadmaps, IEA, Paris.
- NEA (2010), *The Security of Energy Supply and the Contribution of Nuclear Energy*, Nuclear Development, OECD Publishing.
- NEA, International Atomic Energy Agency (IAEA) (2010), *Uranium 2009: Resources, Production and Demand*, OECD Publishing.

Websites

- Nuclear Energy Agency, *www.oecd-nea.org*.

Nuclear electricity generation and nuclear power plants

	2009		Number, as at 1 June 2011	
	Terawatt hours	As a percentage of total electricity generation	Plants connected to the grid	Plants under construction
Australia	-	-	-	-
Austria	-	-	-	-
Belgium	45.0	51.7	7	-
Canada	85.3	14.8	17	-
Chile	-	-	-	-
Czech Republic	25.7	35.8	6	-
Denmark	-	-	-	-
Estonia	-	-	-	-
Finland	22.6	33.1	4	1
France	390.0	75.1	58	1
Germany	127.8	22.8	17	-
Greece	-	-	-	-
Hungary	14.6	44.9	4	-
Iceland	-	-	-	-
Ireland	-	-	-	-
Israel	-	-	-	-
Italy	-	-	-	-
Japan	263.0	29.2	50	2
Korea	141.0	34.7	21	5
Luxembourg	-	-	-	-
Mexico	10.1	4.4	2	-
Netherlands	3.9	3.2	1	-
New Zealand	-	-	-	-
Norway	-	-	-	-
Poland	-	-	-	-
Portugal	-	-	-	-
Slovak Republic	13.1	54.4	4	2
Slovenia	5.5	38.2	1	-
Spain	50.5	17.5	8	-
Sweden	50.0	37.4	10	-
Switzerland	26.1	39.2	5	-
Turkey	-	-	-	-
United Kingdom	62.9	17.9	19	-
United States	798.7	20.2	104	1
EU27 total	847.7	27.3	143	6
OECD total	2 135.8	21.8	338	12
Brazil	13.0	2.9	2	1
China	70.1	1.9	14	27
India	14.7	2.2	20	5
Indonesia	-	-	-	-
Russian Federation	153.0	17.8	32	11
South Africa	11.6	4.8	2	-

StatLink http://dx.doi.org/10.1787/888932504899

Nuclear electricity generation

As a percentage of total electricity generation, 2009

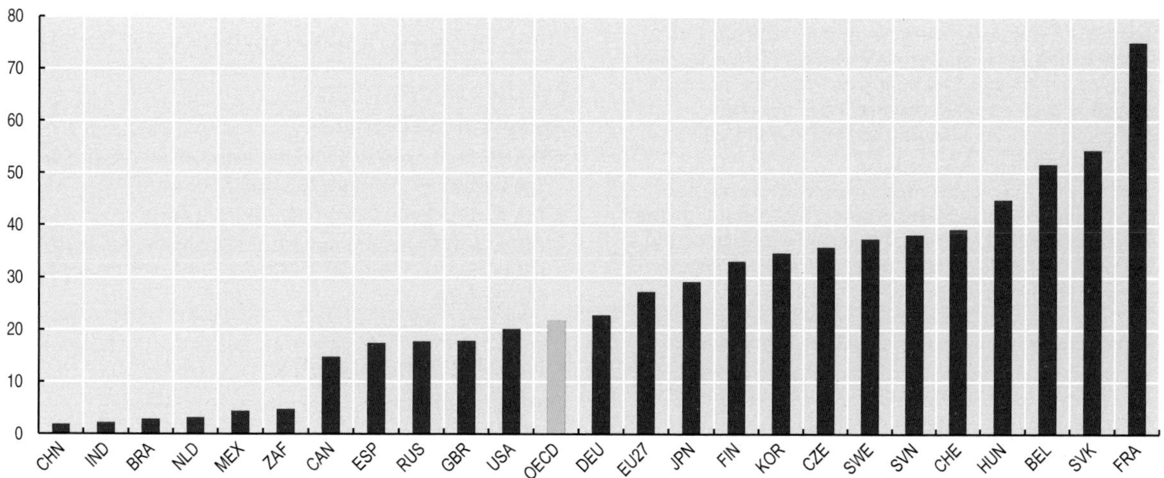

StatLink http://dx.doi.org/10.1787/888932504918

RENEWABLE ENERGY

More and more governments are recognising the importance of promoting sustainable development and combating climate change when setting out their energy policies. Higher energy use has contributed to higher greenhouse gas emissions and higher concentration of these gases in the atmosphere. One way to reduce greenhouse gas emissions is to replace energy from fossil fuels by energy from renewables.

Definition

The table refers to the contribution of renewables to total primary energy supply (TPES) in OECD countries. Renewables include the primary energy equivalent of hydro (excluding pumped storage), geothermal, solar, wind, tide and wave. It also includes energy derived from solid biofuels, biogasoline, biodiesels, other liquid biofuels, biogases, and the renewable fraction of municipal waste. Biofuels are defined as fuels derived directly or indirectly from biomass (material obtained from living or recently living organisms). Included here are wood, vegetal waste (including wood waste and crops used for energy production), ethanol, animal materials/wastes and sulphite lyes. Municipal waste comprises wastes produced by the residential, commercial and public service sectors that are collected by local authorities for disposal in a central location for the production of heat and/or power.

Comparability

Biofuels and waste data are often based on small sample surveys or other incomplete information. Thus, the data give only a broad impression of developments and are not strictly comparable between countries. In some cases, complete categories of vegetal fuel are omitted due to lack of information.

Contribution of renewables to energy supply

As a percentage of total primary energy supply, 2010

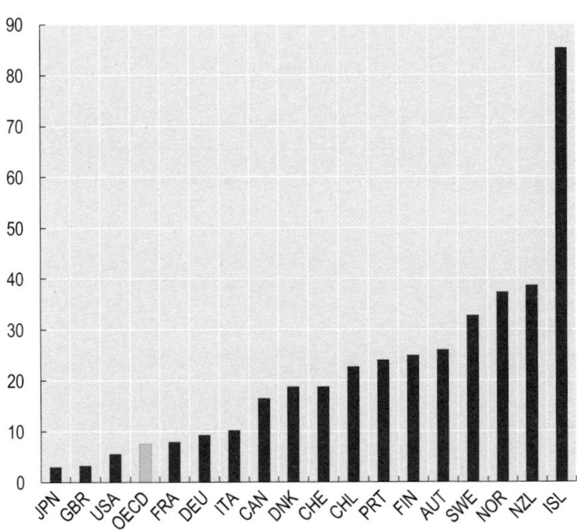

StatLink http://dx.doi.org/10.1787/888932535033

Overview

In OECD countries, total renewables supply grew by 2.4% per annum between 1971 and 2010 as compared to 1.2% per annum for total primary energy supply. Annual growth for hydro (1.1%) was lower than for other renewables such as geothermal (5.3%) and biofuels and waste (2.9%). Due to a very low base in 1971, solar and wind experienced the most rapid growth in OECD member countries, especially where government policies have stimulated expansion of these energy sources.

For the OECD as a whole, the contribution of renewables to energy supply increased from 4.8% in 1971 to 7.6% in 2010. The contribution of renewables varied greatly by country. On the high end, renewables represented 85% of energy supply in Iceland, 39% in New Zealand and 37% in Norway. On the low end, renewables contributed 3% or less of the energy supply for Japan, Korea, Luxembourg and the United Kingdom.

In general, the contribution of renewables to the energy supply in non-OECD countries is higher than in OECD countries. In 2009, renewables contributed 46% to the energy supply of Brazil, 34% in Indonesia, 26% in India, 12% in China, 10% in South Africa and 3% in the Russian Federation.

Sources

- IEA (2011), *Energy Balances of Non-OECD Countries*, IEA, Paris.
- IEA (2011), *Energy Balances of OECD Countries*, IEA, Paris.

Further information

Analytical publications

- IEA (2011), *Harnessing Variable Renewables: A Guide To The Balancing Challenge*, IEA, Paris.
- IEA (2011), *World Energy Outlook*, IEA, Paris.
- Ölz, S. and M. Beerepoot (2010), "Deploying Renewables in Southeast Asia: Trends and Potentials", *IEA Energy Papers*, No. 2010/06.

Statistical publications

- IEA (2011), *Renewables Information*, IEA, Paris.

Online databases

- *IEA World Energy Statistics and Balances*.

Websites

- International Energy Agency, *www.iea.org*.

Contribution of renewables to energy supply

As a percentage of total primary energy supply

	1971	1990	1999	2000	2001	2002	2003	2004	2005	2006	2007	2008	2009	2010
Australia	8.8	5.9	5.9	5.9	6.1	6.1	5.8	5.7	5.4	5.4	5.5	5.6	5.6	5.2
Austria	11.0	20.2	23.1	23.0	21.9	21.2	18.7	19.8	21.1	22.1	24.1	25.3	27.8	26.0
Belgium	-	1.0	1.0	1.1	1.2	1.3	1.5	1.6	2.0	2.3	2.7	3.1	3.9	4.1
Canada	15.3	16.1	16.8	16.9	15.9	16.9	15.6	15.6	15.9	15.7	16.3	16.6	16.9	16.5
Chile	20.8	25.4	21.3	23.7	25.0	24.8	23.4	22.9	24.0	24.8	23.6	23.7	25.1	22.7
Czech Republic	0.2	1.8	3.7	3.3	3.5	3.7	3.4	3.8	4.0	4.2	4.7	5.0	5.8	6.4
Denmark	1.8	6.2	8.7	9.8	10.3	11.2	12.1	13.8	15.1	14.3	16.3	16.8	17.4	18.8
Estonia	..	1.9	10.8	10.8	11.0	11.7	11.2	11.4	11.4	10.5	10.7	11.9	15.2	14.4
Finland	27.3	19.3	22.3	23.9	22.6	22.2	21.2	23.4	23.6	23.3	23.5	25.7	23.8	24.9
France	8.6	6.8	6.6	6.3	6.4	5.8	5.9	5.9	5.8	6.1	6.6	7.3	7.7	7.9
Germany	1.2	1.5	2.4	2.7	2.8	3.2	3.8	4.4	4.9	5.8	7.8	7.9	8.7	9.3
Greece	7.8	5.1	5.5	5.2	4.7	4.9	5.3	5.3	5.4	5.9	5.7	5.6	6.4	7.5
Hungary	2.9	2.6	3.3	3.3	3.4	3.4	3.5	3.6	4.3	4.5	5.1	6.0	7.4	7.6
Iceland	46.7	67.0	74.0	74.2	75.6	75.0	75.2	74.8	75.9	78.4	80.8	82.9	84.3	85.3
Ireland	0.6	1.7	1.7	1.7	1.6	1.8	1.7	1.9	2.5	2.9	3.1	3.8	4.5	4.0
Israel	-	3.1	3.3	3.3	3.3	3.5	3.5	3.8	3.7	3.6	3.5	4.8	5.0	4.9
Italy	5.6	4.4	5.8	5.9	6.0	5.8	6.0	6.6	6.3	6.9	6.7	7.7	9.7	10.2
Japan	2.7	3.5	3.2	3.2	3.1	3.2	3.4	3.3	3.2	3.3	3.2	3.3	3.3	3.0
Korea	0.6	1.1	0.4	0.4	0.4	0.4	0.5	0.5	0.5	0.6	0.6	0.6	0.7	0.7
Luxembourg	-	0.6	1.0	1.2	1.1	1.1	1.0	1.2	1.6	1.6	2.6	2.9	3.0	2.9
Mexico	16.8	12.2	11.4	11.7	10.9	10.2	10.2	10.4	10.4	10.0	10.0	10.1	9.6	10.3
Netherlands	-	1.1	1.6	1.7	1.8	1.9	1.8	2.1	2.7	3.0	3.0	3.5	4.0	3.6
New Zealand	32.0	32.7	28.4	29.6	27.6	29.7	30.0	31.6	31.2	31.2	32.1	33.3	36.1	38.6
Norway	40.9	54.3	45.2	51.2	42.5	49.5	38.3	40.0	48.5	42.6	46.5	44.8	43.3	37.3
Poland	1.4	1.5	4.0	4.3	4.5	4.7	4.6	4.7	4.8	4.8	5.0	5.7	6.7	6.9
Portugal	19.6	19.6	13.6	15.2	16.2	13.7	16.9	14.7	13.1	17.1	17.7	17.7	19.7	24.0
Slovak Republic	2.3	1.5	2.6	2.8	4.1	4.0	3.5	4.0	4.3	4.5	5.4	5.4	7.2	6.7
Slovenia	..	9.1	8.6	12.3	11.6	10.5	10.3	11.5	10.6	10.5	10.1	11.0	12.8	12.7
Spain	6.5	6.9	5.2	5.7	6.5	5.5	6.9	6.4	5.9	6.5	6.9	7.7	9.6	11.4
Sweden	20.4	24.4	26.6	31.0	28.2	25.3	24.5	25.0	28.8	28.7	30.5	31.5	34.8	32.7
Switzerland	15.5	15.0	18.6	17.7	18.3	16.8	16.8	16.4	15.9	15.4	17.7	17.8	17.7	18.8
Turkey	31.0	18.3	15.2	13.2	13.3	13.5	12.9	13.3	12.0	11.1	9.6	9.5	10.2	11.0
United Kingdom	0.1	0.5	1.0	1.0	1.0	1.2	1.2	1.5	1.8	1.9	2.2	2.6	3.2	3.3
United States	3.7	5.0	4.7	4.5	4.0	4.0	4.3	4.4	4.5	4.8	4.7	5.1	5.4	5.6
EU27 total	..	4.3	5.5	5.8	5.8	5.7	5.9	6.3	6.5	7.0	7.7	8.2	9.2	..
OECD total	4.8	5.9	6.0	6.0	5.7	5.7	5.8	6.0	6.2	6.4	6.6	7.0	7.5	7.6
Brazil	56.4	46.8	40.3	39.1	37.6	39.4	42.1	42.4	43.0	43.4	44.5	44.5	45.8	..
China	40.0	24.5	20.5	20.5	21.0	19.5	17.1	15.1	14.2	13.3	12.8	12.3	11.9	..
India	62.8	44.1	34.3	34.0	33.9	33.2	32.9	31.6	31.1	30.2	29.0	28.2	26.1	..
Indonesia	75.3	45.3	35.5	37.5	38.2	37.0	37.1	35.1	34.5	34.0	34.4	35.2	34.4	..
Russian Federation	..	3.0	3.1	2.9	3.0	2.8	2.7	2.9	2.9	2.8	2.9	2.6	2.8	..
South Africa	10.4	11.2	10.8	11.1	11.4	11.8	11.0	10.3	10.5	10.7	10.1	9.4	10.0	..
World	13.2	12.8	13.0	13.0	12.9	12.8	12.7	12.5	12.5	12.5	12.6	12.7	13.1	..

StatLink http://dx.doi.org/10.1787/888932504937

OECD renewable energy supply

Million tonnes of oil equivalent (Mtoe)

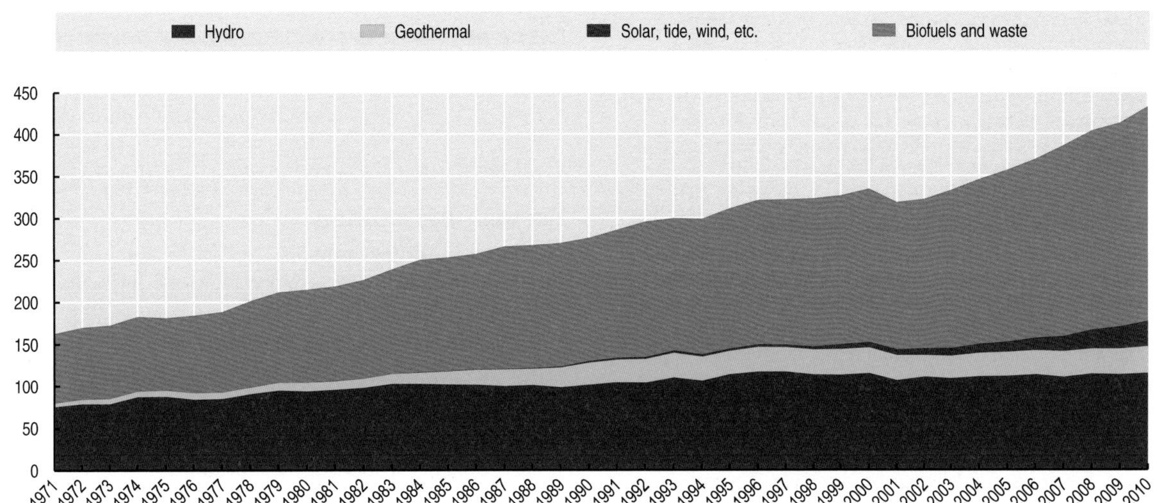

StatLink http://dx.doi.org/10.1787/888932504956

ENERGY PRODUCTION

Energy production is a function of the natural resources of each country and of the economic incentives to exploit those resources. Countries will also take into consideration energy security and environmental protection when making decisions on how much and what type of energy to produce.

Definition

Production refers to the quantities of fuels extracted from the ground after the removal of inert matter or impurities (*e.g.* sulphur from natural gas). For non-combusted energy such as nuclear, hydro and solar, the primary energy equivalent is calculated using the physical energy content method, which expresses the energy content of each source in million tonnes of oil equivalent (Mtoe) energy.

Comparability

In general, data on energy production are of high quality. In some instances, information is based on secondary sources or estimated by the International Energy Agency.

Total energy production by product

As a percentage of total energy production

1971

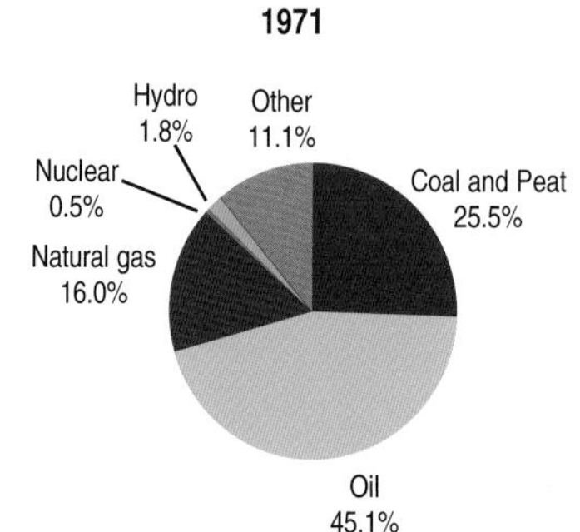

2009

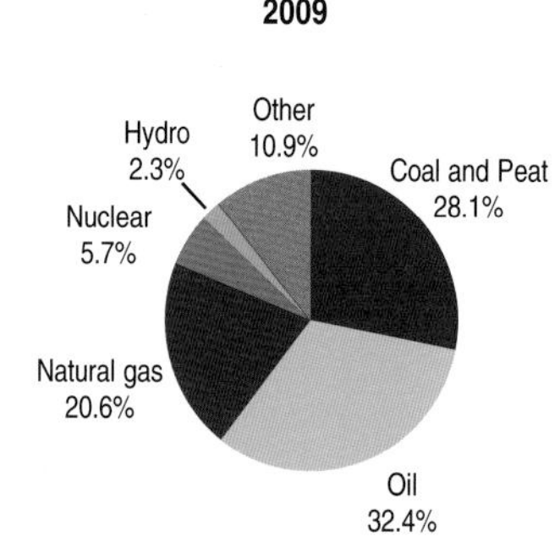

StatLink http://dx.doi.org/10.1787/888932505013

Overview

World energy production increased by 2.1% per year between 1971 and 2009, reaching 12 268 million tonnes of oil equivalent (Mtoe). The OECD, with a 31% share of world production, was the main energy producing region in 2009. China accounted for 17% of world energy production, the United States for 14%, the Middle East region for 13% and the Russian Federation for 10%. Since 1971, the shares of the OECD, Middle East and non-OECD Europe and Eurasia decreased, while those of Latin America and Africa remained stable. On the other hand, the share of energy production in China (as well as the rest of Asia) increased dramatically since 1971, with China overtaking the United States as the largest energy producer in 2006.

The energy mix has changed significantly between 1971 and 2009. Nuclear energy, which experienced an annual average growth of 8.8% since 1971, increased its share of production from 0.5% in 1971 to 6.8% in 1999 to 2002. However, the share of nuclear in production has been falling steadily since 2002 and was 5.7% in 2009. In absolute terms, renewable energy also experienced a high growth rate over the last 38 years, but its share of total production has remained low since it was starting from a very low base. The share of natural gas in total production increased from 16.0% in 1971 to 20.6% in 2009, while the share of oil fell from 45.1% to 32.4%. The share of coal and peat production increased slightly to 28.1%.

Sources

- IEA (2011), *Energy Balances of Non-OECD Countries*, IEA, Paris.
- IEA (2011), *Energy Balances of OECD Countries*, IEA, Paris.

Further information

Analytical publications

- IEA (2011), *Energy Policies of IEA Countries*, series, IEA, Paris.
- IEA (2011), *Harnessing Variable Renewables: A Guide To The Balancing Challenge*, IEA, Paris.
- IEA (2011), *Medium-Term Oil and Gas Markets 2011*, IEA, Paris.

Online databases

- *IEA World Energy Statistics and Balances.*

Websites

- International Energy Agency, *www.iea.org*.

Indices of price levels

OECD = 100

	1997	1998	1999	2000	2001	2002	2003	2004	2005	2006	2007	2008	2009	2010
Australia	97	84	85	81	77	81	90	99	104	106	115	117	111	135
Austria	103	105	100	89	92	94	103	107	109	108	115	118	115	110
Belgium	102	105	100	88	89	91	102	109	110	111	117	121	118	112
Canada	86	82	82	89	88	87	90	93	99	107	109	109	103	115
Chile	64	61	56	56	51	48	46	52	59	69	69	66	65	77
Czech Republic	40	44	42	39	42	49	51	55	59	62	66	76	70	70
Denmark	126	128	124	111	114	117	133	138	141	140	146	149	146	138
Estonia	45	49	48	45	48	50	56	59	61	65	73	76	71	68
Finland	113	114	109	98	102	105	117	119	120	119	124	127	124	118
France	108	110	104	93	92	95	109	115	113	113	118	123	120	113
Germany	111	113	106	95	96	99	107	109	106	105	110	112	110	105
Greece	78	78	77	68	67	69	80	85	87	88	95	97	97	93
Hungary	45	45	43	41	43	50	55	61	63	61	69	71	62	62
Iceland	104	112	112	115	102	111	127	132	155	153	170	127	102	110
Ireland	101	101	101	95	100	105	118	123	124	124	127	131	123	111
Israel	91	90	86	90	91	81	82	77	82	83	85	94	93	97
Italy	92	92	89	81	81	89	99	106	106	105	108	109	106	104
Japan	138	130	145	154	138	128	124	122	116	107	99	107	121	123
Korea	78	57	65	71	66	69	69	68	76	81	80	67	62	70
Luxembourg	107	108	102	93	95	98	109	112	117	115	122	125	123	118
Mexico	54	56	60	69	76	76	65	63	64	66	65	63	56	61
Netherlands	102	103	98	88	91	95	108	111	110	109	113	117	116	108
New Zealand	95	80	77	70	69	76	89	98	106	97	107	99	91	106
Norway	127	127	122	111	115	127	132	131	136	136	145	146	138	145
Poland	46	49	45	45	51	50	49	50	57	60	64	73	59	60
Portugal	76	79	76	69	71	74	82	87	84	83	87	90	86	82
Slovak Republic	40	41	37	37	36	39	47	52	54	56	64	71	70	67
Slovenia	69	72	69	61	63	65	73	75	75	76	83	87	86	82
Spain	81	82	80	72	74	77	87	92	94	92	96	100	97	93
Sweden	121	121	115	107	102	107	119	122	124	123	127	126	115	122
Switzerland	129	133	127	117	122	127	136	138	138	132	129	135	138	141
Turkey	49	52	49	48	39	45	53	56	61	59	64	65	59	64
United Kingdom	103	109	108	103	101	105	108	114	114	115	125	111	98	98
United States	99	102	102	107	112	111	103	98	98	100	97	94	98	97
EU27 total	96	98	94	86	86	90	98	103	102	102	107	108	103	99
OECD total	100	100	100	100	100	100	100	100	100	100	100	100	100	100
Brazil	77	76	52	56	49	42	41	44	55	64	71	78	78	93
China	41	42	41	43	45	44	41	40	41	43	46	52	54	57
India	32	31	31	32	33	32	31	31	33	33	36	35	34	39
Indonesia	46	24	34	35	34	39	40	39	40	48	50	53	55	67
Russian Federation	48	34	23	28	32	33	33	39	44	46	53	54	45	51
South Africa	56	51	49	48	43	38	50	58	60	59	57	51	55	66

StatLink http://dx.doi.org/10.1787/888932504614

Indices of price levels

OECD = 100, 2010

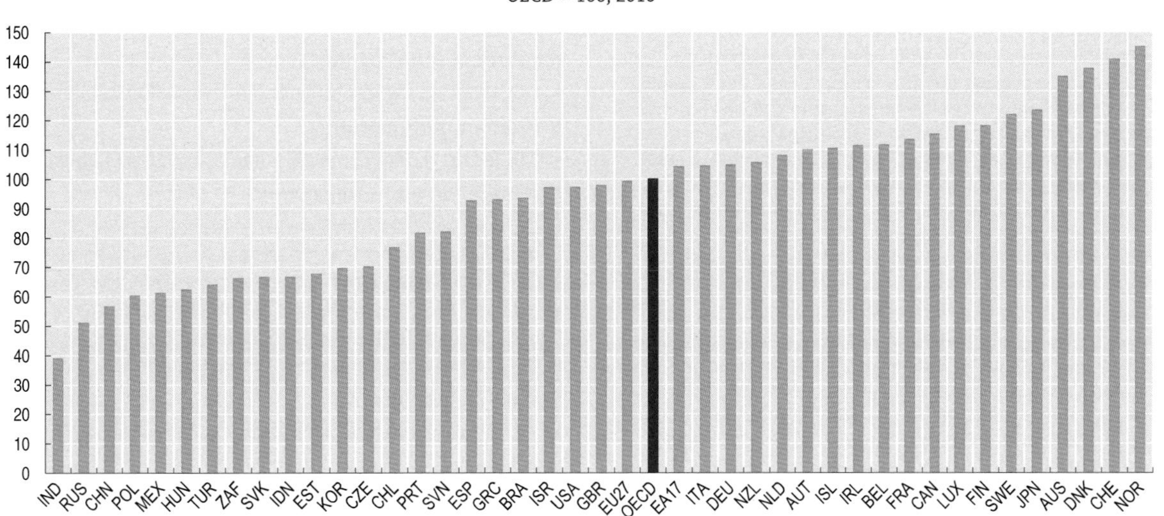

StatLink http://dx.doi.org/10.1787/888932504633

Total production of energy

Million tonnes of oil equivalent (Mtoe)

	1971	1990	1999	2000	2001	2002	2003	2004	2005	2006	2007	2008	2009	2010
Australia	53.9	157.5	213.5	233.6	253.8	263.5	263.6	269.3	280.1	281.5	298.6	301.0	310.7	324.0
Austria	7.4	8.1	9.7	9.8	9.8	9.8	9.6	9.9	10.1	10.1	10.9	11.2	11.4	11.2
Belgium	6.8	13.1	13.9	13.7	13.3	13.5	13.7	13.7	13.9	13.8	14.4	14.5	15.3	15.4
Canada	155.8	273.7	364.4	372.7	377.0	384.1	386.2	397.9	401.1	410.8	416.4	406.1	389.8	395.8
Chile	5.3	7.5	7.5	8.1	8.6	8.6	8.1	8.1	8.9	9.2	8.5	9.1	9.3	9.6
Czech Republic	39.9	40.9	28.8	30.7	31.4	31.4	33.5	34.5	32.9	33.6	33.8	32.8	31.2	31.4
Denmark	0.3	10.1	23.8	27.7	27.1	28.6	28.5	31.1	31.3	29.5	27.1	26.6	23.9	23.2
Estonia	..	5.4	3.0	3.2	3.2	3.4	3.9	3.7	3.9	3.7	4.4	4.2	4.2	4.9
Finland	5.0	12.1	15.4	15.1	15.1	16.1	16.0	15.8	16.7	18.2	16.1	16.5	16.6	17.2
France	47.6	111.9	127.1	130.8	132.1	134.2	135.8	137.0	137.0	137.2	135.3	137.3	129.5	135.8
Germany	175.2	186.2	137.2	135.3	134.7	134.5	135.9	138.0	135.4	136.4	137.5	133.5	127.1	129.2
Greece	2.1	9.2	9.5	10.0	10.0	10.2	9.9	10.3	10.3	10.1	10.2	9.9	10.1	9.2
Hungary	11.8	14.6	11.9	11.6	11.3	11.2	10.4	10.2	10.4	10.3	10.2	10.5	11.0	11.0
Iceland	0.4	1.4	2.2	2.3	2.5	2.5	2.5	2.5	2.6	3.3	4.0	4.4	4.4	4.6
Ireland	1.4	3.5	2.5	2.2	1.8	1.5	1.8	1.9	1.6	1.6	1.4	1.5	1.5	1.9
Israel	5.9	0.4	0.6	0.6	0.7	0.7	0.7	1.7	2.1	2.7	2.9	3.9	3.3	3.7
Italy	19.5	25.3	29.2	28.2	26.9	27.5	27.8	28.4	27.8	27.4	26.4	27.0	27.0	28.8
Japan	35.8	75.2	104.5	105.8	104.8	96.9	84.1	95.1	100.5	101.4	90.6	88.7	93.8	95.1
Korea	6.4	22.6	30.6	34.4	34.9	34.8	37.9	38.3	42.9	43.7	42.6	44.7	44.3	44.6
Luxembourg	-	-	0.1	0.1	0.1	0.1	0.1	0.1	0.1	0.1	0.1	0.1	0.1	0.1
Mexico	43.4	194.7	220.6	222.3	225.8	225.5	236.7	246.9	254.0	250.6	244.1	233.3	220.0	217.7
Netherlands	37.3	60.5	59.5	57.6	61.5	60.7	58.7	68.0	62.2	61.1	61.2	66.6	63.0	69.7
New Zealand	3.4	11.5	13.7	14.1	14.2	14.6	13.4	13.0	12.6	13.1	14.0	15.0	15.2	16.6
Norway	6.0	119.1	209.4	227.0	225.9	234.8	234.4	228.4	223.7	215.0	214.9	219.0	213.6	205.1
Poland	99.2	103.9	83.9	79.6	80.3	80.2	79.9	78.8	78.6	77.6	72.5	71.4	67.5	67.8
Portugal	1.4	3.4	3.4	3.8	4.1	3.6	4.3	3.9	3.6	4.4	4.6	4.5	4.9	6.0
Slovak Republic	2.7	5.3	5.5	6.3	6.7	6.8	6.6	6.5	6.6	6.6	6.0	6.4	5.9	6.1
Slovenia	..	3.1	2.9	3.1	3.2	3.3	3.3	3.5	3.5	3.4	3.5	3.7	3.5	3.5
Spain	10.4	34.6	30.7	31.7	33.5	31.8	33.0	32.6	30.1	31.3	30.3	30.4	29.7	33.9
Sweden	7.4	29.7	33.2	30.5	33.9	31.8	30.9	34.3	34.7	32.8	33.6	33.2	30.3	32.5
Switzerland	2.9	10.3	12.1	12.0	12.6	12.2	12.3	12.1	11.0	12.2	12.7	12.8	12.8	12.7
Turkey	13.8	25.8	27.5	25.9	24.4	24.1	23.6	24.1	23.9	26.3	27.3	29.0	30.3	30.3
United Kingdom	109.8	208.0	281.6	272.5	262.3	258.4	246.6	225.7	205.3	186.9	176.6	166.8	158.9	149.7
United States	1 436.4	1 652.5	1 670.2	1 667.3	1 688.6	1 655.8	1 634.3	1 645.5	1 631.0	1 654.4	1 669.0	1 701.8	1 686.4	1 740.9
EU27 total	..	945.3	955.1	946.4	945.9	945.1	936.9	933.7	900.4	880.6	859.3	853.6	817.3	..
OECD total	2 355.0	3 440.9	3 789.7	3 829.4	3 875.7	3 856.7	3 827.9	3 870.9	3 850.6	3 860.4	3 861.4	3 877.5	3 806.7	3 889.1
Brazil	49.1	104.2	141.5	148.3	152.2	167.4	178.3	182.6	194.8	206.5	216.4	228.2	230.3	..
China	394.1	886.3	1 061.7	1 064.0	1 093.8	1 171.2	1 317.3	1 493.3	1 622.9	1 728.3	1 824.5	1 989.8	2 084.9	..
India	141.6	291.8	359.4	366.4	374.5	383.6	396.4	409.5	422.4	437.9	452.7	468.3	502.5	..
Indonesia	71.7	169.1	244.2	236.3	241.6	248.0	254.9	264.8	280.0	313.7	318.3	323.8	351.8	..
Russian Federation	..	1 293.1	962.1	978.0	1 008.2	1 046.3	1 119.5	1 172.3	1 203.2	1 227.0	1 239.1	1 253.9	1 181.6	..
South Africa	37.8	114.5	145.0	145.6	144.9	143.8	153.4	157.6	157.9	157.4	158.8	162.0	160.6	..
World	5 656.8	8 815.4	9 750.3	9 992.9	10 120.5	10 219.1	10 644.9	11 193.5	11 543.0	11 850.0	12 028.1	12 381.8	12 268.2	..

StatLink http://dx.doi.org/10.1787/888932504975

Total energy production by region

Million tonnes of oil equivalent (Mtoe)

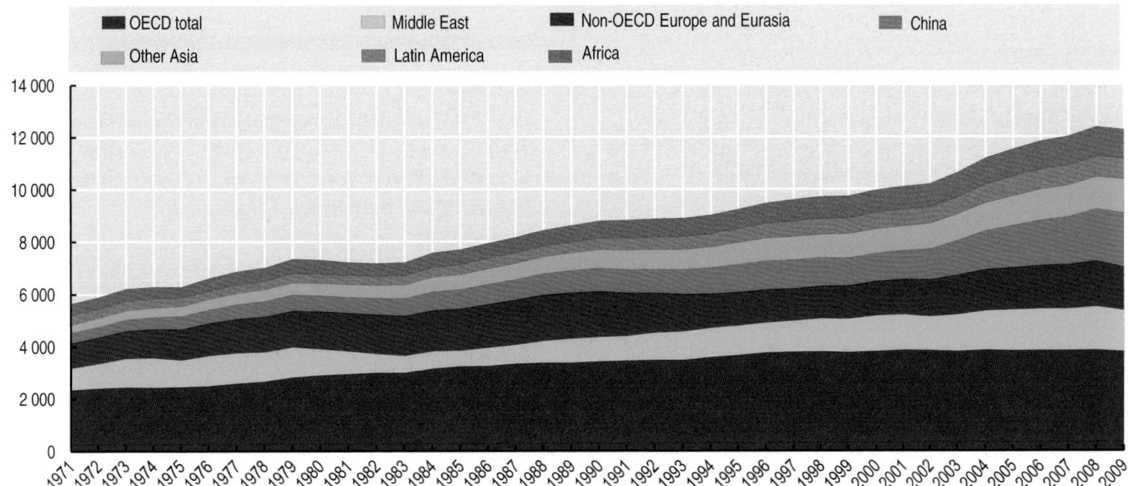

StatLink http://dx.doi.org/10.1787/888932504994

OIL PRODUCTION

The Middle East and North Africa are exceptionally well-endowed with energy resources, holding about 65% of the world's proven conventional oil reserves at the end of 2010. Current oil production is relatively low in comparison to these reserves and further development of them will be critical to meeting global energy needs in the coming decades. Unconventional oil (*e.g.* oil shale and sands, liquid supplies based on coal and biomass, and liquids arising for the chemical processing of natural gas) is also expected to play an increasing role in meeting world demand.

Definition

Crude oil production refers to the quantities of oil extracted from the ground after the removal of inert matter or impurities. It includes crude oil, natural gas liquids (NGLs) and additives. Crude oil is a mineral oil consisting of a mixture of hydrocarbons of natural origin, being yellow to black in colour, of variable density and viscosity. NGLs are the liquid or liquefied hydrocarbons produced in the manufacture, purification and stabilisation of natural gas. Additives are non-hydrocarbon substances added to or blended with a product to modify its properties, for example, to improve its combustion characteristics (*e.g.* MTBE and tetraethyl lead).

Refinery production refers to the output of secondary oil products from an oil refinery.

Comparability

In general, data on oil production are of high quality. In some instances, information has been based on secondary sources or estimated by the International Energy Agency.

Share of refinery production by product

As a percentage of refinery production

1971

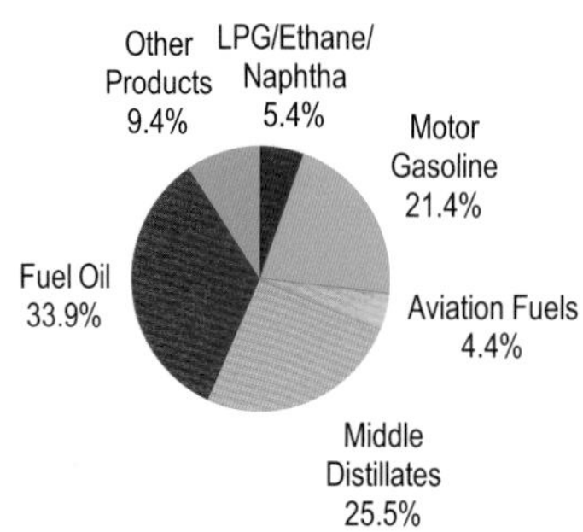

2009

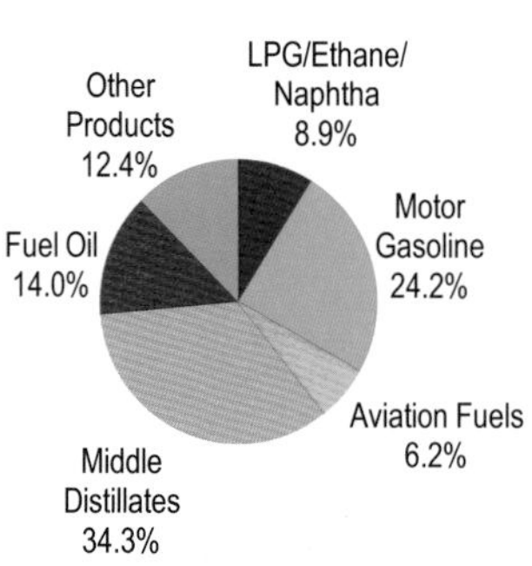

StatLink http://dx.doi.org/10.1787/888932505070

Overview

World crude oil production increased by 60% over the 39 years from 1971 to 2010. In 2010, production reached 3 973 million tonnes or about 86 million barrels per day. Growth was not constant over the period as production declined in the aftermath of two oil shocks in the early and late 1970s.

In 2010, the Middle East region's share of oil production was 30% of the world total. However, both the level of production and its share in the world total varied significantly over the period, from 38% of the world total in 1974 to 19% in 1985. Increased production in the 1980s and 1990s put the OECD on par with the Middle East during that period, but by 2010, the share of OECD oil production had fallen to 22%.

Refinery production of secondary oil products changed significantly between 1971 and 2009. The share of fuel oil in the refinery mix fell from 34% in 1971 to 14% in 2009 whereas the share of middle distillates increased from 25% to 34%.

Sources

- IEA (2011), *Energy Balances of Non-OECD Countries*, IEA, Paris.
- IEA (2011), *Energy Balances of OECD Countries*, IEA, Paris.
- IEA (2011), *Oil Information*, IEA, Paris.

Further information

Analytical publications

- IEA (2011), *Energy Policies of IEA Countries*, series, IEA, Paris.
- IEA (2011), *Medium-Term Oil and Gas Markets 2011*, IEA, Paris.

Online databases

- *IEA World Energy Statistics and Balances.*

Websites

- International Energy Agency, *www.iea.org*.

Production of crude oil

Million tonnes

	1971	1990	1999	2000	2001	2002	2003	2004	2005	2006	2007	2008	2009	2010
Australia	14.3	27.5	23.7	32.1	33.1	31.3	29.1	26.2	22.9	21.9	24.0	22.6	24.2	22.8
Austria	2.6	1.2	1.1	1.1	1.0	1.0	1.0	1.1	1.0	1.0	1.0	1.0	1.0	1.0
Canada	70.6	91.6	119.9	124.8	126.6	132.9	140.4	145.4	143.5	151.3	158.0	153.8	152.6	159.3
Chile	1.7	1.1	0.4	0.4	0.4	0.4	0.4	0.4	0.3	0.3	0.5	0.5	0.6	0.5
Czech Republic	-	0.2	0.4	0.4	0.4	0.4	0.5	0.6	0.6	0.4	0.4	0.3	0.3	0.3
Denmark	-	6.0	14.5	17.8	16.9	18.1	18.1	19.3	18.5	16.8	15.2	14.0	12.9	12.1
Finland	-	-	0.1	0.1	0.1	0.1	0.1	0.1	0.1	0.2	0.1	0.1	0.1	0.1
France	2.5	3.5	2.0	1.9	1.6	1.5	1.6	1.6	1.4	1.2	1.4	1.5	1.2	1.4
Germany	7.6	5.3	3.8	4.3	4.3	4.6	4.8	4.9	5.2	5.2	5.2	4.9	4.5	3.8
Greece	-	0.8	-	0.3	0.2	0.2	0.1	0.1	0.1	0.1	0.1	0.1	0.1	0.1
Hungary	2.0	2.3	1.8	1.7	1.5	1.6	1.6	1.6	1.4	1.3	1.2	1.2	1.2	1.1
Israel	5.7	-	-	-	-	-	-	-	-	-	-	-	-	-
Italy	1.3	4.7	5.2	4.8	4.2	5.8	5.9	5.7	6.4	6.3	6.6	6.0	5.2	5.7
Japan	0.8	0.5	0.6	0.6	0.6	0.6	0.6	0.7	0.7	0.7	0.7	0.7	0.7	0.6
Korea	-	-	0.4	0.7	0.6	0.5	0.5	0.4	0.5	0.6	0.6	0.5	0.7	0.7
Mexico	25.4	151.1	166.9	169.3	175.5	178.3	189.3	191.4	187.6	183.2	172.5	156.9	146.0	144.5
Netherlands	1.7	4.0	2.5	2.4	2.3	3.1	3.1	2.9	2.3	2.0	2.9	2.5	2.2	1.8
New Zealand	-	1.9	2.1	1.9	1.8	1.6	1.3	1.1	1.1	1.0	2.0	2.8	2.6	2.5
Norway	0.3	82.1	149.4	161.0	162.6	157.8	153.7	144.0	133.0	123.8	119.5	114.6	108.3	100.5
Poland	0.4	0.2	0.5	0.7	0.8	0.8	0.8	0.9	0.9	0.8	0.7	0.8	0.7	0.7
Slovak Republic	0.2	0.1	0.1	0.1	0.1	0.1	-	-	-	-	-	-	-	-
Spain	0.1	1.1	0.3	0.2	0.3	0.3	0.3	0.3	0.2	0.1	0.1	0.1	0.1	0.1
Turkey	3.5	3.7	2.9	2.8	2.5	2.4	2.4	2.3	2.3	2.2	2.1	2.2	2.4	2.5
United Kingdom	0.2	91.6	137.2	126.4	116.8	116.1	106.2	95.5	84.7	76.6	76.8	71.7	68.2	62.8
United States	527.7	413.3	354.2	353.0	349.9	348.1	338.4	325.9	310.0	304.4	304.0	299.4	323.1	335.7
EU27 total	..	129.0	176.2	168.7	157.3	161.5	151.7	140.7	129.0	118.1	117.0	109.2	102.4	95.6
OECD total	668.6	893.8	989.9	1 008.5	1 004.1	1 007.6	1 000.3	972.4	924.6	901.4	895.8	858.4	859.0	860.8
Brazil	8.5	32.7	56.8	64.1	67.3	75.4	77.7	77.1	85.1	90.3	92.2	95.5	101.9	107.3
China	39.4	138.3	160.2	163.1	164.1	167.1	169.7	175.9	181.4	184.9	186.4	190.6	189.6	199.9
India	7.3	34.6	36.4	36.4	36.2	37.4	37.7	38.3	36.3	38.1	37.9	37.5	37.7	40.9
Indonesia	44.1	73.2	74.6	70.3	66.6	61.9	56.7	53.4	52.4	48.9	46.6	48.3	47.1	46.9
Russian Federation	..	523.7	303.2	321.7	345.8	377.2	418.6	456.3	466.4	475.8	487.7	486.2	491.2	501.6
South Africa	-	-	0.8	1.0	0.8	1.0	0.7	1.7	0.9	0.8	0.2	0.1	0.1	0.1
World	2 488.7	3 159.1	3 504.9	3 633.3	3 637.0	3 605.5	3 743.4	3 914.9	3 961.4	3 981.7	3 965.0	3 992.8	3 907.9	3 973.4

StatLink http://dx.doi.org/10.1787/888932505032

Production of crude oil by region

Million tonnes

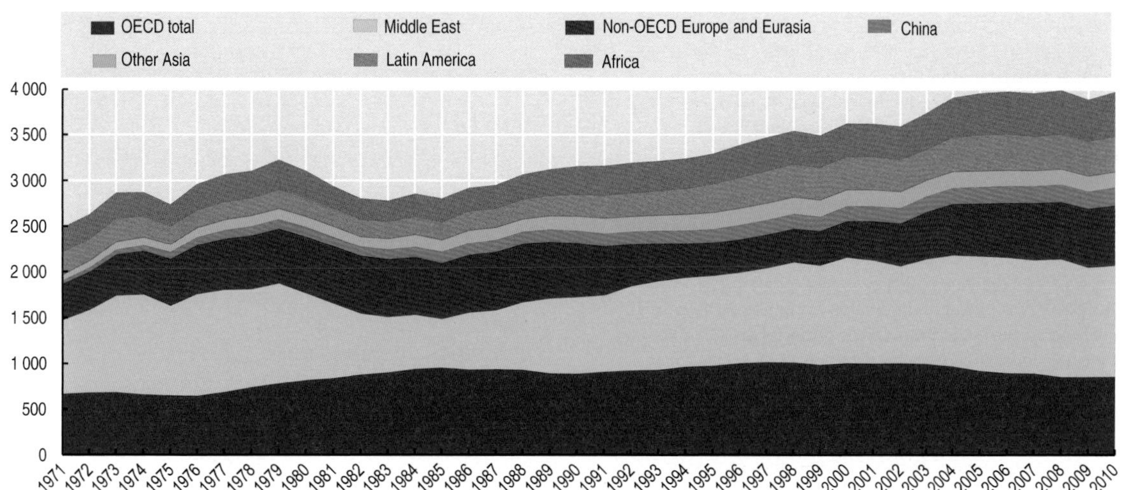

StatLink http://dx.doi.org/10.1787/888932505051

OIL PRICES

The price of crude oil, from which petroleum products such as gasoline are derived, is influenced by a number of factors beyond the traditional movements of supply and demand, notably geopolitics. Some of the lowest cost reserves are located in sensitive areas of the world. There is not one price for crude oil but many. World crude oil prices are established in relation to three market traded benchmarks (West Texas Intermediate [WTI], Brent, Dubai), and are quoted at premiums or discounts to these prices.

Definition

Crude oil import prices come from the Crude Oil Import Register. Information is collected according to type of crude and average prices are obtained by dividing value by volume as recorded by customs administrations for each tariff position. Values are recorded at the time of import and include cost, insurance and freight (c.i.f.) but exclude import duties.

The nominal crude oil spot price from 1985 to 2008 is for Dubai and from 1970 to 1984 for Arabian Light. These nominal spot prices are expressed in US dollars per barrel of oil. The real price was calculated using the deflator for GDP at market prices and rebased with base year 1970 = 100.

Comparability

Average crude oil import prices are affected by the quality of the crude oil that is imported into a country. High quality crude oils such as UK Forties, Norwegian Oseberg and Venezuelan Light are more expensive than lower quality crude oils such as Canadian Heavy and Venezuelan Extra Heavy. For a given country, the mix of crude oils imported each month will affect the average monthly price.

Overview

The 1973 Arab oil embargo had a major price impact as Arabian Light prices surged from USD 1.84/barrel in 1972 to USD 10.77 in 1974. The next spike after 1973 came in 1981, in the wake of the Iranian revolution, when prices rose to a high of nearly USD 40. Prices declined gradually after this crisis. They dropped considerably in 1986 when Saudi Arabia increased its oil production substantially. The first Gulf crisis in 1990 brought a new peak. In 1997, crude oil prices started to decline due to the impact of the Asian financial crisis.

Prices started to increase again in 1999 with OPEC target reductions and tightening stocks. A dip occurred in 2001 and 2002, but the expectation of war in Iraq raised prices to over USD 30 in the first quarter of 2003. Prices remained high in the latter part of 2003 and in 2004. Crude oil prices increased dramatically in late August 2005 after Hurricane Katrina hit the eastern coast of the US Gulf of Mexico. Prices continued to increase throughout 2006 as the demand for oil in emerging economies, especially China, put pressure on the supply/demand balance, averaging 24 per cent higher than the previous year. In 2007, the increase continued with Dubai hitting USD 88.82/barrel at the beginning of November and WTI climbing to USD 96.50/barrel.

In early 2008, prices crossed the symbolic USD 100/barrel threshold and reached a new peak just under USD 150/barrel in July 2008; this brought the real price of oil in 2008 to an all time high. At the beginning of 2009, prices fell to USD 40/barrel as the impact of high prices and the onset of the global financial crisis sharply curbed oil demand. Later in the year, prices ranged between USD 70 and 80/barrel.

Crude oil prices increased steadily throughout 2010 and into 2011. At the end of April 2011, Dubai was trading at USD 119.61/barrel and WTI at USD 113.73/barrel.

Sources

- IEA (2011), *Energy Prices and Taxes*, IEA, Paris.

Further information

Analytical publications

- IEA (2011), *Energy Policies of IEA Countries*, series, IEA, Paris.
- IEA (2011), *Medium-Term Oil and Gas Markets 2011*, IEA, Paris.
- IEA (2011), *Oil Market Report*, IEA, Paris.
- IEA (2011), *World Energy Outlook*, IEA, Paris.

Online databases

- *IEA Energy Prices and Taxes Statistics.*

Websites

- International Energy Agency, *www.iea.org.*

Crude oil import prices

US dollars per barrel, average unit value, c.i.f.

	1976	1990	1999	2000	2001	2002	2003	2004	2005	2006	2007	2008	2009	2010
Australia	..	24.21	18.38	30.79	26.61	25.80	31.24	40.93	56.71	66.71	77.13	107.83	63.40	82.60
Austria	12.85	24.58	17.54	29.39	25.32	24.64	29.59	38.21	53.15	64.44	71.86	103.05	60.69	80.00
Belgium	12.64	21.11	17.33	27.87	24.20	24.35	27.72	35.35	50.06	61.06	70.35	96.01	61.77	79.65
Canada	..	24.15	17.85	29.10	24.87	24.97	29.53	38.13	52.37	64.33	70.04	101.41	60.29	79.14
Czech Republic	..	..	..	26.59	23.74	23.37	28.13	34.82	51.28	62.05	68.54	97.71	60.77	79.04
Denmark	12.98	23.18	17.71	29.66	24.82	24.88	29.68	38.78	54.40	66.92	74.94	96.48	62.87	80.40
Finland	..	..	18.31	28.13	23.49	24.51	27.72	36.09	51.12	63.37	70.48	94.79	61.01	79.10
France	..	..	17.45	28.18	24.13	24.63	28.87	37.61	52.74	63.69	72.22	97.63	61.64	79.78
Germany	13.27	23.17	17.51	28.09	24.15	24.40	28.44	36.65	52.30	63.29	71.60	96.70	61.18	78.49
Greece	12.13	22.42	16.64	26.95	23.22	24.08	27.17	34.53	50.33	60.97	69.93	93.60	60.10	78.97
Hungary	..	..	16.05	26.22	..	..	..	..	..	..	..	..	..	..
Ireland	..	25.55	17.14	29.88	25.31	25.52	29.66	39.24	55.24	66.38	74.16	100.39	62.61	80.95
Italy	12.41	23.23	17.10	27.77	23.87	24.34	28.58	36.60	51.33	62.50	70.20	96.67	60.69	79.29
Japan	12.59	22.64	17.38	28.72	25.01	24.96	29.26	36.59	51.57	64.03	70.09	100.98	61.29	79.43
Korea	..	..	16.91	28.22	24.87	24.12	28.80	36.15	50.19	62.82	70.01	98.11	61.12	78.72
Netherlands	13.06	21.83	16.97	27.59	23.48	23.99	27.67	35.02	50.00	61.47	68.74	97.89	60.54	78.55
New Zealand	..	21.97	18.16	29.95	26.14	25.89	31.00	41.71	56.07	67.36	73.84	105.80	65.85	80.62
Norway	..	18.46	17.46	28.91	23.43	24.46	30.41	39.20	53.08	58.83	70.16	80.22	69.08	81.06
Poland	..	..	..	..	..	..	..	..	..	..	..	94.02	60.83	77.89
Portugal	12.14	22.75	17.38	28.20	24.02	24.27	28.72	37.89	51.94	62.77	70.23	98.83	62.49	79.13
Slovak Republic	..	..	..	..	..	..	..	..	..	..	69.97	90.49	59.37	78.72
Spain	12.54	21.88	16.99	27.16	23.32	23.95	28.13	36.03	50.54	60.99	68.66	94.86	59.78	77.84
Sweden	13.22	23.02	17.68	28.13	24.03	23.86	28.60	36.47	51.78	62.50	70.13	95.09	60.58	79.00
Switzerland	13.87	24.23	18.35	29.53	25.04	25.34	30.26	38.73	55.81	66.76	74.92	101.03	63.27	80.92
Turkey	..	23.11	16.07	26.61	22.98	23.57	27.05	34.90	50.65	61.48	68.59	98.07	61.27	78.26
United Kingdom	12.57	22.92	18.01	28.45	24.45	24.58	29.13	37.75	53.79	65.00	73.80	99.34	62.39	80.60
United States	13.48	21.07	17.06	27.54	22.07	23.52	27.66	35.86	48.82	59.15	66.77	94.97	58.83	76.02

StatLink http://dx.doi.org/10.1787/888932505089

Crude oil spot prices

US dollars per barrel

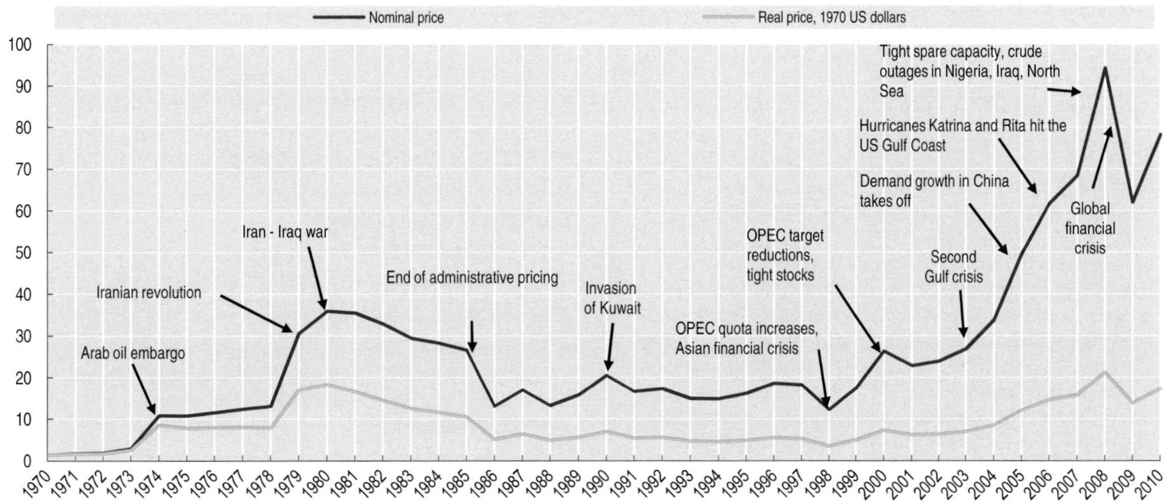

StatLink http://dx.doi.org/10.1787/888932505108

GOODS TRANSPORT

There is an increasing demand for data on the transport sector to assess its various impacts on the economy, the environment and societies. However comparability of transport data between countries is not always possible worldwide due to the lack of harmonised definitions and methods. The Glossary for Transport Statistics (4th edition) provides common definitions to all member states of the European Union, the International Transport Forum and the United Nations Economic Commission for Europe.

Definition

In the following table, goods transport data refer to the total movement of goods using inland transport modes (rail, road, inland waterways and pipelines) on a given network. Data are expressed in tonne-kilometres which represents the transport of one tonne over one kilometre. The distance to be taken into consideration is the distance actually run.

Comparability

Transport is classified as national if both loading and unloading take place in the same country. If one of them occurs in another country then the transport is considered as international. The statistics on international road transport, based on the nationality concept are different for statistics for other modes that are based on the territoriality concept.

Statistics based on the territoriality concept reflect the goods and the vehicles entering or leaving a country irrespective of the nationality of the transporting vehicle. Statistics based on the nationality concept only reflect the performance of the vehicles registered in the reporting country.

Overview

The economic crisis at the end of 2008 and the collapse of world trade in 2009 have had a major impact on freight transport. During 2009, in the European Union goods transported by rail felt by 18% to around 350 billion tonne-kilometres, the lowest level since 1992. In the United States and in the Russian Federation rail freight volumes dropped by 15% and 12% respectively. Road goods transport also suffered in 2009 with an overall drop of 9% in the European Union and of nearly 17% in the Russian Federation. When available, data on inland waterways show a decline in 2009 for almost all countries, with significant drops for the Russian Federation (-17%), Germany (-13%), and the Netherlands (-20%).

Goods transport

Billion tonne-kilometre

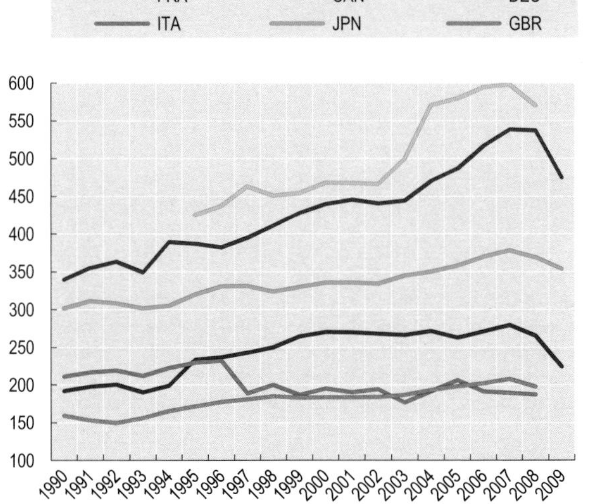

StatLink http://dx.doi.org/10.1787/888932535052

Sources

- International Transport Forum (ITF) (2011), "*Coastal Shipping*", *International Transport Forum* (database).
- ITF (2011), "*Container Transport*", *International Transport Forum* (database).
- ITF (2011), "*Inland Freight Transport*", *International Transport Forum* (database).

Further information

Analytical publications

- Leunig, T. (2011), "Cart or Horse: Transport and Economic Growth", *International Transport Forum Discussion Papers*, No. 2011/04.
- OECD (2011), *Environmental Impacts of International Shipping: The Role of Ports*, OECD Publishing.
- OECD (2010), *Globalisation, Transport and the Environment*, OECD Publishing.

Statistical publications

- ITF (2011), *Trends in the Transport Sector 2011*, OECD Publishing.

Methodological publications

- ITF, Statistical Office of the European Communities and United Nations Economic Commission (2010), *Illustrated Glossary for Transport Statistics, 4th Edition*, OECD Publishing.

Websites

- International Transport Forum, *www.internationaltransportforum.org*.

Goods transport

Million tonne-kilometre

	1970	1980	1990	1999	2000	2001	2002	2003	2004	2005	2006	2007	2008	2009
Australia	60 403	113 320	169 550	258 650	268 756	276 275	296 630	311 047	324 947	349 439	362 383	380 893	388 346	393 418
Austria	17 645	27 543	29 730	41 728	43 763	45 079	45 766	45 049	45 690	44 493	49 900 |	49 842	49 955	43 350
Belgium	27 907	33 965	46 875	62 302	67 634	69 514	70 470	67 655	65 561	62 124	62 149	60 733	57 021	..
Canada	..	..	..	454 100	467 800	467 500	466 200	499 300	570 800	579 200	594 600	598 000	570 300	..
Czech Republic	..	..	..	56 385	58 917	56 508	63 174	64 755	63 413	61 351	69 206	67 422	69 492	60 542
Denmark	9 653	9 470	13 155	16 635	17 715	17 543	18 066	18 151	17 940	18 150	18 251	18 203	16 790	..
Estonia	7 404	10 147	11 489	11 272	12 035	13 234	14 084	16 098	17 325	18 280	19 275	19 090	14 222	12 243
Finland	18 670	26 735	33 827	35 446	37 941	36 635	37 845	37 051	37 553	37 594	36 616	36 498	38 471	33 196
France	174 792	208 403	191 660	264 420	270 351	269 801	267 796	266 155	271 426	262 573 |	271 213 |	279 608	265 506	223 941
Germany	212 432	252 735	339 540 |	428 028	439 698	445 699	440 861	444 320	470 056	486 372	516 835	538 594	536 933	474 856
Greece	7 648	9 973	13 095	14 188	14 717	14 803	15 027	15 156	16 065	16 474	17 172	18 194	17 746	17 345
Hungary	28 441	42 340	39 265	25 163	25 156 |	25 743 |	24 940 |	25 445	27 042	28 191	30 278	31 246	30 771	..
Ireland	545	5 635	5 719	10 801	12 839	12 921	14 874	16 296	17 688	18 455	17 893	19 275	17 393	..
Italy	27 493	150 123	210 745	186 420	194 888	189 990	193 878	176 383	191 176	205 827	191 100	189 164	186 984	..
Japan	198 947	216 329	301 440	329 690	335 254	335 265	334 159	344 656	350 108	357 792	369 726	378 134	368 676	353 263
Korea	..	10 798	13 663	10 072	10 803	101 367	102 778	109 430	111 698	110 977	119 562	116 149	116 788	..
Luxembourg	1 204	1 273	1 428	1 354	1 454	1 486	1 566	1 438	1 503	1 262	1 405	1 219	1 249	1 060
Mexico	65 459	123 577	145 301	245 231	242 386	238 516	244 516	249 332	254 187	276 402 |	283 118	299 560	301 872	280 785
Netherlands	50 924	59 588	66 496	84 147	83 222	82 944	84 070	82 324	89 359	88 032	87 844	90 703	91 741	..
New Zealand	..	..	..	17 244	18 423	19 166	19 976	20 950	22 048	22 231	22 363	23 086	23 391	..
Norway	4 642	6 909	11 919	18 594	18 277	17 965	18 934	19 237	21 389	21 726	22 596	22 521	22 457	22 124
Poland	124 296	198 723	138 744	145 973	150 565 |	147 241	150 045	160 305	188 670 |	196 377	216 938	238 631	248 787	258 858
Portugal	776	12 801	12 510	17 399	17 135	19 312	17 833	16 713	19 727	19 847	20 120	20 960	19 317	16 143
Slovak Republic	..	..	..	30 038	26 958	25 743	25 906	27 520	28 940	32 693	33 038	37 701 |	39 494	35 347
Slovenia	5 425	7 765	9 096	4 678	4 794	4 764	5 023	5 269	5 416 |	5 606	5 652	6 175	6 155	4 944
Spain	63 062	103 787	106 358	153 325	168 350	181 126	199 569	206 775	235 014	248 250	256 613	273 827	258 084	224 269
Sweden	15 084	28 273	36 091	44 260	43 775	42 471	44 208	44 289	45 860	48 807	50 349	52 057	53 908	45 545
Switzerland	13 178	16 324	21 360	22 410	24 201	24 899	24 758	25 106	26 360	26 887	28 232	28 286	28 859	26 156
Turkey	24 960	56 349	136 153	216 044	224 581	202 500	205 827	178 959	178 197	181 719	192 916	204 145 |	229 076	231 892
United Kingdom	112 565	119 178	159 269	182 919	183 438	183 292	183 862	186 394	192 925	197 815	202 042	207 520	197 623	..
United States	227 487	3 470 380	4 028 395	5 157 458	5 165 881	5 186 030	5 302 563	5 379 359	5 588 527	5 649 810	5 729 250	5 718 599	5 712 809	..
India	..	..	..	..	864 278	907 129	959 237	1 045 631	1 125 053	1 471 673	1 329 178	..	..	..
Russian Federation	2 194 921	3 873 007	4 276 002	2 120 059	2 341 894	2 473 485	2 657 937	2 925 424	3 192 426	3 295 161	3 390 146	3 523 107	3 509 073	3 220 801

StatLink http://dx.doi.org/10.1787/888932505127

Goods transport

Average annual growth rate in percentage, 1999-2009 or latest available period

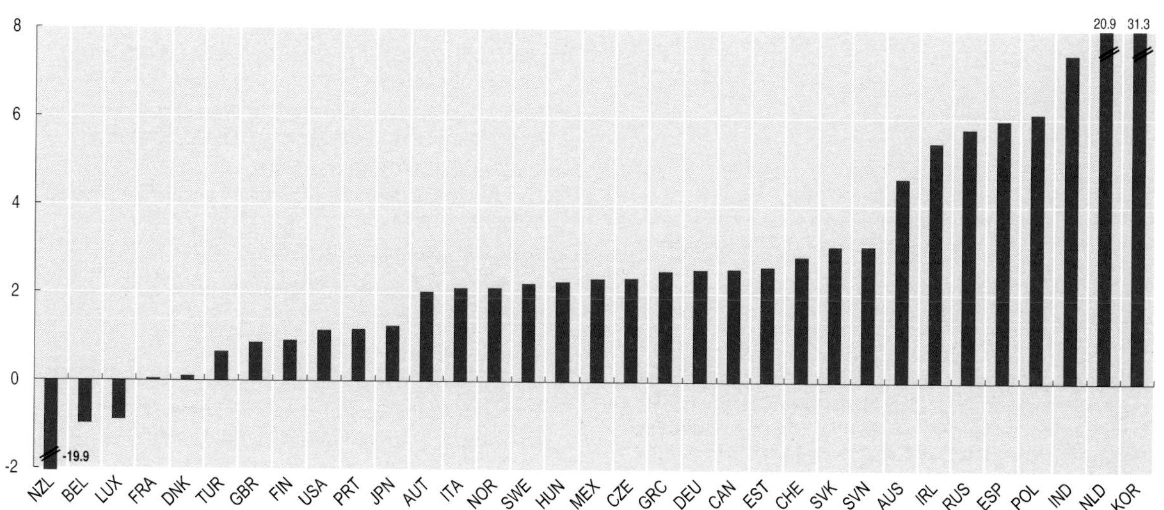

StatLink http://dx.doi.org/10.1787/888932505146

PASSENGER TRANSPORT

Although some studies have suggested a saturation of passenger travel by car in some developed countries, the demand for passenger mobility continues to increase worldwide. There is a need for good and comprehensive data on passenger mobility in order to develop sustainable passenger mobility systems. Comparability of transport data between countries is not always possible worldwide due to the lack of harmonised definitions and methods. The Glossary for Transport Statistics (4th edition) provides common definitions to all member states of the European Union, the International Transport Forum and the United Nations Economic Commission for Europe.

Definition

In the following table, passenger transport data refer to the total movement of passengers using rail or road (passenger cars, buses or coaches) transport modes. Data are expressed in passenger-kilometres which represents the transport of one passenger over one kilometre. The distance to be taken into consideration is the distance actually run.

Comparability

If passenger transport by rail or by regular buses and coaches can be estimated fairly easily, passengers transport by passenger car or by un-schedule coaches are much more difficult to track down. Some countries do not report passenger car transport at all, others carry out different types of surveys to estimate passenger travel on their territory. There is no common methodology for this and since no method provides a complete vision of passenger movements, data are not always comparable between countries.

Overview

The economic crisis had a significant impact on passenger transport in 2009. With the exception of a few countries, rail passenger transport fell in 2009 in most of the International Transport Forum member countries. As far as road passenger transport is concerned, available 2009 figures suggest a slight return to growth of passenger-kilometres travelled by private cars, where as passenger-kilometres travelled by buses and coaches still feel the impact of the crisis in 2009.

Passenger transport

Billion passenger-kilometre

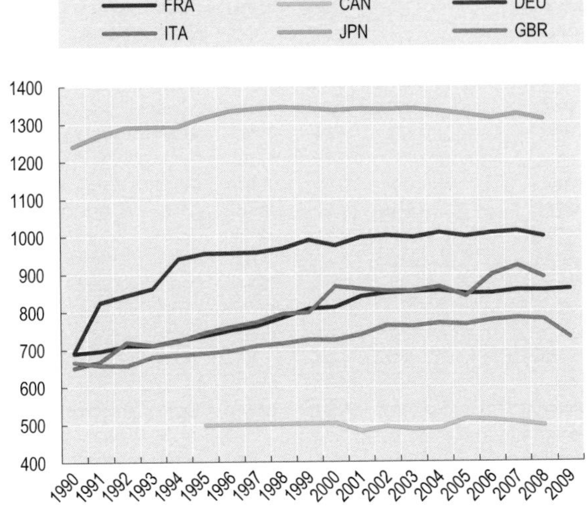

StatLink http://dx.doi.org/10.1787/888932535071

Sources

- International Transport Forum (ITF) (2011), "*Inland passenger transport*", *International Transport Forum* (database).

Further information

Analytical publications

- OECD (2010), *OECD Tourism Trends and Policies 2010*, OECD Publishing.
- OECD (2010), *The Future for Interurban Passenger Transport: Bringing Citizens Closer Together*, OECD Publishing.
- OECD and International Transport Forum (2010), *Improving Reliability on Surface Transport Networks*, OECD Publishing.

Statistical publications

- ITF (2011), *Trends in the Transport Sector 2011*, OECD Publishing.

Methodological publications

- ITF, Statistical Office of the European Communities and United Nations Economic Commission (2010), *Illustrated Glossary for Transport Statistics, 4th Edition*, OECD Publishing.

Websites

- International Transport Forum, *www.internationaltransportforum.org*.

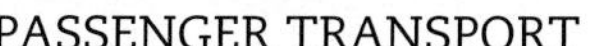

Passenger transport

Million passenger-kilometre

	1970	1980	1990	1999	2000	2001	2002	2003	2004	2005	2006	2007	2008	2009
Australia	120 045	162 825	229 433	264 909	270 235	268 491	274 428	281 095	293 234	294 002	293 284	296 531	297 321	297 509
Austria	41 140	63 365	76 185	7 995	8 206	8 240	8 300	8 249	8 295	8 470	9 296 |	9 580	10 837	10 762
Belgium	66 836	81 414	98 697	123 814	127 155	129 506	132 220	132 995	135 476	136 110	137 597	142 232	141 676	..
Canada	..	..	..	502 498	503 517	482 482	494 525	486 379	489 737	514 164	511 510	504 878	496 000	..
Czech Republic	..	..	..	78 006	80 591	81 377	81 555	83 327	82 676	83 915	86 053	87 959	88 552	88 287
Denmark	3 354	51 248	64 311	70 666	70 544	69 987	70 427	71 404	71 686	72 033	73 282	74 957	75 035	..
Estonia	3 864	5 240	5 964	2 460	2 893	2 903 |	2 780	2 755	2 907	3 186	3 369	3 183	2 950	2 986
Finland	33 356	46 516	63 031	65 915	66 805	67 982	69 318	70 598	71 897	72 928	73 535	75 103	74 992	75 746
France	371 180	545 660	691 040	807 788	812 466 |	840 454	849 200	853 000	855 200	847 800	848 200	856 400	855 300	858 800
Germany	437 683	572 599	693 400	990 196	975 704	997 054	1 001 866	996 493	1 009 071 |	998 909	1 008 248	1 012 485	998 249	..
Greece	6 314	7 281	26 211	41 875	42 086	42 880	43 647	43 603	44 265	44 338	44 120	44 507	43 839	..
Hungary	35 984	76 137	82 507	73 808	74 315	74 511	75 233	75 251	75 402	74 039	74 081	67 038	67 683	..
Iceland	..	..	3 004	4 115	4 250	4 458	4 583	4 711	4 855	5 145	5 455	5 730	5 585	5 646
Ireland	755	1 032	1 226	1 458	1 389	1 515	1 628	1 601	1 582	1 781	1 872	2 007	1 976	1 683
Italy	276 395	421 457	651 258	798 698	867 212 |	860 028	854 634	854 529	865 071	840 297	898 067	921 083	890 773	..
Japan	573 045	746 211	1 240 538	1 340 661	1 335 538	1 339 695	1 337 651	1 339 198	1 333 039	1 324 220	1 313 558	1 324 606	1 310 492	..
Korea	..	..	..	46 790	47 588	326 676	296 884	282 774	242 720	255 420	260 406	260 101	259 336	..
Luxembourg	205	246	208	310	332	346	268	262	266	272	298	316	345	333
Mexico	69 112	159 451	276 848	387 728	381 782	389 396	393 269	399 078	410 074	422 988	437 075	450 001	464 043 |	437 349
Netherlands	85 411	130 192	161 460	171 400 |	171 953	172 583	175 127	176 200	181 628	179 564	179 519	181 229	179 547	..
Norway	23 866	38 069	49 757	55 812	56 444	57 434	58 506	59 240	59 737	60 530	60 961	62 652	62 281	66 298
Poland	66 031	95 548	164 773 |	197 768	201 141	206 904	214 005	222 039	230 244	244 498	265 628	286 143	320 489	328 051
Portugal	21 704	42 676	56 464	97 460	98 038	98 908	99 506	100 126	101 442	101 271	101 078	101 709	100 969	..
Slovak Republic	..	..	..	32 342	35 234	35 114	35 896	35 297	34 442	35 746	35 949	35 896	35 258	33 357
Slovenia	4 140	6 361	21 257 |	24 835	24 532	24 909	25 375	25 554	26 024	26 348	26 932	28 402	28 858	..
Spain	100 249	173 820	224 498	360 984	350 407 |	357 348 |	383 787 |	392 264 |	404 036 |	412 597 |	412 411	424 313	427 444	430 862
Sweden	69 200	81 700	102 200	108 300	109 600	110 700	113 574	114 234	114 558	115 036	115 317	118 361	117 917	119 116
Switzerland	54 211	76 139	91 556	94 689	96 501	97 453	99 035	100 105	101 214	103 260	104 480	106 062	104 011	..
Turkey	46 872	79 138	141 401	181 382	191 513	173 779	168 531	170 189	179 475	187 188	192 870	214 668	211 195	217 838
United Kingdom	373 400	448 750	667 290	726 200	725 200	739 040	762 900	761 000	769 200	765 600	776 800	782 900	778 869	730 700
United States	2 827 740	3 440 680	3 876 662	4 285 112	4 362 729	4 364 672	4 459 461	4 492 268	4 573 337	4 590 940	4 538 784	4 500 156	4 361 400	..
India	..	..	..	..	2 532 500	2 904 000	3 329 700	3 611 400	4 045 000	4 867 300	..	..	..	..
Russian Federation	291 207	436 956	536 592	312 855	338 923	327 025	320 165	319 053	325 996	305 693	304 253	292 220	291 308	258 413

StatLink http://dx.doi.org/10.1787/888932505165

Passenger transport

Average annual growth rate in percentage, 1999-2009 or latest available period

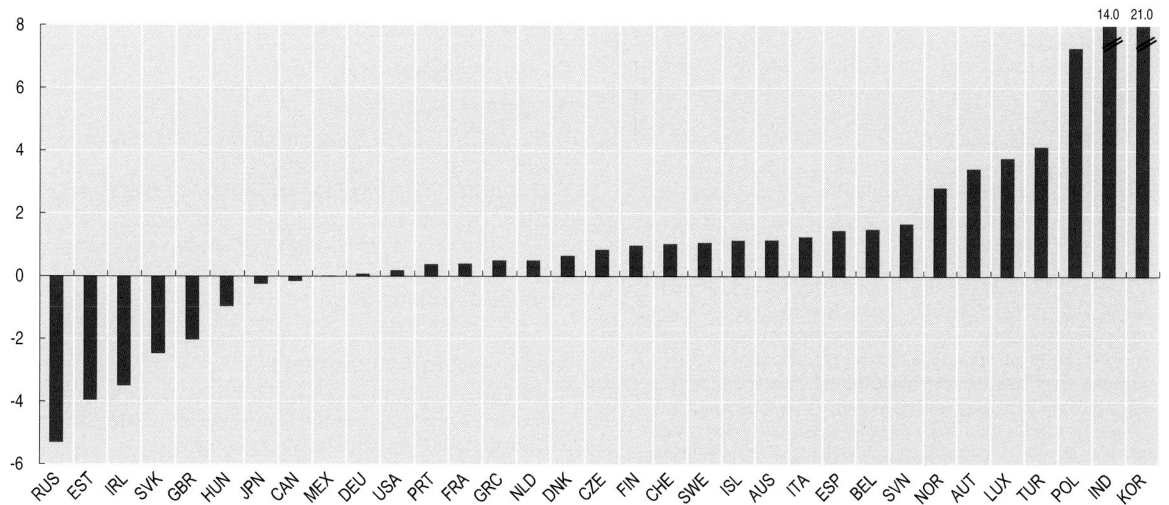

StatLink http://dx.doi.org/10.1787/888932505184

ROAD FATALITIES

The number of road motor vehicles is high amongst member countries of the International Transport Forum and reducing road accidents is a concern for all governments. Such concern becomes more of challenging with increasing needs for more mobility.

Definition

A road motor vehicle is a road vehicle fitted with an engine whence it derives its sole means of propulsion, and which is normally used for carrying persons or goods or for drawing, on the road, vehicles used for the carriage of persons or goods. They include buses, coaches, trolley buses, goods road vehicles and passenger road motor vehicles. Although tramways (street-cars) are rail borne vehicles they are integrated into the urban road network and considered as road motor vehicles.

Road fatality means any person killed immediately or dying within 30 days as a result of a road injury accident. Suicides involving the use of a road motor vehicle are excluded.

Comparability

Road motor vehicles are attributed to the countries where they are registered while deaths are attributed to the countries in which they occur. As a result, ratios of fatalities to million inhabitants and of fatalities to million vehicles cannot strictly be interpreted as indicating the proportion of a country's population that is at risk of suffering a fatal road accident or the likelihood of a vehicle registered in a given country being involved in a fatal accident. In practice, however, this is not a serious problem because discrepancies between the numerators and denominators tend to cancel out.

Fatalities per million inhabitants can be compared with other causes of death in a country (heart diseases, cancer, HIV, etc.) however when comparing countries road fatality risks, this indicator looses it relevance if countries do not have the same level of motorisation. Fatalities per billion vehicle-kilometre provides a better measure of fatality risk on road networks, but there is currently no harmonisation in the methodology to calculate distances travelled, and not all countries collect this indicator.

The numbers of vehicles entering the existing stock is usually accurate, but information on the numbers of vehicles withdrawn from use is less certain. The table in this section shows the numbers of road fatalities per million inhabitants. The chart shows the number of road fatalities per million inhabitants and per million vehicles.

Road fatalities

Per million inhabitants

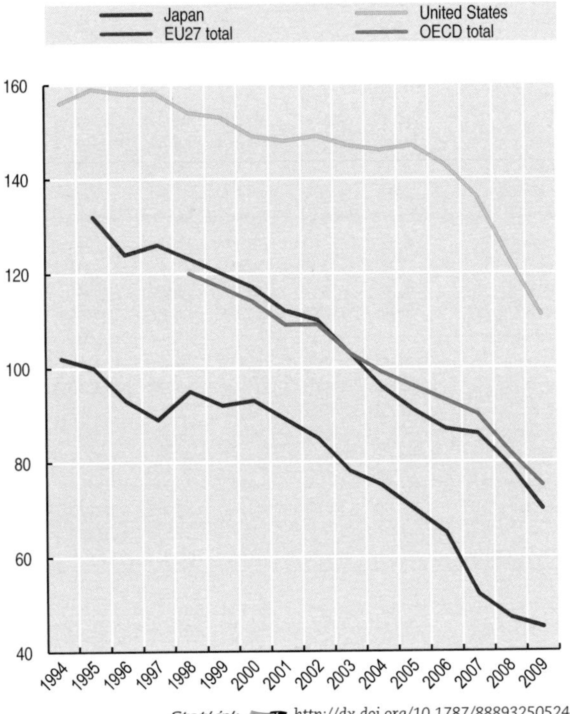

StatLink http://dx.doi.org/10.1787/888932505241

Overview

In 2009, the number of road fatalities fell by almost 10%, following the trend set in 2008 with a drop of nearly 9%. This performance represents the two biggest annual improvements since 1990. In 2009 the number of road fatalities per million inhabitants ranged from 184 per million inhabitants in the Russian Federation to 38 in the United Kingdom. Over the period shown in the table, road fatalities rates have decreased in most countries, with a particularly sharp fall in the Slovak Republic and drops of 25% in Denmark and Estonia.

Road fatality rates per million inhabitants are only a partial indicator of road safety since the number of accidents depends to a great extent on the number of vehicles in each country. The chart shows the number of fatalities per million vehicle together with fatalities per million inhabitants. Both ratios refer to 2009. Road fatality rates per million vehicles are affected by driving habits, traffic legislation and enforcement effectiveness, road design and other factors over which governments may exercise control. In 2009, fatality rates per million vehicles were less than 70 in Sweden, Switzerland, Norway, Iceland and the United Kingdom but exceeded 500 in Turkey and the Russian Federation. Note that low fatality rates per million inhabitants may be associated with very high fatality rates per million vehicles. For example, a country with a small vehicle population (*e.g.* Turkey) may show a low fatality rate per million inhabitants but a high fatality rate per million vehicles.

Sources

- International Transport Forum (ITF) (2011), *Trends in the Transport Sector*, ITF, Paris.

Further information

Analytical publications

- ITF (2008), *Towards Zero: Ambitious Road Safety Targets and the Safe System Approach*, ITF, Paris.
- ITF (2010), *Drugs and Driving: Detection and Deterrence*, OECD Publishing.
- ITF (2010), *IRTAD Road Safety Annual Report 2009*, OECD Publishing.

Statistical publications

- ITF (2011), *Key Transport Statistics 2010*, ITF, Paris.

Methodological publications

- ITF, Statistical Office of the European Communities and United Nations Economic Commission (2010), *Illustrated Glossary for Transport Statistics 4th Edition*, OECD Publishing.

Websites

- International Transport Forum, *www.internationaltransportforum.org*.

Road fatalities

Per million inhabitants

	1996	1997	1998	1999	2000	2001	2002	2003	2004	2005	2006	2007	2008	2009
Australia	108	95	94	93	95	90	87	82	79	81	78	77	68	70
Austria	127	137	121	135	122	119	118	114	108	94	89	83	81	76
Belgium	134	134	147	136	143	144	131	117	112	104	102	100	100	88
Canada	103	101	97	98	95	90	93	87	85	91	89	83	82	73
Chile	132	127	131	109	110	100	98	107	109	100	101	99	106	..
Czech Republic	152	155	132	141	145	130	140	142	136	126	104	118	103	86
Denmark	98	93	94	97	93	80	86	80	68	61	56	74	74	55
Estonia	233	151	200	206	169	149	146	164	121	126	126	146	98	75
Finland	79	85	78	83	76	83	80	73	72	72	64	72	65	53
France	138	136	143	136	129	130	121	96	87	88	77	75	69	69
Germany	107	104	95	95	91	85	83	80	71	65	62	60	55	51
Greece	206	201	207	201	193	178	159	145	151	150	149	141	138	130
Hungary	135	137	136	130	118	122	141	131	129	127	130	123	99	82
Iceland	37	55	98	75	113	84	101	80	79	64	104	48	38	54
Ireland	125	129	124	110	110	107	96	84	94	84	87	77	63	53
Israel	91	91	92	78	73	84	80	67	69	63	57	53	56	42
Italy	115	116	118	116	115	117	117	105	98	94	89	86	79	71
Japan	93	89	95	92	93	89	85	78	75	70	65	52	47	45
Korea	..	..	226	232	218	171	152	151	136	132	131	127	121	120
Luxembourg	170	142	134	133	172	159	140	118	109	101	78	90	72	98
Mexico	52	53	53	53	53	52	49	46	45	46	47	51	51	46
Netherlands	76	74	73	75	73	67	66	67	54	50	50	48	46	44
New Zealand	141	144	132	134	121	118	103	115	107	99	95	100	86	90
Norway	58	69	79	68	76	61	68	61	56	49	52	49	53	45
Poland	165	189	183	174	163	143	152	148	150	143	138	147	143	120
Portugal	241	222	213	200	186	161	165	148	124	118	104	81	83	69
Slovak Republic	119	154	160	125	120	116	116	121	113	111	113	122	112	71
Slovenia	195	180	156	168	157	140	134	121	137	129	130	145	105	84
Spain	139	142	150	144	143	135	129	128	115	89	94	85	68	60
Sweden	61	61	60	65	67	65	63	59	53	49	49	51	43	39
Switzerland	87	83	84	81	82	75	70	74	69	55	50	51	47	46
Turkey	86	81	76	69	58	45	62	56	62	62	62	68	57	58
United Kingdom	65	65	62	62	62	63	63	62	57	55	55	50	43	38
United States	158	158	154	153	149	148	149	147	146	147	143	136	123	111
EU27 total	124	126	123	120	117	112	110	103	96	91	87	86	79	70
OECD total	..	..	120	117	114	109	109	103	99	96	93	90	82	75
India	70	74	77	81	80	80	82	84	91	98	106	115	..	..
Russian Federation	199	188	198	203	203	213	228	248	241	237	230	235	211	184
South Africa	243	235	216	247	196	253	270	268	274	301	325	312	287	..

StatLink http://dx.doi.org/10.1787/888932505203

Road fatalities

2009 or latest available year

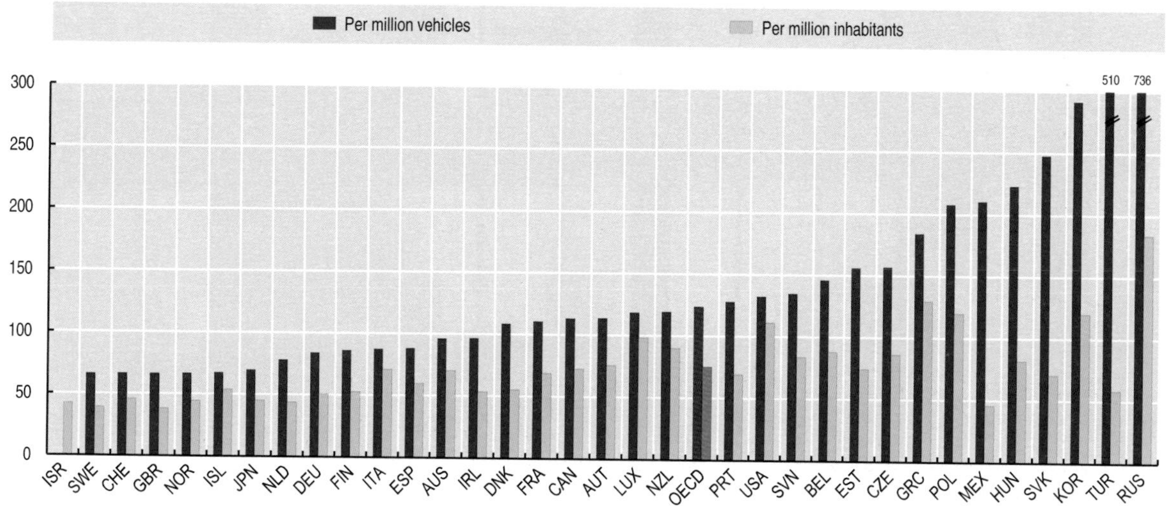

StatLink http://dx.doi.org/10.1787/888932505222

LABOUR

EMPLOYMENT AND HOURS WORKED

UNEMPLOYMENT AND YOUTH INACTIVITY

EMPLOYMENT RATES

Employment rates are a measure of the extent of utilisation of available labour resources. In the short term, these rates are sensitive to the economic cycle, but in the longer term they are significantly affected by government policies with regard to higher education and income support and by policies that facilitate employment of women.

Definition

Employment rates are calculated as the ratio of the employed to the working age population. Employment is generally measured through household labour force surveys. According to the ILO Guidelines, employed persons are defined as those aged 15 or over who report that they have worked in gainful employment for at least one hour in the previous week or who had a job but were absent from work during the reference week. Those not in employment consist of persons who are classified as either unemployed or inactive, in the sense that they are not included in the labour force for reasons of study, incapacity or the need to look after young children or elderly relatives.

The working age population refers to persons aged 15 to 64. Employment rates are here shown for both total employment and for men and women separately.

Comparability

All OECD countries use the ILO Guidelines for measuring employment. Operational definitions used in national labour force surveys may vary slightly from country to country. Employment levels are also likely to be affected by changes in the survey design and the survey conduct. Despite these changes, the employment rates shown here are fairly consistent over time.

Overview

Total employment rates over the three years to 2010 are, in most OECD countries, slightly above the levels achieved in the period 1998 to 2000. In Spain, Germany, Greece, Italy and the Netherlands, the increase in employment rates exceed 5 percentage points, while gains are more moderate for most other OECD countries. However, the United States, Turkey and Iceland recorded modest falls in employment rates over this period. By the end of the period, employment rates ranged between 46% in Turkey and 79% in Iceland. Among the emerging economies shown, employment rates in Brazil and the Russian Federation are slightly above the OECD average, rising by 4 percentage points over the past decade in the Russian Federation. By contrast, employment rates in Chile and Israel are below the OECD average, despite modest rises since the mid-1990s. Estonia experienced an increase of 9 percentage points towards the end of the past decade, followed by a decline by the same amount in 2010.

Employment rates for men are higher than those for women in all OECD countries with an average OECD difference of 16%. While employment rates for men have remained fairly stable in most OECD countries, there are larger differences across countries in how those for women have evolved. In particular, in Luxembourg, the Netherlands, Chile, Italy, Germany and Greece employment rates for women have increased by more than 8 percentage points in this period, while the increase in Spain was as high as 15%, contributing to much of the rise in the total employment. Turkey has by far the lowest women's employment rate, at 26%, with Iceland remaining the highest, despite the recent decrease, at 77%. In the emerging economies, employment rates of men are markedly higher than those of women, by more than 23 points in Brazil and by 7 points in the Russian Federation.

Chile has below OECD-average employment rates for women despite increases (12 percentage points) over the last decade in excess of those recorded for men. By contrast, Estonia, Israel and Slovenia have above OECD-average employment rates for women, rising at a somewhat quicker pace than those of men since 2000.

Sources

- OECD (2011), *OECD Employment Outlook*, OECD Publishing.

Further information

Analytical publications

- Jeaumotte, F. (2003), "Female Labour Force Participation", *OECD Economics Department Working Papers*, No. 376.
- OECD (2007), *Babies and Bosses – Reconciling Work and Family Life*, series, OECD Publishing.

Statistical publications

- OECD (2011), *Labour Force Statistics*, OECD Publishing.

Online databases

- *OECD Employment and Labour Market Statistics*.

Websites

- OECD Labour Statistics Database, *www.oecd.org/statistics/labour*.

Employment rates: total

Share of persons of working age in employment

	1997	1998	1999	2000	2001	2002	2003	2004	2005	2006	2007	2008	2009	2010
Australia	67.4	67.9	68.4	69.3	69.0	69.4	70.0	70.3	71.5	72.2	72.9	73.2	72.0	72.4
Austria	67.8	67.8	68.4	68.3	68.2	68.8	68.9	67.8	68.6	70.2	71.4	72.1	71.6	71.7
Belgium	57.0	57.3	58.9	60.9	59.7	59.9	59.6	60.3	61.1	61.0	62.0	62.4	61.6	62.0
Canada	68.0	68.9	70.0	70.9	70.8	71.4	72.2	72.5	72.4	72.8	73.5	73.6	71.5	71.5
Chile	55.2	55.3	53.4	53.3	52.7	52.6	53.5	53.6	54.4	55.5	56.3	57.3	56.1	59.3
Czech Republic	68.7	67.5	65.9	65.2	65.3	65.7	64.9	64.2	64.8	65.3	66.1	66.6	65.4	65.0
Denmark	75.4	75.3	76.5	76.4	75.9	75.9	75.1	75.7	75.9	77.4	77.1	77.9	75.7	73.4
Estonia	65.7	64.8	62.0	61.0	61.4	62.0	62.8	62.9	64.2	67.9	69.2	69.7	63.5	61.0
Finland	63.5	64.8	66.6	67.5	68.3	68.3	67.9	67.8	68.5	69.6	70.5	71.3	68.4	68.3
France	59.4	59.9	60.4	61.7	62.7	62.9	64.0	63.7	63.7	63.7	64.3	64.9	64.1	64.0
Germany	63.8	64.7	65.2	65.6	65.8	65.3	64.6	65.0	65.5	67.2	69.0	70.2	70.4	71.2
Greece	54.8	55.6	55.4	55.9	55.6	57.5	58.7	59.4	60.1	61.0	61.4	61.9	61.2	59.6
Hungary	52.7	53.6	55.4	56.0	56.2	56.2	57.0	56.8	56.9	57.3	57.3	56.7	55.4	55.4
Iceland	80.0	82.2	84.2	84.6	84.6	82.8	84.1	82.8	84.4	85.3	85.7	84.2	78.9	78.9
Ireland	56.3	60.0	63.0	65.0	65.7	65.2	65.2	65.9	67.5	68.5	69.2	68.1	62.5	60.4
Israel	55.7	55.2	55.5	56.1	55.7	54.8	55.0	55.7	56.7	57.6	58.9	59.8	59.2	60.2
Italy	51.6	52.2	52.9	53.9	54.9	55.6	56.2	57.4	57.5	58.4	58.7	58.7	57.5	56.9
Japan	70.0	69.5	68.9	68.9	68.8	68.2	68.4	68.7	69.3	70.0	70.7	70.7	70.0	70.1
Korea	63.7	59.2	59.6	61.5	62.1	63.3	63.0	63.6	63.7	63.8	63.9	63.8	62.9	63.3
Luxembourg	59.9	60.2	61.6	62.7	63.0	63.6	62.2	62.5	63.6	63.6	64.2	63.4	65.2	65.2
Mexico	60.3	60.4	60.4	60.1	59.4	59.3	58.8	59.9	59.6	61.0	61.1	61.3	59.4	60.4
Netherlands	67.9	69.5	70.8	72.1	72.6	73.0	71.6	71.1	71.5	72.5	74.4	75.9	75.6	74.7
New Zealand	70.1	69.1	69.6	70.4	71.4	72.2	72.2	73.2	74.3	74.9	75.2	74.7	72.9	72.3
Norway	77.0	78.3	78.0	77.9	77.5	77.1	75.8	75.6	75.2	75.5	76.9	78.1	76.5	75.4
Poland	58.8	58.9	57.5	55.0	53.5	51.7	51.4	51.9	53.0	54.5	57.0	59.2	59.3	59.3
Portugal	64.7	66.7	67.3	68.3	68.9	68.7	68.0	67.8	67.5	67.9	67.8	68.2	66.3	65.6
Slovak Republic	61.1	60.5	58.1	56.8	56.9	56.9	57.7	57.0	57.7	59.4	60.7	62.3	60.2	58.8
Slovenia	..	..	..	..	..	63.4	62.6	65.3	66.0	66.6	67.8	68.6	67.5	66.2
Spain	50.7	52.4	55.0	57.4	58.8	59.5	60.7	62.0	64.3	65.7	66.6	65.3	60.6	59.4
Sweden	70.7	71.5	72.9	74.3	75.4	75.2	74.4	73.7	74.0	74.6	75.7	75.8	72.3	72.7
Switzerland	76.9	78.0	78.4	78.4	79.2	78.9	77.9	77.4	77.2	77.9	78.6	79.5	79.0	78.6
Turkey	51.3	51.4	50.8	48.9	47.8	46.7	45.5	44.1	44.4	44.6	44.6	44.9	44.3	46.3
United Kingdom	70.6	71.0	71.5	72.2	72.5	72.3	72.6	72.7	72.6	72.5	72.3	72.7	70.6	70.3
United States	73.5	73.8	73.9	74.1	73.1	71.9	71.2	71.2	71.5	72.0	71.8	70.9	67.6	66.7
OECD total	64.8	65.0	65.2	65.4	65.2	64.9	64.7	65.0	65.3	66.0	66.5	66.5	64.7	64.6
Brazil	..	..	..	..	64.3	65.4	65.0	66.4	67.0	67.4	67.4	68.3	67.6	..
Russian Federation	60.2	58.2	61.7	63.7	63.8	65.1	64.0	64.9	65.9	66.7	68.3	68.6	66.8	67.4

StatLink http://dx.doi.org/10.1787/888932505260

Employment rates: total

Share of persons of working age in employment

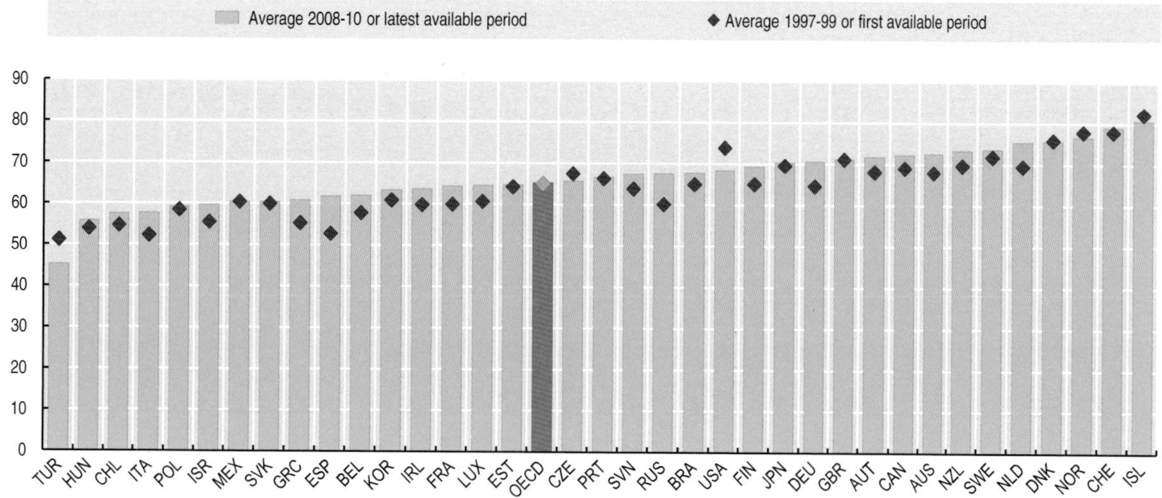

StatLink http://dx.doi.org/10.1787/888932505279

Employment rates: men

Share of men of working age in employment

	1997	1998	1999	2000	2001	2002	2003	2004	2005	2006	2007	2008	2009	2010
Australia	75.8	76.2	76.6	77.1	76.4	76.7	77.0	77.6	78.5	78.8	79.6	79.7	77.8	78.6
Austria	77.2	77.0	77.5	77.3	76.6	76.4	76.4	74.9	75.4	76.9	78.4	78.5	76.9	77.1
Belgium	67.1	67.0	67.5	69.8	68.5	68.3	67.3	67.9	68.3	67.9	68.7	68.6	67.2	67.4
Canada	73.8	74.4	75.4	76.2	75.7	75.9	76.4	76.6	76.6	76.7	77.1	77.2	73.9	74.2
Chile	75.6	75.2	72.2	71.9	71.2	71.0	71.3	70.7	71.1	72.0	72.3	72.6	70.0	72.1
Czech Republic	77.4	76.3	74.3	73.6	73.6	74.2	73.4	72.4	73.3	73.7	74.8	75.4	73.8	73.5
Denmark	81.3	80.2	81.2	80.7	80.2	80.0	79.6	79.7	79.8	81.2	81.0	81.9	78.3	75.8
Estonia	71.4	69.5	66.4	65.4	65.8	66.5	67.2	66.3	66.8	70.9	73.0	73.5	64.1	61.5
Finland	66.6	68.2	69.6	70.5	71.2	70.4	70.1	70.0	70.5	71.8	72.4	73.4	68.9	69.7
France	66.8	67.2	67.5	68.8	69.8	69.6	69.9	69.4	69.2	68.9	69.2	69.6	68.4	68.3
Germany	72.1	72.9	72.8	72.9	72.8	71.7	70.4	70.8	71.4	72.8	74.7	75.9	75.5	76.1
Greece	71.9	71.6	70.9	71.3	70.9	72.2	73.4	73.7	74.2	74.6	74.9	75.0	73.5	70.9
Hungary	60.3	60.3	62.2	62.7	63.0	62.9	63.4	63.1	63.1	63.8	64.0	63.0	61.1	60.4
Iceland	84.2	86.0	88.2	88.2	88.0	85.7	86.8	86.2	87.4	88.7	89.5	87.8	80.6	80.6
Ireland	67.8	71.5	74.2	76.1	76.7	75.1	74.9	75.7	76.6	77.7	77.6	75.7	67.3	64.5
Israel	63.1	61.9	61.3	61.4	60.8	59.5	59.4	60.4	61.0	61.8	63.3	64.1	62.5	63.4
Italy	66.8	67.1	67.6	68.2	68.7	69.2	69.7	69.7	69.7	70.5	70.7	70.3	68.6	67.7
Japan	82.4	81.7	81.0	80.9	80.5	79.9	79.8	80.0	80.4	81.0	81.7	81.6	80.2	80.0
Korea	76.2	71.3	71.3	73.1	73.5	74.9	75.0	75.2	75.0	74.6	74.7	74.4	73.6	73.9
Luxembourg	74.3	74.6	74.4	75.0	74.9	75.5	73.3	72.8	73.3	72.6	72.3	71.5	73.2	73.1
Mexico	83.7	83.5	83.7	82.8	82.3	81.6	80.8	81.0	80.2	81.6	80.9	80.7	77.7	78.4
Netherlands	78.1	79.6	80.3	81.2	81.6	81.4	79.5	78.6	78.7	79.5	81.1	82.4	81.5	80.0
New Zealand	78.1	76.8	76.9	77.9	78.6	79.5	79.3	80.6	81.3	81.9	81.9	80.9	78.6	78.2
Norway	81.7	82.8	82.1	81.7	81.0	80.2	78.7	78.4	78.3	78.6	79.7	80.6	78.4	77.4
Poland	66.1	65.8	63.6	61.2	59.2	57.0	56.7	57.4	59.0	60.9	63.6	66.3	66.1	65.6
Portugal	72.5	75.6	75.5	76.3	76.7	76.3	74.8	74.1	73.4	73.9	73.9	74.0	71.1	70.1
Slovak Republic	68.4	67.8	64.3	62.2	62.1	62.5	63.4	63.2	64.6	67.0	68.4	70.0	67.6	65.2
Slovenia	..	..	..	..	..	68.2	67.4	70.0	70.4	71.1	72.7	72.7	71.0	69.6
Spain	66.1	68.3	70.8	72.7	73.8	73.9	74.5	74.9	76.4	77.3	77.4	74.6	67.5	65.6
Sweden	72.4	73.6	74.8	76.3	77.2	76.9	76.0	75.5	76.2	77.1	78.2	78.3	74.2	75.0
Switzerland	85.9	87.2	87.1	87.3	87.6	86.2	85.1	84.5	83.9	84.7	85.6	85.4	84.4	84.8
Turkey	74.8	74.3	72.7	71.7	69.3	66.9	65.9	66.4	66.9	66.8	66.8	66.6	64.6	66.7
United Kingdom	77.4	78.0	78.3	78.9	79.1	78.6	78.9	78.9	78.8	78.4	78.4	78.5	75.7	75.3
United States	80.1	80.5	80.5	80.6	79.4	78.0	76.9	77.2	77.6	78.1	77.8	76.4	72.0	71.1
OECD total	75.9	76.0	75.9	76.1	75.6	74.9	74.5	74.7	74.9	75.5	75.9	75.6	72.9	72.7
Brazil	..	..	..	..	78.2	78.7	77.9	79.3	79.4	79.6	79.7	80.6	79.7	..
Russian Federation	64.9	62.7	65.8	67.7	67.7	68.6	67.6	68.5	69.5	69.9	71.8	72.9	70.6	71.6

StatLink http://dx.doi.org/10.1787/888932505298

Employment rates: men

Share of men of working age in employment

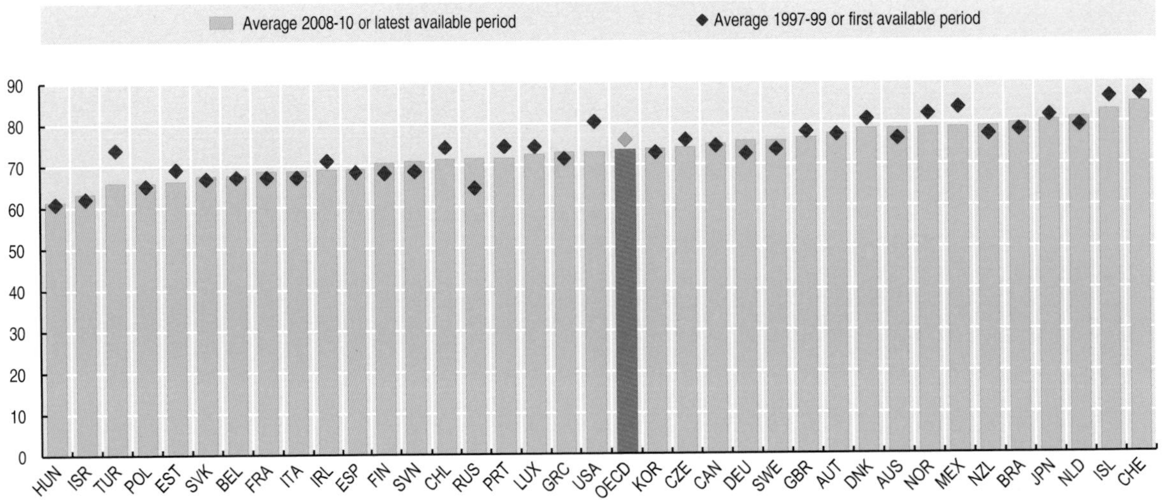

StatLink http://dx.doi.org/10.1787/888932505317

Employment rates: women

Share of women of working age in employment

	1997	1998	1999	2000	2001	2002	2003	2004	2005	2006	2007	2008	2009	2010
Australia	58.9	59.6	60.0	61.4	61.7	62.0	63.0	63.0	64.6	65.5	66.1	66.7	66.3	66.2
Austria	58.4	58.5	59.4	59.4	59.9	61.2	61.6	60.7	62.0	63.5	64.4	65.8	66.4	66.4
Belgium	46.7	47.5	50.2	51.9	50.7	51.4	51.8	52.6	53.8	54.0	55.3	56.2	56.0	56.5
Canada	62.1	63.5	64.6	65.6	65.9	66.9	68.0	68.3	68.2	68.8	69.9	70.1	69.0	68.8
Chile	35.4	35.8	35.0	35.1	34.5	34.5	35.8	36.7	38.0	39.2	40.4	42.1	42.2	46.7
Czech Republic	59.9	58.7	57.4	56.9	57.0	57.1	56.3	56.0	56.3	56.8	57.3	57.6	56.7	56.3
Denmark	69.4	70.3	71.6	72.1	71.4	71.7	70.5	71.6	71.9	73.4	73.2	73.9	73.1	71.1
Estonia	60.5	60.5	57.9	57.0	57.3	57.8	58.8	59.8	61.9	65.1	65.7	66.3	63.0	60.5
Finland	60.4	61.3	63.6	64.5	65.4	66.1	65.7	65.5	66.5	67.3	68.5	69.0	67.9	66.9
France	52.1	52.9	53.5	54.8	55.7	56.4	58.2	58.2	58.4	58.6	59.7	60.4	60.0	59.9
Germany	55.3	56.3	57.4	58.1	58.7	58.8	58.7	59.2	59.6	61.4	63.2	64.3	65.2	66.1
Greece	39.1	40.3	40.7	41.3	41.2	42.9	44.3	45.2	46.1	47.4	47.9	48.7	48.9	48.1
Hungary	45.5	47.3	48.9	49.6	49.8	49.8	50.9	50.7	51.0	51.2	50.9	50.6	49.9	50.6
Iceland	75.6	78.3	80.2	81.0	81.1	79.8	81.2	79.4	81.2	81.6	81.7	80.3	77.2	77.0
Ireland	44.7	48.4	51.8	53.8	54.6	55.2	55.5	56.1	58.2	59.1	60.7	60.5	57.8	56.4
Israel	48.4	48.7	49.8	50.9	50.7	50.2	50.6	51.0	52.5	53.3	54.6	55.6	55.9	56.9
Italy	36.4	37.3	38.3	39.6	41.1	42.0	42.7	45.2	45.3	46.3	46.6	47.2	46.4	46.1
Japan	57.6	57.2	56.7	56.7	57.0	56.5	56.8	57.4	58.1	58.8	59.5	59.7	59.8	60.1
Korea	51.6	47.3	48.1	50.0	50.9	52.0	51.1	52.2	52.5	53.1	53.2	53.2	52.2	52.6
Luxembourg	45.4	45.6	48.5	50.0	50.8	51.5	50.9	51.9	53.7	54.6	56.1	55.1	57.0	57.2
Mexico	39.1	39.3	39.1	39.6	39.0	39.5	39.1	40.9	41.6	42.9	43.6	44.1	43.0	44.1
Netherlands	57.4	59.1	61.1	62.7	63.4	64.5	63.5	63.5	64.1	65.4	67.5	69.3	69.6	69.4
New Zealand	62.3	61.7	62.6	63.2	64.5	65.1	65.5	66.1	67.6	68.2	68.7	68.7	67.4	66.7
Norway	72.2	73.6	73.8	74.0	73.8	73.9	72.7	72.7	72.0	72.3	74.0	75.4	74.4	73.3
Poland	51.8	52.2	51.6	48.9	47.8	46.4	46.2	46.4	47.0	48.2	50.6	52.4	52.8	53.0
Portugal	57.2	58.2	59.4	60.5	61.3	61.4	61.4	61.7	61.7	62.0	61.9	62.5	61.6	61.1
Slovak Republic	54.0	53.5	52.1	51.5	51.8	51.4	52.2	50.9	50.9	51.9	53.0	54.6	52.8	52.3
Slovenia	..	..	..	..	..	58.6	57.6	60.5	61.3	61.8	62.6	64.2	63.8	62.6
Spain	35.2	36.5	39.1	42.0	43.8	44.9	46.8	49.0	51.9	54.0	55.5	55.7	53.5	53.0
Sweden	68.9	69.4	70.9	72.2	73.5	73.4	72.8	71.8	71.8	72.1	73.2	73.2	70.2	70.3
Switzerland	67.8	68.8	69.6	69.4	70.7	71.5	70.7	70.3	70.4	71.1	71.6	73.5	73.6	72.3
Turkey	28.0	28.5	28.9	26.2	26.3	26.6	25.2	22.3	22.3	22.7	22.8	23.5	24.2	26.2
United Kingdom	64.0	64.2	65.0	65.6	66.0	66.3	66.4	66.6	66.7	66.8	66.3	66.9	65.6	65.3
United States	67.1	67.4	67.6	67.8	67.1	66.1	65.7	65.4	65.6	66.1	65.9	65.5	63.4	62.4
OECD total	53.9	54.2	54.6	55.0	55.1	55.1	55.1	55.4	55.9	56.7	57.2	57.6	56.7	56.7
Brazil	..	..	..	..	51.3	52.9	52.9	54.3	55.3	55.9	55.8	56.8	56.4	..
Russian Federation	55.8	54.1	57.8	59.8	60.0	61.8	60.5	61.5	62.6	63.7	65.1	64.7	63.3	63.5

StatLink http://dx.doi.org/10.1787/888932505336

Employment rates: women

Share of women of working age in employment

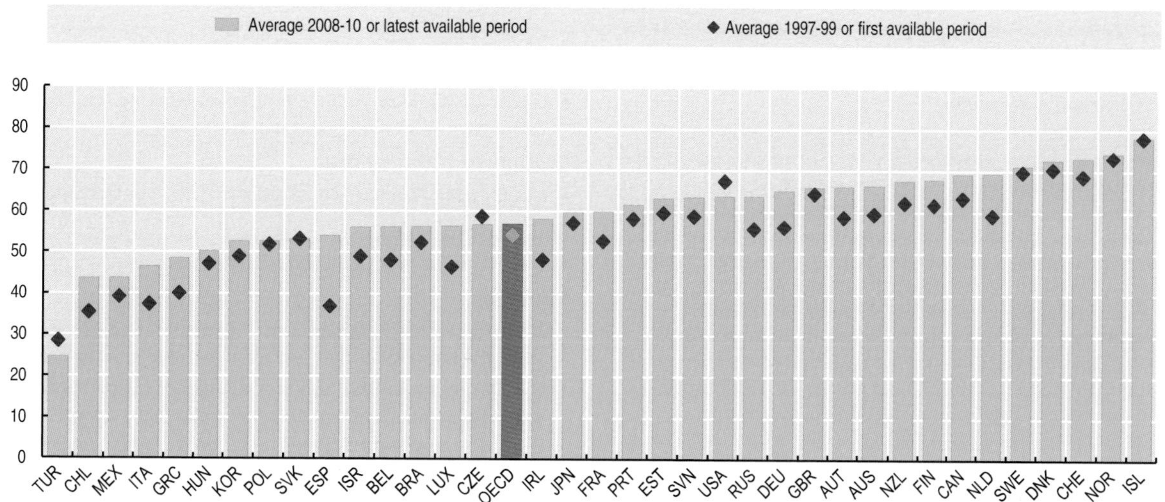

StatLink http://dx.doi.org/10.1787/888932505355

Employment rates by age group

As a percentage of population in that age group

	Persons 15-24 in employment				Persons 25-54 in employment				Persons 55-64 in employment			
	1990	2000	2005	2010	1990	2000	2005	2010	1990	2000	2005	2010
Australia	62.7	62.1	63.3	60.7	76.0	76.3	78.8	79.5	41.5	46.2	53.5	60.6
Austria	..	52.8	53.1	53.6	..	82.5	82.6	84.2	..	28.3	31.8	42.4
Belgium	30.4	30.3	27.5	25.2	71.7	77.9	78.3	80.0	21.4	25.0	31.8	37.3
Canada	61.3	56.2	57.7	55.0	78.1	79.9	81.3	80.5	46.2	48.1	54.7	58.3
Chile	..	26.4	25.4	30.5	..	65.0	67.5	72.1	..	47.5	51.0	58.0
Czech Republic	..	38.3	27.3	25.2	..	81.6	82.0	82.2	..	36.3	44.6	46.5
Denmark	65.0	67.1	62.3	58.1	84.0	84.3	84.5	83.2	53.6	54.6	59.5	57.6
Estonia	51.7	32.9	29.8	26.4	91.8	75.7	79.3	74.6	60.4	44.0	55.7	53.8
Finland	55.2	42.9	42.1	40.5	87.9	80.9	81.7	81.5	42.8	42.3	52.6	56.3
France	35.7	28.3	30.5	30.8	77.3	78.4	80.7	81.8	30.7	29.3	38.5	39.7
Germany	56.4	47.2	42.6	46.8	73.6	79.3	77.4	81.5	36.8	37.6	45.5	57.7
Greece	30.3	26.9	25.0	20.4	68.5	70.2	74.0	73.3	40.8	39.0	41.6	42.3
Hungary	..	32.5	21.8	18.3	..	73.0	73.7	72.5	..	21.9	33.0	34.4
Iceland	..	68.2	71.6	62.1	..	90.6	88.2	83.7	..	84.2	84.8	80.5
Ireland	41.4	49.4	47.9	30.7	60.0	75.5	77.8	70.8	38.6	45.2	51.6	50.8
Israel	23.6	28.2	26.6	27.0	66.5	70.4	70.6	73.9	48.5	46.6	52.4	59.8
Italy	29.8	27.8	25.5	20.5	68.2	68.0	72.2	71.1	32.6	27.7	31.4	36.6
Japan	42.2	42.7	40.9	39.2	79.6	78.6	79.0	79.9	62.9	62.8	63.9	65.2
Korea	32.5	29.4	29.9	23.0	73.2	72.2	73.4	73.8	61.9	57.8	58.7	60.9
Luxembourg	43.3	31.8	24.9	21.2	71.8	78.2	80.7	82.3	28.2	27.2	31.7	39.6
Mexico	..	48.9	43.7	42.7	..	67.4	68.8	70.0	..	51.7	52.6	54.5
Netherlands	54.5	66.5	61.7	63.0	71.2	81.0	81.5	84.6	29.7	37.6	44.8	54.1
New Zealand	59.1	54.2	56.4	50.1	76.3	78.3	81.6	80.0	41.8	56.9	69.5	73.3
Norway	53.4	58.1	52.9	52.0	82.2	85.3	83.2	84.7	61.5	67.1	67.6	68.6
Poland	..	24.5	20.9	26.3	..	70.9	69.5	77.1	..	28.4	29.1	34.0
Portugal	54.8	41.8	36.1	28.5	78.4	81.8	80.8	79.2	47.0	50.7	50.5	49.2
Slovak Republic	..	29.0	25.6	20.5	..	74.7	75.3	75.8	..	21.3	30.4	40.6
Slovenia	..	..	34.1	34.1	..	..	83.8	83.7	..	..	30.7	35.0
Spain	38.3	36.3	41.9	27.4	61.4	68.4	74.4	69.6	36.9	37.0	43.1	43.6
Sweden	66.1	46.7	43.3	38.5	91.6	83.8	83.9	85.0	69.5	65.1	69.6	70.6
Switzerland	..	65.1	59.9	61.7	..	85.4	85.1	86.0	..	63.3	65.1	68.3
Turkey	45.9	37.0	30.2	30.0	61.6	56.7	53.0	55.4	42.7	36.4	28.0	29.6
United Kingdom	70.1	61.5	58.6	50.9	79.1	80.2	81.1	79.8	49.2	50.4	56.7	56.7
United States	59.8	59.7	53.9	45.0	79.7	81.5	79.3	75.1	54.0	57.8	60.8	60.3
OECD total	49.1	45.5	42.7	39.5	75.8	75.9	75.8	75.3	47.7	47.6	51.7	54.0
Brazil	..	..	52.7	..	..	..	75.9	..	..	..	54.1	..
Russian Federation	..	35.0	32.9	36.0	..	80.2	82.8	83.3	..	35.3	43.8	44.4

StatLink http://dx.doi.org/10.1787/888932505374

Employment rates for age group 15-24

Persons in employment as a percentage of population in that age group

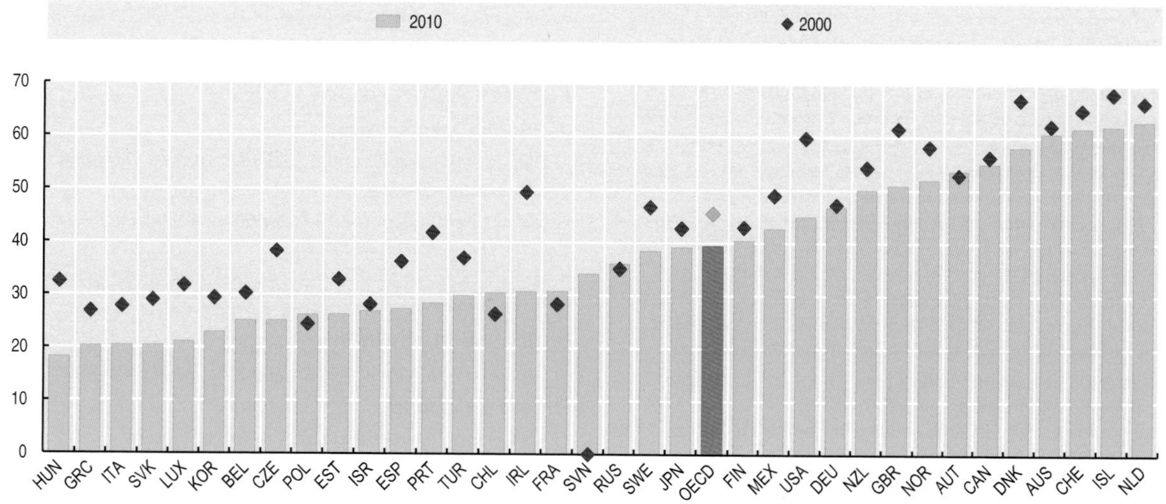

StatLink http://dx.doi.org/10.1787/888932505393

PART-TIME EMPLOYMENT

Opportunities for part-time work are especially important for people whose family obligations prevent them from working full-time, such as women with young children and those caring for elderly relatives. Indeed, recent surveys in a large number of OECD countries show that most people who work part-time do so from choice. This suggests that countries with little part-time employment could foster increased employment by policies that promote the availability of part-time jobs.

Definition

Part-time employment refers to persons who usually work less than 30 hours per week in their main job. This definition has the advantage of being comparable across countries as national definitions of part-time employment vary greatly from one country to another. Part-time workers include both employees and the self-employed.

Employment is generally measured through household labour force surveys. According to the ILO Guidelines, employed persons are those aged 15 or over who report that they have worked in gainful employment for at least one hour in the previous week or who had a job but were absent from work in the reference week. The rates shown here refer to the number of persons who usually work less than 30 hours per week as a percentage of the total number of those in employment.

Comparability

All OECD countries use the ILO Guidelines for measuring employment. Operational definitions used in national labour force surveys may, however, vary slightly across countries. Employment levels are also likely to be affected by changes in the survey design and the survey conduct. Despite these changes, the employment rates shown here are fairly consistent over time. Information on the number of hours usually worked is collected in household labour force surveys. The part-time rates shown here are considered to be of good comparability.

Overview

The incidence of part-time employment for the OECD area as a whole was 17% in 2010. But this incidence differed significantly across countries. In the Netherlands and Switzerland over 25% of all those in employment were working part-time, while this share was under 10% in one third of OECD countries, and especially low in Hungary, the Slovak Republic and the Czech Republic, as well as in Estonia and Slovenia. In the Russian Federation this rate is around 5%.

In recent years, part-time work has accounted for a substantial share of overall employment growth in many OECD countries. For the OECD as a whole, the incidence of part-time employment rates increased by 5 percentage points between 2000 and 2010. Part-time employment rates grew by more than 5 percentage points in Austria, Ireland, Mexico and the Netherlands, with the largest increase in Chile at 13%. Part-time employment rates fell by more than 1 percentage point in Iceland and Poland, as well as in the Russian Federation.

The growth of part-time employment has been especially important for groups that are often under-represented in the labour force such as women – over 5 percentage points in Chile, Austria, Korea, Italy, Spain, Ireland and Greece; youths – over 15 percentage points in Korea, Spain, Ireland and Chile; and, to a lesser extent, older workers.

Sources

- OECD (2011), *OECD Employment Outlook*, OECD Publishing.
- For non-member countries: National sources.

Further information

Analytical publications

- OECD (2007), *Babies and Bosses – Reconciling Work and Family Life*, series, OECD Publishing.
- OECD (2003), *The Sources of Economic Growth in OECD Countries*, OECD Publishing.
- OECD (1999), *Implementing the OECD Jobs Strategy: Assessing Performance and Policy*, OECD Publishing.

Statistical publications

- OECD (2011), *Labour Force Statistics*, OECD Publishing.

Online databases

- *OECD Employment and Labour Market Statistics.*

Websites

- OECD Employment Policies, *www.oecd.org/els/employment.*
- OECD Labour Statistics, *www.oecd.org/statistics/labour.*

Incidence of part-time employment

As a percentage of total employment

	1997	1998	1999	2000	2001	2002	2003	2004	2005	2006	2007	2008	2009	2010
Australia	..	..	..	..	23.7	24.0	24.3	23.8	24.0	23.9	23.8	23.8	24.7	24.9
Austria	10.8	11.5	12.3	12.2	12.4	13.3	13.7	15.4	16.3	16.8	17.3	17.7	18.5	19.0
Belgium	15.0	15.6	19.9	19.0	17.0	17.6	18.3	18.5	18.5	18.7	18.1	18.3	18.2	18.3
Canada	19.1	18.8	18.4	18.1	18.1	18.8	19.0	18.6	18.4	18.2	18.3	18.5	19.3	19.4
Chile	4.7	4.1	4.6	4.7	5.6	5.2	5.7	6.6	7.2	7.7	8.0	9.1	10.5	17.4
Czech Republic	3.4	3.3	3.4	3.2	3.2	2.9	3.2	3.1	3.3	3.3	3.5	3.5	3.9	4.3
Denmark	17.2	17.1	15.3	16.1	14.7	15.5	16.2	17.0	17.3	17.9	17.3	17.8	18.9	19.5
Estonia	..	..	..	7.1	7.1	..	..	..	..	..	..	..	..	8.7
Finland	9.3	9.7	9.9	10.4	10.5	11.0	11.3	11.3	11.2	11.4	11.7	11.5	12.2	12.5
France	14.8	14.7	14.6	14.2	13.8	13.8	13.0	13.2	13.2	13.2	13.3	12.9	13.3	13.6
Germany	15.8	16.6	17.1	17.6	18.3	18.8	19.6	20.1	21.5	21.8	22.0	21.8	21.9	21.7
Greece	8.3	9.1	8.0	5.5	4.9	5.4	5.6	5.9	6.4	7.4	7.7	7.9	8.4	8.8
Hungary	2.9	3.2	3.2	2.9	2.5	2.6	3.2	3.3	3.2	2.7	2.8	3.1	3.6	3.6
Iceland	22.4	23.2	21.2	20.4	20.4	20.1	16.0	16.6	16.4	16.0	15.9	15.1	17.5	18.4
Ireland	15.0	17.6	17.9	18.1	17.9	18.4	18.9	18.9	19.3	19.3	19.8	20.8	23.7	24.8
Israel	13.2	14.3	14.6	14.3	15.1	15.2	15.0	15.0	15.0	15.0	14.6	14.5	14.6	13.8
Italy	11.3	11.2	11.8	12.2	12.2	11.6	11.7	14.7	14.6	15.0	15.2	15.9	15.8	16.3
Japan	..	..	..	..	..	17.7	18.2	18.1	18.3	18.0	18.9	19.6	20.3	20.3
Korea	5.0	6.7	7.7	7.0	7.3	7.6	7.7	8.4	9.0	8.8	8.9	9.3	9.9	10.7
Luxembourg	11.0	12.6	12.1	12.4	13.3	12.5	13.3	13.2	13.9	12.7	13.1	13.4	16.4	15.8
Mexico	15.5	15.0	13.7	13.5	13.7	13.5	13.4	15.1	16.8	17.0	17.6	17.6	17.9	18.7
Netherlands	29.1	30.0	30.4	32.1	33.0	33.9	34.5	35.0	35.6	35.4	35.9	36.1	36.7	37.1
New Zealand	22.3	22.7	23.0	22.2	22.3	22.5	22.2	21.9	21.6	21.2	22.0	22.2	22.5	21.9
Norway	21.0	20.8	20.7	20.2	20.1	20.6	21.0	21.1	20.8	21.1	20.4	20.3	20.4	20.1
Poland	11.9	11.8	14.0	12.8	11.6	11.7	11.5	12.0	11.7	10.8	10.1	9.3	8.7	8.7
Portugal	10.2	10.0	9.4	9.4	9.2	9.6	9.9	9.6	9.4	9.3	9.9	9.7	9.6	9.3
Slovak Republic	2.0	2.0	1.8	1.9	1.9	1.6	2.3	2.8	2.6	2.5	2.6	2.7	3.0	3.7
Slovenia	..	..	..	..	..	4.9	5.0	7.5	7.4	7.8	7.8	7.5	8.3	9.4
Spain	7.9	7.7	7.8	7.7	7.8	7.6	7.8	8.4	11.0	10.8	10.7	11.1	11.9	12.4
Sweden	14.2	13.5	14.5	14.0	13.9	13.8	14.1	14.4	13.5	13.4	14.4	14.4	14.6	14.0
Switzerland	24.0	24.2	24.8	24.4	24.8	24.8	25.1	24.9	25.1	25.5	25.4	25.9	26.5	26.3
Turkey	6.1	6.0	7.7	9.4	6.2	6.6	6.0	6.1	5.6	7.6	8.1	8.5	11.1	11.5
United Kingdom	22.9	23.0	22.9	23.0	22.7	23.2	23.5	23.6	23.0	23.2	22.9	23.0	23.9	24.6
United States	13.5	13.4	13.3	12.6	12.8	13.1	13.2	13.2	12.8	12.6	12.6	12.8	14.1	13.5
OECD total	11.7	11.8	12.0	11.9	12.0	14.4	14.6	15.0	15.2	15.2	15.4	15.6	16.4	16.6
Brazil	..	..	..	..	16.8	17.9	18.0	18.2	19.0	19.2	18.3	18.1	17.8	..
Russian Federation	4.4	4.6	8.2	7.4	5.2	3.8	5.3	5.5	5.6	5.3	5.1	5.0	4.8	4.3

StatLink http://dx.doi.org/10.1787/888932505412

Incidence of part-time employment

As a percentage of total employment

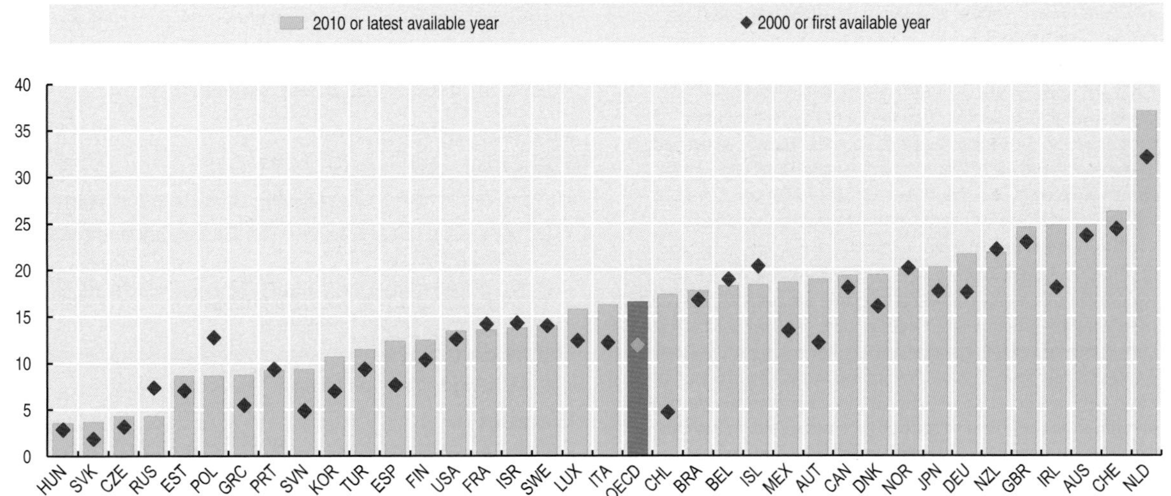

StatLink http://dx.doi.org/10.1787/888932505431

SELF-EMPLOYMENT

Self-employment may be seen either as a survival strategy for those who cannot find any other means of earning an income or as evidence of entrepreneurial spirit and a desire to be one's own boss. The self-employment rates shown here reflect these various motives.

Definition

Employment is generally measured through national labour force surveys. According to the ILO Guidelines, employed persons are defined as those aged 15 or over who report that they have worked in gainful employment for at least one hour in the previous week or who had a job but were absent from work in the reference week.

Self-employed persons include employers, own-account workers, members of producers' co-operatives, and unpaid family workers. People in the last of these groups do not have a formal contract to receive a fixed amount of income at regular intervals, but they share in the income generated by the enterprise; unpaid family workers are particularly important in farming and retail trade. Note that all persons who work in corporate enterprises, including company directors, are considered to be employees.

The rates shown here are the percentages of the self-employed in total civilian employment *i.e.* total employment less military employees.

Comparability

All OECD countries use ILO Guidelines for measuring employment. Operational definitions used in national labour force surveys may, however, vary slightly across countries. Only unincorporated self-employed are included in self-employed in Australia, Canada and the United States. Employment levels are also likely to be affected by changes in the survey design, questions sequencing and/or the ways in which surveys are conducted. Despite this, self-employment rates are likely to be fairly consistent over time.

Overview

In 2010, the share of self-employed workers in the total (men and women together) ranged from under 8% in the United States, and Norway to well over 30% in Greece, Mexico, and Turkey. In general, self-employment rates are highest in countries with low per capita income although Italy, with a self-employment rate of around 25.5%, is an exception. Ireland and Spain also combine high per capita incomes and high self-employment rates.

Over the period 1990-2010, self-employment rates have been falling in most countries. However the Czech Republic, the Netherlands, and the United Kingdom saw moderate increases and the Slovak Republic sharp increases, albeit from low levels in the latter country. Conversely, there have been sharp declines in self-employment rates in Turkey, Greece, Korea, Poland, New Zealand, Spain, Portugal, and Mexico, starting from a higher level.

Levels and changes in total self-employment rates conceal significant differences between men and women. While most men would tend to be employers or own account workers, a larger share of self-employed women play a supporting role in unpaid family jobs. In 2010, considering those countries with data, only two countries, Mexico and Turkey recorded female self-employment rates larger than the male rate. In the case of Turkey, almost half of all woman with a paid job are self-employed, down from 78.4% recorded in 1990.

Sources

- OECD (2011), *Labour Force Statistics*, OECD Publishing.
- For non-member countries: National sources.

Further information

Analytical publications

- OECD (2011), *OECD Employment Outlook*, OECD Publishing.
- OECD (2010), *OECD Studies on SMEs and Entrepreneurship*, OECD Publishing.
- OECD (2005), *OECD SME and Entrepreneurship Outlook – 2005 Edition*, OECD Publishing.

Online databases

- *OECD Employment and Labour Market Statistics.*

Websites

- OECD Employment Policies, *www.oecd.org/els/employment.*
- OECD Centre for Entrepreneurship, SMEs and Local Development, *www.oecd.org/cfe.*

Self-employment rates

As a percentage of total employment by gender

	Total				Men				Women			
	1990	2000	2005	2010	1990	2000	2005	2010	1990	2000	2005	2010
Australia	14.4	13.6 |	12.7	11.6	16.4	16.1 |	15.2	13.9	11.6	10.4 |	9.7	8.9
Austria	14.2 |	13.1 |	13.3	13.8	..	13.9 |	15.3	16.0	..	12.2 |	10.9	11.3
Belgium	18.1 |	15.8	15.2	14.4	18.5 |	17.5	17.5	17.3	17.5 |	13.5	12.3	10.8
Canada	9.5	10.6	9.5	9.2	10.8	11.8	10.6	10.2	7.8	9.2	8.2	8.1
Chile	..	29.8	30.4	26.5	..	32.4	32.8	27.5	..	24.5	25.8	24.9
Czech Republic	..	15.2	16.1	17.8	..	19.1	20.4	22.0	..	10.2	10.4	12.2
Denmark	11.7 |	8.7	8.7	8.8	..	11.7	11.6	11.7	..	5.5	5.3	5.5
Estonia	..	9.1	8.1	8.3	..	11.6	11.3	11.5	..	6.4	5.1	5.3
Finland	15.6	13.7	12.7	13.5	19.5	17.8	16.7	17.7	11.3	9.2	8.5	9.0
France	13.2	9.3	9.1	..	15.0	11.0	10.9	..	10.9	7.3	6.9	..
Germany	..	11.0 |	12.4	11.6	..	13.4 |	14.9	14.4	..	7.9 |	9.4	8.4
Greece	47.7	42.0	36.4	35.5	47.5	43.7	39.1	38.6	48.0	38.9	32.0	31.0
Hungary	..	15.2	13.8	12.3	..	19.1	17.3	15.4	..	10.5	9.9	8.8
Iceland	..	18.0 |	14.2	12.6	..	24.0 |	20.1	16.4	..	11.0 |	7.4	8.4
Ireland	24.9 |	18.8	17.7	17.4	32.3 |	25.8	25.1	25.8	10.9 |	8.7	7.6	7.8
Israel	..	14.2	13.1	12.8	..	18.3	17.3	17.0	..	9.3	8.2	8.0
Italy	28.7 |	28.5	27.0	25.5	31.1 |	32.3	31.2	30.3	24.1 |	22.0	20.6	18.5
Japan	22.3	16.6	14.7	12.3	18.9	15.5	14.5	12.9	27.4	18.3	14.9	11.4
Korea	39.5 |	36.8	33.6	28.8	36.9 |	35.7	34.0	30.0	43.2 |	38.4	32.9	27.1
Luxembourg	9.1	7.4	6.5	..	9.1	7.7	7.4	..	9.1	6.9	5.3	..
Mexico	31.9 |	36.0 |	35.5	34.3	35.5 |	36.4 |	35.7	33.8	20.4 |	35.2 |	35.3	35.1
Netherlands	12.4 |	11.2	12.4	..	11.8 |	12.6	14.6	..	13.4	9.4	9.7	..
New Zealand	19.8	20.6	18.3	..	24.7	25.6	22.7	..	13.4	14.5	13.3	..
Norway	11.3	7.4	7.4 |	7.7	14.6	9.8	10.2 |	10.8	7.4	4.8	4.4 |	4.4
Poland	27.2 |	27.4	25.8	22.8	..	29.5	27.9	25.1	..	24.8	23.1	19.9
Portugal	29.4 |	26.0	25.1	22.9	..	27.4	26.7	25.3	..	24.4	23.3	20.1
Slovak Republic	..	8.0	12.6	16.0	..	10.8	17.2	21.3	..	4.6	6.9	9.4
Slovenia	..	16.1	15.1	17.3	..	18.6	17.2	20.0	..	13.0	12.7	14.0
Spain	25.8	20.2 |	18.2	16.9	25.8	22.2 |	20.8	20.5	25.9	16.6 |	14.5	12.4
Sweden	9.2	10.3 |	9.8	10.9	12.9	14.5 |	14.0	15.0	5.2	5.7 |	5.3	6.4
Switzerland	..	13.2	11.2	..	..	13.9	11.7	..	..	12.3	10.6	..
Turkey	61.0 |	51.4 |	43.0	39.1	53.5 |	46.5 |	40.0	35.1	78.4 |	64.7 |	51.7	49.3
United Kingdom	15.1 |	12.8 |	12.9	13.9	19.9 |	16.7 |	17.4	18.2	8.9 |	8.3 |	7.7	8.9
United States	8.8 |	7.4 |	7.5	7.0	10.5 |	8.6 |	8.8	8.3	6.7 |	6.1 |	5.9	5.6
EU27 total	..	18.3	17.3	..	..	20.9	20.5	..	..	14.8	13.2	..
OECD total	..	17.7 |	16.8 |	..	..	19.1	18.4	..	..	14.8	13.5	..
Russian Federation	..	10.1	7.8	6.9	..	10.5	8.3	7.7	..	9.7	7.3	6.0

StatLink http://dx.doi.org/10.1787/888932505450

Self-employment rates: total

As a percentage of total employment

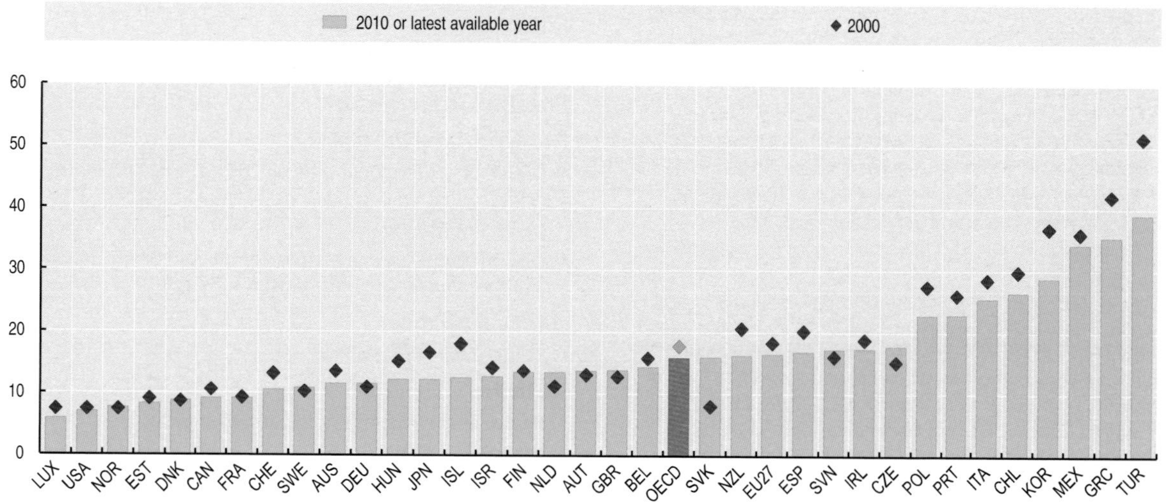

StatLink http://dx.doi.org/10.1787/888932505469

EMPLOYMENT BY REGION

Inequalities in economic performance across regions partly reflect the extent to which each region is able to utilise its available labour resources, and especially to increase job opportunities for under-represented groups.

Definition

Employed persons are all persons who during the reference week of the survey worked at least one hour for pay or profit, or were temporarily absent from such work. The employment rate is the number of employed persons as a percentage of the working age (15-64) population.

Comparability

As for the other regional statistics, comparability is affected by differences in the meaning of the word "region". The word "region" can mean very different things both within and among countries, with significant differences in terms of area and population. To address this issue, the OECD has classified regions within each country based on two levels: territorial level 2 (TL2, large regions) and territorial level 3 (TL3, small regions). Labour market data for Canada refers to a different regional grouping, labelled non-official grids (NOG) comparable to the small regions. For Brazil, China, India, the Russian Federation and South Africa only large regions have been defined so far.

Data on employment growth refer to period 1999-2009 for all countries except for the Czech Republic (2003-09); Finland and Norway (1999-2008); Mexico (2000-09) and Switzerland (2001-09). Denmark and Turkey are excluded for lack of data on comparable years. Data on employment increase contributed by the top 10% of TL3 regions include only countries with average positive growth of employment over 1999-2009. Hungary and Japan are excluded.

Data on employment growth refer to small (TL3) regions for all countries except Portugal. Data on employment growth for women refer to large (TL2) regions.

Overview

Differences in employment growth within countries are larger than across countries. During 1999-2009, international differences in annual employment growth rates across OECD countries were as large as 2.9 percentage points, ranging from -0.4% in Turkey to 2.5% in Spain.

Over the same period, differences in regional employment growth rates across regions were above three percentage points in almost half of the countries. The widest differences in regional employment growth rates are found in Sweden, Spain, the Russian Federation and Canada.

A small number of regions drives employment creation at the national level. On average, 54% of overall employment creation in OECD countries between 1999 and 2009 was accounted for by just 10% of regions. The regional contribution to national employment creation was particularly concentrated in certain countries. In Sweden, the United States and Greece as well as South Africa, more than 60% of employment growth was spurred by 10% of regions.

The last two years have seen an increase in the regional concentration of employment creation in 20 of the 31 countries, resulting in higher differences in employment among regions.

The employment rate for women steadily increased in OECD countries up to 2007, when it reached 57.2% and then declined to 56.7% in 2009 as a result of the job losses following the economic recession. However, in around 25% of OECD regions, less than one out of two women was employed in 2009. Regional differences in employment for women were the largest in Italy, Spain, the United States, France, Portugal, Mexico and the Slovak Republic.

Sources

- OECD (2011), *OECD Regions at a Glance*, OECD Publishing.

Further information

Analytical publications

- OECD (2011), *Regional Outlook 2011*, OECD Publishing.
- OECD (2009), *How Regions Grow: Trends and Analysis*, OECD Publishing.
- OECD (2009), *Regions Matter: Economic Recovery, Innovation and Sustainable Growth*, OECD Publishing.

Online databases

- *OECD Regional Database.*

Websites

- Regional Development, *www.oecd.org/gov/regionaldevelopment*.
- Regional Statistics and Indicators, *www.oecd.org/gov/regional/statisticsindicators*.

Differences in annual employment growth across regions

Percentage, 1999-2009 or latest available period

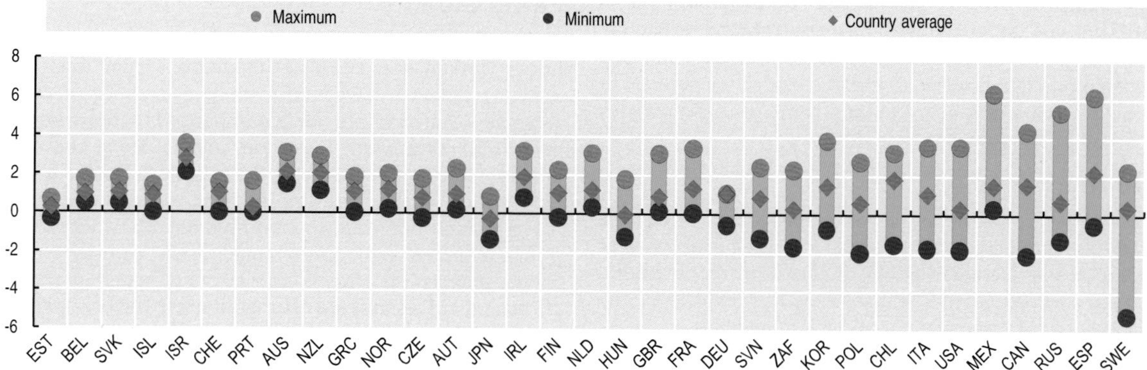

StatLink http://dx.doi.org/10.1787/888932505488

Share of national employment growth due to the 10% of most dynamic regions

Percentage

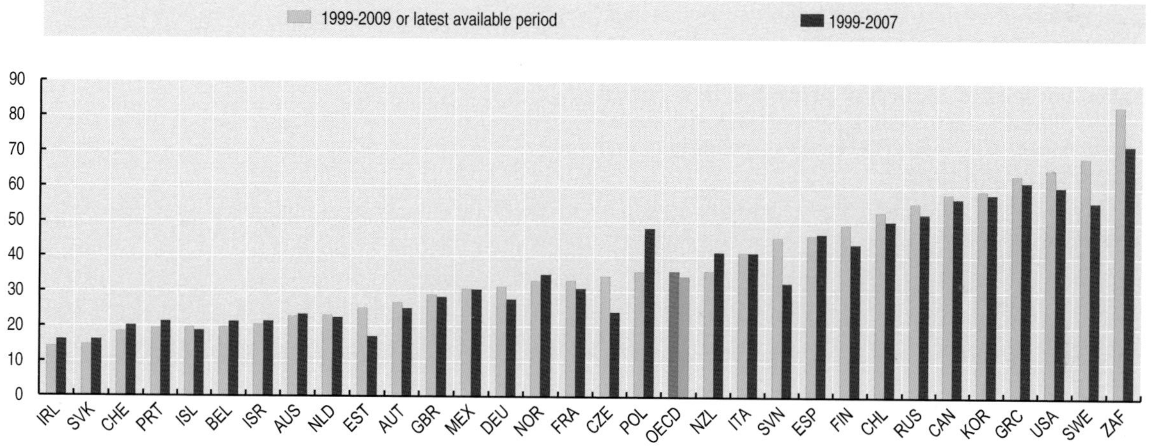

StatLink http://dx.doi.org/10.1787/888932505507

Regional differences in the employment rate of women

Percentage, 2009 or latest available year

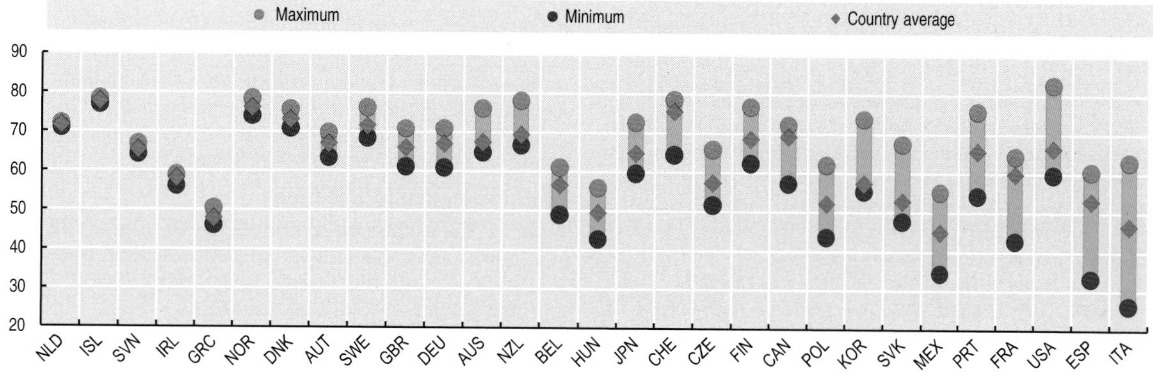

StatLink http://dx.doi.org/10.1787/888932505526

HOURS WORKED

Lower hours worked is one of the forms in which the benefits of productivity growth have been shared by people. In recent years, governments of several OECD countries have also pursued policies to make it easier for parents to reconcile work and family life, and some of these policies have tended to reduce working time.

Definition

The average number of hours worked per year is calculated as the total numbers of hours actually worked over the year divided by the average number of people in employment. The data cover employees and self-employed workers; they include both full-time and part-time employment.

Employment is generally measured through household labour force surveys. In accordance with the ILO Guidelines, employed persons are defined as those aged 15 years or over who report that they have worked in gainful employment for at least one hour in the previous week or were temporarily absent from work.

Estimates of the hours actually worked are based on national labour force surveys in most countries, while others use establishment surveys, administrative records or a combination of sources. Actual hours worked include regular work hours of full-time and part-time workers, overtime (paid and unpaid), hours worked in additional jobs, and time not worked because of public holidays, annual paid leave, illness, maternity and parental leave, strikes and labour disputes, bad weather, economic conditions and several other minor reasons.

Comparability

National statisticians and the OECD work to ensure that hours worked data are as comparable as possible. These data are however based on a range of sources of varying reliability. For example, for a number of EU countries, data are OECD estimates based on results from the *Spring European Labour Force Survey*; these results reflect a single observation in the year, and have to be supplemented by information from other sources on hours not worked due to public holidays and annual paid leave. Annual working hours reported for other countries are provided by national statistical offices and are estimated using the best available sources. These national data are intended for comparisons of trends in productivity and labour inputs and are not fully suitable for inter-country comparisons of the level of hours worked because of differences in their sources and other uncertainties about their international comparability.

Overview

In the large majority of OECD countries, average hours worked per employed person have fallen over the period from 2000 to 2010. However, this decline was rather small in most countries, as compared to the decline in earlier decades. Part of the observed decline in average hours worked between these two years may reflect business cycle effects.

For the OECD as a whole, the average hours worked per employed person fell from 1 818 annual hours in 2000 to 1 749 in 2010; this is equivalent to a reduction of around one and a half hours over a 40-hour work-week. Annual working hours fell in a majority of countries, increasing only in Belgium and Greece. Reductions in annual hours worked over this period were most marked in Chile, Iceland, the Czech Republic and Estonia, where they declined by over 100 hours, with Korea showing the largest decrease of 319 hours.

Although one should exercise caution when comparing levels across countries, actual hours worked are significantly above the OECD average in Korea, Greece, Chile, Hungary, the Czech Republic, Poland, Estonia, Turkey and Mexico, and significantly below the OECD average in the Netherlands, Norway, Germany, Belgium, Austria, Luxembourg and the United Kingdom. The Russian Federation is also significantly above the OECD average with 227 more hours.

Sources

- OECD (2011), *OECD Employment Outlook*, OECD Publishing.

Further information

Analytical publications

- Durand, M., J. Martin and A. Saint-Martin (2004), "The 35 Hour Week: Portrait of a French Exception", *OECD Observer*, No. 244, September, OECD Publishing.
- Evans, J.M., D. Lippoldt and P. Marianna (2001), "Trends in Working Hours in OECD Countries", *OECD Labour Market and Social Policy Occasional Papers*, No. 45.

Methodological publications

- OECD (2004), "Recent Labour Market Developments and Prospects: Clocking In (and Out): Several Facets of Working Time", *OECD Employment Outlook 2004*, OECD Publishing. See also Annex I.A1.

Websites

- OECD Employment Policies, *www.oecd.org/els/employment*.
- OECD Labour Statistics, *www.oecd.org/statistics/labour*.

Average hours actually worked

Hours per year per person in employment

	1997	1998	1999	2000	2001	2002	2003	2004	2005	2006	2007	2008	2009	2010
Australia	1 784	1 775	1 777	1 780	1 739	1 732	1 737	1 732	1 727	1 719	1 712	1 717	1 690	1 686
Austria	1 667	1 668	1 656	1 658	1 657	1 652	1 658	1 663	1 652	1 642	1 632	1 620	1 581	1 587
Belgium	1 567	1 578	1 581	1 545	1 577	1 580	1 575	1 549	1 565	1 566	1 560	1 568	1 550	1 551
Canada	1 780	1 779	1 778	1 775	1 768	1 747	1 736	1 754	1 739	1 738	1 738	1 728	1 700	1 702
Chile	2 256	2 299	2 277	2 263	2 242	2 250	2 235	2 232	2 157	2 165	2 128	2 095	2 074	2 068
Czech Republic	2 067	2 075	2 088	2 092	2 000	1 980	1 972	1 986	2 002	1 997	1 985	1 992	1 942	1 947
Denmark	1 544	1 559	1 569	1 581	1 587	1 579	1 577	1 579	1 579	1 586	1 570	1 570	1 559	..
Estonia	..	..	..	1 987	1 978	1 983	1 985	1 996	2 010	2 001	1 999	1 969	1 831	1 879
Finland	1 771	1 761	1 764	1 751	1 733	1 726	1 719	1 723	1 716	1 709	1 706	1 704	1 673	1 697
France	1 649	1 637	1 630	1 591	1 579	1 537	1 533	1 561	1 557	1 536	1 556	1 560	1 554	..
Germany	1 509	1 503	1 492	1 473	1 458	1 445	1 439	1 442	1 434	1 430	1 430	1 426	1 390	1 419
Greece	2 065	2 063	2 107	2 121	2 121	2 109	2 103	2 082	2 086	2 148	2 116	2 116	2 119	..
Hungary	2 059	2 052	2 067	2 057	2 011	2 019	1 990	1 993	1 993	1 989	1 985	1 986	1 968	1 961
Iceland	1 839	1 817	1 873	1 885	1 847	1 812	1 807	1 810	1 794	1 795	1 807	1 807	1 716	1 697
Ireland	1 832	1 754	1 725	1 719	1 713	1 698	1 671	1 668	1 654	1 645	1 634	1 601	1 549	1 664
Israel	..	..	..	..	..	..	..	1 905	1 989	1 887	1 921	1 898	1 889	..
Italy	1 863	1 880	1 876	1 861	1 843	1 831	1 826	1 826	1 819	1 815	1 816	1 803	1 772	1 778
Japan	1 865	1 842	1 810	1 821	1 809	1 798	1 799	1 787	1 775	1 784	1 785	1 771	1 714	1 733
Korea	2 582	2 488	2 495	2 512	2 499	2 464	2 424	2 392	2 351	2 346	2 306	2 246	2 232	2 193
Luxembourg	1 678	1 672	1 669	1 662	1 646	1 635	1 630	1 586	1 570	1 580	1 515	1 555	1 601	1 616
Mexico	1 927	1 878	1 922	1 888	1 864	1 888	1 857	1 849	1 909	1 883	1 871	1 893	1 857	1 866
Netherlands	1 451	1 440	1 437	1 435	1 424	1 408	1 401	1 399	1 393	1 392	1 388	1 379	1 378	1 377
New Zealand	1 821	1 824	1 837	1 828	1 817	1 817	1 813	1 828	1 811	1 788	1 766	1 750	1 738	1 758
Norway	1 478	1 476	1 473	1 455	1 429	1 414	1 399	1 417	1 420	1 414	1 419	1 423	1 407	1 414
Poland	..	..	..	1 988	1 974	1 979	1 984	1 983	1 994	1 985	1 976	1 969	1 948	1 939
Portugal	1 812	1 799	1 812	1 765	1 769	1 767	1 742	1 763	1 752	1 757	1 727	1 745	1 719	1 714
Slovak Republic	1 834	1 848	1 845	1 844	1 833	1 780	1 734	1 774	1 785	1 779	1 793	1 790	1 738	1 786
Slovenia	..	..	..	..	..	..	..	..	1 698	1 669	1 655	1 687	..	..
Spain	1 728	1 732	1 732	1 731	1 727	1 721	1 706	1 690	1 668	1 656	1 636	1 647	1 653	1 663
Sweden	1 658	1 656	1 665	1 642	1 618	1 595	1 582	1 605	1 605	1 599	1 618	1 617	1 602	1 624
Switzerland	1 665	1 672	1 694	1 688	1 650	1 630	1 643	1 673	1 667	1 652	1 643	1 640	..	..
Turkey	1 878	1 884	1 925	1 937	1 942	1 943	1 943	1 918	1 936	1 944	1 911	1 900	1 881	1 877
United Kingdom	1 731	1 726	1 716	1 700	1 705	1 684	1 674	1 674	1 673	1 668	1 670	1 665	1 643	1 647
United States	1 846	1 846	1 847	1 836	1 814	1 810	1 800	1 802	1 799	1 800	1 798	1 792	1 768	1 778
OECD total	1 841	1 827	1 827	1 818	1 802	1 794	1 785	1 783	1 782	1 779	1 773	1 767	1 741	1 749
Russian Federation	1 951	1 946	1 964	1 982	1 980	1 982	1 994	1 994	1 990	1 999	2 000	1 997	1 973	1 976

StatLink http://dx.doi.org/10.1787/888932505545

Average hours actually worked

Hours per year per person in employment

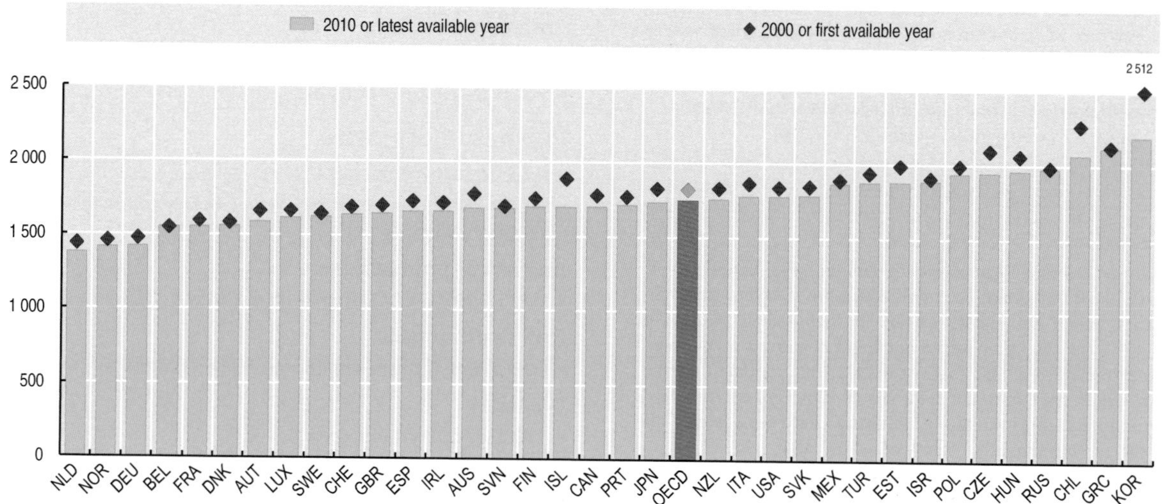

StatLink http://dx.doi.org/10.1787/888932505564

UNEMPLOYMENT RATES

The unemployment rate is one measure of the extent of labour market slack, as well as being an important indicator of economic and social well-being. Breakdowns of unemployment by gender show how certain groups are faring compared to others and to the overall population.

Definition

Unemployed persons are defined as those who report that they are without work, that they are available for work and that they have taken active steps to find work in the last four weeks. The ILO Guidelines specify what actions count as active steps to find work; these include answering vacancy notices, visiting factories, construction sites and other places of work, and placing advertisements in the press as well as registering with labour offices.

The unemployment rate is defined as the number of unemployed persons as a percentage of the labour force, where the latter consists of the unemployed plus those in paid employment.

The unemployment rates shown here differ from rates derived from registered unemployed at labour offices that are often published in individual countries. Data on registered unemployment have limited international comparability, as the rules for registering at labour offices vary from country to country.

When unemployment is high, some persons become discouraged and stop looking for work; they are then excluded from the labour force. This implies that the unemployment rate may fall, or stop rising, even though there has been no underlying improvement in the labour market.

Comparability

All OECD countries use the ILO Guidelines for measuring unemployment. The operational definitions used in national labour force surveys may, however, vary slightly across countries. Unemployment levels are also likely to be affected by changes in the survey design and the survey conduct. Despite these limits, the unemployment rates shown here are fairly consistent over time.

Overview

When looking at total unemployment rates averaged over the three years ending in 2010, countries can be divided into three groups: a low unemployment group with rates below 5% (Austria, Korea, Luxembourg, Norway, the Netherlands and Switzerland); a middle group with unemployment rates between 5% and 10%; and a high unemployment group with unemployment rates of 10% and above (Estonia, Greece, Hungary, Ireland, Portugal, Spain and Turkey).

In most OECD countries, unemployment rates grew over the last three years, with marked increases in Estonia, Ireland and Spain. This increase could be explained by the global recession of 2008-09.

From the breakdown of unemployment by gender, it can be observed that unemployment rates for men and women have increased in the past three years. The unemployment rate for men rose faster than for women in the beginning of the recent economic crisis. This could be explained by the fact that job losses in predominantly male sectors – namely construction, manufacturing mining and quarrying – have been particularly severe. Nevertheless, recent data shows that, the men to women unemployment ratio has slightly decreased in some countries within the last year.

Sources

- OECD (2011), *Main Economic Indicators*, OECD Publishing.
- For non-member countries: National sources.

Further information

Analytical publications

- OECD (2011), *Society at a Glance: OECD Social Indicators*, OECD Publishing.

Statistical publications

- OECD (2011), *OECD Employment Outlook*, OECD Publishing.

Online databases

- *OECD Employment and Labour Market Statistics.*

Websites

- OECD Employment Data, *www.oecd.org/els/employment/data*.
- OECD Employment Policies, *www.oecd.org/els/employment*.
- OECD Labour Statistics, *www.oecd.org/statistics/labour*.

Unemployment rates: total

As a percentage of labour force

	1997	1998	1999	2000	2001	2002	2003	2004	2005	2006	2007	2008	2009	2010
Australia	8.5	7.7	6.9	6.3	6.8	6.4	5.9	5.4	5.0	4.8	4.4	4.2	5.6	5.2
Austria	4.4	4.5	3.9	3.6	3.6	4.2	4.3	4.9	5.2	4.7	4.4	3.8	4.8	4.4
Belgium	9.2	9.3	8.5	6.9	6.6	7.5	8.2	8.4	8.5	8.3	7.5	7.0	7.9	8.3
Canada	9.1	8.3	7.6	6.8	7.2	7.7	7.6	7.2	6.8	6.3	6.0	6.1	8.3	8.0
Chile	6.1	6.4	10.1	9.7	9.9	9.8	9.5	10.0	9.2	7.8	7.1	7.8	10.8	8.2
Czech Republic	4.8 |	6.4	8.6	8.7	8.0	7.3	7.8	8.3	7.9	7.2	5.3	4.4	6.7	7.3
Denmark	5.2	4.9	5.1	4.3	4.5	4.6	5.4	5.5	4.8	3.9	3.8	3.3	6.0	7.4
Estonia	9.7	9.2	11.4	13.6	12.6	10.2	10.0	9.7	7.8	5.9	4.6	5.6	13.8	16.8
Finland	12.7	11.4	10.3	9.6	9.1	9.1	9.1	8.9	8.3	7.7	6.9	6.4	8.2	8.4
France	11.4	11.0	10.4	9.0	8.3	8.6	9.0	9.2	9.3	9.2	8.4	7.8	9.5	9.8
Germany	9.7	9.4	8.6	8.0	7.9	8.7	9.8	10.5	11.2	10.2	8.8	7.6	7.7	7.1
Greece	9.6	11.1	12.0	11.2	10.7	10.3	9.7	10.5	9.9	8.9	8.3	7.7	9.5	12.6
Hungary	9.0	8.4	6.9	6.4	5.7	5.8	5.9	6.1	7.2	7.4	7.4	7.8	10.0	11.2
Iceland	3.9	2.7	2.0	2.3	2.3	3.3 |	3.4	3.1	2.6	2.9	2.3	3.0	7.2	7.5
Ireland	9.9	7.6	5.7	4.2	4.0	4.5	4.6	4.5	4.4	4.5	4.6	6.3	11.9	13.7
Israel	..	..	..	..	9.3	10.3	10.7	10.4	9.0	8.4	7.3	6.1 |	7.5	6.7
Italy	11.2	11.3	10.9	10.1	9.1	8.6	8.5	8.0	7.7	6.8	6.1	6.8	7.8	8.4
Japan	3.4	4.1	4.7	4.7	5.0	5.4	5.3	4.7	4.4	4.1	3.9	4.0	5.1	5.1
Korea	2.6	7.0	6.6 |	4.4	4.0	3.3	3.6	3.7	3.7	3.5	3.2	3.2	3.6	3.7
Luxembourg	2.7	2.7	2.4	2.3	1.9	2.6	3.8	4.9	4.6	4.6	4.2	4.9	5.1	4.5
Mexico	3.7	3.2	2.5	2.5 |	2.8	3.0	3.4	3.9	3.6	3.6	3.7	4.0	5.5	5.4
Netherlands	5.4	4.3	3.6	3.0	2.6	3.1	4.1	5.1	5.3	4.3	3.6	3.1	3.7	4.5
New Zealand	6.8	7.7	7.1	6.2	5.5	5.3	4.8	4.1	3.8	3.9	3.7	4.2	6.1	6.5
Norway	3.9	3.1	3.0	3.2	3.4	3.7	4.2	4.3	4.5	3.4	2.5	2.5	3.2	3.5
Poland	10.9	10.2	13.4	16.2	18.3	20.0	19.7	19.0	17.8	13.9	9.6	7.2	8.2	9.6
Portugal	6.7 |	5.6	5.0	4.5	4.6	5.7	7.1	7.5	8.6	8.6	8.9	8.5	10.6	12.0
Slovak Republic	11.8 |	12.6	16.3	18.8	19.3	18.7	17.6	18.2	16.2	13.4	11.1	9.5	12.0	14.4
Slovenia	6.9	7.4	7.4	6.7	6.2	6.3	6.7	6.3	6.5	6.0	4.9	4.4	5.9	7.3
Spain	16.7	15.0	12.5	11.1	10.4	11.1	11.1	10.6	9.2	8.5	8.3	11.4	18.0	20.1
Sweden	9.9	8.2	6.7	5.6 |	5.9	6.0	6.6	7.4	7.7 |	7.1	6.1	6.2	8.3	8.4
Switzerland	3.9	3.3	2.8	2.5	2.2	2.9	3.9	4.1	4.2	3.8	3.4	3.2	4.1	4.2
Turkey	..	..	..	..	..	..	..	..	9.2	8.7	8.8	9.7	12.5	10.6
United Kingdom	6.8	6.1	5.9	5.4	5.0	5.1	5.0	4.7	4.8	5.4	5.3	5.7	7.6	7.8
United States	4.9	4.5	4.2 |	4.0	4.7	5.8	6.0	5.5	5.1	4.6	4.6	5.8	9.3	9.6
EU27 total	..	9.5	9.3	8.8	8.6	9.0	9.1	9.2	9.0	8.3	7.2	7.1	9.0	9.7
OECD total	6.9	6.8	6.8	6.3	6.6	7.1	7.3	7.1	6.8	6.2	5.8	6.1	8.4	8.6
Brazil	10.1	13.6	13.5	12.7	11.2	11.7	12.3	11.5	9.8	10.0	9.3	7.9	8.1	6.7
Indonesia	4.7	5.5	6.4	6.1	8.1	9.1	9.7	9.9 |	10.8	10.4	9.4	8.4	8.0	7.3
Russian Federation	10.8	11.9	12.9	10.5	9.0	8.0	8.6	8.2	7.6	7.2	6.1	6.4	8.4	7.5
South Africa	..	..	..	23.3	26.2	26.6	24.8	23.0	23.5	22.1	21.0 |	22.9	23.9 |	24.9

StatLink http://dx.doi.org/10.1787/888932505583

Unemployment rates: total

As a percentage of labour force

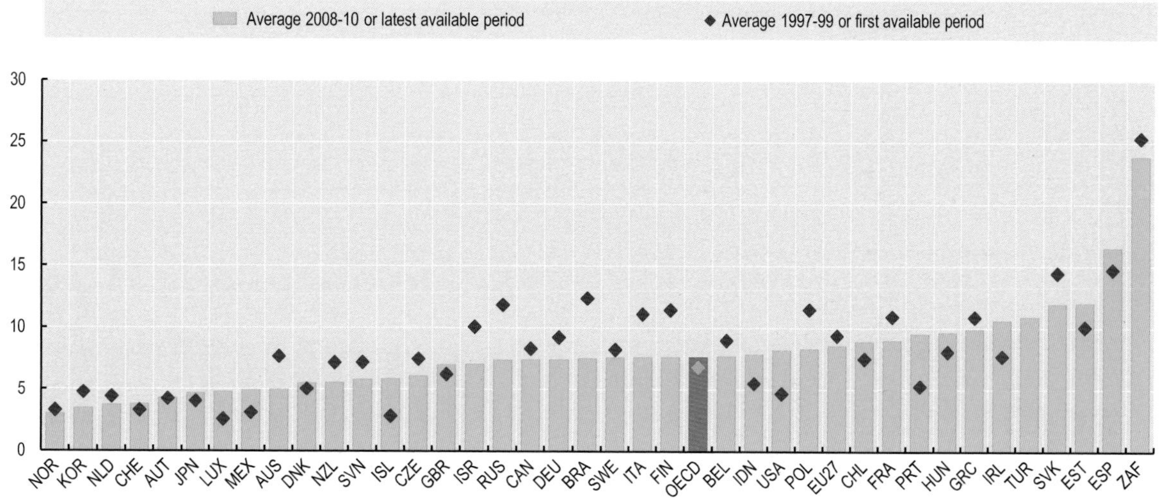

StatLink http://dx.doi.org/10.1787/888932505602

Unemployment rates: men

As a percentage of men in the labour force

	1997	1998	1999	2000	2001	2002	2003	2004	2005	2006	2007	2008	2009	2010
Australia	8.7	8.0	7.1	6.5	7.0	6.5	5.9	5.3	4.9	4.7	4.0	4.0	5.7	5.1
Austria	3.6	3.8	3.3	3.0	3.2	4.0	4.0	4.5	4.9	4.3	3.9	3.6	5.0	4.6
Belgium	7.3	7.6	7.2	5.6	5.9	6.7	7.7	7.5	7.7	7.4	6.7	6.5	7.7	8.1
Canada	9.3	8.5	7.8	6.9	7.5	8.1	7.9	7.5	7.0	6.5	6.4	6.6	9.4	8.7
Chile	5.4	5.8	9.8	9.3	9.7	9.6	9.1	9.4	8.5	6.9	6.3	6.8	9.8	7.2
Czech Republic	4.0 |	5.0	7.3	7.3	6.7	6.0	6.2	7.1	6.5	5.8	4.2	3.5	5.9	6.4
Denmark	4.5	3.9	4.5	3.9	4.1	4.3	4.9	5.1	4.4	3.4	3.4	3.0	6.6	8.2
Estonia	10.4	9.9	12.5	14.6	13.0	10.8	10.3	10.4	8.6	6.1	5.3	6.0	17.0	19.4
Finland	12.4	10.9	9.7	8.7	8.7	9.1	9.3	8.8	8.1	7.4	6.6	6.2	8.9	9.1
France	10.0	9.4	8.9	7.5	7.0	7.7	8.1	8.4	8.4	8.5	7.8	7.3	9.3	9.4
Germany	9.0	8.9	8.2	7.7	7.8	8.9	10.1	10.8	11.5	10.2	8.7	7.5	8.1	7.6
Greece	6.3	7.3	8.0	7.4	7.2	6.8	6.2	6.6	6.2	5.7	5.2	5.1	6.9	10.0
Hungary	9.7	9.0	7.4	7.0	6.3	6.2	6.1	6.1	7.0	7.2	7.1	7.7	10.3	11.6
Iceland	3.3	2.2	1.4	1.8	2.1	3.6 |	3.6	3.2	2.6	2.7	2.3	3.3	8.6	8.3
Ireland	9.9	7.7	5.7	4.3	4.1	4.8	4.9	4.9	4.6	4.6	4.9	7.5	14.9	16.9
Israel	..	..	..	..	8.9	10.1	10.2	9.5	8.6	7.9	6.8	5.8 |	7.6	6.8
Italy	8.7	8.8	8.5	7.8	7.0	6.7	6.5	6.4	6.2	5.4	4.9	5.6	6.8	7.5
Japan	3.4	4.2	4.8	4.9	5.2	5.5	5.5	4.9	4.6	4.3	3.9	4.1	5.3	5.4
Korea	2.8	7.8	7.4 |	5.0	4.5	3.7	3.8	3.9	4.0	3.8	3.7	3.6	4.1	4.0
Luxembourg	2.0	1.9	1.8	1.8	1.6	2.0	3.0	3.6	3.6	3.6	3.4	4.1	4.6	3.9
Mexico	..	..	..	..	2.4	2.6	2.9	3.3	3.4	3.4	3.5	3.9	5.5	5.4
Netherlands	4.4	3.5	2.8	2.4	2.1	2.8	4.1	4.9	4.9	3.9	3.1	2.8	3.7	4.4
New Zealand	6.9	7.8	7.3	6.3	5.5	5.2	4.5	3.6	3.6	3.6	3.4	4.1	6.1	6.2
Norway	3.7	3.0	3.2	3.4	3.5	3.8	4.5	4.6	4.7	3.5	2.6	2.7	3.6	4.0
Poland	9.1	8.5	11.8	14.4	16.9	19.1	19.0	18.2	16.6	13.0	9.0	6.5	7.8	9.3
Portugal	6.0 |	4.8	4.7	3.8	3.9	5.1	6.7	7.2	8.1	8.0	8.0	7.9	10.7	11.8
Slovak Republic	11.1 |	12.2	16.3	18.9	19.8	18.6	17.4	17.4	15.4	12.2	9.9	8.4	11.4	14.2
Slovenia	6.8	7.3	7.2	6.5	5.7	5.9	6.4	5.9	6.1	4.9	4.0	4.0	5.9	7.5
Spain	13.1	11.2	9.0	7.9	7.5	8.1	8.2	8.0	7.1	6.3	6.4	10.1	17.7	19.8
Sweden	10.2	8.4	6.6	5.9 |	6.1	6.3	6.9	7.6	7.7 |	6.9	5.9	5.9	8.6	8.5
Switzerland	4.0	3.0	2.5	2.1	1.6	2.6	3.6	3.8	3.7	3.2	2.7	2.7	3.7	3.8
Turkey	..	..	..	..	..	..	..	..	9.2	8.6	8.7	9.6	12.5	10.4
United Kingdom	7.7	6.8	6.5	5.9	5.5	5.7	5.5	5.1	5.2	5.8	5.6	6.2	8.6	8.6
United States	4.9	4.4	4.1 |	3.9	4.8	5.9	6.3	5.6	5.1	4.6	4.7	6.1	10.3	10.5
EU27 total	..	8.5	8.3	7.8	7.8	8.3	8.5	8.6	8.4	7.6	6.7	6.7	9.1	9.7
OECD total	6.5	6.6	6.5	6.1	6.5	7.1	7.3	7.1	6.7	6.2	5.7	6.2	8.9	9.0
Brazil	..	..	..	..	..	..	10.1	9.1	7.8	8.2	7.4	6.1	6.5	5.2
Indonesia	..	..	..	..	..	..	..	..	..	..	..	7.7	..	..
Russian Federation	12.1	13.5	13.2	10.6	9.3	8.1	8.4	8.0	7.3	7.5	6.4	6.6	9.0	8.0
South Africa	..	..	..	20.4	23.3	22.6	21.7	19.9	19.7	17.8	18.2 |	20.0	22.1 |	22.8

StatLink http://dx.doi.org/10.1787/888932505621

Unemployment rates: men

As a percentage of men in the labour force

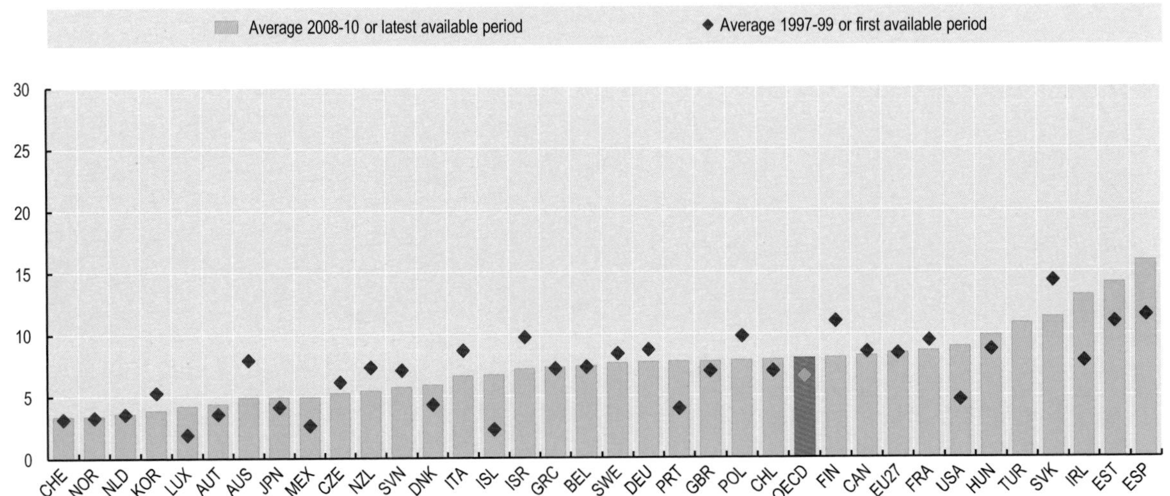

StatLink http://dx.doi.org/10.1787/888932505640

Unemployment rates: women

As a percentage of women in the labour force

	1997	1998	1999	2000	2001	2002	2003	2004	2005	2006	2007	2008	2009	2010
Australia	8.2	7.4	6.7	6.1	6.4	6.2	6.0	5.5	5.2	4.9	4.8	4.6	5.4	5.4
Austria	5.4	5.4	4.7	4.3	4.2	4.4	4.7	5.4	5.5	5.3	5.0	4.1	4.6	4.2
Belgium	11.9	11.6	10.2	8.5	7.5	8.7	8.8	9.5	9.5	9.3	8.4	7.6	8.1	8.5
Canada	8.9	8.0	7.3	6.7	6.9	7.1	7.2	6.9	6.5	6.1	5.6	5.7	7.0	7.2
Chile	7.7	7.6	10.8	10.3	10.1	10.1	10.3	11.2	10.6	9.5	8.6	9.5	12.5	9.7
Czech Republic	5.9 |	8.0	10.3	10.3	9.7	9.0	9.9	9.9	9.8	8.9	6.8	5.6	7.7	8.5
Denmark	6.2	6.0	5.7	4.8	5.0	5.0	6.1	6.0	5.3	4.5	4.2	3.7	5.4	6.6
Estonia	8.9	8.4	10.2	12.7	12.2	9.7	9.8	8.9	7.0	5.6	3.9	5.3	10.6	14.3
Finland	13.0	11.9	10.8	10.5	9.7	9.1	8.9	9.0	8.5	8.1	7.2	6.7	7.6	7.7
France	13.2	12.8	12.1	10.8	9.9	9.8	10.0	10.2	10.3	10.1	9.0	8.4	9.8	10.2
Germany	10.6	10.2	9.1	8.3	8.0	8.5	9.4	10.2	10.9	10.0	8.9	7.7	7.3	6.5
Greece	14.8	17.0	18.1	17.1	16.1	15.7	15.0	16.2	15.3	13.6	12.8	11.4	13.2	16.2
Hungary	8.1	7.8	6.3	5.6	5.0	5.5	5.6	6.1	7.4	7.8	7.7	8.0	9.7	10.7
Iceland	4.5	3.2	2.6	2.9	2.5	2.9 |	3.1	2.9	2.6	3.1	2.3	2.6	5.7	6.7
Ireland	9.9	7.3	5.5	4.1	3.8	4.1	4.1	4.0	4.1	4.2	4.1	4.8	8.0	9.7
Israel	..	..	..	..	9.9	10.6	11.3	11.4	9.5	9.0	7.9	6.5 |	7.5	6.5
Italy	15.3	15.4	14.8	13.6	12.2	11.5	11.4	10.5	10.0	8.8	7.9	8.6	9.3	9.7
Japan	3.4	4.0	4.5	4.5	4.7	5.1	4.9	4.4	4.2	3.9	3.7	3.8	4.8	4.6
Korea	2.3	5.7	5.3 |	3.6	3.3	2.7	3.3	3.4	3.4	2.9	2.6	2.6	3.0	3.3
Luxembourg	3.9	4.0	3.3	2.9	2.4	3.4	4.9	6.8	6.0	6.0	5.2	5.8	5.9	5.3
Mexico	..	..	..	..	3.5	3.7	4.3	5.1	4.0	3.9	4.1	4.1	5.5	5.3
Netherlands	6.8	5.5	4.5	3.9	3.3	3.5	4.3	5.3	5.8	5.0	4.1	3.4	3.8	4.5
New Zealand	6.9	7.6	6.7	6.0	5.4	5.5	5.1	4.6	4.1	4.2	4.0	4.2	6.2	6.9
Norway	4.1	3.2	2.9	3.1	3.3	3.5	3.9	3.9	4.3	3.4	2.5	2.3	2.6	3.0
Poland	13.0	12.2	15.2	18.2	19.9	20.9	20.5	20.0	19.2	15.0	10.4	8.0	8.7	10.0
Portugal	7.6 |	6.6	5.4	5.3	5.4	6.4	7.7	8.0	9.1	9.3	10.0	9.2	10.5	12.3
Slovak Republic	12.8 |	13.2	16.4	18.6	18.7	18.7	17.8	19.2	17.2	14.7	12.7	10.9	12.8	14.6
Slovenia	7.1	7.5	7.6	7.0	6.8	6.8	7.1	6.8	7.1	7.2	5.9	4.8	5.8	7.1
Spain	22.6	21.2	18.1	16.1	14.8	15.7	15.3	14.3	12.2	11.6	10.9	13.1	18.4	20.5
Sweden	9.5	8.0	6.8	5.3 |	5.6	5.6	6.2	7.1	7.6 |	7.2	6.4	6.5	8.0	8.3
Switzerland	3.9	3.7	3.2	3.1	3.0	3.2	4.2	4.6	4.8	4.5	4.2	3.8	4.5	4.7
Turkey	..	..	..	..	..	..	..	..	9.3	9.1	9.1	10.1	12.6	11.4
United Kingdom	5.8	5.3	5.2	4.8	4.4	4.5	4.3	4.2	4.3	5.0	5.0	5.1	6.4	6.8
United States	5.0	4.6	4.3 |	4.1	4.7	5.6	5.7	5.4	5.1	4.6	4.5	5.4	8.1	8.6
EU27 total	..	10.9	10.5	10.0	9.6	9.9	9.9	10.0	9.8	9.0	7.9	7.6	9.0	9.6
OECD total	7.7	7.6	7.4	7.0	7.0	7.5	7.6	7.5	7.3	6.7	6.2	6.3	8.0	8.4
Brazil	..	..	..	..	..	..	15.2	14.4	12.4	12.2	11.6	10.0	9.9	8.5
Indonesia	..	..	..	..	..	..	..	..	..	..	..	9.5	..	..
Russian Federation	11.5	13.0	12.9	10.4	8.6	7.6	8.0	7.5	7.0	6.8	5.8	6.1	7.9	7.0
South Africa	..	..	..	26.5	29.4	31.1	28.4	26.6	27.8	27.0	24.3 |	26.3	26.1 |	27.5

StatLink http://dx.doi.org/10.1787/888932505659

Unemployment rates: women

As a percentage of women in the labour force

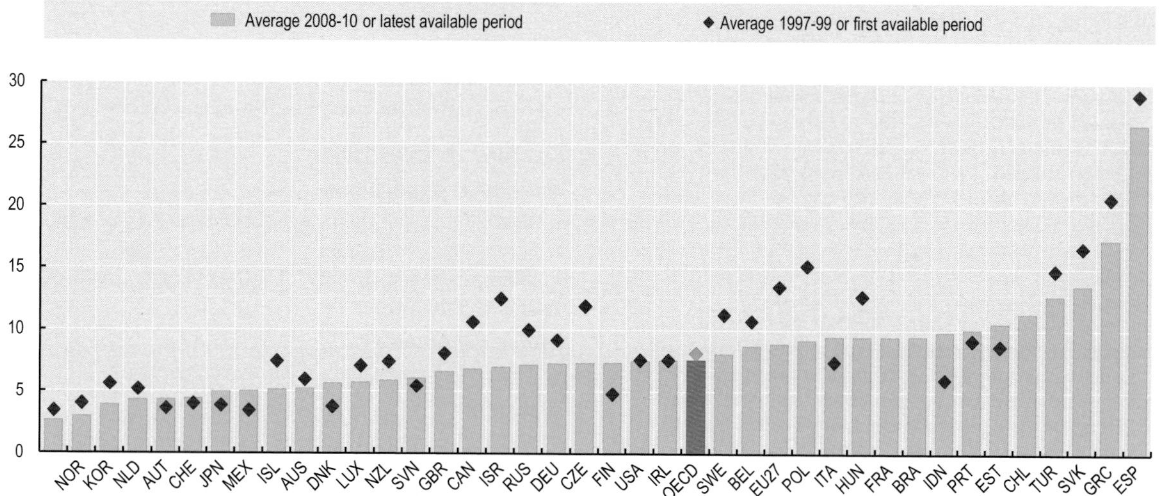

StatLink http://dx.doi.org/10.1787/888932505678

LONG-TERM UNEMPLOYMENT

Long-term unemployment is of particular concern to the people affected and to policy makers. Quite apart from the mental stress caused to the unemployed and their families, high rates of long-term unemployment indicate that labour markets are operating inefficiently. In countries that pay generous unemployment benefits, the existence of long-term unemployment is also a significant burden on government finances.

Definition

Long-term unemployment is here defined as referring to people who have been unemployed for 12 months or more. The ratios calculated here show the proportion of these long-term unemployed among all unemployed, hereafter called long-term unemployment rates. Lower duration limits (*e.g.* six months or more) are sometimes considered in national statistics on the subject.

Unemployment is defined in most OECD countries in accordance with the ILO Guidelines. Unemployment is usually measured by national labour force surveys and refer to persons who report that they have worked in gainful employment for less than one hour in the previous week, who are available for work and who have taken actions to seek employment in the previous four weeks. The ILO Guidelines specify the kinds of actions that count as seeking work.

Comparability

All OECD countries use the ILO Guidelines for measuring unemployment. Operational definitions used in national labour force surveys may vary slightly across countries. Unemployment levels may also be affected by changes in the survey design and the survey conduct. Despite these caveats the long-term unemployment rates shown here are fairly consistent over time.

In comparing rates of long-term unemployment, it is important to bear in mind differences in institutional arrangements between countries. Rates of long-term unemployment will generally be higher in countries where unemployment benefits are relatively generous and are available for long periods of unemployment. In countries where benefits are low and of limited duration, unemployed persons will more quickly lower their wage expectations or consider taking jobs that are in other ways less attractive than those which they formerly held.

Overview

Rates of long-term unemployment are generally lower in countries that have enjoyed high GDP growth rates in recent years. There appears to be a two-way causal relationship here; on the one hand, jobs are easier to find in a faster growing economy; on the other, in economies that grow faster, unemployment will become increasingly unattractive relative to having a paid job. Lower rates of long-term unemployment may also occur at the onset of an economic downturn due to rising inflow of newly unemployed persons, as witnessed during the first years of the current jobs crisis.

In 2010, rates of long-term unemployment varied from 10% or less in Korea, Mexico, Norway and New Zealand, to 50% or more in Hungary, Portugal and the Slovak Republic. Estonia and Slovenia have experienced long-term unemployment rates over 10% above the OECD average, whereas Israel is 10% lower than the OECD average.

Over the period 2000-2010, long-term unemployment rates increased by 1.2 percentage for the OECD as a whole. Gradually falling until 2007, long-term unemployment rates receded markedly the first two years at the onset of the current crisis, while increasing by more than 8 percentage points between 2009 and 2010. Country patterns differ depending on how deeply national labour markets were affected by the current crisis. Since 2000, sharp rises, of 5 percentage points or more, were recorded in Ireland, Japan, Israel, Iceland, Portugal, Turkey, Luxembourg and Switzerland, with a remarkable increase of 23 percentage points in the United States. Falls of over 5 per cent occurred in just under one third of countries, with Italy, Poland, Slovenia, Greece and New Zealand recording the steepest fall of over 10 percentage points. In the new OECD member countries, long-term unemployment rates have almost doubled over the 10 years to 2010 in Israel, while they have receded markedly in Slovenia (since 2005) and very slightly in Estonia. The delayed impact of rising inflows into unemployment during the first two years of the current crisis is witnessed by rising long-term unemployment rates in all countries, except Korea, since 2009. Rises of 10 percentage points or more are visible in Ireland, Estonia, Spain, Iceland, Slovenia, the Czech Republic, the United States and Denmark.

Sources

- OECD (2011), *Labour Force Statistics*, OECD Publishing.
- For non-member countries: National sources.

Further information

Analytical publications

- OECD (2011), *OECD Employment Outlook*, OECD Publishing.
- OECD (2002), "The Ins and Outs of Long-term Unemployment", in OECD, *OECD Employment Outlook 2002*, OECD Publishing.

Online databases

- *OECD Employment and Labour Market Statistics*.

Websites

- OECD Employment Outlook (supplementary material), *www.oecd.org/els/employmentoutlook*.
- OECD Employment Policies, *www.oecd.org/els/employment*.
- OECD Labour Statistics, *www.oecd.org/statistics/labour*.

Long-term unemployment

Persons unemployed for 12 months or more as a percentage of total unemployed

	1997	1998	1999	2000	2001	2002	2003	2004	2005	2006	2007	2008	2009	2010
Australia	31.2	32.9	31.3	28.3	23.9	22.4	21.5	20.6	18.3	18.1	15.4	14.9	14.7	18.5
Austria	27.5	30.3	29.2	25.8	23.3	19.2	24.5	27.6	25.3	27.3	26.8	24.2	21.3	25.2
Belgium	60.5	61.7	60.5	56.3	51.7	48.8	45.4	49.0	51.7	51.2	50.4	47.6	44.2	48.8
Canada	16.1	13.8	11.7	11.3	9.5	9.6	10.0	9.5	9.6	8.7	7.4	7.1	7.8	12.0
Czech Republic	30.5	31.2	37.1	48.8	52.7	50.7	49.9	51.8	53.6	55.2	53.4	50.2	31.2	43.3
Denmark	27.2	26.9	20.5	20.0	22.2	19.1	20.4	21.5	23.4	20.8	16.2	13.1	9.1	19.1
Estonia	49.0	49.7	48.9	46.3	48.3	52.9	45.9	52.2	53.4	48.2	49.5	30.9	27.4	45.4
Finland	29.8	27.5	29.6	29.0	26.2	24.4	24.7	23.4	24.9	24.8	23.0	18.2	16.6	23.6
France	39.6	41.6	38.7	39.6	36.8	32.7	39.2	40.6	41.1	41.9	40.2	37.5	35.2	40.1
Germany	50.1	52.6	51.7	51.5	50.4	47.9	50.0	51.8	53.0	56.4	56.6	52.6	45.5	47.4
Greece	55.7	54.9	55.3	56.4	52.8	51.3	54.9	53.1	52.1	54.3	50.0	47.5	40.8	45.0
Hungary	51.3	50.1	49.4	48.9	46.5	44.8	42.2	45.1	46.1	46.1	47.5	47.6	42.6	50.6
Iceland	16.3	16.1	11.7	11.8	12.5	11.1	8.1	11.2	13.3	7.3	8.0	4.1	6.9	21.3
Ireland	57.0	..	55.3	..	33.1	30.1	32.8	34.9	33.4	31.6	29.5	27.1	29.0	49.0
Israel	6.4	7.3	11.3	12.0	11.8	13.5	18.0	24.2	25.3	27.3	24.9	22.7	20.3	22.4
Italy	66.3	59.6	61.4	61.3	63.4	59.6	58.1	49.2	49.9	49.6	47.3	45.7	44.4	48.5
Japan	21.8	20.3	22.4	25.5	26.6	30.8	33.5	33.7	33.3	33.0	32.0	33.3	28.5	37.6
Korea	2.6	1.5	3.8	2.3	2.3	2.5	0.6	1.1	0.8	1.1	0.6	2.7	0.5	0.3
Luxembourg	34.6	31.3	32.3	22.4	28.4	27.4	24.7	21.0	26.4	29.5	28.7	32.4	23.1	29.3
Mexico	1.8	0.8	1.5	1.2	1.0	0.9	0.9	1.1	2.3	2.5	2.7	1.7	1.9	2.4
Netherlands	49.1	47.9	43.5	..	..	26.5	27.8	34.2	40.2	43.0	39.4	34.4	24.8	27.6
New Zealand	19.8	19.6	21.1	19.8	17.2	14.8	13.6	11.7	9.7	7.8	6.1	4.4	6.3	9.0
Norway	12.4	8.3	7.1	5.3	5.5	6.4	6.4	9.2	9.5	14.5	8.8	6.0	7.7	9.5
Poland	38.0	37.4	34.8	37.9	43.1	48.4	49.7	47.9	52.2	50.4	45.9	29.0	25.2	25.5
Portugal	55.6	44.7	41.2	42.9	38.1	34.6	35.0	44.3	48.2	50.2	47.1	47.4	44.1	52.3
Slovak Republic	51.6	51.3	47.7	54.6	53.7	59.8	61.1	60.6	68.1	73.1	70.8	66.0	50.9	59.3
Slovenia	..	..	..	..	..	55.6	52.8	51.5	47.3	49.3	45.7	42.2	30.1	43.3
Spain	55.7	54.3	51.2	47.6	44.0	40.2	39.8	37.7	32.6	29.5	27.6	23.8	30.2	45.1
Sweden	33.4	33.5	30.1	26.4	22.3	20.9	17.8	18.9	..	..	13.0	12.4	12.8	16.6
Switzerland	28.2	34.8	39.6	29.0	29.9	21.8	26.1	33.5	39.0	39.1	40.8	34.3	30.1	34.3
Turkey	41.6	40.3	28.2	21.1	21.3	29.4	24.4	39.2	39.4	35.7	30.3	26.9	25.3	28.6
United Kingdom	38.6	32.7	29.6	28.0	27.8	21.7	21.5	20.6	21.0	22.3	23.7	24.1	24.5	32.6
United States	8.7	8.0	6.8	6.0	6.1	8.5	11.8	12.7	11.8	10.0	10.0	10.6	16.3	29.0
OECD total	34.8	32.9	31.6	31.2	29.5	29.3	30.4	31.6	32.4	31.8	29.0	25.5	24.2	32.4

StatLink http://dx.doi.org/10.1787/888932505697

Long-term unemployment

Persons unemployed for 12 months or more as a percentage of total unemployed

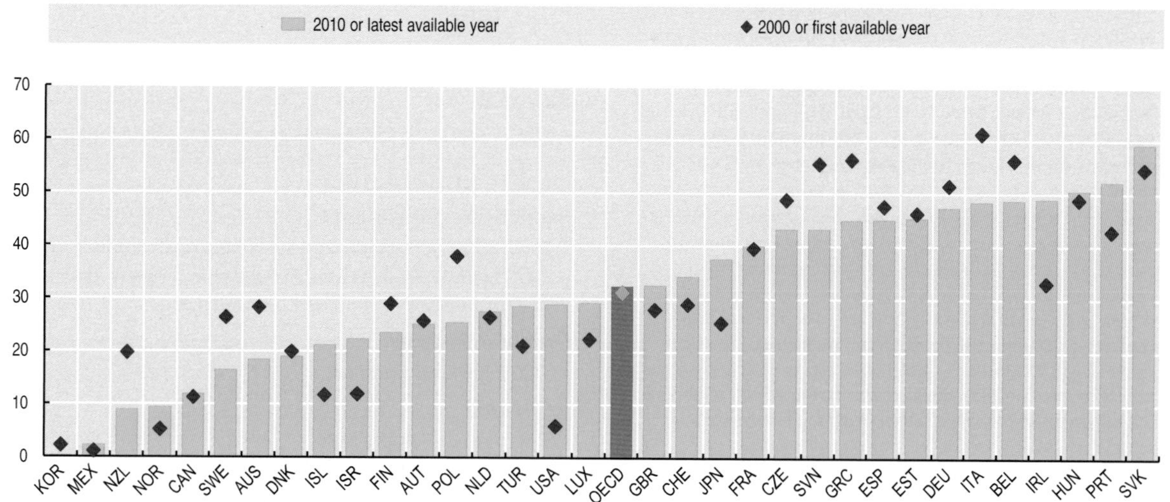

StatLink http://dx.doi.org/10.1787/888932505716

UNEMPLOYMENT BY REGION

Unemployment rates vary significantly among countries but large international differences hide even larger differences among regions within each country.

Definition

Unemployed persons are defined as those who are without work, who are available for work and have taken active steps to find work in the last four weeks. The unemployment rate is defined as the ratio between unemployed persons and labour force, where the latter is composed of unemployed and employed persons.

The long-term unemployment rate is defined as the ratio of those unemployed for 12 months or more out of the total labour force.

The Gini index is a measure of inequality among all regions of a given country. The index takes on values between 0 and 1, with zero interpreted as no disparity. It assigns equal weight to each region regardless of its size; therefore differences in the values of the index among countries may be partially due to differences in the average size of regions in each country.

Comparability

As for the other regional statistics, the comparability of unemployment rates is affected by differences in the meaning of the word "region". The word "region" can mean very different things both within and among countries, with significant differences in terms of area and population. To address this issue, the OECD has classified regions within each country based on two levels: territorial level 2 (TL2, large regions) and territorial level 3 (TL3, small regions). Labour market data for Canada refers to a different regional grouping, labelled non-official grids (NOG), which is comparable to the small regions. For Brazil, China, India, the Russian Federation and South Africa only large regions have been defined so far.

Data on unemployment refer to small (TL3) regions. Data on youth and long-term unemployment refer to large (TL2) regions.

Overview

Unemployment has soared in OECD countries in recent years, from 5.6% in 2007 to 8.3% in 2009. Recent OECD analysis suggests a further rise in the past two years. In 2009, regional differences in unemployment rates within OECD countries were almost two times higher (28 percentage points) than differences among OECD countries (15 percentage points).

Regional disparities in unemployment were already high before the economic crisis in countries such as Canada, Germany, Italy, Spain and the Slovak Republic. Overall the economic downturn has aggravated problems of the most fragile regions. The Gini index gives a measure of differences in unemployment rates among all regions in a country. According to this measure Belgium, Germany, Italy and the Slovak Republic displayed the highest inequalities among OECD countries. Large regional differences were also found in China and the Russian Federation.

Young people have been hit hardest by the economic crisis: youth employment fell by 8% between the end of 2008 and the end of 2009, nearly four times the decline in overall employment.

Youth unemployment is of particular concern in Italy, France, the Slovak Republic, Turkey, Poland and Spain, where regional differences are high and some regions display a youth unemployment rate over 30%.These regions display also higher than average early leavers from education and training, suggesting that specific policies to improve the employability of these people through training and apprenticeship are needed.

Among the unemployed, the long-term unemployed (*i.e.* those who have been unemployed for 12 months or more) are of particular concern to policy makers both for their impact on social cohesion and because those individuals become increasingly unattractive to employers. The regional long-term unemployment is, therefore, an indicator of labour-market rigidity. Moreover, it highlights areas with individuals whose inadequate skills prevent them from getting a job. The long-term unemployment rate showed large regional variations not only in dual economies such as Italy or Germany, but also in Spain, the Slovak Republic, Belgium, Turkey and Hungary.

Sources

- OECD (2011), *OECD Regions at a Glance*, OECD Publishing.

Further information

Analytical publications

- OECD (2011), *Regional Outlook 2011*, OECD Publishing.
- OECD (2009), *Regions Matter: Economic Recovery, Innovation and Sustainable Growth*, OECD Publishing.

Online databases

- *OECD Regional Database.*

Websites

- Regional Development, *www.oecd.org/gov/regionaldevelopment.*
- Regional Statistics and Indicators, *www.oecd.org/gov/regional/statisticsindicators.*

Gini index of regional unemployment rates

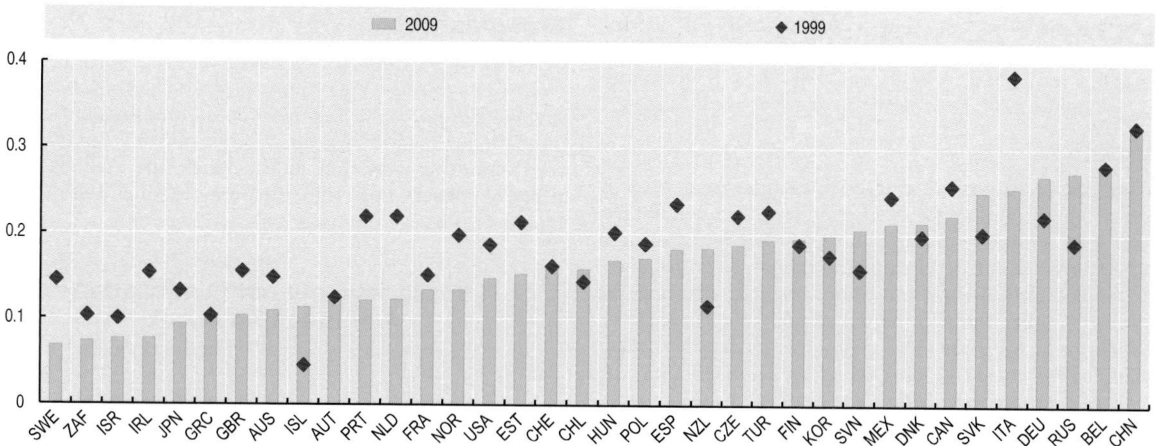

StatLink http://dx.doi.org/10.1787/888932505735

Regional variation of the youth unemployment rate

Percentage, 2009

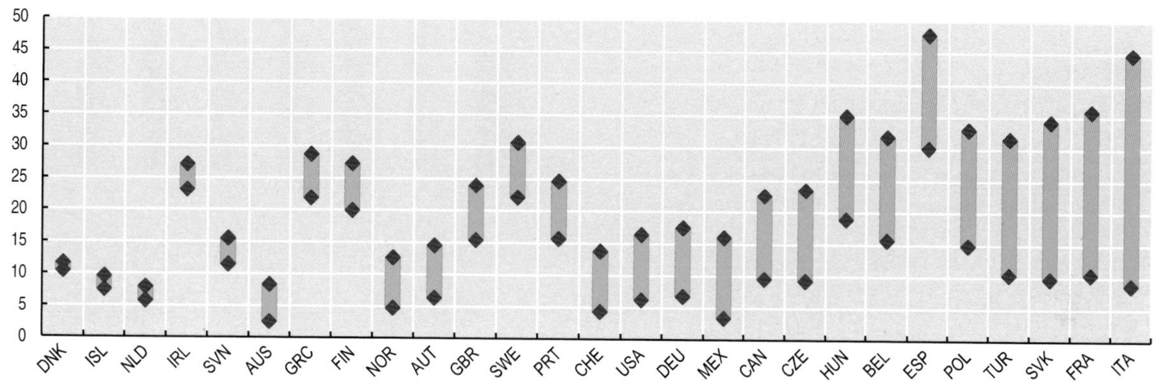

StatLink http://dx.doi.org/10.1787/888932505754

Regional variation of the long-term unemployment rate

Percentage, 2009

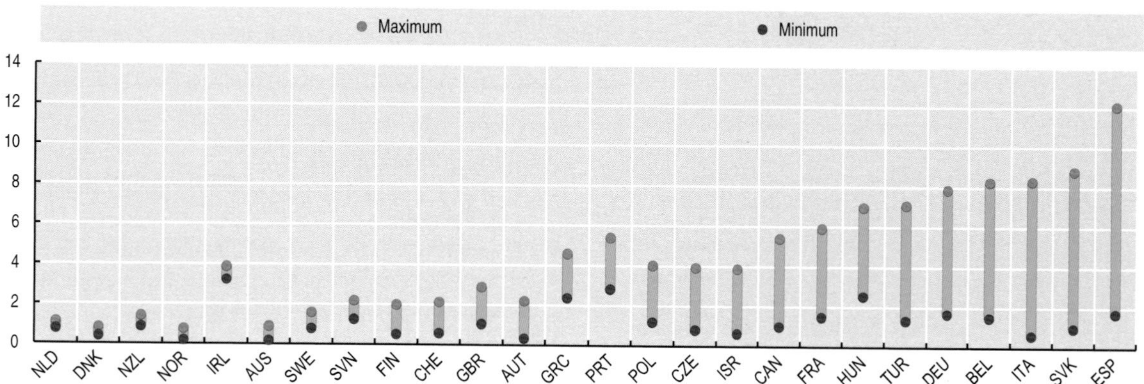

StatLink http://dx.doi.org/10.1787/888932505773

YOUTH INACTIVITY

Young people who are neither in employment nor in education and training are at risk of becoming socially excluded – individuals with income below the poverty-line and lacking the skills to improve their economic situation.

Definition

The indicator presents the share of youth who are neither in education and training nor in employment, as a percentage of the total number of youths in the corresponding age group. Youths in education include those attending part-time as well as full-time education, but exclude those in non-formal education and in educational activities of very short duration. Employment is defined according to the ILO Guidelines and covers all those who have worked for pay for at least one hour in the reference week of the survey or were temporarily absent from such work.

Comparability

The main problem of comparability is that, in some countries, youths performing compulsory military service are considered as being neither in employment nor in education. However, the duration of military services is in most countries generally short; hence, the reallocation of military conscripts to the employment/education category would not change the figures shown here by much.

Overview

On average across OECD countries, 17.7% of the 20-to-24-year-olds and 8.4% of the 15-to-19-year-olds were neither in school nor at work in 2009. The share of youth who are neither in education nor in employment was twice as high for youths aged 20 to 24 than those aged 15 to 19. This ratio has been relatively constant between 1997 and 2009.

The proportion of the 20-to-24-year-olds who were neither in school nor out work increased by 2.2 percentage points between 2008 and 2009, whereas it decreased by 3.5 percentage points between 1997 and 2008. For OECD countries as a whole, the share of youth aged 20-to-24-year-old who are not in employment nor in education declined up to 2008, mainly reflecting the fact that young people, particularly women, spend more time in education than they did a decade ago. This share is even higher among people aged 25 to 29 (19.1% in 2009).

Differences across countries are large: in Japan, Luxembourg and the Netherlands less than 9% of youth were in this situation. The ratio is substantially higher in Hungary, Ireland, Israel, Italy, Mexico, Spain, the United States and Brazil, where this figure exceeded 20%, and in Turkey, where the share exceeded 40%.

In most countries, a smooth transition from school to work is highly dependent on the business cycle and on economic conditions. As these conditions worsen, youths making the transition from school to work will be among the first affected. This is because, when employers are shedding workers, it is often difficult for young individuals to get a foothold in the labour market as they will be competing for jobs with more experienced workers. Also, when employment rates drop, people's incentive to stay in school longer becomes stronger as the potential earnings that students forego while studying will in many cases be close to zero. In this context, it is important for education systems to ease conditions of access to education and training to make additional resources available to educational institutions.

Youth who are not in education nor in employment

As a percentage of persons in that age group, 2009

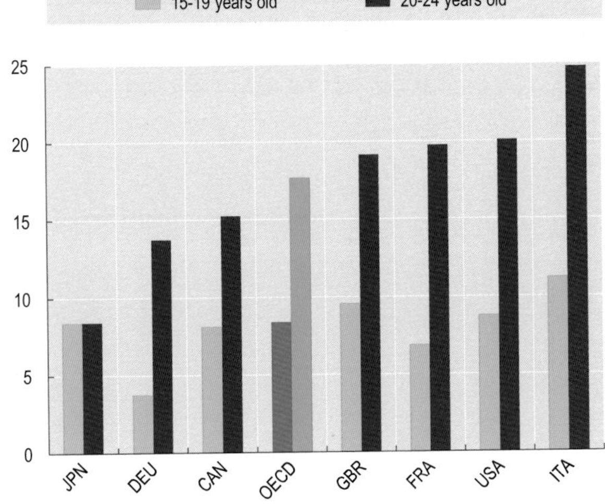

StatLink http://dx.doi.org/10.1787/888932535090

Sources

- OECD (2011), *Education at a Glance*, OECD Publishing.
- OECD (2011), *OECD Economic Outlook*, OECD Publishing.

Further information

Analytical publications

- OECD (2011), *Society at a Glance: OECD Social Indicators*, OECD Publishing.
- OECD (2010), *Jobs for Youth*, OECD Publishing.
- OECD (2000), *From Initial Education to Working Life: Making Transitions Work*, OECD Publishing.

Websites

- OECD Education at a Glance (supplementary material), *www.oecd.org/edu/eag2011*.
- Youth Employment Summit, *www.yesweb.org*.

Youths who are not in education nor in employment

As a percentage of persons in that age group

	Youth ages between 15 and 19							Youths aged between 20 and 24						
	1997	2000	2005	2006	2007	2008	2009	1997	2000	2005	2006	2007	2008	2009
Australia	8.1	6.8	7.4	7.1	6.5	6.3	8.3	17.5	13.3	11.6	11.5	10.7	10.7	11.6
Austria	..	..	6.9	6.6	5.3	5.6	6.5	..	..	12.4	12.5	11.0	11.4	11.8
Belgium	9.0	6.5	6.2	7.1	5.2	5.5	5.7	18.3	16.0	18.3	16.9	15.4	14.1	16.1
Canada	7.7	8.2	7.0	7.3	7.3	7.3	8.1	17.9	15.7	14.4	13.0	13.7	13.1	15.2
Czech Republic	..	7.9	5.3	4.5	2.9	2.7	3.5	..	20.3	16.6	14.1	11.0	10.6	13.1
Denmark	1.4	2.7	4.3	4.4	3.9	2.8	2.9	6.5	6.6	8.3	5.9	8.2	7.7	9.8
Estonia	..	..	5.2	3.7	5.7	4.9	8.0	..	..	16.3	15.4	15.3	10.7	19.8
Finland	..	..	5.2	3.6	3.5	5.1	5.1	..	..	13.0	13.3	13.3	12.0	15.1
France	5.7	6.2	5.4	5.4	6.3	7.0	6.9	21.3	20.5	16.7	18.8	17.8	19.0	19.8
Germany	5.0	5.7	4.4	4.2	4.2	3.7	3.8	18.4	16.9	18.7	16.7	15.2	14.0	13.7
Greece	9.6	9.3	11.7	7.8	8.5	8.4	7.9	27.5	25.9	21.6	18.4	17.7	17.1	18.2
Hungary	8.9	8.6	6.4	6.0	5.0	5.7	5.6	29.2	22.0	18.9	18.5	16.9	18.4	20.9
Iceland	..	..	..	..	..	..	..	6.6	..	10.0	..	6.4	..	9.4
Ireland	..	4.4	4.5	5.0	5.1	8.5	11.0	..	9.7	12.3	11.8	12.1	14.6	20.8
Israel	..	..	24.7	24.3	25.7	22.2	24.7	..	..	40.3	40.6	39.6	37.5	37.5
Italy	..	13.1	11.2	11.8	10.2	9.6	11.2	..	27.5	24.1	22.8	22.6	22.0	24.8
Japan	7.7	8.8	8.8	9.1	7.6	7.4	8.4	7.7	8.8	8.8	9.1	7.6	7.4	8.4
Luxembourg	5.6	..	2.2	4.1	2.9	2.1	2.7	10.3	8.2	9.3	10.3	9.2	9.8	8.7
Mexico	19.0	18.3	..	..	..	..	18.4	28.7	27.1	..	..	..	..	27.6
Netherlands	2.8	3.7	3.9	3.0	3.6	2.1	3.6	7.1	8.2	9.1	7.3	6.9	5.6	7.9
New Zealand	..	..	8.0	9.1	9.7	8.4	12.4	..	..	14.4	13.7	14.2	15.2	18.3
Norway	1.6	..	2.5	3.4	3.7	4.0	4.2	11.7	8.0	9.6	9.1	8.8	7.0	9.4
Poland	5.3	4.5	1.7	3.8	2.5	2.4	3.6	25.3	30.8	20.1	20.7	18.3	15.6	16.4
Portugal	9.8	7.7	8.4	7.8	8.6	7.1	6.9	14.2	11.0	14.1	13.3	15.2	13.5	15.7
Slovak Republic	16.7	26.3	6.3	6.7	5.4	5.7	4.5	25.5	33.1	25.2	22.8	19.9	16.6	17.1
Slovenia	..	..	4.9	4.2	4.3	4.4	2.5	..	..	13.0	13.7	10.4	10.3	11.4
Spain	10.9	8.0	10.8	10.1	10.9	10.5	13.4	22.1	15.0	19.4	16.9	17.2	19.4	26.3
Sweden	4.6	3.6	4.7	5.3	5.4	4.4	5.5	16.3	10.7	13.4	15.2	13.1	12.9	16.5
Switzerland	7.4	7.9	7.5	7.6	8.2	9.4	7.9	10.4	5.9	11.9	10.8	10.4	9.1	10.7
Turkey	30.2	31.2	36.1	35.0	34.5	37.1	28.7	48.4	44.2	49.7	48.8	46.3	46.1	46.1
United Kingdom	..	8.0	9.3	10.9	10.7	9.8	9.6	..	15.4	16.8	18.2	18.1	18.3	19.1
United States	7.1	7.0	6.1	6.3	6.3	7.2	8.8	15.1	14.4	15.5	15.6	16.2	17.2	20.1
OECD average	8.8	9.4	7.9	7.8	7.7	7.6	8.4	19.0	17.8	17.2	16.8	15.7	15.5	17.7
Brazil	..	..	..	..	14.7	13.8	14.0	..	..	..	..	23.4	22.5	23.3

StatLink http://dx.doi.org/10.1787/888932505792

Youths aged between 20 and 24 who are not in education nor in employment

As percentage of persons in that age group

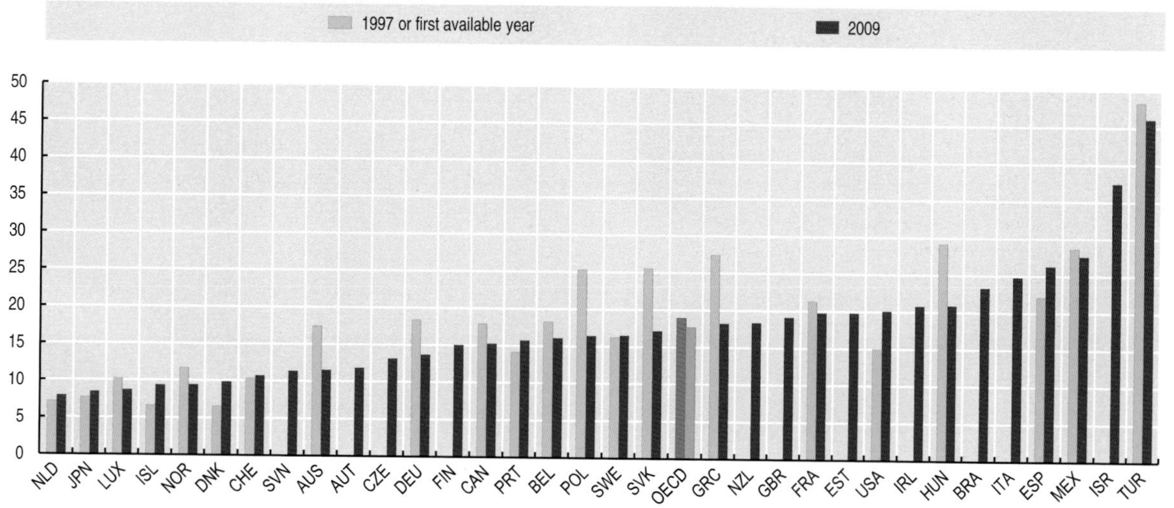

StatLink http://dx.doi.org/10.1787/888932505811

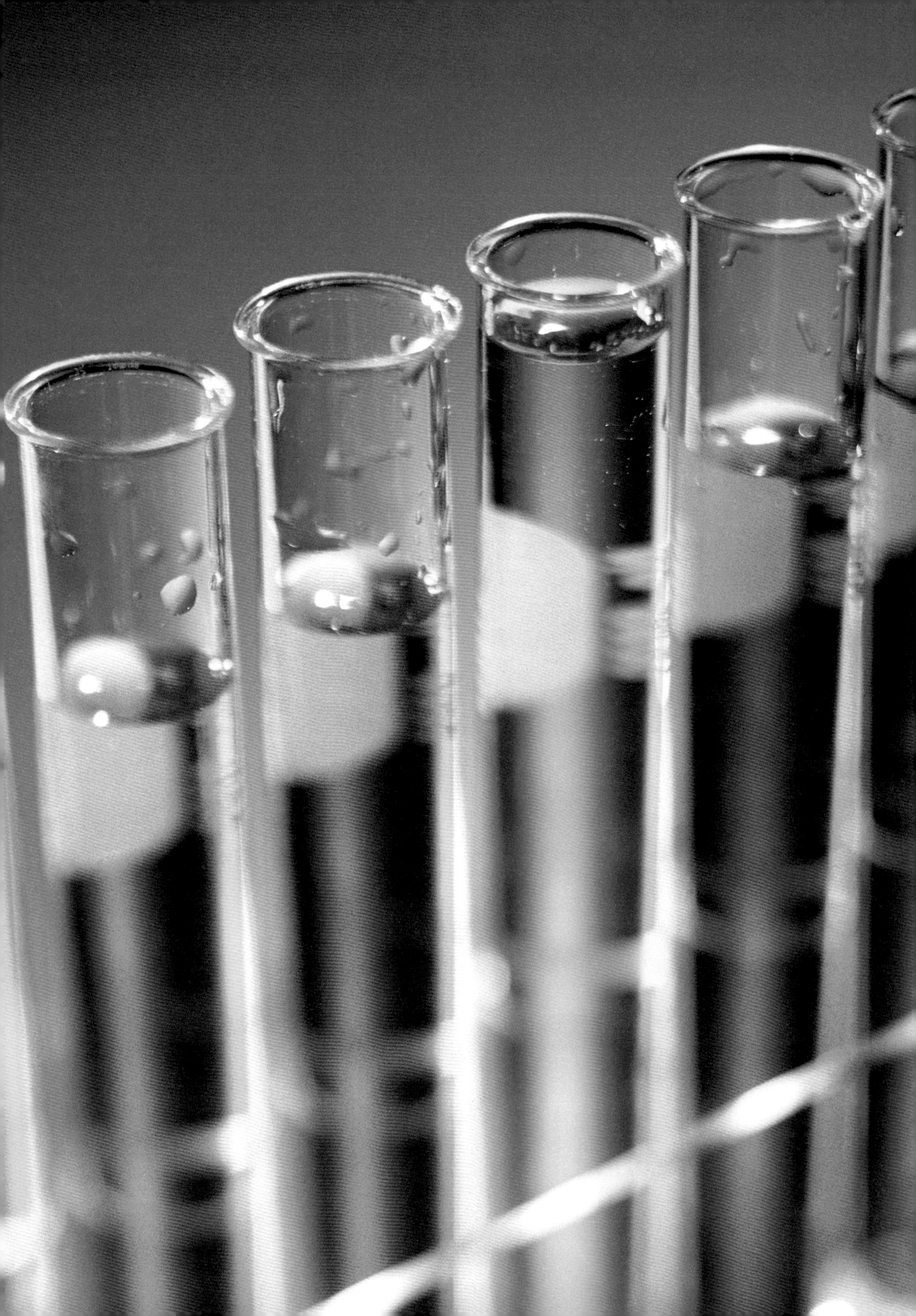

SCIENCE AND TECHNOLOGY

EXPENDITURE ON R&D

Expenditure on research and development (R&D) is a key indicator of government and private sector efforts to obtain competitive advantage in science and technology.

Definition

Research and development (R&D) comprise creative work undertaken on a systematic basis in order to increase the stock of knowledge (including knowledge of man, culture and society) and the use of this knowledge to devise new applications. R&D covers three activities: basic research, applied research, and experimental development. Basic research is experimental or theoretical work undertaken primarily to acquire new knowledge of the underlying foundation of phenomena and observable facts, without any particular application or use in view. Applied research is also original investigation undertaken in order to acquire new knowledge; it is, however, directed primarily towards a specific practical aim or objective. Experimental development is systematic work, drawing on existing knowledge gained from research and/or practical experience, which is directed to producing new materials, products or devices, to installing new processes, systems and services, or to improving substantially those already produced or installed.

The main aggregate used for international comparisons is gross domestic expenditure on R&D (GERD). This consists of the total expenditure (current and capital) on R&D by all resident companies, research institutes, university and government laboratories, etc. It excludes R&D expenditures financed by domestic firms but performed abroad. GERD is here expressed as a share of GDP.

Comparability

The R&D data shown here have been compiled according to the guidelines of the OECD *Frascati Manual*. Estimates of the resources allocated to R&D are affected by national characteristics such as the periodicity and coverage of national R&D surveys across institutional sectors and industries (and the inclusion of firms and organisations of different sizes); and the use of different sampling and estimation methods. R&D typically involves a few large performers, hence R&D surveys use various techniques to maintain up-to-date registers of known performers, while attempting to identify new or occasional performers.

Data for Israel exclude defence. Those for Korea, prior to 2007, exclude social sciences and the humanities. Those for the United States, exclude capital expenditure.

Overview

In 2008, research and development amounted to 2.3% of GDP for the OECD as a whole. Denmark (since 2009), Finland, Israel, Japan, Korea, Sweden and Switzerland were the only OECD countries in which the R&D-to-GDP ratio exceeded 3%, well above the OECD average. Since 2000, R&D expenditure relative to GDP has increased significantly in the EU and Japan and only slightly in the United States. In China, R&D intensity increased from 0.9% in 2000 to 1.7% in 2009.

Since the mid-1990s, R&D expenditure in real terms has been growing the fastest (among OECD countries) in Turkey and Portugal, both with average annual growth rates above 10%. In China, growth in real R&D spending since 2000 has exceeded 18% per year.

Sources

- OECD (2011), *Main Science and Technology Indicators*, OECD Publishing.

Further information

Analytical publications

- OECD (2010), *OECD Science, Technology and Industry Outlook 2010*, OECD Publishing.
- OECD (2011), *OECD Science, Technology and Industry Scoreboard 2011*, OECD Publishing.

Statistical publications

- OECD (2011), *OECD Science, Technology and R&D Statistics*, OECD Publishing.

Methodological publications

- OECD (2002), *Frascati Manual 2002: Proposed Standard Practice for Surveys on Research and Experimental Development*, The Measurement of Scientific and Technological Activities, OECD Publishing.

Websites

- OECD Science, Technology and Industry, *www.oecd.org/sti*.

Gross domestic expenditure on R&D

As a percentage of GDP

	1997	1998	1999	2000	2001	2002	2003	2004	2005	2006	2007	2008	2009	2010
Australia	..	1.43	..	1.47	..	1.64	..	1.72	..	2.00	..	2.21	..	..
Austria	1.70	1.78	1.90	1.94	2.07	2.14	2.26	2.26	2.48	2.46	2.52	2.67	2.75	2.75
Belgium	1.83	1.86	1.94	1.97	2.07	1.94	1.88	1.86	1.83	1.86	1.90	1.96	1.96	..
Canada	1.66	1.76	1.80	1.91	2.09	2.04	2.04	2.07	2.04	2.00	1.96	1.87	1.92	1.80
Chile	..	..	..	..	..	..	..	..	..	..	0.33	0.39	..	..
Czech Republic	1.08	1.15	1.14	1.21	1.20	1.20	1.25	1.25	1.41	1.55	1.54	1.47	1.53	..
Denmark	1.92	2.04	2.18	..	2.39	2.51	2.58	2.48	2.46	2.48	2.58 |	2.87	3.02	..
Estonia	..	0.57	0.68	0.60	0.70	0.72	0.77	0.85	0.93	1.13	1.10	1.29	1.42	1.44
Finland	2.71	2.88	3.17	3.35	3.32	3.37	3.44	3.45	3.48	3.48	3.47	3.72	3.96	3.84
France	2.19 |	2.14	2.16	2.15 |	2.20	2.23	2.17	2.15 |	2.10	2.10	2.07	2.11	2.21	..
Germany	2.24	2.27	2.40	2.45	2.46	2.49	2.52	2.49	2.49	2.53	2.53	2.68	2.78	..
Greece	0.45	..	0.60	..	0.58	..	0.57	0.55	0.59	0.58	0.59	..	..	..
Hungary	0.70	0.66	0.67	0.79	0.92	1.00	0.93	0.87 |	0.95	1.00	0.97	1.00	1.15	..
Iceland	1.83	2.00	2.30	2.67	2.95	2.95	2.82	..	2.77	2.99	2.68	2.64	..	..
Ireland	1.27	1.24	1.18	1.12	1.10	1.10	1.17	1.23	1.25	1.25	1.29	1.45	1.79	..
Israel	2.97	3.08	3.52	4.27	4.55	4.56	4.28	4.28	4.41	4.43	4.76	4.68	4.28	4.25
Italy	1.03 |	1.05	1.02	1.05	1.09	1.13	1.11	1.10	1.09	1.13	1.18	1.23	1.27	..
Japan	2.87	3.00	3.02	3.04	3.12	3.17	3.20	3.17	3.32	3.40	3.44	3.44 |	3.33	..
Korea	2.41	2.26	2.17	2.30	2.47	2.40	2.49	2.68	2.79	3.01	3.21 |	3.36	..	..
Luxembourg	..	..	..	1.65	..	..	1.65	1.63	1.56	1.66	1.58	1.56	1.68	..
Mexico	0.31	0.34	0.39	0.34	0.36	0.40	0.40	0.40 |	0.41	0.39	0.37	..	..	..
Netherlands	1.99	1.90	1.98 |	1.94	1.93	1.88	1.92	1.93	1.90	1.88	1.81	1.76	1.82	..
New Zealand	1.08	..	0.98	..	1.12 |	..	1.17	..	1.14	..	1.17	..	..	..
Norway	1.63	..	1.64	..	1.59	1.66	1.71	1.59	1.52	1.52	1.62	1.61	1.76	..
Poland	0.65	0.67	0.69	0.64	0.62	0.56	0.54	0.56	0.57	0.56	0.57	0.60	0.68	..
Portugal	0.57	0.63	0.69	0.73	0.77	0.73	0.71	0.75	0.78	0.99	1.17	1.50 |	1.66	..
Slovak Republic	1.08 |	0.78	0.66	0.65	0.63	0.57	0.57	0.51	0.51	0.49	0.46	0.47	0.48	..
Slovenia	1.28	1.34	1.37	1.39	1.50	1.47	1.27	1.40	1.44	1.56	1.45	1.65 |	1.86	..
Spain	0.80	0.87	0.86	0.91	0.91	0.99	1.05	1.06	1.12	1.20	1.27	1.35 |	1.38	..
Sweden	3.47	..	3.58	..	4.13	..	3.80	3.58	3.56 |	3.68	3.40	3.70	3.62	..
Switzerland	..	..	..	2.53	..	..	..	2.90	..	..	..	3.00	..	..
Turkey	0.37	0.37	0.47	0.48	0.54	0.53	0.48	0.52	0.59	0.58	0.72	0.73	0.85	..
United Kingdom	1.77	1.76	1.82	1.81	1.79	1.79	1.75	1.68	1.73	1.75	1.78	1.77	1.85	1.82
United States	2.57	2.60 |	2.64	2.71	2.72	2.62	2.61	2.54	2.57	2.61	2.67	2.79	..	..
EU27 total	1.66	1.67	1.72	1.74	1.76	1.77	1.76	1.73	1.74	1.77	1.77	1.84	1.90	..
OECD total	2.10	2.12	2.16	2.20	2.24	2.21	2.21	2.18	2.21	2.24	2.27	2.33	..	..
China	0.64	0.65	0.76	0.90 |	0.95	1.07	1.13	1.23	1.32	1.39	1.40	1.47	1.70	..
Russian Federation	1.04	0.95	1.00	1.05	1.18	1.25	1.29	1.15	1.07	1.07	1.12	1.04	1.24	..
South Africa	0.60	..	..	..	0.73	..	0.79	0.85	0.90	0.93	0.92	0.93	..	..

StatLink http://dx.doi.org/10.1787/888932505830

Gross domestic expenditure on R&D

As a percentage of GDP

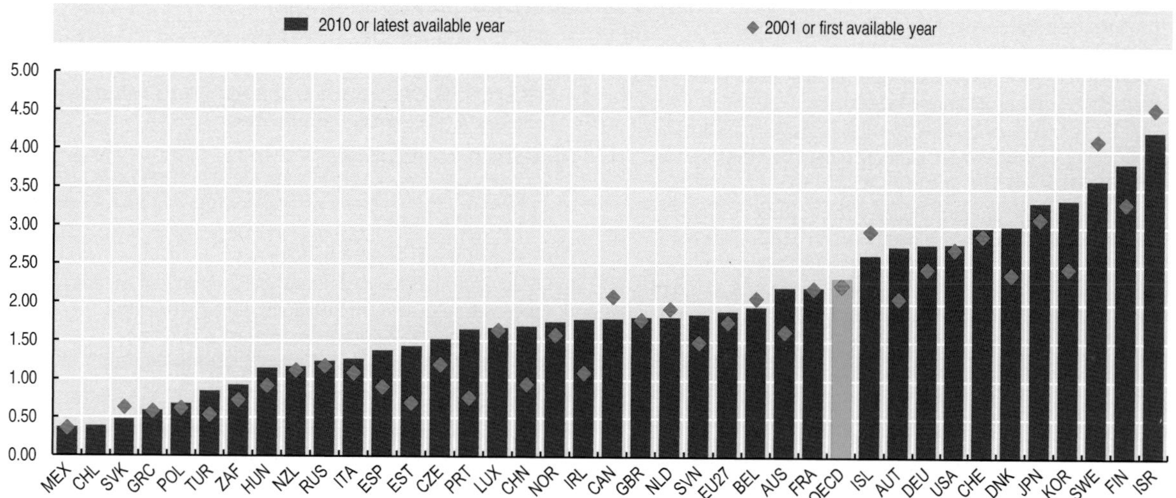

StatLink http://dx.doi.org/10.1787/888932505849

RESEARCHERS

Researchers are the central element of the research and development system.

Definition

Researchers are professionals engaged in the conception and creation of new knowledge, products, processes, methods and systems, as well as those who are directly involved in the management of projects. They include researchers working in both civil and military research in government, universities and research institutes as well as in the business sector.

The number of researchers is measured in full-time equivalent (*i.e.* a person working half-time on R&D is counted as 0.5 person-year) and expressed per thousand people employed in each country. The number of researchers includes staff engaged in R&D during the course of one year.

Comparability

The data on researchers have been compiled on the basis of the methodology of the OECD *Frascati Manual*. Comparability over time is affected to some extent by improvements in the coverage of national R&D surveys and by the efforts of countries to improve the international comparability of their data.

For the United States beginning 2000, the total numbers of researchers are OECD estimates. Also, data for the United States since 1985 exclude military personnel. For China, researcher data are collected according to the OECD *Frascati Manual* definition of researcher from 2009.

Researchers

Per thousand employed, full-time equivalent

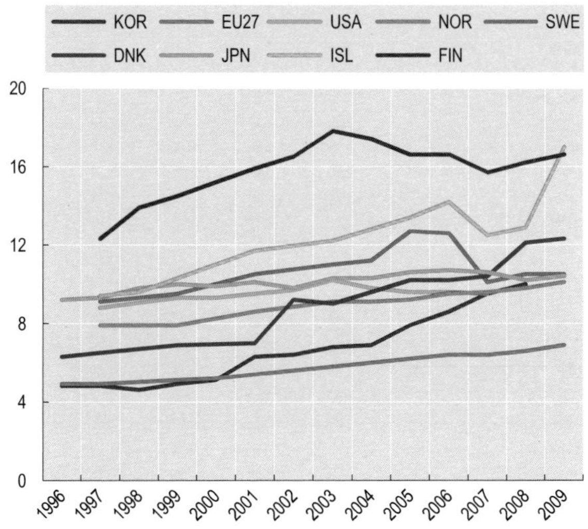

StatLink http://dx.doi.org/10.1787/888932535109

Overview

In the OECD area, around 4.2 million persons were employed as researchers in 2007. Approximately two-thirds of these were engaged in the business sector.

In 2007, there were about 7.6 researchers per thousand of employed people in the OECD area, compared with 5.9 per thousand employed in 1995. This indicator has steadily increased over the last two decades.

Among the major OECD areas, Japan has the highest number of researchers relative to total employment, followed by the United States and the European Union.

Finland, Iceland, Denmark and New Zealand have the highest number of research workers per thousand persons employed. Rates are also high in Japan, Korea, Sweden, Norway and the United States. Conversely, research workers per thousand of employed people are low in Chile, Mexico and Turkey.

Among the major non-member countries, growth in the number of researchers has been steady in China although the overall level, at 1.5 per thousand of people employed in 2009, still remains well below the OECD average. The number of researchers per thousand of people employed for the Russian Federation has been falling since 1994 but this level, at 6.4 researchers per thousand employed in 2009, is similar to that of EU countries.

Sources

- OECD (2011), *Main Science and Technology Indicators*, OECD Publishing.

Further information

Analytical publications

- OECD (2010), *OECD Science, Technology and Industry Outlook 2010*, OECD Publishing.
- OECD (2011), *OECD Science, Technology and Industry Scoreboard 2011*, OECD Publishing.

Statistical publications

- OECD (2011), *OECD Science, Technology and R&D Statistics*, OECD Publishing.

Methodological publications

- OECD (2002), *Frascati Manual 2002: Proposed Standard Practice for Surveys on Research and Experimental Development*, The Measurement of Scientific and Technological Activities, OECD Publishing.

Websites

- OECD Measuring Science and Technology, *www.oecd.org/sti/measuring-scitech*.
- OECD Science, Technology and Industry, *www.oecd.org/sti*.
- OECD Science, Technology and Industry Scoreboard (supplementary material), *www.oecd.org/sti/scoreboard*.

Researchers

Per thousand employed, full-time equivalent

	1996	1997	1998	1999	2000	2001	2002	2003	2004	2005	2006	2007	2008	2009
Australia	7.3	..	7.3	..	7.3	..	7.8	..	8.3	..	8.5	..	8.4	..
Austria	..	..	5.1	..	..	..	6.3	..	6.7	7.3	7.3	7.8	8.4	8.5
Belgium	6.5	6.7	6.9	7.4	7.4	7.7	7.4	7.4	7.7	7.8	8.1	8.3	8.4	8.4
Canada	6.6	6.6	6.6	6.7	7.2	7.5	7.4	7.7	8.1	8.3	8.4	8.7	8.6	..
Chile	..	..	..	..	..	..	..	..	..	..	..	0.9	0.9	..
Czech Republic	2.5	2.4	2.5	2.7	2.8	3.0	3.0	3.2	3.3	4.8 |	5.2	5.3	5.6	5.5
Denmark	6.3	6.5	..	6.9	..	7.0	9.2 |	9.0	9.6	10.2	10.2	10.4 |	12.1	12.3
Estonia	..	..	4.9	5.2	4.7	4.6	5.2	5.1	5.7	5.5	5.4	5.6	6.1	7.2
Finland	..	12.3 |	13.9	14.5	15.2	15.9	16.5	17.8	17.4 |	16.6	16.6	15.7	16.2	16.6
France	6.8	6.8 |	6.7	6.8	7.1 |	7.2	7.5	7.7	8.1	8.1	8.3	8.6	8.9	..
Germany	6.1	6.3	6.3	6.6	6.6	6.7	6.8	6.9	6.9	7.0	7.2	7.3	7.5	7.7
Greece	..	2.7	..	3.5	..	3.4	..	3.5	..	4.3	4.2	4.4	..	..
Hungary	2.6	2.8	2.9	3.0	3.4	3.5	3.5	3.6	3.6 |	3.8	4.2	4.2	4.5	5.0
Iceland	..	9.4	9.6	10.3	..	11.7	..	12.2	..	13.4	14.2	12.5	12.9	17.0
Ireland	4.8	5.0	5.1	4.9	5.0	5.1	5.3	5.5	5.9	5.9	6.0	6.0	6.9	7.7
Italy	3.5	3.0 |	2.9	2.9	2.9	2.9	3.0	2.9	3.0	3.4	3.6	3.7	3.8	4.1
Japan	9.2 |	9.3	9.8	10.0	9.9	10.1	9.8	10.3	10.3	10.6	10.7	10.6	10.2 |	10.4
Korea	4.8	4.8	4.6	4.9	5.1	6.3	6.4	6.8	6.9	7.9	8.6	9.5 |	10.0	..
Luxembourg	..	..	..	..	6.2	..	..	6.7	6.8	7.2	6.4	6.6	6.6	6.8
Mexico	0.6	0.6	0.6	0.6	..	..	..	0.9	1.0 |	1.1	0.9	0.9	..	..
Netherlands	4.9 |	5.0	5.1	5.3	5.2	5.5	5.3 |	5.3 |	5.9	5.8	6.3	5.9	5.8	5.4
New Zealand	..	6.2	..	6.2	..	9.1 |	..	10.4	..	10.5	..	10.8	..	..
Norway	..	7.9	..	7.9	..	8.6	..	9.1	9.1	9.2	9.5	9.6	9.8	10.1
Poland	3.6	3.7	3.7	3.8	3.8	4.0	4.1	4.3	4.4	4.4	4.1	4.0	3.9	3.9
Portugal	2.7	2.9	3.0	3.2	3.3	3.5	3.7	4.0	4.0	4.1	4.8	5.5	7.8 |	9.1
Slovak Republic	4.7	4.7 |	4.8	4.5	4.9	4.7	4.5	4.7	5.2	5.2	5.5	5.7	5.6	6.1
Slovenia	5.0	4.6	4.9	5.0	4.8	4.9	5.0	4.1	4.4	5.7	6.3	6.5	7.1 |	7.7
Spain	3.7	3.8	4.0	3.9	4.7	4.7	4.8	5.2	5.5	5.7	5.8	5.9	6.4 |	7.0
Sweden	..	9.1	..	9.5	..	10.5	..	11.0	11.2	12.7 |	12.6	10.1 |	10.5	10.5
Switzerland	5.6	..	..	..	6.4	..	..	..	6.1	..	..	..	5.6	..
Turkey	0.9	1.0	1.0	1.0	1.2	1.2	1.2	1.7	1.7	2.0	2.1	2.4	2.5	2.7
United Kingdom	5.1	5.1	5.5	5.7	5.8	6.1	6.6	7.1	7.5	8.0 |	8.1	8.0	8.0	8.3
United States	..	8.8	..	9.3	9.3	9.5	9.7	10.2	9.8	9.6	9.6	9.5	..	..
EU27 total	4.9	4.9	5.0	5.1	5.2	5.4	5.6	5.8	6.0	6.2	6.4	6.4	6.6	6.9
OECD total	..	6.2	..	6.6	6.7	6.9	7.0	7.4	7.3	7.5	7.6	7.6	..	..
China	0.8	0.8	0.7	0.7	1.0 |	1.0	1.1	1.2	1.2	1.5	1.6	1.8	2.1	1.5
Russian Federation	9.2	8.9	8.4	7.9	7.8	7.8	7.4	7.3	7.1	6.8	6.7	6.6	6.4	6.4
South Africa	..	0.9	..	..	..	1.3	..	1.2	1.5	1.4	1.5	1.5	1.4	..

StatLink http://dx.doi.org/10.1787/888932505868

Researchers

Per thousand employed, full-time equivalent

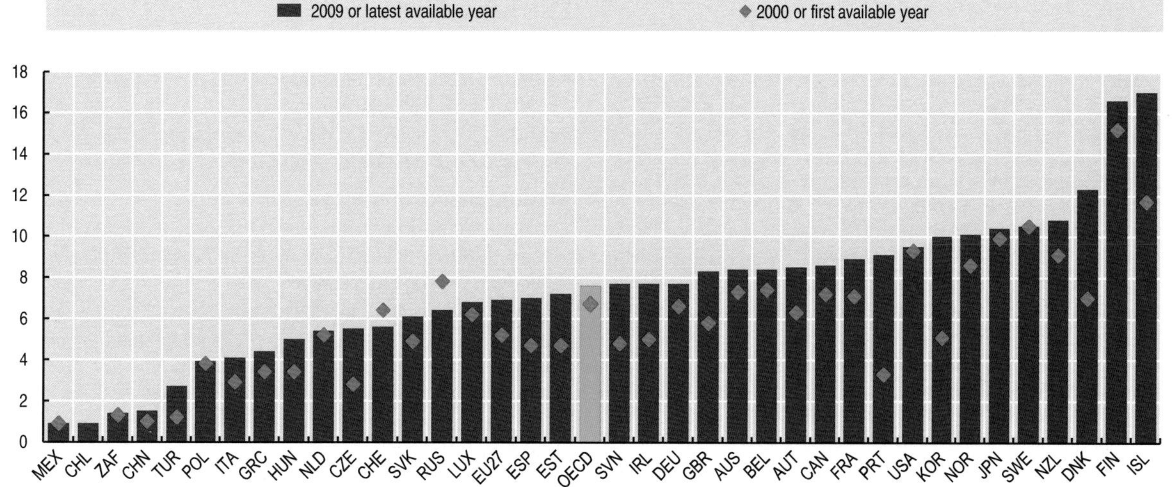

StatLink http://dx.doi.org/10.1787/888932505887

PATENTS

Patent-based indicators provide a measure of the output of a country's R&D, *i.e.* its inventions. The methodology used for counting patents can however influence the results, as simple counts of patents filed at a national patent office are affected by various kinds of limitations (such as weak international comparability) and highly heterogeneous patent values. To overcome these limits, the OECD has developed triadic patent families, which are designed to capture all important inventions and to be internationally comparable.

Definition

A patent family is defined as a set of patents registered in various countries (*i.e.* patent offices) to protect the same invention. Triadic patent families are a set of patents filed at three of these major patent offices: the European Patent Office (EPO), the Japan Patent Office (JPO) and the United States Patent and Trademark Office (USPTO).

Triadic patent family counts are attributed to the country of residence of the inventor and to the date when the patent was first registered.

Triadic patent families are expressed as numbers and per million inhabitants.

Comparability

The concept of triadic patent families has been developed in order to improve the international comparability and quality of patent-based indicators. Indeed, only patents registered in the same set of countries are included in the family: home advantage and influence of geographical location are therefore eliminated. Furthermore, patents included in the triadic family are typically of higher economic value: patentees only take on the additional costs and delays of extending the protection of their invention to other countries if they deem it worthwhile.

Share of countries in triadic patent families

Percentage, 2009

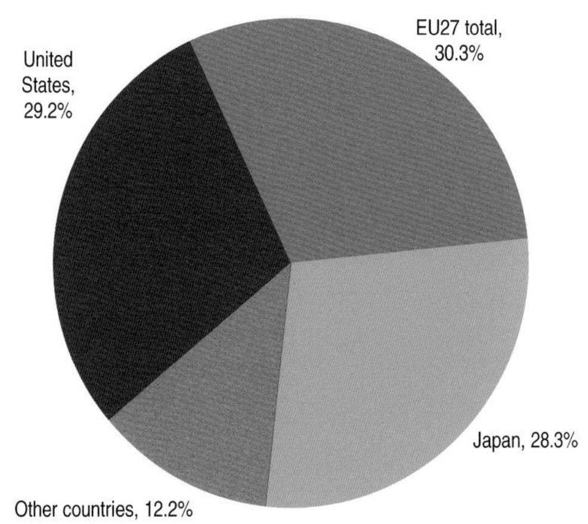

StatLink http://dx.doi.org/10.1787/888932505944

Overview

Growth in the number of triadic patent families during the second half of the 1990s was at a steady 4.5% a year. The beginning of the 21st century was marked by a slowdown, with patent families increasing by 0.5% a year on average. The United States, the European Union and Japan show a similar declining trend.

About 47 000 triadic patent families were filed in 2009, compared to nearly 45 000 registered in 1999. The United States accounts for 29.2% of patent families, a lower share compared to the one recorded in 1999 (32.6%). The share of triadic patent families originating from Europe has also tended to decrease, losing almost 2 percentage points between 1999 and 2009 (to 30.3% in 2009). The origin of patent families has shifted towards Asian countries. The most spectacular growth was observed by Korea, whose share of all triadic patent families increased from 1.3% in 1999 to 4.2% in 2009. Strong rises are also observed for China and India, with an average growth in the number of triadic patents of more than 15% a year between 1999 and 2009.

When triadic patent families are expressed relative to the total population, Switzerland, Japan, Sweden and Germany were the four most inventive countries in 2007, with the highest values recorded in Switzerland (113) and Japan (104). Ratios for Austria, Denmark, Finland, France, Germany, Israel, Korea, the Netherlands and the United States are also above the OECD average (37). Conversely, China has less than 0.5 patent families per million population.

Sources

- *OECD Patent Statistics.*

Further information

Analytical publications

- OECD (2010), *OECD Science, Technology and Industry Outlook 2010*, OECD Publishing.
- OECD (2011), *OECD Science, Technology and Industry Scoreboard 2011*, OECD Publishing.

Methodological publications

- Dernis, H. and M. Khan (2004), "Triadic Patent Families Methodology", *OECD Science, Technology and Industry Working Papers*, No. 2004/2.
- Maraut, S. *et al.* (2008), "The OECD REGPAT Database: A Presentation", *OECD Science, Technology and Industry Working Papers*, No. 2008/2.
- OECD (2009), *OECD Patent Statistics Manual*, OECD Publishing.

Websites

- OECD Work on Patents, *www.oecd.org/sti/ipr-statistics*.

Triadic patent families

Number

	1996	1997	1998	1999	2000	2001	2002	2003	2004	2005	2006	2007	2008	2009
Australia	236	279	300	292	364	321	343	336	359	357	348	310	290	288
Austria	214	259	270	258	273	256	320	337	381	426	443	424	413	416
Belgium	362	435	397	374	327	336	342	326	412	410	444	420	397	376
Canada	430	533	534	521	520	531	588	571	647	665	675	642	598	602
Chile	3	-	2	2	2	5	5	3	5	5	6	5	6	9
Czech Republic	12	11	16	10	9	11	14	15	14	14	19	21	21	21
Denmark	227	217	271	237	218	221	228	244	292	309	276	301	300	279
Estonia	4	2	2	1	1	2	1	4	-	1	6	7	6	8
Finland	357	449	452	446	343	347	273	300	337	341	348	355	347	336
France	2 159	2 216	2 286	2 341	2 118	2 179	2 205	2 255	2 394	2 384	2 491	2 471	2 453	2 456
Germany	5 529	5 692	6 157	6 004	5 763	5 632	5 486	5 427	5 615	5 757	6 076	6 047	5 859	5 764
Greece	13	9	12	6	5	6	8	13	9	15	14	14	13	11
Hungary	25	32	18	41	27	31	29	41	44	41	44	49	47	44
Iceland	7	4	6	7	11	4	8	4	2	4	4	3	3	4
Ireland	30	37	38	74	31	50	51	65	68	75	74	75	78	76
Israel	215	289	299	278	317	314	263	290	345	452	420	375	361	339
Italy	705	739	677	662	632	706	708	705	750	741	770	752	735	718
Japan	10 691	11 316	11 722	12 974	14 471	13 952	14 125	14 372	14 079	13 828	13 729	13 861	13 744	13 322
Korea	323	388	468	581	728	910	1 207	1 686	1 961	2 120	2 121	2 053	1 863	1 959
Luxembourg	16	16	22	22	20	26	13	20	23	20	24	17	19	16
Mexico	10	9	10	11	9	13	10	15	16	14	17	16	15	13
Netherlands	812	838	853	913	1 015	1 051	959	969	986	970	1 034	948	964	926
New Zealand	31	40	52	47	46	42	61	57	63	59	60	53	47	43
Norway	76	101	95	106	100	89	106	98	105	123	124	117	115	122
Poland	10	9	4	9	9	11	11	11	16	13	13	19	21	23
Portugal	4	8	5	5	3	6	6	7	6	12	16	24	21	21
Slovak Republic	1	5	3	3	2	2	3	5	1	2	2	3	3	3
Slovenia	5	5	12	4	8	6	14	14	12	17	12	18	18	15
Spain	92	108	127	124	144	157	161	155	216	219	213	221	225	226
Sweden	922	984	852	878	608	667	692	671	694	828	938	943	928	900
Switzerland	816	823	804	767	804	804	802	839	871	863	895	899	883	879
Turkey	4	4	7	3	4	9	8	8	13	12	20	22	22	24
United Kingdom	1 669	1 646	1 789	1 633	1 604	1 593	1 639	1 653	1 648	1 656	1 655	1 666	1 641	1 618
United States	13 050	13 933	14 499	14 548	13 720	13 567	14 423	14 760	15 136	15 311	15 166	14 505	13 923	13 715
EU27 total	13 174	13 723	14 266	14 055	13 168	13 301	13 172	13 261	13 936	14 271	14 933	14 808	14 530	14 269
OECD total	39 057	41 435	43 061	44 184	44 256	43 856	45 112	46 274	47 522	48 063	48 498	47 654	46 379	45 571
Brazil	20	29	29	26	29	45	42	42	48	52	62	64	61	58
China	22	44	48	59	71	103	153	216	223	308	421	484	503	667
India	15	24	32	39	53	86	122	130	113	126	143	145	146	161
Indonesia	1	2	3	1	4	2	2	2	2	2	2	1	1	1
Russian Federation	59	70	96	62	73	51	51	52	50	66	65	65	63	63
South Africa	31	33	37	27	37	23	27	32	29	35	33	31	29	27
World	39 385	41 799	43 503	44 622	44 758	44 424	45 838	47 080	48 362	49 063	49 670	48 915	47 658	47 022

StatLink http://dx.doi.org/10.1787/888932505906

Triadic patent families

Number per million inhabitants, 2009

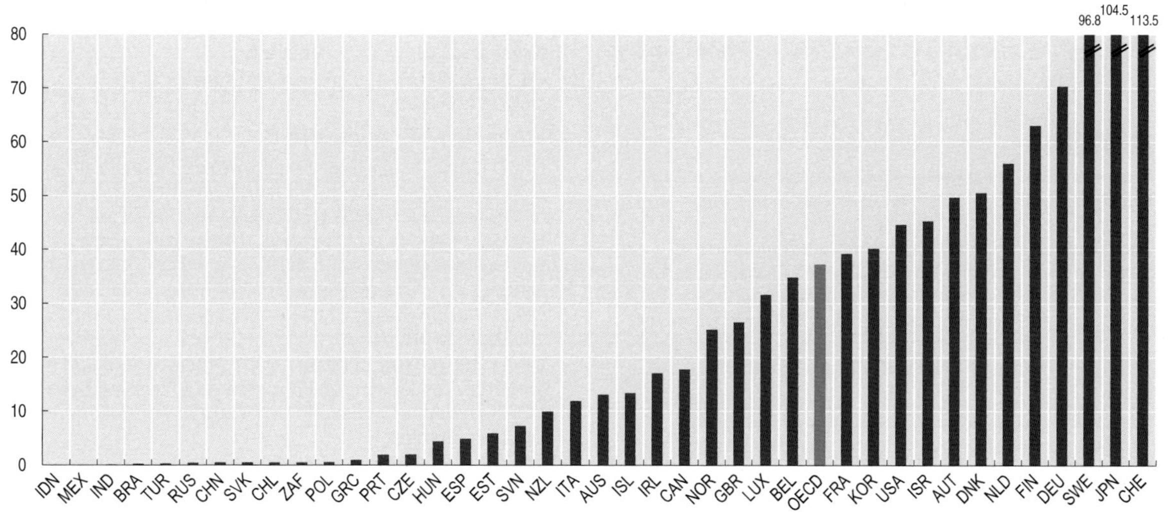

StatLink http://dx.doi.org/10.1787/888932505925

BIOTECHNOLOGY

The amount that is spent on biotechnology research and development (R&D) by the business enterprise sector within a county, is a measure of its research focus on biotechnology.

Definition

The OECD developed both a single definition and a list-based definition of biotechnology. The single definition is deliberately broad: "The application of science and technology to living organisms, as well as parts, products and models thereof, to alter living or non-living materials for the production of knowledge, goods and services." This definition covers all modern biotechnology but also many traditional or borderline activities. For this reason, the single definition should always be accompanied by the list-based definition.

The (indicative, not exhaustive) list-based definition, which serves as an interpretative guideline to the single definition includes seven categories. Respondents are usually given a write-in option for new biotechnologies that do not fit any of the categories. A firm that reports activity in one or more categories is defined as a biotechnology firm. The seven categories include:

i) DNA/RNA: Genomics, pharmacogenomics, gene probes, genetic engineering, DNA/RNA sequencing/synthesis/amplification, gene expression profiling, and use of antisense technology;

ii) Proteins and other molecules: Sequencing/synthesis/engineering of proteins and peptides (including large molecule hormones); improved delivery methods for large molecule drugs; proteomics, protein isolation and purification, signalling, identification of cell receptors;

iii) Cell and tissue culture and engineering: Cell/tissue culture, tissue engineering (including tissue scaffolds and biomedical engineering), cellular fusion, vaccine/immune stimulants, embryo manipulation;

iv) Process biotechnology techniques: Fermentation using bioreactors, bioprocessing, bioleaching, biopulping, biobleaching, biodesulphurisation, bioremediation, biofiltration and phytoremediation;

v) Gene and RNA vectors: Gene therapy, viral vectors;

vi) Bioinformatics: Construction of databases on genomes, protein sequences; modelling complex biological processes, including systems biology; and

vii) Nanobiotechnology: Applies the tools and processes of nano/microfabrication to build devices for studying biosystems and applications in drug delivery, diagnostics, etc.

Comparability

Data availability and comparability depends on how each country collects biotechnology statistics. Biotechnology activities can be measured in three ways: dedicated surveys of firms active in biotechnology; adding questions on biotechnology to the national R&D survey of firms; and, constructing databases with information on biotechnology firms from secondary sources, and/or data-linking exercises.

A biotechnology firm is a firm engaged in biotechnology using at least one biotechnology technique (as defined in the OECD list-based definition of biotechnology) to produce goods or services and/or to perform biotechnology R&D. Some firms may be large, with only a small share of total economic activity attributable to biotechnology. These firms are captured by biotechnology firm surveys. Two subgroups of biotechnology firms are largely defined by the data collection method:

i) Dedicated biotechnology firm; firms whose main activity involves the application of biotechnology techniques to produce goods or services and/or to perform biotechnology R&D. These firms are captured by biotechnology firm surveys; and

ii) Biotechnology R&D firm: Firms that perform biotechnology R&D. Dedicated biotechnology R&D firms, a subset of this group, are firms that devote 75% or more of their total R&D to biotechnology R&D. These firms are captured by R&D surveys.

Countries that collect biotechnology statistics through their R&D surveys may underestimate biotechnology activity, as firms that use biotechnology but do not perform biotechnology R&D are excluded.

Although every effort has been made to maximise comparability across countries, caution must be used in comparing biotechnology activities among countries when the data are obtained from studies with very different methodologies. Factors such as differences in the definition of biotechnology, whether or not all firms innovate, low response rates, whether or not results were imputed to account for non-respondents or extrapolated to the total population will affect comparability.

Overview

The United States spends the most on biotechnology BERD, USD 22 030 million in PPPs, over 7% of total US Business Enterprise R&D (BERD). This accounts for almost 70% of total biotechnology BERD expenditures in the 23 countries for which data are available. Biotechnology BERD as a share of total BERD is an indicator of country's research focus on biotechnology. On average, biotechnology BERD accounted for 5.7% of total BERD. Ireland spends the most as a percentage of BERD (15.1%). Belgium and Switzerland follow with 12.6% of BERD.

Biotechnology R&D intensity (biotechnology R&D as a percentage of industry value added) is highest in Denmark (0.389%), followed by Switzerland (0.384%) and Belgium (0.264%).

Sources

- Key biotechnology indicators, *www.oecd.org/sti/biotechnology/indicators*.

Further information

Analytical publications

- OECD (2011), *OECD Science, Technology and Industry Scoreboard 2011*, OECD Publishing.
- OECD (2009), *OECD Biotechnology Statistics 2009*, OECD Publishing.

Methodological publications

- OECD (2009), "*Guidelines for a Harmonised Statistical Approach to Biotechnology Research and Development in the Government and Higher Education Sectors*", OECD Working Party of National Experts on Science and Technology Indicators, unclassified document DSTI/EAS/STP/NESTI(2009)1/FINAL.
- OECD (2005), "*A Framework for Biotechnology Statistics*", OECD Working Party of National Experts on Science and Technology Indicators.
- OECD (2002), *Frascati Manual 2002: Proposed Standard Practice for Surveys on Research and Experimental Development*, The Measurement of Scientific and Technological Activities, OECD Publishing.

Websites

- OECD Key Biotechnology Indicators, *www.oecd.org/sti/biotechnology/indicators*.

Biotechnology R&D expenditures in the business sector

2009 or latest available year

	Million US dollars, current prices and PPPs	As a percentage of total business enterprise R&D	As a percentage of industry value added
Australia	133.4	1.2	0.023
Belgium	574.0	12.6	0.264
Canada	944.5	7.2	0.110
Czech Republic	50.7	2.2	0.027
Denmark	463.7	11.0	0.389
Estonia	17.1	10.2	0.097
Finland	115.6	2.5	0.098
France	2 454.9	9.1	0.200
Germany	1 262.6	2.2	0.067
Ireland	301.6	15.1	0.263
Italy	360.1	3.2	0.031
Korea	957.5	2.8	0.106
Netherlands	395.7	6.6	0.093
Norway	148.7	5.8	0.084
Poland	16.8	1.4	0.004
Portugal	37.1	1.8	0.024
Slovak Republic	2.4	1.1	0.003
Slovenia	15.4	2.3	0.042
Spain	682.4	6.4	0.068
Sweden	411.3	4.9	0.196
Switzerland	922.3	12.6	0.384
United States	22 030.0	7.6	0.252
South Africa	19.0	0.8	0.006

StatLink http://dx.doi.org/10.1787/888932505963

Total biotechnology R&D expenditures in the business sector

2009 or latest available year

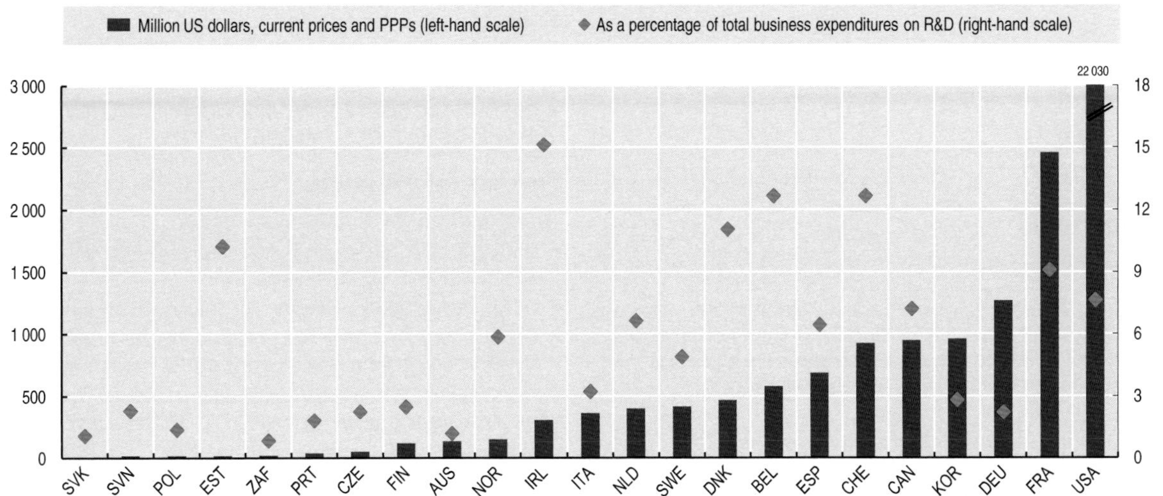

StatLink http://dx.doi.org/10.1787/888932505982

SIZE OF THE ICT SECTOR

Information and communication technologies (ICT) have been at the heart of economic changes for more than a decade. ICT-producing sectors and ICT employment contribute to technological progress and productivity growth.

Definition

The industry-based definition of the ICT sector is based on Revision 3 of the International Standard Industrial Classification (ISIC Rev. 3).

The principles underlying this definition are the following. For manufacturing industries, an ICT product must fulfil the function of information processing and communication, including transmission and display; and they must use electronic processing to detect, measure and/or record physical phenomena or control a physical process. For services industries, ICT products must enable information processing and communication by electronic means. These two measures of ICT production are expressed as a share of the total value added in the manufacturing and business services.

Two measures of ICT employment are shown here: a narrow measure, comprising ICT specialists whose job is directly focused on ICT such as software engineers; and a broader measure including jobs that regularly use ICT but are not focused on ICT per se (these occupations include scientists and engineers, as well as office workers, but exclude teachers and medical specialists for whom the use of ICT is not essential for their tasks). These two measures of ICT employment are expressed as a share of total employment.

Comparability

The existence of a widely accepted definition of the ICT sector is the first step towards making comparisons across time and countries possible. However, this definition is not yet consistently applied. Data provided by OECD countries have been combined with different data sources to estimate ICT aggregates compatible with national accounts totals. For this reason, statistics presented here may differ from data contained in national reports and in previous OECD publications.

Data on ICT employment for EU countries are based on the International Standard Classification of Occupations (ISCO 88) while data for non-EU countries are based on national classification systems. The classification and the selection of occupations are not harmonised internationally. This implies that the level of the indicators is not directly comparable across countries. Furthermore, there may be differences in ICT usage in occupations, both within and between countries, even when they are based on the same classification.

Overview

In 2008, the ICT sector accounted for between 3.7% (Switzerland) and 13.9% (Finland) of value added in manufacturing and business services of the 28 OECD countries with available data. The average share for the OECD was 8.2%. Over 1995-2008 the ICT share in value added has increased in all OECD countries except Austria (-1.3%), Australia and Canada (-0.8% both).

In 2010, the narrow definition of ICT employment (ICT specialists) accounted for between 1.7% (Turkey) and 5.4% (Sweden) of total employment of the OECD countries with available data. Over 1995-2010 this share has been rising in most countries, despite the stagnation of employment in the ICT sector. The broader group of ICT-using occupations (specialists, advanced and basic users) accounts for over 20% of total employment in most countries, ranging from 10.9% (Turkey) and 35.3% (Luxembourg).

Sources

- OECD (2010), *OECD Science, Technology and Industry Outlook 2010*, OECD Publishing.
- OECD (2011), *OECD Science, Technology and Industry Scoreboard 2011*, OECD Publishing.

Further information

Analytical publications

- OECD (2011), *OECD Guide to Measuring the Information Society 2011*, OECD Publishing.
- OECD (2010), *OECD e-Government Studies*, OECD Publishing.
- OECD (2006), *OECD Reviews of Risk Management Policies: Norway 2006: Information Security*, OECD Publishing.
- OECD (2003), *ICT and Economic Growth: Evidence from OECD Countries, Industries and Firms*, OECD Publishing.

Statistical publications

- OECD (2004), *Understanding Economic Growth: A Macro-level, Industry-level, and Firm-level Perspective*, OECD Publishing.

Websites

- OECD Key ICT indicators, *www.oecd.org/sti/ictindicators*.
- OECD Science, Technology and Industry, *www.oecd.org/sti*.
- OECD Telecommunications and Internet Policy, *www.oecd.org/sti/telecom*.

Share of ICT in value added and in employment

Percentage

	Share of ICT value added in business sector value added		Share of ICT-related occupations in total employment			
			ICT specialists *As a percentage of total employment*		ICT specialists, advanced and basic users *As a percentage of total employment*	
	2008	Percentage point change 1995-2008	2010	Percentage point change 1995-2010	2010	Percentage point change 1995-2010
Australia	6.7	-0.8	3.6	0.5	22.1	0.4
Austria	5.9	-1.3	3.2	0.6	20.8	5.8
Belgium	7.1	1.1	3.1	1.1	22.7	4.0
Canada	5.8	-0.8	4.4	1.4	21.2	0.5
Czech Republic	9.0	3.5	4.7	0.8	22.8	4.2
Denmark	8.1	1.7	4.4	1.5	27.3	6.9
Estonia	..	..	3.2	3.2	24.1	24.1
Finland	13.9	5.8	4.5	1.8	25.5	5.5
France	7.8	0.7	3.1	0.2	20.7	2.1
Germany	7.1	0.0	3.5	1.3	22.5	2.1
Greece	6.2	1.2	2.2	0.0	15.2	4.9
Hungary	9.9	3.8	2.7	2.7	22.5	22.5
Iceland	5.7	1.1	3.5	3.5	23.0	23.0
Ireland	13.0	1.3	2.8	0.1	24.0	9.5
Israel	..	..	..	..	..	..
Italy	6.3	1.0	3.1	0.6	20.4	-0.5
Japan	8.8	1.1	..	..	..	..
Korea	12.2	2.0	..	..	..	..
Luxembourg	7.0	2.6	4.4	1.5	35.3	12.4
Mexico	5.0	0.6	..	..	..	..
Netherlands	8.8	1.4	4.0	0.8	23.5	0.4
Norway	8.2	2.0	4.7	4.7	24.1	24.1
Poland	5.7	..	2.8	2.8	19.5	19.5
Portugal	7.2	0.8	2.6	-0.2	15.0	-1.4
Slovak Republic	7.5	2.6	2.9	2.9	20.8	20.8
Slovenia	..	..	3.0	3.0	24.0	24.0
Spain	6.4	0.3	3.1	0.9	19.5	3.7
Sweden	10.4	2.1	5.4	1.6	26.5	6.1
Switzerland	3.7	0.7	5.0	5.0	23.6	23.6
Turkey	..	..	1.7	1.7	10.9	10.9
United Kingdom	9.6	0.6	3.3	0.4	28.1	0.3
United States	9.0	0.0	4.0	0.7	20.3	-0.9
OECD average	8.2	0.5	..	..	..	..

StatLink http://dx.doi.org/10.1787/888932506001

Share of ICT in value added

As a percentage of business sector value added

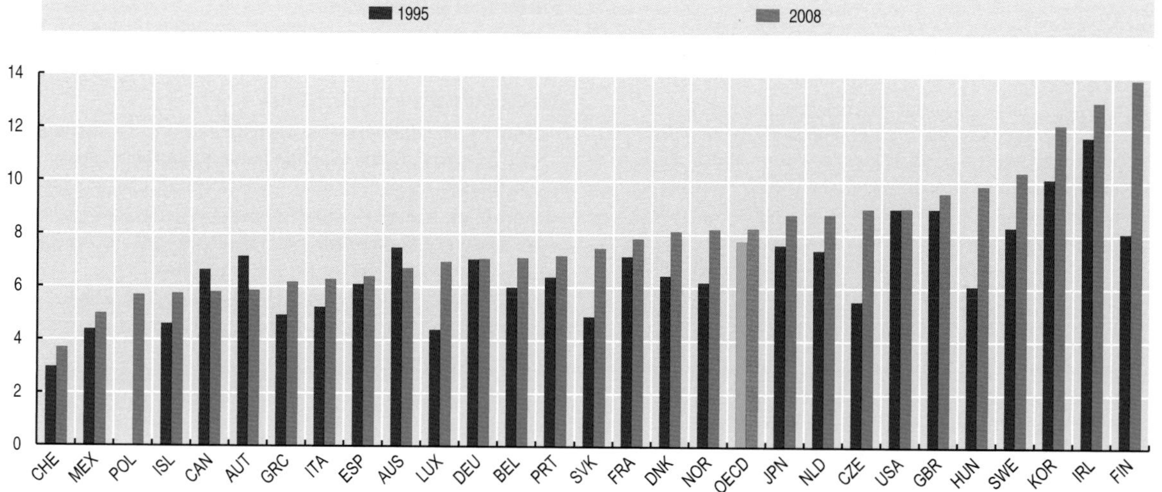

StatLink http://dx.doi.org/10.1787/888932506020

INVESTMENT IN ICT

Investment in information and communication technology (ICT) has been the most dynamic component of investment in late 1990s and early 2000s. This investment has enabled new technologies to enter the production process, to expand and renew the capital stock, and to sustain economic growth.

Definition

Investment is defined in accordance with the 1993 System of National Accounts. ICT investment covers the acquisition of equipment and computer software that is used in production for more than one year. ICT has three components: information technology equipment (computers and related hardware); communications equipment; and software. Software includes acquisition of pre-packaged software, customised software and software developed in-house.

The investment shares shown in the table and graph are percentages of each country's gross fixed capital formation, excluding residential construction.

Comparability

Data availability and measurement of ICT investment vary considerably across OECD countries, especially in terms of measurement of investment in software, deflators applied, breakdown by institutional sector and temporal coverage.

In the national accounts, expenditure on ICT is considered as investment only if the products can be physically isolated (*i.e.* ICT embodied in equipment is considered not as investment but as intermediate consumption). This means that ICT investment may be underestimated, with the size of the underestimation differing depending on how intermediate consumption and investment are treated in each country's accounts. In particular, it is only recently that expenditure on software has started being treated as investment in the national accounts, and methodologies still vary across countries. The difficulties of measuring software investment are also linked to the ways in which software can be acquired, *e.g.* via rental and licences or embedded in hardware. Moreover, software is often developed on own account. International comparability of ICT investment has improved over the recent years but some differences remain across OECD countries.

Note that ICT components that are incorporated in other products, such as motor vehicles or machine tools, are included in the value of those other products and excluded from ICT investment as defined here.

Overview

ICT shares in total non-residential investment in 2009 (or the latest year available) differ significantly among OECD countries but were particularly high (at 20% or more of the total) in the United States, Sweden, Japan and New Zealand, while they were below 10% in Ireland, and below 12% in Italy, Korea and Spain.

Software has been the main component of ICT investment in many countries, its share in non-residential investment in 2009 (or the latest year available) was highest in Sweden, the United States, Denmark, New Zealand and the United Kingdom while it was below 5% in Portugal and Ireland. The share of IT equipment was highest in Belgium, Denmark and the United Kingdom but lowest in Korea, Ireland and Spain.

In 2009, communication equipment was the major component of ICT investment in Portugal, while IT equipment was the major component in Belgium.

Sources

- OECD (2010), *OECD Productivity Statistics* (database).

Further information

Analytical publications

- OECD (2011), *OECD Communications Outlook*, OECD Publishing.
- OECD (2011), *OECD Information Technology Outlook*, OECD Publishing.
- OECD (2011), *OECD Science, Technology and Industry Scoreboard 2011*, OECD Publishing.
- OECD (2008), *Broadband Growth and Policies in OECD Countries*, OECD Publishing.
- OECD (2003), *ICT and Economic Growth: Evidence from OECD countries, industries and firms*, OECD Publishing.

Statistical publications

- OECD (2011), *National Accounts of OECD Countries*, OECD Publishing.

Methodological publications

- Ahmad, N. (2003), "Measuring Investment in Software", *OECD Science, Technology and Industry Working Papers*, No. 2003/6.
- Lequillier, F. *et al.* (2003), "Report of the OECD Task Force on Software Measurement in the National Accounts", *OECD Statistics Working Papers*, No. 2003/1.
- OECD (2010), *Handbook on Deriving Capital Measures of Intellectual Property Products*, OECD Publishing.

Online databases

- *STAN: OECD Structural Analysis Statistics.*

Websites

- OECD Compendium of Patents Statistics 2007, *www.oecd.org/sti/ipr-statistics.*
- OECD Productivity Database, *www.oecd.org/statistics/productivity*.

Shares of ICT investment in non-residential gross fixed capital formation

As a percentage of total non-residential gross fixed capital formation, total economy

	1996	1997	1998	1999	2000	2001	2002	2003	2004	2005	2006	2007	2008	2009
Australia	19.2	20.4	20.2	21.5	24.0	22.5	19.9	19.7	17.3	15.3	14.6	14.2	13.8	..
Austria	10.8	11.2	12.6	13.5	13.4	14.0	14.5	13.1	12.4	11.9	12.1	12.3	..	..
Belgium	18.4	19.4	21.5	21.7	24.2	23.3	20.3	19.9	20.1	..	..	..	..	..
Canada	18.0	17.5	18.8	19.9	20.6	20.2	19.2	18.8	18.5	17.6	16.8	16.7	15.9	17.0
Denmark	18.5	19.8	19.5	21.6	19.9	19.2	22.0	22.1	23.7	24.8	24.5	24.6	..	..
Finland	17.5	17.5	18.7	19.4	19.5	17.9	18.5	20.1	19.2	15.0	15.4	14.3	12.8	12.7
France	15.5	17.5	18.7	19.9	19.2	20.5	19.2	18.6	17.6	17.5	17.0	16.2	16.2	16.3
Germany	14.1	14.5	15.3	16.6	17.5	17.8	17.0	15.3	14.8	15.2	15.3	14.1	13.0	13.2
Ireland	11.4	9.6	11.0	10.1	10.1	9.9	8.2	7.9	7.9	7.5	9.0	8.9	7.5	9.1
Italy	13.6	14.8	14.1	13.8	14.6	13.6	12.3	11.6	11.4	11.7	10.9	10.7	10.4	10.9
Japan	12.6	12.1	12.0	13.0	15.0	15.1	14.8	14.8	14.6	14.3	13.4	13.2	22.5	..
Korea	10.0	10.9	12.8	15.8	18.0	17.0	15.7	13.2	11.9	12.2	12.4	12.1	11.7	11.1
Netherlands	16.4	17.9	18.9	19.1	19.9	19.9	19.1	20.0	21.3	22.0	22.3	19.5	..	..
New Zealand	18.9	20.6	24.4	23.3	26.1	22.3	21.1	21.8	21.7	21.6	22.3	22.4	22.9	23.3
Portugal	12.2	12.0	13.0	13.4	12.4	13.1	11.9	13.6	12.9	12.7	..	..	..	..
Spain	14.6	14.5	14.7	14.9	14.7	14.3	13.8	13.6	13.3	12.7	12.7	13.1	13.6	11.8
Sweden	23.3	24.8	27.1	28.7	31.3	28.7	26.3	24.7	24.3	25.1	24.4	23.0	21.9	24.7
Switzerland	16.2	17.9	18.0	19.1	18.9	19.3	20.7	20.7	21.9	19.0	18.5	18.2	18.3	19.3
United Kingdom	25.1	23.8	25.6	27.2	30.0	28.0	26.5	24.5	25.0	24.6	24.7	23.8	..	..
United States	27.8	28.9	29.1	30.6	32.0	30.3	29.1	28.9	28.1	27.8	26.7	26.3	26.7	31.5

StatLink http://dx.doi.org/10.1787/888932506039

Shares of ICT investment in non-residential gross fixed capital formation

As a percentage of total non-residential gross fixed capital formation, total economy, 2009 or latest available year

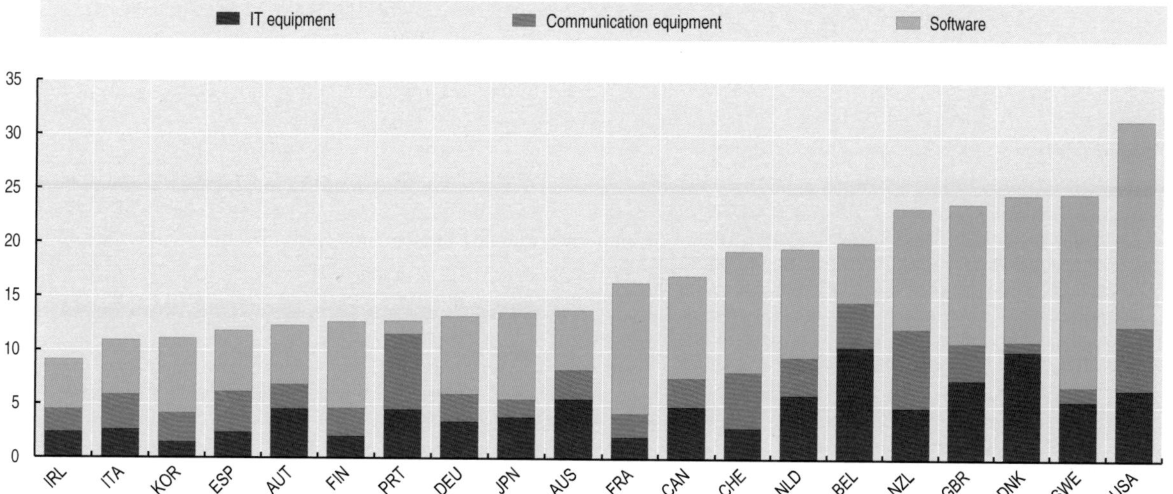

StatLink http://dx.doi.org/10.1787/888932506058

EXPORTS OF ICT GOODS

Information and communication (ICT) goods have been among the most dynamic components of international trade over the last decade.

Definition

The ICT commodities trade list is defined according to the OECD definition based on the 2002 version of the World Customs Organisation's Harmonized System (HS). Data in this section refer to the value of ICT exports in US dollars.

Comparability

The data for this table are taken from the statistics on international trade. These are compiled according to internationally agreed standards and are generally considered to assure good comparability.

It is however difficult to compare values of the OECD ICT goods trade in 2007 with those for earlier years owing to the new HS classification adopted in 2007, which differs radically from earlier revisions. The OECD is developing a correspondence between the HS 2002 and the HS 2007 for ICT goods. Further efforts will be also required to quantify and adjust for the impact of Missing Trader Intra-Community (MTIC) VAT Fraud from the mid-2000s, which mainly affected the movements of ICT goods within the EU.

Exports of ICT goods

Billion US dollars

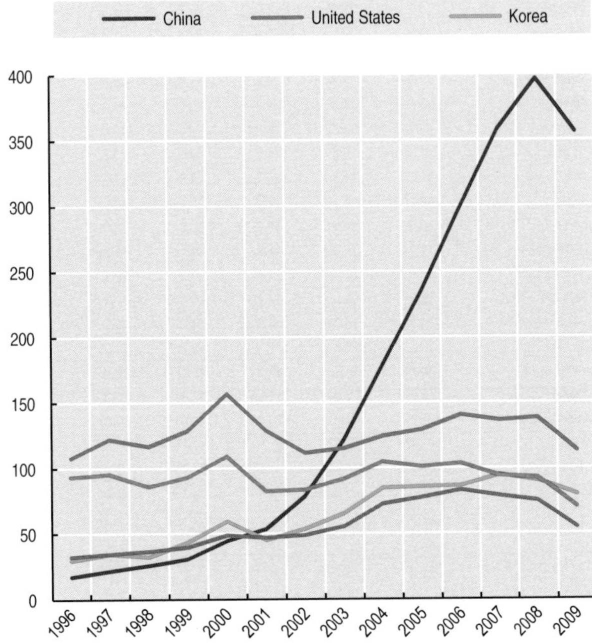

StatLink http://dx.doi.org/10.1787/888932506115

Overview

Exports of ICT goods by all OECD countries and the emerging economies listed reached about 1 trillion USD in 2009. OECD countries accounted for 62% of total ICT exports while China alone accounted for 36%. OECD countries can be divided into three groups; a first group includes the United States, Japan, Germany, Korea, the Netherlands and Mexico, countries with high exports of ICT goods; a second group includes the United Kingdom, France, Ireland, Hungary, Canada and the Czech Republic, with intermediate levels of ICT exports; the last groups includes all other countries, which are characterised by low values of ICT exports.

Over 1995-2006, growth of ICT exports has been steady for most OECD countries – particularly the Slovak Republic, the Czech Republic, Poland and Hungary – but it has started to level off as from 2006-07. The financial crisis in 2008-09 has accelerated this trend and has resulted in a sharp decrease in ICT exports worldwide.

China has experienced a spectacular growth in exports of ICT goods. Between 1998 and 2008, the value of ICT exports from China has been growing at an average rate of 31% per year. By 2004, China's ICT exports had surpassed those from the United States. However, Chinese exports of ICT goods have dropped by over 10% in 2009.

Sources

- OECD (2011), *International Trade by Commodity Statistics*, OECD Publishing.

Further information

Analytical publications

- OECD (2011), *OECD Communications Outlook*, OECD Publishing.
- OECD (2011), *OECD Information Technology Outlook*, OECD Publishing.

Methodological publications

- OECD (2011), *OECD Guide to Measuring the Information Society 2011*, OECD Publishing.

Websites

- OECD Key ICT indicators, *www.oecd.org/sti/ictindicators*.

Exports of ICT goods

Million US dollars

	1996	1997	1998	1999	2000	2001	2002	2003	2004	2005	2006	2007	2008	2009
Australia	1 920	1 967	1 562	1 562	1 727	1 619	1 372	1 571	1 713	1 781	1 788	1 943	2 076	1 647
Austria	2 092	2 460	2 774	3 176	3 941	4 006	4 533	5 002	5 908	6 467	6 710	7 318	7 494	5 271
Belgium	7 770	7 604	8 619	8 963	10 825	11 453	9 734	11 591	12 527	13 458	12 300	11 603	12 388	9 296
Canada	10 995	13 606	13 218	14 317	20 967	13 094	10 163	10 052	11 845	13 990	14 878	15 065	14 129	10 944
Chile	20	26	26	31	30	33	36	32	33	44	52	76	90	72
Czech Republic	644	575	991	752	1 334	2 582	4 148	5 207	7 907	8 668	12 330	16 806	20 614	16 305
Denmark	2 855	3 105	3 250	3 385	3 654	3 470	4 692	4 282	4 662	5 783	5 248	5 089	3 936	3 108
Estonia	150	319	427	408	967	853	579	820	1 126	1 405	1 310	730	743	494
Finland	5 266	6 157	7 849	8 499	10 781	8 526	8 944	10 026	10 412	13 238	13 243	14 047	14 419	6 746
France	22 335	24 526	28 446	29 015	31 939	26 310	23 629	23 277	26 864	27 331	31 584	26 122	25 360	19 762
Germany	32 289	34 389	36 554	39 677	48 717	46 634	48 601	55 200	72 250	77 168	82 809	78 319	74 643	54 601
Greece	116	178	233	280	466	347	338	389	511	490	629	562	667	496
Hungary	491	3 065	4 335	5 521	7 231	7 244	8 804	10 899	15 694	15 944	17 841	21 301	24 522	19 517
Iceland	1	-	1	1	2	2	2	3	2	3	5	8	9	3
Ireland	15 657	17 357	21 152	25 589	27 697	31 638	27 430	22 524	23 482	24 675	24 140	22 784	19 989	12 801
Israel	3 008	3 665	4 044	4 745	6 668	5 842	4 367	4 228	5 133	3 210	3 527	1 470	6 299	7 854
Italy	10 742	9 571	9 742	9 712	10 675	10 612	9 239	9 851	11 455	11 581	11 376	11 143	10 340	8 092
Japan	93 237	95 373	85 710	92 974	108 795	81 953	82 922	91 436	104 335	100 814	103 139	94 022	92 513	70 164
Korea	29 710	34 563	32 273	43 453	59 426	44 871	53 500	65 323	84 555	85 314	86 167	94 694	90 337	79 508
Luxembourg	..	..	..	707	889	1 179	945	720	859	998	840	757	524	408
Mexico	15 023	18 630	22 599	27 472	34 771	34 943	33 345	31 845	37 003	38 533	46 916	48 149	56 897	50 499
Netherlands	24 392	26 773	30 136	33 805	38 160	34 286	28 578	42 666	53 615	58 717	62 308	67 740	63 156	50 265
New Zealand	199	183	227	148	158	141	152	284	351	369	374	414	402	348
Norway	970	1 112	1 149	1 149	1 104	1 165	952	1 015	1 169	1 268	1 471	1 669	2 245	1 757
Poland	588	833	1 185	1 162	1 290	1 619	1 980	2 339	2 819	3 558	5 519	7 858	11 949	9 510
Portugal	1 110	1 107	1 155	1 472	1 492	1 701	1 711	2 364	2 545	2 972	3 673	4 041	3 843	1 757
Slovak Republic	..	232	323	354	388	487	492	852	1 698	2 991	5 267	8 454	11 823	9 410
Slovenia	186	161	170	130	169	204	220	251	275	229	291	384	618	519
Spain	4 201	4 392	5 032	5 367	5 355	5 270	5 000	6 523	7 014	7 197	7 347	6 688	6 820	5 428
Sweden	10 309	11 722	12 295	14 079	15 487	8 485	9 228	10 153	13 640	14 613	15 115	14 533	15 734	11 788
Switzerland	2 529	2 327	2 476	2 816	3 080	2 680	1 910	2 204	2 595	3 408	3 015	3 034	3 368	2 746
Turkey	347	497	904	840	1 024	1 056	1 603	1 988	2 933	3 227	3 178	2 884	2 407	2 032
United Kingdom	38 149	38 851	43 215	44 529	50 419	47 999	46 747	37 280	37 736	42 777	50 761	29 493	27 856	23 411
United States	107 890	121 872	116 598	128 678	156 670	128 513	111 448	114 860	124 097	128 943	140 314	136 219	138 001	113 157
OECD total	445 041	486 880	498 242	554 359	665 331	569 962	546 763	586 237	687 636	719 756	774 156	754 690	765 469	609 222
Brazil	868	1 021	995	1 243	2 232	2 329	2 178	2 106	2 013	3 701	3 969	2 975	3 139	2 859
China	17 287	21 626	25 646	30 522	44 135	53 221	78 243	121 365	177 742	234 086	297 653	357 974	396 424	356 301
India	736	656	441	501	714	858	781	957	1 082	1 113	1 344	1 567	1 770	6 099
Indonesia	3 219	2 862	2 313	3 069	7 573	6 095	6 301	5 687	6 527	6 944	6 138	6 025	6 517	6 921
Russian Federation	436	547	299	441	411	284	311	324	451	423	771	778	784	838
South Africa	294	314	375	432	417	442	390	462	578	587	745	846	805	677

StatLink http://dx.doi.org/10.1787/888932506077

Exports of ICT goods

Million US dollars, 2009

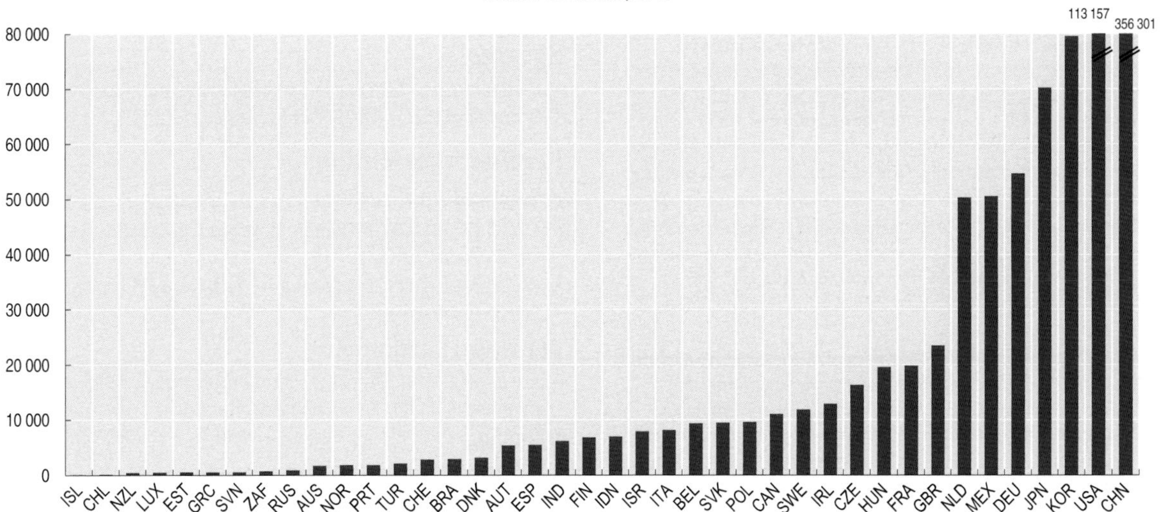

StatLink http://dx.doi.org/10.1787/888932506096

EMPLOYMENT RATES BY AGE GROUP

Labour markets differ in how they allocate employment opportunities among people of different ages. Employment rates for people of different ages are significantly affected by government policies with regard to higher education, pensions and retirement age.

Definition

The employment rate for a given age group is measured as the number of employed people of a given age as a ratio of the total number of people in that same age group.

Employment is generally measured through national labour force surveys. In accordance with the ILO Guidelines, employed persons are those aged 15 or over who report that they have worked in gainful employment for at least one hour in the previous week or who had a job but were absent from work in the reference week. Those not in employment consist of persons who are classified as either unemployed or inactive, in the sense that they are not included in the labour force for reasons of study, incapacity or the need to look after young children or elderly relatives.

Employment rates are shown for three age groups: persons aged 15 to 24 are those just entering the labour market following education; persons aged 25 to 54 are those in their prime working lives; persons aged 55 to 64 are those who are approaching retirement.

Comparability

All OECD countries use the ILO Guidelines for measuring employment. Operational definitions used in national labour force surveys may, however, vary slightly from country to country. Employment levels are also likely to be affected by changes in the survey design and the survey conduct. Despite these changes, the employment rates shown here are fairly consistent over time.

Overview

Employment rates for people aged 25 to 54 are relatively similar between OECD countries, with rates in all countries except Turkey ranging between 70% and 86% in 2010. Cross-country differences are larger when looking at the youngest age group where, in 2010, employment rates ranged between less than 26% in Hungary, Greece, Italy, the Slovak Republic, Luxembourg, Korea, Belgium and the Czech Republic and over 60% in the Netherlands, Iceland, Switzerland and Australia. Employment rates for the oldest age group also vary considerably, between 70% or more in Iceland, New Zealand and Sweden and less than 35% in Turkey, Poland, Hungary and Slovenia. Chile, Estonia and Israel have prime-age rates below the OECD average, whereas Slovenia is 8 points above the average. Youth rates for all new members are below the OECD average. In the emerging economies, employment rates for youths and older workers are above the OECD average only in Brazil, while those for people of prime working age exceed the OECD average by more than 8 percentage points in the Russian Federation.

Over the period from 1990 to 2010, employment rates for the youngest age group have declined by 10 percentage points for the OECD as a whole, with large decreases in Sweden, Portugal, Estonia, Luxembourg, the United Kingdom, Turkey, Finland and the United States (between 15 and 27 percentage points). This partly reflects government policies to encourage young people to increase their educational qualifications and general employment conditions, but also the difficulties experienced by youths to get a foothold in the labour market. For people in their prime working age, employment rates have remained stable for the OECD as a whole, with significant falls in Estonia, and large gains in the Netherlands, Ireland, Luxembourg, Belgium and Spain. The employment rates for older workers increased by 6 percentage points on average, with the largest increases recorded in New Zealand, the Netherlands, Germany, Australia, Belgium and Finland, while they fell in Turkey.

Sources

- OECD (2011), *OECD Employment Outlook*, OECD Publishing.
- For non-member countries: National sources.

Further information

Analytical publications

- Burniaux, J.M., R. Duval and F. Jaumotte (2004), "Coping with Ageing", *OECD Economics Department Working Papers*, No. 371.
- OECD (2010), *Off to a Good Start? Jobs for Youth*, OECD Publishing.
- OECD (2006), *Ageing and Employment Policies*, OECD Publishing.
- OECD (2000), *From Initial Education to Working Life: Making Transitions Work*, OECD Publishing.

Statistical publications

- OECD (2011), *Labour Force Statistics*, OECD Publishing.

Online databases

- *OECD Employment and Labour Market Statistics.*

Websites

- Meetings of National Economic Research Organisations (NERO) – Labour Market Issues, *www.oecd.org/eco/nero*.
- OECD Ageing and Employment Policies (supplementary material), *www.oecd.org/els/employment/olderworkers*.
- OECD Employment Policies, *www.oecd.org/els/employment*.
- OECD Jobs for Youth Project (supplementary material), *www.oecd.org/employment/youth*.
- OECD Labour Statistics, *www.oecd.org/statistics/labour*.
- Youth Employment Summit, *www.yesweb.org*.

COMPUTER, INTERNET AND TELECOMMUNICATION

Communication access and computers are increasingly present in homes in OECD countries, both in countries that already have high penetration rates and in those where adoption has lagged.

Definition

For access to home computers, the table shows the number of households that reported having at least one personal computer in working order in their home. The second part of the table shows the percentage of households who reported that they had access to the Internet. In almost all cases this access is via a personal computer either using a dial-up, ADSL or cable broadband access.

The table also shows total communication access paths. For OECD countries and China, these refer to the total number of fixed lines (standard analogue access lines and ISDN lines), DSL, Cable modem subscribers and mobile telephone subscribers. For Brazil, India, the Russian Federation and South Africa, total communication access paths are the sum of main telephone lines in operation, ISDN lines, DSL and cable modem subscribers and cellular mobile telephone subscribers.

Comparability

The OECD has addressed issues of international comparability by developing a model survey on ICT used in households and by individuals. The model survey uses modules addressing different topics so that additional components can be added reflecting usage practices and policy interests. The ICT access and use by households and individuals model survey is available on the OECD website.

Statistics on ICT use by households may run into problems of international comparability because of structural differences in the composition of households. On the other hand, statistics on ICT use by individuals may refer to people of different ages, and age is an important determinant of ICT use. Household- and person-based measures yield different figures in terms of levels and growth rates of ICT use. Such differences complicate international comparisons and make benchmarking exercises based on a single indicator of Internet access or use misleading, since country rankings change according to the indicator used.

For telecommunications access, data for OECD countries are collected according to agreed definitions and are highly comparable. The data shown for the nine non-OECD countries were partly collected according to the OECD definitions and partly provided by the International Telecommunication Union (ITU). The definition used by ITU is slightly narrower than the one used by the OECD, although data reported for the two sets of countries can be regarded as broadly comparable.

Mobile cellular subscribers

OECD and non-OECD share in the world total

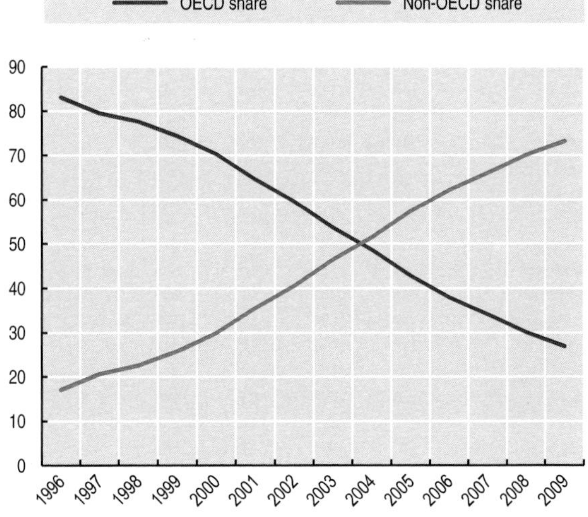

StatLink http://dx.doi.org/10.1787/888932506172

Overview

ICT penetration rates are the highest in Iceland, the Netherlands, Luxembourg, Norway, Sweden, Japan, and Denmark, where over 85% of households had access to a home computer by 2009. Penetration rates in Mexico and Turkey remain below 30%. Between 2000 and 2009, the share of households with access to a home computer increased by over 40 percentage points in the United Kingdom, France, Austria and Ireland.

The picture with regard to Internet access is similar. In Korea, the Netherlands, Iceland, Luxembourg, Sweden, and Norway, over 85% of all households had Internet access in 2009. In Mexico, less than 20% of all households had Internet access in the same year.

Access to telecommunications networks continues to expand in all OECD countries. Over 1999-2009, access more than doubled in the OECD area as a whole, going from 80.2 to 162.7 telecommunications paths per 100 inhabitants. Growth rates in telecommunication paths were even higher in India (with a growth in access penetration of over 1600%), China (over 600%), Mexico and Brazil (over 400%).

Sources

- OECD (2011), *OECD Science, Technology and Industry Scoreboard 2011*, OECD Publishing.

Further information

Analytical publications

- OECD (2011), *OECD Communications Outlook*, OECD Publishing.
- OECD (2011), *OECD Information Technology Outlook*, OECD Publishing.

Statistical publications

- Eurostat (2011), *Eurostat community survey on ICT usage in households and by individuals*, Eurostat, Luxembourg.

Websites

- OECD Science, Technology and Industry, *www.oecd.org/sti*.
- OECD Telecommunications and Internet Policy, *www.oecd.org/sti/telecom*.

Households with access to home computers, Internet and telephone

	Percentage of households with access to a home computer				Percentage of households with access to the Internet				Number of telecommunication access paths per 100 inhabitants			
	2000	2005	2008	2009	2000	2005	2008	2009	1995	2000	2005	2009
Australia	53.0	70.0	78.0	..	32.0	60.0	72.0	..	62.3	96.1	152.5	173.5
Austria	34.0	63.1	75.9	74.5	19.0	46.7	68.9	69.8	51.6	120.2	152.7	190.6
Belgium	..	..	70.0	71.1	..	50.2	63.6	67.4	48.3	100.0	149.4	179.8
Canada	55.2	72.0	79.4	..	42.6	64.3	74.6	..	68.8	96.7	132.8	155.6
Chile	17.5	30.1	40.0	..	8.4	16.7	23.8	..	..	43.5	90.3	128.0
Czech Republic	..	30.0	52.4	59.6	..	19.1	45.9	54.2	23.7	80.3	149.6	168.8
Denmark	65.0	83.8	85.5	86.2	46.0	74.9	81.9	82.5	77.2	124.4	177.1	201.9
Estonia	..	..	59.6	65.1	..	38.7	58.1	63.0	..	79.7	148.9	253.2
Finland	47.0	64.0	75.8	80.1	30.0	54.1	72.4	77.8	75.5	131.7	168.4	197.7
France	27.0	..	68.4	69.2	11.9	..	62.3	63.0	57.8	97.9	135.8	158.2
Germany	47.3	69.9	81.8	84.1	16.4	61.6	74.9	79.1	53.7	107.2	156.3	202.7
Greece	..	32.6	44.0	47.3	..	21.7	31.0	38.1	51.1	107.1	163.2	243.9
Hungary	..	42.3	58.8	63.0	..	22.1	48.4	55.1	24.1	65.3	128.5	166.1
Iceland	..	89.3	91.9	92.5	..	84.4	87.7	89.6	67.2	134.4	180.0	185.2
Ireland	32.4	54.9	70.3	72.8	20.4	47.2	63.0	66.7	40.1	96.1	149.4	163.4
Israel	47.1	62.4	71.0	74.4	19.8	48.9	61.8	66.0	..	116.0	147.7	196.1
Italy	29.4	45.7	56.0	61.3	18.8	38.6	46.9	53.5	50.7	117.5	175.3	195.7
Japan	50.5	80.5	85.9	87.2	..	57.0	63.9	67.1	58.5	101.9	139.1	147.0
Korea	71.0	78.9	80.9	81.4	49.8	92.7	94.3	95.9	45.6	113.4	156.0	173.1
Luxembourg	..	74.5	82.8	87.9	..	64.6	80.1	87.2	62.7	125.7	221.7	229.6
Mexico	..	18.6	25.7	26.8	..	9.0	13.5	18.4	10.4	26.9	66.4	104.6
Netherlands	..	77.9	87.7	90.8	41.0	78.3	86.1	89.7	55.5	122.1	161.5	184.8
New Zealand	..	..	..	80.0	..	..	..	75.0	56.7	102.7	140.2	176.4
Norway	..	74.2	85.8	87.6	..	64.0	84.0	85.6	78.6	125.8	167.0	170.9
Poland	..	40.1	58.9	66.1	..	30.4	47.6	58.6	15.2	18.0	109.6	152.0
Portugal	27.0	42.5	49.8	56.0	8.0	31.5	46.0	47.9	39.2	102.3	152.0	197.8
Slovak Republic	..	46.7	63.2	64.0	..	23.0	58.3	62.2	21.1	55.4	109.0	131.8
Slovenia	..	..	65.1	71.2	..	48.2	58.9	63.9	..		134.9	149.6
Spain	30.4	54.6	63.6	66.3	..	35.5	51.0	54.0	40.7	103.7	154.7	177.1
Sweden	59.9	79.7	87.1	87.6	48.2	72.5	84.4	86.0	91.0	141.1	181.5	200.8
Switzerland	57.7	76.5	81.0	..	..	..	77.0	..	70.2	122.2	166.0	200.0
Turkey	..	12.2	..	..	6.9	7.7	..	..	23.7	52.1	93.5	119.3
United Kingdom	38.0	70.0	78.0	81.2	19.0	60.2	71.1	76.7	58.4	122.1	175.8	205.4
United States	51.0	..	..	..	41.5	..	..	68.7	71.4	106.1	144.9	162.8
EU27 total	..	..	67.9	71.2	..	48.4	60.4	65.2	..	..	..	..
OECD average	..	..	..	..					51.7	93.9	137.4	162.7
Brazil	..	16.9	..		..	12.9	..		9.2	31.1	69.3	117.5
China	..	..	..		..	..	..	..	..	18.2	58.8	85.1
India	..	..	..	..	..	..	..	..	1.3	3.5	12.5	47.5
Russian Federation	..	26.0	..	..	..	25.0	..	..	16.9	24.2	112.7	..
South Africa	..	..	..	..	..	..	..	..	11.1	29.6	82.2	..

StatLink http://dx.doi.org/10.1787/888932506134

Households with access to home computers

As a percentage of all households

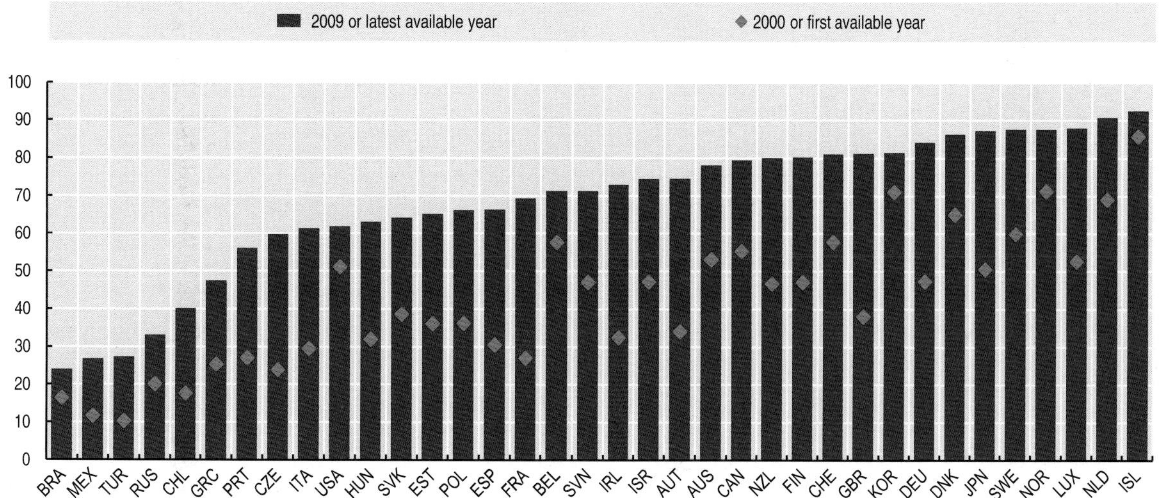

StatLink http://dx.doi.org/10.1787/888932506153

ENVIRONMENT

WATER CONSUMPTION

Freshwater resources are of major environmental and economic importance. Their distribution varies widely among and within countries. In arid regions, freshwater resources may at times be limited to the extent that demand for water can be met only by going beyond sustainable use, leading to reductions in terms of freshwater quantities.

Freshwater abstractions, particularly for public water supplies, irrigation, industrial processes and cooling of electric power plants, exert a major pressure on water resources, with significant implications for their quantity and quality. Main concerns relate to the inefficient use of water and to its environmental and socio-economic consequences: low river flows, water shortages, salinisation of freshwater bodies in coastal areas, human health problems, loss of wetlands, desertification and reduced food production.

Definition

Water abstractions refer to freshwater taken from ground or surface water sources, either permanently or temporarily, and conveyed to the place of use. If the water is returned to a surface water source, abstraction of the same water by the downstream user is counted again in compiling total abstractions: this may lead to double counting.

Mine water and drainage water are included, while water used for hydroelectricity generation (which is considered an in situ use) is excluded.

Comparability

Definitions and estimation methods employed by countries to compile data on water abstractions and supply may vary considerably and change over time. In general, data availability and quality are best for water abstractions for public supply, which represent about 15% of the total water abstracted in OECD countries.

Overview

Most OECD countries increased their total water abstractions over the 1960s and 1970s in response to higher demand by the agricultural and energy sectors. However, since the 1980s, some countries have succeeded in stabilising their total water abstractions through more efficient irrigation techniques, the decline of water-intensive industries (*e.g.* mining, steel), the increased use of cleaner production technologies and reduced losses in pipe networks. More recently, this stabilisation of water abstractions has partly reflected the consequences of droughts (with population growth continuing to drive increases in public supply).

At world level, it is estimated that, over the last century, the growth in water demand was more than double the rate of population growth, with agriculture being the largest user of water.

Water abstractions in OECD countries

1980 = 100

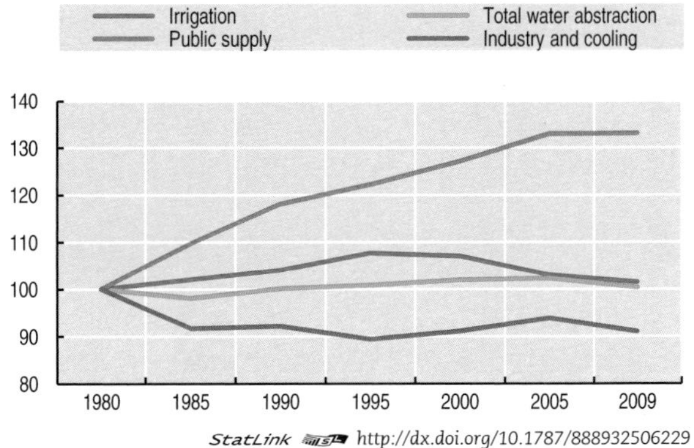

StatLink http://dx.doi.org/10.1787/888932506229

Sources

- OECD (2008), *OECD Environmental Data Compendium*, OECD Publishing.
- OECD (2006), *Environment at a Glance: OECD Environmental Indicators*, OECD Publishing.

Further information

Analytical publications

- OECD (2011), *OECD Environmental Outlook*, OECD Publishing.
- OECD (2009), *Managing Water for All: An OECD Perspective on Pricing and Financing*, OECD Publishing.
- OECD (2006), *Environment, Water Resources and Agricultural Policies: Lessons from China and OECD Countries*, China in the Global Economy, OECD Publishing.
- OECD (2006), *Financing Water and Environment Infrastructure: The Case of Eastern Europe, the Caucasus and Central Asia*, OECD Publishing.
- OECD (2006), *Water and Agriculture: Sustainability, Markets and Policies*, OECD Publishing.
- OECD (2003), *Social Issues in the Provision and Pricing of Water Services*, OECD Publishing.
- OECD (2003), *Water: Performance and Challenges in OECD Countries*, OECD Environmental Performance Reviews, OECD Publishing.
- OECD (2003), *Improving Water Management: Recent OECD Experience*, OECD Publishing.
- OECD and The World Bank (2006), *Liberalisation and Universal Access to Basic Services: Telecommunications, Water and Sanitation, Financial Services, and Electricity*, OECD Trade Policy Studies, OECD Publishing.
- OECD and World Health Organisation (2003), *Assessing Microbial Safety of Drinking Water: Improving Approaches and Methods*, OECD Publishing.
- Strange, T. and A. Bayley (2008), *Sustainable Development: Linking Economy, Society, Environment*, OECD Insights, OECD Publishing.

Websites

- OECD Environmental Indicators, *www.oecd.org/env/indicators*.
- The Water Challenge: OECD's Response, *www.oecd.org/water*.

Water abstractions

	Water abstractions per capita m^3/capita							Total abstractions Millions m^3
	1980	1985	1990	1995	2000	2005	2009 or latest available year	Latest available year
Australia	740	920	..	1 300	1 120	920	640	14 100
Austria	440	470	490	430	450	..	..	3 816
Belgium	..	..	..	810	740	610	590	6 220
Canada	1 510	1 620	1 610	1 430	..	1 280	1 130	37 250
Chile	..	..	..	..	..	1 950	2 200	36 510
Czech Republic	350	360	350	270	190	190	190	1 950
Denmark	240	..	250	170	140	120	120	660
Estonia	..	..	2 050	1 240	1 070	1 170	1 030	1 380
Finland	770	820	470	510	450	..	..	2 320
France	570	630	660	710 |	550	550	510	31 620
Germany	540	530 |	600	530	490	430	390	32 300
Greece	520	550	780	810	910	870	850	9 470
Hungary	450	590	610	580 |	650	490	570	5 740
Iceland	470	460	640	620	580	560	..	170
Ireland	310	..	..	330	..	..	..	..
Israel	..	..	380	330	270	250	220	1 600
Italy	..	..	..	..	740	..	..	..
Japan	730	720	720	710	690	650	650	83 100
Korea	460	460	480	520	560	610	..	29 160
Luxembourg	..	180	160	140	140	..	100	50
Mexico	800	..	..	800	720 |	740	750	79 760
Netherlands	650	640	530	420	560	700	640	10 610
New Zealand	..	..	..	..	820	1 170	1 200	5 200
Norway	..	490	..	550	530	620	640	3 030
Poland	430	440	400	340	310	300	300	11 520
Portugal	1 080	..	860	1 080	860	..	..	9 150
Slovak Republic	450	400	400	260	220	170	120	630
Slovenia	..	..	..	..	450	460	470	940
Spain	1 060	1 200	950	850	910	820	710	32 470
Sweden	490	360	350	310	300	290	..	2 630
Switzerland	410	410	400	370	360	340	360	2 660
Turkey	360	390	510	560	680	650	630	40 560
United Kingdom	270	230	240 |	190 |	210	200 |	150	8 350
United States	2 280	1 960	1 880	1 770	1 690	1 630	..	482 390
OECD total	1 030	930	950	920	900	870	840	994 100
China	..	..	..	..	430	430	440	579 300
Russian Federation	820	820	750	620	550	520	500	69 920

StatLink http://dx.doi.org/10.1787/888932506191

Water abstractions

m^3/capita, 2009 or latest available year

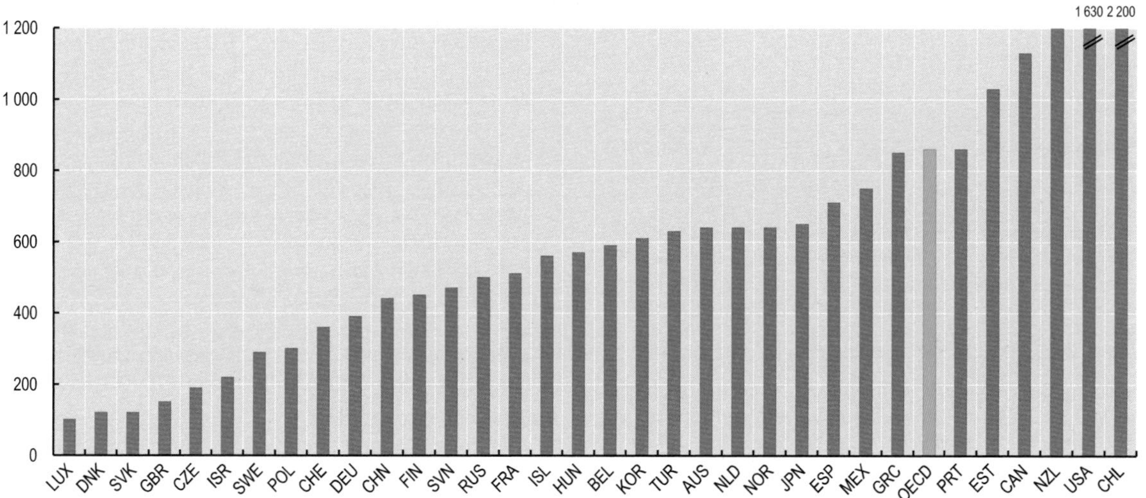

StatLink http://dx.doi.org/10.1787/888932506210

FISHERIES

Fisheries make an important contribution to sustainable incomes, employment opportunities and overall food protein intake. On the other hand, overfishing of some species in some areas is threatening stocks with depletion. In certain countries, including at least two OECD countries – Iceland and Japan – fish is the main source of animal protein intake.

Definition

The figures refer to the tonnage of landed catches of marine fish, and to cultivated fish and crustaceans taken from marine and inland waters and sea tanks. Landed catches of marine fish for each country cover landings in both foreign and domestic ports. The table distinguishes between marine capture fisheries and aquaculture because of their different production systems and growth rates.

Comparability

The time series presented are relatively comprehensive and consistent across the years, but some of the variation over time may reflect changes in national reporting systems. In one case, the data shown are estimated by the OECD Secretariat.

Overview

Marine capture fisheries landings in the OECD countries amounted to around 22.5 million tons in 2008, which is roughly 28% of the total world marine capture production. There has been a nearly constant downward trend in OECD catches since the late 1980s. The principal reason for this downward trend is overexploitation, and underscores the importance for environmental, social and economic reasons that governments make an effort in rebuilding fisheries.

Global aquaculture production has grown by roughly 8% per year over the last two decades. At the same time growth in the aquaculture production in the OECD has been much slower; at around 3.6% per year. OECD countries produced around 10% of the world aquaculture production in 2008 with the largest producers being Korea, Japan, Chile and Norway.

Fish landings in domestic and foreign ports

As a percentage of OECD total, 2008

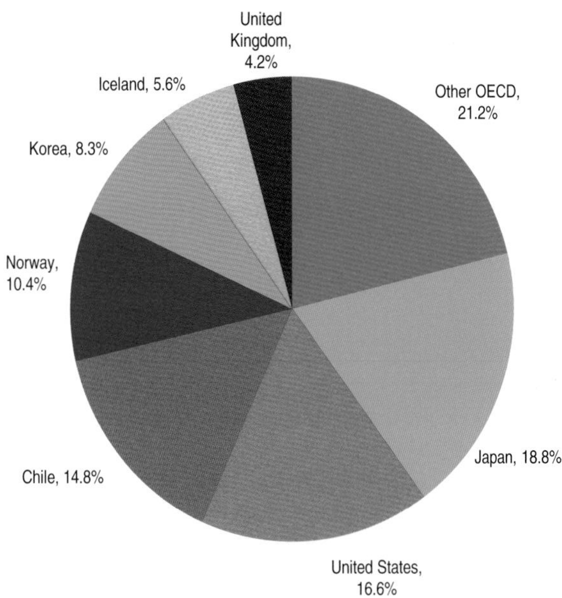

StatLink http://dx.doi.org/10.1787/888932506286

Sources

- OECD (2010), *Review of Fisheries in OECD Countries: Policies and Summary Statistics*, OECD Publishing.

Further information

Analytical publications

- OECD (2011), *Fisheries and Aquaculture Certification*, OECD Publishing.
- OECD (2011), *The Economics of Adapting Fisheries to Climate Change*, OECD Publishing.
- OECD (2010), *Advancing the Aquaculture Agenda: Workshop Proceedings*, OECD Publishing.
- OECD (2010), *Globalisation in Fisheries and Aquaculture: Opportunities and Challenges*, OECD Publishing.
- OECD (2007), *Structural Change in Fisheries: Dealing with the Human Dimension*, OECD Publishing.
- OECD (2006), *Financial Support to Fisheries: Implications for Sustainable Development*, OECD Publishing.
- OECD (2006), *Fishing for Coherence: Proceedings of the Workshop on Policy Coherence for Development in Fisheries*, The Development Dimension, OECD Publishing.
- OECD (2006), *Using Market Mechanisms to Manage Fisheries: Smoothing the Path*, OECD Publishing.
- OECD and Food and Agriculture Organization of the United Nations (FAO) (2008), *Globalisation and Fisheries – Proceedings of an OECD-FAO Workshop*, OECD Publishing.

Statistical publications

- OECD (2009), *Reducing Fishing Capacity: Best Practices for Decommissioning Schemes*, OECD Publishing.

Websites

- OECD Fisheries, *www.oecd.org/fisheries*.

Marine capture and aquaculture production

Thousand tonnes

	Fish landings in domestic and foreign ports							Aquaculture						
	1995	2000	2005	2006	2007	2008	2009	1995	2000	2005	2006	2007	2008	2009
Australia	201	185	236	189	182	172	..	24	37	47	61	64	70	..
Austria	..	..	..	..	..	..	..	4	..	..	..	..	..	..
Belgium	29	27	22	20	22	20	19	2	2	..	..	..	..	..
Canada	854	1 008	1 079	1 060	1 002	915	936	66	127	154	172	153	144	141
Chile	7 684	4 032	4 462	4 133	3 687	3 460	3 379	206	425	739	836	804	-	..
Czech Republic	..	..	..	..	..	..	..	19	19	20	20	20	20	20
Denmark	2 025	1 524	899	857	645	682	769	45	44	40	38	42	43	42
Estonia	129	101	90	88	97	100	..	..	..	..	1	1	1	..
Finland	106	92	77	101	117	111	116	17	15	14	13	13	13	14
France	616	682	606	602	474	-	..	281	267	238	238	..	..	..
Germany	241	194	247	259	262	243	211	40	45	46	35	45	44	39
Greece	153	93	92	94	95	87	83	33	88	110	113	155	115	118
Hungary	..	..	..	..	..	..	..	9	..	..	14	15	15	..
Iceland	1 603	1 930	1 411	1 323	1 419	1 305	1 151	4	4	8	10	5	5	6
Ireland	379	291	282	282	219	202	227	27	41	..	..	53	45	47
Israel	5	6	4	4	3	3	3	14	20	22	22	21	..	..
Italy	301	387	268	286	276	227	242	225	228	234	242	247	238	..
Japan	7 450	5 092	4 511	4 511	4 436	4 400	..	1 390	1 292	1 254	1 224	1 284	1 188	..
Korea	2 322	2 090	1 829	1 311	1 862	1 951	1 839	1 017	667	1 057	1 280	1 386	1 381	1 313
Luxembourg	..	..	..	..	..	..	..	..	..	..	..	..	..	..
Mexico	1 222	1 193	1 203	1 244	1 312	..	..	158	46	102	123	128	..	..
Netherlands	463	312	547	469	464	401	380	84	92	70	41	41	36	53
New Zealand	567	536	633	442	427	270	-	69	87	105	108	42	38	..
Norway	2 701	2 894	2 546	2 401	2 539	2 437	2 529	278	492	662	712	842	848	960
Poland	241	200	136	126	133	..	..	25	32	38	35	..	..	..
Portugal	242	172	172	181	197	202	178	5	8	7	8	7	8	..
Slovak Republic	..	..	..	..	..	..	..	..	..	1	1	1	1	1
Slovenia	2	2	1	1	1	1	1	-	-	-	-	-	-	-
Spain	1 075	1 002	717	677	752	802	677	224	312	273	273	285	253	268
Sweden	379	341	239	262	246	219	197	8	6	7	9	6	9	9
Switzerland	..	..	..	..	..	..	..	1	..	..	..	..	..	..
Turkey	577	461	523	489	589	443	-	22	79	118	129	140	152	..
United Kingdom	912	748	670	614	610	980	840	92	144	165	152	157	148	147
United States	4 783	4 245	4 463	4 371	4 294	3 890	..	413	373	358	363	373	351	..
OECD total	37 061	29 654	27 730	26 208	26 180	23 368	13 770	4 801	4 989	5 888	5 998	6 277	5 121	..
Russian Federation	..	4 289	..	..	..	..	..	..	205	..	..	..	..	..

StatLink http://dx.doi.org/10.1787/888932506248

Share of aquaculture in total fish capture and production

Percentage, average 2006-08

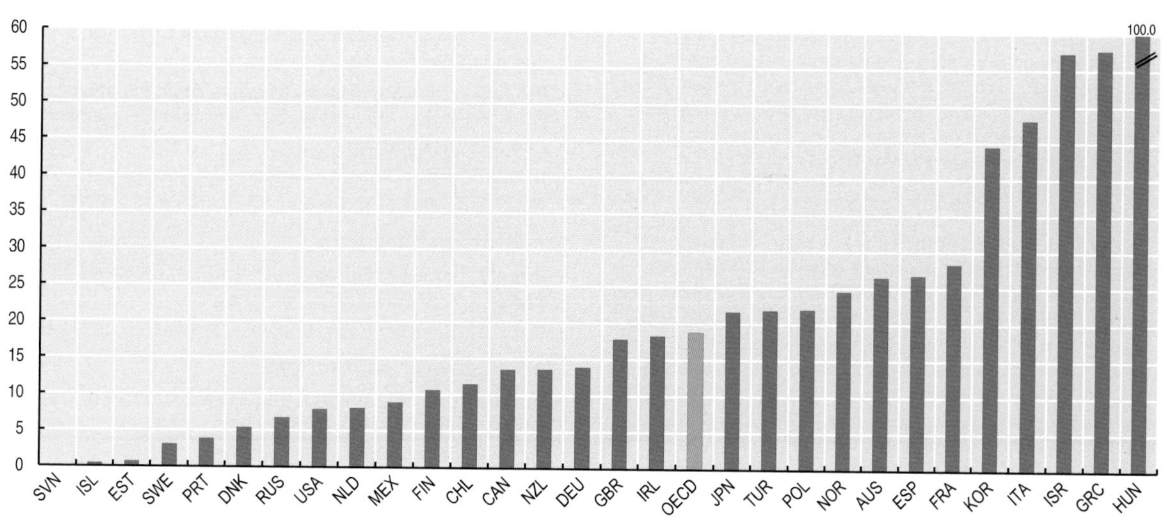

StatLink http://dx.doi.org/10.1787/888932506267

EMISSIONS OF CARBON DIOXIDE

Carbon dioxide (CO_2) makes up the largest share of greenhouse gases. The addition of man-made greenhouse gases to the atmosphere disturbs the earth's radiative balance (i.e. the balance between the solar energy that the earth absorbs and radiates back into space). This is leading to an increase in the earth's surface temperature and to related effects on climate, sea level and world agriculture.

Definition

The table refers to emissions of CO_2 from burning oil, coal and natural gas for energy use. Carbon dioxide also enters the atmosphere from burning wood and waste materials and from some industrial processes such as cement production. However, emissions of CO_2 from these other sources are a relatively small part of global emissions, and are not included in the statistics shown here. The *Revised 1996 IPCC Guidelines for National Greenhouse Gas Inventories* provide a fuller, technical definition of how CO_2 emissions have been estimated for this table.

Comparability

These emissions estimates are affected by the quality of the underlying energy data. For example, some countries, both OECD and non-OECD, have trouble reporting information on bunker fuels and incorrectly define bunkers as fuel used abroad by their own ships and planes. Since emissions from bunkers are excluded from the national totals, this affects the comparability of the estimates across countries. On the other hand, since these estimates have been made using the same method and emission factors for all countries, in general, the comparability across countries is quite good.

These data are preliminary and differ slightly from those published in the 2011 edition of the CO_2 *Emissions from Fuel Combustion*.

Overview

Global emissions of carbon dioxide have risen by 106%, or on average 1.9% per year, since 1971. In 1971, the current OECD countries were responsible for 67% of the world CO_2 emissions. As a consequence of rapidly rising emissions in the developing world, the OECD contribution to the total fell to 42% in 2009. By far, the largest increases in non-OECD countries occurred in Asia, where China's emissions of CO_2 from fuel combustion have risen by 5.8% per annum between 1971 and 2009. The use of coal in China increased the levels of CO_2 emissions by 5.0 billion tonnes over the 38 years to 2009.

Two significant downturns in OECD CO_2 emissions occurred following the oil shocks of the mid-1970s and early 1980s. Emissions from the economies in transition declined over the last decade, helping to offset the OECD increases between 1990 and the present. However, this decline did not stabilise global emissions as emissions in developing countries continued to grow. With the economic crisis in 2008-09, world CO_2 emissions declined by 1.5% in 2009. However, early indicators suggest that growth in CO_2 emissions rebounded in 2010.

Disaggregating the emissions estimates shows substantial variations within individual sectors. Between 1971 and 2009, the combined share of electricity and heat generation and transport shifted from one-half to two-thirds of the total. The share of fossil fuels in overall emissions changed slightly during the period. The weight of coal in global emissions has remained at approximately 40% since the early 1970s, while the share of natural gas increased from 15% in 1971 to 20% in 2009. The share of oil decreased from 49% to 37%. Fuel switching and the increasing use of non-fossil energy sources reduced the CO_2/total primary energy supply (TPES) ratio by 6% over the past 38 years.

Sources

- International Energy Agency (IEA) (2011), CO_2 *Emissions from Fuel Combustion*, IEA, Paris.

Further information

Analytical publications

- IEA (2011), *Climate and Electricity Annual 2011: Data and Analyses*, IEA, Paris.
- IEA (2011), *IEA Scoreboard 2011: Implementing Energy Efficiency Policy: Progress and challenges in IEA member countries*, IEA, Paris.
- IEA (2011), *World Energy Outlook*, IEA, Paris.
- IEA (2010), *Energy Technology Perspectives*, IEA, Paris.

Statistical publications

- IEA (2011), *Energy Balances of Non-OECD Countries*, IEA, Paris.
- IEA (2011), *Energy Balances of OECD Countries*, IEA, Paris.

Methodological publications

- Intergovernmental Panel on Climate Change (IPCC) (1996), *Revised 1996 IPCC Guidelines for National Greenhouse Gas Inventories*, Institute for Global Environmental Strategies (IGES), Japan.

Online databases

- IEA CO_2 *Emissions from Fuel Combustion*.

CO_2 emissions from fuel combustion

Million tonnes

	1971	1990	1998	1999	2000	2001	2002	2003	2004	2005	2006	2007	2008	2009
Australia	144	260	323	333	339	352	359	362	372	389	393	389	393	395
Austria	49	56	63	61	62	66	68	73	73	75	72	70	70	63
Belgium	117	108	121	117	119	119	112	120	117	113	110	106	111	101
Canada	339	432	500	511	533	526	533	556	554	559	544	568	551	521
Chile	21	31	54	57	53	50	51	53	58	58	60	67	68	65
Czech Republic	151	155	118	111	122	121	117	121	122	120	121	122	117	110
Denmark	55	50	58	55	51	52	52	57	52	48	56	51	48	47
Estonia	..	36	16	15	15	15	15	17	17	17	16	19	18	15
Finland	40	54	57	56	54	59	62	72	67	55	67	65	57	55
France	432	352	385	378	377	384	376	385	385	388	380	374	371	354
Germany	979	950	861	829	827	845	833	842	843	812	824	800	804	750
Greece	25	70	80	80	87	90	90	94	93	95	94	98	94	90
Hungary	60	67	57	57	54	56	55	57	56	56	56	54	53	48
Iceland	1	2	2	2	2	2	2	2	2	2	2	2	2	2
Ireland	22	30	38	39	41	43	42	42	42	44	45	44	44	39
Israel	14	33	49	50	55	56	59	61	60	60	62	67	66	65
Italy	293	397	421	425	426	429	435	452	459	461	464	447	435	389
Japan	759	1 064	1 129	1 169	1 184	1 170	1 205	1 213	1 212	1 221	1 205	1 242	1 153	1 093
Korea	52	229	351	385	438	451	445	448	469	468	476	490	502	515
Luxembourg	15	10	7	7	8	9	9	10	11	11	11	11	11	10
Mexico	97	265	338	334	349	350	356	363	369	386	395	410	404	400
Netherlands	130	156	174	169	172	178	178	183	185	183	178	181	183	176
New Zealand	14	23	28	30	31	32	32	33	33	34	34	32	34	31
Norway	24	28	37	38	34	35	34	37	38	36	37	38	38	37
Poland	287	342	313	303	291	290	279	290	293	293	304	304	299	287
Portugal	14	39	53	60	59	59	63	58	60	63	56	56	53	53
Slovak Republic	39	57	40	39	37	38	38	38	37	38	37	37	36	33
Slovenia	..	13	15	14	14	15	15	15	15	16	16	16	17	15
Spain	120	206	249	269	284	285	302	310	327	340	332	344	318	283
Sweden	82	53	58	57	53	52	54	55	54	50	48	46	45	42
Switzerland	39	41	43	43	43	43	42	44	44	45	44	42	44	42
Turkey	41	127	178	177	201	182	192	202	207	216	240	265	264	256
United Kingdom	623	549	518	515	524	537	522	534	534	533	534	521	512	466
United States	4 291	4 869	5 479	5 506	5 698	5 678	5 605	5 680	5 758	5 772	5 685	5 763	5 587	5 195
EU27 total	..	4 052	3 878	3 812	3 831	3 905	3 877	3 994	4 010	3 979	3 996	3 942	3 868	3 577
OECD total	9 370	11 158	12 214	12 293	12 634	12 669	12 635	12 880	13 019	13 056	12 999	13 142	12 799	12 045
Brazil	91	194	283	292	303	309	309	300	320	322	327	342	361	338
China	800	2 211	3 156	3 047	3 037	3 083	3 308	3 828	4 552	5 062	5 603	6 028	6 507	6 832
India	200	582	872	939	972	984	1 015	1 041	1 117	1 160	1 252	1 357	1 431	1 586
Indonesia	25	142	229	261	264	292	302	326	334	336	356	366	343	376
Russian Federation	..	2 179	1 433	1 468	1 506	1 508	1 494	1 531	1 513	1 516	1 580	1 579	1 593	1 533
South Africa	174	255	309	291	298	284	295	321	337	330	331	357	388	369
World	14 085	20 966	22 769	22 947	23 493	23 671	24 064	25 117	26 369	27 195	28 093	29 037	29 449	28 994

StatLink http://dx.doi.org/10.1787/888932506305

World CO_2 emissions from fuel combustion, by region

Million tonnes

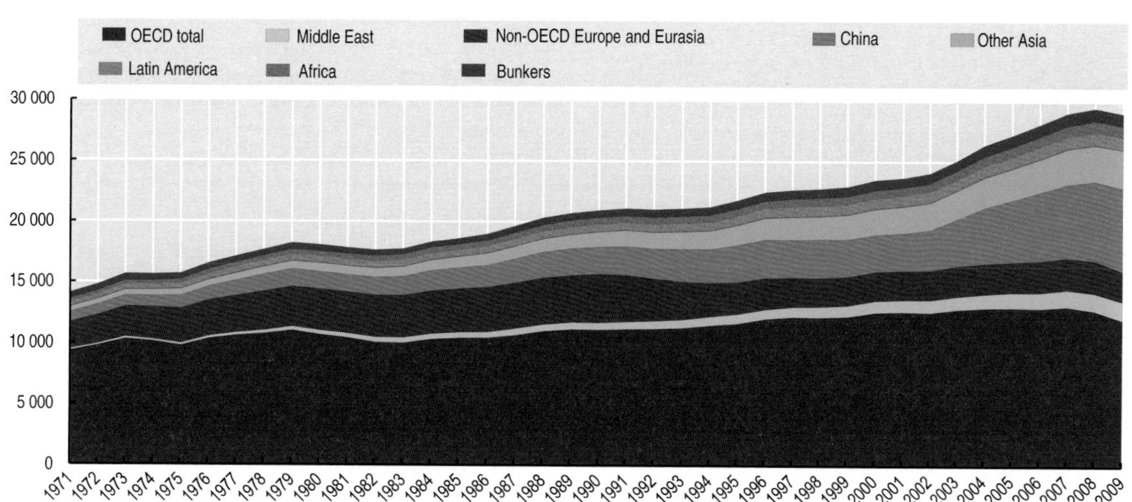

StatLink http://dx.doi.org/10.1787/888932506324

AIR QUALITY BY REGION

The urgency of the climate change challenge requires a rapid, sustained, and effective transition to lower carbon regional economies. Apart from necessary reduction in greenhouse gases, there is also a need to cut emissions of other pollutants like toxic gases or fine particles that can severely threaten people's health. Regional and city-level policies have a key role to play in this transition.

Definition

CO_2 regional emissions are imputed from national emission data allocated to grids of around 10 km × 10 km square. It includes emissions from all sources with the exception of air transport, international aviation and shipping.

Population exposure to air pollution is calculated by taking the weighted average value of 2.5 micrometers for the grid cells present in each region, with the weight given by the estimated population count in each cell.

Comparability

While it is increasingly clear that urban areas emanate a growing percentage of the world carbon emissions, we still lack statistics suited for global comparison and monitoring of the carbon footprints of cities. Even if many cities around the world have started collecting inventories of their carbon emissions, differences in the methodologies (techniques, input data, sources included) used to compute total CO_2 make any comparison of their performance very difficult. Another problem is that cities "delimit" themselves in different ways, so that inventories in different countries can refer to a very narrow (the core municipality) or a very extended (the functional area of influence) definition of city. While supporting international efforts to harmonise urban carbon inventory, the OECD is also using estimates for small geographic units, derived from national data downscaled through the use of spatial datasets. Time-varying statistics for large and medium-sized cities in the OECD are obtained by applying these estimates to urban areas that are defined through a harmonised methodology.

Overview

A look at interregional disparities gives a first rationale for spatially targeted interventions. In fact, it is possible to observe large disparities in carbon dioxide (CO_2) per capita produced in different regions. Regions with the highest levels of emissions per capita are located in the United States, the Czech Republic and Canada. For Canada, this result is largely explained by the low levels of population in these regions. Similarly, relative low population explains in part the very high levels observed in Wyoming (United States). The significant degree of geographical concentration of CO_2 emissions per capita is evident in several countries, where some regions have a value more than twice the country average.

A positive correlation is found between levels of regional gross domestic product (GDP) and CO_2 emissions, but there are significant differences in the "carbon intensity" of production across regions. In fact, when looking at the ratio of GDP over CO_2, it is clear that the production of some regions is much more efficient, in terms of embodied CO_2, than the national average. This is particularly evident in Turkey, the United States, Mexico, the Russian Federation and Brazil. In general, the regions with the highest GDP/CO_2 host the national capital (where service-intensive industries are concentrated). However, this is not always the case (for example, Bolzano in Italy or Shikogu in Japan). Relatively low values of GDP/CO_2 indicate a potential for decoupling emissions from the economic growth of the region.

Internationally comparable measures of air quality in regions can be derived from satellite-based measurement of particulate matter finer than 2.5 micrometers (PM 2.5), which can cause cardiovascular and other diseases when inhaled. While these estimates can be less precise than ground-based measurement, they have the advantage of being available for the large areas of the globe that are still without air monitoring stations. By overlaying these data on fine particulate matter with data on population distribution at 1 km resolution, it is possible to conclude that large fractions of the world population breathe air whose pollution exceeds the World Health Organization's recommended level of 10 micrograms of PM 2.5 per cubic meter. It is important to emphasise that the measured PM 2.5 concentration comes from both natural and human sources, with the fraction imputable to human activity varying significantly among regions. The share of people living in areas with health-damaging levels of pollution is worryingly high in several countries (particularly in China, India and Italy).

There are large regional variations in the extent of population exposure to high levels of particulate matters. Regional peaks are clear in China, Italy, India, Mexico and Chile, while a more equitable distribution across regions appears in Japan and Korea.

Sources

- OECD (2011), *OECD Regions at a Glance*, OECD Publishing.

Further information

Analytical publications

- Donkelaar A. van *et al.* (2010) "*Global Estimates of Ambient Fine Particulate Matter Concentrations from Satellite-Based Aerosol Optical Depth: Development and Application*", *Environmental Health Perspective*, 118(6), US National Institute of Environmental Health Sciences, USA.
- Hunt, A. (2011), "*Policy Interventions to Address Health Impacts Associated with Air Pollution, Unsafe Water Supply and Sanitation, and Hazardous Chemicals*", *OECD Environment Working Papers*, No. 35.
- OECD (2011), *OECD Environmental Outlook*, OECD Publishing.

Statistical publications

- OECD (2011), *Towards Green Growth: Monitoring Progress: OECD Indicators*, OECD Green Growth Studies, OECD Publishing.

Online databases

- *OECD Regional Database.*

Websites

- Regional Development, *www.oecd.org/gov/regionaldevelopment.*
- Regional Statistics and Indicators, *www.oecd.org/gov/regional/statisticsindicators.*

Regional range in CO_2 emissions per capita

Tonnes of CO_2 per capita, 2005

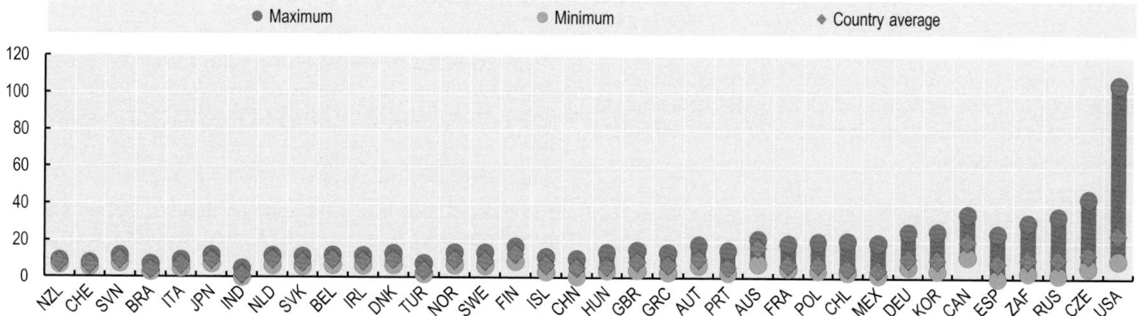

StatLink http://dx.doi.org/10.1787/888932506343

Large region with highest GDP to CO_2 ratio and country average

2005

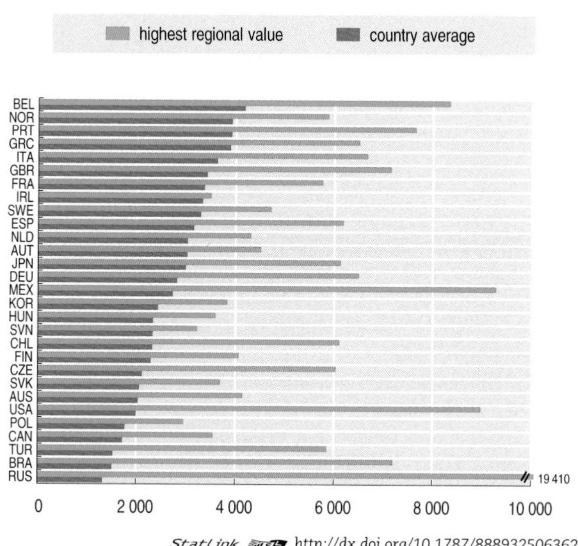

StatLink http://dx.doi.org/10.1787/888932506362

Population exposed to air pollution, PM2.5 thresholds

Percentage, average 2001-06

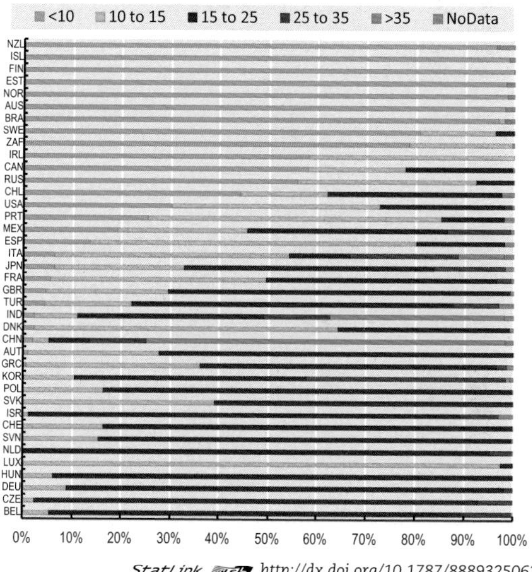

StatLink http://dx.doi.org/10.1787/888932506381

Regional range of population exposure to air pollution

Percentage, average 2001-06

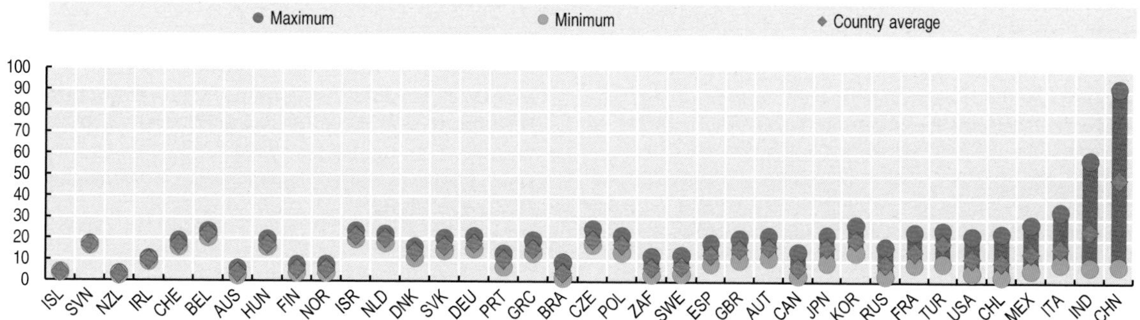

StatLink http://dx.doi.org/10.1787/888932506400

MUNICIPAL WASTE

The amount of municipal waste generated in a country is related to the rate of urbanisation, the types and patterns of consumption, household revenue and lifestyles. While municipal waste is only one part of total waste generated in each country, its management and treatment often absorbs more than one third of the public sector's financial efforts to abate and control pollution.

The main concerns raised by municipal waste are the potential impact from inappropriate waste management on human health and the environment (soil and water contamination, air quality, land use and landscape).

Definition

Municipal waste is waste collected and treated by or for municipalities. It covers waste from households, including bulky waste, similar waste from commerce and trade, office buildings, institutions and small businesses, yard and garden waste, street sweepings, the contents of litter containers, and market cleansing waste. The definition excludes waste from municipal sewage networks and treatment, as well as waste from construction and demolition activities.

The kilogrammes of municipal waste per capita produced each year – or "waste generation intensities" – provide one broad indicator of the potential environmental and health pressures from municipal waste. They should be complemented with information on waste management practices and costs, and on consumption levels and patterns.

Overview

The quantity of municipal waste generated in the OECD area has risen strongly since 1980, and exceeded an estimated 650 million tonnes in 2009 (540 kg per capita).

In most countries for which data are available, increased affluence, associated with economic growth, and changes in consumption patterns tend to generate higher rates of waste per capita. Over the past twenty years, waste generation has however risen at a lower rate than private final consumption expenditure and GDP, with a slowdown in recent years.

The amount and composition of municipal waste going to final disposal depends on national waste management practices. Despite improvements in these practices, only a few countries have succeeded in reducing the quantity of solid waste to be disposed of.

Comparability

The definition of municipal waste and the surveying methods used to collect information vary from country to country.

The main problems in terms of data comparability relate to the coverage of waste from commerce and trade, and of separate waste collections carried out by private companies.

Depending on the data availability, in some cases the reference year refers to the closest available year (*e.g.* 2005 might refer to 2004 data).

Data for Australia and Canada refer to household waste only. Data for New Zealand refer to the amount going to landfill only. Portugal includes Azores and Madeira Islands. Data for China do not cover waste produced in rural areas.

Time series data for the OECD total exclude Estonia, Israel and Slovenia.

Sources

- OECD (2011), *OECD Environmental Outlook*, OECD Publishing.
- OECD (2008), *OECD Environmental Data Compendium*, OECD Publishing.
- OECD (2006), *Environment at a Glance: OECD Environmental Indicators*, OECD Publishing.

Further information

Analytical publications

- OECD (2011), *Greening Household Behaviour: The Role of Public Policy*, OECD Publishing.
- OECD (2008), *Conducting Sustainability Assessments*, OECD Sustainable Development Studies, OECD Publishing.
- OECD (2004), *Addressing the Economics of Waste*, OECD Publishing.
- OECD (2004), *Economic Aspects of Extended Producer Responsibility*, OECD Publishing.
- OECD (2004), "*Toward Waste Prevention Performance Indicators*", Unclassified Working Document, Environment Directorate, ENV/EPOC/WGWPR/SE(2004)1/FINAL.
- Strange, T. and A. Bayley (2008), *Sustainable Development: Linking Economy, Society, Environment*, OECD Insights, OECD Publishing.

Websites

- OECD Environmental Indicators, *www.oecd.org/env/indicators*.
- OECD Waste Prevention and Management, *www.oecd.org/env/waste*.

Municipal waste generation

	Generation intensities kg/capita							Total amount generated Thousand tonnes
	1980	1985	1990	1995	2000	2005	2009 or latest available year	2009 or latest available year
Australia	..	..	400	..	400	..	600	12 730
Austria	..	..	420	430	530	560	580	4 850
Belgium	280	310	340	450	480	480	490	5 280
Canada	..	..	310 |	240	370	390	390	12 900
Chile	200	230	250	280	330	350	380	6 520
Czech Republic	..	250 |	..	300	330	290	310	3 310
Denmark	400	480	..	570	660	740	830	4 590
Estonia	..	..	..	370	460 |	440	350	460
Finland	..	..	..	410	500	480	480	2 560
France	..	..	450	480	510	530	530	34 500
Germany	..	..	630 |	620	640	560	590	48 100
Greece	260	300	300	300	410	440	480	5 390
Hungary	..	..	530	460 |	450	460	430	4 310
Iceland	..	..	..	430	460	520	550	180
Ireland	190	310	..	510	600 |	730	660	2 950
Israel	..	..	..	..	630	590	610	4 560
Italy	250	270	350 |	450	510	540	540	32 500
Japan	380	350	410	420	430	410	380	48 110
Korea	..	510	710 |	390	360	370	390	19 010
Luxembourg	350	360	580 |	580	650	680	710	350
Mexico	..	..	250 |	330	310	340	360	39 060
Netherlands	490	480	500	550	610	620	610	10 110
New Zealand	650	..	990	870	770	770	580	2 500
Norway	550	590	550 |	640	620 |	430	470	2 270
Poland	280	300	290	290	320 |	320	320	12 050
Portugal	200	230	300	390	440	450	520	5 500
Slovak Republic	..	360	300	300	320 |	270	300	1 650
Slovenia	..	..	..	600	510 |	420	400	810
Spain	..	..	..	480	610	600	560	25 340
Sweden	300	320	370	400	430	480	480	4 490
Switzerland	440	530	610	600	660	660	710	5 460
Turkey	270	360	400	460	480 |	460	390	28 010
United Kingdom	..	..	470	500	580	590	540	32 600
United States	610	630	760	740	780	770	720	220 410
OECD total	..	430	500	520	560	560	540	650 000
Brazil	..	..	..	..	330	320	270	51 430
China	..	..	210	280	260	280	250	157 340
India	..	..	..	..	..	..	..	17 570
Indonesia	..	..	..	..	..	..	..	9 600
Russian Federation	160	170	190	340	350	400	440	63 080

StatLink http://dx.doi.org/10.1787/888932506419

Municipal waste generation

Kg per capita, 2009 or latest available year

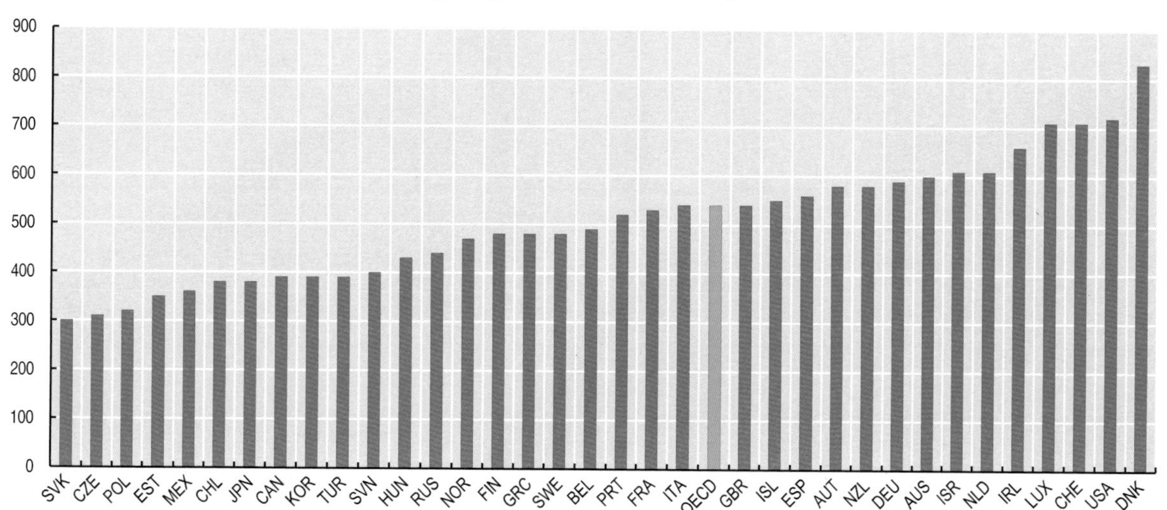

StatLink http://dx.doi.org/10.1787/888932506438

EDUCATION

OUTCOMES

INTERNATIONAL STUDENT ASSESSMENT
TRENDS IN READING
ENJOYMENT OF READING
HOW MANY STUDENTS STUDY ABROAD?
EDUCATION ATTAINMENT

RESOURCES

INCENTIVES TO INVEST IN EDUCATION
EDUCATIONAL EXPENDITURE PER STUDENT
PRIVATE EXPENDITURE IN TERTIARY EDUCATION
EDUCATION EXPENDITURE

INTERNATIONAL STUDENT ASSESSMENT

How effective are school systems at providing young people with a solid foundation in the knowledge and skills that will equip them for life and learning beyond school? The OECD Programme for International Student Assessment (PISA) assesses student knowledge and skills at age 15, i.e. toward the end of compulsory education. The PISA 2009 survey focused on reading, including students' attitudes towards reading; for the first time, PISA also assessed the ability of students to read, understand and use digital texts.

Definition

The PISA survey covers reading, mathematics and science. In the 2009 round of PISA, one hour of testing time was devoted to reading, half an hour was devoted to mathematics and half an hour to science. Each student spent two hours on the assessment items. In 19 countries, students were given additional questions via computer to assess their capacity to read digital texts.

Reading literacy is the capacity to understand, use and reflect on written texts in order to achieve one's goals, develop one's knowledge and potential, and participate in society. Mathematical literacy is the capacity to identify and understand the role that mathematics plays in the world, make well-founded judgements, and use mathematics in ways that meet the needs of concerned and reflective citizens. Scientific literacy is the capacity to use scientific knowledge to identify questions, acquire new knowledge, explain scientific phenomena, and draw evidence-based conclusions about science-related issues.

Overview

The graph shows the difference between the OECD average score in reading (493 score points, left axis) and the mean scores of individual countries. As it did in PISA 2006, Korea tops all participating OECD countries in reading. The reading scores of the United States, Sweden, Germany, Ireland, France, Denmark, the United Kingdom, Hungary and Portugal are not significantly different from the OECD average. The graph also shows results for mathematics relative to the OECD average (496 score points). While most countries that do well in one subject also do well in the other, some countries show significant differences: Switzerland, for example, has better scores in mathematics than in reading, while the opposite is true for Indonesia.

The table presents scores by gender. As in PISA 2006, girls do significantly better in reading than boys in all countries, with an average gender gap of 39 score points. Conversely, in all countries, boys outperform girls in mathematics by an average of 12 score points. On average, there is no gender gap in science performance, although in some countries, there are significant differences. For example, in the United States, boys perform significantly better in science than girls, while in Finland the opposite is true.

Comparability

Leading experts in countries participating in PISA advise on the scope and nature of the assessments, with final decisions taken by OECD governments. Substantial efforts and resources are devoted to achieving cultural and linguistic breadth and balance in the assessment materials. Stringent quality assurance mechanisms are applied in translation, sampling and data collection.

Over 520 000 15-year-old students in 75 participating countries were assessed in PISA 2009. Because the results are based on probability samples, standard errors (S.E.) are shown in the tables.

Sources

- OECD (2010), *PISA 2009 Results: What Students Know and Can Do: Student Performance in Reading, Mathematics and Science (Volume I)*, PISA, OECD Publishing.
- OECD (2007), *PISA 2006: Science Competencies for Tomorrow's World: Volume 1: Analysis*, PISA, OECD Publishing.

Further information

Analytical publications

- OECD (2011), *PISA 2009 Results: Students on Line: Reading and Using Digital Information (Volume VI)*, PISA, OECD Publishing.
- OECD (2010), *PISA 2009 Results: Learning to Learn: Student Engagement, Strategies and Practices (Volume III)*, PISA, OECD Publishing.
- OECD (2010), *PISA 2009 Results: Learning Trends: Changes in Student Performance Since 2000 (Volume V)*, PISA, OECD Publishing.
- OECD (2010), *PISA 2009 Results: Overcoming Social Background: Equity in Learning Opportunities and Outcomes (Volume II)*, PISA, OECD Publishing.
- OECD (2010), *PISA 2009 Results: What Makes a School Successful?: Resources, Policies and Practices (Volume IV)*, PISA, OECD Publishing.

Statistical publications

- OECD (2010), *PISA 2009 at a Glance*, OECD Publishing.

Methodological publications

- OECD (2009), *PISA 2009 Assessment Framework: Key Competencies in Reading, Mathematics and Science*, PISA, OECD Publishing.

Online databases

- *OECD PISA Database*.

Websites

- Programme for International Student Assessment (PISA), *www.pisa.oecd.org*.

Mean scores and gender differences in PISA 2009

	Reading scale				Mathematics scale				Science scale			
	Males		Females		Males		Females		Males		Females	
	Mean score	S.E.	Mean score	S.E.	Mean score	S.E.	Mean score	S.E.	Mean score	S.E.	Mean score	S.E.
Australia	496	2.9	533	2.6	519	3.0	509	2.8	527	3.1	528	2.8
Austria	449	3.8	490	4.0	506	3.4	486	4.0	498	4.2	490	4.4
Belgium	493	3.4	520	2.9	526	3.3	504	3.0	510	3.6	503	3.2
Canada	507	1.8	542	1.7	533	2.0	521	1.7	531	1.9	526	1.9
Chile	439	3.9	461	3.6	431	3.7	410	3.6	452	3.5	443	3.5
Czech Republic	456	3.7	504	3.0	495	3.9	490	3.0	498	4.0	503	3.2
Denmark	480	2.5	509	2.5	511	3.0	495	2.9	505	3.0	494	2.9
Estonia	480	2.9	524	2.8	516	2.9	508	2.9	527	3.1	528	3.1
Finland	508	2.6	563	2.4	542	2.5	539	2.5	546	2.7	562	2.6
France	475	4.3	515	3.4	505	3.8	489	3.4	500	4.6	497	3.5
Germany	478	3.6	518	2.9	520	3.6	505	3.3	523	3.7	518	3.3
Greece	459	5.5	506	3.5	473	5.4	459	3.3	465	5.1	475	3.7
Hungary	475	3.9	513	3.6	496	4.2	484	3.9	503	3.8	503	3.5
Iceland	478	2.1	522	1.9	508	2.0	505	1.9	496	2.1	495	2.0
Ireland	476	4.2	515	3.1	491	3.4	483	3.0	507	4.3	509	3.8
Israel	452	5.2	495	3.4	451	4.7	443	3.3	453	4.4	456	3.2
Italy	464	2.3	510	1.9	490	2.3	475	2.2	488	2.5	490	2.0
Japan	501	5.6	540	3.7	534	5.3	524	3.9	534	5.5	545	3.9
Korea	523	4.9	558	3.8	548	6.2	544	4.5	537	5.0	539	4.2
Luxembourg	453	1.9	492	1.5	499	2.0	479	1.3	487	2.0	480	1.6
Mexico	413	2.1	438	2.1	425	2.1	412	1.9	419	2.0	413	1.9
Netherlands	496	5.1	521	5.3	534	4.8	517	5.1	524	5.3	520	5.9
New Zealand	499	3.6	544	2.6	523	3.2	515	2.9	529	4.0	535	2.9
Norway	480	3.0	527	2.9	500	2.7	495	2.8	498	3.0	502	2.8
Poland	476	2.8	525	2.9	497	3.0	493	3.2	505	2.7	511	2.8
Portugal	470	3.5	508	2.9	493	3.3	481	3.1	491	3.4	495	3.0
Slovak Republic	452	3.5	503	2.8	498	3.7	495	3.4	490	4.0	491	3.2
Slovenia	456	1.6	511	1.4	502	1.8	501	1.7	505	1.7	519	1.6
Spain	467	2.2	496	2.2	493	2.3	474	2.5	492	2.5	485	2.3
Sweden	475	3.2	521	3.1	493	3.1	495	3.3	493	3.0	497	3.2
Switzerland	481	2.9	520	2.7	544	3.7	524	3.4	520	3.2	512	3.0
Turkey	443	3.7	486	4.1	451	4.6	440	5.6	448	3.8	460	4.5
United Kingdom	481	3.5	507	2.9	503	3.2	482	3.3	519	3.6	509	3.2
United States	488	4.2	513	3.8	497	4.0	477	3.8	509	4.2	495	3.7
OECD average	474	0.6	513	0.5	501	0.6	490	0.6	501	0.6	501	0.6
Brazil	397	2.9	425	2.8	394	2.4	379	2.6	407	2.6	404	2.6
Russian Federation	437	3.6	482	3.4	469	3.7	467	3.5	477	3.7	480	3.5
Indonesia	383	3.8	420	3.9	371	4.1	372	4.0	378	4.2	387	4.0

StatLink http://dx.doi.org/10.1787/888932506457

Performance on the mathematics and reading scales in PISA 2009

Mean score

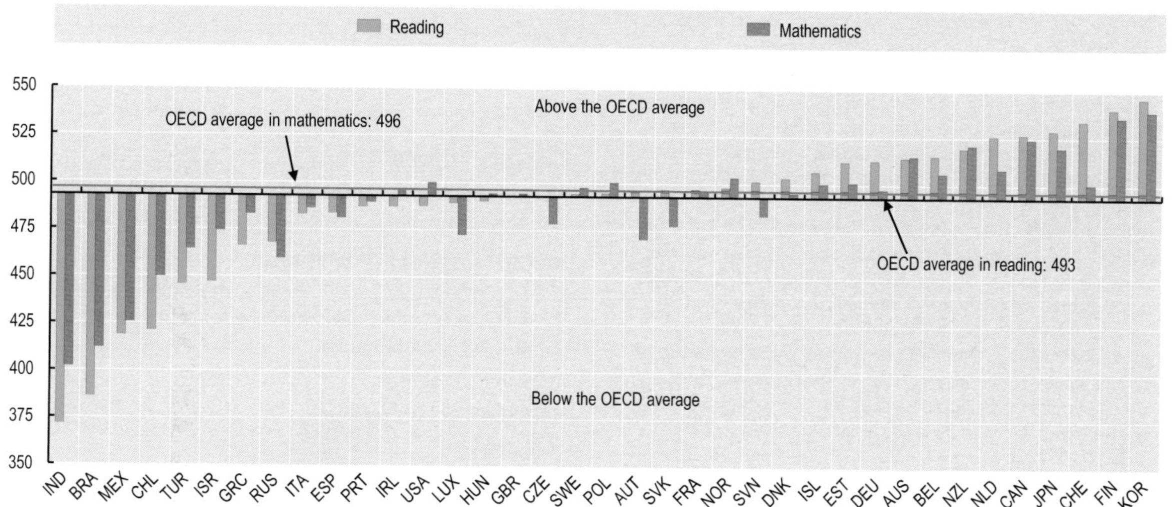

StatLink http://dx.doi.org/10.1787/888932506476

TRENDS IN READING

Since the PISA surveys have now been conducted for a decade, it is not only possible to see not just where countries stand in terms of student performance but also how learning outcomes have changed since the assessments were first administered. Every three years, PISA measures student knowledge and skills in reading, mathematics and science, covering each of these areas once as a major focus and twice as a minor area across a nine-year cycle. The 2009 round marks the first time that reading has been re-assessed in detail.

Definition

Only 29 countries with comparable results in both the 2000 and 2009 PISA reading assessments, and 31 countries with comparable results in both the 2003 and 2009 PISA mathematics assessments are discussed below. For reading, the reference point is the OECD average for the 26 OECD countries that participated in both PISA 2000 and PISA 2009. For mathematics, the main reference point is the OECD average for the 28 OECD countries that participated in both PISA 2003 and PISA 2009.

Level 2 is considered the baseline level of proficiency in reading, at which students begin to demonstrate the competencies that will enable them to participate effectively and productively in life. PISA tasks at this level may involve comparisons or contrasts based on a single feature in a text. They may also require students to make a comparison or several connections between the text and outside knowledge by drawing on personal experience and attitudes. Top performers are those students who attain proficiency Level 5 or above, the highest levels of performance.

Comparability

Leading experts in countries participating in PISA advise on the scope and nature of the assessments, with final decisions taken by OECD governments. Substantial efforts and resources are devoted to achieving cultural and linguistic breadth and balance in the assessment materials. Stringent quality assurance mechanisms are applied in translation, sampling and data collection.

Over 520 000 15-year-old students in 75 participating countries were assessed in PISA 2009. Because the results are based on probability samples, standard errors are shown in the tables.

Overview

Between PISA 2000 and PISA 2009, reading performance improved in 9 countries, deteriorated in 4 and was unchanged in 16. Among the countries that performed above the OECD average in 2000, Korea's reading scores improved, while those of Australia, the Czech Republic, Ireland and Sweden declined; both Ireland and Australia had been among the top five performers in PISA 2000. Chile and Indonesia show the greatest improvement in reading scores; both performed far below the OECD average in 2000.

In most countries where reading performance improved overall, girls' performance improved more than boys' did. In addition, improvements in mean country scores were more often driven by a reduction in the proportion of low-performing students than by an increase in the proportion of top performers. The percentage of students who did not reach the baseline proficiency Level 2 fell in 10 countries. However, only six countries showed a rise in the number of students reaching Level 5 or above; and in only Israel, Japan and Korea was this rise greater than one percentage point.

The graph shows changes in both reading and mathematics performance. Between PISA 2003 and PISA 2009, mathematics performance improved in 7 countries, deteriorated in 9, and was unchanged in 15. All countries that showed better performance in mathematics were well below the OECD average in both 2003 and 2009, except Germany, which was below the OECD average in 2000 but above it in 2009. All of the declines in mathematics performance occurred in countries that had scored at or above the OECD average in 2003. Despite a slight drop, the Netherlands remains among the highest-scoring countries in the PISA mathematics survey. In Australia, Belgium, Denmark and Iceland, mean scores also remained above the OECD average in 2009. However, in the Czech Republic, France and Sweden, mean performance in mathematics declined from above-average levels in 2003 to around the OECD average in 2009. In Ireland, performance declined from around the OECD average to below average.

Sources

- OECD (2010), *PISA 2009 Results: Learning Trends: Changes in Student Performance Since 2000 (Volume V)*, PISA, OECD Publishing.
- OECD (2010), *PISA 2009 Results: What Students Know and Can Do: Student Performance in Reading, Mathematics and Science (Volume I)*, PISA, OECD Publishing.
- OECD (2007), *PISA 2006: Science Competencies for Tomorrow's World: Volume 1: Analysis*, PISA, OECD Publishing.

Further information

Statistical publications

- OECD (2010), *PISA 2009 at a Glance*, OECD Publishing.

Methodological publications

- OECD (2009), *PISA 2009 Assessment Framework: Key Competencies in Reading, Mathematics and Science*, PISA, OECD Publishing.

Online databases

- *OECD PISA Database*.

Websites

- Programme for International Student Assessment (PISA), *www.pisa.oecd.org*.

Changes in reading performance

	Mean score in reading	All students	Males	Females	Share of students below proficiency Level 2	Share of students at proficiency Level 5 or above
	2009	Changes over the period 2000-09				
Australia	515	-13.4	-16.5	-13.4	1.8	-4.9
Belgium	506	-1.2	0.3	-5.4	-1.2	-0.8
Canada	524	-10.1	-11.7	-9.6	0.7	-4.0
Chile	449	39.8	42.1	39.5	-17.6	0.8
Czech Republic	478	-13.4	-17.1	-6.1	5.6	-1.9
Denmark	495	-2.0	-5.1	-1.1	-2.7	-3.4
Finland	536	-10.6	-11.7	-7.9	1.2	-4.0
France	496	-9.1	-15.3	-3.9	4.6	1.1
Germany	497	13.3	10.3	15.4	-4.2	-1.2
Greece	483	9.0	3.1	13.2	-3.1	0.6
Hungary	494	14.2	10.9	17.1	-5.1	1.0
Iceland	500	-6.6	-10.4	-5.9	2.3	-0.5
Ireland	496	-31.0	-36.5	-26.0	6.2	-7.3
Israel	474	21.8	8.6	35.3	-6.7	3.3
Italy	486	-1.4	-5.4	2.2	2.1	0.5
Japan	520	-2.4	-6.2	3.0	3.5	3.6
Korea	539	14.5	4.0	25.3	0.0	7.2
Mexico	425	3.3	1.2	5.8	-4.0	-0.5
New Zealand	521	-7.9	-8.3	-8.4	0.6	-3.0
Norway	503	-2.1	-5.5	-1.4	-2.5	-2.8
Poland	500	21.4	14.3	27.8	-8.2	1.3
Portugal	489	19.2	12.2	25.6	-8.6	0.6
Spain	481	-11.5	-14.4	-9.6	3.3	-0.9
Sweden	497	-18.9	-23.6	-15.0	4.9	-2.2
Switzerland	501	6.1	1.4	10.2	-3.6	-1.1
United States	500	-4.6	-1.9	-5.7	-0.3	-2.4
Brazil	412	15.7	8.9	20.9	-6.2	0.8
Indonesia	402	31.1	23.0	39.3	-15.2	..
Russian Federation	459	-2.4	-6.0	0.5	-0.1	0.0

StatLink http://dx.doi.org/10.1787/888932506495

Performance on the reading and mathematics scales

Changes over the period 2000-09 for reading scale and 2003-09 for mathematics scale

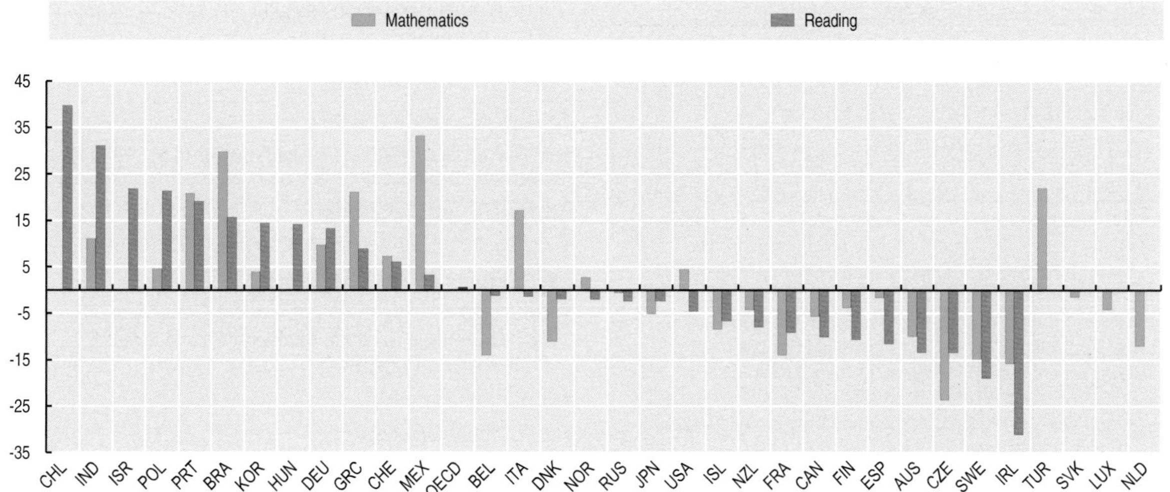

StatLink http://dx.doi.org/10.1787/888932506514

ENJOYMENT OF READING

Being interested in and enjoying a particular subject affects both the degree and the continuity of engagement in learning and the depth of understanding achieved, an effect that research has shown to operate largely independently of students' motivation to learn. Students who enjoy reading, and therefore make it a regular part of their lives, build their reading skills through practice.

Definition

Reading enjoyment is measured on an index based on student responses to a questionnaire. PISA asked students how strongly they agreed with statements about their attitudes toward reading, such as "I only read if I have to", "I enjoy going to a bookstore or a library" and "I cannot sit still and read for more than a few minutes".

Time spent reading for enjoyment measures how frequently and for how long students read. The amount of time students spend reading for enjoyment indicates their interest in reading.

Comparability

Leading experts in countries participating in PISA advise on the scope and nature of the assessments, with final decisions taken by OECD governments. Substantial efforts and resources are devoted to achieving cultural and linguistic breadth and balance in the assessment materials. Stringent quality assurance mechanisms are applied in translation, sampling and data collection.

Over 520 000 15-year-old students in 75 participating countries were assessed in PISA 2009. Because the results are based on probability samples, standard errors (S.E.) are shown in the tables.

Overview

Students in the top quarter of the index of enjoyment of reading are significantly more likely to be good readers than students in the bottom quarter. On average in OECD countries, the performance difference between students who enjoy reading and those who don't is 103 score points. Across OECD countries, variations in how much students enjoy reading explain 18% of the differences in reading performance. The link between reading performance and enjoyment of reading tends to be strongest in countries where students do best in reading overall. In Australia and Finland, two of the best-performing countries overall, over 25% of differences in reading performance are associated with how much students enjoy reading. On average across OECD countries, a difference of one unit on the index of enjoyment of reading corresponds to 40 score points on the PISA reading scale.

On average across OECD countries, over one-third of students – and 40% or more in Austria, the Netherlands, Luxembourg, Switzerland, Belgium, Japan, the Czech Republic, the United States, Ireland, Germany, the Slovak Republic and Norway – reported that they did not read for enjoyment at all. The average performance among these students, 460 score points, is well below the average for the OECD as a whole. In more than two-thirds of countries that participated in PISA, the score point difference associated with at least some daily reading for enjoyment is far greater than the score point difference associated with increasing amounts of time spent reading. This may mean that the more time students spend reading for enjoyment, the fewer the returns on their investment; or it could mean that poor readers need more time to read a text.

Sources

- OECD (2010), *PISA 2009 Results: What Students Know and Can Do: Student Performance in Reading, Mathematics and Science (Volume I)*, PISA, OECD Publishing.
- OECD (2010), *PISA 2009 Results: Learning to Learn: Student Engagement, Strategies and Practices (Volume III)*, PISA, OECD Publishing.
- OECD (2010), *PISA 2009 Results: Learning Trends: Changes in Student Performance Since 2000 (Volume V)*, PISA, OECD Publishing.

Further information

Analytical publications

- OECD (2003), *Learners for Life: Student Approaches to Learning: Results from PISA 2000*, PISA, OECD Publishing.

Statistical publications

- OECD (2010), *PISA 2009 at a Glance*, OECD Publishing.

Methodological publications

- OECD (2009), *PISA 2009 Assessment Framework: Key Competencies in Reading, Mathematics and Science*, PISA, OECD Publishing.

Online databases

- *OECD PISA Database.*

Websites

- Programme for International Student Assessment (PISA), *www.pisa.oecd.org.*

Index of enjoyment of reading and relationship between performance in reading and time spent reading for enjoyment in PISA 2009

	Index of enjoyment of reading						Relationship between performance in reading and time spent reading for enjoyment per day					Score point difference between students who read up to 30 minutes and students who don't read for enjoyment
	All students		Males		Females		Do not read for enjoyment	30 minutes or less	Between 30 to less than 60 minutes	Between 1 to 2 hours	More than 2 hours	
	Mean index	S.E.	Mean index	S.E.	Mean index	S.E.	Mean score					
Australia	0.00	0.02	-0.33	0.02	0.31	0.02	469	524	560	570	563	55
Austria	-0.13	0.03	-0.55	0.03	0.26	0.03	437	494	517	530	504	57
Belgium	-0.20	0.02	-0.45	0.02	0.07	0.02	469	532	547	548	523	63
Canada	0.13	0.01	-0.28	0.02	0.55	0.02	481	530	555	565	559	49
Chile	-0.06	0.01	-0.28	0.02	0.16	0.02	437	449	472	478	499	12
Czech Republic	-0.13	0.02	-0.44	0.02	0.22	0.02	441	489	520	532	522	48
Denmark	-0.09	0.02	-0.35	0.02	0.17	0.02	464	503	518	537	536	39
Estonia	-0.03	0.02	-0.38	0.02	0.33	0.02	469	514	525	530	527	45
Finland	0.05	0.02	-0.41	0.02	0.50	0.02	492	545	569	572	568	54
France	0.01	0.03	-0.23	0.03	0.24	0.03	450	512	538	546	543	62
Germany	0.07	0.02	-0.38	0.02	0.52	0.03	457	513	545	548	532	55
Greece	0.07	0.02	-0.24	0.02	0.36	0.02	450	480	490	492	507	29
Hungary	0.14	0.02	-0.15	0.03	0.43	0.02	453	490	517	533	536	37
Iceland	-0.06	0.02	-0.38	0.02	0.25	0.02	455	621	544	542	533	166
Ireland	-0.08	0.02	-0.30	0.03	0.15	0.03	458	505	540	550	549	48
Israel	0.06	0.02	-0.26	0.03	0.35	0.03	460	483	498	492	484	23
Italy	0.06	0.01	-0.27	0.01	0.41	0.01	449	489	516	521	528	40
Japan	0.20	0.02	0.02	0.03	0.38	0.02	492	536	550	552	537	44
Korea	0.13	0.02	0.00	0.02	0.27	0.02	518	550	558	560	535	32
Luxembourg	-0.16	0.02	-0.51	0.02	0.20	0.03	437	493	516	524	519	56
Mexico	0.14	0.01	-0.04	0.01	0.32	0.01	421	420	444	430	437	-1
Netherlands	-0.32	0.03	-0.66	0.03	0.02	0.03	478	534	552	541	514	57
New Zealand	0.13	0.02	-0.17	0.02	0.44	0.02	472	525	558	574	573	52
Norway	-0.19	0.02	-0.50	0.02	0.13	0.03	465	523	540	542	528	58
Poland	0.02	0.02	-0.36	0.02	0.39	0.03	463	498	526	544	549	35
Portugal	0.21	0.02	-0.15	0.02	0.54	0.02	459	490	519	530	538	32
Slovak Republic	-0.10	0.02	-0.36	0.02	0.15	0.02	445	486	514	523	516	41
Slovenia	-0.20	0.01	-0.53	0.02	0.14	0.02	446	499	526	520	521	53
Spain	-0.01	0.01	-0.28	0.02	0.26	0.01	453	484	510	515	517	31
Sweden	-0.11	0.02	-0.47	0.02	0.26	0.03	455	515	539	539	532	60
Switzerland	-0.04	0.02	-0.44	0.02	0.37	0.03	461	521	548	558	533	60
Turkey	0.64	0.02	0.34	0.02	0.95	0.02	444	468	480	473	472	24
United Kingdom	-0.12	0.02	-0.37	0.02	0.13	0.02	458	505	531	549	539	47
United States	-0.04	0.03	-0.35	0.03	0.28	0.03	467	514	532	541	544	47
OECD average	0.00	0.00	-0.31	0.00	0.31	0.00	460	504	527	532	527	44
Brazil	0.27	0.01	0.05	0.01	0.47	0.01	396	403	428	431	429	7
Indonesia	0.43	0.01	0.32	0.01	0.55	0.01	380	390	414	412	429	10
Russian Federation	0.07	0.01	-0.15	0.02	0.29	0.02	427	452	472	489	498	25

StatLink http://dx.doi.org/10.1787/888932506533

Relationship between time spent reading for enjoyment and performance in reading

Mean score

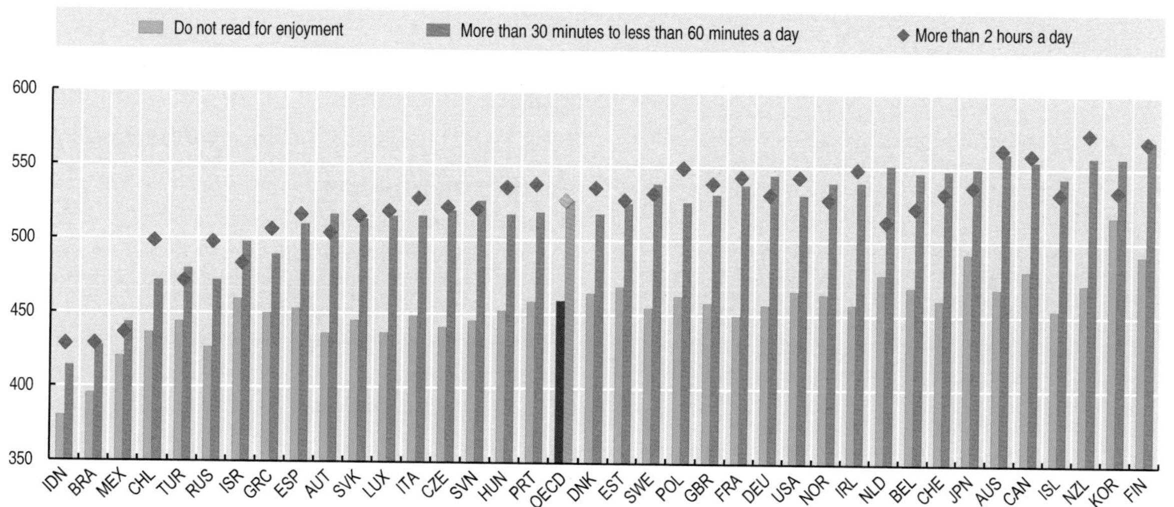

StatLink http://dx.doi.org/10.1787/888932506552

HOW MANY STUDENTS STUDY ABROAD?

As national economies become more interconnected, governments and individuals are looking to higher education to broaden students' horizons. It is through the pursuit of high level studies in countries other than their own that students may expand their knowledge of other cultures and languages, and to better equip themselves in an increasingly globalised labour market. Some countries, particularly in the European Union, have established policies and schemes that promote such mobility to foster intercultural contacts and help build social networks.

Overview

Over the past three decades (particularly since the late 1990s) the number of students enrolled outside their country of citizenship has risen dramatically, a more than fourfold increase (from 0.8 million in 1975 to almost 3.7 million in 2009) that exceeds that for global tertiary enrolment. This trend mirrors the globalisation of economies and societies, universities' expanded capacity and a substantial increase in global access to tertiary education .

Language as well as cultural considerations, quality of programmes, geographic proximity and similarity of education systems are determining factors driving student mobility. The destinations of international students highlight the attractiveness of specific education systems, whether because of their academic reputation or because of subsequent immigration opportunities.

Foreign students enrolled in G20 countries account for 83% of total foreign students, and students in the OECD area represent 77% of the total foreign students enrolled worldwide. European countries in the OECD were the destination for 38% of foreign students in 2009 followed by North American countries (23%). Despite the strong increase in absolute numbers, these proportions have remained stable during the last decade. In the OECD area, the number of foreign students in tertiary education is nearly three times as high as the number of national citizens enrolled abroad. In the 21 European countries who are OECD members there is a ratio of 2.6 foreign students per each citizen from an European country studying abroad.

More than 9 out of 10 OECD students enrol in another OECD country when pursuing tertiary studies outside their country of citizenship. Students from other G20 countries not in OECD also prefer to study in OECD countries, with 84% of them enroled in an OECD country. European citizens from OECD countries are also mostly enrolled in another European country (72%), while in North America a large majority of students are citizens of a country in a different region.

Tertiary-type A programmes (largely theory-based) are far more internationalised than tertiary-type B (shorter, and vocationally oriented) programmes in most OECD. The large presence of international students also has a significant impact on graduation rates in some countries. When international students are excluded, Australia's first time tertiary-type A graduation rate drops by 15 percentage points and New Zealand's rate drops by 9 percentage points. This effect is also evident in second-degree programmes, such as master's degrees, in Australia and the United Kingdom, where graduation rates drop by 11 and 7 percentage points, respectively, when international graduates are excluded.

Definition

Students are classified as "international" if they left their country of origin only for the purpose of study. Students are classified as "foreign" when they are not citizens of the country where they are enrolled. This includes some students who are permanent residents, albeit not citizens, of the countries in which they are studying as young people from immigrant families. Consequently, foreign graduation rates are not comparable with data on international graduation rates and are therefore presented separately.

Comparability

Data on international and foreign students refer to the academic year 2008/2009, based on data collected on education statistics, annually by the OECD. Additional data from the UNESCO Institute for Statistics are also included. Data on the impact of international students on tertiary graduation rates are based on a special survey conducted by the OECD in December 2010.

Sources

- OECD (2011), *Education at a Glance*, OECD Publishing.

Further information

Analytical publications

- OECD (2008), *Tertiary Education for the Knowledge Society*, OECD Review of Tertiary Education, OECD Publishing.
- OECD (2004), *Internationalisation and Trade in Higher Education: Opportunities and Challenges*, OECD Publishing.

Online databases

- *OECD Education Statistics*.

Websites

- OECD Education at a Glance, *www.oecd.org/edu/eag2011*

Evolution by region of destination in the number of students enrolled outside their country of citizenship

Thousand of persons

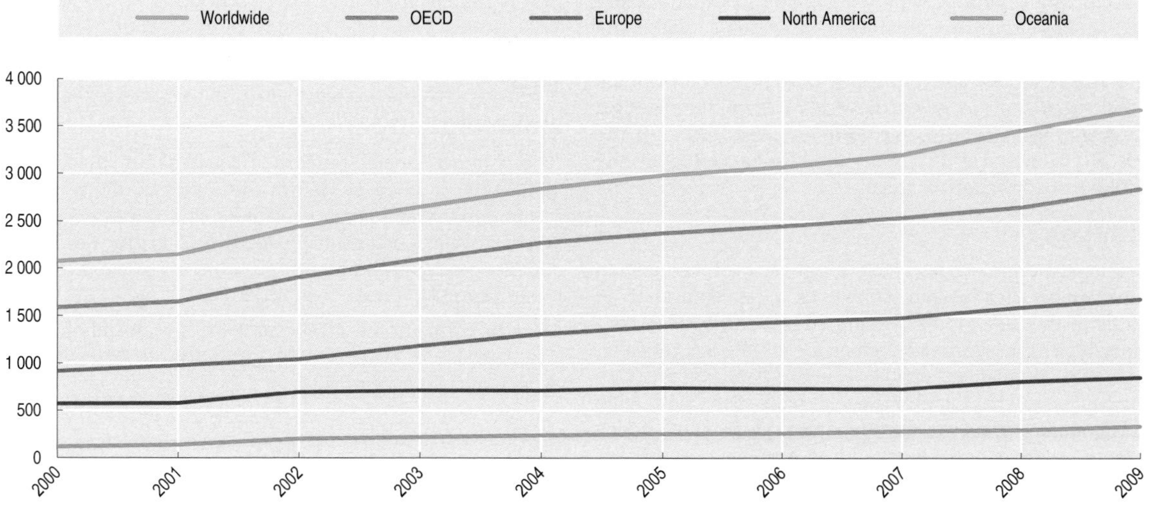

StatLink http://dx.doi.org/10.1787/888932506571

The impact of international/foreign students on graduation rate at tertiary-type A level

Percentage, 2009 or latest available year

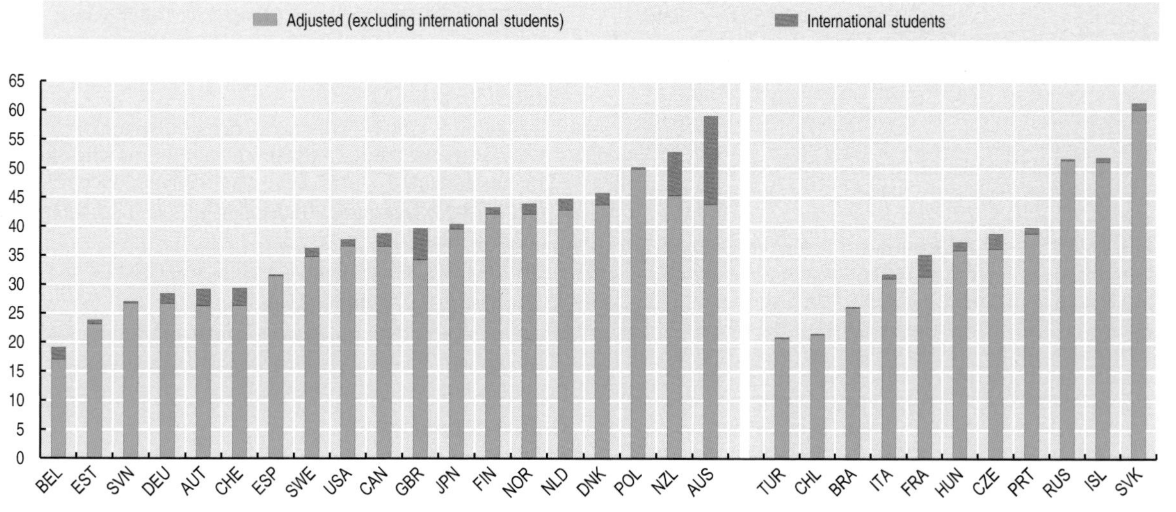

StatLink http://dx.doi.org/10.1787/888932506590

EDUCATION ATTAINMENT

A well-educated and well-trained population is essential for the social and economic well-being of countries. Education plays a key role in providing individuals with the knowledge, skills and competencies needed to participate effectively in society and in the economy. It also contributes to the expansion of scientific and cultural knowledge. Educational attainment is a commonly used proxy for the stock of "human capital", *i.e.* the skills available in the population and the labour force.

Definition

Educational attainment refers to the highest level of education completed by each person, shown as a percentage of all persons in that age group. Tertiary education includes both tertiary-type "A programmes", which are largely theoretically-based and designed to provide qualifications for entry to advanced research programmes and professions with high skill requirements; and tertiary-type "B programmes", which are more occupationally-oriented and lead to direct labour market access. Upper secondary education typically follows completion of lower secondary schooling. Lower secondary education completes provision of basic education, usually in a more subject-oriented way and with more specialised teachers.

Comparability

The International Standard Classification of Education (ISCED-97) is used to define the levels of education in a comparable way across countries. The *OECD Handbook for Internationally Comparative Education Statistics* describes of ISCED-97 education programmes and attainment levels and their mappings for each country.

Data on educational attainment of 25-year-olds and older are based on UNESCO for Argentina, Indonesia, Saudi Arabia and South Africa.

Overview

OECD countries have experienced significant increases in the proportion of the adult population attaining tertiary education over the last decades. In 2009, over 30% of the population aged between 25 and 64 has attained tertiary level education, in more than half of OECD countries. In Canada, Israel, Japan, New Zealand and the United States, this share is significantly higher, while in the Russian Federation this figure exceeds 50%. Conversely, in Italy, Portugal and Turkey, as well as some of the other G20 countries (Argentina, Brazil, China, Indonesia, Saudi Arabia and South Africa), the share of the population between the ages of 25 to 64 with tertiary attainment is below 15%.

An indication of long-term trends in educational attainment can be obtained by comparing the current attainment levels of younger and older age cohorts. For instance, comparing tertiary attainment levels, in almost all countries the proportion of 25-34 year-olds is greater than that among the generation about to leave the labour market (55-64 year olds). Korea shows the largest increase in tertiary attainment over the past 30 years with almost 50 percentage points of the difference between the proportion of young adults and older adults with tertiary education; this is more than 30 percentage points higher than the OECD average. In contrast, other OECD countries over the same period experienced only marginal increases (Germany and the United States), or even declines (Israel).

On average across OECD countries, 27% of adults now have only primary or lower secondary levels of education, 44% have upper secondary education and 30% have a tertiary qualification. Over the past decade most of the changes in educational attainment have occurred at the low and high ends of the attainment distribution. Between 1999 and 2009 the share of those who have not attained an upper secondary education decreased by 10 percentage points while the proportion with tertiary education increased by 8.9 percentage points across OECD countries. This largely reflects the fact that older workers with low levels of education have moved out of the labour force, and that many countries have expanded their focus on higher education in recent years.

Sources

- OECD (2011), *Education at a Glance*, OECD Publishing.

Further information

Analytical publications

- Hansson, B. (2007), "Effects of Tertiary Expansion: Crowding-out effects and labour market matches for the higher educated", *OECD Education Working Papers*, No. 10.
- OECD (2011), *Reviews of National Policies for Education*, OECD Publishing.
- OECD (2010), *Trends Shaping Education*, OECD Publishing.

Methodological publications

- OECD (2004), *OECD Handbook for Internationally Comparative Education Statistics: Concepts, Standards, Definitions and Classifications*, OECD Publishing.

Online databases

- *OECD Education Statistics.*

Websites

- OECD Centre for Educational Research and Innovation (CERI), *www.oecd.org/edu/ceri*.
- OECD Education at a Glance, *www.oecd.org/edu/eag2011*.

Education attainment

As a percentage of total population in that age group

	Population with tertiary education					Population aged 25-64								
	25-64	25-34	35-44	45-54	55-64	Below upper secondary			Upper secondary and post-secondary non-tertiary			Tertiary education		
	2009 or latest available year					1998	1999	2009 or latest available year	1998	1999	2009 or latest available year	1998	1999	2009 or latest available year
Australia	36.9	44.8	38.0	33.6	29.3	44.0	42.6	29.0	30.6	30.7	34.1	25.4	26.7	36.9
Austria	19.0	21.1	20.3	18.3	15.9	25.8	24.9	18.1	60.5	61.4	62.8	13.7	13.7	19.0
Belgium	33.4	42.5	36.9	30.3	23.4	43.3	42.6	29.4	31.4	30.7	37.2	25.3	26.7	33.4
Canada	49.5	56.1	55.7	45.1	40.7	21.4	20.5	12.4	40.4	40.2	38.1	38.2	39.3	49.5
Chile	24.4	34.9	24.2	20.2	16.6	..	..	31.0	..	..	44.7	..	..	24.4
Czech Republic	15.5	20.2	14.8	15.6	10.8	14.7	14.0	8.6	74.9	75.2	75.9	10.4	10.8	15.5
Denmark	34.3	44.7	39.0	28.3	25.8	21.5	20.4	23.7	53.2	53.1	42.0	25.4	26.5	34.3
Estonia	36.0	36.6	36.3	37.7	32.8	..	..	11.1	..	..	53.0	..	..	36.0
Finland	37.3	39.4	44.5	37.5	29.0	31.0	28.5	18.0	38.8	40.2	44.7	30.2	31.3	37.3
France	28.9	43.2	32.3	22.2	18.0	39.3	38.1	30.0	40.1	40.4	41.1	20.6	21.5	28.9
Germany	26.4	25.7	27.8	26.4	25.3	16.2	18.8	14.5	60.8	58.3	59.1	23.0	22.9	26.4
Greece	23.5	29.4	26.4	21.6	15.0	53.9	52.2	38.8	29.3	30.4	37.7	16.8	17.3	23.5
Hungary	19.9	25.1	19.0	18.3	16.3	36.7	32.6	19.4	50.1	53.8	60.7	13.2	13.5	19.9
Iceland	32.8	35.8	38.2	31.7	22.8	44.6	44.0	34.1	34.4	33.6	33.1	21.0	22.4	32.8
Ireland	35.9	47.6	39.4	28.2	20.2	48.7	44.9	28.5	30.2	34.7	35.7	21.1	20.5	35.9
Israel	44.9	42.9	47.1	44.9	45.0	..	..	18.2	..	..	36.9	..	..	44.9
Italy	14.5	20.2	15.4	11.8	10.3	59.3	57.8	45.7	32.1	33.0	39.8	8.6	9.3	14.5
Japan	43.8	55.7	48.7	44.7	27.4	20.0	19.0	..	49.4	49.1	56.2	30.6	31.8	43.8
Korea	38.8	63.1	44.3	25.8	13.2	33.6	32.6	20.1	43.9	44.3	41.2	22.5	23.1	38.8
Luxembourg	34.8	44.5	37.9	29.0	24.9	..	44.1	22.7	..	37.5	42.5	..	18.3	34.8
Mexico	15.9	20.2	14.9	15.1	9.8	72.0	72.8	64.8	14.5	14.0	19.3	13.5	13.2	15.9
Netherlands	32.8	40.1	33.6	30.8	27.4	35.7	45.3	26.6	40.1	32.1	40.6	24.2	22.6	32.8
New Zealand	40.1	46.7	41.2	37.8	33.7	38.6	38.0	27.8	33.7	33.5	32.2	27.6	28.5	40.0
Norway	36.7	46.8	39.7	32.8	27.2	15.4	15.1	19.3	57.2	57.4	44.0	27.4	27.5	36.7
Poland	21.2	35.4	20.9	13.1	12.6	21.7	21.5	12.0	67.4	67.2	66.8	10.9	11.3	21.2
Portugal	14.7	23.3	15.1	11.0	7.4	82.1	81.2	70.1	9.5	10.2	15.2	8.3	8.7	14.7
Slovak Republic	15.8	20.6	14.6	14.1	12.1	19.8	17.6	9.1	69.9	72.4	75.2	10.3	10.1	15.8
Slovenia	23.3	30.4	26.0	19.4	16.7	..	..	16.7	..	..	60.0	..	..	23.3
Spain	29.7	38.2	33.5	25.2	16.6	67.1	64.9	48.2	13.2	14.1	22.1	19.7	21.0	29.7
Sweden	33.0	42.3	34.6	28.7	26.9	24.4	23.7	14.2	53.9	54.2	52.7	21.7	22.1	33.0
Switzerland	35.0	40.0	37.9	33.0	28.3	16.3	16.1	13.1	60.8	60.3	51.7	22.9	23.6	35.2
Turkey	12.7	16.6	11.3	9.7	9.9	78.2	77.5	68.9	14.4	14.4	18.3	7.5	8.1	12.7
United Kingdom	36.9	44.9	38.9	34.1	28.7	39.9	38.4	26.3	36.3	36.7	36.8	23.8	24.9	36.9
United States	41.2	41.1	43.1	39.9	40.8	13.5	13.1	11.4	51.6	51.2	47.4	34.9	35.8	41.2
OECD average	30.0	37.1	32.1	26.9	22.4	37.2	36.8	26.7	42.2	42.1	44.1	20.6	21.1	30.0
Brazil	10.9	11.6	11.3	10.7	8.9	..	..	59.3	..	..	29.8	..	..	10.9
China	4.6	6.1	4.8	3.0	3.1	..	..	..	..	..	..	..	..	..
Indonesia	4.5	..	..	..	..	..	..	..	..	..	..	..	..	..
Russian Federation	54.0	55.5	58.1	54.3	44.5	..	..	..	..	..	..	..	..	..
South Africa	4.3	..	..	..	..	..	..	..	..	..	..	..	..	..

StatLink http://dx.doi.org/10.1787/888932506609

Population that has attained at least tertiary education

Percentage, 2009 or latest available year

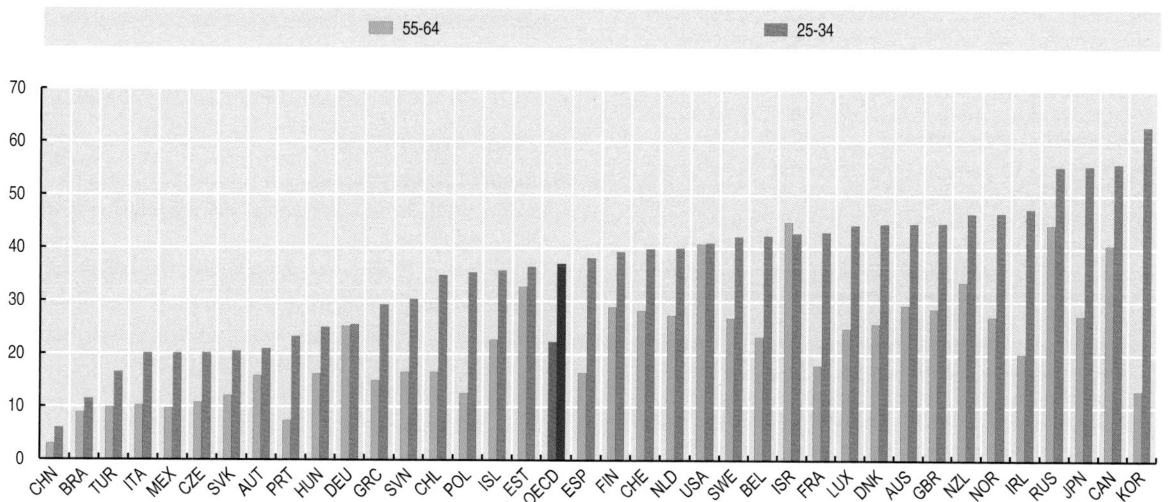

StatLink http://dx.doi.org/10.1787/888932506628

INCENTIVES TO INVEST IN EDUCATION

The economic benefits of education flow not just to individuals but also to governments through additional tax receipts as people enter the labour market. These public returns, which take into account the fact that providing education is also a cost to governments, offer an additional perspective on the overall returns to education. Of course, they must be understood in the wider context of the benefits that economies and societies gain from increasing levels of education. From a policy perspective, awareness of economic incentives is crucial to understanding how individuals move through the education system. In shaping policies, it is important to consider the balance between private and public returns.

Definition

The economic returns to education are measured by the net present value. Public costs include lost income tax receipts during the schooling years, and public expenditures (such as paying teachers' salaries), both of these investment streams take into account the duration of studies. On the benefit side, age-earnings profiles are used to calculate the earnings differential between different educational groups (below upper secondary education; upper secondary or post-secondary non-tertiary education; and tertiary education). The benefits for the public sector are additional tax and social contribution receipts associated with higher earnings and savings from transfers (housing benefits and social assistance) that the public sector does not have to pay because of higher levels of earnings.

Comparability

The calculations involve a number of restrictive assumptions needed for international comparability. In calculating the investments in education, foregone earnings have been standardised at the level of the legal minimum wage or the equivalent in countries in which earnings data include part-time work. When no national minimum wage was available, the level was selected from wages set in collective agreements. This assumption aims to counterbalance the very low earnings recorded for 15-24 year-olds that led to excessively high estimates in earlier estimates. In the Czech Republic, Hungary, Japan, the Netherlands, Portugal and the United Kingdom, actual earnings are used in calculating foregone earnings and taxes, as part-time work is excluded in these earnings data collections.

Overview

Investments in education generate public returns from higher income levels in the form of income taxes, increased social insurance payments and lower social transfers. The public returns for a man investing in upper secondary or post-secondary non-tertiary education are positive in most countries. On average across OECD countries, this level of education generates a net return of USD 36 000. For Austria, the United Kingdom and the United States, it generates a net return of more than USD 70 000. The benefits are more than twice as large, on average, as the overall public costs for upper secondary or post-secondary non-tertiary education.

The public returns to tertiary education are substantially larger than the returns to upper secondary or post-secondary non-tertiary education, in part because a larger share of the investment costs are borne by the individuals themselves. The main contributing factors are, however, the higher taxes and social contributions that flow from the higher income levels of those with tertiary qualifications. In Belgium, Germany and the United States, these benefits exceed USD 190 000 over an individual's working life.

Direct costs for tertiary education are generally borne by the public sector, except in Australia, Japan, Korea, and the United States, where private direct costs such as tuition fees constitute over half of the overall direct investment costs. Together with foregone public benefits in the form of taxes and social contributions, direct and indirect public investment costs for a man with a tertiary education is on average USD 34 000 among OECD countries. It exceeds USD 50 000 in Austria, Denmark, the Netherlands and Sweden, whereas in Korea and Turkey it is below USD 15 000. Such public costs are large, but they are surpassed by private investment costs in most countries. On average across OECD countries, the total benefits for a man investing in tertiary education (USD 129 000) is almost four times the total costs (USD 34 000).

Sources

- OECD (2011), *Education at a Glance*, OECD Publishing.

Further information

Analytical publications

- OECD (2011), *Reviews of National Policies for Education*, OECD Publishing.
- OECD (2010), *Trends Shaping Education*, OECD Publishing.

Methodological publications

- OECD (2011), "A User's Guide to Indicator A9 – Incentives to Invest in Education", *Education at a Glance 2011: OECD Indicators* website.

Online databases

- *OECD Education Statistics.*

Websites

- OECD Education at a Glance, *www.oecd.org/edu/eag2011*.

Public investment and return in education for men

US dollars, 2007 or latest available year

	Upper secondary non tertiary education					Tertiary education				
	Direct cost	Foregone taxes on earning	Total cost	Total benefits	Net present value	Direct cost	Foregone taxes on earning	Total cost	Total benefits	Net present value
Australia	-14 757	-4 357	-19 114	46 632	27 518	-13 209	-7 002	-20 211	104 749	84 532
Austria	-39 507	-9 061	-48 568	128 205	79 637	-51 546	-10 354	-61 900	160 578	98 678
Belgium	..	..	..	..	..	-20 552	-8 132	-28 684	196 786	167 241
Canada	-20 114	-2 859	-22 974	51 178	28 204	-24 166	-3 234	-27 400	108 278	79 774
Czech Republic	-18 306	-6 804	-25 110	47 037	21 927	-14 749	-8 735	-23 485	104 791	81 307
Denmark	-28 705	-12 076	-40 781	99 870	59 089	-64 272	-18 007	-82 279	136 583	28 621
Finland	-19 061	-3 568	-22 629	40 991	18 362	-34 358	-6 565	-40 923	149 831	100 177
France	-29 063	-5 660	-34 722	32 221	-2 501	-28 412	-8 841	-37 253	104 057	63 701
Germany	-23 597	-7 812	-31 410	88 089	56 680	-29 854	-12 292	-42 146	216 069	168 649
Hungary	-14 543	-6 026	-20 569	53 507	32 938	-13 612	-8 763	-22 375	190 446	166 872
Ireland	-20 729	-7 054	-27 784	71 408	43 624	-21 467	-9 833	-31 301	120 773	85 917
Italy	-30 614	-8 568	-39 181	81 343	42 162	-18 847	-11 023	-29 870	116 469	82 932
Japan	..	..	..	..	..	-17 897	-15 254	-33 151	100 562	67 411
Korea	..	..	..	..	..	-5 185	-2 923	-8 108	97 141	89 034
Netherlands	..	..	..	..	..	-34 104	-34 351	-68 454	179 600	95 030
New Zealand	-16 527	-4 015	-20 542	54 096	33 553	-17 470	-4 756	-22 227	70 332	46 482
Norway	-34 470	-10 723	-45 193	91 904	46 711	-31 963	-13 333	-45 296	113 029	61 507
Poland	-12 824	-7 216	-20 040	26 050	6 010	-10 791	-9 092	-19 883	115 750	94 125
Portugal	-19 937	-3 854	-23 791	76 420	52 629	-11 848	-4 706	-16 553	106 018	89 464
Slovenia	-20 398	-5 164	-25 562	48 543	22 981	-19 911	-5 848	-25 759	181 623	155 664
Spain	-17 532	-1 048	-18 580	26 317	7 738	-30 308	-2 429	-32 737	62 319	29 582
Sweden	-26 133	-7 755	-33 888	64 944	31 056	-36 490	-14 668	-51 158	97 340	37 542
Turkey	-4 776	-4 551	-9 327	20 699	11 371	-9 567	-3 814	-13 381	35 106	21 724
United Kingdom	-15 838	-3 817	-19 655	91 815	72 161	-24 919	-16 257	-41 176	138 199	95 322
United States	-30 470	-1 063	-31 533	102 029	70 497	-32 281	-1 776	-34 057	227 641	193 584
OECD average	-21 805	-5 860	-27 664	63 967	36 302	-24 711	-9 680	-34 391	129 363	91 395

StatLink http://dx.doi.org/10.1787/888932506647

Public cost and benefits for a man obtaining upper secondary or post-secondary non-tertiary education and tertiary education

Thousand US dollars, 2007 or latest available year

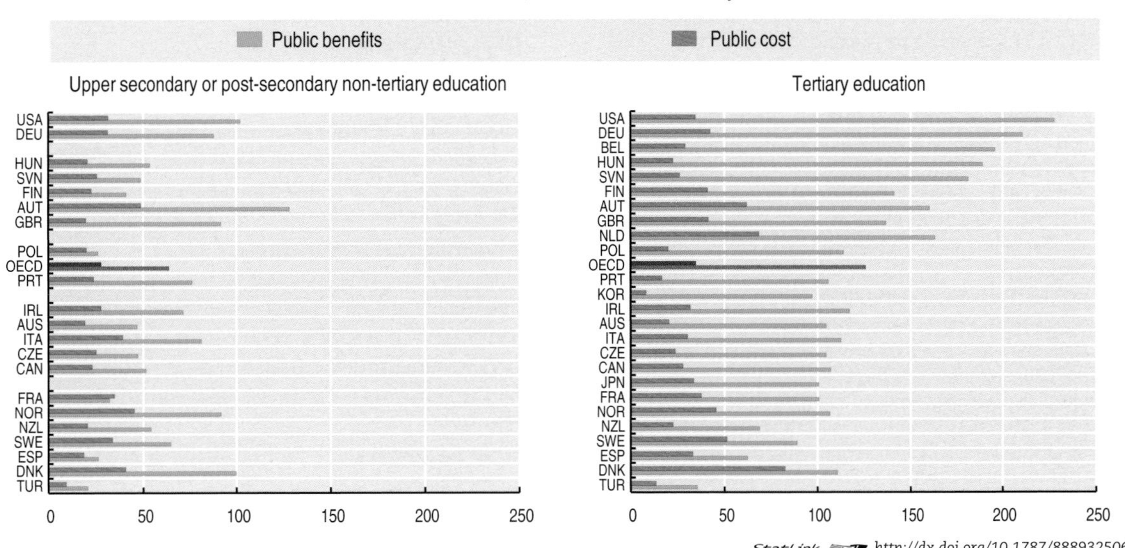

StatLink http://dx.doi.org/10.1787/888932506666

EDUCATIONAL EXPENDITURE PER STUDENT

Policy makers must balance the importance of improving the quality of educational services with the desirability of expanding access to educational opportunities, specifically at the tertiary level. In many OECD countries the expansion of enrolments, particularly in tertiary education, has not been paralleled by similar rises in educational expenditures. In primary, secondary and post-secondary non-tertiary education, enrolments are stable but expenditure has increased more than at the tertiary level.

Definition

The indicator shows change in expenditure on educational institutions in relation to the number of full-time equivalent students enrolled in these institutions. The indicator includes only those educational institutions and programmes, both public and private, for which both enrolment and expenditure data are available. Public subsidies for students' living expenses are excluded to ensure international comparability of the data.

Educational expenditure in national currency for 2008 is converted into equivalent USD by dividing the national currency figure by the purchasing power parity (PPP) index for GDP. PPP exchange rates are used because market exchange rates are affected by many factors (*e.g.* interest rates, trade policies, expectations of economic growth, etc.) that are unrelated to the purchasing power of currencies in different countries.

Comparability

The data on expenditures were obtained by a special survey conducted in 2010 which applied consistent methods and definitions. Expenditure data are based on the definitions and coverage of the UNESCO-OECD-Eurostat data collection programme on education; they have been adjusted to 2008 prices using the GDP price deflator. The use of a common survey and definitions ensures good comparability of results across countries.

Overview

In 2008, the average level of expenditure per tertiary student, across OECD countries, was 13 717 USD. Spending per student at tertiary level ranged from 5 780 USD in Estonia to more than 20 000 USD in Canada, Sweden, Switzerland and the United States. OECD countries in which most R&D is performed by tertiary educational institutions tend to report higher tertiary expenditure per student than countries in which a large part of research and development is performed in other public institutions or by industry.

The expenditure for tertiary education increased in real terms across OECD countries by an average of 40% between 2000 and 2008, when student enrolment at this level increased by an average of 24%. Spending per student at tertiary level increased by 14% on average. However, spending per student fell in Chile, Israel, the Netherlands and the United States, and public expenditure per student fell also in Brazil, Hungary and Switzerland (data on private expenditure are not available). In all of these countries the decline was mainly the result of a rapid increase (by 20% or more) in the number of tertiary students. Japan and Spain were the only countries in which the number of tertiary students decreased between 2000 and 2008.

In 2008, the OECD average level of annual expenditure per student for primary, secondary and post-secondary education was 8 169 USD. Between 2000 and 2008, a period of relatively stable student enrolment at these levels, spending per students increased in every country, rising by 34% on average. Over this period, expenditure per student increased by at least 15% in 23 of the 30 OECD and partner countries with available data. The rise exceeded 40% in Brazil, the Czech Republic, Estonia, Hungary, Ireland, Korea, Poland, the Slovak Republic and the United Kingdom.

Sources

- OECD (2011), *Education at a Glance*, OECD Publishing.

Further information

Analytical publications

- OECD (2011), *Reviews of National Policies for Education*, OECD Publishing.
- OECD (2010), *Trends Shaping Education*, OECD Publishing.
- OECD (2008), *Higher Education Management and Policy*, OECD Publishing.
- OECD (2006), *Education Policy Analysis: Focus on Higher Education*, OECD Publishing.
- OECD (2004), *Internationalisation and Trade in Higher Education: Opportunities and Challenges*, OECD Publishing.
- OECD (2004), *Quality and Recognition in Higher Education: The Cross-border Challenge*, OECD Publishing.

Methodological publications

- OECD (2004), *OECD Handbook for Internationally Comparative Education Statistics: Concepts, Standards, Definitions and Classifications*, OECD Publishing.
- UNESCO Institute for Statistics (UIS), OECD and Eurostat (2011), *UOE Data Collection on Education Systems*, UIS, Montreal.

Online databases

- *OECD Education Statistics.*

Websites

- OECD Education at a Glance, *www.oecd.org/edu/eag2011*.

Expenditure on educational institutions per student and change in expenditure due to different factors

	Primary, secondary and post-secondary non-tertiary education							Tertiary education						
	Expenditure per student, US dollars, 2008 constant prices and PPPs	Index of change, 2000 = 100						Expenditure per student, US dollars, 2008 constant prices and PPPs	Index of change, 2000 = 100					
		Expenditure		Number of students		Expenditure per student			Expenditure		Number of students		Expenditure per student	
	2008 or latest available year	1995	2008 or latest available year	1995	2008 or latest available year	1995	2008 or latest available year	2008 or latest available year	1995	2008 or latest available year	1995	2008 or latest available year	1995	2008 or latest available year
Australia	7 814	81	133	94	108	85	123	15 043	90	134	83	123	109	108
Austria	10 994	93	108	..	97	..	112	15 043	97	148	91	115	107	129
Belgium	9 706	..	124	..	106	..	117	15 020	..	120	..	109	..	110
Canada	8 388	106	122	..	101	..	121	20 903	75	126	..	110	..	114
Chile	2 635	54	132	88	98	62	135	6 829	61	149	76	194	80	77
Czech Republic	5 236	116	137	107	86	109	159	8 318	101	202	64	164	159	124
Denmark	10 429	84	115	96	104	87	111	17 634	91	119	96	102	95	116
Estonia	6 054	78	163	96	75	81	219	5 780	69	154	60	116	115	132
Finland	8 068	89	133	93	105	95	126	15 402	90	126	89	103	101	122
France	8 559	90	103	..	98	..	105	14 079	91	121	..	103	..	117
Germany	7 859	94	100	97	93	97	107	15 390	95	122	104	113	91	107
Greece	..	64	..	107	..	60	..	..	66	..	68	..	97	..
Hungary	4 626	100	139	105	86	95	162	7 327	78	131	58	149	135	88
Iceland	9 745	..	146	99	107	..	136	10 429	..	164	79	162	..	101
Ireland	8 915	82	197	105	108	78	183	16 284	56	136	85	118	66	115
Israel	5 780	84	127	89	111	94	115	12 568	71	110	74	125	96	88
Italy	9 071	101	108	102	102	99	106	9 553	79	120	99	111	80	108
Japan	8 301	98	103	113	89	86	115	14 890	87	115	99	99	88	117
Korea	6 723	..	167	107	96	..	175	9 081	..	162	68	110	..	147
Luxembourg	16 909	..	..	..	..	..	..	..	..	..	..	..	..	..
Mexico	2 284	81	128	93	109	87	117	7 504	77	155	77	133	101	117
Netherlands	9 251	82	127	97	105	84	121	17 245	95	128	96	129	99	99
New Zealand	6 496	71	109	..	..	..	..	10 526	104	156	..	..	..	..
Norway	12 070	83	127	89	108	93	118	18 942	93	126	100	113	93	112
Poland	4 682	70	129	110	76	64	169	7 063	59	195	55	119	107	163
Portugal	6 276	76	98	105	90	72	109	10 373	73	152	77	112	96	136
Slovak Republic	4 006	97	157	105	83	92	189	6 560	81	185	72	174	113	106
Slovenia	8 555	..	..	..	..	..	..	9 263	..	..	..	..	..	..
Spain	8 522	99	123	119	95	84	129	13 366	72	135	100	98	72	138
Sweden	9 524	81	117	86	98	94	119	20 014	81	121	83	114	97	107
Switzerland	13 775	101	120	95	101	107	119	21 648	74	122	95	146	78	84
Turkey	..	57	..	..	..	..	..	..	55	..	..	..	..	..
United Kingdom	9 169	86	139	87	89	99	156	15 310	97	143	89	110	109	130
United States	10 995	80	125	95	108	84	116	29 910	71	117	92	120	77	98
OECD average	8 169	85	129	99	98	87	134	13 717	80	140	83	124	98	114
Brazil	2 098	82	216	85	98	96	221	11 610	78	148	79	157	98	94
Russian Federation	4 071	..	198	..	..	..	..	6 758	..	328	..	..	..	..

StatLink http://dx.doi.org/10.1787/888932506685

Changes in expenditure on educational institutions in tertiary education by factor

Changes in 2000-08 or latest available period, 2000 = 100

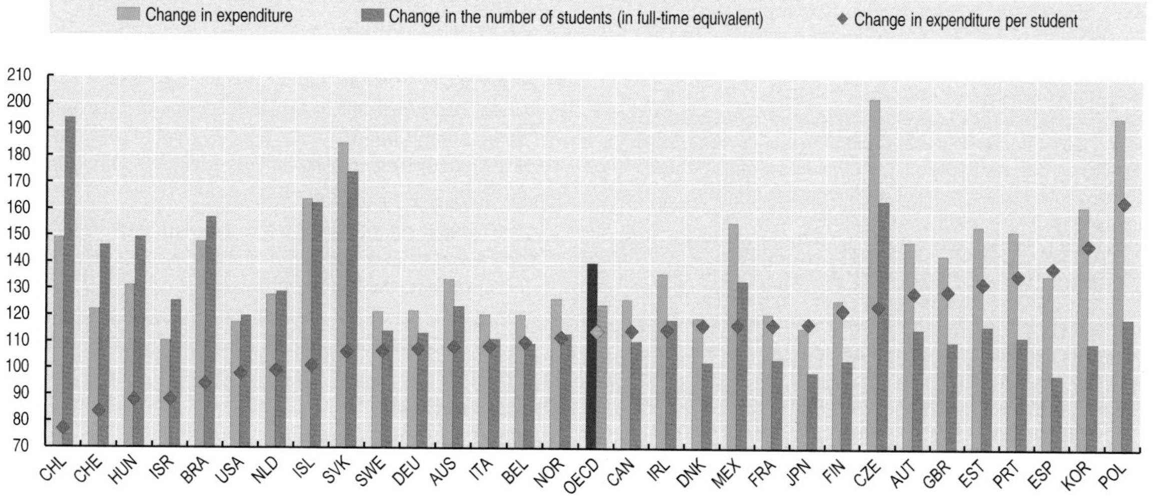

StatLink http://dx.doi.org/10.1787/888932506704

PRIVATE EXPENDITURE IN TERTIARY EDUCATION

Educational institutions in OECD countries are mainly publicly funded, although there are substantial and growing levels of private funding at the tertiary level. At this level, the contribution to the costs of education by individuals and other private entities is more and more considered an effective way to ensure funding is available to students regardless of their economic backgrounds.

Definition

This indicator covers private expenditure on schools, universities and other private institutions delivering or supporting educational services. Other private entities include private businesses and non-profit organisations, *e.g.* religious organisations, charitable organisations and business and labour associations. Expenditure by private companies on the work-based element of school- and work-based training of apprentices and students is also taken into account.

Private expenditure is recorded net of public subsidies attributable to educational institutions; it also includes expenditures made outside educational institutions.

Comparability

The broad definition of educational institutions used here ensures that expenditures on services are covered by schools and universities (as it occurs in many OECD countries) or by agencies other than schools (as it happens in other countries).

The data on expenditure were obtained by a survey conducted in 2010 which applied consistent methods and definitions. Expenditure data are based on the definitions and coverage for the UNESCO-OECD-Eurostat data collection programme on education; they have been adjusted to 2008 prices using the GDP price deflator. The use of a common survey and definitions ensures good comparability of results across countries.

Overview

In all countries, the proportion of private expenditure on education is far higher for tertiary education – an average of 31% of total expenditure at this level – than it is for primary, secondary and post-secondary non-tertiary education (9%).

The share of expenditure on tertiary institutions covered by individuals, businesses and other private sources, including subsidised private payments, ranges from less than 5% in Denmark, Finland and Norway, to more than 40% in Australia, Canada, Israel, Japan, the United Kingdom and the United States, to over 75% in Chile and Korea. In Korea, around 80% of tertiary students are enrolled in private universities, and more than 70% of the budget comes from tuition fees.

On average across OECD countries, contribution from private entities other than households to financing educational institutions is higher for tertiary education than for other levels of education. In Australia, Canada, the Czech Republic, Israel, Japan, Korea, the Netherlands, the Russian Federation, the Slovak Republic, Sweden, the United Kingdom and the United States, 10% or more of expenditure on tertiary institutions is covered by private entities other than households. For example, in Sweden these contributions are largely directed to sponsoring research and development.

Between 2000 and 2008, 20 out of the 26 countries for which comparable data are available showed an increase in the share of private funding for tertiary education. The share increased by six percentage points, on average, and by more than ten percentage points in Austria, Portugal, the Slovak Republic and the United Kingdom. While the share of private funding for tertiary education rose substantially in some countries during the period, this was not the case for other levels of education.

Sources

- OECD (2011), *Education at a Glance*, OECD Publishing.

Further information

Analytical publications

- OECD (2011), *Reviews of National Policies for Education*, OECD Publishing.
- OECD (2010), *Trends Shaping Education*, OECD Publishing.

Methodological publications

- OECD (2004), *OECD Handbook for Internationally Comparative Education Statistics: Concepts, Standards, Definitions and Classifications*, OECD Publishing.
- UNESCO Institute for Statistics (UIS), OECD and Eurostat (2011), *UOE Data Collection on Education Systems*, UIS, Montreal.

Online databases

- *OECD Education Statistics*.

Websites

- OECD Education at a Glance, *www.oecd.org/edu/eag2011*.

Public and private expenditure on tertiary educational institutions

Percentage

	As a percentage of total expenditure							Index of change, 2000 = 100	
	Public sources		Private sources					Public sources	Private sources
			Total	Household expenditure	Expenditure of other private entities	Total	*Of which:* Subsidised		
	2000	2008 or latest available year	2000	2008 or latest available year				2008 or latest available year	2008 or latest available year
Australia	49.6	44.8	50.4	39.8	15.4	55.2	0.4	121	146
Austria	96.3	84.7	3.7	5.9	9.4	15.3	8.4	130	611
Belgium	91.5	89.8	8.5	5.5	4.7	10.2	3.8	118	144
Canada	61.0	58.7	39.0	19.9	21.4	41.3	..	121	133
Chile	19.5	14.6	80.5	79.3	6.1	85.4	7.1	112	158
Czech Republic	85.4	79.1	14.6	9.4	11.5	20.9	..	187	289
Denmark	97.6	95.5	2.4	..	..	4.5	..	114	218
Estonia	..	78.8	..	19.3	1.9	21.2	7.2	154	..
Finland	97.2	95.4	2.8	..	..	4.6	..	124	209
France	84.4	81.7	15.6	9.6	8.7	18.3	2.4	116	141
Germany	88.2	85.4	11.8	..	..	14.6	..	117	150
Greece	99.7	..	0.3	..	..	..	..	..	..
Hungary	..	..	..	..	..	..	..	131	..
Iceland	91.8	92.2	8.2	7.2	0.6	7.8	..	165	156
Ireland	79.2	82.6	20.8	15.0	2.5	17.4	1.1	142	114
Israel	58.5	51.3	41.5	33.7	15.0	48.7	6.2	97	130
Italy	77.5	70.7	22.5	21.5	7.8	29.3	6.7	108	155
Japan	38.5	33.3	61.5	50.7	16.0	66.7	..	100	125
Korea	23.3	22.3	76.7	52.1	25.6	77.7	2.3	155	164
Mexico	79.4	70.1	20.6	29.5	0.4	29.9	1.1	137	225
Netherlands	76.5	72.6	23.5	15.1	12.3	27.4	0.3	120	147
New Zealand	..	70.4	..	29.6	..	29.6	..	156	..
Norway	96.3	96.9	3.7	3.1	..	3.1	..	126	106
Poland	66.6	69.6	33.4	23.7	6.7	30.4	..	202	176
Portugal	92.5	62.1	7.5	28.3	9.6	37.9	..	98	739
Slovak Republic	91.2	73.1	8.8	10.5	16.4	26.9	2.0	145	557
Slovenia	..	83.8	..	16.0	0.2	16.2	..	..	..
Spain	74.4	78.9	25.6	17.0	4.2	21.1	1.7	144	112
Sweden	91.3	89.1	8.7	..	10.9	10.9	..	117	151
Switzerland	..	..	..	..	..	..	..	122	..
Turkey	95.4	..	4.6	..	..	..	..	..	..
United Kingdom	67.7	34.5	32.3	51.5	14.0	65.5	16.3	112	278
United States	31.1	37.4	68.9	41.2	21.5	62.6	..	141	107
OECD average	75.1	68.9	24.9	..	..	31.1	3.3	131	217
Brazil	..	..	..	..	..	..	..	148	..
Russian Federation	..	64.3	..	20.1	15.6	35.7	..	328	..

StatLink http://dx.doi.org/10.1787/888932506723

Share of private expenditure on tertiary educational institutions

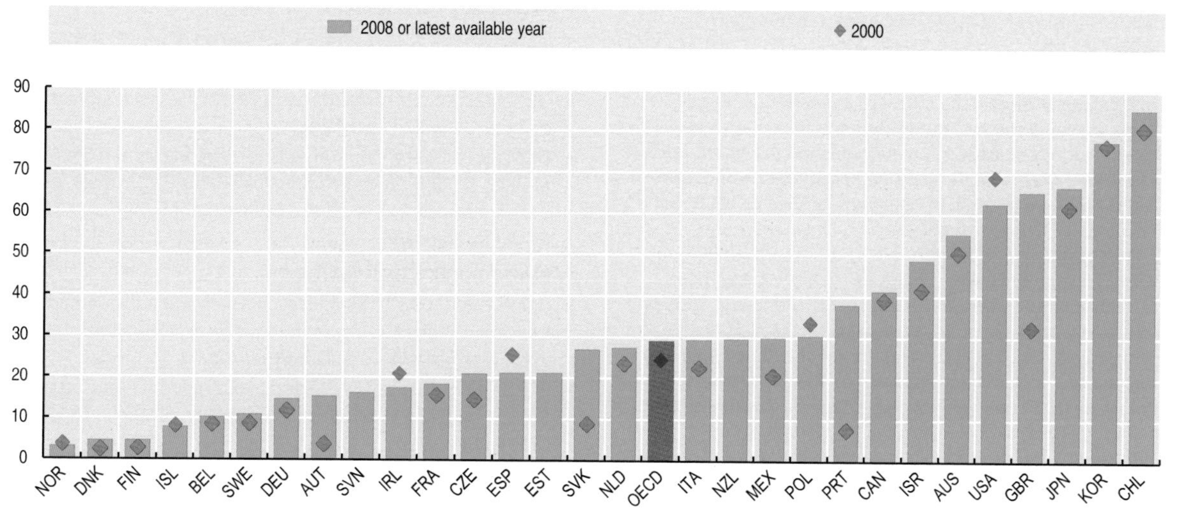

StatLink http://dx.doi.org/10.1787/888932506742

EDUCATION EXPENDITURE

Expenditure on education is an investment that can foster economic growth, enhance productivity, contribute to personal and social development and reduce social inequality. The proportion of total financial resources devoted to education is one of the key choices made by governments, enterprises, students and their families.

Definition

The indicator covers expenditure on schools, universities and other public and private institutions delivering or supporting educational services. Expenditure on institutions is not limited to expenditure on instruction services but includes public and private expenditure on ancillary services for students and their families, where these services are provided through educational institutions. At the tertiary level, spending on research and development can also be significant and is included in this indicator, to the extent that the research is performed by educational institutions.

In principle, public expenditure includes both direct expenditure on educational institutions and educational-related public subsidies to households administered by educational institutions. Private expenditure is recorded net of these public subsidies attributable to educational institutions; it also excludes expenditure made outside educational institutions (such as textbooks purchased by families, private tutoring for students and student living cost).

Comparability

The broad definition of educational institutions used here ensures coverage of expenditures on services by schools and universities (as it occurs in many OECD countries) or by agencies other than schools (as it happens in other countries).

The data on expenditure were obtained by a special survey conducted in 2010 which applied consistent methods and definitions. Expenditure data are based on the definitions and coverage for the UNESCO-OECD-Eurostat data collection programme on education; they have been adjusted to 2008 prices using the GDP price deflator. The use of a common survey and definitions ensures good comparability of results across countries.

No data for private expenditure are currently collected for countries ranked separately on the left-hand side of the chart.

Data for Indonesia are based on UNESCO Institute for Statistics (World Education Indicators Programme).

Overview

Expenditure on educational institutions represents a financial burden for society as a whole. This burden, however, does not fall on public funding alone. In 2008, taking into account both public and private sources, OECD countries spent 6.1% of their GDP on educational institutions at the pre-primary, primary, secondary and tertiary levels. More than three-quarters of this amount came from public sources. The highest spending on educational institutions is in Chile, Denmark, Iceland, Israel, Korea, Norway and the Unites States, with at least 7% of GDP accounted for by public and private spending on educational institutions. Nine out of 36 countries with available data spent 5% or less of GDP on educational institutions; in China, Indonesia and the Slovak Republic these shares are at or below 4.0%.

Nearly one-third of OECD expenditure on educational institutions is accounted for by tertiary education. At this level, the pathways available to students, the tuition fees paid by student, the duration of programmes and the organisation of teaching vary greatly among OECD countries, resulting in significant differences in the expenditure allocated to tertiary education. On the one hand, Canada, Chile, Israel, Korea, the United States spend between 1.7% and 2.7% of their GDP on tertiary institutions; these countries are also among those with the highest proportion of private expenditure on tertiary education. On the other hand, in Belgium, Brazil, Estonia, France, Iceland, Ireland, Switzerland and the United Kingdom expenditure on tertiary institutions, as a portion of GDP, is below the OECD average; yet, these countries are among those with a share of GDP spent on primary, secondary and post-secondary non-tertiary education higher than the OECD average.

Sources

- OECD (2011), *Education at a Glance*, OECD Publishing.

Further information

Analytical publications

- OECD (2010), *Trends Shaping Education*, OECD Publishing.
- OECD (2006), *Schooling for Tomorrow*, OECD Publishing.
- OECD (2006), *Starting Strong II: Early Childhood Education and Care*, OECD Publishing.
- OECD and Edebé Ediciones Internacionales S.A de C.V. Mexico (2008), *Students with Disabilities, Difficulties and Disadvantages: Statistics and Indicators of OAS Countries*, OECD Publishing.

Methodological publications

- OECD (2004), *OECD Handbook for Internationally Comparative Education Statistics: Concepts, Standards, Definitions and Classifications*, OECD Publishing.
- UNESCO Institute for Statistics (UIS), OECD and Eurostat (2011), *UOE Data Collection on Education Systems*, UIS, Montreal.

Websites

- OECD Education at a Glance, *www.oecd.org/edu/eag2011*.

Public and private expenditure on education

2008 or latest available year

	As a percentage of GDP						Index of change, 2000 = 100					
	Primary, secondary and post-secondary non-tertiary education		Tertiary education		All levels of education		Primary, secondary and post-secondary non-tertiary education		Tertiary education		All levels of education	
	Public	Private	Public	Private	Public	Private	Public	Private	Public	Private	Public	Private
Australia	3.0	0.6	0.7	0.8	3.7	1.4	131	142	121	146	128	145
Austria	3.5	0.1	1.2	0.1	5.2	0.2	109	105	130	611	112	180
Belgium	4.3	0.2	1.3	0.1	6.3	0.3	125	113	118	144	125	123
Canada	3.1	0.4	1.5	1.0	4.6	1.4	117	182	121	133	113	142
Chile	3.3	0.9	..	..	4.3	2.7	152	91	..	..	156	134
Czech Republic	2.5	0.3	0.9	0.2	3.9	0.6	136	158	187	289	146	190
Denmark	4.2	0.1	1.6	0.1	6.5	0.6	115	126	114	218	113	229
Estonia	3.8	..	1.1	0.2	5.5	0.2	163	..	154	..	164	..
Finland	3.8	..	1.6	0.1	5.7	0.1	133	197	124	209	131	167
France	3.7	0.2	1.2	0.2	5.5	0.5	102	107	116	141	106	122
Germany	2.6	0.4	1.0	0.2	4.1	0.7	100	101	117	150	107	114
Hungary	3.0	..	0.9	..	4.8	..	139	..	131	..	140	..
Iceland	4.9	0.2	1.2	0.1	7.2	0.7	146	146	165	156	155	139
Ireland	4.0	0.1	1.2	0.2	5.2	0.3	200	115	142	114	181	113
Israel	4.0	0.2	0.9	0.7	5.9	1.4	126	151	97	130	121	135
Italy	3.2	0.1	0.8	0.2	4.5	0.3	110	147	108	155	107	167
Japan	2.5	0.3	0.5	1.0	3.3	1.7	103	100	100	125	102	127
Korea	3.4	0.8	0.6	1.9	4.7	2.8	161	193	155	164	175	173
Luxembourg	2.8	0.1	..	..	..	..	..	..	..	..	..	..
Mexico	3.1	0.6	0.9	0.4	4.7	1.1	123	158	137	225	131	182
Netherlands	3.3	0.4	1.1	0.4	4.8	0.8	128	121	120	147	126	131
New Zealand	3.8	0.6	1.1	0.5	5.4	1.2	109	..	156	..	121	..
Norway	5.0	..	1.6	0.1	7.3	..	127	..	126	106	139	..
Poland	3.4	0.2	1.0	0.4	5.0	0.7	128	151	202	176	140	167
Portugal	3.4	..	0.9	0.5	4.7	0.5	98	90	98	739	99	718
Slovak Republic	2.2	0.4	0.7	0.2	3.5	0.6	135	992	145	557	136	768
Slovenia	3.4	0.3	1.0	0.2	4.8	0.6	..	..	..	..	..	..
Spain	2.9	0.2	1.0	0.2	4.5	0.6	124	121	144	112	136	141
Sweden	4.0	..	1.4	0.2	6.1	0.2	117	85	117	151	122	110
Switzerland	3.8	0.5	1.3	..	5.3	..	117	145	122	..	116	145
United Kingdom	4.2	..	0.6	0.6	5.1	0.6	122	273	112	278	109	276
United States	3.8	0.3	1.0	1.7	5.1	2.1	126	120	141	107	129	108
OECD average	3.5	0.3	1.0	0.5	5.0	0.9	127	170	131	217	130	198
OECD total	3.4	0.3	0.9	1.0	4.7	1.4	..	..	..	..	..	..
Brazil	4.1	..	0.8	..	5.3	..	216	..	148	..	197	..
Indonesia	2.9	..	0.3	..	3.3	..	..	..	..	..	..	..
Russian Federation	2.0	0.1	0.9	0.5	4.1	0.7	198	..	328	..	229	..

StatLink http://dx.doi.org/10.1787/888932506761

Public and private expenditure on education for all levels of education

As a percentage of GDP, 2008 or latest available year

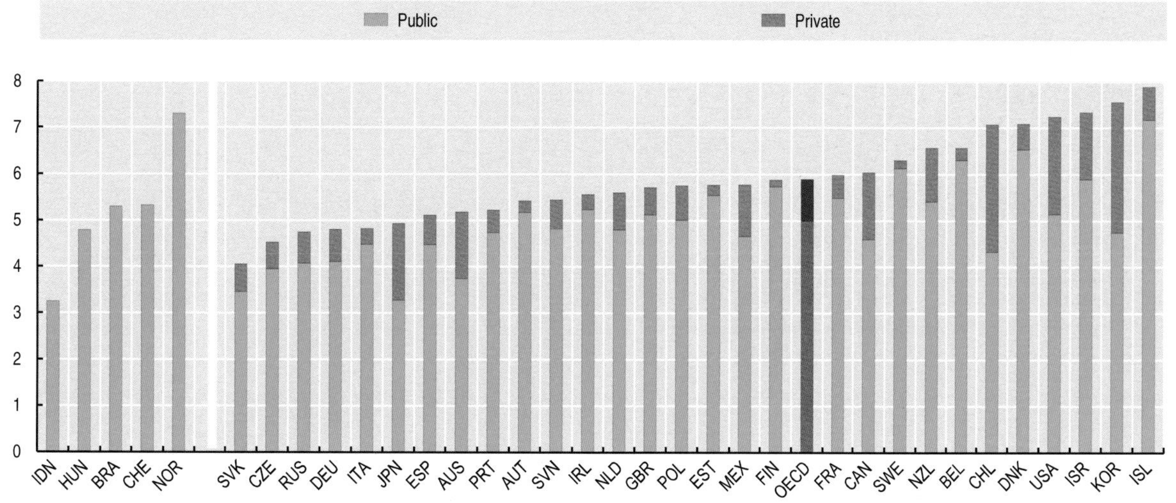

StatLink http://dx.doi.org/10.1787/888932506780

PUBLIC FINANCE

GOVERNMENT DEFICITS AND DEBT

GOVERNMENT EXPENDITURE, REVENUES AND DEFICITS

GOVERNMENT DEBT

GENERAL GOVERNMENT

DISTRIBUTION OF EXPENDITURES ACROSS LEVELS OF GOVERNMENT

GENERAL GOVERNMENT EXPENDITURES AND REVENUES PER CAPITA

GENERAL GOVERNMENT PRODUCTION COSTS

TRANSPARENCY IN GOVERNMENT DECISION MAKING

PUBLIC EXPENDITURE

SOCIAL EXPENDITURE

PENSION EXPENDITURE

LAW, ORDER AND DEFENCE EXPENDITURE

AGRICULTURAL SUPPORT AND FOREIGN AID

GOVERNMENT SUPPORT FOR AGRICULTURE

GOVERNMENT SUPPORT FOR FISHING

OFFICIAL DEVELOPMENT ASSISTANCE

TAXES

TOTAL TAX REVENUE

TAXES ON THE AVERAGE WORKER

General government net lending

As a percentage of GDP

	1997	1998	1999	2000	2001	2002	2003	2004	2005	2006	2007	2008	2009	2010
Australia	-1.0	0.8	1.2	0.4	-0.5	0.7	1.3	1.0	1.2	1.3	1.4	-0.2	-4.9	-5.9
Austria	-2.0	-2.5	-2.4	-1.9	-0.2	-0.9	-1.7	-4.6	-1.8	-1.7	-1.0	-1.0	-4.2	-4.6
Belgium	-2.3	-1.0	-0.7	-0.1	0.4	-0.2	-0.2	-0.4	-2.8	0.1	-0.4	-1.3	-6.0	-4.2
Canada	0.2	0.1	1.6	2.9	0.7	-0.1	-0.1	0.9	1.5	1.6	1.4	0.0	-5.5	-5.5
Czech Republic	-3.8	-5.0	-3.7	-3.7	-5.6	-6.8	-6.6	-2.9	-3.6	-2.6	-0.7	-2.7	-5.8	-4.7
Denmark	-0.6	-0.1	1.3	2.2	1.2	0.3	-0.1	1.9	5.0	5.0	4.8	3.3	-2.8	-2.9
Estonia	2.2	-0.7	-3.5	-0.2	-0.1	0.3	1.7	1.6	1.6	2.4	2.5	-2.9	-1.8	0.1
Finland	-1.4	1.5	1.6	6.8	5.0	4.0	2.3	2.1	2.5	3.9	5.2	4.2	-2.9	-2.8
France	-3.3	-2.6	-1.8	-1.5	-1.6	-3.2	-4.1	-3.6	-3.0	-2.3	-2.7	-3.3	-7.5	-7.0
Germany	-2.6	-2.2	-1.5	1.3	-2.8	-3.6	-4.0	-3.8	-3.3	-1.6	0.3	0.1	-3.0	-3.3
Greece	-5.9	-3.8	-3.1	-3.7	-4.4	-4.8	-5.7	-7.4	-5.3	-6.0	-6.7	-9.8	-15.6	-10.4
Hungary	-6.0	-7.9	-5.4	-3.0	-4.0	-8.9	-7.2	-6.4	-7.9	-9.3	-5.0	-3.6	-4.4	-4.2
Iceland	0.0	-0.4	1.1	1.7	-0.7	-2.6	-2.8	0.0	4.9	6.3	5.4	-13.5	-10.0	-7.8
Ireland	1.4	2.3	2.6	4.8	1.0	-0.3	0.4	1.4	1.6	2.9	0.1	-7.3	-14.3	-32.4
Israel	..	-8.0	-6.3	-4.0	-6.4	-8.2	-8.3	-6.1	-4.9	-2.5	-1.5	-3.7	-6.4	-5.0
Italy	-2.7	-3.1	-1.8	-0.9	-3.1	-3.0	-3.5	-3.6	-4.4	-3.3	-1.5	-2.7	-5.3	-4.5
Japan	-4.0	-11.2	-7.4	-7.6	-6.3	-8.0	-7.9	-6.2	-6.7	-1.6	-2.4	-2.2	-8.7	-8.1
Korea	3.0	1.3	2.4	5.4	4.3	5.1	0.5	2.7	3.4	3.9	4.7	3.0	-1.1	0.0
Luxembourg	3.7	3.4	3.4	6.0	6.1	2.1	0.5	-1.1	0.0	1.4	3.7	3.0	-0.9	-1.7
Netherlands	-1.2	-0.9	0.4	2.0	-0.3	-2.1	-3.2	-1.8	-0.3	0.5	0.2	0.5	-5.5	-5.3
New Zealand	0.9	0.0	-0.2	1.8	1.5	3.6	3.8	4.1	4.7	5.3	4.5	0.4	-2.6	-4.6
Norway	7.6	3.3	6.0	15.4	13.3	9.2	7.3	11.1	15.1	18.4	17.5	19.1	10.5	10.5
Poland	-4.6	-4.3	-2.3	-3.0	-5.3	-5.0	-6.2	-5.4	-4.1	-3.6	-1.9	-3.7	-7.4	-7.9
Portugal	-3.4	-3.5	-2.7	-2.9	-4.3	-2.9	-3.1	-3.4	-5.9	-4.1	-3.2	-3.6	-10.1	-9.2
Slovak Republic	-6.3	-5.3	-7.4	-12.3	-6.5	-8.2	-2.8	-2.4	-2.8	-3.2	-1.8	-2.1	-8.0	-7.9
Slovenia	-2.4	-2.4	-3.0	-3.7	-4.0	-2.5	-2.7	-2.3	-1.5	-1.4	-0.1	-1.8	-6.0	-5.6
Spain	-3.4	-3.2	-1.4	-1.0	-0.7	-0.5	-0.2	-0.4	1.0	2.0	1.9	-4.2	-11.1	-9.2
Sweden	-1.6	0.9	0.8	3.6	1.6	-1.5	-1.3	0.4	1.9	2.2	3.6	2.2	-0.9	-0.3
Switzerland	-2.8	-1.9	-0.5	0.1	-0.1	-1.2	-1.7	-1.8	-0.7	0.8	1.7	2.3	1.2	0.5
Turkey	..	..	..	..	..	..	..	..	..	0.8	-1.2	-2.2	-6.7	-4.6
United Kingdom	-2.2	-0.1	0.9	3.7	0.6	-2.0	-3.7	-3.6	-3.3	-2.7	-2.8	-4.8	-10.8	-10.3
United States	-0.9	0.3	0.7	1.5	-0.6	-4.0	-5.0	-4.4	-3.3	-2.2	-2.9	-6.3	-11.3	-10.6
OECD total	-1.9	-2.2	-1.0	0.1	-1.4	-3.3	-4.1	-3.4	-2.8	-1.3	-1.3	-3.3	-8.2	-7.7

StatLink http://dx.doi.org/10.1787/888932506799

General government net lending

As a percentage of GDP

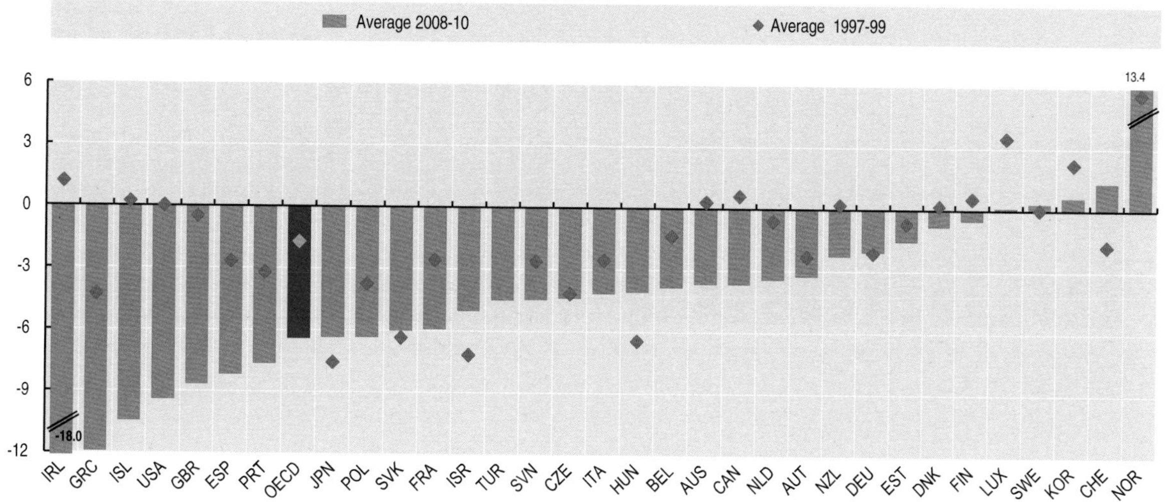

StatLink http://dx.doi.org/10.1787/888932506818

General government revenues

As a percentage of GDP

	1997	1998	1999	2000	2001	2002	2003	2004	2005	2006	2007	2008	2009	2010
Australia	34.3	35.4	35.6	35.2	34.8	35.4	35.4	35.5	35.2	34.8	34.8	34.0	28.2	30.4
Austria	51.8	51.6	51.3	50.4	51.5	50.0	50.0	49.7	48.6	47.9	48.0	48.5	49.0	48.3
Belgium	49.0	49.5	49.6	49.0	49.5	49.7	51.0	49.1	49.3	48.7	48.1	48.9	48.2	48.9
Canada	44.5	44.9	44.3	44.1	42.6	41.1	41.1	40.7	40.8	41.1	40.8	39.8	38.5	38.3
Czech Republic	39.4	38.2	38.6	38.1	38.7	39.5	40.7	42.2	41.4	41.1	41.8	40.2	40.1	40.6
Denmark	56.1	56.2	56.8	55.8	55.4	54.8	55.0	56.4	57.8	56.6	55.6	55.2	55.6	55.3
Estonia	39.6	38.5	36.7	35.9	34.7	36.0	36.5	35.6	35.2	36.0	36.9	37.0	43.4	40.1
Finland	55.2	54.4	53.2	55.2	52.8	52.9	52.5	52.1	52.7	52.8	52.4	53.5	53.3	52.4
France	50.8	50.0	50.8	50.1	50.0	49.4	49.1	49.6	50.5	50.3	49.6	49.6	48.7	49.1
Germany	45.7	45.9	46.7	46.4	44.7	44.4	44.4	43.5	43.6	43.7	43.8	43.9	44.5	43.4
Greece	39.0	40.5	41.3	43.0	40.9	40.3	39.0	38.1	38.6	39.2	40.0	39.9	37.3	39.1
Hungary	43.0	42.2	43.0	43.7	42.7	41.9	41.9	42.3	42.0	42.3	44.6	45.1	45.8	44.4
Iceland	40.7	40.9	43.2	43.6	41.9	41.7	42.8	44.1	47.1	48.0	47.7	44.1	41.1	42.3
Ireland	38.1	36.8	36.7	36.1	34.1	33.1	33.6	35.0	35.6	37.4	36.8	35.5	33.9	34.6
Israel	..	47.0	47.4	47.5	47.4	47.6	46.0	44.8	44.4	45.1	44.7	42.2	39.2	40.5
Italy	47.6	46.2	46.5	45.3	44.9	44.4	44.7	44.2	43.8	45.3	46.4	46.1	46.5	46.1
Japan	31.7	31.3	31.2	31.4	32.2	30.8	30.5	30.9	31.7	34.5	33.5	35.1	33.3	32.5
Korea	24.8	25.5	25.5	27.9	28.3	28.7	29.4	28.8	30.0	31.7	33.3	33.4	31.9	30.9
Luxembourg	44.3	44.4	42.6	43.6	44.2	43.6	42.2	41.5	41.5	39.9	39.8	39.8	41.3	39.5
Netherlands	46.3	45.8	46.4	46.1	45.1	44.1	43.9	44.3	44.5	46.1	45.4	46.6	45.9	45.9
New Zealand	42.6	40.6	40.0	40.0	39.3	40.6	41.3	41.2	42.9	44.9	44.1	42.3	40.2	38.4
Norway	54.5	52.5	53.7	57.7	57.5	56.3	55.5	56.7	57.3	59.0	58.7	59.7	56.9	56.5
Poland	41.9	40.2	40.6	38.1	38.5	39.2	38.4	37.3	39.4	40.3	40.3	39.6	37.2	37.9
Portugal	37.8	37.3	38.3	38.2	38.2	39.4	40.7	41.3	39.9	40.5	41.1	41.1	39.7	41.5
Slovak Republic	42.6	40.5	40.7	39.9	38.0	36.8	37.4	35.3	35.2	33.4	32.5	32.9	33.6	33.1
Slovenia	42.5	43.3	43.4	43.0	43.6	43.9	43.7	43.6	43.8	43.2	42.4	42.3	43.1	43.4
Spain	38.2	37.8	38.4	38.1	38.0	38.4	38.2	38.5	39.4	40.4	41.1	37.1	34.7	35.7
Sweden	59.0	59.7	58.9	58.7	56.1	54.1	54.4	54.6	55.8	54.9	54.5	53.9	54.2	52.7
Switzerland	32.7	33.8	33.8	35.2	34.7	35.0	34.6	34.2	34.6	34.3	34.0	34.5	34.9	34.2
Turkey	..	..	..	..	..	..	..	..	..	34.0	33.4	32.0	32.7	32.5
United Kingdom	38.4	39.4	39.8	40.3	40.6	39.0	38.7	39.6	40.8	41.5	41.2	42.6	40.3	40.7
United States	34.6	34.9	34.9	35.4	34.4	31.9	31.3	31.6	33.0	33.8	33.9	32.6	30.9	31.6
OECD total	38.6	38.7	38.8	38.9	38.4	37.1	36.8	36.8	37.6	38.5	38.5	38.1	36.7	36.8

StatLink http://dx.doi.org/10.1787/888932506837

General government revenues

As a percentage of GDP

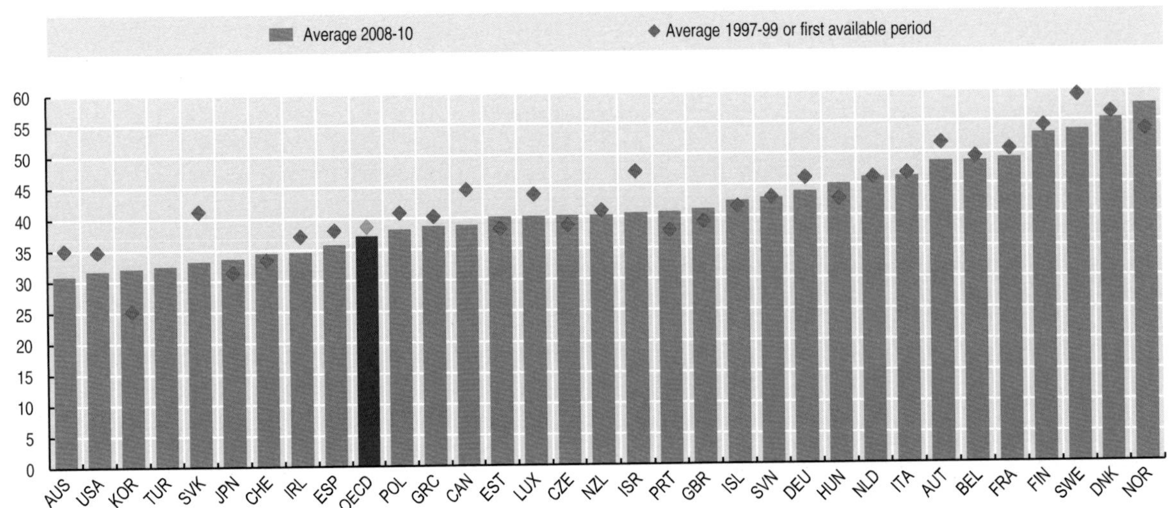

StatLink http://dx.doi.org/10.1787/888932506856

General government expenditures

As a percentage of GDP

	1997	1998	1999	2000	2001	2002	2003	2004	2005	2006	2007	2008	2009	2010
Australia	35.4	34.6	34.5	34.8	35.3	34.7	34.1	34.6	34.0	33.5	33.4	34.2	33.1	36.3
Austria	53.7	54.1	53.8	52.2	51.7	50.9	51.7	54.3	50.4	49.6	49.0	49.5	53.1	53.0
Belgium	51.2	50.4	50.2	49.1	49.2	49.9	51.1	49.5	52.1	48.6	48.4	50.2	54.1	53.1
Canada	44.3	44.8	42.7	41.1	42.0	41.2	41.2	39.9	39.3	39.4	39.4	39.8	44.1	43.8
Czech Republic	43.2	43.2	42.3	41.8	44.3	46.3	47.3	45.2	45.0	43.7	42.4	42.9	45.9	45.2
Denmark	56.7	56.3	55.5	53.7	54.2	54.6	55.1	54.6	52.8	51.6	50.8	51.9	58.4	58.2
Estonia	37.4	39.2	40.1	36.1	34.8	35.8	34.8	34.0	33.6	33.6	34.4	39.9	45.2	40.0
Finland	56.6	52.9	51.7	48.3	47.8	48.9	50.2	50.0	50.2	49.0	47.3	49.3	56.2	55.1
France	54.1	52.7	52.6	51.6	51.6	52.6	53.2	53.3	53.4	52.7	52.4	52.9	56.2	56.2
Germany	48.3	48.1	48.2	45.1	47.5	48.0	48.4	47.2	46.9	45.3	43.5	43.8	47.5	46.7
Greece	44.9	44.3	44.4	46.7	45.3	45.1	44.7	45.5	44.0	45.2	46.6	49.7	52.9	49.5
Hungary	49.0	50.1	48.4	46.7	46.8	50.7	49.0	48.7	49.9	51.6	49.5	48.8	50.2	48.6
Iceland	40.7	41.3	42.0	41.9	42.6	44.3	45.6	44.1	42.2	41.6	42.3	57.6	51.0	50.0
Ireland	36.7	34.5	34.1	31.3	33.1	33.4	33.2	33.6	34.0	34.5	36.7	42.8	48.2	67.0
Israel	..	55.0	53.7	51.5	53.7	55.7	54.3	50.9	49.3	47.6	46.2	46.0	45.6	45.5
Italy	50.2	49.3	48.2	46.1	48.0	47.4	48.3	47.8	48.1	48.7	47.9	48.8	51.8	50.6
Japan	35.7	42.5	38.6	39.0	38.6	38.8	38.4	37.0	38.4	36.2	35.9	37.2	42.0	40.7
Korea	21.8	24.1	23.2	22.4	23.9	23.6	28.9	26.1	26.6	27.7	28.7	30.4	33.1	30.9
Luxembourg	40.7	41.1	39.2	37.6	38.1	41.5	41.8	42.6	41.5	38.6	36.2	36.9	42.2	41.2
Netherlands	47.5	46.7	46.0	44.2	45.4	46.2	47.1	46.1	44.8	45.5	45.3	46.0	51.4	51.2
New Zealand	41.6	40.6	40.2	38.3	37.8	36.9	37.5	37.1	38.2	39.6	39.6	41.9	42.8	43.0
Norway	46.9	49.2	47.7	42.3	44.2	47.1	48.3	45.6	42.3	40.6	41.2	40.6	46.4	46.0
Poland	46.6	44.5	42.9	41.2	43.7	44.2	44.6	42.7	43.5	43.9	42.2	43.2	44.6	45.8
Portugal	41.1	40.8	41.0	41.1	42.5	42.3	43.8	44.7	45.8	44.5	44.4	44.7	49.8	50.7
Slovak Republic	48.9	45.8	48.1	52.1	44.5	45.1	40.1	37.7	38.0	36.6	34.3	35.0	41.5	41.0
Slovenia	44.8	45.7	46.5	46.7	47.6	46.3	46.4	45.9	45.3	44.6	42.5	44.1	49.0	49.0
Spain	41.6	41.1	39.9	39.1	38.6	38.9	38.4	38.9	38.4	38.4	39.2	41.3	45.8	45.0
Sweden	60.7	58.8	58.1	55.1	54.5	55.6	55.7	54.2	53.9	52.7	51.0	51.7	55.2	53.1
Switzerland	35.5	35.8	34.3	35.1	34.8	36.2	36.4	35.9	35.3	33.5	32.3	32.2	33.7	33.7
Turkey	..	..	..	..	..	..	..	..	..	33.2	34.5	34.2	39.4	37.1
United Kingdom	40.6	39.5	38.8	36.6	39.9	40.9	42.4	43.1	44.0	44.3	44.1	47.4	51.2	51.0
United States	35.4	34.6	34.2	33.9	35.0	35.9	36.3	36.0	36.2	36.0	36.8	39.0	42.2	42.3
OECD total	40.5	40.8	39.8	38.9	39.9	40.4	40.9	40.2	40.4	39.7	39.8	41.4	44.9	44.5

StatLink http://dx.doi.org/10.1787/888932506875

General government expenditures

As a percentage of GDP

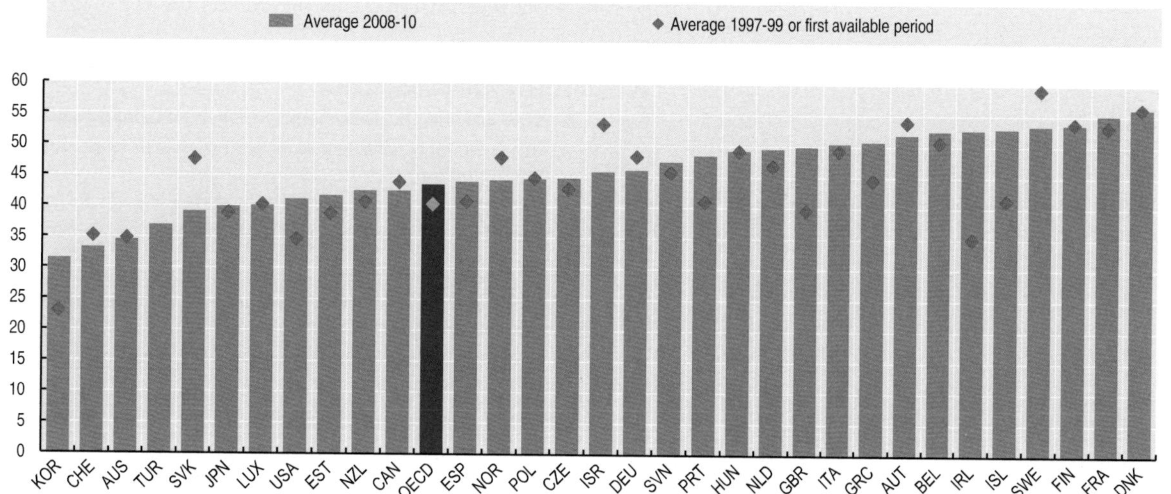

StatLink http://dx.doi.org/10.1787/888932506894

GOVERNMENT DEBT

Government debt is one of the key indicators in assessing sustainability of public finances.

Definition

Subject to data availability, debt refers to general government consolidated gross financial liabilities as a percentage of GDP, based on the 1993 *System of National Accounts* (SNA) or on the 1995 *European System of Accounts* (ESA). The general government sector consists of central, state and local government units together with social security funds controlled by those units. In principle, debts within and between different levels of government are consolidated. In other terms, a loan from one level of government to another represents both an asset for the first level and a liability for the second, and they cancel out for the general government sector as a whole (*i.e.* are "consolidated"). The SNA/ESA definition differs from the definition of debt applied under the Maastricht Treaty. First, gross debt according to the Maastricht definition excludes trade credits and advances, as well as shares and insurance technical reserves. Second, government debt according to the Maastricht definition is valued at face (*i.e.* at issue prices) rather than market value as required by the SNA93. The United States and Canada also value government bonds at their face value.

Comparability

The comparability of data on government debt can be affected both across countries, through national differences in implementing SNA93/ESA95 definitions, and within a country, due to changes in how SNA93/ESA95 definitions are implemented over time.

General government debt

As a percentage of GDP

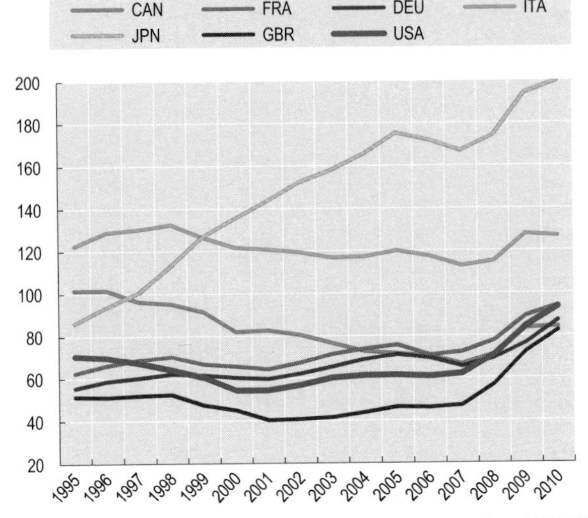

StatLink http://dx.doi.org/10.1787/888932535147

Overview

Gross general government debt as a share of GDP for the OECD area has been gradually on the rise since the 1970s, reaching a record level of nearly 100% in 2010. The rapid increase in debt in past three years reflects mainly crisis related high budget deficits. Debt-to-GDP ratios in 2010 varied considerably among OECD countries, ranging from 12% in Estonia to 200% in Japan.

Sources

- OECD (2011), *OECD Economic Outlook*, OECD Publishing.

Further information

Analytical publications

- OECD (2011), *OECD Economic Surveys*, OECD Publishing.
- OECD (2006), *Credit Risk and Credit Access in Asia*, OECD Publishing.
- OECD (2002), *Debt Management and Government Securities Markets in the 21st Century*, OECD Publishing.

Statistical publications

- OECD (2011), *Central Government Debt: Statistical Yearbook*, OECD Publishing.
- OECD (2011), *National Accounts of OECD Countries*, OECD Publishing.

Methodological publications

- OECD (2008), *OECD Glossary of Statistical Terms*, OECD Publishing.

Online databases

- *OECD National Accounts Statistics*.
- *OECD Economic Outlook: Statistics and Projections*.

Websites

- OECD Economic Outlook – Sources and Methods, *www.oecd.org/eco/sources-and-methods*.

General government gross financial liabilities

As a percentage of GDP

	1997	1998	1999	2000	2001	2002	2003	2004	2005	2006	2007	2008	2009	2010
Australia	37.0	32.0	27.6	24.6	21.8	19.8	18.3	16.5	16.1	15.3	14.2	13.6	19.4	25.3
Austria	66.7	68.4	71.2	71.1	72.1	73.0	71.2	70.8	70.9	66.6	63.1	67.3	72.6	78.6
Belgium	128.0	123.2	119.7	113.7	112.0	108.4	103.5	98.5	95.9	91.7	88.1	93.3	100.5	100.7
Canada	96.3	95.2	91.4	82.1	82.7	80.6	76.6	72.6	71.6	70.3	66.5	71.3	83.4	84.2
Czech Republic	..	..	..	..	..	32.8	34.7	34.5	34.3	33.9	33.7	36.3	42.4	46.6
Denmark	74.8	72.4	67.1	60.4	58.4	58.2	56.6	54.0	45.9	41.2	34.3	42.6	52.4	55.5
Estonia	11.3	10.0	10.9	9.4	8.9	10.2	10.8	8.5	8.2	8.0	7.3	8.3	12.4	12.1
Finland	64.8	61.2	54.9	52.5	50.0	49.6	51.5	51.5	48.4	45.5	41.4	40.6	52.1	57.4
France	68.8	70.3	66.8	65.6	64.3	67.3	71.4	73.9	75.7	70.9	72.3	77.8	89.2	94.1
Germany	60.3	62.2	61.5	60.4	59.8	62.2	65.4	68.8	71.2	69.3	65.3	69.3	76.4	87.0
Greece	100.0	97.7	101.5	115.3	118.1	117.6	112.3	114.8	121.2	115.6	112.9	116.1	131.6	147.3
Hungary	..	..	..	..	59.1	60.2	61.3	65.0	68.5	71.7	71.8	76.3	84.7	85.6
Iceland	..	77.3	73.6	72.9	75.0	72.0	71.0	64.5	52.6	57.4	53.3	102.0	120.0	120.2
Ireland	..	62.1	51.2	39.4	36.9	35.2	34.1	32.8	32.6	28.8	28.8	49.6	71.6	102.4
Israel	99.3	100.9	94.9	84.5	89.0	96.6	99.2	97.4	93.5	84.3	77.7	76.7	79.2	76.1
Italy	130.3	132.6	126.4	121.6	120.8	119.4	116.8	117.3	120.0	117.4	112.8	115.2	127.8	126.8
Japan	100.5	113.2	127.0	135.4	143.7	152.3	158.0	165.5	175.3	172.1	167.0	174.1	194.1	199.7
Korea	..	..	..	..	..	19.2	19.3	22.6	24.6	27.7	27.9	29.6	32.5	33.9
Luxembourg	10.2	11.2	10.0	9.2	8.2	8.4	7.9	8.6	7.6	12.1	11.7	16.4	14.7	19.7
Netherlands	82.2	80.8	71.6	63.9	59.4	60.3	61.4	61.9	60.7	54.5	51.5	64.5	67.6	71.4
New Zealand	41.7	41.6	39.0	36.9	34.9	33.0	30.9	28.2	26.9	26.6	25.7	28.9	34.5	38.7
Norway	29.7	28.0	29.1	32.7	31.6	38.8	48.2	51.0	47.9	59.4	57.4	54.9	48.0	49.5
Poland	48.4	44.0	46.8	45.4	43.7	55.0	55.3	54.8	54.7	55.2	51.7	54.5	58.4	62.4
Portugal	65.3	63.3	60.5	60.2	61.7	65.0	66.8	69.3	72.8	77.6	75.4	80.6	93.1	103.1
Slovak Republic	39.0	41.2	53.5	57.6	57.1	50.2	48.2	47.6	39.1	34.1	32.8	31.8	39.9	44.5
Slovenia	..	..	..	..	33.7	34.8	34.2	35.0	33.9	33.8	30.0	29.7	44.2	47.5
Spain	75.0	75.3	69.4	66.5	61.9	60.3	55.3	53.4	50.4	45.9	42.1	47.4	62.3	66.1
Sweden	83.0	82.0	73.2	64.3	62.7	60.2	59.3	60.0	60.8	53.9	49.3	49.6	52.0	49.1
Switzerland	52.1	54.8	51.9	52.4	51.2	57.2	57.0	57.9	56.4	50.2	46.8	43.7	41.5	40.2
United Kingdom	52.0	52.5	47.4	45.1	40.4	40.8	41.5	43.8	46.4	46.1	47.2	57.0	72.4	82.4
United States	67.4	64.2	60.5	54.5	54.4	56.8	60.2	61.2	61.4	60.8	62.0	71.0	84.3	93.6
OECD total	73.5	74.2	72.5	69.8	69.6	71.6	73.4	74.9	76.3	74.5	73.1	79.3	90.9	97.6

StatLink http://dx.doi.org/10.1787/888932506913

General government gross financial liabilities

As a percentage of GDP

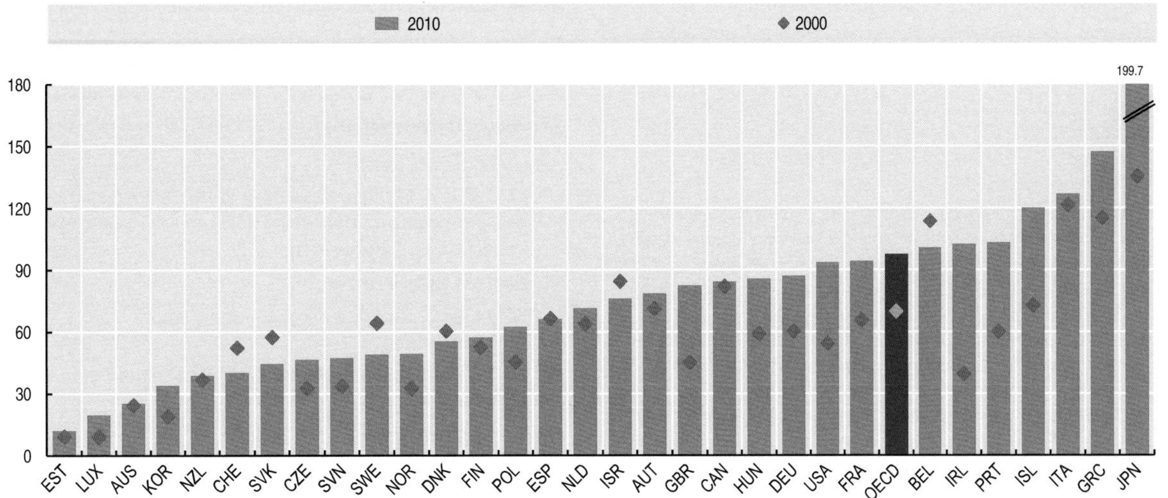

StatLink http://dx.doi.org/10.1787/888932506932

DISTRIBUTION OF EXPENDITURES ACROSS LEVELS OF GOVERNMENT

The responsibility for the provision of public goods and services and redistribution of income is divided between different levels of government. In some countries, local and regional governments play a larger role in delivering services, such as providing public housing or running schools. Data on the distribution of government spending by both level and function provide an indication of the extent to which key government activities are decentralised to sub-national governments.

Definition

Government expenditures data are derived from the *OECD Annual National Accounts*, which are based on the System of National Accounts, a set of internationally agreed concepts, definitions, classifications and rules for national accounting. The general government sector consists of central, state and local governments and the social security funds controlled by these units. Data on the distribution of general government expenditures across levels of government exclude transfers between levels of government and thus provide a rough proxy of the overall responsibility for providing goods and services borne by each level of government. For the central level of government, data on expenditures are shown here according to the Classification of the Functions of Government (COFOG), which divides spending into ten functions: general public services; defence; public order and safety; economic affairs; environmental protection; housing and community amenities; health; recreation, culture and religion; education; and social protection. Data on central government expenditures by function include transfers between the different levels of government.

Comparability

Data are based on the *1993 System of National Accounts* or on the *1995 European System of Accounts* so that all countries are using a common set of definitions. Data for Australia and Japan on the distribution of general government expenditures across levels of government include transfers between levels of government. The state government category is only applicable to the nine OECD countries that are federal states: Australia, Austria, Belgium, Canada, Germany, Mexico, Spain (considered a de facto federal state in the national accounts data), Switzerland and the United States. Local government is included in state government for the United States. Social security funds are included in central government in New Zealand, Norway, the United Kingdom and the United States. Australia does not operate government social insurance schemes; central government refers to commonwealth and multijurisdictional data. Data for Australia, Japan, Israel, Korea and New Zealand refer to 2008 instead of 2009. The OECD average excludes Chile, Mexico and Turkey (and Australia and Japan for central government expenditures by function). Data on central government expenditures by function for Canada and New Zealand refer to 2006 and 2005 respectively.

Overview

Across the OECD, in 2009, 46% of general government expenditures were undertaken by central government. Sub-central governments (state and local) covered 32%, and social security funds accounted for the remaining share. However, the level of fiscal decentralisation varies considerably across countries. For example, in New Zealand (a unitary state), almost 90% of total spending is by central government. In contrast, central government accounts for less than 15% of total expenditures in Switzerland, a federal state where regional and local governments play a much larger role in financing the public goods and services that they deliver themselves.

In the past decade, some countries have become more fiscally decentralised. Between 2000 and 2009, the share of expenditures attributed to sub-central governments rose in several countries including Canada, the Czech Republic, Denmark, Finland, Poland, the Slovak Republic, Slovenia, Spain, Sweden and Switzerland. The Slovak Republic, for example, transferred responsibilities for the execution of certain policies and programmes from central to local governments beginning in 2002 accompanied by fiscal decentralisation in 2005.

In general, central governments spend a relatively larger proportion of their budgets on social protection (*e.g.* pensions and unemployment benefits), general public services (*e.g.* executive and legislative organs, public debt transactions) and defence compared to sub-central governments. Expenditures on social protection represent the largest share of central government budgets for over half of OECD countries. The central governments of Spain and Belgium allocate most of their budgets to general public services, accounting for over 50% of total expenditures. Defence accounts for 6% of central government expenditures on average. Education, recreation, environmental protection, and housing and community amenities are mostly financed by sub-central governments. Responsibility for health, police and economic affairs (*e.g.* agriculture, mining, transportation and communications) programmes are often mixed responsibilities and vary by country.

Sources

- OECD (2011), *Government at a Glance*, OECD Publishing.

Further information

Analytical publications

- OECD (2011), *Making the Most of Public Investment in a Tight Fiscal Environment: Multi-level Governance Lessons from the Crisis*, OECD Publishing.

Statistical publications

- OECD (2011), *National Accounts at a Glance*, OECD Publishing.
- OECD (2011), *National Accounts of OECD Countries*, OECD Publishing.

Online databases

- "*General Government Accounts: Government expenditure by function*", *OECD National Accounts Statistics*.
- "*National Accounts at a Glance*", *OECD National Accounts Statistics*.

Websites

- Government at a Glance (supplementary material), *www.oecd.org/gov/indicators/govataglance*.

Structure of central government expenditures by function

Percentage, 2008

	General public services	Defence	Public order and safety	Economic affairs	Environmental protection	Housing and community amenities	Health	Recreation, culture and religion	Education	Social protection
Austria	18.4	3.9	4.9	11.6	0.4	2.3	4.3	1.3	13.3	39.6
Belgium	67.9	3.8	4.2	6.1	0.1	0.0	3.5	0.3	4.3	9.7
Canada	33.2	6.6	3.8	7.9	0.7	1.5	10.2	2.1	2.6	31.6
Czech Republic	11.7	3.8	6.3	16.2	0.7	1.8	5.2	1.5	11.9	41.0
Denmark	39.2	4.1	2.7	4.4	0.7	0.6	0.4	2.1	10.0	35.7
Estonia	14.1	6.0	9.2	12.9	2.8	0.0	8.0	4.2	9.1	33.8
Finland	20.2	6.1	4.4	13.5	0.8	0.8	12.1	1.7	13.5	27.0
France	30.0	8.1	4.4	13.5	0.4	1.4	0.9	2.0	19.3	20.0
Germany	30.7	7.8	1.1	9.5	0.2	1.3	0.0	0.3	1.2	47.9
Greece	24.1	8.4	4.5	39.5	0.3	0.6	1.2	1.3	11.1	9.0
Hungary	29.1	2.8	6.2	16.7	1.6	0.3	6.7	3.0	11.0	22.7
Iceland	12.8	0.1	3.1	39.9	0.8	0.2	17.1	2.8	7.6	15.6
Ireland	10.8	1.4	4.9	14.5	1.5	1.2	22.3	1.5	15.4	26.5
Israel	15.9	18.8	4.0	6.4	0.4	0.9	13.5	2.4	17.0	20.8
Italy	33.5	5.2	6.1	6.6	0.8	1.1	13.3	1.5	13.0	19.0
Korea	13.9	16.8	5.3	37.2	1.0	1.8	11.9	1.5	7.2	3.4
Luxembourg	18.0	0.9	3.1	13.1	1.5	1.6	1.5	4.4	13.6	42.3
Netherlands	31.4	4.9	6.5	9.5	0.7	0.8	1.3	1.2	16.3	27.5
New Zealand	12.0	2.8	5.4	8.3	1.1	1.1	18.5	1.6	20.8	28.4
Norway	17.9	5.0	2.4	9.3	0.4	0.1	16.2	1.4	5.7	41.6
Poland	18.5	5.8	7.3	13.5	0.5	0.9	4.5	1.6	19.6	27.9
Portugal	33.9	3.8	6.0	4.7	0.3	0.0	18.6	1.3	17.6	13.6
Slovak Republic	18.3	7.1	11.4	23.7	2.0	1.8	9.0	3.3	11.8	11.8
Slovenia	15.4	5.3	5.4	14.2	1.6	1.2	11.8	3.7	17.8	23.8
Spain	61.1	6.6	7.2	11.4	0.5	0.3	1.6	2.2	1.0	8.1
Sweden	25.7	5.1	4.0	10.1	0.5	0.4	4.5	1.2	6.3	42.4
Switzerland	29.8	8.0	1.5	19.2	0.7	0.2	0.4	0.8	7.5	31.9
United Kingdom	15.4	5.9	4.4	9.5	0.9	1.2	17.3	1.3	12.1	32.0
United States	11.8	20.1	1.6	7.2	0.0	2.0	24.2	0.1	2.4	30.6
OECD average	24.6	6.4	4.9	14.1	0.8	0.9	9.0	1.8	11.0	26.4

StatLink http://dx.doi.org/10.1787/888932506951

Distribution of general government expenditures across levels of government

Percentage, 2009

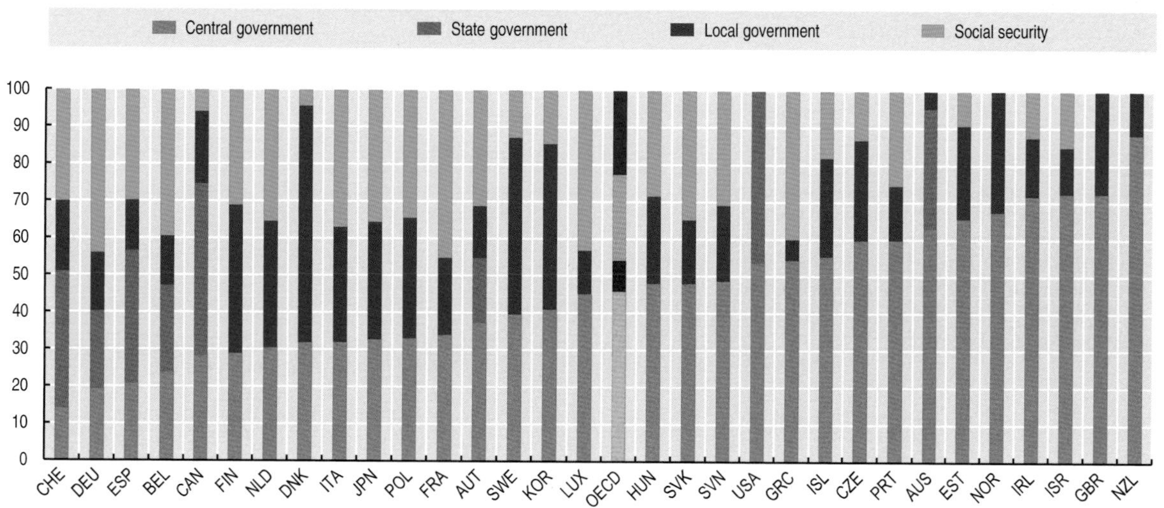

StatLink http://dx.doi.org/10.1787/888932506970

GENERAL GOVERNMENT EXPENDITURES AND REVENUES PER CAPITA

Governments spend money to provide goods and services and redistribute income. To finance these activities governments raise money in the form of revenues (*e.g.* taxation) and/or borrowing. The amount of revenues collected or the expenditures spent per capita are two ways of comparing the size of government across countries. Variations across countries however can also reflect different approaches to the delivery of public services (*e.g.* such as the use of tax breaks rather than direct expenditures). Additionally, both revenues and expenditures are heavily influenced by economic fluctuations. The recent global and financial crisis had a strong negative impact on government revenues in many OECD countries.

Definition

The general government sector consists of central, state and local governments and the social security funds controlled by these units. Data on government expenditures and revenues are derived from the *OECD National Accounts Statistics*, which are based on the System of National Accounts, a set of internationally agreed concepts, definitions, classifications and rules for national accounting. The underlying population estimates are based on the System of National Accounts notion of residency. They include persons who are resident in a country for one year or more, regardless of their citizenship, and also include foreign diplomatic personnel, and defence personnel, together with their families, and students studying and patients seeking treatment abroad, even if they stay abroad for more than one year. The "one year" rule means that usual residents who live abroad for less than one year are included in the population, while foreign visitors (for example, vacationers) who are in the country for less than one year are excluded.

Government revenues and expenditures per capita were calculated by converting these data to USD 2009 using the OECD/Eurostat purchasing power parities (PPP) for GDP and dividing by the population. For the countries whose source is the *IMF Economic Outlook*, an implied PPP conversion rate was used. PPP is the number of units of country B's currency needed to purchase the same quantity of goods and services in country A.

Comparability

Data are based on the 1993 *System of National Accounts* or on the 1995 *European System of Accounts* so that all countries are using a common set of definitions. Differences in the amounts of government revenues and expenditures per capita in some countries can be related to the fact that individuals may feature as employees of one country (contributing to the GDP of that country via production), but residents of another (with their wages and salaries reflected in the Gross National Income of their resident country). Data for Australia, Japan, Korea, New Zealand and the Russian Federation refer to 2008 rather than 2009.

Overview

On average in the OECD area, governments collected nearly USD 14 000 per capita in revenues in 2009, while spending about USD 15 000 per capita in the same year.

Luxembourg and Norway collected the most government revenues per capita in the OECD, topping more than USD 30 000 per person, reflecting the importance of cross-border workers and corporate tax in Luxembourg, and of oil revenues in Norway. These countries also spent the most per citizen (about USD 26 000 and 36 000 respectively) in terms of government expenditures.

The governments of Turkey, Mexico and Chile collected the least revenues per capita; below USD 5 000 in 2009. Likewise, government expenditures in these countries were also much lower than average (under USD 6 000 per capita). In general central European countries also collect comparatively less revenues per capita, and also spend less than most OECD countries.

All countries except Israel experienced increases in government expenditures per capita between 2000 and 2009. Estonia and Korea experienced real annual growth in government revenues and expenditures per capita of over 6% between 2000 and 2009. During this same period, the United States, Canada, Israel, Italy and Spain reduced revenues collected per capita.

Sources

- OECD (2011), *Government at a Glance*, OECD Publishing.

Further information

Analytical publications

- OECD (2011), *Making the Most of Public Investment in a Tight Fiscal Environment: Multi-level Governance Lessons from the Crisis*, OECD Publishing.

Statistical publications

- OECD (2011), *National Accounts at a Glance*, OECD Publishing.
- OECD (2011), *National Accounts of OECD Countries*, OECD Publishing.

Online databases

- *"General Government Accounts: Main aggregates", OECD National Accounts Statistics.*
- *"National Accounts at a Glance", OECD National Accounts Statistics.*

Websites

- Government at a Glance (supplementary material), *www.oecd.org/gov/indicators/govataglance.*

General government revenues per capita

Thousand US dollars, current prices and PPPs, 2009

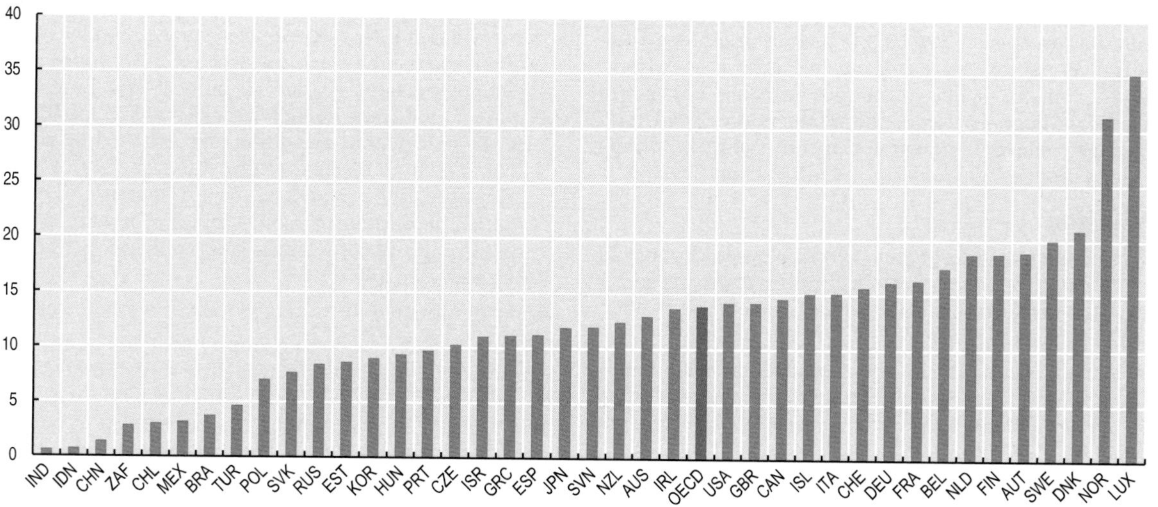

StatLink http://dx.doi.org/10.1787/888932506989

General government expenditures per capita

Thousand US dollars, current prices and PPPs, 2009

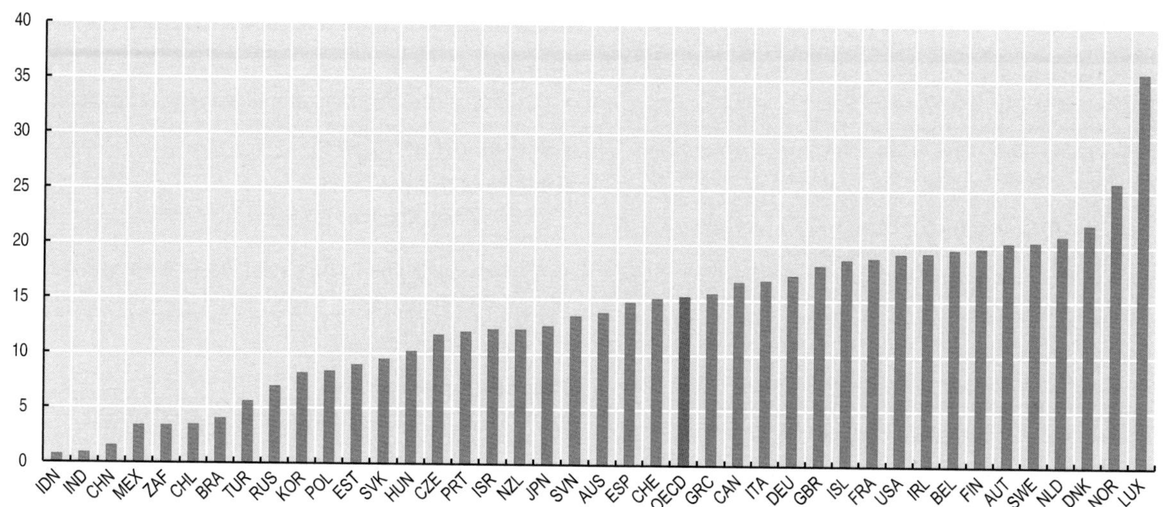

StatLink http://dx.doi.org/10.1787/888932507008

GENERAL GOVERNMENT PRODUCTION COSTS

Decisions on the amount and type of goods and services to produce, as well as on how best to produce them, are often political in nature and based on a country's social and cultural context. While some governments choose to outsource a large portion of the production of goods and services to non-governmental or private entities, others decide to produce the goods and services themselves.

Definition

Governments use a mix of their own employees, capital and outside contractors (non-profit institutions or private sector entities) to produce goods and services. The latter is often referred to as "outsourcing".

The concept and methodology of production costs builds on the existing classification of public expenditures in the 1993 *System of National Accounts*. Specifically, government production costs include:

i) Compensation costs of general government employees, including cash and in-kind remuneration plus all mandatory employer (and imputed) contributions to social insurance and voluntary contributions paid on behalf of employees;

ii) Costs of goods and services produced by non-government entities paid for by government (these include goods and services provided to both government and citizens). This includes intermediate consumption (procurement of intermediate products required for government production such as accounting or information technology services) and social transfers in kind via market producers (including those that are initially paid for by citizens but are ultimately refunded by government, such as medical treatments refunded by public social security payments). Social transfers in kind via market producers are used as a proxy for when governments pay a firm to deliver goods or services *directly* to the end user; and

iii) Consumption of fixed capital (depreciation of capital).

The data include government employment and intermediate consumption for output produced by the government for its own use, such as roads and other capital investment projects built by government employees. The production costs presented here are not equal to the value of output in the system of national accounts.

Comparability

Data are based on the *1993 System of National Accounts* or on the *1995 European System of Accounts* so that all countries are using a common set of definitions. However, cross-country differences in how employee pension schemes are funded can impair the comparison of compensation costs. In addition, some countries do not account separately for social transfers in-kind via market producers in their national accounts. Thus, the costs of goods and services produced by non-government entities paid for by government may be understated in these countries.

Data for Australia, Japan, Korea, New Zealand and the Russian Federation are for 2008 rather than 2009. Data for Mexico are for 2003 rather than 2000. Data for the Russian Federation are for 2002 rather than 2000. The OECD average for production costs as percentage of GDP does not include Turkey.

Overview

In 2009, the proportion of the economy devoted to producing government services and goods represented on average almost a quarter of GDP, varying significantly among OECD countries. For example, production costs of government services and goods as a percentage of GDP in Denmark were roughly three times higher than in Mexico reflecting, in part, the different roles for government in these countries.

On average, production by own employees is still more prevalent than outsourcing: compensation of employees accounts for 49% of the cost of producing goods and services, compared to 43% paid to non-governmental actors for intermediate goods and services or to deliver services directly to households. Consumption of fixed capital represents the remaining 9% of total production costs. The Netherlands and Germany, where close to 60% of the value of government goods and services is outsourced, rely more on corporations and non-profit institutions to produce goods and services than other OECD countries. Relatively higher expenditures in this area in the Netherlands could be due, in part, to the country's system of scholastic grants as well as the country's mandatory health insurance system whereby the government subsidises individuals' purchase of coverage from private providers.

Total production costs as a share of GDP increased in all but five OECD countries (Israel, Austria, the Slovak Republic, Australia and Poland) between 2000 and 2009. This increase was primarily driven by increases in outsourcing (the costs of goods and services produced by corporations and non-profit providers rose by 1.5 percentage points) and to a lesser extent by increases in compensation costs of government employees (0.8 percentage points). These increases could reflect that governments are providing more goods and services and/or that input costs have increased.

Sources

- OECD (2011), *Government at a Glance*, OECD Publishing.

Further information

Analytical publications

- OECD (2008), *The State of the Public Service*, OECD Publishing.
- Pilichowski, E. and E. Turkisch (2008), "Employment in Government in the Perspective of the Production Costs of Goods and Services in the Public Domain", *OECD Working Papers on Public Governance*, No. 8.

Statistical publications

- OECD (2011), *National Accounts of OECD Countries*, OECD Publishing.

Online databases

- *"General Government Accounts: Main aggregates", OECD National Accounts Statistics.*

Websites

- Government at a Glance (supplementary material), *www.oecd.org/gov/indicators/govataglance.*

Production costs for general government

As a percentage of GDP, 2009

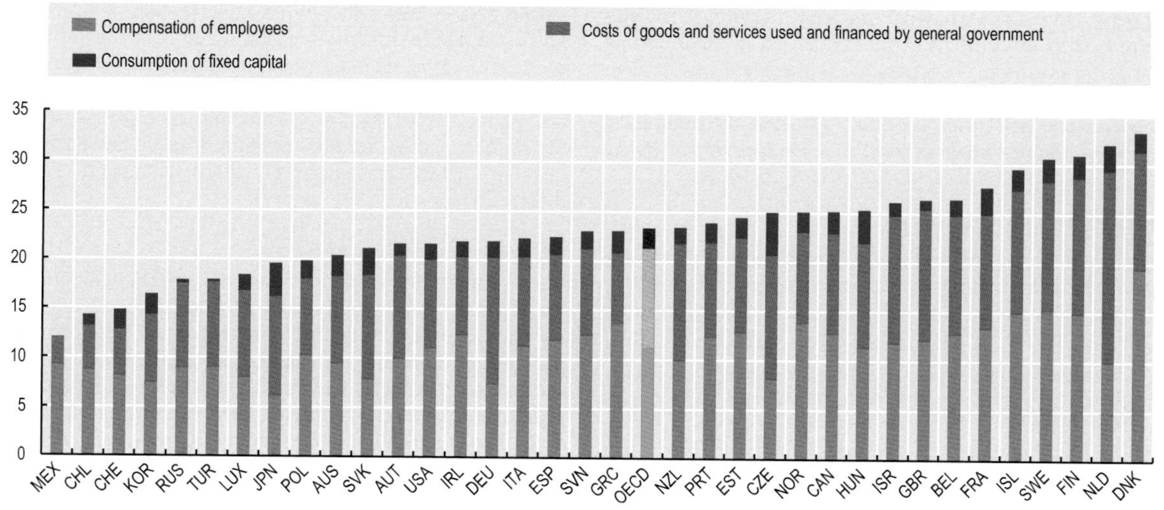

StatLink http://dx.doi.org/10.1787/888932507027

Structure of general government production costs

Percentage, 2009

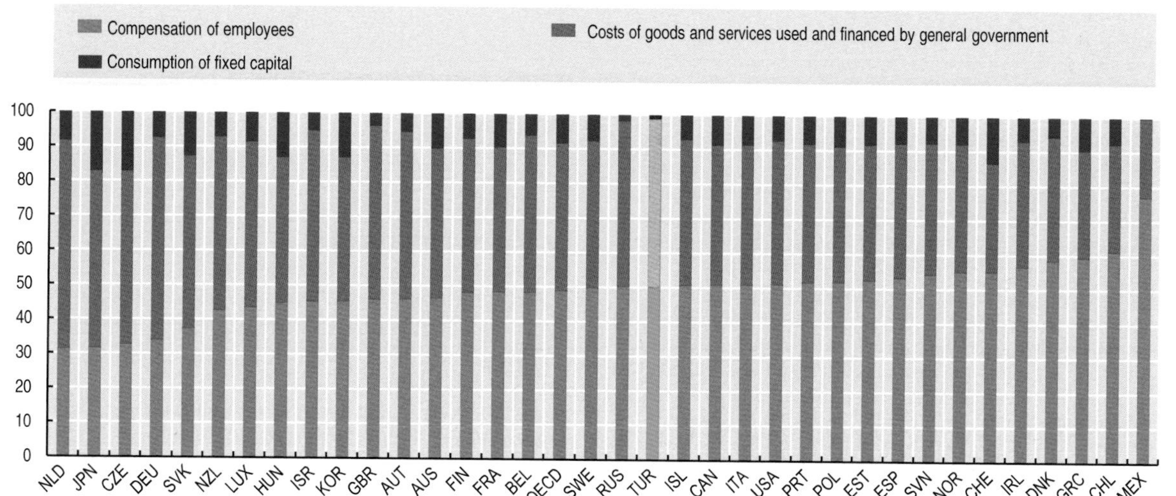

StatLink http://dx.doi.org/10.1787/888932507046

TRANSPARENCY IN GOVERNMENT DECISION MAKING

Ensuring that government decision making is not compromised by conflicts of interest is key to maintaining trust in government. Transparency is therefore essential to hold governments to account and maintain confidence in public institutions. It improves policy outcomes by minimising the risk of fraud, corruption and mismanagement of public funds, and supports a level playing field for business.

Definition

Laws on access to information (FOI laws) grant and regulate the right of individuals to access information held by government. Proactive disclosure (also known as "affirmative publication") ensures that information seekers get immediate access to public information and avoid the costs of filing a request or engaging in administrative procedures. For public organisations, proactive disclosure can reduce the burden of complying with Freedom of Information (FOI) requests. In some cases, governments are compelled by law (either FOI laws or others) to proactively disclose certain types of information.

Comparability

Data were collected through the 2010 OECD Open Government Survey. This survey focused on collecting data on the scope and the implementation of freedom of (or access to) information laws at the central level of government. A section of the survey explored the extent to which information is proactively disseminated and is available electronically. Respondents to the survey were central government officials responsible for implementing open government initiatives. The survey was completed by 32 OECD countries as well as Brazil and the Russian Federation. Data are not available for Germany and Greece, although these countries do have freedom of information legislation in place. Luxembourg and Brazil are currently drafting laws on access to information. Freedom of information procedures in Austria are required to be published by the general law for administrative procedures.

Overview

All OECD countries are proactively publishing public information, and in 72% of them, proactive disclosure is required by FOI laws for certain categories of information. The type of information proactively disclosed varies across countries. While a majority of countries proactively disclose budget documents (94%), annual Ministry reports (84%), and audit reports (72%), only a smaller number (28%) proactively publish lists of public servants and their salaries. Chile, Estonia and Israel publish information on the salaries of all public servants, whereas Hungary, Italy, Mexico, the Netherlands, Turkey and the United Kingdom publish salary information for some public servants, such as managers at the top of salary scales.

Applying the principle of proactive disclosure is facilitated by the use of information and communication technologies (ICTs). Some 81% of OECD countries have developed central portals as a means of proactively disseminating information from a single location. In addition, ICTs provide opportunities to create new added-value services through the re-use of government-held information (such as geo-spatial data). Some 63% of OECD countries publish administrative data sets, and a majority have established provisions in laws or policies requiring electronic information to be published in formats that allow for re-use and manipulation of the information (*e.g.* open formats). Countries like Australia, New Zealand, the United Kingdom and the United States are providing access to public data in a reusable format through a central website (*e.g. data.gov*), and other countries (such as Chile and Spain) have taken steps in this direction.

Freedom of information laws–also referred to as access to information laws–allow the public to access information that is not proactively made available by governments. These laws contribute to strengthening transparency, enhancing government accountability and promoting informed participation in policy making. Today, all OECD member countries except Luxembourg have FOI legislation that covers the actions of at least the central government. However, the scope of these laws varies in terms of the institutions covered, reflecting different institutional and legal systems across countries. In about half of OECD countries, the laws extend to all branches of central government (legislative, judicial and executive) and in the majority of countries, all bodies that form the executive branch of the central government (*e.g.* Ministries/Departments and executive agencies) are subject to FOI legislation. Private entities managing public funds, such as those contracted by the government to provide services to citizens, are subject to FOI laws in over half of member countries.

Sources

- OECD (2011), *Government at a Glance*, OECD Publishing.

Further information

Analytical publications

- OECD (2011), *The Call for Innovative and Open Government: An Overview of Country Initiatives*, OECD Publishing.
- OECD (2009), *Focus on Citizens: Public Engagement for Better Policies and Services*, OECD Studies on Public Engagement, OECD Publishing.
- OECD (2005), "*Public Sector Modernisation: Open Government*", Policy Brief, OECD Publishing.
- OECD (2003), *Open Government: Fostering Dialogue with Civil Society*, OECD Publishing.

Websites

- Public Engagement, *www.oecd.org/gov/publicengagement*.
- Fighting Corruption in the Public Sector, *www.oecd.org/gov/ethics*.
- Government at a Glance (supplementary material), *www.oecd.org/gov/indicators/govataglance*.

Proactive disclosure of information by central government

2010

	Budget documents	Annual ministry reports, including accounts	Audit reports	All government policy reports	Commercial contracts over a stipulated threshold	List of public servants and their salaries	Administrative data sets	Information describing the types of records systems and their contents and uses	Information on internal procedures, manuals and guidelines	Description of the structure and function of government institutions	Annual report on freedom of information law	Freedom of information procedural information
Australia	⊙	●	⊙	○	⊙	○	⊙	●	●	●	⊙	●
Austria	⊙	○	⊙	○	○	○	⊙	○	⊙	⊙	○	⊙
Belgium	⊙	○	○	⊙	○	○	⊙	○	○	●	⊙	⊙
Canada	●	●	●	○	●	○	⊙	●	●	●	●	⊙
Chile	●	⊙	●	○	●	●	○	○	○	●	⊙	⊙
Czech Republic	●	●	○	○	○	○	○	○	●	●	●	●
Denmark	⊙	⊙	⊙	⊙	○	○	⊙	⊙	⊙	⊙	○	○
Estonia	●	●	●	●	●	●	●	●	●	●	●	●
Finland	●	●	●	●	●	○	●	●	⊙	⊙	○	●
France	●	●	○	⊙	○	○	○	○	○	●	●	●
Hungary	●	●	●	●	●	○	●	●	●	●	●	●
Iceland	⊙	⊙	⊙	⊙	○	⊙	⊙	○	⊙	⊙	⊙	⊙
Ireland	○	⊙	○	○	⊙	○	○	⊙	⊙	●	●	⊙
Israel	●	●	⊙	○	○	⊙	○	⊙	●	●	●	●
Italy	●	●	●	●	●	●	⊙	⊙	⊙	●	●	●
Japan	⊙	○	⊙	○	⊙	○	○	⊙	○	⊙	⊙	⊙
Korea	●	●	●	●	●	○	●	●	●	●	●	●
Luxembourg	⊙	⊙	○	○	○	○	○	⊙	○	⊙	○	○
Mexico	●	●	●	●	●	●	⊙	●	●	●	●	⊙
Netherlands	⊙	⊙	⊙	⊙	○	⊙	⊙	○	⊙	⊙	⊙	⊙
New Zealand	●	●	○	○	●	○	⊙	○	○	○	●	●
Norway	⊙	○	○	⊙	○	○	○	⊙	⊙	⊙	○	⊙
Poland	○	●	○	○	○	○	●	○	○	●	○	●
Portugal	●	●	●	⊙	●	○	○	●	●	●	●	○
Slovak Republic	●	○	○	●	○	○	⊙	⊙	⊙	●	○	●
Slovenia	●	●	●	●	○	○	●	●	●	●	●	●
Spain	●	●	●	○	●	○	⊙	⊙	●	●	○	○
Sweden	⊙	⊙	⊙	⊙	○	○	⊙	⊙	○	⊙	○	⊙
Switzerland	⊙	⊙	⊙	○	○	○	○	○	⊙	⊙	⊙	⊙
Turkey	●	●	●	⊙	○	●	○	●	○	●	●	●
United Kingdom	⊙	⊙	⊙	○	⊙	⊙	⊙	⊙	○	⊙	●	●
United States	⊙	⊙	⊙	⊙	⊙	○	⊙	●	●	●	●	●
OECD total												
● Required to be proactively published by FOI law	17	17	12	8	11	5	6	11	12	19	16	16
⊙ Not required by FOI law, but routinely published	13	10	11	10	5	4	15	11	10	11	7	12
○ Neither required nor routintely published	2	5	9	14	16	23	11	10	10	2	9	4
Brazil	⊙	⊙	⊙	⊙	⊙	⊙	⊙	⊙	⊙	⊙	○	○
Russian Federation	●	○	○	●	○	●	●	●	●	○	●	●

StatLink http://dx.doi.org/10.1787/888932507065

Breadth of central government freedom of information laws

2010

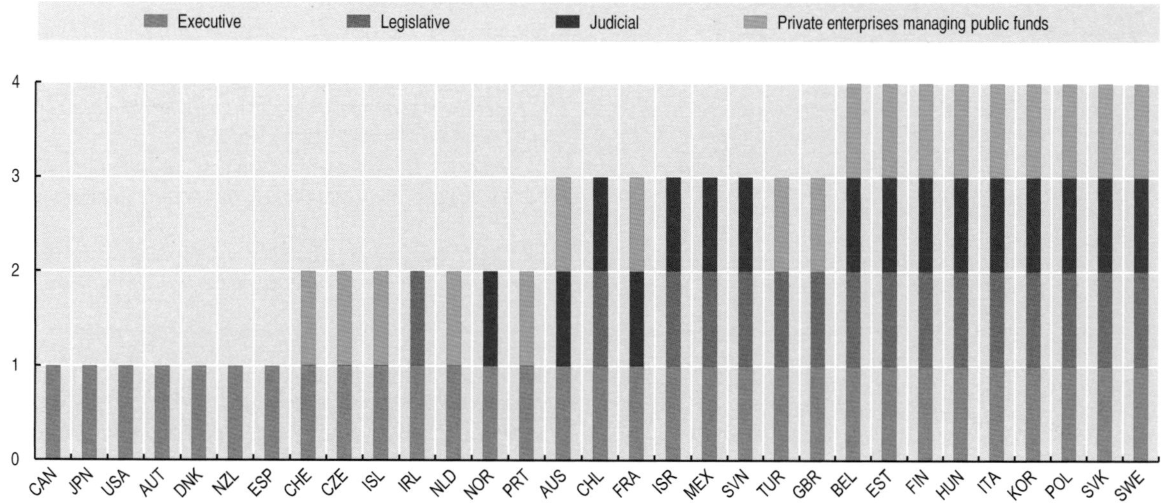

StatLink http://dx.doi.org/10.1787/888932507084

SOCIAL EXPENDITURE

Social expenditures are a measure of the extent to which countries assume responsibility for supporting the standard of living of disadvantaged or vulnerable groups.

Definition

Social expenditure comprises cash benefits, direct in-kind provision of goods and services, and tax breaks with social purposes. Benefits may be targeted at low-income households, the elderly, disabled, sick, unemployed, or young persons. To be considered "social", programmes have to involve either redistribution of resources across households or compulsory participation. Social benefits are classified as public when general government (that is central, state, and local governments, including social security funds) controls the relevant financial flows. All social benefits not provided by general government are considered private. Private transfers between households are not considered as "social" and not included here.

Comparability

For cross-country comparisons, the most commonly used indicator of social support is gross (before tax) public social expenditure relative to GDP. Measurement problems do exist, particularly with regard to spending by lower tiers of government, which may be underestimated in some countries. Data on private social spending are often of lesser quality than for public spending.

No data for private expenditure are currently collected for countries ranked separately on the left-hand side of the chart.

Overview

In 2007, on average, public social expenditure amounted to 19% of GDP. In France, public social spending is about 28% of GDP while it is 7% in Mexico.

Gross public social expenditure increased from about 16% in 1980 to 18% in 1990 and to 19% of GDP in 2007 across OECD countries. On average, public social spending-to-GDP ratios increased the most in the early 1980s, early 1990s and in the beginning of this millennium. In between these decennial turning points, spending-to-GDP ratios changed little; during the 1980s the average OECD public social spending to GDP ratio oscillated just below 17% of GDP while during the 1990s it was generally just below 20% of GDP after the economic downturn in the early 1990s.

The three biggest categories of social transfers are pensions (on average 7% of GDP), health (6%) and income transfers to the working-age population (4%). Public spending on other social services exceeds 5% of GDP only in the Nordic countries, where the public role in providing services to the elderly, the disabled and families is the most extensive.

There are also considerable differences across countries in the extent to which social protection systems rely on private provision. In 2007, gross private social spending was highest (at just over 10% of GDP) in the United States and lowest (at less than 1% of GDP) in the Czech Republic, Estonia, Hungary, Israel, Mexico, New Zealand, Poland, Spain and Turkey. In some OECD countries, the role of private social benefits has increased in recent years, especially in Canada, the Netherlands and the United States. Reductions in the generosity of public employment-related social benefits (sickness and incapacity related income support) since the 1980s have encouraged the growth of private benefits to top-up public programmes. In Denmark, the Netherlands and Sweden, governments have legislated increased employer's responsibility for the provision of sickness benefits during the first part of the 1990s.

Sources

- OECD (2011), *Social Expenditure Statistics* (database).

Further information

Analytical publications

- Adema, W., P. Fron and M. Ladaique (2011), *Is The European Welfare State Really more Expensive? Indicators on Social Spending, 1980-2012; and a Manual to the OECD Social Expenditure Database (SOCX)*, *OECD Social, Employment and Migration Working Papers*, No. 124.
- OECD (2011), *Doing Better for Families*, OECD Publishing.
- OECD (2011), *Society at a Glance: OECD Social Indicators*, OECD Publishing.
- OECD (2010), *Sickness, Disability and Work: Breaking the Barriers: A Synthesis of Findings across OECD Countries*, OECD Publishing.

Websites

- Social Expenditure (supplementary material), *www.oecd.org/els/social/expenditure*.
- Sickness, Disability and Work (supplementary material), *www.oecd.org/els/disability*.
- Statistics, Data and Indicators on Social and Welfare Issues, *www.oecd.org/social/statistics*.

Public and private social expenditure

As a percentage of GDP

	Public expenditure							Private expenditure						
	1990	1995	2000	2004	2005	2006	2007	1990	1995	2000	2004	2005	2006	2007
Australia	13.1	16.2	17.3	17.1	16.5	16.1	16.0	0.8	3.6	4.4	2.8	2.9	2.9	3.8
Austria	23.8	26.6	26.7	27.7	27.4	27.0	26.4	2.2	2.1	1.9	1.9	1.9	1.8	1.8
Belgium	24.9	26.3	25.4	26.5	26.4	26.4	26.3	1.6	2.1	2.4	4.1	4.5	5.3	4.7
Canada	18.1	18.9	16.5	17.1	17.0	16.9	16.9	3.3	4.4	5.0	5.5	5.5	5.5	5.3
Chile	10.2	11.4	13.2	11.7	11.2	10.5	10.6	0.6	1.2	1.2	1.5	1.4	1.3	1.2
Czech Republic	16.0	18.2	19.8	19.7	19.5	19.1	18.8	..	0.1	0.4	0.3	0.4	0.4	0.4
Denmark	25.1	28.9	25.7	27.7	27.2	26.6	26.1	2.1	2.4	2.4	2.6	2.6	2.5	2.6
Estonia	..	-	14.1	13.5	13.2	12.8	13.0	..	..	..	-	-	-	-
Finland	24.1	30.7	24.2	25.9	26.0	25.8	24.8	1.1	1.3	1.2	1.2	1.1	1.1	1.1
France	24.9	28.5	27.7	29.0	29.0	28.6	28.4	1.9	2.3	2.6	2.9	3.0	3.0	2.9
Germany	21.7	26.8	26.6	27.1	27.2	26.1	25.2	3.0	3.1	3.0	3.0	3.0	2.9	2.9
Greece	16.5	17.3	19.2	19.9	21.0	21.3	21.3	2.1	1.9	2.1	1.8	1.7	1.6	1.5
Hungary	..	..	20.3	21.6	22.6	22.9	22.9	..	..	-	0.1	0.1	0.2	0.2
Iceland	13.7	15.2	15.2	17.4	16.3	15.9	14.6	3.0	3.5	4.2	4.9	4.9	4.9	5.1
Ireland	14.9	15.7	13.3	16.0	15.8	15.8	16.3	1.4	1.7	1.4	1.5	1.5	1.5	1.5
Israel	..	16.7	17.1	17.1	16.5	15.9	15.5	..	..	0.2	0.4	0.4	0.5	0.5
Italy	20.0	19.9	23.3	24.7	25.0	25.1	24.9	4.0	4.1	2.2	2.1	2.0	2.1	2.1
Japan	11.3	14.3	16.5	18.2	18.6	18.4	18.7	0.3	0.5	3.8	3.5	3.0	2.9	3.6
Korea	2.8	3.2	4.8	6.0	6.4	7.4	7.6	0.4	2.3	2.8	2.2	2.3	2.5	2.6
Luxembourg	19.1	20.8	19.8	23.9	23.0	21.8	20.6	..	..	0.1	1.2	1.1	1.0	0.9
Mexico	3.3	4.3	5.3	6.6	6.9	7.0	7.2	0.1	0.1	0.1	0.2	0.2	0.2	0.2
Netherlands	25.6	23.8	19.8	21.1	20.7	20.3	20.1	6.1	6.7	7.3	8.2	8.2	7.0	6.9
New Zealand	21.5	18.7	19.1	17.7	18.1	19.0	18.4	0.2	0.5	0.5	0.4	0.4	0.5	0.4
Norway	22.3	23.3	21.3	23.3	21.7	20.4	20.8	1.9	1.7	2.0	2.3	2.1	2.0	2.0
Poland	14.9	22.6	20.5	21.4	21.0	20.8	19.8	..	..	..	-	-	-	-
Portugal	12.5	16.5	18.9	22.4	22.9	22.9	22.5	0.9	1.1	1.5	1.8	1.9	1.9	1.9
Slovak Republic	..	18.8	17.9	16.5	16.3	16.0	15.7	..	0.7	0.8	1.3	1.0	0.9	1.0
Slovenia	-	-	22.9	22.2	21.9	21.5	20.3	..	..	-	1.1	1.1	1.1	1.0
Spain	19.9	21.4	20.4	21.2	21.4	21.4	21.6	0.2	0.3	0.3	0.5	0.5	0.5	0.5
Sweden	30.2	32.0	28.4	29.5	29.1	28.4	27.3	1.2	2.4	2.6	2.9	3.0	2.9	2.9
Switzerland	13.5	17.5	17.8	20.2	20.2	19.2	18.5	5.3	7.6	8.3	8.6	8.4	8.2	8.3
Turkey	5.7	5.6	..	..	9.9	10.0	10.5	-	-	-	-	-	-	-
United Kingdom	16.8	19.9	18.6	20.5	20.6	20.4	20.5	5.1	6.6	7.5	5.9	6.1	6.1	5.8
United States	13.5	15.4	14.5	15.9	15.8	16.0	16.2	7.6	8.3	9.1	10.0	10.0	10.2	10.5
OECD total	17.6	19.4	18.9	19.9	19.8	19.5	19.2	1.8	2.3	2.4	2.5	2.5	2.5	2.5

StatLink http://dx.doi.org/10.1787/888932507103

Public and private social expenditure

As a percentage of GDP, 2007

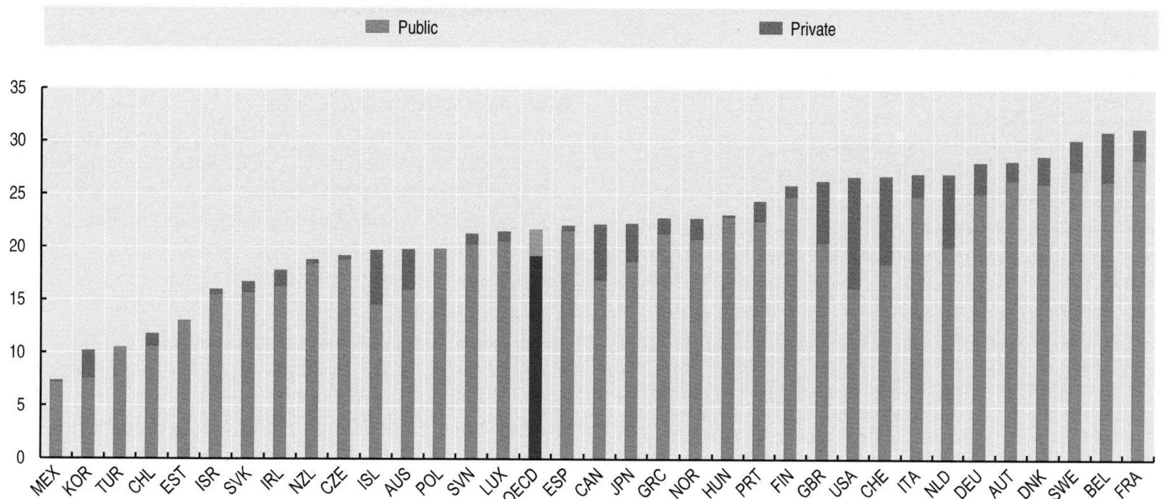

StatLink http://dx.doi.org/10.1787/888932507122

PENSION EXPENDITURE

Pension systems vary across countries and no single model fits all. Generally, there is a mix of public and private provision. Public pensions are statutory, most often financed on a pay-as-you-go (PAYG) basis – where current contributions pay for current benefits – and managed by public institutions. Private pensions are in some cases mandatory but more usually voluntary, funded, employment-based (occupational) pension plans or individual retirement savings plans (personal pensions).

Definition

Old-age pension benefits are treated as public when relevant financial flows are controlled by general government (*i.e.* central and local governments or social security funds). Pension benefits provided by governments to their own employees and paid directly out of the government's current budget are also considered to be public. Public pensions are generally financed on a PAYG basis, but also include some funded arrangements. All pension benefits not provided by general government are within the private domain.

Private expenditures on pensions include payments made to private pension plan members (or dependants) after retirement. All types of plans are included (occupational and personal, mandatory and voluntary, funded and book reserved), covering persons working in both the public and private sectors.

Outlays on public and private pension benefits are expressed as a percentage of GDP. The data are shown for old-age and survivors cash benefits.

Comparability

Public pension expenditures come from the *OECD Social Expenditure* (SOCX) *Database* while pension expenditures for private pension arrangements come from the *OECD Global Pension Statistics* (GPS) *Database*. The GPS database provides information on funded pension arrangements, which includes both private and public pension plans that are funded. However, only private expenditures are considered for this indicator. At the time of writing, only data up until 2007 were available in the SOCX Database.

The GPS Database does not cover all types of private pension arrangements for all countries: the private pension data for Austria, Canada, Germany, Luxembourg and the United States include only autonomous pension funds. The break in series for Mexico reflects the inclusion of occupational pension plans registered by CONSAR since 2005.

No data for private expenditure are currently collected for countries ranked separately on the left-hand side of the chart.

Overview

Public spending on old-age benefits averaged 7.0% of GDP in 2007, compared with private pension benefits of an average of 1.9% of GDP in the same year (in the countries for which data are available). Public spending on old-age pensions is highest – greater than 10% of GDP – in Austria, France, Germany, Greece, Italy, Poland and Portugal. By contrast, Australia, Iceland, Ireland, Korea and Mexico spend 4% of GDP or less on public old-age pensions.

Private expenditure on old-age benefits is the highest in Australia, Denmark, Iceland, the Netherlands and Switzerland, where it exceeds 3.5% of GDP. However, private benefit spending is negligible in around a third of OECD countries.

The share of private pensions in total expenditures on old-age benefits exceeds 50% only in Australia and Iceland. The average share of private pensions in the total is 21%.

Over time, public pension expenditures have grown a little faster than national income: from an average of 6.4% of GDP in 1990 to 7.0% in 2007.

Expenditure in private pensions has also grown between 2001 and 2009, from an average of 1.8% of GDP in 2001 to 2.3% in 2009.

In recent years, there has been a shift towards funding and private sector management within statutory pension systems. This trend has been especially strong in Latin America and Central and Eastern Europe. Although negligible now, private pension expenditures in the future will be much higher in Hungary, Mexico, Poland and the Slovak Republic, for example. Other OECD countries with mandatory private pensions include Australia, Iceland, Norway, Sweden and Switzerland.

Sources

- OECD (2011), *OECD Pensions Statistics* (database).
- OECD (2011), *OECD Social Expenditure Statistics* (database).

Further information

Analytical publications

- OECD (2011), *OECD Pensions at a Glance*, OECD Publishing.
- OECD (2009), *Pensions at a Glance: Asia/Pacific*, OECD Publishing.
- OECD (2008), *Complementary and Private Pensions throughout the World 2008*, OECD Publishing.
- OECD (2008), *OECD Private Pensions Outlook*, OECD Publishing.

Methodological publications

- Adema, W. and M. Einerhand (1998), "The Growing Role of Private Social Benefits", *OECD Labour Market and Social Policy Occasional Papers*, No. 32.
- OECD (2005), *Private Pensions: OECD Classification and Glossary*, OECD Publishing.

Websites

- Pension Markets in Focus, *www.oecd.org/daf/pensions/pensionmarkets*.
- OECD Pensions at a Glance (supplementary material), *www.oecd.org/els/social/pensions/PAG*.
- OECD Private Pensions Outlook (supplementary material), *www.oecd.org/daf/pensions/outlook*.
- Social Expenditure Database (SOCX), *www.oecd.org/els/social/expenditure*.

Public and private expenditure on pension

As a percentage of GDP

	Public expenditure							Private expenditure						
	1990	1995	2000	2004	2005	2006	2007	2003	2004	2005	2006	2007	2008	2009
Australia	3.0	3.6	3.8	3.5	3.3	3.3	3.4	4.3	3.6	3.7	3.9	3.4	5.5	4.6
Austria	11.4	12.3	12.3	12.7	12.5	12.4	12.3	0.2	0.2	0.2	0.2	0.3	0.2	0.2
Belgium	9.1	9.4	8.9	9.0	9.0	8.9	8.9	1.4	1.4	1.3	1.3	2.8	2.6	3.3
Canada	4.2	4.7	4.3	4.2	4.2	4.2	4.2	2.1	2.2	2.0	2.2	2.2	2.3	2.7
Chile	8.3	6.9	7.5	6.4	5.9	5.4	5.2	2.0	2.0	1.8	1.6	0.9	1.9	..
Czech Republic	6.1	6.3	7.5	7.1	7.3	7.2	7.4	0.2	0.2	..	..	0.3	0.3	0.4
Denmark	5.1	6.2	5.3	5.3	5.4	5.5	5.6	3.2	3.2	3.4	3.8	3.3	4.1	4.3
Estonia	..	..	6.0	5.5	5.3	5.3	5.2	..	..	..	..	..	..	0.0
Finland	7.3	8.8	7.7	8.3	8.4	8.5	8.3	..	..	..	0.5	0.5	0.5	0.7
France	10.6	12.0	11.8	12.2	12.3	12.4	12.5	..	..	..	..	..	..	..
Germany	9.7	10.7	11.2	11.6	11.5	11.1	10.7	0.1	0.1	0.1	0.1	0.1	0.1	0.3
Greece	9.9	9.6	10.7	11.1	11.7	11.8	11.9	..	..	..	..	0.0	0.0	0.0
Hungary	..	..	7.4	8.0	8.6	8.7	9.1	0.1	0.1	0.2	0.1	0.2	0.2	0.2
Iceland	2.2	2.4	2.2	2.1	2.0	1.8	1.9	3.4	3.4	3.4	3.5	3.7	3.8	6.3
Ireland	3.9	3.5	3.1	3.4	3.4	3.4	3.6	..	..	..	..	..	..	..
Israel	..	4.7	4.9	5.4	5.1	4.9	4.8	1.8	1.7	1.7	1.8	1.7	1.7	1.7
Italy	10.1	11.3	13.6	13.8	14.0	14.0	14.1	..	..	0.2	0.2	0.2	0.3	0.2
Japan	4.9	6.1	7.4	8.5	8.7	8.7	8.8	..	..	..	..	..	..	..
Korea	0.7	1.2	1.4	1.4	1.5	1.6	1.7	1.0	0.6	0.8	0.9	1.0	0.8	0.7
Luxembourg	8.2	8.8	7.5	7.3	7.2	6.8	6.5	..	..	0.1	0.1	0.1	0.1	0.1
Mexico	0.5	0.7	0.9	1.1	1.2	1.2	1.4	0.1	0.1	0.1	0.2	0.3	0.3	0.2
Netherlands	6.7	5.8	5.0	5.0	5.0	4.8	4.7	3.2	3.4	3.5	3.6	3.6	3.6	3.9
New Zealand	7.4	5.7	5.0	4.3	4.3	4.3	4.3	1.8	1.4	1.3	1.5	1.3	1.4	1.9
Norway	5.6	5.5	4.8	5.1	4.8	4.6	4.7	..	..	1.4	1.4	2.0	1.5	..
Poland	5.1	9.4	10.5	11.7	11.4	11.5	10.6	..	..	0.0	0.0	0.0	0.0	0.0
Portugal	4.9	7.2	7.9	9.9	10.3	10.6	10.8	0.9	0.9	0.9	1.0	1.0	1.4	1.0
Slovak Republic	..	6.3	6.3	6.2	6.2	6.0	5.9	..	..	..	..	..	..	..
Slovenia	..	..	10.6	10.2	9.9	10.0	9.6	..	..	..	..	0.0	0.0	0.0
Spain	7.9	9.0	8.6	8.1	8.1	8.0	8.0	0.4	0.5	0.5	0.6	0.5	0.6	0.6
Sweden	7.7	8.2	7.2	7.7	7.6	7.3	7.2	..	..	1.0	1.1	1.3	1.2	..
Switzerland	5.6	6.7	6.6	6.8	6.8	6.5	6.4	5.1	5.3	5.3	5.3	5.4	5.3	5.5
Turkey	2.4	2.7	..	..	5.9	5.8	6.1	..	0.0	0.0	0.0	0.0	0.1	0.1
United Kingdom	4.8	5.4	5.3	5.5	5.6	5.3	5.4	2.9	2.8	3.0	3.1	2.8	2.9	3.2
United States	6.1	6.3	5.9	6.0	6.0	5.9	6.0	2.8	2.9	2.9	3.1	3.3	3.0	..
OECD average	6.4	6.9	6.9	7.1	7.1	7.0	7.0	1.8	1.8	1.8	1.9	1.9	2.1	2.3

StatLink http://dx.doi.org/10.1787/888932507141

Public and private pension expenditure

As a percentage of GDP, 2007

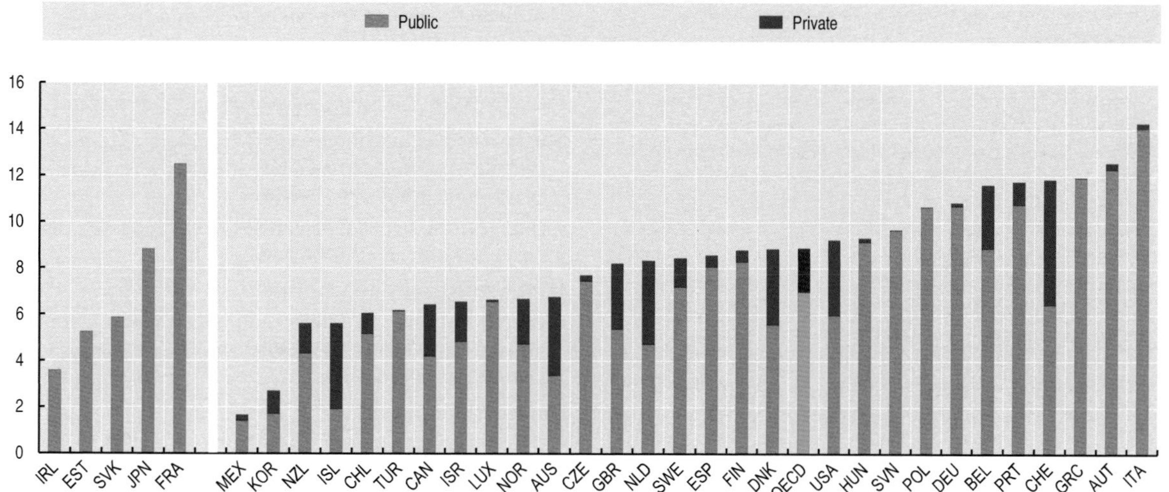

StatLink http://dx.doi.org/10.1787/888932507160

LAW, ORDER AND DEFENCE EXPENDITURE

Two essential tasks of every government are to protect its citizens from external aggression and maintain law and public order within its frontiers.

Definition

Data on public expenditures on law, order and defence are taken from national accounts sources, compiled according to the Classification of the Functions of Government (COFOG). These data cover all expenditures, whether current or capital, undertaken by general government.

Law and order covers expenditure for police forces, intelligence services, prisons and other correctional facilities, the judicial system, and ministries of internal affairs. Defence expenditures are those related to military and civil defence, military aid in the form of grants (in cash or in kind), loans (including equipment) and contributions to international peacekeeping forces, and research and development expenditures related to defence.

Comparability

National accounts data conform to the definitions of the 1993 *System of National Accounts* (SNA) and are broadly comparable across countries.

In the case of Japan, expenditure data on law, order and defence refer to fiscal years whereas GDP refers to calendar year. Data for New Zealand refer to fiscal years. Data for Australia are based on the 2008 SNA.

Public expenditure on defence

As a percentage of GDP

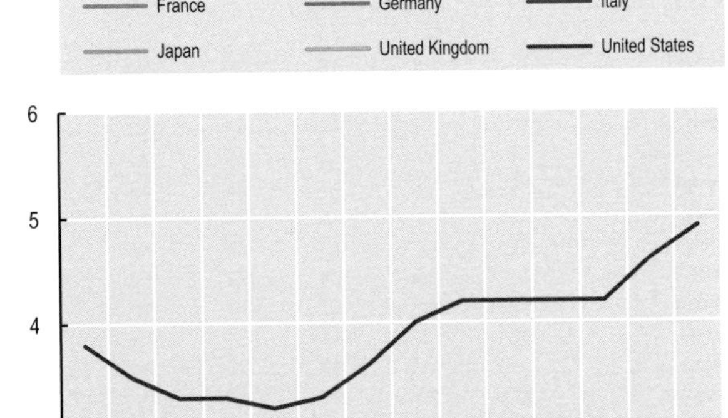

StatLink http://dx.doi.org/10.1787/888932507217

Overview

In 2009 – the latest year for which most countries can supply data – public expenditure on defence, as a share of GDP, was highest in Israel, the United States, Greece and Korea and lowest in Iceland, Luxembourg, Ireland, Austria, Hungary and Switzerland who spent less than 1% of GDP on defence. For the majority of OECD countries these shares have been either falling or have remained steady since 2003 (the earliest data point presented in the table).

For public order and safety, in 2009 – the latest year for which most countries can supply data – the United Kingdom, the Slovak Republic, Estonia, the United States, Portugal, the Czech Republic and Spain recorded a ratio above 2% of GDP. At the other end of the spectrum, Luxembourg, and Norway, at 1% of GDP, spent the lowest amount.

Sources

- OECD (2011), *National Accounts of OECD Countries*, OECD Publishing.

Further information

Analytical publications

- OECD (2004), *The Security Economy*, OECD Publishing.

Statistical publications

- OECD (2011), *National Accounts at a Glance*, OECD Publishing.
- OECD (2011), *National Accounts of OECD Countries, General Government Accounts*, OECD Publishing.

Methodological publications

- United Nations, OECD, International Monetary Fund and Eurostat (eds.) (2010), *System of National Accounts 2008*, United Nations, Geneva.

Online databases

- *OECD National Accounts Statistics*.

GOVERNMENT EXPENDITURE, REVENUES AND DEFICITS

The government budget deficit provides information on how much government revenues fall short of government spending. It is an important indicator for assessing fiscal performance and more generally imbalances in the economy.

Definition

The net lending of the general government is the balancing item of the non-financial account for this sector and is equal to the difference between total revenue and total expenditure. A negative figure indicates a deficit. Data are based on the 1993 *System of National Accounts* (SNA) or – for the EU countries – on the 1995 *European System of Accounts* (ESA). The ESA definition of net lending differs from the Maastricht definition; therefore the numbers reported here may differ from those used in the European Union for the Excessive Deficit Procedure.

The general government sector consists of central, state and local government units together with social security funds controlled by those units. Revenues include taxes (on corporations and households, and those on income, wealth, production and imports), social security contributions, property income and others. Expenditure includes among others the compensation of civil servants, social security benefits, interest on public debt and subsidies.

Comparability

For OECD countries data are based on the SNA or ESA so that all countries are using a common set of definitions.

Overview

Over the last four decades, the fiscal balance in the OECD as a whole has been typically in deficit, oscillating around 3% of GDP. This, however, masks diversified levels and trends among the OECD countries. Following the global recession of 2008-09, the OECD fiscal balance increased to a record level in 2009. This reflected an increase in government expenditure from around 40% of GDP in the previous decade and a fall in revenues. As with the fiscal balance, there is a big variation in the shares of expenditure and revenues in the GDP across the OECD countries and over time.

General government revenues and expenditures

As a percentage of GDP

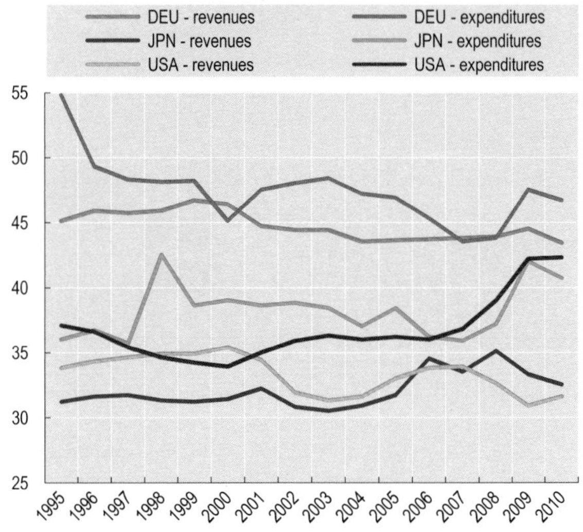

StatLink http://dx.doi.org/10.1787/888932535128

Sources

- OECD (2011), *OECD Economic Outlook*, OECD Publishing.

Further information

Analytical publications

- OECD (2011), *OECD Economic Surveys*, OECD Publishing.

Statistical publications

- OECD (2011), *National Accounts of OECD Countries*, OECD Publishing.

Methodological publications

- OECD (2008), *OECD Glossary of Statistical Terms*, OECD Publishing.

Online databases

- *OECD National Accounts Statistics.*
- *OECD Economic Outlook: Statistics and Projections.*

Websites

- OECD Economic Outlook – Sources and Methods, *www.oecd.org/eco/sources-and-methods.*

Public expenditure on law, order and defence

As a percentage of GDP

	Defence							Public order and safety						
	2004	2005	2006	2007	2008	2009	2010	2004	2005	2006	2007	2008	2009	2010
Austria	0.9	0.9	0.8	0.9	1.0	0.8	..	1.5	1.5	1.5	1.4	1.5	1.6	..
Belgium	1.1	1.1	1.0	1.0	1.1	1.1	..	1.7	1.7	1.7	1.7	1.8	1.9	..
Canada	1.0	1.1	1.0	..	..	..	..	1.6	1.6	1.6	..	..	..	..
Czech Republic	1.4	1.6	1.2	1.2	1.1	1.1	..	2.2	2.2	2.2	2.1	2.1	2.2	..
Denmark	1.6	1.5	1.7	1.6	1.5	1.5	1.4	1.0	1.0	1.0	1.0	1.1	1.2	1.1
Estonia	1.4	1.4	1.3	1.3	1.7	2.2	..	2.2	2.1	2.1	2.2	2.7	2.4	..
Finland	1.5	1.6	1.5	1.4	1.5	1.7	..	1.3	1.4	1.3	1.2	1.3	1.5	..
France	2.0	1.9	1.9	1.8	1.7	1.9	..	1.3	1.3	1.3	1.3	1.3	1.3	..
Germany	1.1	1.1	1.1	1.0	1.1	1.2	..	1.7	1.6	1.6	1.6	1.6	1.7	..
Greece	3.2	2.9	2.6	2.7	3.1	3.6	..	1.7	1.6	1.5	1.6	1.7	1.9	..
Hungary	1.3	1.3	1.4	1.3	0.9	0.8	..	2.1	2.0	2.2	2.0	2.0	2.0	..
Iceland	0.0	0.0	0.1	0.1	0.1	0.0	..	1.5	1.4	1.4	1.5	1.5	1.6	..
Ireland	0.5	0.4	0.4	0.4	0.5	0.5	..	1.5	1.5	1.5	1.6	1.9	2.0	..
Israel	8.1	8.0	8.0	7.5	7.3	6.7	..	1.7	1.7	1.6	1.7	1.7	1.7	..
Italy	1.4	1.4	1.3	1.3	1.4	1.6	..	1.9	1.9	1.9	1.8	1.9	2.0	..
Japan	1.0	1.0	0.9	0.9	0.9	1.0	..	1.4	1.5	1.4	1.4	1.4	1.5	..
Korea	2.3	2.5	2.5	2.5	2.7	2.8	..	1.2	1.2	1.3	1.3	1.3	1.4	..
Luxembourg	0.3	0.2	0.2	0.2	0.2	0.3	0.5	1.1	1.0	0.9	0.9	0.9	1.0	1.0
Netherlands	1.5	1.4	1.4	1.4	1.3	1.5	..	1.8	1.7	1.8	1.8	1.8	2.0	..
New Zealand	1.1	1.0	..	..	..	..	..	1.6	1.9	..	..	..	..	..
Norway	1.8	1.6	1.6	1.7	1.6	1.8	..	1.1	0.9	0.9	0.9	0.9	1.0	..
Poland	0.9	1.0	1.1	1.4	1.4	1.1	..	1.6	1.7	1.8	1.8	1.9	2.0	..
Portugal	1.3	1.4	1.3	1.2	1.2	1.4	..	1.9	2.0	1.9	1.8	2.0	2.2	..
Slovak Republic	1.9	1.6	1.7	1.5	1.3	1.5	..	2.3	2.0	2.1	2.0	2.2	2.6	..
Slovenia	1.3	1.3	1.5	1.5	1.4	1.5	..	1.9	1.7	1.7	1.6	1.6	1.7	..
Spain	1.1	1.1	1.0	1.0	1.0	1.0	..	1.8	1.8	1.8	1.9	2.0	2.1	..
Sweden	1.9	1.7	1.7	1.5	1.5	1.5	..	1.3	1.3	1.3	1.3	1.3	1.4	..
Switzerland	..	..	..	0.9	0.9	0.9	..	..	..	..	1.6	1.6	1.7	..
United Kingdom	2.5	2.5	2.5	2.4	2.5	2.7	..	2.5	2.6	2.5	2.5	2.6	2.8	..
United States	4.2	4.2	4.2	4.2	4.6	4.9	..	2.1	2.1	2.1	2.1	2.2	2.3	..

StatLink http://dx.doi.org/10.1787/888932507179

Public expenditure on law, order and defence

As a percentage of GDP

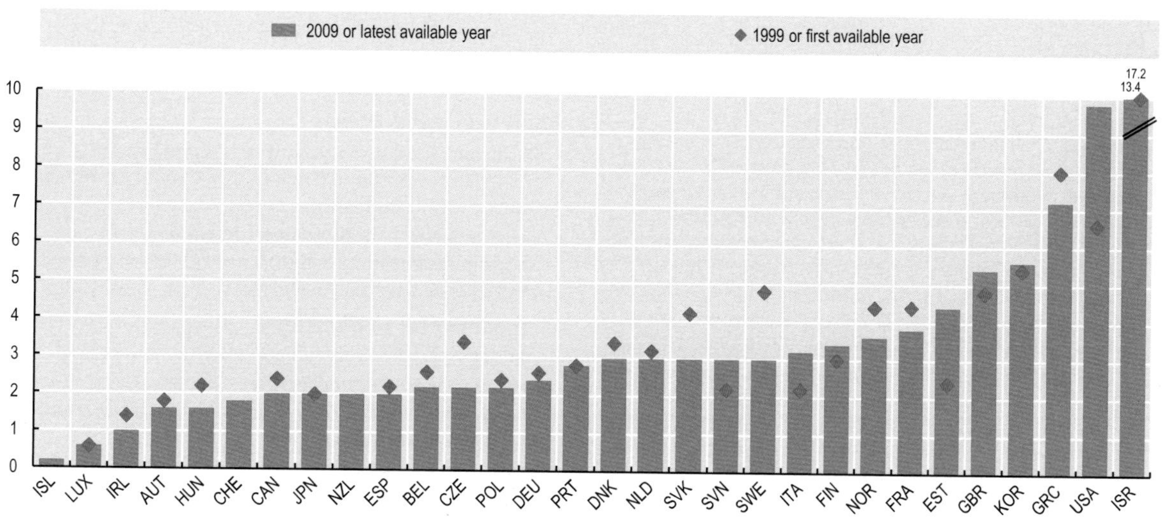

StatLink http://dx.doi.org/10.1787/888932507198

GOVERNMENT SUPPORT FOR AGRICULTURE

Governments provide support to agriculture through a variety of means, ranging from budgetary transfers financed by taxpayers to policies such as border protection and administered pricing that, by raising farm prices above the levels that would otherwise prevail, are equivalent to an implicit tax on consumers. While some of these measures may pursue commendable goals such as sustaining rural communities and encouraging more environmentally-friendly agricultural practices, they may also lead to production and trade distortions and environmental damage.

Definition

The OECD producer support estimate (PSE) is an indicator of the annual monetary value of gross transfers from consumers and taxpayers to agricultural producers, measured at the farmgate level, arising from policy measures that support agriculture, regardless of their nature, objectives or impacts on farm production or income. PSE can be expressed as a total monetary amount, but is usually quoted as a percentage of gross farm receipts. This is the measure used here.

The measure is agreed by OECD member countries and is widely recognised as the only reliable indicator for comparing support across countries and over time. The producer support estimate indicator is available on a timely and comprehensive basis for all OECD countries (the European Union is treated as a single entity) and selected emerging economies.

Comparability

Continuous efforts are made to ensure consistency in the treatment and completeness of coverage of policies in all OECD countries through the annual preparation of the *Monitoring and Evaluation* report. Each year, PSE provisional estimates are reviewed and approved by representatives of OECD's member countries, as are all methodological developments.

In the table, data are not shown for individual EU member countries. The level of support is calculated for EU12 for 1986-94, including ex-GDR from 1990; EU15 for 1995-2003; EU25 for 2004-06; and EU27 from 2007. The OECD total does not include the non-OECD EU member states.

Agricultural producer support estimate for selected countries

As a percentage of gross farm receipts

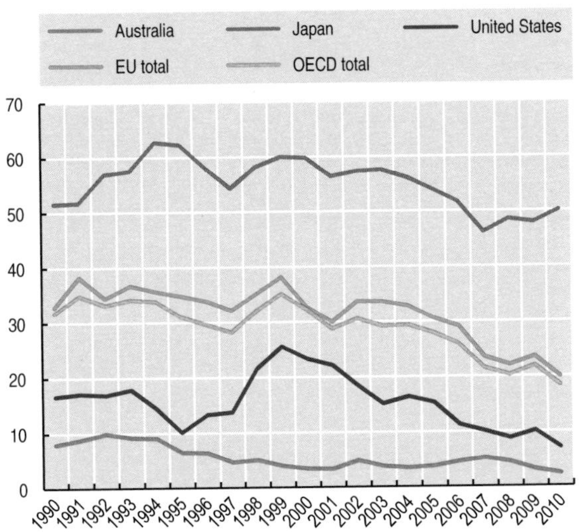

StatLink http://dx.doi.org/10.1787/888932507274

Overview

There are large differences in the levels of agricultural support among OECD countries. Producer support estimates as a percentage of gross farm receipts currently range from almost zero to 60%. These differences reflect, among other things, variations in policy objectives, different historical uses of policy instruments, and the varying pace and degrees of progress in agricultural policy reform. Over the longer term, the level of producer support has fallen in most OECD countries. The average support as a share of gross farm receipt in 2008-10, at 20%, is lower than the 1986-88 average of 37% and has fallen in most countries. There has also been some change in the way support is delivered to the sector. Support known to be the most distorting in terms of production and trade is also less dominant today (51% of total support during the 2008-10 period) than in the past (over 82% in 1986-1988).

For the emerging economies covered here producer support estimates as a percentage of farm receipts has been lower than the OECD average for Brazil, China, and South Africa, but higher for the Russian Federation, where it reached 22% and was above the OECD average in 2008-10. Trends in the level of producer support vary between economies. While in South Africa the level of producer support has fallen, in Brazil, China, and the Russian Federation it has increased since the mid-1990s.

Sources

- OECD (2011), *Agricultural Policy Monitoring and Evaluation 2011*, OECD Publishing.

Further information

Analytical publications

- OECD and Food and Agriculture Organization of the United Nations (FAO) (2011), *OECD-FAO Agricultural Outlook*, OECD Publishing.
- van Tongeren, F. (2008), "Agricultural Policy Design and Implementation: A Synthesis", *OECD Food, Agriculture and Fisheries Working Papers*, No. 7.

Methodological publications

- OECD (2010), "*Producer Support Estimate and Related Indicators of Agricultural Support: Concepts, Calculations, Interpretation and Use (The PSE Manual)*", OECD Trade and Agriculture Directorate.

Online databases

- *OECD Agriculture Statistics*.

Websites

- Producer and Consumer Support Estimates (supplementary material), *www.oecd.org/agriculture/pse*.

Agricultural producer support estimate by country

As a percentage of value of gross farm receipts

	1997	1998	1999	2000	2001	2002	2003	2004	2005	2006	2007	2008	2009	2010
Australia	4.6	4.9	3.9	3.3	3.3	4.7	3.7	3.4	3.7	4.5	5.1	4.4	3.0	2.2
Canada	13.9	16.0	17.2	19.3	15.5	20.5	24.4	20.3	21.3	20.8	16.4	13.1	17.3	17.7
Chile	8.0	10.5	10.4	11.2	6.2	9.3	5.3	4.9	5.0	4.2	6.3	3.2	4.4	2.9
Iceland	59.4	71.4	72.5	69.6	62.6	66.4	65.0	65.8	66.8	64.7	55.3	51.6	48.0	44.8
Israel	20.7	19.0	20.1	22.7	20.5	16.1	11.8	10.3	10.6	7.9	1.7	15.2	12.0	9.9
Japan	54.3	58.2	59.9	59.7	56.3	57.2	57.5	56.0	53.8	51.6	46.1	48.5	47.9	50.0
Korea	63.6	56.9	65.5	66.7	57.7	59.8	56.7	61.3	59.7	58.6	57.4	45.5	51.2	44.6
Mexico	14.6	17.6	17.3	23.4	18.2	26.8	19.2	11.6	12.9	13.2	12.9	12.0	12.8	12.1
New Zealand	0.9	0.8	0.8	0.3	0.6	0.3	0.7	0.7	1.3	0.9	0.7	0.6	0.4	0.5
Norway	68.3	70.8	71.2	66.5	65.3	73.7	71.1	66.4	65.9	64.1	54.6	59.3	60.9	60.6
Switzerland	69.1	71.6	75.2	69.8	67.3	70.6	69.2	69.3	66.2	65.4	48.6	54.4	59.5	53.9
Turkey	27.7	31.3	33.2	29.2	16.2	26.6	32.0	33.6	36.9	37.8	31.0	24.8	28.7	27.9
United States	13.7	21.6	25.5	23.3	22.1	18.4	15.1	16.3	15.3	11.2	10.0	8.8	10.1	7.0
EU total	32.1	35.2	38.2	32.7	30.0	33.6	33.6	32.8	30.5	29.1	23.4	22.0	23.5	19.8
OECD total	28.1	32.1	35.1	32.2	28.7	30.5	29.1	29.3	27.8	25.8	21.4	20.2	21.9	18.3
Brazil	-1.5	7.0	1.3	6.4	4.2	4.9	5.8	4.5	6.8	6.1	4.9	4.1	6.5	4.5
China	1.7	1.2	-2.6	3.0	4.7	8.4	10.1	7.5	8.5	12.3	10.1	3.3	13.2	17.4
Russian Federation	22.0	15.8	0.9	5.5	10.7	12.7	19.2	22.3	14.6	17.2	18.2	21.9	22.1	21.4
South Africa	10.8	10.5	8.0	5.8	3.7	10.1	7.1	7.9	6.2	9.2	4.2	3.1	4.3	2.2

StatLink http://dx.doi.org/10.1787/888932507236

Agricultural producer support estimate by country

As a percentage of value of gross farm receipts

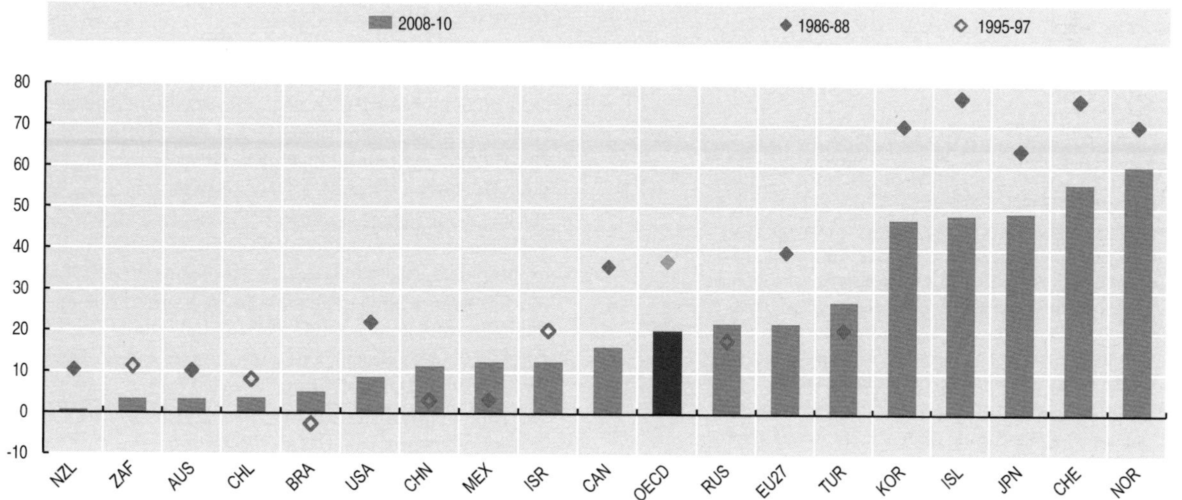

StatLink http://dx.doi.org/10.1787/888932507255

GOVERNMENT SUPPORT FOR FISHING

OECD governments provide financial support to the fishing industry, typically for the purposes of management, including surveillance and research. This financial support is important to ensure a sustainable and responsible fisheries sector.

Definition

The indicator on "Government financial transfers (GFTs)" provides a measure of the financial support provided by governments to the fisheries sector. GFT consists of direct revenue enhancing transfers (direct payments), *i.e.* transfers that reduce the operating costs and the costs of general services provided to the fishing industry. These general services consist mainly of fishery protection services and fisheries management; in some cases they also include the costs of local area weather forecasting and the costs of navigation and satellite surveillance systems designed to assist fishing fleets.

Comparability

The data are relatively comprehensive and consistent across the years. However, some year-to-year variations may reflect changes in national statistical systems. General services provided by governments may also include large and irregular capital investments. It should also be noted that some types of GFT (*e.g.* maritime surveillance) may be provided by another agency than fisheries agencies (*e.g.* in some countries maritime surveillance is carried out by the navy); some of these data may not be available. Also, some figures, in particular for later years, are still preliminary.

Overview

Total government support for fishing peaked at USD 6.7 billion in 2007, the last year for which comprehensive data are available. Overall, transfers to the fishing industry in OECD countries have been fluctuating at around the USD 6 to 7 billion mark over the past decade. The majority of GFTs are categorized as general services, accounting for around three quarters of the total GFTs. General services include in particular management and enforcement, and fisheries research. Other types of general services covered by GFTs include harbour construction and maintenance, as well as stock enhancement and habitat conservation.

Direct payments represent 15% of total GFTs. In 2007, USD 287 million were dedicated to decommissioning schemes, while USD 25 million were used to construct or modernize fishing vessels. Other direct payments include unemployment insurance (USD 244 million) and disaster relief (USD 266 million). The third category of GFTs, cost reducing transfers, accounted for 6% of the total GFTs.

GFT to fishing for selected countries

Million US dollars

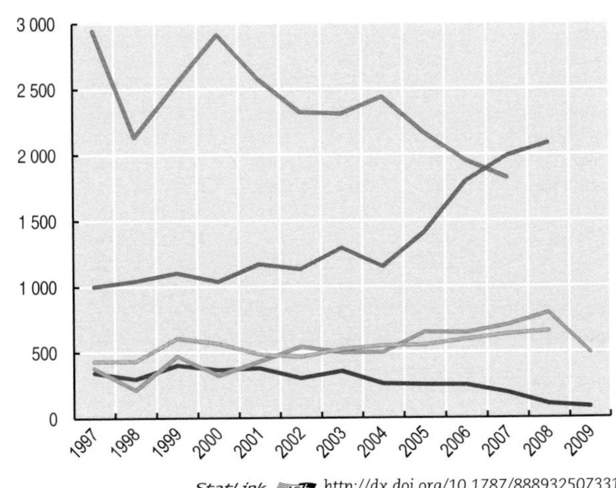

StatLink http://dx.doi.org/10.1787/888932507331

Sources

- OECD (2010), *Review of Fisheries in OECD Countries: Policies and Summary Statistics*, OECD Publishing.
- OECD (2007), *Review of Fisheries in OECD Countries: Country Statistics*, OECD Publishing.

Further information

Analytical publications

- Love, P. (2010), *Fisheries: While Stocks Last?*, OECD Insights, OECD Publishing.
- OECD (2009), *Reducing Fishing Capacity: Best Practices for Decommissioning Schemes*, OECD Publishing.
- OECD (2007), *Structural Change in Fisheries: Dealing with the Human Dimension*, OECD Publishing.
- OECD (2006), *Financial Support to Fisheries: Implications for Sustainable Development*, OECD Publishing.
- OECD (2006), *OECD Sustainable Development Studies – Subsidy Reform and Sustainable Development: Economic, Environmental and Social Aspects*, OECD Publishing.
- OECD (2005), *Environmentally Harmful Subsidies: Challenges for Reform*, OECD Publishing.
- OECD (2000), *Transition to Responsible Fisheries: Economic and Policy Implications*, OECD Publishing.
- OECD and Food and Agriculture Organization of the United Nations (FAO) (2008), *Globalisation and Fisheries – Proceedings of an OECD-FAO Workshop*, OECD Publishing.

Websites

- OECD Fisheries, *www.oecd.org/fisheries*.

Government financial transfers to fishing

Thousand US dollars

	1997	1998	1999	2000	2001	2002	2003	2004	2005	2006	2007	2008	2009
Australia	41 230	..	..	82 272	75 902	78 038	95 558	95 560	38 420	45 772	57 954	66 959	..
Belgium	4 949	..	4 473	6 849	2 830	1 607	1 668	6 328	8 613	7 132	3 288	1 268	9 132
Canada	433 309	..	606 443	564 497	483 982	464 257	522 581	547 923	553 193	595 220	634 525	657 050	..
Chile	..	..	..	..	..	..	..	..	..	..	39 351	48 247	64 462
Czech Republic	..	..	..	..	..	..	..	..	..	3 801	8 836	29 234	36 844
Denmark	82 030	90 507	27 765	16 316	..	68 769	37 659	28 505	58 108	89 991	63 717	82 139	81 722
Estonia	..	..	..	..	..	..	..	..	..	11 579	9 002	4 047	..
Finland	26 198	26 888	19 236	13 908	16 510	16 025	20 231	19 397	24 816	17 569	20 877	20 900	17 066
France	140 807	..	71 665	166 147	141 786	155 283	179 740	236 811	126 194	36 535	35 229	..	..
Germany	63 215	16 488	31 276	29 834	28 988	28 208	33 890	6 088	17 284	4 899	6 815	5 129	4 817
Greece	46 958	26 908	43 030	87 315	86 957	88 334	119 045	35 500	61 013	57 188	56 276	66 744	60 795
Iceland	38 678	36 954	39 763	41 978	28 310	28 955	48 348	55 705	64 326	51 331	61 459	45 489	31 043
Ireland	98 880	..	143 184	..	..	63 632	64 960	21 448	22 144	19 743	..	..	..
Italy	91 811	..	200 470	217 679	231 680	159 630	149 270	170 055	74 524	194 696	123 276	56 855	..
Japan	2 945 785	2 135 946	2 537 536	2 913 149	2 574 086	2 323 601	2 310 744	2 437 934	2 165 198	1 952 853	1 821 144	..	..
Korea	378 994	211 927	471 556	320 449	428 313	538 695	495 280	495 280	649 387	644 000	702 990	793 569	490 126
Mexico	16 808	..	..	..	..	..	177 000	114 000	84 973	88 760	85 267	..	..
Netherlands	35 849	..	..	1 389	12 779	12 443	6 569	5 218	13 685	18 501	5 635	42 726	3 206
New Zealand	40 397	29 412	29 630	27 273	15 126	18 981	38 325	29 973	37 147	37 926	40 545	41 805	..
Norway	163 437	153 046	180 962	104 564	99 465	156 340	139 200	142 315	149 521	188 488	237 347	261 244	253 826
Poland	7 927	..	..	..	..	..	..	..	97 327	34 264	28 326	..	..
Portugal	65 077	..	28 674	25 578	25 066	24 899	26 930	26 930	32 769	29 219	30 896	..	..
Spain	344 581	296 642	399 604	364 096	376 614	301 926	353 290	257 730	249 047	247 647	188 082	102 699	78 979
Sweden	53 452	26 960	31 053	25 186	22 505	24 753	30 650	51 129	49 780	50 057	89 310	92 766	66 789
Turkey	15 114	..	1 277	26 372	17 721	16 167	16 300	59 500	98 072	135 931	144 927	199 858	..
United Kingdom	128 066	90 833	75 968	81 394	73 738	64 743	81 997	87 863	90 579	103 347	..	..	..
United States	1 002 580	1 041 000	1 103 100	1 037 710	1 169 590	1 130 810	1 290 440	1 147 521	1 407 813	1 793 833	1 985 497	2 084 409	..
OECD total	6 258 205	4 183 511	6 046 665	6 153 955	5 949 321	5 734 867	6 307 763	6 080 611	6 173 933	6 456 480	6 671 916	4 919 816	..

StatLink http://dx.doi.org/10.1787/888932507293

Government financial transfers to fishing

Average annual growth in percentage, 1999-2009 or latest available period

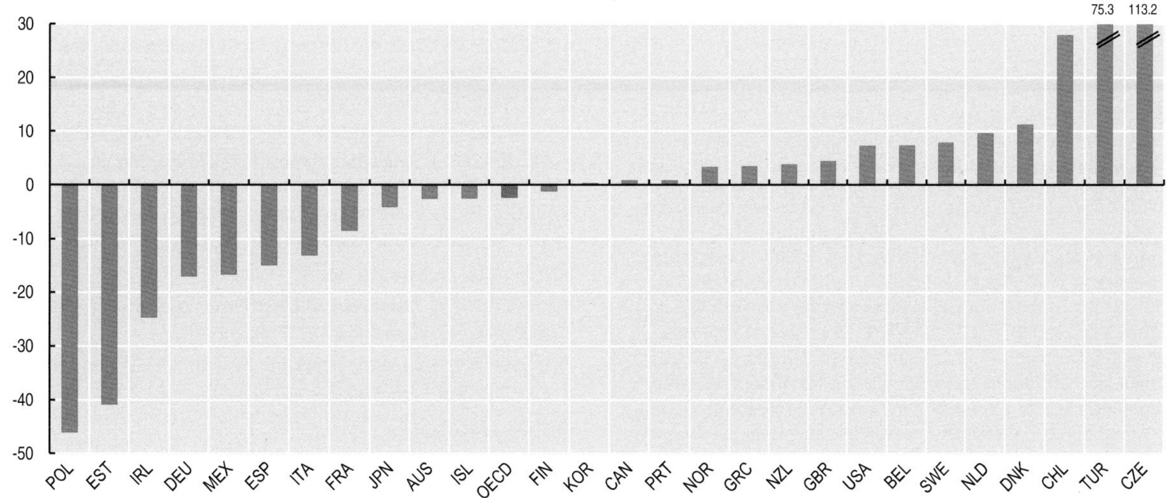

StatLink http://dx.doi.org/10.1787/888932507312

OFFICIAL DEVELOPMENT ASSISTANCE

Promoting economic and social development in non-member countries has been a principal objective of the OECD since its foundation. The share of national income devoted to official development assistance (ODA) is a test of a country's commitment to international development. A long-standing United Nations target is that developed countries should devote 0.7% of their gross national income (GNI) to ODA.

Definition

This section shows total net ODA as shares of GNI as well as the distribution by geographical region and income group of ODA.

ODA is defined as government aid designed to promote the economic development and welfare of developing countries. Loans and credits for military purposes are excluded. Aid may be provided bilaterally, from donor to recipient, or channelled through a multilateral development agency such as the United Nations or the World Bank. Aid includes grants, "soft" loans and the provision of technical assistance. Soft loans are those where the grant element is at least 25% of the total.

The OECD maintains a list of developing countries and territories; only aid to these countries counts as ODA. The list is periodically updated and currently contains over 150 countries or territories with per capita incomes below USD 11 456 in 2007. Data on ODA flows are provided by the 24 OECD members of the Development Assistance Committee (DAC).

Comparability

Statistics on ODA are compiled according to directives drawn up by the DAC. Each country's statistics are subject to regular peer reviews by other DAC members.

Overview

In 2010, total net ODA from DAC members reached the highest value ever recorded (USD 128.7 billion), representing an increase of 6.5% in real terms compared to 2009. The weighted average of total ODA as a percentage of their combined GNI, was 0.32% in 2010; the unweighted average, measuring "average country effort", was 0.49%. The decline in both the weighted and unweighted averages recorded since 1990 was halted in 1999 and then reversed as DAC members took steps to meet the commitments they made at the Monterrey 2002 Financing for Development Conference and at the Gleneagles G8 and UN Millennium +5 summits in 2005.

The volume of bilateral ODA development projects and programmes has been on a rising trend in recent years and increased significantly between 2007 and 2009, indicating that donors are considerably scaling up their core aid programmes.

Sources

- OECD (2011), *OECD International Development Statistics*, OECD Publishing.

Further information

Analytical publications

- OECD (2010), *Development Co-operation Report*, OECD Publishing.
- OECD (2010), *OECD Journal on Development*, OECD Publishing.
- OECD (2009), *Aid Effectiveness: A Progress Report on Implementing the Paris Declaration*, Better Aid, OECD Publishing.
- OECD (2009), *Natural Resources and Pro-Poor Growth: The Economics and Politics*, DAC Guidelines and Reference Series, OECD Publishing.
- OECD (2008), *2008 Survey on Monitoring the Paris Declaration: Making Aid More Effective by 2010*, Better Aid, OECD Publishing.
- OECD (2008), *Governance, Taxation and Accountability: Issues and Practice*, OECD Development Co-operation Directorate.

Statistical publications

- OECD (2011), *Geographical Distribution of Financial Flows to Developing Countries*, OECD Publishing.
- OECD (2010), *Creditor Reporting System*, OECD Publishing.
- OECD (2009), *Development Aid at a Glance*, OECD Publishing.

Online databases

- *OECD International Development Statistics*.

Websites

- OECD Aid Statistics, *www.oecd.org/dac/stats*.
- OECD Calculation of the Grant Element of Loans, *www.oecd.org/dac/stats/methodology*.

Net official development assistance

As a percentage of gross national income

	1997	1998	1999	2000	2001	2002	2003	2004	2005	2006	2007	2008	2009	2010
Australia	0.27	0.27	0.26	0.27	0.25	0.26	0.25	0.25	0.25	0.30	0.32	0.32	0.29	0.32
Austria	0.24	0.22	0.24	0.23	0.34	0.26	0.20	0.23	0.52	0.47	0.50	0.43	0.30	0.32
Belgium	0.31	0.35	0.30	0.36	0.37	0.43	0.60	0.41	0.53	0.50	0.43	0.48	0.55	0.64
Canada	0.34	0.30	0.28	0.25	0.22	0.28	0.24	0.27	0.34	0.29	0.29	0.33	0.30	0.33
Denmark	0.97	0.99	1.01	1.06	1.03	0.96	0.84	0.85	0.81	0.80	0.81	0.82	0.88	0.90
Finland	0.32	0.31	0.33	0.31	0.32	0.35	0.35	0.37	0.46	0.40	0.39	0.44	0.54	0.55
France	0.44	0.38	0.38	0.30	0.31	0.37	0.40	0.41	0.47	0.47	0.38	0.39	0.47	0.50
Germany	0.28	0.26	0.26	0.27	0.27	0.27	0.28	0.28	0.36	0.36	0.37	0.38	0.35	0.38
Greece	0.14	0.15	0.15	0.20	0.17	0.21	0.21	0.16	0.17	0.17	0.16	0.21	0.19	0.17
Ireland	0.31	0.30	0.31	0.29	0.33	0.40	0.39	0.39	0.42	0.54	0.55	0.59	0.54	0.53
Italy	0.11	0.20	0.15	0.13	0.15	0.20	0.17	0.15	0.29	0.20	0.19	0.22	0.16	0.15
Japan	0.21	0.27	0.27	0.28	0.23	0.23	0.20	0.19	0.28	0.25	0.17	0.19	0.18	0.20
Korea	0.04	0.05	0.07	0.04	0.06	0.05	0.06	0.06	0.10	0.05	0.07	0.09	0.10	0.12
Luxembourg	0.55	0.65	0.66	0.70	0.77	0.78	0.86	0.79	0.79	0.89	0.92	0.97	1.04	1.09
Netherlands	0.81	0.80	0.79	0.84	0.82	0.81	0.80	0.73	0.82	0.81	0.81	0.80	0.82	0.81
New Zealand	0.26	0.27	0.27	0.25	0.25	0.22	0.23	0.23	0.27	0.27	0.27	0.30	0.28	0.26
Norway	0.84	0.89	0.88	0.76	0.80	0.89	0.92	0.87	0.94	0.89	0.95	0.89	1.06	1.10
Portugal	0.25	0.24	0.26	0.26	0.25	0.27	0.22	0.63	0.21	0.21	0.22	0.27	0.23	0.29
Spain	0.24	0.24	0.23	0.22	0.30	0.26	0.23	0.24	0.27	0.32	0.37	0.45	0.46	0.43
Sweden	0.79	0.72	0.70	0.80	0.77	0.84	0.79	0.78	0.94	1.02	0.93	0.98	1.12	0.97
Switzerland	0.34	0.32	0.35	0.34	0.34	0.33	0.37	0.40	0.43	0.39	0.38	0.44	0.45	0.41
United Kingdom	0.26	0.27	0.24	0.32	0.32	0.31	0.34	0.36	0.47	0.51	0.36	0.43	0.51	0.56
United States	0.09	0.10	0.10	0.10	0.11	0.13	0.15	0.17	0.23	0.18	0.16	0.18	0.21	0.21
DAC total	0.22	0.23	0.22	0.22	0.22	0.23	0.24	0.25	0.32	0.30	0.27	0.30	0.31	0.32
***of which:** EU members*	0.33	0.33	0.31	0.32	0.33	0.35	0.35	0.35	0.44	0.43	0.39	0.43	0.44	0.46

StatLink http://dx.doi.org/10.1787/888932507350

Net official development assistance

2010

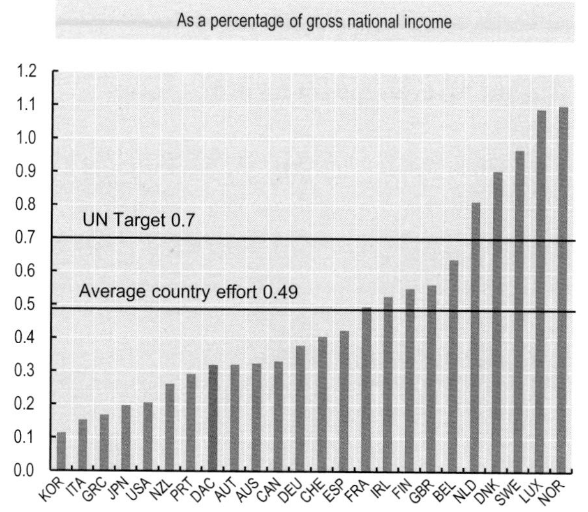

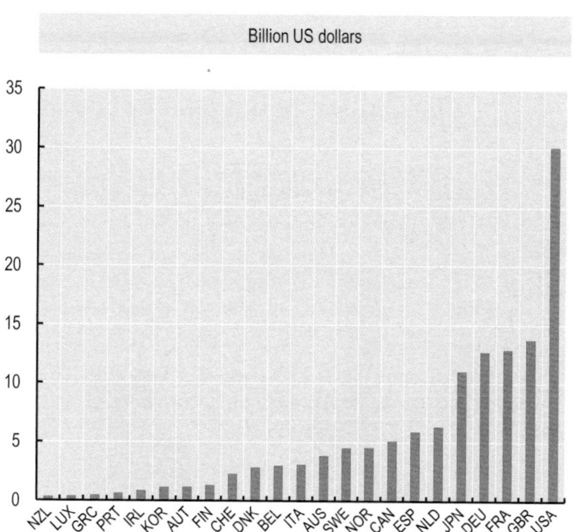

StatLink http://dx.doi.org/10.1787/888932507369

Distribution of net bilateral ODA from all sources by income group and by region

Million US dollars

	2005	2006	2007	2008	2009
Distribution of bilateral ODA by income group					
Least Developed Countries	25 967	28 476	32 973	38 627	39 940
Other Low-Income Countries	13 338	19 128	10 937	10 645	16 042
Lower Middle-Income Countries	43 411	28 916	29 023	31 769	26 452
Upper Middle-Income Countries	4 457	6 136	6 125	8 490	7 682
More Advanced Developing Countries and Territories	30	23	-116	-	-
Unallocated	21 238	23 869	27 832	37 125	37 410
Distribution of bilateral ODA by region					
Sub-Saharan Africa	32 368	40 379	34 661	39 229	42 266
Middle East and North Africa	28 129	16 886	17 459	23 193	13 639
South and Central Asia	11 611	11 360	13 059	15 945	18 213
Other Asia and Oceania	10 597	8 638	9 574	9 808	10 999
Europe	4 044	5 035	4 186	5 371	5 788
Latin America and Caribbean	6 708	7 340	6 987	9 288	9 089
Unspecified	14 985	16 910	20 849	23 821	27 532
Developing countries total	108 441	106 549	106 775	126 656	127 527

StatLink http://dx.doi.org/10.1787/888932507388

Distribution of net bilateral ODA from all sources by region

Million US dollars

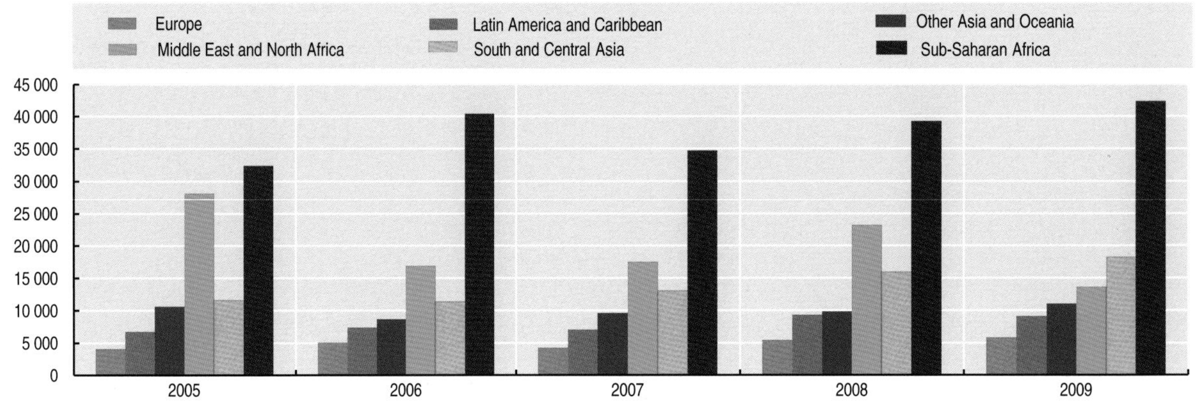

StatLink http://dx.doi.org/10.1787/888932507407

Distribution of net bilateral country ODA from all sources by income group

Million US dollars

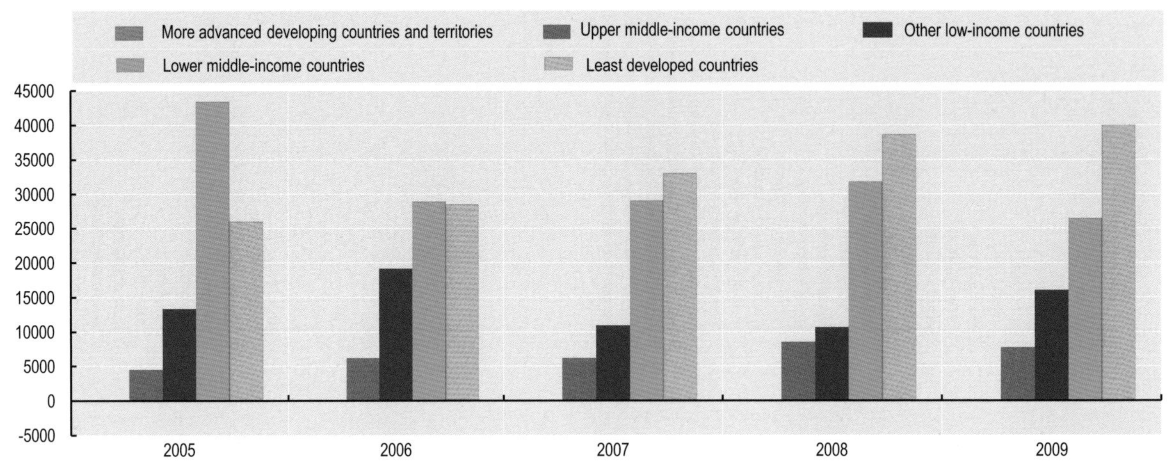

StatLink http://dx.doi.org/10.1787/888932507426

Distribution of gross bilateral ODA from DAC countries by income group

Million US dollars, 2008-09 average

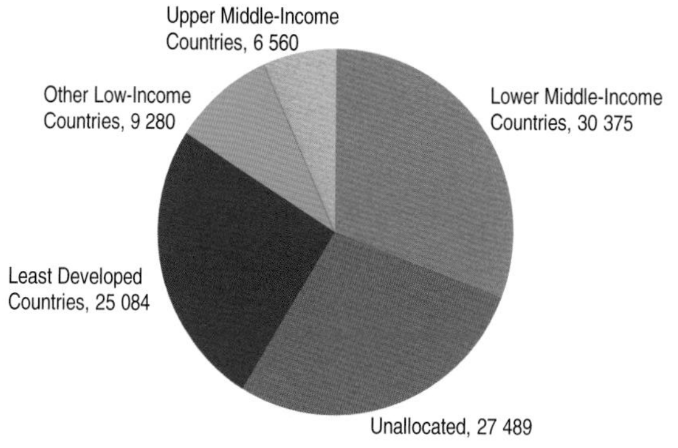

StatLink http://dx.doi.org/10.1787/888932507445

Distribution of gross bilateral ODA from DAC countries by region

Million US dollars, 2008-09 average

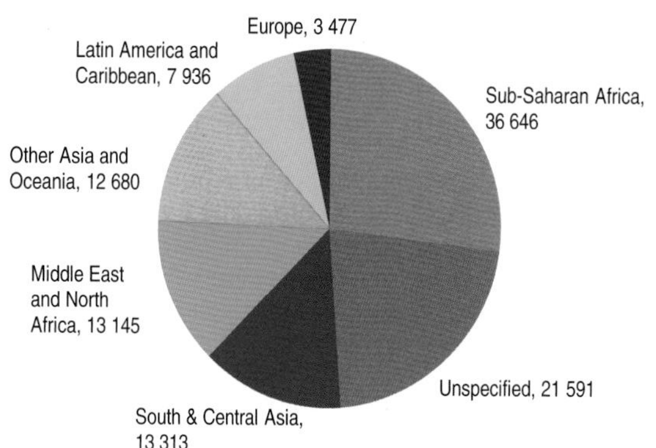

StatLink http://dx.doi.org/10.1787/888932507464

Top recipients of gross bilateral ODA

2008-09 average

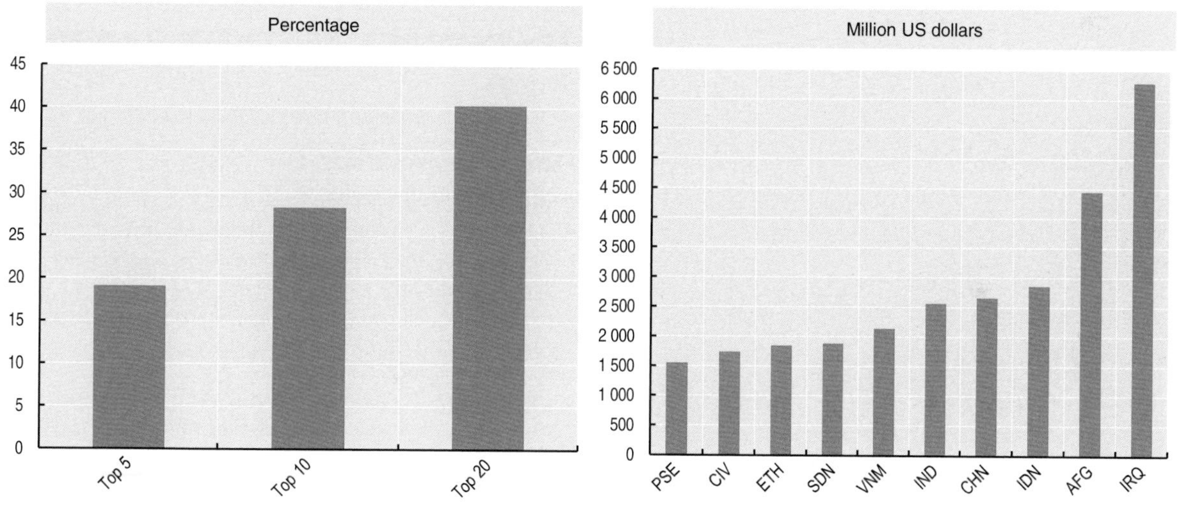

StatLink http://dx.doi.org/10.1787/888932507483

Distribution of gross bilateral ODA from DAC countries by sector

As a percentage of gross bilateral ODA, 2008-09 average

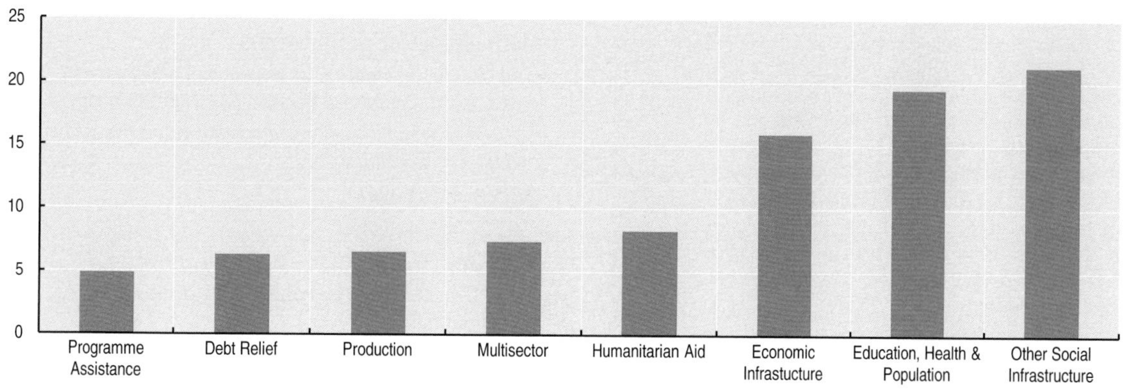

StatLink http://dx.doi.org/10.1787/888932507502

TOTAL TAX REVENUE

Total tax revenue as a percentage of GDP indicates the share of a country's output that is collected by the government through taxes. It can be regarded as one measure of the degree to which the government controls the economy's resources.

Definition

Taxes are defined as compulsory, unrequited payments to general government. They are unrequited in the sense that benefits provided by government to taxpayers are not normally in proportion to their payments. The data on total tax revenue shown here refer to the revenues collected from taxes on income and profits, social security contributions, taxes levied on goods and services, payroll taxes, taxes on the ownership and transfer of property, and other taxes.

Taxes on incomes and profits cover taxes levied on the net income or profits (gross income minus allowable tax reliefs) of individuals and enterprises. They also cover taxes levied on the capital gains of individuals and enterprises, and gains from gambling.

Taxes on goods and services cover all taxes levied on the production, extraction, sale, transfer, leasing or delivery of goods, and the rendering of services, or on the use of goods or permission to use goods or to perform activities. They consist mainly of value added and sales taxes.

Note that the sum of taxes on goods and services and taxes on income and profits is less than the figure for total tax revenues.

Comparability

The tax revenue data are collected in a way that makes them as internationally comparable as possible. Country representatives have agreed on the definitions of each type of tax and how they should be measured in all OECD countries, and they are then responsible for submitting data to the OECD that conform to these rules. The rules are set out in "The OECD Interpretative Guide" shown at the end of each edition of *Revenue Statistics*.

Overview

In 2009, total tax revenues as a percentage of GDP fell in 17 OECD countries and rose in 7. The OECD average of total revenues fell by about 1% of GDP from the level of 34.8% reached in 2008. The slow upward trend in this ratio recorded in almost all OECD countries during the 1990s stopped in 2000. Since then, the total tax revenue as a percentage of GDP for all OECD countries has fallen by between one and two percentage points.

Revenue collected from taxes on income and profit accounted for 12.5% of GDP on average in 2008. This ratio showed an upward trend in the second half of the 1990s reaching a peak in 2000. After declining slightly in the following years, the average ratio in 2007 rose above the 2000 peak but has now fallen back again.

The OECD average for tax revenues on goods and services has been remarkably stable since 1995 at a level of around 11% of GDP.

Sources

- OECD (2011), *Revenue Statistics*, OECD Publishing.

Further information

Analytical publications

- OECD (2010), *Consumption Tax Trends*, OECD Publishing.
- OECD (2010), *Tax Co-operation: Towards a Level Playing Field*, OECD Publishing.
- OECD (2006), *Encouraging Savings through Tax-Preferred Accounts*, OECD Tax Policy Studies, No. 15, OECD Publishing.
- OECD (2006), *Tax Administration in OECD and Selected Non-OECD Countries: Comparative Information Series (2006)*, OECD Publishing.
- OECD (2006), *The Political Economy of Environmentally Related Taxes*, OECD Publishing.
- OECD (2004), *Recent Tax Policy Trends and Reforms in OECD Countries*, OECD Tax Policy Studies, No. 9, OECD Publishing.

Statistical publications

- OECD (2011), *Taxing Wages*, OECD Publishing.

Methodological publications

- OECD (2010), *Model Tax Convention on Income and on Capital: Condensed Version*, OECD Publishing.
- OECD (2008), *Model Tax Convention on Income and on Capital 2008*, OECD Publishing.

Online databases

- *OECD Tax Statistics.*

Websites

- OECD Centre for Tax Policy and Administration, *www.oecd.org/ctp*.
- Global Forum on Transparency and Exchange of Information for Tax Purposes, *www.oecd.org/tax/transparency*.

Total tax revenue

As a percentage of GDP

	1996	1997	1998	1999	2000	2001	2002	2003	2004	2005	2006	2007	2008	2009
Australia	28.7	28.5	29.3	29.7	30.3	28.7	29.6	29.8	30.1	29.8	29.3	29.5	27.1	..
Austria	42.9	44.4	44.4	44.0	43.2	45.3	44.0	43.8	43.4	42.4	41.9	42.1	42.7	42.8
Belgium	43.9	44.4	45.1	45.0	44.7	44.7	44.8	44.3	44.5	44.6	44.3	43.8	44.2	43.2
Canada	35.9	36.7	36.7	36.4	35.6	34.8	33.7	33.7	33.6	33.4	33.3	33.0	32.3	31.1
Chile	20.1	19.5	19.3	18.6	19.4	19.7	19.7	19.3	19.8	21.6	23.2	24.0	22.5	18.2
Czech Republic	36.0	36.3	34.9	35.9	35.3	35.6	36.3	37.3	37.8	37.5	37.0	37.3	36.0	34.8
Denmark	49.2	48.9	49.3	50.1	49.4	48.5	47.9	48.0	49.0	50.8	49.6	49.0	48.2	48.2
Finland	47.1	46.4	46.3	45.9	47.2	44.8	44.7	44.1	43.5	43.9	43.8	43.0	43.1	43.1
France	44.1	44.4	44.2	45.1	44.4	44.0	43.4	43.2	43.5	43.9	44.0	43.5	43.2	41.9
Germany	36.5	36.2	36.4	37.1	37.2	36.1	35.4	35.5	34.8	34.8	35.4	36.0	37.0	37.0
Greece	35.9	30.3	32.0	32.9	34.0	32.9	33.6	32.0	31.1	31.8	31.7	32.3	32.6	29.4
Hungary	39.5	37.8	37.5	38.2	38.5	37.9	37.8	37.8	37.4	37.4	37.2	39.7	40.2	39.1
Iceland	32.3	32.2	34.5	36.9	37.2	35.4	35.3	36.7	38.0	40.6	41.5	40.6	36.8	34.1
Ireland	32.5	31.8	31.3	31.5	31.3	29.1	27.9	28.4	29.9	30.4	31.8	30.9	28.8	27.8
Israel	36.0	37.3	36.0	36.0	36.8	36.7	36.3	35.4	35.4	35.5	35.9	36.3	33.8	31.4
Italy	41.8	43.3	41.7	42.5	42.2	41.9	41.3	41.7	41.0	40.8	42.3	43.4	43.3	43.5
Japan	26.8	27.2	26.8	26.3	27.0	27.3	26.2	25.7	26.3	27.4	28.0	28.3	28.1	..
Korea	20.6	20.3	20.3	20.7	22.6	23.0	23.2	24.0	23.3	24.0	25.0	26.5	26.5	25.6
Luxembourg	37.6	39.3	39.4	38.3	39.1	39.7	39.3	38.1	37.3	37.6	35.6	35.7	35.5	37.5
Mexico	15.3	15.9	15.1	15.8	16.9	17.1	16.5	17.4	17.1	18.1	18.2	17.9	21.0	17.5
Netherlands	40.9	40.9	39.0	40.1	39.6	38.1	37.4	36.9	37.2	38.4	39.1	38.7	39.1	..
New Zealand	34.4	34.6	33.0	33.0	33.2	32.7	34.0	33.8	34.8	36.7	36.1	35.1	33.7	31.0
Norway	40.8	41.5	42.4	42.7	42.6	42.9	43.1	42.3	43.3	43.5	44.0	43.8	42.6	41.0
Poland	37.4	36.6	35.6	35.1	32.8	32.6	33.1	32.6	31.7	33.0	34.0	34.8	34.3	..
Portugal	31.8	31.8	31.9	32.7	32.8	32.6	33.3	33.6	32.8	33.7	34.4	35.2	35.2	..
Slovak Republic	..	..	36.8	35.4	34.1	33.1	33.3	33.1	31.7	31.5	29.4	29.4	29.3	29.3
Slovenia	38.1	37.0	37.8	38.2	37.5	37.7	38.0	38.2	38.3	38.6	38.3	37.8	37.2	37.9
Spain	31.9	32.9	33.2	34.1	34.2	33.8	34.2	34.2	34.6	35.7	36.6	37.3	33.3	30.7
Sweden	49.4	50.5	50.7	51.1	51.4	49.4	47.5	47.8	48.1	48.9	48.3	47.4	46.3	46.4
Switzerland	28.1	27.6	28.5	28.7	30.0	29.5	29.9	29.2	28.8	29.2	29.3	28.9	29.1	30.3
Turkey	18.9	20.7	21.1	23.1	24.2	26.1	24.6	25.9	24.1	24.3	24.5	24.1	24.2	24.6
United Kingdom	33.8	34.3	35.5	35.7	36.4	36.2	34.6	34.3	34.8	35.7	36.5	36.2	35.7	34.3
United States	28.2	28.7	29.1	29.1	29.5	28.4	26.0	25.5	25.7	27.1	27.9	27.9	26.1	24.0
OECD average	34.9	34.9	35.0	35.3	35.5	35.0	34.7	34.7	34.6	35.2	35.4	35.4	34.8	..

StatLink http://dx.doi.org/10.1787/888932507521

Total tax revenue

As a percentage of GDP

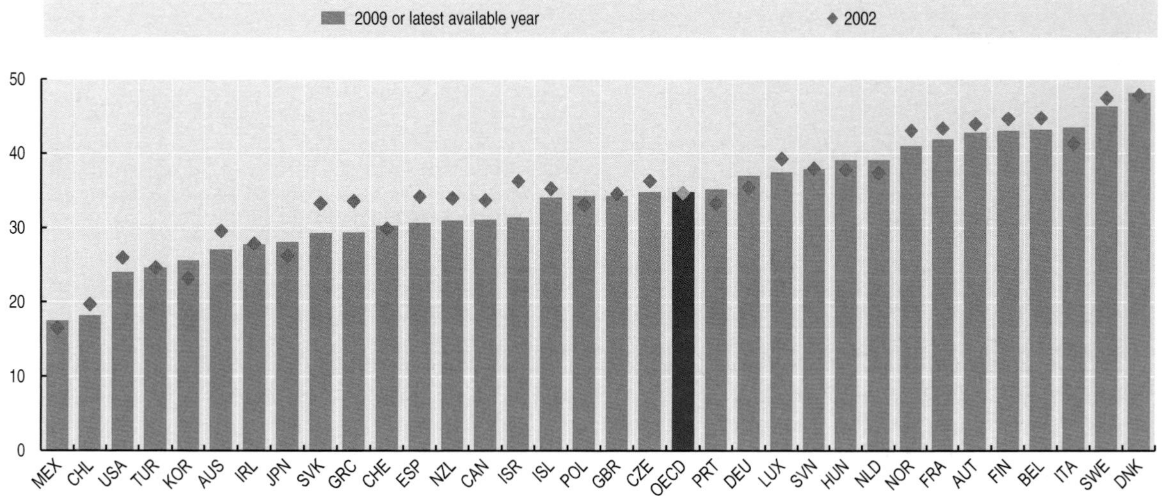

StatLink http://dx.doi.org/10.1787/888932507540

Taxes on income and profits

As a percentage of GDP

	1996	1997	1998	1999	2000	2001	2002	2003	2004	2005	2006	2007	2008	2009
Australia	16.2	16.1	17.3	17.8	17.6	16.2	16.7	16.8	17.6	17.6	17.4	17.7	16.0	..
Austria	11.9	12.7	12.8	12.5	12.3	14.1	13.0	12.8	12.6	12.0	12.1	12.6	13.1	11.9
Belgium	16.6	17.0	17.5	17.1	17.2	17.5	17.2	16.8	16.9	17.1	16.7	16.5	16.8	15.5
Canada	16.9	17.9	17.7	18.1	17.8	16.7	15.4	15.4	15.7	15.8	16.2	16.2	15.9	14.2
Chile	5.1	4.7	4.2	3.7	4.5	4.6	4.8	4.9	5.9	7.8	10.5	11.0	8.4	5.6
Czech Republic	8.1	8.7	8.1	8.3	8.0	8.6	9.0	9.5	9.5	9.1	9.1	9.4	7.9	7.4
Denmark	30.2	29.8	29.4	29.6	29.8	28.8	28.6	28.8	29.6	31.2	29.9	29.4	29.2	29.5
Finland	18.2	17.8	18.2	17.8	20.4	18.3	18.1	17.1	16.8	16.8	16.7	16.9	16.8	15.5
France	7.4	8.1	10.2	10.8	11.1	11.2	10.4	10.0	10.2	10.3	10.7	10.4	10.4	8.7
Germany	10.5	10.2	10.7	11.1	11.2	10.4	9.9	9.7	9.5	9.8	10.7	11.2	11.5	10.7
Greece	6.4	6.8	8.1	8.4	9.3	8.0	8.1	7.4	7.5	8.0	7.5	7.5	7.3	7.4
Hungary	8.7	8.2	8.4	8.9	9.3	9.7	10.0	9.3	8.8	8.8	9.1	10.0	10.4	9.6
Iceland	11.3	11.5	13.0	14.2	14.8	15.3	15.3	16.0	16.1	17.5	18.3	18.4	17.8	16.7
Ireland	13.2	13.2	12.9	13.2	13.2	12.2	11.1	11.3	11.8	11.7	12.5	12.1	10.8	10.0
Israel	12.1	13.2	12.9	12.7	14.6	14.5	12.8	12.0	11.7	12.0	13.3	13.2	11.1	9.4
Italy	14.5	15.3	13.6	14.4	14.0	14.3	13.4	12.9	12.9	12.9	13.9	14.6	14.9	14.2
Japan	10.2	10.1	9.0	8.4	9.4	9.1	8.0	7.9	8.4	9.3	9.9	10.3	9.5	7.7
Korea	5.9	5.3	6.2	5.1	6.5	6.1	5.9	6.7	6.5	7.0	7.4	8.4	8.2	7.3
Luxembourg	14.9	15.6	15.1	13.9	14.1	14.3	14.4	13.9	12.4	12.9	12.4	12.4	12.8	13.2
Mexico	3.7	4.2	4.3	4.6	4.6	4.8	4.8	4.6	4.2	4.4	4.6	5.0	5.2	5.0
Netherlands	11.1	10.7	10.3	10.2	10.0	10.1	10.2	9.4	9.2	10.7	10.6	10.9	10.6	..
New Zealand	20.4	20.7	19.2	19.1	19.9	19.3	20.3	20.1	21.3	23.1	22.4	22.1	20.4	17.6
Norway	14.8	15.7	15.7	16.0	19.2	19.3	18.8	18.5	20.1	21.4	22.0	21.1	21.6	18.4
Poland	10.7	10.4	10.3	7.4	6.8	6.4	6.3	6.0	5.9	6.4	7.0	8.0	8.1	..
Portugal	8.3	8.4	8.3	8.7	9.2	8.8	8.6	8.1	8.0	7.9	8.3	9.1	9.3	..
Slovak Republic	..	..	8.6	8.6	7.0	7.1	6.6	6.7	5.7	5.6	5.7	5.8	6.2	5.6
Slovenia	7.0	7.1	6.9	6.9	6.9	7.1	7.4	7.6	7.8	8.3	8.7	8.8	8.4	7.9
Spain	9.2	9.8	9.4	9.6	9.7	9.5	10.0	9.6	9.8	10.5	11.2	12.4	10.3	9.2
Sweden	19.3	19.9	19.8	20.6	21.0	18.7	17.0	17.6	18.3	19.1	19.1	18.4	16.8	16.3
Switzerland	12.3	11.9	12.5	12.0	13.2	12.4	12.9	12.5	12.5	13.0	13.4	13.3	13.9	14.5
Turkey	5.0	5.7	7.0	7.3	7.1	7.5	6.1	6.1	5.3	5.3	5.3	5.7	5.8	5.9
United Kingdom	12.4	12.7	13.8	13.8	14.2	14.3	13.2	12.6	12.8	13.7	14.5	14.3	14.3	13.2
United States	13.4	13.9	14.3	14.4	14.9	13.8	11.5	11.0	11.2	12.7	13.5	13.6	11.8	9.8
OECD average	12.1	12.3	12.3	12.3	12.7	12.4	12.0	11.8	11.9	12.4	12.7	12.9	12.5	..

StatLink http://dx.doi.org/10.1787/888932507559

Taxes on income and profits

As a percentage of GDP

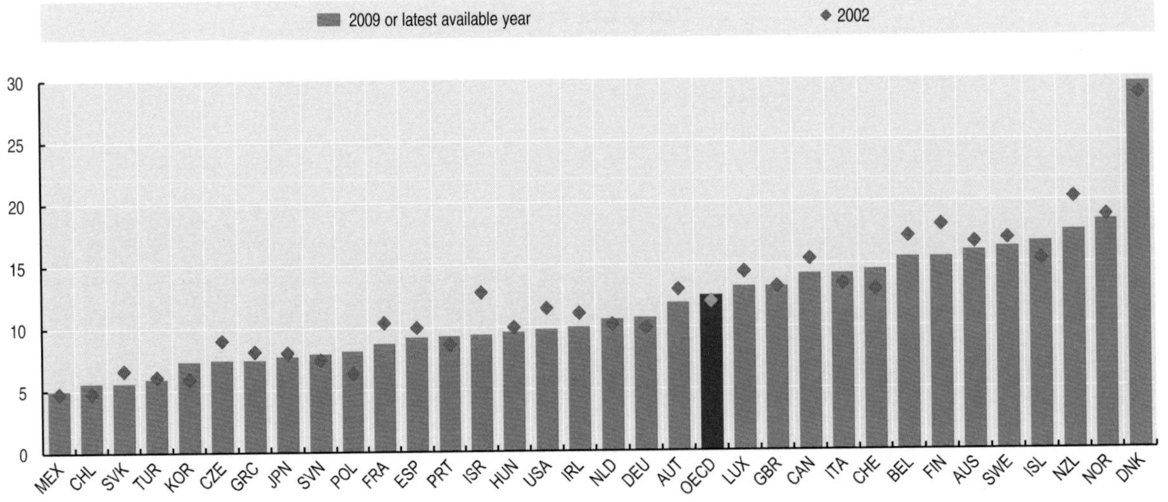

StatLink http://dx.doi.org/10.1787/888932507578

Taxes on goods and services

As a percentage of GDP

	1996	1997	1998	1999	2000	2001	2002	2003	2004	2005	2006	2007	2008	2009
Australia	8.0	7.8	8.0	7.8	8.7	8.7	9.0	8.8	8.6	8.3	8.0	7.9	7.4	..
Austria	12.3	12.8	12.5	12.6	12.3	12.4	12.6	12.4	12.3	12.1	11.7	11.6	11.6	12.0
Belgium	11.5	11.6	11.1	11.5	11.4	10.9	11.0	10.9	11.2	11.3	11.3	11.0	10.8	10.9
Canada	9.0	9.0	9.1	8.8	8.6	8.8	8.9	8.9	8.7	8.5	8.1	7.9	7.6	7.7
Chile	12.7	12.4	12.5	12.1	12.4	12.2	12.2	11.7	11.2	11.1	10.0	10.5	11.4	10.0
Czech Republic	11.8	11.3	10.8	11.5	11.2	10.8	10.8	11.1	11.8	11.8	11.2	11.1	11.5	11.6
Denmark	16.1	16.1	16.4	16.5	15.9	15.9	16.0	15.8	16.0	16.3	16.4	16.3	15.6	15.3
Finland	14.1	14.7	14.2	14.2	13.7	13.3	13.5	14.1	13.8	13.8	13.6	12.9	13.0	13.6
France	12.3	12.1	11.9	12.0	11.4	11.1	11.1	11.0	11.1	11.1	10.8	10.7	10.6	10.5
Germany	10.3	10.1	9.9	10.4	10.4	10.4	10.3	10.4	10.1	10.1	10.0	10.5	10.5	11.0
Greece	12.2	12.3	12.0	12.2	12.0	12.5	12.3	11.4	11.0	11.0	11.5	11.5	11.4	10.6
Hungary	16.1	14.9	14.6	15.4	15.6	14.7	14.2	14.9	15.3	14.8	14.3	15.0	14.9	15.4
Iceland	15.6	15.3	15.9	17.0	16.4	14.3	14.4	15.1	16.0	17.1	17.6	16.4	13.6	11.9
Ireland	13.0	12.6	12.3	12.2	11.7	10.6	10.8	10.7	11.2	11.4	11.4	11.2	10.7	9.7
Israel	13.5	13.5	12.8	13.0	12.3	12.2	13.0	12.9	13.0	12.7	12.4	12.8	12.6	12.3
Italy	10.8	11.2	11.5	11.7	11.8	11.2	11.2	10.7	10.8	10.8	11.1	11.0	10.6	10.6
Japan	4.3	4.7	5.3	5.4	5.2	5.3	5.3	5.2	5.3	5.3	5.2	5.1	5.1	5.1
Korea	8.6	8.7	7.7	8.3	8.7	9.1	9.0	8.9	8.4	8.2	8.1	8.3	8.4	8.2
Luxembourg	9.9	10.6	10.5	10.4	10.6	10.5	10.6	10.5	11.2	10.9	10.0	9.8	9.9	10.4
Mexico	8.5	8.6	7.5	7.9	8.9	8.8	8.1	9.1	9.5	10.2	10.3	9.5	12.4	8.8
Netherlands	11.6	11.3	11.3	11.7	11.5	11.8	11.6	11.7	11.9	12.2	12.1	12.0	11.8	..
New Zealand	12.0	12.0	12.0	11.9	11.5	11.6	11.9	11.9	11.8	11.8	11.8	11.1	11.4	11.4
Norway	15.5	15.4	15.8	15.6	13.5	13.3	13.3	12.9	12.7	12.1	12.0	12.4	10.9	11.6
Poland	13.7	13.1	12.3	12.8	11.8	11.4	12.1	12.2	11.9	12.7	13.3	13.0	13.0	..
Portugal	12.8	12.5	12.6	12.7	12.2	12.3	12.6	12.8	12.7	13.4	13.7	13.2	12.9	..
Slovak Republic	..	..	12.7	12.2	12.3	11.2	11.4	12.0	12.3	12.6	11.4	11.3	10.5	10.5
Slovenia	14.9	13.9	14.5	15.0	14.1	13.7	13.9	14.0	13.8	13.6	13.3	13.2	13.2	14.1
Spain	9.3	9.5	9.8	10.2	10.1	9.7	9.6	9.7	9.8	9.9	9.9	9.5	8.3	7.1
Sweden	12.9	12.9	12.7	12.5	12.7	12.6	12.7	12.7	12.6	12.8	12.6	12.6	12.8	13.5
Switzerland	6.0	6.0	6.2	6.6	6.7	6.8	6.8	6.8	6.8	6.9	6.8	6.6	6.3	6.3
Turkey	7.2	7.7	7.6	8.3	10.1	10.5	11.5	12.8	11.5	12.0	11.9	11.5	11.0	11.2
United Kingdom	12.0	11.9	11.7	11.8	11.6	11.3	11.3	11.2	11.1	10.8	10.6	10.5	10.3	10.0
United States	4.9	4.8	4.8	4.8	4.7	4.6	4.6	4.7	4.7	4.8	4.8	4.7	4.6	4.4
OECD average	11.4	11.3	11.2	11.4	11.3	11.0	11.1	11.2	11.2	11.3	11.1	11.0	10.8	..

StatLink http://dx.doi.org/10.1787/888932507597

Taxes on goods and services

As a percentage of GDP

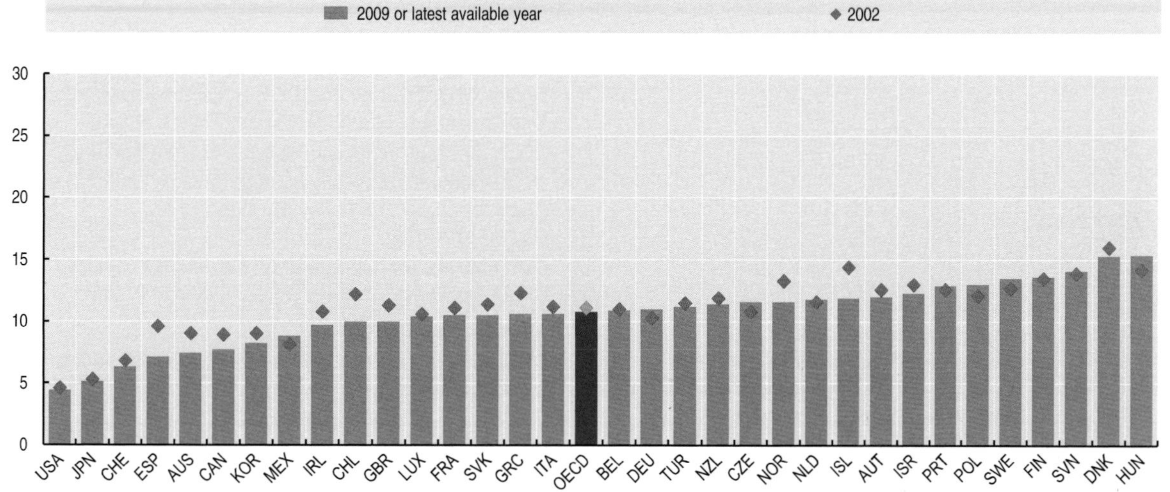

StatLink http://dx.doi.org/10.1787/888932507616

TAXES ON THE AVERAGE WORKER

Taxes on the average worker measures the ratio between the amount of taxes paid by an average single worker without children and the corresponding total labour cost for the employer. This tax wedge measures the extent to which the tax system on labour income discourages employment.

Definition

The taxes included in the measure are personal income taxes, employees' social security contributions and employers' social security contributions. For the few countries that have them, it also includes payroll taxes. The amount of these taxes paid in relation to the employment of one average worker is expressed as a percentage of their labour cost (gross wage plus employers' social security contributions and payroll tax).

An average worker is defined as somebody who earns the average income of full-time workers of the country concerned in Sectors B-N of the International Standard Industrial Classification (ISIC Rev. 4). The average worker is single, meaning that he or she does not receive any tax relief in respect of a spouse, unmarried partner or child.

Comparability

The types of taxes included in the measure are fully comparable across countries. They are based on common definitions agreed by all OECD countries and published in OECD *Revenue Statistics*.

While the income levels of workers in Sectors B-N differ across countries, they can be regarded as corresponding to comparable types of work in each country.

The information on the average worker's income level is supplied by the Ministries of Finance in all OECD countries and is based on national statistical surveys. The amount of taxes paid by the single worker is calculated by applying the tax laws in each country. These tax wedge measures are therefore derived from a modelling exercise rather than from the direct observation of taxes actually paid by workers and their employers.

Taxes on the average worker

As a percentage of labour cost

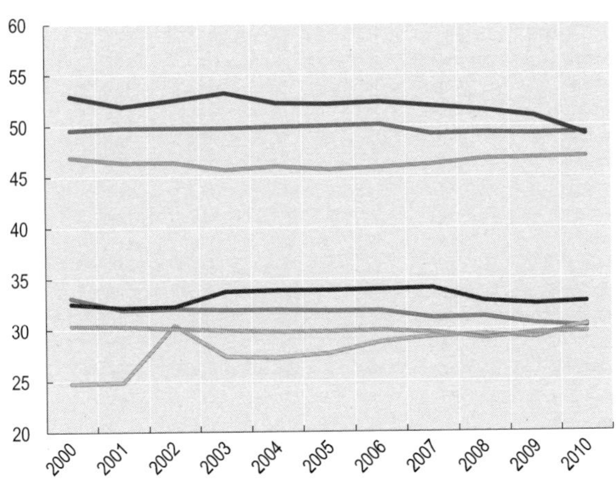

StatLink http://dx.doi.org/10.1787/888932535166

Overview

In 2010, taxes on an average worker, on average, represented around 35% of their total labour costs across OECD countries. This tax wedge ranged between 7% in Chile and 55% in Belgium.

On average, taxes on an average worker for the OECD as a whole have decreased by nearly two percentage points since 2000. However, there are important differences between countries. Of the 34 OECD member countries, 9 countries experienced an overall increase in the taxes on an average worker since 2000. The countries with the largest increases were Iceland and Japan. Of the 23 countries that have experienced an overall decline, the largest decreases were for Hungary, Israel and Sweden.

Sources

- OECD (2011), *Taxing Wages*, OECD Publishing.

Further information

Analytical publications

- Immervoll, H. (2004), "Average and Marginal Effective Tax Rates Facing Workers in the EU: A Micro-Level Analysis of Levels, Distributions and Driving Factors", *OECD Social Employment and Migration Working Papers*, No. 19.
- OECD (2007), *Benefits and Wages*, OECD Publishing.
- OECD (2006), *Encouraging Savings through Tax-Preferred Accounts*, OECD Tax Policy Studies, No. 15, OECD Publishing.
- OECD (2006), *The Taxation of Employee Stock Options*, OECD Tax Policy Studies, No. 11, OECD Publishing.

Statistical publications

- OECD (2011), *OECD Latin American Economic Outlook*, OECD Publishing.
- OECD (2011), *Revenue Statistics*, OECD Publishing.

Websites

- OECD Benefits and Wages: OECD Indicators, *www.oecd.org/els/social/workincentives*.
- OECD Centre for Tax Policy and Administration, *www.oecd.org/ctp*.
- OECD Tax Policy Analysis, *www.oecd.org/ctp/tpa*.

Taxes on the average worker

As a percentage of labour cost

	2000	2001	2002	2003	2004	2005	2006	2007	2008	2009	2010
Australia	30.4	27.3	28.0	28.3	28.2	28.2	27.9	27.3	26.5	26.2	26.2
Austria	47.3	46.9	47.1	47.4	48.1	48.0	48.3	48.6	48.8	47.8	47.9
Belgium	57.1	56.7	56.3	55.7	55.4	55.5	55.5	55.6	55.9	55.4	55.4
Canada	33.2	32.0	32.1	32.0	32.0	31.9	31.9	31.2	31.3	30.6	30.3
Chile	7.0	7.0	7.0	7.0	7.0	7.0	7.0	7.0	7.0	7.0	7.0
Czech Republic	42.6	42.6	43.0	43.2	43.5	43.7	42.5	42.9	43.4	42.0	42.2
Denmark	44.1	43.3	42.4	42.4	41.0	40.9	41.0	41.1	40.9	39.5	38.3
Estonia	41.3	41.0	42.1	42.3	41.5	39.9	39.0	39.0	38.4	39.2	40.0
Finland	47.8	46.4	45.9	45.0	44.5	44.6	44.0	43.9	43.8	42.3	42.0
France	49.6	49.8	49.8	49.8	49.9	50.0	50.1	49.2	49.3	49.2	49.3
Germany	52.9	51.9	52.5	53.2	52.2	52.1	52.3	51.9	51.5	50.9	49.1
Greece	35.2	34.7	35.1	35.2	35.8	35.2	35.8	37.0	37.0	38.2	36.6
Hungary	54.6	55.8	53.7	50.8	51.8	51.1	52.0	54.5	54.1	53.1	46.4
Iceland	26.2	26.9	28.5	29.3	29.8	29.7	29.5	28.1	28.3	28.0	31.3
Ireland	35.2	31.3	29.7	29.8	30.7	31.0	29.2	27.2	26.8	29.0	29.3
Israel	29.0	29.5	30.0	27.1	25.3	25.0	23.5	24.1	21.7	20.2	20.2
Italy	46.9	46.4	46.4	45.7	46.0	45.7	45.9	46.2	46.7	46.8	46.9
Japan	24.8	24.9	30.5	27.4	27.3	27.7	28.8	29.3	29.5	29.2	30.5
Korea	16.3	16.4	16.1	16.3	17.0	17.3	18.1	19.7	19.9	19.3	19.8
Luxembourg	37.5	35.8	32.9	33.5	33.9	34.7	35.3	36.3	34.7	33.8	34.0
Mexico	12.6	13.2	15.8	16.8	15.3	14.7	15.0	15.9	15.1	15.3	15.5
Netherlands	39.7	37.2	37.4	37.1	38.8	38.9	38.3	38.7	39.2	38.0	38.4
New Zealand	19.4	19.4	19.4	19.5	19.6	19.9	20.2	20.8	20.3	17.7	16.9
Norway	38.6	39.2	38.6	38.1	38.1	37.2	37.4	37.5	37.5	36.9	36.8
Poland	38.2	38.0	38.0	38.2	38.4	38.7	39.0	38.2	34.7	34.2	34.3
Portugal	37.3	36.4	37.6	37.4	37.4	36.8	37.1	37.7	37.6	37.5	37.7
Slovak Republic	41.9	42.5	42.1	42.5	42.2	38.0	38.3	38.4	38.8	37.7	37.8
Slovenia	46.3	46.2	46.1	46.2	46.3	45.6	45.3	43.3	42.9	42.2	42.4
Spain	38.6	38.9	39.1	38.6	38.8	39.0	39.1	39.0	38.0	38.3	39.6
Sweden	50.1	49.1	47.8	48.2	48.4	48.1	47.8	45.3	44.8	43.2	42.7
Switzerland	21.6	21.6	21.7	21.2	20.9	20.9	20.9	21.1	20.6	20.8	20.8
Turkey	40.4	43.6	42.5	42.2	42.8	42.8	42.7	42.7	39.9	37.4	37.4
United Kingdom	32.6	32.2	32.3	33.8	33.9	33.9	34.0	34.1	32.8	32.5	32.7
United States	30.4	30.3	30.1	29.9	29.8	29.8	29.9	29.7	29.1	29.6	29.7
OECD average	36.7	36.3	36.4	36.2	36.2	36.0	36.0	36.0	35.5	35.0	34.9

StatLink http://dx.doi.org/10.1787/888932507635

Taxes on the average worker

As a percentage of labour cost

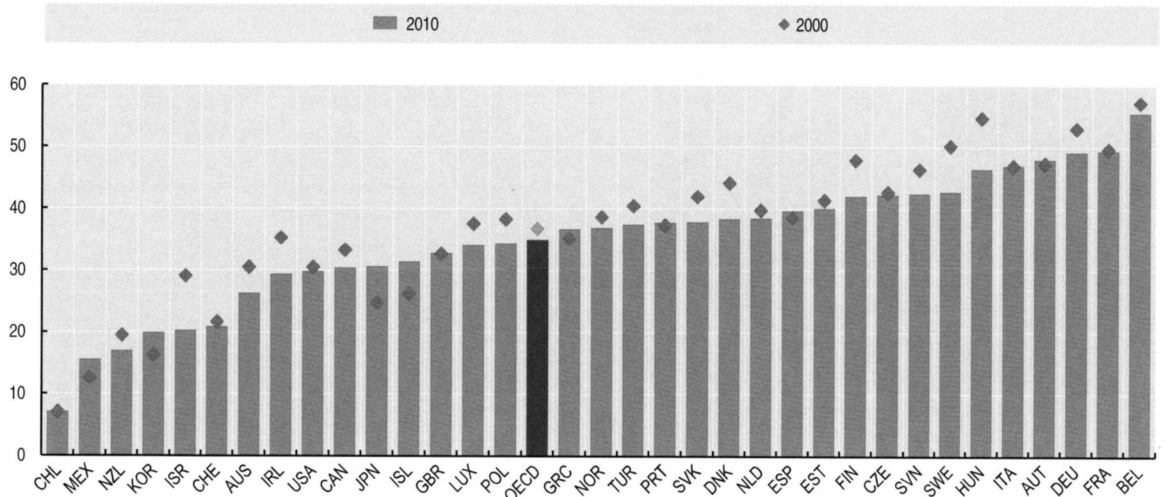

StatLink http://dx.doi.org/10.1787/888932507654

HEALTH

HEALTH STATUS

LIFE EXPECTANCY

INFANT MORTALITY

SUICIDES

RISK FACTOR

SMOKING

ALCOHOL CONSUMPTION

OVERWEIGHT AND OBESITY

RESOURCES

DOCTORS

NURSES

HEALTH EXPENDITURE

LIFE EXPECTANCY

Life expectancy at birth remains one of the most frequently used health status indicators. Gains in life expectancy at birth in OECD countries in recent decades can be attributed to a number of factors, including rising living standards, improved lifestyle and better education, as well as greater access to quality health services. Other factors, such as better nutrition, sanitation and housing also played a role, particularly in countries with emerging economies.

Definition

Life expectancy at birth measures how long on average a newborn can expect to live, if current death rates do not change. However, the actual age-specific death rate of any particular birth cohort cannot be known in advance. If rates are falling (as has been the case over the past decades in OECD countries), actual life spans will be higher than life expectancy calculated using current death rates.

Comparability

The methodology used to calculate life expectancy can vary slightly between countries. These differences can affect the comparability of reported life expectancy estimates, as different methods can change a country's estimates by a fraction of a year. Life expectancy at birth for the total population is calculated by the OECD Secretariat for all countries, using the unweighted average of life expectancy of men and women.

Overview

On average across OECD countries, life expectancy at birth for the whole population reached 79.5 years in 2009, a gain of more than 11 years since 1960. Japan leads a large group (including almost two-thirds of OECD countries) in which the total life expectancy at birth is currently 80 years or more. A second group, including Portugal, the United States and a number of central and eastern European countries have a life expectancy of between 75 and 80 years. Life expectancy among OECD countries was lowest in Turkey, followed by Hungary. However, while life expectancy in Hungary has increased only modestly since 1960, it has increased sharply in Turkey, and is rapidly catching up with the OECD average.

Nearly all OECD and emerging countries have experienced large gains in life expectancy over the past 50 years. Life expectancy at birth in Korea, Turkey and Chile has increased by twenty years or more over the period 1960-2009. Mexico, Portugal and Japan, as well as emerging countries such as Indonesia, China, India and Brazil also show strong gains. Other countries such as the Russian Federation and South Africa are still characterised by high mortality rates and by a length of life well below the OECD average.

The gender gap in life expectancy stood at 5.5 years on average across OECD countries in 2009, with life expectancy reaching 76.7 years among men and 82.2 years among women. While the gender gap in life expectancy increased substantially in many countries during the 1960s and the 1970s, it narrowed during the past 30 years, reflecting higher gains in life expectancy among men than among women in most OECD countries. This can be attributed at least partly to the narrowing of differences in risk-increasing behaviours between men and women, such as smoking, accompanied by sharp reductions in mortality rates from cardiovascular diseases among men.

Higher national income (as measured by GDP per capita) is generally associated with higher life expectancy at birth, although the relationship is less pronounced at higher levels of national income.

Sources

- OECD (2011), *OECD Health Statistics*, OECD Publishing.

Further information

Analytical publications

- Colombo, F. *et al.* (2011), *Help Wanted?: Providing and Paying for Long-Term Care*, OECD Health Policy Studies, OECD Publishing.
- OECD (2010), *Health Care Systems: Efficiency and Policy Settings*, OECD Publishing.
- OECD (2009), *Achieving Better Value for Money in Health Care*, OECD Publishing.
- OECD (2004), *The OECD Health Project: Towards High-Performing Health Systems*, OECD Publishing.

Statistical publications

- OECD (2011), *Health at a Glance: OECD indicators*, OECD Publishing.
- OECD (2011), *Society at a Glance: OECD Social Indicators*, OECD Publishing.

Online databases

- *OECD Health Statistics.*

Websites

- OECD Health Data, *www.oecd.org/health/healthdata*.
- OECD Health at a Glance, *www.oecd.org/health/healthataglance*.

Life expectancy at birth: total

Number of years

	1960	1970	1980	1990	1995	2000	2002	2003	2004	2005	2006	2007	2008	2009
Australia	70.9	70.8	74.5	77.0	77.9	79.3	80.0	80.3	80.5	80.9	81.1	81.3	81.5	81.6
Austria	68.7	70.0	72.6	75.6	76.7	78.2	78.7	78.7	79.2	79.4	79.9	80.2	80.5	80.4
Belgium	69.8	71.0	73.3	76.1	76.9	77.8	78.2	78.2	79.0	79.0	79.5	79.8	79.8	80.0
Canada	71.3	72.8	75.3	77.6	78.0	79.0	79.5	79.7	79.9	80.1	80.4	80.7	..	..
Chile	..	..	..	72.9	74.8	76.8	77.4	77.4	77.4	77.9	78.4	77.8	77.8	78.2
Czech Republic	70.6	69.6	70.4	71.5	73.3	75.1	75.4	75.3	75.9	76.0	76.7	77.0	77.3	77.3
Denmark	72.4	73.3	74.3	74.9	75.3	76.8	77.1	77.4	77.8	78.2	78.4	78.4	78.8	79.0
Estonia	..	69.7	69.2	69.6	67.7	70.6	71.0	71.5	72.0	72.7	72.9	72.9	73.9	75.0
Finland	69.0	70.8	73.6	75.0	76.6	77.7	78.3	78.5	78.9	79.1	79.5	79.6	79.9	80.0
France	70.3	72.2	74.3	76.8	77.8	79.0	79.3	79.3	80.3	80.3	80.7	80.9	81.0	81.0
Germany	69.1	70.5	72.9	75.3	76.6	78.2	78.5	78.6	79.2	79.4	79.8	80.0	80.2	80.3
Greece	..	73.8	75.3	77.1	77.5	78.0	78.7	78.8	79.0	79.2	79.5	79.5	80.0	80.3
Hungary	68.0	69.2	69.1	69.4	69.9	71.7	72.5	72.5	72.8	72.8	73.2	73.3	73.8	74.0
Iceland	72.8	74.3	76.7	78.0	78.0	80.1	80.6	81.2	81.0	81.2	81.2	81.2	81.3	81.5
Ireland	70.0	71.2	72.8	74.9	75.5	76.6	77.9	78.3	78.8	79.4	79.7	79.8	80.1	80.0
Israel	..	71.8	73.9	76.7	77.5	78.8	79.5	79.7	80.2	80.2	80.6	80.5	81.0	81.6
Italy	69.8	72.0	74.0	77.1	78.3	79.8	80.3	79.9	80.9	80.8	81.3	81.5	81.8	..
Japan	67.8	72.0	76.1	78.9	79.6	81.2	81.8	81.8	82.1	82.0	82.4	82.6	82.7	83.0
Korea	52.4	62.1	65.9	71.4	73.5	76.0	77.0	77.3	78.0	78.5	79.0	79.4	79.9	80.3
Luxembourg	69.3	69.7	72.8	75.5	76.8	78.0	78.1	77.8	79.2	79.5	79.3	79.5	80.6	80.7
Mexico	57.5	60.9	67.2	70.6	72.5	73.9	74.3	74.5	74.5	74.6	74.8	75.0	75.1	75.3
Netherlands	73.5	73.7	75.8	77.0	77.5	78.0	78.3	78.5	79.2	79.4	79.8	80.2	80.3	80.6
New Zealand	71.1	71.5	73.2	75.5	76.8	78.3	79.0	79.3	79.5	79.8	80.1	80.2	80.4	80.8
Norway	73.8	74.3	75.9	76.7	77.9	78.8	79.0	79.6	80.0	80.3	80.5	80.6	80.8	81.0
Poland	67.8	70.0	70.2	70.7	72.0	73.8	74.5	74.7	75.0	75.1	75.3	75.3	75.6	75.8
Portugal	63.9	66.7	71.4	74.1	75.4	76.7	77.2	77.4	78.3	78.1	78.9	79.0	79.3	79.5
Slovak Republic	70.5	69.8	70.5	71.0	72.3	73.3	73.8	73.8	74.0	74.0	74.3	74.3	74.8	75.0
Slovenia	..	..	..	73.3	74.0	75.5	76.1	76.9	77.3	77.7	78.4	78.2	78.8	79.0
Spain	69.8	72.0	75.4	77.0	78.1	79.4	79.8	79.7	80.3	80.3	81.1	81.0	81.3	81.8
Sweden	73.0	74.7	75.8	77.6	78.8	79.7	79.9	80.2	80.5	80.6	80.8	81.0	81.2	81.4
Switzerland	71.4	73.1	75.6	77.5	78.6	79.9	80.5	80.6	81.2	81.3	81.7	82.0	82.2	82.3
Turkey	48.3	54.1	58.0	67.5 |	69.3	71.0	71.8	72.2	72.5	73.0	73.2	73.3	73.6	73.8
United Kingdom	70.8	71.8	73.2	75.7	76.6	77.9	78.3	78.3	79.0	79.2	79.5	79.7	79.8	80.4
United States	69.8	70.9	73.7	75.3	75.7	76.7	76.9	77.0	77.4	77.4	77.7	77.9	78.0	78.2
OECD average	68.9	70.5	72.6	74.9	75.7	77.1	77.6	77.8	78.3	78.5	78.8	78.9	79.2	79.5
Brazil	54.5	58.6	62.6	66.4	68.4	70.3	70.9	71.2	71.5	71.7	72.0	72.2	72.5	72.7
China	46.6	62.0	66.0	68.1	69.7	71.3	71.9	72.2	72.4	72.6	72.8	73.0	73.2	73.3
India	42.4	48.8	55.1	58.2	59.7	61.3	61.9	62.2	62.5	62.8	63.1	63.4	63.8	64.1
Indonesia	41.2	47.6	54.5	61.6	64.4	67.4	68.4	68.8	69.3	69.7	70.1	70.5	70.8	71.2
Russian Federation	68.7	68.3	67.3	69.0	65.0	65.7	65.3	65.2	65.6	65.6	66.8	67.6	68.0	68.7
South Africa	49.1	52.9	56.9	61.5	60.6	55.9	53.8	52.9	52.3	51.8	51.6	51.5	51.5	51.7

StatLink http://dx.doi.org/10.1787/888932507673

Life expectancy at birth: total

Number of years

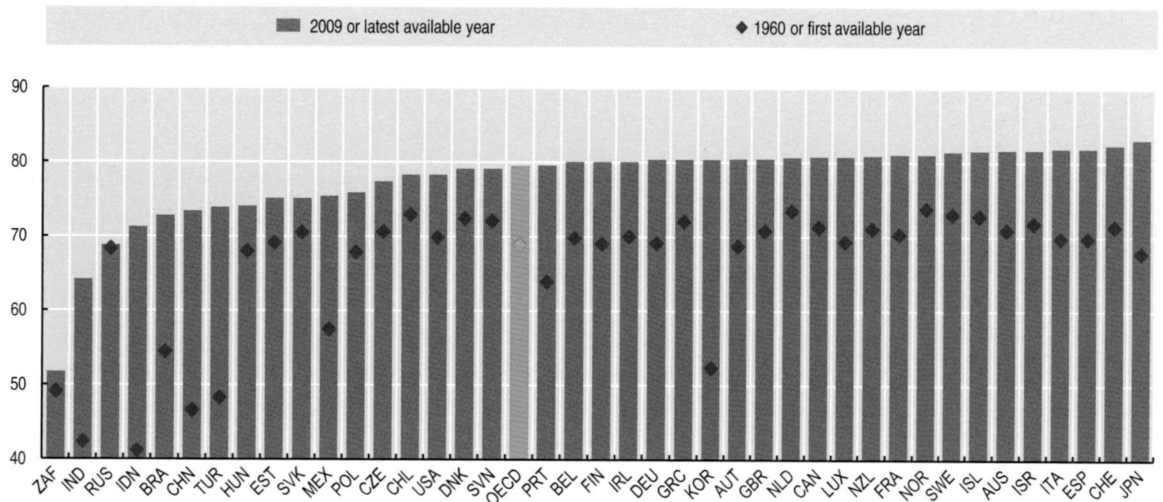

StatLink http://dx.doi.org/10.1787/888932507692

Life expectancy at birth: men

Number of years

	1960	1970	1980	1990	1995	2000	2002	2003	2004	2005	2006	2007	2008	2009
Australia	67.9	67.4	71.0	73.9	75.0	76.6	77.4	77.8	78.1	78.5	78.7	79.0	79.2	79.3
Austria	65.4	66.5	69.0	72.3	73.3	75.2	75.8	75.9	76.4	76.6	77.1	77.4	77.8	77.6
Belgium	66.8	67.8	69.9	72.7	73.5	74.6	75.1	75.3	76.0	76.2	76.6	77.1	76.9	77.3
Canada	68.4	69.3	71.7	74.4	75.0	76.3	77.0	77.2	77.5	77.7	78.0	78.3	..	..
Chile	..	..	..	69.4	71.5	73.7	74.1	74.3	74.4	74.9	75.5	75.0	75.1	75.6
Czech Republic	67.8	66.1	66.9	67.6	69.7	71.7	72.1	72.0	72.6	72.9	73.5	73.8	74.1	74.2
Denmark	70.4	70.7	71.2	72.0	72.7	74.5	74.8	75.0	75.4	76.0	76.1	76.2	76.5	76.9
Estonia	65.2	65.4	64.2	64.5	61.3	65.1	65.1	66.0	66.3	67.3	67.4	67.1	68.6	69.8
Finland	65.5	66.5	69.3	71.0	72.8	74.2	74.9	75.1	75.4	75.6	75.9	76.0	76.5	76.6
France	67.0	68.4	70.2	72.8	73.8	75.2	75.7	75.8	76.7	76.7	77.1	77.4	77.6	77.7
Germany	66.5	67.5	69.6	72.0	73.3	75.1	75.7	75.8	76.5	76.7	77.2	77.4	77.6	77.8
Greece	70.2	71.6	73.0	74.7	75.0	75.5	76.2	76.5	76.6	76.8	77.2	77.1	77.7	77.8
Hungary	65.9	66.3	65.5	65.1	65.3	67.4	68.4	68.4	68.6	68.6	69.0	69.2	69.8	70.0
Iceland	70.7	71.2	73.7	75.4	75.9	78.4	78.7	79.7	79.2	79.2	79.4	79.4	79.6	79.7
Ireland	68.1	68.8	70.1	72.1	72.8	74.0	75.2	75.8	76.4	77.2	77.3	77.4	77.8	77.4
Israel	..	70.1	72.1	74.9	75.5	76.7	77.5	77.6	78.0	78.2	78.7	78.7	79.0	79.7
Italy	67.2	69.0	70.6	73.8	75.0	76.9	77.4	77.1	77.9	78.0	78.5	78.7	79.1	..
Japan	65.3	69.3	73.3	75.9	76.4	77.7	78.3	78.4	78.6	78.6	79.0	79.2	79.3	79.6
Korea	51.1	58.7	61.8	67.3	69.6	72.3	73.4	73.9	74.5	75.1	75.7	76.1	76.5	76.8
Luxembourg	66.5	66.2	70.0	72.4	73.0	74.6	74.6	74.8	76.0	76.7	76.8	76.7	78.1	78.1
Mexico	55.8	58.5	64.1	67.7	69.7	71.3	71.8	72.0	72.0	72.2	72.4	72.6	72.7	72.9
Netherlands	71.5	70.8	72.5	73.8	74.6	75.5	76.0	76.2	76.9	77.2	77.6	78.0	78.3	78.5
New Zealand	68.4	68.4	70.1	72.5	74.1	75.9	76.6	77.0	77.3	77.7	78.0	78.2	78.4	78.8
Norway	71.6	71.2	72.4	73.5	74.8	76.0	76.4	77.1	77.6	77.8	78.2	78.3	78.4	78.7
Poland	64.9	66.6	66.0	66.2	67.6	69.7	70.4	70.5	70.7	70.8	70.9	71.0	71.3	71.5
Portugal	61.1	63.6	67.9	70.6	71.7	73.2	73.8	74.2	75.0	74.9	75.5	75.9	76.2	76.5
Slovak Republic	68.4	66.7	66.8	66.6	68.4	69.1	69.8	69.9	70.3	70.1	70.4	70.5	70.9	71.3
Slovenia	..	..	..	69.4	70.3	71.9	72.3	73.2	73.5	74.1	74.8	74.6	75.4	75.8
Spain	67.4	69.2	72.3	73.4	74.4	75.8	76.3	76.3	76.9	77.0	77.7	77.8	78.2	78.6
Sweden	71.2	72.2	72.8	74.8	76.2	77.4	77.7	77.9	78.4	78.4	78.7	78.9	79.1	79.4
Switzerland	68.7	70.0	72.3	74.0	75.4	77.0	77.9	78.0	78.6	78.7	79.2	79.5	79.8	79.9
Turkey	46.3	52.0	55.8	65.4 |	67.2	69.0	69.8	70.1	70.5	70.9	71.1	71.1	71.4	71.5
United Kingdom	67.9	68.7	70.2	72.9	74.0	75.5	76.0	76.2	76.8	77.1	77.3	77.6	77.8	78.3
United States	66.6	67.1	70.0	71.8	72.5	74.1	74.3	74.5	74.9	74.9	75.1	75.4	75.5	75.7
OECD average	66.3	67.3	69.2	71.6	72.4	74.0	74.6	74.9	75.3	75.6	75.9	76.1	76.4	76.7
Brazil	52.7	56.5	59.8	62.6	64.5	66.4	67.1	67.4	67.7	68.0	68.3	68.6	68.8	69.1
China	45.4	61.3	65.0	66.7	68.2	69.8	70.3	70.6	70.8	71.0	71.1	71.3	71.5	71.6
India	43.3	49.5	55.2	58.0	59.0	60.3	60.8	61.0	61.2	61.5	61.7	62.0	62.3	62.6
Indonesia	40.4	46.5	53.0	59.8	62.6	65.6	66.5	67.0	67.4	67.8	68.2	68.5	68.8	69.2
Russian Federation	63.7	63.0	61.5	63.8	58.3	59.1	58.7	58.5	58.9	58.9	60.4	61.3	61.8	62.8
South Africa	47.3	50.3	53.6	57.8	56.9	52.9	51.3	50.6	50.1	49.8	49.7	49.8	50.0	50.3

StatLink http://dx.doi.org/10.1787/888932507711

Life expectancy at birth: men

Number of years

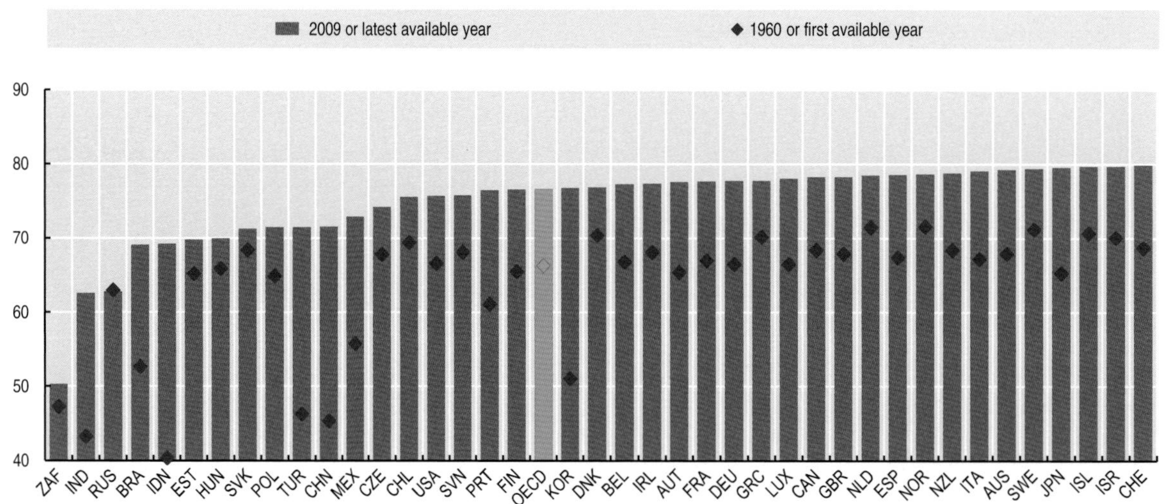

StatLink http://dx.doi.org/10.1787/888932507730

Life expectancy at birth: women

Number of years

	1960	1970	1980	1990	1995	2000	2002	2003	2004	2005	2006	2007	2008	2009
Australia	73.9	74.2	78.1	80.1	80.8	82.0	82.6	82.8	83.0	83.3	83.5	83.7	83.7	83.9
Austria	71.9	73.5	76.1	79.0	80.1	81.2	81.7	81.5	82.1	82.2	82.8	83.1	83.3	83.2
Belgium	72.8	74.3	76.7	79.5	80.4	81.0	81.2	81.1	81.9	81.9	82.3	82.6	82.6	82.8
Canada	74.2	76.4	78.9	80.8	81.0	81.7	82.0	82.2	82.3	82.5	82.8	83.0	..	..
Chile	..	..	..	76.5	78.2	80.0	80.7	80.5	80.5	80.9	81.4	80.7	80.6	80.9
Czech Republic	73.5	73.1	74.0	75.5	76.8	78.5	78.7	78.6	79.2	79.2	79.9	80.2	80.5	80.5
Denmark	74.4	75.9	77.3	77.8	77.9	79.2	79.3	79.8	80.2	80.5	80.7	80.6	81.0	81.1
Estonia	73.0	74.0	74.2	74.7	74.1	76.0	77.0	76.9	77.8	78.1	78.5	78.7	79.2	80.1
Finland	72.5	75.0	78.0	79.0	80.4	81.2	81.6	81.9	82.5	82.5	83.1	83.1	83.3	83.5
France	73.6	75.9	78.4	80.9	81.9	82.8	83.0	82.9	83.8	83.8	84.2	84.4	84.3	84.4
Germany	71.7	73.6	76.2	78.5	79.9	81.2	81.3	81.3	81.9	82.0	82.4	82.7	82.7	82.8
Greece	73.8	76.0	77.5	79.5	80.0	80.6	81.1	81.2	81.3	81.6	81.9	81.8	82.3	82.7
Hungary	70.1	72.1	72.7	73.7	74.5	75.9	76.7	76.7	76.9	76.9	77.4	77.3	77.8	77.9
Iceland	75.0	77.3	79.7	80.5	80.0	81.8	82.5	82.7	82.7	83.1	83.0	82.9	83.0	83.3
Ireland	71.9	73.5	75.6	77.7	78.3	79.2	80.5	80.8	81.3	81.6	82.1	82.1	82.4	82.5
Israel	..	73.4	75.7	78.4	79.5	80.9	81.5	81.8	82.4	82.2	82.5	82.4	83.0	83.5
Italy	72.3	74.9	77.4	80.3	81.5	82.8	83.2	82.8	83.8	83.6	84.2	84.2	84.5	..
Japan	70.2	74.7	78.8	81.9	82.8	84.6	85.2	85.3	85.6	85.5	85.8	86.0	86.0	86.4
Korea	53.7	65.6	70.0	75.5	77.4	79.6	80.5	80.8	81.4	81.9	82.4	82.7	83.3	83.8
Luxembourg	72.2	73.0	75.6	78.7	80.6	81.3	81.5	80.8	82.4	82.3	81.9	82.2	83.1	83.3
Mexico	59.2	63.2	70.2	73.5	75.2	76.5	76.8	77.0	77.0	77.0	77.2	77.4	77.5	77.6
Netherlands	75.4	76.5	79.2	80.1	80.4	80.5	80.7	80.9	81.4	81.6	81.9	82.3	82.3	82.7
New Zealand	..	74.5	76.2	78.4	79.5	80.8	81.3	81.5	81.8	82.0	82.2	82.2	82.4	82.7
Norway	76.0	77.5	79.3	79.9	80.9	81.5	81.6	82.1	82.5	82.7	82.9	82.9	83.2	83.2
Poland	70.6	73.3	74.4	75.2	76.4	78.0	78.7	78.8	79.2	79.4	79.6	79.7	80.0	80.0
Portugal	66.7	69.7	74.9	77.5	79.0	80.2	80.6	80.6	81.5	81.3	82.3	82.2	82.4	82.6
Slovak Republic	72.7	72.9	74.3	75.4	76.3	77.4	77.7	77.8	77.8	77.9	78.2	78.1	78.7	78.7
Slovenia	..	..	..	77.2	77.8	79.1	79.9	80.7	81.1	81.3	81.9	81.8	82.3	82.3
Spain	72.2	74.8	78.5	80.6	81.8	82.9	83.2	83.0	83.7	83.7	84.4	84.3	84.5	84.9
Sweden	74.9	77.1	78.8	80.4	81.4	82.0	82.1	82.5	82.7	82.8	82.9	83.0	83.2	83.4
Switzerland	74.1	76.2	79.0	80.9	81.9	82.8	83.2	83.2	83.8	84.0	84.2	84.4	84.6	84.6
Turkey	50.3	56.3	60.3	69.5 |	71.3	73.1	73.9	74.3	74.6	75.0	75.3	75.6	75.8	76.1
United Kingdom	73.7	75.0	76.2	78.5	79.3	80.3	80.6	80.5	81.2	81.3	81.7	81.8	81.9	82.5
United States	73.1	74.7	77.4	78.8	78.9	79.3	79.5	79.6	79.9	79.9	80.2	80.4	80.5	80.6
OECD average	71.5	73.6	75.9	78.3	79.0	80.2	80.6	80.7	81.2	81.3	81.7	81.8	82.0	82.2
Brazil	56.4	60.7	65.3	70.1	72.3	74.2	74.7	75.0	75.2	75.5	75.7	75.9	76.2	76.4
China	47.8	62.7	67.0	69.5	71.1	72.9	73.5	73.8	74.0	74.3	74.5	74.7	74.9	75.1
India	41.5	48.1	55.0	58.5	60.3	62.3	63.1	63.4	63.8	64.2	64.5	64.9	65.2	65.6
Indonesia	42.0	48.8	56.0	63.3	66.2	69.3	70.3	70.7	71.2	71.6	72.0	72.5	72.8	73.3
Russian Federation	72.3	73.5	73.1	74.3	71.7	72.3	71.9	71.8	72.3	72.4	73.2	73.9	74.2	74.7
South Africa	50.8	55.6	60.2	65.2	64.2	58.8	56.3	55.3	54.4	53.8	53.4	53.2	53.1	53.1

StatLink http://dx.doi.org/10.1787/888932507749

Life expectancy at birth: women

Number of years

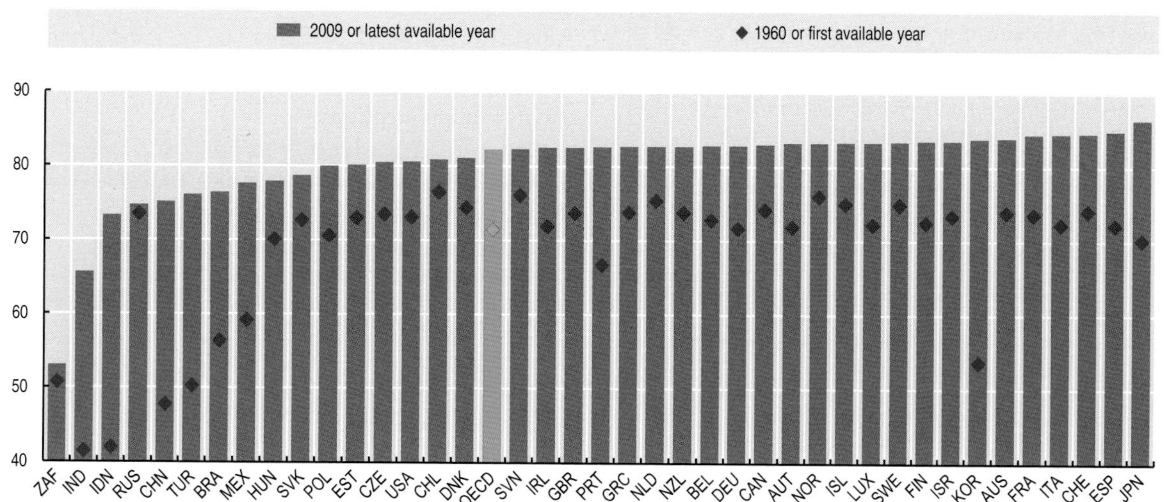

StatLink http://dx.doi.org/10.1787/888932507768

INFANT MORTALITY

Infant mortality reflects the effect of economic and social conditions of mothers and newborns, the social environment, individual lifestyles as well as the characteristics of health systems. Some countries have low levels of infant mortality and also low levels of health expenditure, suggesting that higher spending is not necessarily a precondition to improve outcomes in this area.

Definition

The infant mortality rate is the number of deaths of children under one year of age in a year, expressed per 1 000 live births. Neonatal mortality refers to the death of children during the first four weeks of life. Post neonatal mortality refers to deaths occurring between the second and the twelfth months of life.

Comparability

Some of the international variation in infant and neonatal mortality rates may be due to variations among countries in registering practices for premature infants. Most countries have no gestational age or weight limits for mortality registration. Limits exist for Norway (where the gestational age required to be counted as a death following a live birth must exceed 12 weeks) and in the Czech Republic, France, the Netherlands and Poland (which apply a minimum gestational age of 22 weeks and/or a weight threshold of 500 g).

Overview

In most OECD countries, infant mortality is low and there is little difference in rates. A small group of OECD and emerging countries, however, have infant mortality rates above 10 deaths per 1 000 live births. In 2009, rates among OECD countries ranged from less than three deaths per 1 000 live births in Nordic countries (Iceland, Sweden, Finland), Japan, Slovenia, Luxembourg and the Czech Republic, up to a high of 13 and 15 in Turkey and Mexico respectively. Infant mortality rates were also relatively high (six or more deaths per 1 000 live births) in the United States and in Chile. The average across all OECD countries was 4.4 in 2009.

Around two-thirds of the deaths that occur during the first year of life are neonatal deaths (i.e. during the first four weeks). Birth defects, prematurity and other conditions arising during pregnancy are the principal factors contributing to neonatal mortality in developed countries. With an increasing number of women deferring childbearing and the rise in multiple births linked with fertility treatments, the number of pre-term births has tended to increase. In a number of higher-income countries, this has contributed to a levelling-off of the downward trend in infant mortality rates over the past few years. For deaths beyond a month (post neonatal mortality), there tends to be a greater range of causes – the most common being SIDS (Sudden Infant Death Syndrome), birth defects, infections and accidents.

All OECD countries have achieved remarkable progress in reducing infant mortality rates from the levels of 1970, when the average was approaching 30 deaths per 1 000 live births. This equates to a cumulative reduction of 85% since 1970. Portugal has seen its infant mortality rate reduced by nearly 7% per year on average since 1970, moving from the country with the highest rate in Europe to an infant mortality rate among the lowest in the OECD in 2009. Large reductions in infant mortality rates have also been observed in Korea, Israel and Turkey. On the other hand, the reduction in infant mortality rates has been slower in the Netherlands and the United States. The infant mortality rates in the United States used to be well below the OECD average, but it is now above average.

Sources

- OECD (2011), *OECD Health Statistics*, OECD Publishing.

Further information

Analytical publications

- OECD (2011), *Doing Better for Families*, OECD Publishing.
- OECD (2009), *Doing Better for Children*, OECD Publishing.

Statistical publications

- OECD (2011), *Health at a Glance: OECD Indicators*, OECD Publishing.
- OECD (2011), *Society at a Glance 2011: OECD Social Indicators*, OECD Publishing.
- OECD (2006), *Economic Valuation of Environmental Health Risks to Children*, OECD Publishing.

Online databases

- *OECD Health Statistics*.

Websites

- OECD Health Data, *www.oecd.org/health/healthdata*.

Infant mortality

Deaths per 1 000 live births

	1970	1980	1990	1995	2000	2001	2002	2003	2004	2005	2006	2007	2008	2009
Australia	17.9	10.7	8.2	5.7	5.2	5.3	5.0	4.8	4.7	5.0	4.7	4.2	4.1	4.3
Austria	25.9	14.3	7.8	5.4	4.8	4.8	4.1	4.5	4.5	4.2	3.6	3.7	3.7	3.8
Belgium	21.1	12.1	8.0	6.0	4.8	4.5	4.4	4.1	3.9	3.7	4.0	3.9	3.7	3.4
Canada	18.8	10.4	6.8	6.1	5.3	5.2	5.4	5.3	5.3	5.4	5.0	5.1	..	..
Chile	79.3	33.0	16.0	11.1	8.9	8.3	7.8	7.8	8.4	7.9	7.6	8.3	7.8	7.9
Czech Republic	20.2	16.9	10.8	7.7	4.1	4.0	4.1	3.9	3.7	3.4	3.3	3.1	2.8	2.9
Denmark	14.2	8.4	7.5	5.1	5.3	4.9	4.4	4.4	4.4	4.4	3.5	4.0	4.0	3.1
Estonia	17.7	17.1	12.3	14.9	8.4	8.8	5.7	7.0	6.4	5.4	4.4	5.0	5.0	3.6
Finland	13.2	7.6	5.6	3.9	3.8	3.2	3.0	3.1	3.3	3.0	2.8	2.7	2.6	2.6
France	18.2	10.0	7.3	5.0	4.5	4.6	4.2	4.2	4.0	3.8	3.8	3.8	3.8	3.9
Germany	22.5	12.4	7.0	5.3	4.4	4.3	4.2	4.2	4.1	3.9	3.8	3.9	3.5	3.5
Greece	29.6	17.9	9.7	8.1	5.9	5.1	5.1	4.0	4.1	3.8	3.7	3.5	2.7	3.1
Hungary	35.9	23.2	14.8	10.7	9.2	8.1	7.2	7.3	6.6	6.2	5.7	5.9	5.6	5.1
Iceland	13.2	7.7	5.9	6.1	3.0	2.7	2.2	2.4	2.8	2.3	1.4	2.0	2.5	1.8
Ireland	19.5	11.1	8.2	6.4	6.2	5.7	5.1	5.1	4.8	4.0	3.6	3.1	3.8	3.2
Israel	..	15.6	9.9	6.8	5.5	5.1	5.4	4.9	4.6	4.4	4.0	3.9	3.8	3.8
Italy	29.6	14.6	8.1	6.1	4.3	4.4	4.1	3.9	3.9	3.8	3.6	3.5	3.3	3.7
Japan	13.1	7.5	4.6	4.3	3.2	3.1	3.0	3.0	2.8	2.8	2.6	2.6	2.6	2.4
Korea	45.0	17.0	10.0	7.7	6.2	..	5.3	..	..	4.7	4.1	3.6	3.5	..
Luxembourg	24.9	11.5	7.3	5.5	5.1	5.9	5.1	4.9	3.9	2.6	2.5	1.8	1.8	2.5
Mexico	80.9	52.6	39.2	27.7	19.4	18.3	18.1	17.3	17.6	16.8	16.2	15.7	15.2	14.7
Netherlands	12.7	8.6	7.1	5.5	5.1	5.4	5.0	4.8	4.4	4.9	4.4	4.1	3.8	3.8
New Zealand	16.7	13.0	8.4	6.7	6.3	5.6	6.2	5.4	5.9	5.0	5.1	4.8	5.0	4.7
Norway	11.3	8.1	6.9	4.0	3.8	3.9	3.5	3.3	3.2	3.1	3.2	3.1	2.7	3.1
Poland	36.7	25.5	19.3	13.6	8.1	7.7	7.5	7.0	6.8	6.4	6.0	6.0	5.6	5.6
Portugal	55.5	24.3	10.9	7.4	5.5	5.0	5.0	4.1	3.8	3.5	3.3	3.4	3.3	3.6
Slovak Republic	25.7	20.9	12.0	11.0	8.6	6.2	7.6	7.9	6.8	7.2	6.6	6.1	5.9	5.7
Slovenia	24.5	15.3	8.4	5.5	4.9	4.2	3.8	4.0	3.7	4.1	3.4	2.8	2.4	2.4
Spain	28.1	12.3	7.6	5.5	4.4	4.1	4.1	3.9	4.0	3.8	3.5	3.5	3.3	3.3
Sweden	11.0	6.9	6.0	4.1	3.4	3.7	3.3	3.1	3.1	2.4	2.8	2.5	2.5	2.5
Switzerland	15.1	9.1	6.8	5.1	4.9	5.0	4.5	4.3	4.2	4.2	4.4	3.9	4.0	4.3
Turkey	145.0	117.5	51.5 |	45.2	31.6	28.3	25.4	22.8	20.5	18.4	16.9	15.9	14.9	13.1
United Kingdom	18.5	12.1	7.9	6.2	5.6	5.5	5.2	5.2	5.1	5.1	5.0	4.8	4.7	4.6
United States	20.0	12.6	9.2	7.6	6.9	6.9	7.0	6.8	6.8	6.9	6.7	6.8	6.5	..
OECD average	29.3	18.2	9.9	8.6	6.7	6.3	5.9	5.7	5.5	5.2	4.9	4.7	4.6	4.4
Brazil	95.2	72.0	46.0	36.1	28.2	..	..	..	..	21.5	20.4	19.3	18.3	17.3
China	82.8	46.1	36.8	36.4	32.2	..	..	..	..	21.5	..	..	14.9	13.8
India	126.2	103.2	83.8	77.0	67.6	66.0	64.0	..	..	57.2	55.4	53.6	51.9	50.3
Indonesia	103.0	78.1	56.4	45.6	39.5	..	..	..	..	33.7	32.6	31.7	30.7	29.8
Russian Federation	23.0	22.1	17.3	18.1	15.4	14.6	13.4	12.6	11.8	11.0	10.2	9.4	8.5	8.2
South Africa	..	68.1	47.8	48.2	54.3	..	..	..	..	52.4	48.9	46.9	44.7	43.1

StatLink http://dx.doi.org/10.1787/888932507787

Infant mortality

Deaths per 1 000 live births

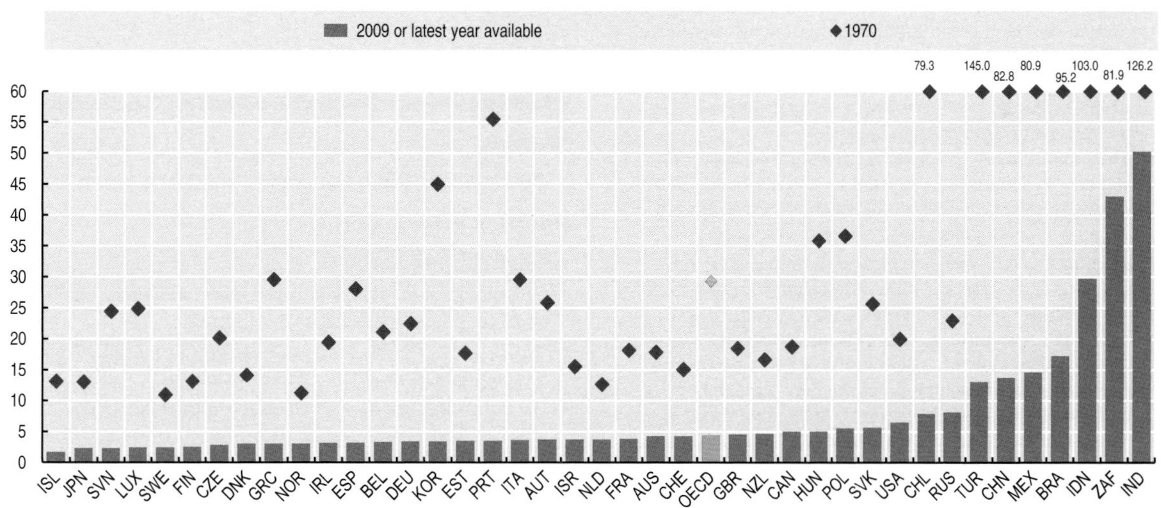

StatLink http://dx.doi.org/10.1787/888932507806

SUICIDES

The intentional killing of oneself can be evidence not only of personal breakdown, but also of a deterioration of the social context in which an individual lives. Suicide may be the end-point of a number of different contributing factors. It is more likely to occur during crisis periods associated with upheavals in personal relationships, alcohol and drug abuse, unemployment, clinical depression and other forms of mental illness. Because of this, suicide is often used as a proxy indicator of the mental health status of a population.

Definition

The World Health Organisation defines suicide as an act deliberately initiated and performed by a person in the full knowledge or expectation of its fatal outcome. Data on suicide rates are based on official registers of causes of death.

Mortality rates are based on numbers of deaths registered in a country in a year divided by the size of the corresponding population. The rates have been age-standardised to the 1980 OECD population to remove variations arising from differences in age structures across countries and over time. The source is the WHO Mortality Database.

Comparability

Comparability of data between countries is affected by a number of reporting criteria, including how a person's intention of killing themselves is ascertained, who is responsible for completing the death certificate, whether a forensic investigation is carried out, and the provisions for confidentiality of the cause of death. The number of suicides in certain countries may be under-estimated because of the stigma that is associated with the act, or because of data issues associated with reporting criteria. Caution is required therefore in interpreting variations across countries.

Overview

Suicide is a significant cause of death in many OECD countries, with almost 150 000 such deaths in 2009. There were fewest suicides in southern European countries (Greece, Italy and Spain) and in Mexico and Israel, at six or less deaths per 100 000 population. Suicides rates were highest in Korea, the Russian Federation, Hungary, and Japan, at more than 19 deaths per 100 000 population. There is a ten-fold difference between Korea and Greece, the countries with the lowest and highest suicide rates.

In general, death rates from suicide are three to four times greater for men than for women across OECD countries, and this gender gap has been fairly stable over time. The exception is Korea, where women are much more likely to take their own lives than in other OECD countries. Suicide is also related to age, with young people aged under 25 and elderly people especially at risk. While suicide rates among the latter have generally declined over the past two decades, less progress has been observed among younger people.

Since 1995, suicide rates have decreased in many OECD countries, with declines of 35% or more in Estonia, Luxembourg and Austria. On the other hand, suicide rates have increased in Korea, Chile, Mexico, Japan and Portugal, although in Mexico rates remain at low levels, and in Japan rates have been static since the late 1990s. In Korea and Japan, suicide rates are well above the OECD average.

In Korea, male suicide rates more than doubled from 17 per 100 000 in 1995 to 39 in 2009, and rates among women are the highest in the OECD, at 20 per 100 000. Between 2006 and 2010, the number of persons treated for depression and bipolar disease in Korea rose sharply (increases of 17 and 29 per cent respectively), with those in low socioeconomic groups more likely to be affected. Economic downturn, weakening social integration and the erosion of the traditional family support base for the elderly have all been implicated in Korea's recent increase in suicide rates.

Suicide is often linked with depression and the abuse of alcohol and other substances. Early detection of these psycho-social problems in high-risk groups by families and health professionals is an important part of suicide prevention campaigns, together with the provision of effective support and treatment. Many countries are promoting mental health and developing national strategies for prevention, focussing on at-risk groups. In Germany, as well as Finland and Iceland, suicide prevention programmes have been based on efforts to promote strong multisectoral collaboration and networking.

Sources

- OECD (2011), *Health at a Glance*, OECD Publishing.

Further information

Analytical publications

- OECD (2011), *Mental Health and Work: Evidence, Challenges and Policy Directions*, OECD Publishing.
- OECD (2010), "New social challenges", in OECD, *Trends Shaping Education 2010*, OECD Publishing.
- OECD (2008), "Are All Jobs Good for Your Health? The Impact of Work Status and Working Conditions on Mental Health", in OECD, *OECD Employment Outlook 2008*, OECD Publishing.
- OECD (2011), *Health at a Glance: OECD Indicators*, OECD Publishing.

Trends in suicide rates

Per 100 000 persons

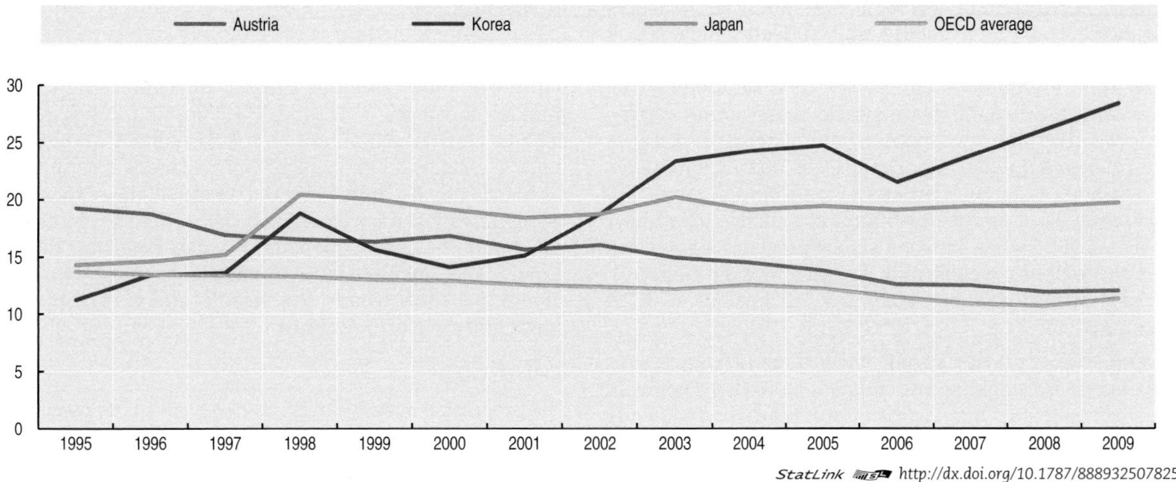

StatLink http://dx.doi.org/10.1787/888932507825

Suicide rates by gender

Per 100 000 persons, 2009 or latest available year

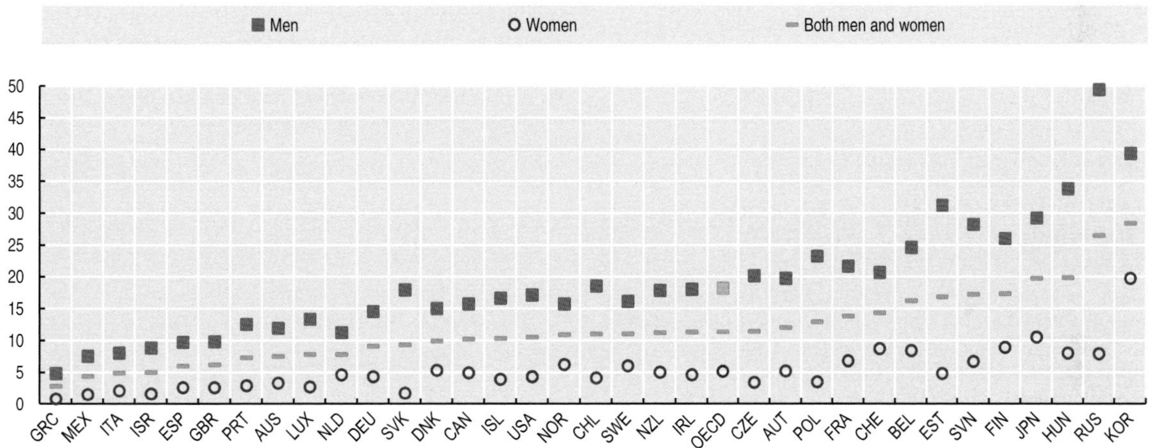

StatLink http://dx.doi.org/10.1787/888932507844

Change in suicide rates

Percentage, 1995-2009 or latest available period

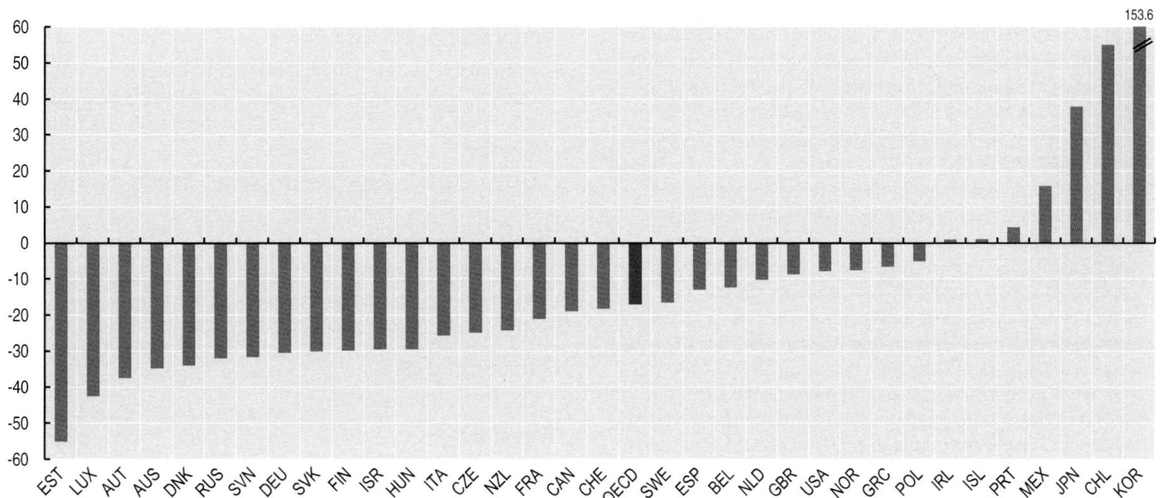

StatLink http://dx.doi.org/10.1787/888932507863

SMOKING

Tobacco is responsible for about one-in-ten adult deaths worldwide, equating to about 6 million deaths each year. It is a major risk factor for at least two of the leading causes of premature mortality – circulatory disease and cancer, increasing the risk of heart attack, stroke, lung cancer, cancers of the larynx and mouth, and pancreatic cancer. It also causes peripheral vascular disease and hypertension. In addition, it is an important contributory factor for respiratory diseases such as chronic obstructive pulmonary disease (COPD), while smoking among pregnant women can lead to low birth weight and illnesses among infants. It remains the largest avoidable risk to health in OECD countries.

Several studies provide strong evidence of socio-economic differences in smoking and related mortality. People in lower social groups have a greater prevalence and intensity of smoking. The influence of smoking as a determinant of overall health inequalities is such that, in a non-smoking population, mortality differences between social groups would be halved.

In the post-war period, most OECD countries tended to follow a general pattern marked by very high smoking rates among men (50% or more) through to the 1960s and 1970s, while the 1980s and the 1990s were characterised by a marked downturn in tobacco consumption. Much of this decline can be attributed to policies aimed at reducing tobacco consumption through public awareness campaigns, advertising bans and increased taxation, in response to rising rates of tobacco-related diseases. In addition to government policies, actions by anti-smoking interest groups were very effective in reducing smoking rates by changing beliefs about the health effects of smoking, particularly in North America.

Definition

The proportion of daily smokers is defined as the percentage of the population aged 15 years and over reporting smoking every day.

Comparability

International comparability is limited due to the lack of standardisation in the measurement of smoking habits in health interview surveys across OECD countries. Variations remain in the age groups surveyed, wording of questions, response categories and survey methodologies. For example in a number of countries, respondents are asked if they smoke regularly, rather than daily.

Overview

The proportion of daily smokers among the adult population varies greatly across countries, even between neighbouring countries. Thirteen of 34 OECD countries had less than 20% of the adult population smoking daily in 2009. Rates among OECD countries were lowest in Mexico, Sweden, Iceland, the United States, Canada and Australia. Although large disparities remain, smoking rates across most OECD countries have shown a marked decline. On average, smoking rates have decreased by about one-fifth over the past ten years, with a higher decline for men than for women. Large declines occurred in Denmark (from 31% to 19%), Iceland (from 25% to 16%), Norway (from 32% to 21%), Canada (from 24% to 16%) and New Zealand (from 26% to 18%). Greece maintains the highest level of smoking (40%), along with Chile and Ireland among OECD countries, with around 30% or more of the adult population smoking daily. Smoking rates are also high in the Russian Federation. Greece and the Czech Republic are the only two OECD countries where smoking rates have increased over the past ten years.

Smoking prevalence among men is higher in all OECD countries except Sweden. Rates for men and women are nearly equal in Iceland, Norway and the United Kingdom. Smoking rates for women continue to decline in most OECD countries, and in a number of cases (Canada, Ireland, the Netherlands, New Zealand and the United States) at an even faster pace than rates for men. However, in three countries for women smoking rates have been increasing over the last ten years (the Czech Republic, Greece and Korea), but even in these countries women are still less likely to smoke than men. In 2009, the gender gap in smoking rates was particularly large in Korea, Japan and Turkey, as well as in the Russian Federation, Indonesia and China.

Sources

- OECD (2011), *OECD Health Statistics*.

Further information

Analytical publications

- Joumard, I., et al. (2008), "Health Status Determinants: Lifestyle, Environment, Health Care Resources and Efficiency", *OECD Economics Department Working Papers*, No. 627.
- OECD (2010), *Health Care Systems: Efficiency and Policy Settings*, OECD Publishing.

Statistical publications

- OECD (2011), *Health at a Glance*, OECD Publishing.
- OECD (2010), *Health at a Glance: Europe 2010*, OECD Publishing.

Online databases

- *OECD Health Statistics*.

Websites

- OECD Health Data, *www.oecd.org/health/healthdata*.
- Health at a Glance 2011, *www.oecd.org/health/healthataglance*.

Adult population smoking daily

As a percentage of adult population, 2009 or latest available year

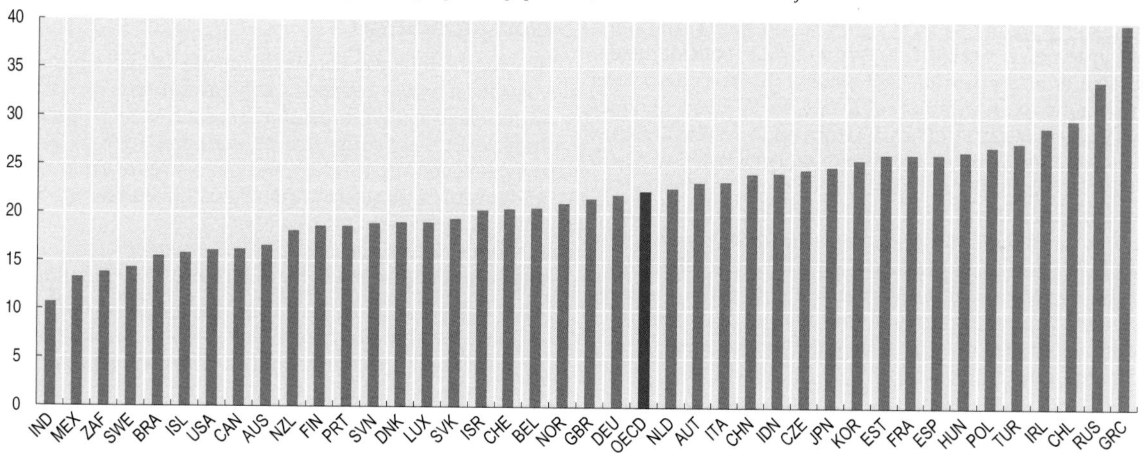

StatLink http://dx.doi.org/10.1787/888932507882

Change in smoking rates

Percentage change over the period 1999-2009 or latest available period

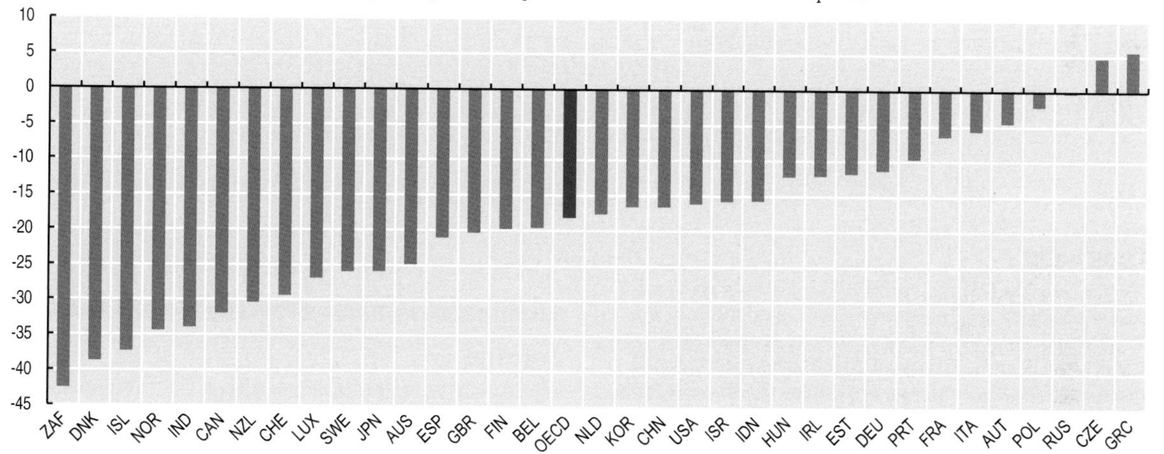

StatLink http://dx.doi.org/10.1787/888932507901

Adult population smoking daily by gender

Percentage, 2009 or latest available year

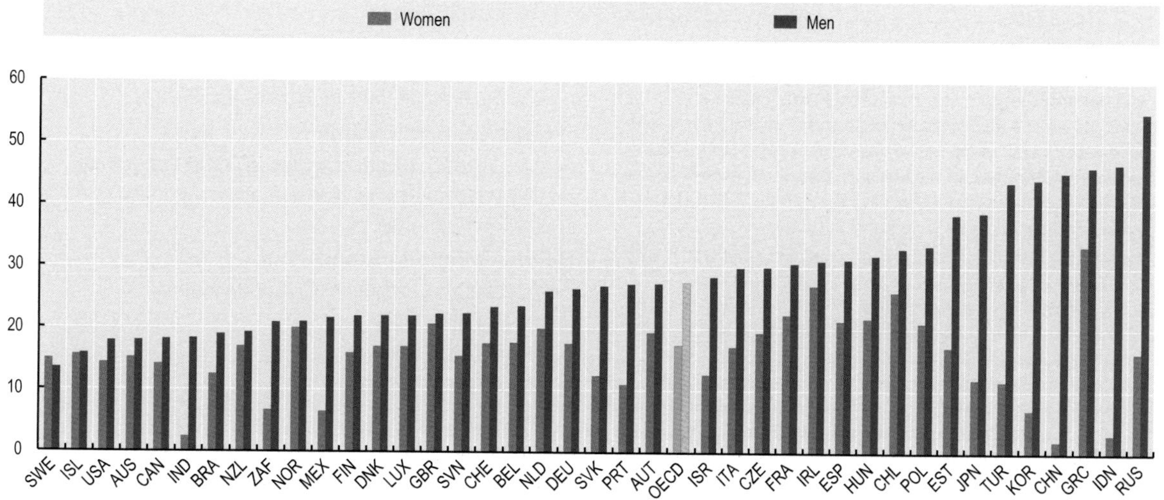

StatLink http://dx.doi.org/10.1787/888932507920

ALCOHOL CONSUMPTION

The health burden related to excessive alcohol consumption, both in terms of morbidity and mortality, is considerable in most parts of the world. High alcohol intake is associated with numerous harmful health and social consequences, such as increased risk of heart, stroke and vascular diseases, as well as liver cirrhosis and certain cancers. Foetal exposure to alcohol increases the risk of birth defects and intellectual impairments. Alcohol also contributes to death and disability through accidents injuries, assault, violence, homicide and suicide. It is estimated to cause more than 2 million deaths worldwide per year. In the Russian Federation, the sharp rise in premature mortality and decline in life expectancy during the 1990s was due, in part, to excessive alcohol consumption.

In 2010, the World Health Organization endorsed a global strategy to combat the harmful use of alcohol, through direct measures such as medical services for alcohol-related health problems, and indirect measures such as policy options for the availability, marketing and pricing of alcohol.

Definition

Alcohol consumption is defined as annual sales of pure alcohol in litres per person aged 15 years and over.

Comparability

The methodology to convert alcoholic drinks to pure alcohol may differ across countries. Official statistics do not include unrecorded alcohol consumption, such as home production. Italy reports consumption for the population 14 years and over, Sweden for 16 years and over, and for Japan 20 years and over. In some countries (*e.g.* Luxembourg), national sales do not accurately reflect actual consumption by residents, since purchases by non-residents may create a significant gap between national sales and consumption.

Although adult alcohol consumption per capita gives useful evidence of long-term trends, it does not identify sub-populations at risk from harmful drinking patterns. The consumption of large quantities of alcohol at a single session, termed "binge drinking", is a particularly dangerous pattern of consumption, which is on the rise in some countries and social groups, especially among young males.

Overview

Alcohol consumption as measured by annual sales stands at 9.1 litres per adult on average across OECD countries, using the most recent data available. France, Austria, Portugal, the Czech Republic and Estonia reported the highest consumption of alcohol, with 12.0 litres or more per adult per year in 2009. Low alcohol consumption was recorded in Indonesia, India, Turkey and Israel where religious and cultural traditions restrict the use of alcohol among some population groups, as well as in China, Mexico and some of the Nordic countries (Norway, Iceland and Sweden).

Although average alcohol consumption has gradually fallen in many OECD countries over the past three decades, it has risen in some others such as Iceland, Finland and Mexico. There has been a degree of convergence in drinking habits across OECD countries, with wine consumption increasing in many traditional beer-drinking countries and *vice versa*. The traditional wine-producing countries of Italy, France and Spain, as well as the Slovak Republic and Germany have seen per capita consumption fall by one third or more since 1980. Alcohol consumption in the Russian Federation, as well as in Brazil and China has risen substantially, although in the latter two countries per capita consumption is still low.

Variations in alcohol consumption across countries and over time reflect not only changing drinking habits but also the policy responses to control alcohol use. Curbs on advertising, sales restrictions and taxation have all proven to be effective measures to reduce alcohol consumption. Strict controls on sales and high taxation are mirrored by overall lower consumption in most Nordic countries, while falls in consumption in France, Italy and Spain may also be associated with the voluntary and statutory regulation of advertising, following a 1989 European directive.

Sources

- OECD (2011), *OECD Health Statistics*, OECD Publishing.

Further information

Analytical publications

- OECD (2011), *Consumption Tax Trends 2010: VAT/GST and Excise Rates, Trends and Administration Issues*, OECD Publishing.
- OECD (2010), *Drugs and Driving: Detection and Deterrence*, OECD Publishing.
- Huerta, M. and F. Borgonovi (2010), "Education, Alcohol Use and Abuse Among Young Adults in Britain", *OECD Education Working Papers*, No. 50.

Statistical publications

- OECD (2011), *Health at a Glance*, OECD Publishing.
- OECD (2010), *Health at a Glance: Europe 2010*, OECD Publishing.

Methodological publications

- OECD (2011), *A System of Health Accounts*, OECD Publishing.

Online databases

- *OECD Health Statistics*.

Websites

- OECD Health Data, *www.oecd.org/health/healthdata*.
- Health at a Glance 2011, *www.oecd.org/health/healthataglance*.

Alcohol consumption among population aged 15 and over

Litres per capita, 2009 or latest available year

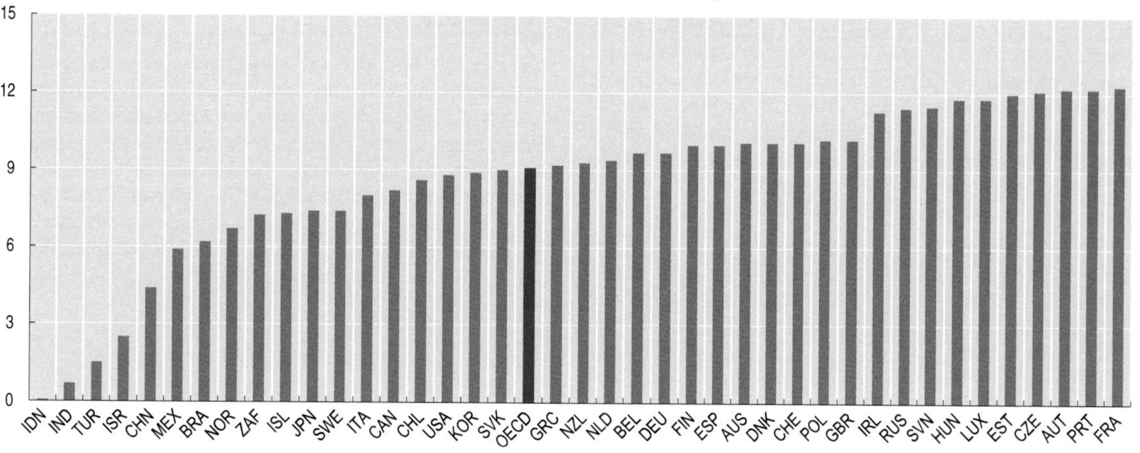

StatLink http://dx.doi.org/10.1787/888932507939

Change in alcohol consumption in litres per capita among population aged 15 and over

Percentage change in litres per capita over the period 1980-2009 or latest available period

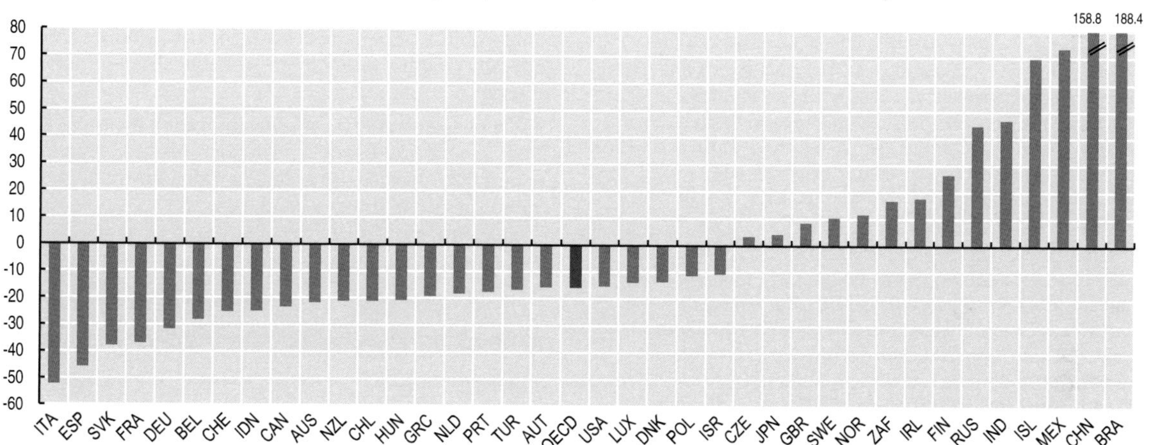

StatLink http://dx.doi.org/10.1787/888932507958

Trends in alcohol consumption among population aged 15 and over

Litres per capita

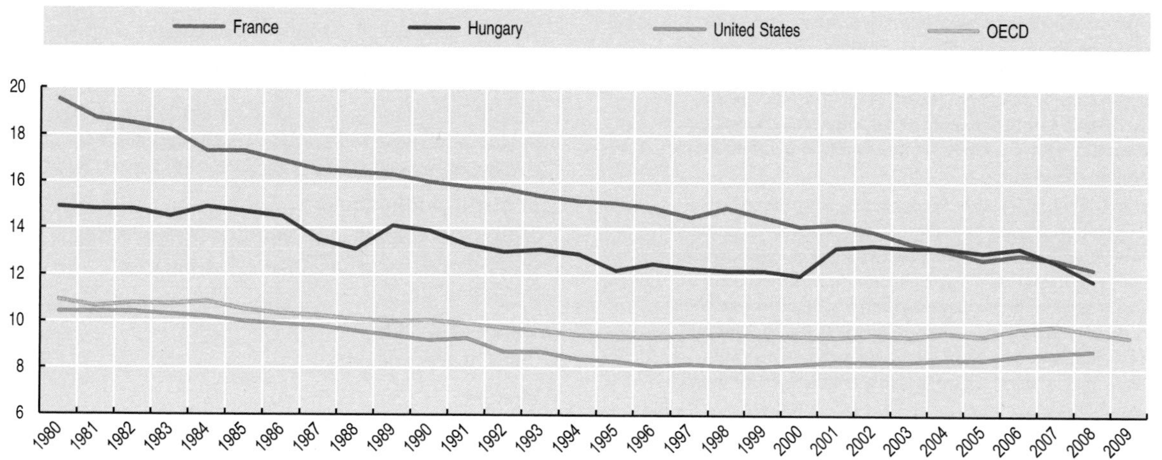

StatLink http://dx.doi.org/10.1787/888932507977

OVERWEIGHT AND OBESITY

The rise in overweight and obesity is a major public health concern. Obesity is a known risk factor for numerous health problems, including hypertension, high cholesterol, diabetes, cardiovascular diseases, respiratory problems (asthma), musculoskeletal diseases (arthritis) and some forms of cancer. At an individual level, several factors can lead to obesity, including excessive calorie consumption, lack of physical activity, genetic predisposition and disorders of the endocrine system.

Because obesity is associated with higher risks of chronic illnesses, it is linked to significant additional health care costs. There is a time lag between the onset of obesity and related health problems, suggesting that the rise in obesity over the past two decades will mean higher health care costs in the future. Mortality also increases sharply once the overweight threshold is crossed.

Overview

Based on latest available surveys, more than half (50.3%) of the adult population in the OECD report that they are overweight or obese. Among those countries where height and weight were measured, the proportion was even greater, at 55.8%. The prevalence of overweight and obesity among adults exceeds 50% in no less than 19 of 34 OECD countries. In contrast, overweight and obesity rates are much lower in Japan and Korea and in some European countries (France and Switzerland), although even in these countries rates are increasing.

The prevalence of obesity, which presents even greater health risks than overweight, varies tenfold among OECD countries, from a low of 4% in Japan and Korea, to 30% or more in the United States and Mexico. Across the entire OECD region, 17% of the adult population are obese. Average obesity rates among men and women are similar, although there are disparities in some countries. In Chile, Turkey and Mexico, a greater proportion of women are obese, whereas in the Russian Federation, Luxembourg and Spain men are more likely to be obese.

Obesity prevalence has more than doubled over the past 20 years in Australia and New Zealand, and increased by half in the United Kingdom and the United States. Some 20-24% of adults in Australia, Canada, the United Kingdom and Ireland are obese, about the same rate as in the United States in the early 1990s. Obesity rates in many western European countries have also increased substantially over the past decade. The rapid rise occurred regardless of where levels stood two decades ago. Obesity almost doubled in both the Netherlands and the United Kingdom, even though the current rate in the Netherlands is around half that in the United Kingdom.

In most countries, the rise in obesity has affected all population groups, regardless of sex, age, race, income or education level, but to varying extents. Evidence from a number of countries (Australia, Austria, Canada, France, Italy, Korea, Spain, the United Kingdom and the United States) indicates that obesity tends to be more common among individuals in disadvantaged socio-economic groups, especially women. There is also a relationship between the number of years spent in full-time education and obesity, with the most educated individuals displaying lower rates. Again, the gradient in obesity is stronger in women than in men.

Definition

Overweight and obesity are defined as excessive weight presenting health risks because of the high proportion of body fat. The most frequently used measure is based on the body mass index (BMI), which is a single number that evaluates an individual's weight in relation to height (weight/height^2, with weight in kilograms and height in metres). Based on the WHO classification, adults with a BMI between 25 and 30 are defined as overweight, and those with a BMI over 30 as obese.

Comparability

The BMI classification may not be suitable for all ethnic groups, who may be exposed to different levels of health risk for the same level of BMI. The thresholds for adults are also not suitable to measure overweight and obesity among children.

For most countries, overweight and obesity rates are self-reported through estimates of height and weight from population-based health interview surveys. However, around one-third of OECD countries derive their estimates from health examinations. These differences limit data comparability. Estimates from health examinations are generally higher and more reliable than from health interviews.

The following countries use measured data: Australia, Canada, Chile, the Czech Republic, Finland, Ireland, Japan, Korea, Luxembourg, Mexico, New Zealand, the Slovak Republic, the United Kingdom and the United States.

Sources

- OECD (2011), *OECD Health Statistics*, OECD Publishing.

Further information

Analytical publications

- OECD (2010), *Obesity and the Economics of Prevention: Fit not Fat*, OECD Publishing.
- Sassi, F. *et al.* (2009), "Education and Obesity in Four OECD Countries", *OECD Health Working Papers*, No. 46.
- Sassi, F. *et al.* (2009), "Improving Lifestyles, Tackling Obesity: The Health and Economic Impact of Prevention Strategies", *OECD Health Working Papers*, No. 48.
- Sassi, F. *et al.* (2009), "The Obesity Epidemic: Analysis of Past and Projected Future Trends in Selected OECD Countries", *OECD Health Working Papers*, No. 45.

Statistical publications

- OECD (2011), *Health at a Glance*, OECD Publishing.
- OECD (2010), *Health at a Glance: Europe 2010*, OECD Publishing.

Online databases

- *OECD Health Statistics*.

Websites

- OECD Health Data, *www.oecd.org/health/healthdata*.
- OECD Health at a Glance, *www.oecd.org/health/healthataglance*.

Overweight and obese population aged 15 and above

As a percentage of population aged 15 and above, 2009 or latest available year

	Women			Men			Total		
	Overweight	Obese	Overweight and obese	Overweight	Obese	Overweight and obese	Overweight	Obese	Overweight and obese
Australia	31.0	23.6	54.7	42.2	25.5	67.7	36.7	24.6	61.2
Austria	29.9	12.7	42.6	44.9	12.0	56.9	35.3	12.4	47.7
Belgium	26.0	14.4	40.4	40.6	13.1	53.7	33.1	13.8	46.9
Canada	30.7	23.2	54.0	40.9	25.2	66.1	35.8	24.2	60.0
Chile	33.6	30.7	64.3	45.3	19.2	64.6	39.3	25.1	64.5
Czech Republic	29.0	17.0	46.0	42.0	18.0	60.0	35.0	17.0	52.0
Denmark	26.3	13.1	39.4	40.5	13.7	54.3	33.3	13.4	46.7
Estonia	26.3	18.3	44.6	38.8	17.5	56.3	31.6	18.0	49.6
Finland	31.3	21.1	52.4	46.6	19.3	65.9	39.0	20.2	59.1
France	22.3	11.5	33.8	32.2	10.9	43.1	27.0	11.2	38.2
Germany	29.1	13.8	42.9	44.4	15.7	60.1	36.7	14.7	51.4
Greece	34.8	18.5	53.3	47.2	17.7	64.9	40.7	18.1	58.9
Hungary	30.2	18.3	48.5	38.6	20.8	59.4	34.1	19.5	53.6
Iceland	32.2	21.3	53.5	47.7	18.9	66.6	40.1	20.1	60.2
Ireland	32.0	24.0	56.0	45.0	22.0	67.0	38.0	23.0	61.0
Israel	29.1	14.4	43.5	39.0	13.2	52.2	33.9	13.8	47.7
Italy	27.7	9.3	37.0	45.2	11.3	56.5	36.1	10.3	46.3
Japan	17.3	3.5	20.8	26.1	4.3	30.5	21.2	3.9	25.1
Korea	22.4	4.1	26.4	30.9	3.6	34.5	26.6	3.8	30.5
Luxembourg	29.2	21.0	50.2	42.6	23.6	66.2	36.7	22.5	59.1
Mexico	37.4	34.5	71.9	42.5	24.2	66.7	39.5	30.0	69.5
Netherlands	29.5	12.4	41.9	41.3	11.2	52.5	35.4	11.8	47.2
New Zealand	30.6	27.0	57.6	41.7	26.0	67.7	36.2	26.5	62.6
Norway	27.0	8.0	36.0	43.0	11.0	55.0	35.0	10.0	46.0
Poland	26.6	12.5	39.1	39.5	12.6	52.1	32.8	12.5	45.3
Portugal	31.4	16.1	47.5	41.4	14.6	56.0	36.2	15.4	51.6
Slovak Republic	31.0	16.7	47.7	40.7	17.1	57.8	34.6	16.9	51.5
Slovenia	29.6	15.8	45.4	47.9	17.0	64.9	38.7	16.4	55.1
Spain	29.9	14.7	44.6	45.5	17.3	62.8	37.6	16.0	53.6
Sweden	27.6	10.7	38.3	42.4	11.7	54.1	35.1	11.2	46.3
Switzerland	20.9	7.7	28.6	37.8	8.6	46.3	29.2	8.1	37.3
Turkey	27.4	18.5	45.9	36.9	12.3	49.2	32.4	15.2	47.6
United Kingdom	32.8	23.9	56.7	43.7	22.1	65.8	38.3	23.0	61.3
United States	28.6	35.5	64.1	40.1	32.2	72.3	34.2	33.8	68.0
OECD average	28.8	17.2	46.1	41.3	16.7	58.0	34.9	16.9	51.8
Brazil	28.3	14.0	42.3	37.3	13.7	51.0	32.7	13.9	46.6
China	15.4	3.4	18.8	16.7	2.4	19.1	16.0	2.9	18.9
India	9.8	2.8	12.6	8.0	1.3	9.3	8.9	2.0	10.9
Indonesia	3.6	3.6	..	1.1	1.1	..	2.4	2.4	..
Russian Federation	25.0	20.1	45.1	31.1	11.8	42.9	28.1	15.9	44.0
South Africa	27.5	27.4	54.9	21.0	8.8	29.8	24.3	18.1	42.4

StatLink http://dx.doi.org/10.1787/888932507996

Obese population aged 15 and above

As a percentage of population aged 15 and above, 2009 or latest available year

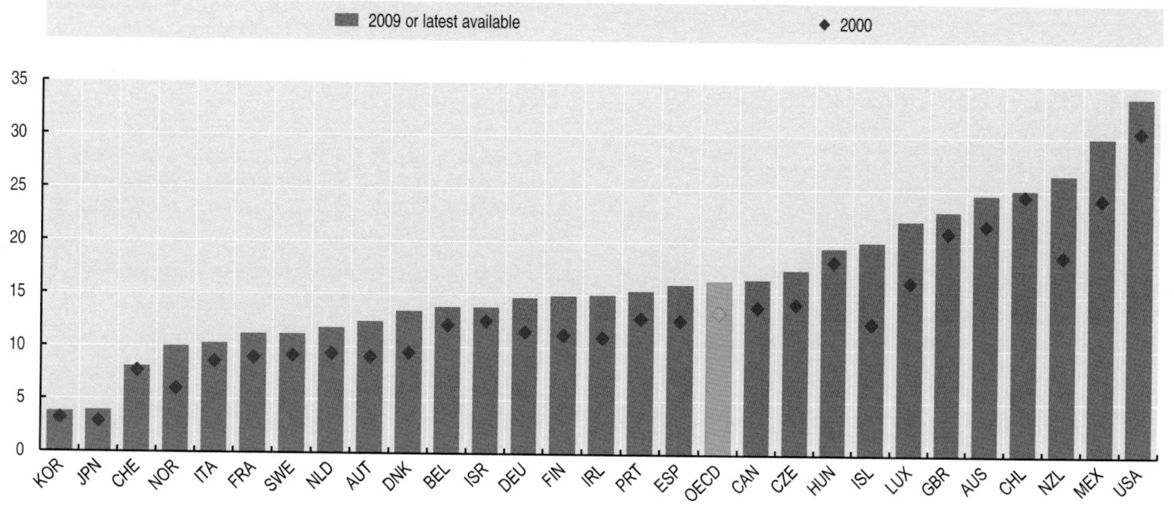

StatLink http://dx.doi.org/10.1787/888932508015

DOCTORS

Access to high-quality health services depends crucially on the size, skill mix, geographic distribution and productivity of the health workforce. Health workers, and in particular doctors and nurses, are the cornerstone of health systems.

Many OECD countries are concerned about current or looming doctor shortages. Forecasting the future supply and demand of doctors is difficult, because of uncertainties concerning overall economic growth, changes in physician productivity, advances in medical technologies, changing roles of physicians versus other care providers, as well as changes in the health needs of the population.

Definition

Practising physicians are defined as the number of doctors providing care to patients. General practitioners include doctors assuming responsibility for the provision of continuing care to individuals and families, as well as other generalist/non-specialist medical practitioners. Specialists include paediatricians, obstetricians/gynaecologists, psychiatrists, medical specialists and surgical specialists. Other physicians include interns/residents if not reported in the field in which they are training, and doctors not elsewhere classified. The numbers are based on head counts.

Comparability

In several countries (Canada, France, Greece, Iceland, Ireland, the Netherlands, and Turkey), the data include not only physicians providing direct care to patients, but also those working in the health sector as managers, educators, researchers, etc. This can add another 5-10% of doctors. Data for Portugal refer to all physicians who are licensed to practice (resulting in a large overestimation). Data for Spain include dentists and stomatologists, while data for Belgium include stomatologists. Data for Chile include only doctors working in the public sector.

Not all countries are able to report all their practising physicians in the two broad categories of specialists and generalists. For example, specialty-specific data may not be available for doctors in training or for those working in private practice.

Overview

In 2009, there were just over three doctors per 1 000 population across OECD countries. Greece had by far the highest number of doctors per capita, followed by Austria, Chile, Turkey, Korea and Mexico had the lowest number, with between one and two doctors per 1 000 population. The number of doctors per capita is lower in some of the major emerging economies, with less than one doctor per 1 000 population in Indonesia, India and South Africa.

From 2000 to 2009, the ratio of practising physicians per 1 000 population has grown in most OECD countries. On average across OECD countries, physician density grew at a rate of 1.7% per year. The growth rate was particularly rapid in countries which started with lower levels in 2000 (Turkey, Chile, Korea and Mexico) as well as in the United Kingdom and Greece. There was no growth in the number of physicians per capita in Estonia, France, Israel and Poland, and there was a marked decline in the Slovak Republic. The decline in the Slovak Republic can be explained at least partly by a reduction in the number of medical graduates since the late 1990s. In France, following the reduction in the number of new entrants into medical schools during the 1980s and 1990s, the number of doctors per capita began to decline since 2006. This downward trend is expected to continue.

In 2009, 43% of doctors on average across OECD countries were women, up from 29% in 1990. This ranged from highs of more than half in central and eastern European countries (Estonia, Slovenia, Poland, the Slovak Republic, the Czech Republic and Hungary) and Finland to lows of less than 20% in Korea. The share of women physicians increased in all OECD countries over this time period with particularly high increases in the United States, Spain and Denmark.

The balance in the physician workforce between general practitioners and specialists has changed over the past few decades, with the number of specialists increasing much more rapidly. Although health policy and research emphasises the importance and cost-effectiveness of generalist primary care, on average across OECD countries, general practitioners made up only a quarter of all physicians in 2009. There were more than two specialists for every general practitioner in 2009, while this ratio was one-and-a-half in 1990. Specialists greatly out-number generalists in central and eastern European countries and in Greece. However, some countries have maintained a more equal balance between specialists and generalists, such as Australia, Canada, France, and Portugal, where generalists made up nearly half of all doctors. In some countries, for example in the United States, general internal medicine doctors are categorised as specialists although their practice can be very similar to that of general practitioners, resulting in some underestimation of the capacity of these countries to provide generalist care.

Sources

- OECD (2011), *OECD Health Statistics*, OECD Publishing.
- WHO-Europe for Russian Federation, and national sources for other non-OECD countries.

Further information

Analytical publications

- Chaloff, J. (2008), "Mismatches in the Formal Sector, Expansion of the Informal Sector: Immigration of Health Professionals to Italy", *OECD Health Working Papers*, No. 34.
- Colombo, F. *et al.* (2011), *Help Wanted?: Providing and Paying for Long-Term Care*, OECD Health Policy Studies, OECD Publishing.
- Fujisawa, R. and G. Lafortune (2008), "The Remuneration of General Practitioners and Specialists in 14 OECD Countries: What are the Factors Influencing Variations across Countries?", *OECD Health Working Papers*, No. 41.
- OECD (2008), *The Looming Crisis in the Health Workforce: How Can OECD Countries Respond?*, OECD Health Policy Studies, OECD Publishing.
- OECD (2007), "Immigrant Health Workers in OECD Countries in the Broader Context of Highly Skilled Migration", in OECD, *International Migration Outlook 2007*, OECD Publishing.

Statistical publications

- OECD (2011), *Health at a Glance*, OECD Publishing.
- OECD (2010), *Health at a Glance: Europe 2010*, OECD Publishing.

Online databases

- *OECD Health Statistics*.

Websites

- OECD Health Data (supplementary material), *www.oecd.org/health/healthdata*.
- OECD Health at a Glance (supplementary material), *www.oecd.org/health/healthataglance*.

Practising physicians

Per 1 000 inhabitants

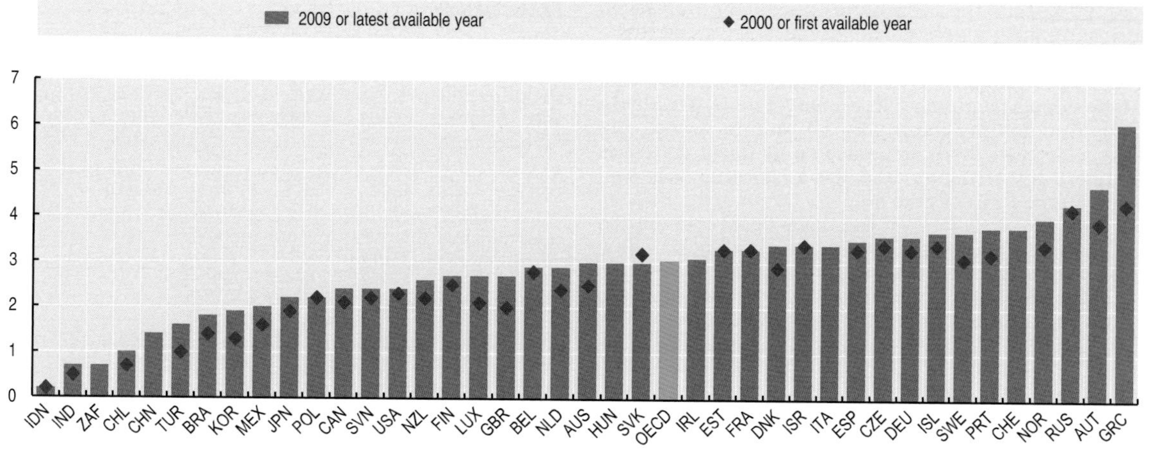

StatLink http://dx.doi.org/10.1787/888932508034

Distribution of physicians

As a percentage of total physicians, 2009 or latest available year

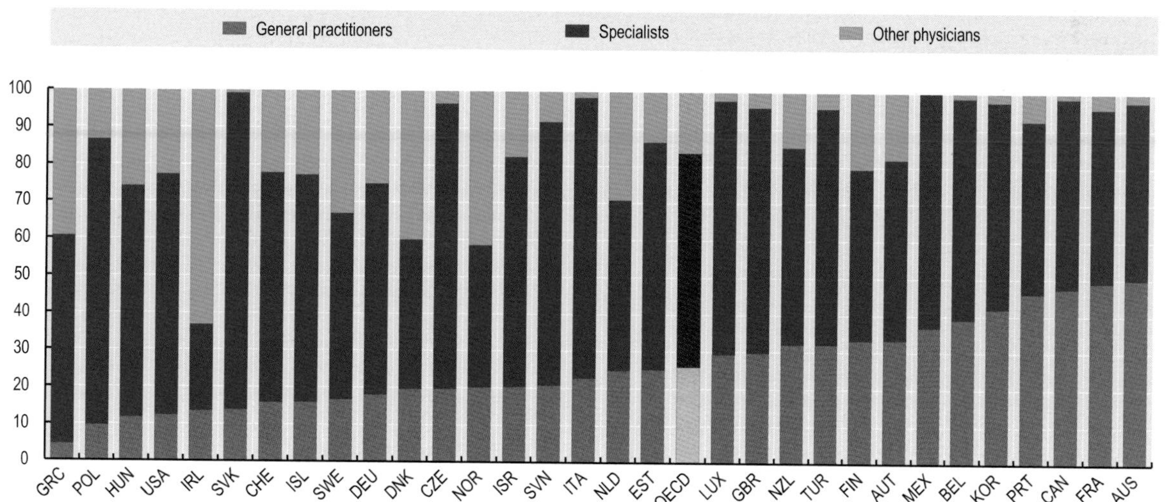

StatLink http://dx.doi.org/10.1787/888932508072

NURSES

Nurses are usually the most numerous health profession, greatly outnumbering physicians in most OECD countries. Nurses play a critical role in providing health care not only in traditional settings such as hospitals and long-term care institutions but increasingly in primary care (especially in offering care to the chronically ill) and in home care settings. However, there are concerns in many countries about shortages of nurses, and these concerns may well intensify in the future as the demand for nurses continues to increase and the ageing of the "baby-boom" generation precipitates a wave of retirements among nurses. These concerns have prompted actions in many countries to increase the training of new nurses combined with efforts to increase the retention of nurses in the profession.

Overview

On average across OECD countries, there were 8.4 nurses per 1 000 population in 2009. The number of nurses per capita was highest in several Nordic countries, with 14 to 15 nurses per 1 000 population. It was also high in Belgium, although the data relate to all nurses who are licensed to practice, resulting in a large overestimation. The number of nurses per capita in OECD countries was lowest in Chile (although the number is underestimated, because it only takes into account nurses working in the public sector), as well as in Turkey, Mexico and Greece. The number of nurses per capita was also low compared with the OECD average in major emerging economies, such as India, Brazil, Indonesia and China, where there were fewer than 1.5 nurses per 1 000 population in 2009. This ratio has however been growing quite rapidly in some of these countries in recent years.

The number of nurses per capita increased in almost all OECD countries over the past decade. Across OECD countries, the number of nurses per 1 000 population increased at an average rate of 1.8% per year between 2000 and 2009. Chile saw the largest increase in the number of nurses per 1 000 population among OECD countries in this time period, with an increase of 12% per year, although the number of nurses per capita remains very low. Portugal and Korea also had strong increases in the number of nurses. On the other hand, in Israel, the number of nurses per capita declined between 2000 and 2009. In Australia and the Netherlands, the number of nurses per capita declined between 2000 and 2007, but has risen since then.

In 2009, the nurse-to-doctor ratio ranged from five nurses per doctor in Ireland to less than one nurse per doctor in Chile, Greece and Turkey. The number of nurses per doctor is also relatively low in Italy, Mexico, Israel, Portugal and Spain. The average across OECD countries is just below three nurses per doctor, with most countries reporting between two to four nurses per doctor. In Greece and Italy, there is evidence of an over-supply of doctors and under-supply of nurses, resulting in an inefficient allocation of resources.

In response to shortages of doctors and to ensure proper access to care, some countries have in recent years developed more advanced roles for nurses. Evaluations of nurse practitioners from the United States, Canada, the United Kingdom show that these advanced practice nurses can improve access to services and reduce waiting times, while delivering the same quality of care as doctors for a range of patients, including those with minor illnesses and those requiring routine follow-up. Most evaluations find a high patient satisfaction rate, while the impact on cost is either cost reducing or cost neutral.

Definition

The number of nurses includes all those employed in public and private settings providing services to patients ("practising"), including the self-employed. In those countries where there are different levels of nurses, the data include both "professional nurses" who have a higher level of education and perform higher level tasks and "associate professional nurses" who have a lower level of education but are nonetheless recognised and registered as nurses. Midwives and nursing aids who are not recognised as nurses should normally be excluded.

Comparability

In several countries (France, Greece, Iceland, Ireland, Portugal, the Slovak Republic, Turkey and the United States), the data include not only nurses providing direct care to patients, but also those working in the health sector as managers, educators, researchers, etc. Data for Belgium and Italy refer to all nurses who are licensed to practice (resulting in a large overestimation). Austria reports only nurses employed in hospitals. Chile includes only nurses working in the public sector.

About half of OECD countries include midwives because they are considered as a specialist nurse. Data for Germany does not include about 250 000 nurses (representing an additional 30% of nurses) who have three years of education and are providing services for the elderly.

Sources

- OECD (2011), *OECD Health Statistics*, OECD Publishing.
- WHO-Europe for Russian Federation, and national sources for other non-OECD countries.

Further information

Analytical publications

- Buchan, J. and S. Black (2011), "The Impact of Pay Increases on Nurses' Labour Market: A Review of Evidence from Four OECD Countries", *OECD Health Working Papers*, No. 57.
- Colombo, F. *et al.* (2011), *Help Wanted?: Providing and Paying for Long-Term Care*, OECD Health Policy Studies, OECD Publishing.
- Delamaire, M. and G. Lafortune (2010), "Nurses in Advanced Roles: A Description and Evaluation of Experiences in 12 Developed Countries", *OECD Health Working Papers*, No. 54.
- OECD (2008), *The Looming Crisis in the Health Workforce: How Can OECD Countries Respond?*, OECD Health Policy Studies, OECD Publishing.

Statistical publications

- OECD (2011), *Health at a Glance*, OECD Publishing.
- OECD (2010), *Health at a Glance: Europe 2010*, OECD Publishing.

Online databases

- *OECD Health Statistics.*

Websites

- OECD Health Data (supplementary material), *www.oecd.org/health/healthdata.*
- OECD Health at a Glance (supplementary material), *www.oecd.org/health/healthataglance.*

Practising nurses

Per 1 000 inhabitants

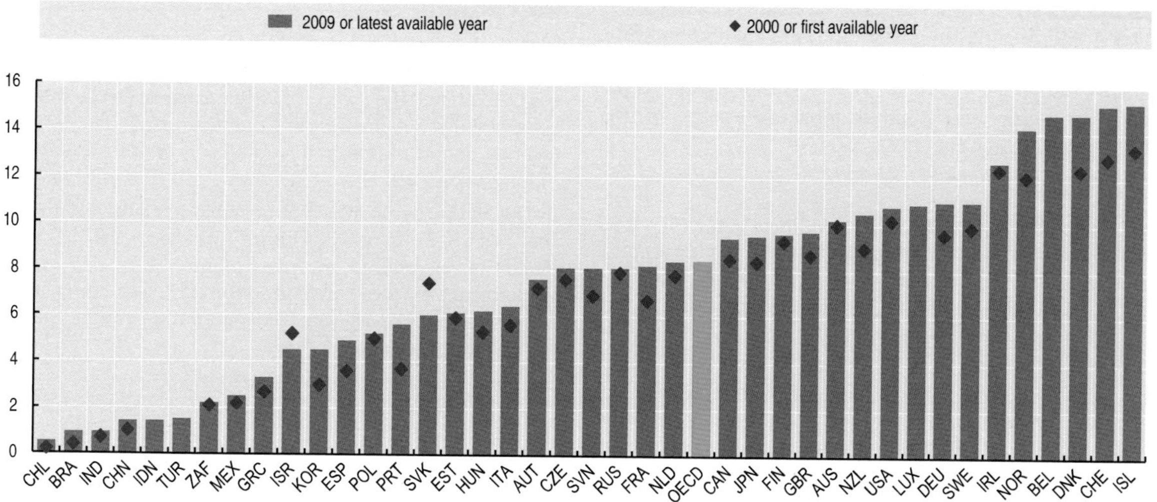

StatLink http://dx.doi.org/10.1787/888932508091

Ratio of nurses to physicians

2009 or latest available year

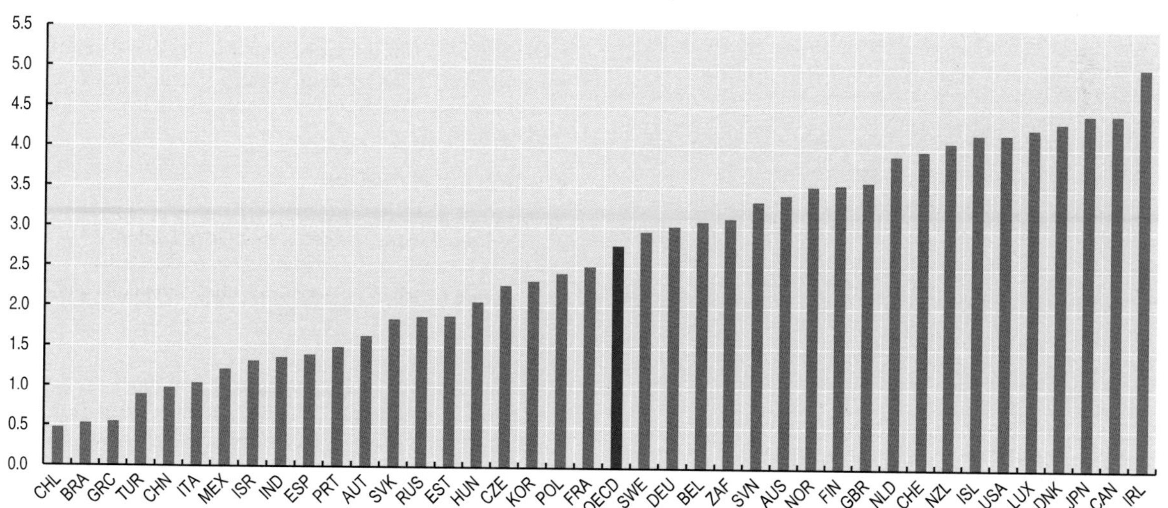

StatLink http://dx.doi.org/10.1787/888932508110

HEALTH EXPENDITURE

In most OECD countries, spending on health is a large and growing share of both public and private expenditure. Health spending as a share of GDP varies widely across countries, reflecting market and social factors as well as the diverse financing and organisational structures of the health system in each country.

Definition

Total expenditure on health care measures the final consumption of health goods and services plus capital investment in health care infrastructure. It includes spending by both public and private sources (including households) on medical goods and services, on public health and prevention programmes, and on administration.

For a more comprehensive assessment of health spending, the health spending to GDP ratio should be considered together with per capita health spending. Countries having a relatively high health spending to GDP ratio might have relatively low health expenditure per capita, while the converse also holds. For example, Portugal and Sweden both spent a similar proportion of their GDP on health at around 10% of GDP; however, per capita spending (adjusted to USD PPP) was close to 50% higher in Sweden.

Comparability

OECD countries are at varying stages of reporting health expenditure data according to the definitions proposed in the OECD manual *A System of Health Accounts* (SHA). While the comparability of health expenditure data has improved recently, some limitations do remain, *e.g.* on the measurement of long-term care.

In the Netherlands, it is not possible to clearly distinguish the public and private share for the part of health expenditures related to investments. For Belgium, total expenditure excludes investments. In Luxembourg, health expenditure is for the insured population rather than the resident population.

Overview

Trends in the health spending to GDP ratio are the result of the combined effect of trends in GDP and health expenditure. Apart from Luxembourg, health spending grew more quickly than GDP since 2000 resulting in a higher share of GDP allocated to health. In 2009, OECD countries devoted 9.6% of their GDP to health spending, a sharp increase from 8.8% in 2008, following the recession that started in many countries in 2008 and became widespread in 2009. The rise in the health spending share of GDP was particularly marked in Ireland, where the percentage of GDP devoted to health increased from 7.7% in 2007 to 9.5% in 2009, and in the United Kingdom, where it rose from 8.4% in 2007 to 9.8% in 2009.

In 2009, there were large variations in how much OECD countries spent on health as a share of GDP. The United States spent 17.4% on health in 2009, 5 percentage points more than in the next two countries, the Netherlands and France (which allocated 12.0% and 11.8% of their GDP to health). Of the OECD countries, Korea and Mexico spent less than 7.0% of their GDP on health. The fast-growing economies of China and India spent on health 4.6% and 4.2% of their GDP respectively in 2009, while South Africa and Brazil allocated 8.5% and 9.0% of GDP to health. The share of public expenditure on health to GDP also varies among OECD countries from a high of 9.8% in Denmark to a low of 3.1% in Mexico.

Since 2000, after an initial period of growth in the health spending to GDP ratio, there was a period of relative stability until 2009. The subsequent reduction in GDP, due to the economic downturn, has led to rises in the health spending to GDP ratios. Previous recessions show that, in many countries, the health spending share of GDP has tended to go up strongly during periods of economic downturn, and then stabilise or go down only slightly during periods of economic growth.

Sources

- OECD (2011), *OECD Health Statistics*, OECD Publishing.
- For non-OECD member countries: World Health Organization (WHO) (2011), *Global Health Expenditure* (database).

Further information

Analytical publications

- OECD (2010), *Value for Money in Health Spending*, OECD Health Policy Studies, OECD Publishing.
- Scherer, P. and M. Devaux (2010), "*The Challenge of Financing Health Care in the Current Crisis: An Analysis Based on the OECD Data*", OECD Health Working Papers, No. 49.
- Oliveira Martins, J. and C. Maisonneuve (2007), "The drivers of public expenditure on health and long-term care: An integrated approach", *OECD Economic Studies*, Vol. 2006/2.

Statistical publications

- OECD (2011), *Government at a Glance 2011*, OECD Publishing.
- OECD (2011), *Health at a Glance*, OECD Publishing.

Methodological publications

- OECD (2011), *A System of Health Accounts*, OECD Publishing.

Online databases

- *OECD Health Statistics*.

Websites

- OECD Health Data (supplementary material), *www.oecd.org/health/healthdata*.

Public and private expenditure on health

As a percentage of GDP

	Public expenditure							Private expenditure						
	1980	1990	2000	2005	2008	2009	2010	1980	1990	2000	2005	2008	2009	2010
Australia	3.8	4.4 |	5.4	5.6	5.9	..	..	2.3	2.3 |	2.7	2.8	2.8	..	..
Austria	5.1 |	6.1	7.6	7.9	8.0	8.6	..	2.3 |	2.2	2.3	2.5	2.4	2.5	..
Belgium	..	..	6.1 |	7.6	7.6	8.2	..	..	..	2.1 |	2.4	2.5	2.7	..
Canada	5.3	6.6 |	6.2	6.9	7.2	8.1	8.0	1.7	2.3 |	2.6	2.9	3.0	3.4	3.3
Chile	..	..	3.4	2.8	3.3	4.0	..	..	..	3.2	4.1	4.2	4.4	..
Czech Republic	..	4.6 |	5.9 |	6.3	5.9	6.9	..	..	0.1 |	0.6 |	0.9	1.2	1.3	..
Denmark	7.9	6.9	7.3 |	8.3	8.7	9.8	..	1.1	1.4	1.4 |	1.5	1.6	1.7	..
Estonia	..	..	4.1	3.9	4.8	5.3	..	..	..	1.2	1.2	1.3	1.8	..
Finland	5.0	6.3 |	5.1	6.4	6.2	6.8	6.7	1.3	1.5 |	2.1	2.1	2.1	2.3	2.2
France	5.6	6.4 |	8.0	8.8	8.6	9.2	..	1.4	2.0 |	2.1	2.4	2.5	2.6	..
Germany	6.6	6.3 |	8.2	8.2	8.2	8.9	..	1.8	2.0 |	2.1	2.5	2.5	2.7	..
Greece	3.3	3.5 |	4.7	5.8	..	..	..	2.6	3.1 |	3.2	3.8	..	..	..
Hungary	..	..	5.0 |	6.0	5.1	5.2	..	..	..	2.1 |	2.3	2.1	2.3	..
Iceland	5.5	6.8	7.7 |	7.7	7.5	7.9	7.5	0.7	1.0	1.8 |	1.8	1.6	1.7	1.8
Ireland	6.8 |	4.4	4.6	5.9	6.8	7.2	..	1.5 |	1.7	1.5	1.8	2.1	2.4	..
Israel	..	..	4.7	4.6	4.5	4.6	..	..	..	2.8	3.2	3.1	3.2	..
Italy	..	6.1	5.8	6.8	7.0	7.4	7.4	..	1.6	2.2	2.1	2.0	2.1	2.1
Japan	4.6	4.6 |	6.2	6.7	6.9	..	..	1.9	1.3 |	1.5	1.5	1.6	..	..
Korea	0.8	1.5	2.2	3.0	3.6	4.0	4.1	2.9	2.5	2.3	2.7	2.8	2.9	2.9
Luxembourg	4.8	5.0 |	6.4	6.7	5.7	6.5	..	0.4	0.4 |	1.1	1.2	1.1	1.2	..
Mexico	..	1.8 |	2.4	2.6	2.7	3.1	2.9	..	2.6 |	2.7	3.2	3.1	3.3	3.2
Netherlands	5.1	5.4 |	5.0 |	5.9	7.4 |	9.5	..	2.3	2.6 |	2.9 |	3.1	1.6 |	1.7	..
New Zealand	5.1	5.6	5.9	6.7	7.7	8.3	..	0.7	1.2	1.7	2.0	1.9	2.0	..
Norway	5.9	6.3 |	6.9	7.6	7.3	8.1	..	1.0	1.3 |	1.5	1.5	1.4	1.5	..
Poland	..	4.4	3.9 |	4.3	5.1	5.3	..	..	0.4	1.7 |	1.9	1.9	2.0	..
Portugal	3.3	3.7 |	6.2	7.0	6.5	..	..	1.8	2.0 |	3.2	3.4	3.5	..	..
Slovak Republic	..	..	4.9	5.2	5.4	6.0	..	..	..	0.6	1.8	2.6	3.1	..
Slovenia	..	..	6.1 |	6.1	6.1	6.8	6.0	..	..	2.2 |	2.3	2.2	2.5	..
Spain	4.2	5.1 |	5.2 |	5.8	6.5	7.0	..	1.1	1.4 |	2.0 |	2.4	2.5	2.5	..
Sweden	8.3	7.4 |	6.9 |	7.4	7.5	8.2	..	0.7	0.8	1.2 |	1.7	1.7	1.9	..
Switzerland	..	4.3 |	5.6	6.7	6.4	6.8	6.9	..	3.9 |	4.5	4.5	4.4	4.6	4.8
Turkey	0.7	1.6 |	3.1	3.7	4.4	..	..	1.8	1.1 |	1.8	1.8	1.6	..	..
United Kingdom	5.0	4.9 |	5.6	6.7	7.2	8.2	..	0.6	1.0 |	1.5	1.5	1.6	1.6	..
United States	3.7	4.9	5.9	6.9	7.6	8.3	..	5.3	7.5	7.8	8.8	8.9	9.1	..
OECD average	4.8	5.0	5.5	6.1	6.3	6.9	..	1.7	1.9	2.2	2.5	2.5	2.7	..
Brazil	..	..	2.9	3.3	3.7	4.1	..	..	..	4.3	4.9	4.7	4.9	..
China	..	..	1.8	1.8	2.0	2.3	..	..	..	2.9	2.9	2.3	2.3	..
India	..	..	1.1	1.0	1.1	1.4	..	..	..	3.3	3.2	2.9	2.8	..
Indonesia	..	..	0.7	1.0	1.2	1.2	..	..	..	1.3	1.1	1.0	1.1	..
Russian Federation	..	..	3.2	3.2	3.1	3.5	..	..	..	2.2	2.0	1.7	1.9	..
South Africa	..	..	3.4	3.4	3.3	3.4	..	..	..	5.0	5.4	5.0	5.1	..

StatLink http://dx.doi.org/10.1787/888932508129

Public and private expenditure on health

As a percentage of GDP, 2009 or latest available year

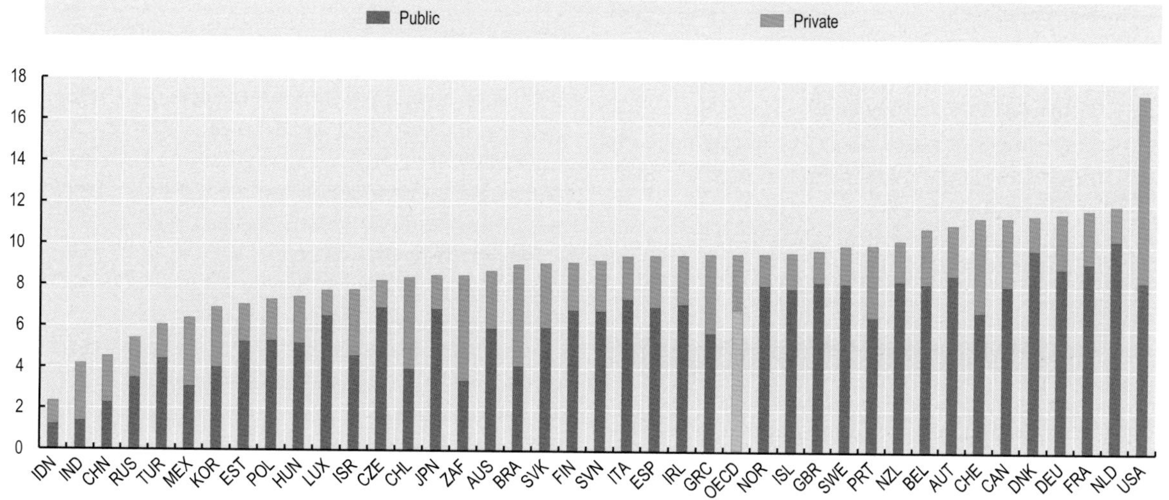

StatLink http://dx.doi.org/10.1787/888932508148

Analytical index

E

F

G

H

I

L

M

N

R

S

T

U

V

W

Y

ORGANISATION FOR ECONOMIC CO-OPERATION AND DEVELOPMENT

The OECD is a unique forum where governments work together to address the economic, social and environmental challenges of globalisation. The OECD is also at the forefront of efforts to understand and to help governments respond to new developments and concerns, such as corporate governance, the information economy and the challenges of an ageing population. The Organisation provides a setting where governments can compare policy experiences, seek answers to common problems, identify good practice and work to co-ordinate domestic and international policies.

The OECD member countries are: Australia, Austria, Belgium, Canada, Chile, the Czech Republic, Denmark, Estonia, Finland, France, Germany, Greece, Hungary, Iceland, Ireland, Israel, Italy, Japan, Korea, Luxembourg, Mexico, the Netherlands, New Zealand, Norway, Poland, Portugal, the Slovak Republic, Slovenia, Spain, Sweden, Switzerland, Turkey, the United Kingdom and the United States. The European Union takes part in the work of the OECD.

OECD Publishing disseminates widely the results of the Organisation's statistics gathering and research on economic, social and environmental issues, as well as the conventions, guidelines and standards agreed by its members.

OECD PUBLISHING, 2, rue André-Pascal, 75775 PARIS CEDEX 16
(30 2011 04 1 P) ISBN 978-92-64-11150-9 – No. 59671 2011-05